# IVY LEAGUE FOOTBALL

*Since 1872*

**BOOKS by JOHN McCALLUM**

*Big Ten Football: Since 1895*

*College Football, U.S.A.*

*This Was Football*

*We Remember Rockne*

*The World Heavyweight Boxing Championship: A History*

*The Encyclopedia of World Boxing Champions*

*Dumb Dan*

*Boxing Fans' Almanac*

*Ty Cobb*

*The Tiger Wore Spikes*

*Everest Diary*

*That Kelly Family*

*Six Roads From Abilene*

*Going Their Way*

*How You Can Play Little League Baseball*

BROWN

COLUMBIA

CORNELL

DARTMOUTH

# IVY LEAGUE

HARVARD

PENNSYLVANIA

PRINCETON

YALE

*John McCallum*

# IVY LEAGUE FOOTBALL

## *Since 1872*

*Stein and Day/Publishers/New York*

First published in 1977

Designed by Herb Johnson
Printed in the United States of America
Stein and Day/*Publishers*/Scarborough House, Briarcliff Manor, NY 10510

*Library of Congress Cataloging in Publication Data*

McCallum, John Dennis, 1924-
Ivy League football since 1872.

Includes index.
1. Ivy League (Football Conference)—History.
I. Title.
GV958.5.I9M3 796.33'278'0973 77-5450
ISBN 0-8128-2258-7

*To*

*Chester J. LaRoche*

*and*

*F. Peavey Heffelfinger,*

*Two Loyal Sons of*

*Ivy League*

*Football,*

*and to*

*Lee Knight Moffett*

# Acknowledgments

In addition to the material I gathered from personally covering Ivy League football for the NEA syndicate in the late 1940s and 1950s, I am indebted to a number of people who shared with me private memories of the conference. The names include F. Peavey Heffelfinger, nephew of the legendary Pudge and whose own football experience at Yale as student manager dates back to the days of Tad Jones; Chet LaRoche, Yale quarterback 1916, a founder and chairman of the National Football Foundation and Hall of Fame, who for years was one of America's leading advertising executives and part owner of ABC network; Lloyd McGovern, football historian, Palo Alto, California, and his brother, Reginald; professors George H. Hildebrand and Paul M. O'Leary, Cornell; Roger Kittinger, Colgate; Jay Barry, Brown Alumni Association; DeLaney Kiphuth, former athletic director, Yale; the late Charley Loftus, long-time Yale sports information chief; and the following sports information directors: Jack DeGange, Dartmouth; Phil Langan, Princeton; Dave Matthews, Harvard; Ben Mintz, Cornell; Edwin Fabricius, Pennsylvania; Rod Commons, Brown; Kevin DeMarrais, Columbia; and Peter Easton, Yale. Permission to reprint the photos was graciously granted by all eight of the league schools.

I especially want to thank my editor, Benton Arnovitz, a Cornell man, who encouraged me to write this book.

—John McCallum

# *Contents*

# *Foreword*

At a time when people are thinking of the moon as a landing field, it may be out of place for me, in this introduction, to talk about the importance to the nation of college football and the possible influence on the game of John McCallum's story of the Ivy League. Yet in large measure, that's what follows. You may feel I've overemphasized Yale's part.

But there is a reason for emphasis on Yale, for it was that mutual interest which brought John McCallum and me together. John is far more than a gifted author of sports; he is an *historian* of college football, and particularly interested in the game as an educational discipline.

He grew up in the Pacific Northwest, I in Boston. I'm thirty years his senior, but our love of football was the same—intense, concerned, and involved. He lettered in athletics at Washington State University. I played football for Yale in 1916, coached there in 1920 and '21, and was chairman of the Football Committee for seven years.

I set down these details for a good reason. As old as the game of football seems to most of the country, John and I got to know better than almost anyone else, the men who *started* football: Pudge Heffelfinger (or "Big Heff" as he was called), Camp, Stagg, Dr. Williams (one of Minnesota's greatest coaches), Frank Hinkey, Shevlin, and "Billy" Bull, probably the game's greatest kicker.

These men not only helped to develop the game, but they and 67 other Yale ex-players were often called on as volunteers to teach the game from coast to coast. As football manager of Stanford, Herbert Hoover called on Walter Camp to come out to Palo Alto and indoctrinate them, and when Knute Rockne was asked where Notre Dame "learned" the game—"Where did it all come from?"—he said, in effect, "from Yale, where else?—from Stagg, when he came West and coached at Chicago."

John McCallum got to know some of them well; he inherited the game's history and folklore because of Pudge Heffelfinger. John had come to live and work in New York for 12 years. He became known nationally as an authoritative writer. Those were the days of such great sports writers as Grantland Rice, Frank Graham, Dan Parker, Harry Grayson, Allison Danzig, and Joe Williams.

It's not so peculiar that I knew all the old Yalies well. I even played against some in scrimmage in 1915 and 1916, just before the First World War. They were all still around then, and 30 or 40 would come back during the fall, but those were the last years they dominated Yale's play.

Big Heff had become a close friend and we were often on the field together, and because I was a quarterback, he spent a lot of time with me. Many years later, in 1953, he decided to write a book, *This Was Football*, and John McCallum was to set it down from Heff's dictation. It was this that brought the three of us together, for Pudge insisted I write the Introduction; Grant Rice, the Preface; and Joe Williams, the Postscript.

Now the reason for this lengthy prelude is to explain why in the book there is a dimension of football seldom discussed. It is *not* known to many. To most, football is a sport, winning is the goal, the stars national heroes—these are its accepted dimensions. But what was it that made Yale its philosophical leader for the first 20 years? Followed closely —not by Harvard, as so many think—but by Princeton. Why is it that today the Ivy League, and many other eastern schools set the pattern for the rest of the country in awarding scholarships based on need, not on other extraneous considerations?

This philosophy is set forth by a scholarly West Pointer, Colonel Alexander M. (Babe) Weyand, who played 37 football games for West Point and never took time out. See his book *The Saga of American Football,* probably one of the most authoritative ever written because of his intensive research. He talked to them "all," from Stagg, Rockne, Williams, and Heisman, to Don Fourot, "Biff" Jones, Grant Rice, and maybe most important, Henry W. Twombly, Yale '84, who had kept the most complete records. Here's what you would read:

> Eugene VonVoy Baker, a back from Wilbraham, Massachusetts, was Yale's football captain in 1876; it was he who laid the foundation of Yale's future greatness. At that time, college men followed the English "ideal" and played for sports' sake; but under Baker, Yale took football seriously. He instilled in his players the will to win, based on a doctrine of work and sacrifice and a determination to conquer, regardless of the odds or the cost. Eventually this peculiar ardor became known as Yale Spirit. Walter Camp played on this team and for the following four years.

I knew this spirit, for in 1916 it was pounded into me. And partially as a consequence, we beat Haughton and Harvard for the first time, scored the first touchdown against them in the Yale Bowl, and were rated one of the three or four best teams in the country.

That was the year, too, just before we went on the field against Harvard, that Tad Jones made the statement often quoted, often ridiculed: "This is the most important thing you will ever do in your life." People make fun of it, but we didn't—we knew what he meant. This was a time of decision—whether we were going to be men who put everything we had and more into an effort that was not only a test of skill, but a test of heart and spirit.

I followed Yale's 1976 team, beaten only in their first game, against Brown. As I watched the Blues beat Harvard in 1976, saw 250- and 270-pound guards and tackles for the first time in years, and one of the greatest halfbacks in the country, I felt that Yale was "back" and could take on the Southern Cals, Penn States, Alabamas, Pittsburghs. Now we are once again in a strong position to advance the spirit advocated by Eugene Baker as the one suited to healthy college football and to the American tradition.

*Chester J. LaRoche*
FORMER CHAIRMAN
NATIONAL FOOTBALL FOUNDATION
AND HALL OF FAME

# *The Ivy Eight*

*There's a cradle of Autumn Ivy*
*Rallied by memories since born*
*Where legions of athletes are marching*
*To a roll of thunder and song.*

*Sweet are the fieldstones of wisdom*
*The keystones of gridiron fame*
*Harvard, Princeton and Yale*
*Surrounded by brothers we name.*

*Hail Columbia, Dartmouth, Cornell*
*Give cheer Pennsylvania and Brown*
*To the mighty thunders in Heaven*
*To the great men of Ivy renown.*

*—by David L. Stidolph, 1976*

# Playing Gentlemen's Football

OCTOBER THIRTY FIRST 1959 FIFTY CENTS
DARTMOUTH
OFFICIAL
PENNSYLVANIA
THANKSGIVING DAY 1929
THE GAME
NOVEMBER 22, 1975
$1.50
SOUTH IS STILL ON TOP
CORNELL VS DARTMOUTH
WEST POINT
YALE
OCTOBER-22ND 1921
OFFICIAL SOUVENIR PROGRAM
GROUNDS, NEW YORK
50th Anniversary · 1925 National Championship
PENNSYLVANIA
DARTMOUTH
OFFICIAL PRINCETON UNIVERSITY PROGRAM
PRINCETON
YALE
FOOTBALL NEWS
Ivy League Champions 1962
October 26, 1963
ONE DOLLAR
HARVARD
OCTOBER 27, 1928
PRINCETON
HARVARD
HARVARD A·A·NEWS
YALE Game
PRINCETON
YALE
OFFICIAL PROGRAM
Harvard - Yale

# *Once Lightly Around the Ivy*

Chet LaRoche, who was there, testifies that this actually happened. "Gentlemen," Coach Tad Jones said to his Yale troops in the cathedral hush of the locker room just before sending them into the 1916 Harvard game, "you are now going out to play football against Harvard. Never again in your whole life will you do anything so important."

Tad Jones believed that, and he was of such transparent sincerity that his players believed him when he said it. Corny as it may sound, they went out and won the game for dear old Yale, 6 to 3.

There are still a great passel of incorrigible Old Blues who feel that Coach Jones was right. For more than 100 years, the Yale-Harvard football rivalry has been known only as The Game, a matchup bathed in tradition and legend and intrigue enough to stir the blood in the most sluggish of veins. Before the 1977 season, the series stood with Yale ahead, 50 wins, 35 losses, 8 ties.

Down the decades, barbershop strategists have poked a lot of fun at Harvard. Wise guys used to say that you had to be born on Beacon Hill or belong to Porcellian to make the Harvard varsity, except that a few South Boston Irishmen were recruited to do the tackling. In one of the long-ago Yale-Harvard games, Captain Charles Coolidge of the Crimson called his teammates together after the Elis had penetrated to the 1-yard line.

"Gentlemen of Harvard," he said with all dignity, "in this frightful expediency, I really think that you men should be introduced. Mr. Saltonstall, shake hands with Murphy here. And Mr. Bacon, say hello to O'Brien from South Boston."

When I told that purely apocryphal story at the New York Harvard Club some years ago, an indignant old Cantab protested. "I assure you, sir," he told me, "Harvard is the most democratic institution in America. I was coxswain of the Harvard crew for three years and knew every man in the boat by his first name—except the two in the bow."

The Crimson and the Bulldogs began playing against each other in 1875; they were, you could say, the original traditional rivalry. Until the mid-1920s, few teams outside of a small, select group of Eastern schools—mainly Yale, Harvard, Princeton, and Penn—ever impressed Walter Camp enough to gain a rating among his Big Four at the season's end. Walter Camp was the original Associated Press (AP) poll.

One reason Yale and Harvard may have quit competing in big-time college football is that they grew weary of turning out legendary names. Yale, after all, produced Walter Camp himself, "the father of American football," who gave us the down system, the idea of 11 players to a side, and modern scoring. Yale also spawned Amos Alonzo Stagg, Pudge Heffelfinger, T.A.D. Jones, Ted Coy, Bill Mallory, Albie Booth, Larry Kelley, and Clint Frank, along with an occasional Archibald MacLeish and John Hersey.

Harvard was just as busy. Coming out of Cambridge were the likes of Charles Daly, Hamilton Fish, Charlie Brickley, Eddie Mahan, Edward Casey, Barry Wood, and a guard with the most perfect Ivy League name of all—Endicott Peabody. There were also a few Kennedys along the way.

One of them, U.S. Senator Edward, scored Harvard's only touchdown in the 21-7 loss to Yale in 1955.

Times have changed for The Game. Fifty years ago, even 40 or 30, the men who played were considered the noblest examples of manhood. There was nothing bestial about them. They were gentlemen of courage, bravery, and daring, who lured 70,000 spectators at a time into Yale Bowl. A star was instantly taken into the social elite, and the Old Grads liked nothing better than to sit around the fires of their private clubs and dredge up memories of the day in 1913 when Charlie Brickley booted five field goals to beat Yale, 15-5, or discuss, cut by cut, every touchdown scamper of "Little Boy Blue," Albie Booth.

In more recent times, it seems different. The nostalgic hero for present-day students is more apt to be a man like little Charlie Yeager, the Yale football manager of 1952 who slipped into The Game late in the last quarter, as preplanned by Coach Jordan Olivar, to catch a pass for a conversion against poor Harvard. It is someone like the impulsive young girl in 1960, who dashed into the end zone to embrace Harvard's Charlie Ravenel as he scored his last touchdown. It is someone like the Harvard student who arranged to let loose several greased pigs in the Yale Bowl during the 1955 Harvard game—and did. And, finally, it is someone like the small boy who picked up the ball after a kick conversion in the end zone and beat it like hell through one of the tunnels for what was undoubtedly the longest run of the season.

For all of its deterioration as a game of importance to the outside world, there is still a color and an atmosphere to a Yale-Harvard weekend that few other rivalries can match. No one enjoys college football more. The station wagons will begin streaming into the parking areas around Yale Bowl before noon, the tailgates will be let down, and jugs of martinis will be set out on plaid blankets beside plates of chicken and deviled eggs. On one of those crackling red-and-gold New England afternoons that helped so much to make football popular in the first place, it reminds you of a convention of John O'Hara characters. Old Grads assemble in turtlenecks and blazers, and the glow of their cheeks illuminates the candy-striped tents where some of them hoarsely sing good old songs the way they used to be sung, with banjo backing and harmony on the favorite lines and nothing that needs plugging into an electric socket.

While the Old Grads whoop it up, there are intercollegiate competitions between the two schools on all levels—varsity, junior varsity, and freshman. There are also tackle games between all dorms. Thus, more than 700 students participate in football either Friday or Saturday, and there is soccer and touch football too. It is difficult to walk down a street in either New Haven or Cambridge without being thrown a pass. And then on Saturday afternoon, between fraternity parties and with the class reunions warming up all over the parking lots, the two varsities get down to the more or less importance of The Game.

Whereas cheerleading is an involved specialty at most schools, the attitude at Yale is extremely informal. Yale cheerleaders don't even have matching uniforms, or pompons, or minitrampolines. They are given real old megaphones, all broken, and sweaters with the letters Y-A-L-E on the chest, and a real tiny cannon (only about 1 foot long) to shoot off when the Bulldogs score a touchdown. That is not the only disillusionment. Facing the banks of alumni and students stretching up to the rim of the Yale Bowl, you must pardon the cheerleaders if they have the impression that they are trying to manipulate a vast class of truants.

"They don't *do* anything," lamented one female cheerleader in her Blue sweater. "They don't know when to cheer. They don't know *what* to cheer. You call for a round of Hold That Line, and they respond with Get That Ball. Of course, a lot of them are polluted and can't do anything. What a contrast! I have cheerleading friends in the Big Ten, and there they practice two hours a day, all week long, and they look at videotapes to see if they can improve, just like the players do. Here at Yale we practice at the game. There's not much to do. We have very few cheers. Things like, 'Bulldog, bulldog, bow, wow, wow.' Then we have one that goes 'Go, go, go.' And we have 'Eat 'em up, eat 'em up, rah, rah, rah.' And that's about it. We tried a pyramid during the Harvard game, and it fell down. No one was hurt. You know what? They like it best when we try something and *miss.*"

Ah, those college songs. They may well be the most intoxicating form of musical enterprise. Any undergraduate who produces one rarely gets over it and spends the rest of his or her life trying—and failing—to compose another hit. Caleb O'Connor, who wrote "Down the Field" for Yale in 1904, followed it with 200 others, none now remembered. The single exception among campus composers was

Cole Porter, who after turning out two good football tunes at Yale went on to true celebrity as a writer of popular songs and musical comedy. Raised in Peru, Indiana, Porter enrolled at Yale in 1909 at the age of 18 (although for some reason he said he was only 16), and he became a campus hero as a sophomore with "Bingo, Eli Yale." The *Yale Daily News* had sponsored a competition for a new football song ("Down the Field" referred to the great tackle Jim Hogan, who had since graduated), and Porter's contribution was outstanding in its avoidance of verse that could become dated. The song also was decidedly easy to memorize:

*Bingo! Bingo!*
*Bingo! Bingo! Bingo!*
*That's the lingo.*

Introduced near the end of Yale's undistinguished 1910 football season (6-2-2 record), "Bingo" became an instant campus favorite when it was sung at baseball games the following spring. It was even published by Remick, the leading New York sheet music company. In 1911, another songwriting competition was held on campus, and this time Porter came up with a more professional effort. It was "Bull Dog," which was in the enduring Yale musical tradition:

*Bull Dog! Bull Dog!*
*Bow wow wow!*
*Eli Yale!*
*Bull Dog! Bull Dog!*
*Bow wow wow!*
*Our team can never fail.*

Another big part of the Yale–Harvard tradition are the bands. In a day when college bands have grown almost as big as Army divisions and when college bandsmen maneuver at half time like zombies in the toils of some master hypnotist, Harvard still maintains a hearteningly old-fashioned and informal attitude toward football music. The Harvard band is usually larded out with ringers from the Cambridge fire department (student bandsmen reciprocate by switching uniforms and playing for the fire department when the need arises), and some years ago a Harvard janitor named Stanley De Pinto was Harvard's drum major. Harvard, however, long boasted a source of half-time entertainment unavailable to more splendiferous musical organizations: the biggest "playable" bass drum in the world (except, perhaps, for one in Japan and a University of Chicago drum which Toscanini could not get into Carnegie Hall back in 1938).

The drum, which was six feet in diameter and mounted on bicycle wheels, was proudly exhibited at football games ever since it was presented to the band by the Associated Harvard Clubs 50 years ago. It was thumped in various ways. In its youth it was clobbered by a drummer who galloped along beside as it was whirled around the field by volunteer coolies. Later a 13-year-old fireman's son rode on top of it, whacking it with one hand while hanging on with the other. But for three years in the early 1950s the drum went unbeaten—it was obvious that age was finally undermining it. The end came in January, 1955. One of the drumheads, strained by a change of weather, suddenly split wide open.

The fact, duly noted in the *Alumni Bulletin,* "War Drum Throbs no Longer," disturbed Harvard men from coast to coast—the more because the University of Florida cheekily acquired a drum of similar size in 1954. None, however, offered to buy a new one. Drum manufacturers protested, moreover, that it would be exceedingly difficult to find two cows with hides big enough to make new drumheads and that tanning and curing them properly would be harder yet.

Harvard students themselves, however, rallied sternly and started a "dimes for the drum" campaign. Arnold Aronson, the Band Manager, found a manufacturer, The Slingerland Drum Company of Chicago, willing to build a new drum six feet in diameter and 24 inches wide for $800. The new instrument was strongly built. To satisfy tradition, it had to be. Harvard men still happily remembered the Yale undergraduate who ran out on the field in 1947, dove head first at the old drum in an attempt to sail clean through it—and simply bounced off, knocking himself as cold as a salt herring in the process.

Ivy League bands are a community unto themselves. Where they sit during football games is described as The Pit. There is very little conformity of dress. Their sector is the noisiest in the stadium, but it is the roar of conversation that drifts out of it, rather than shouts in support of the team. Whatever interest there has been in the game wanes almost completely after the first half. The backs of many of the band members always seem to be to the field.

George Plimpton is a seasoned band-watcher and can describe in most intricate detail what goes on there:

The great gold bells of a pair of tubas bellow at each other; the two instuments seem to lock, rocking back and forth obscenely to the accompaniment of the peeps and squawks of detached mouthpieces and the rhythm of whiskey flasks and beer bottles clinked against each other. They have their own private cheers— a "confetti" cheer in which they rip up their programs and toss them in the air. Obscenity abounds. A trumpet player will rise and call out, "Give me a C." The band members respond: "C!" "An O!" "O!" "A P!" "P!" "A U!" "U!" "An L!" "L!" "An A!" "A!" . . . until the word is done, and around the perimeter of the band, lips compress and the more traditional of the alumni start composing letters in their minds to be posted to the alumni bulletin on Monday morning.

But the music is often so good that many people are willing to overlook the rowdy iconoclasm. The Harvard band even had a trumpet cheer adapted from the classics, the notes rising out of all that rumpus with such purity that, across the field, even the Yale musicians themselves seem to quiet down to hear what their Crimson counterparts can do.

The half-time show is usually representative of the band itself—7½ minutes for each side to do its thing. On the field, the band performing stands in ill-formed lines, and the members never seem to take off on the downbeat, stepping ever so smartly, without the glockenspiel player dropping the music off the little stand on his instrument. The effect of his stopping to pick it up seems to sweep through the band so that whatever precision exists breaks down almost immediately into the chaos of a crowd moving out of a subway.

Yale and Harvard compete, of course, in a league called the Ivy. One of the ironic twists about the conference is that whereas its member universities are among the oldest on the continent, the Ivy League itself is one of the youngest in American intercollegiate athletics. From 1869 to 1955, Ivy standings were kept haphazardly and unofficially by newspapers. In fact, most Ivy opponents scheduled one another periodically, instead of annually, if at all. It wasn't until 1954 that the presidents of the eight schools—Brown, Columbia, Cornell, Dartmouth, Harvard, Penn, Princeton, and Yale—responded to criticism that football had grown out of hand by getting together on what they called the "presidents' agreement" that is the Ivy League charter. To this day, it is not so much a league as a federation by agreement. There is no commissioner to enforce the rules. The university presidents have instead jointly and separately accepted this responsibility.

Like the many others in college football leagues, the eight Ivy schools are dissimilar types. Enrollments range from about 17,000 (Penn) to 4,000 (Dartmouth), and undergraduate enrollments from about 10,000 (Cornell) to 2,500 (Columbia). Their educational focus also differs. Harvard, for instance, has some 10,000 graduate students, Dartmouth only 500. Another diversity is shown in their geographical moorings. Some are urban, some rural. In the beginning they were all rural, then Boston and Cambridge grew up beside Harvard, New Haven beside Yale, and Providence beside Brown. New York grew out to Columbia and Philadelphia to the University of Pennsylvania, which, incidentally, is not *the* university of Pennsylvania. Penn State is. Penn is a private school.

Of the Ivy's rural sites, Princeton, New Jersey, sits squarely between New York and Philadelphia—and halfway between Boston and Washington—and never grew up. There is something about the pastoral setting of Princeton that blends in perfectly with football in the autumn, that grand time of year when, as Will Rogers once observed, "you can take a girl under one arm, a blanket under the other, and walk along without having some cop ask a lot of foolish questions." No college building in America has the historic associations of ivy-covered Nassau Hall, from which George Washington's tattered Continentals drove the British Redcoats in 1776. Behind the graystone hall sits the famous cannon, around which bonfires flare after each Princeton victory. In the past, Tiger football history ran to glorified individual heroes: Alex Moffat, Snake Ames, Tilly Lamar, Arthur Poe, John DeWitt, and Sam White, to name a few. They made a habit of grabbing a loose ball and running the length of the field for a touchdown. In 1898, when Spanish War guns were thundering elsewhere, Arthur Poe, nephew of the famous poet, stole the ball from a Yale halfback on the Princeton 1-yard line and raced 99 yards for the only points of the game. A year later, he kicked a last-second field goal to beat the Elis, 11-10 at New Haven. It was the first time he had ever attempted a dropkick.

Cornell, another of the rural schools, is located at Ithaca, New York, a town that is smaller than the Greek island for which it was named. Cornell sits in lordly grandeur far above the blue finger of water that is Lake Cayuga. Without a doubt, this youngest of the Ivies has the most breathtaking setting. The heart lifts at the sight of those tall, silver-leafed poplar trees along the ribbon-white roads, flanked by red barns; the soaring, cloud-shadowed uplands, checkerboarded with cultivated fields, and the rugged limestone glens, two of which cut across the campus. Heinie Schoellkopf, one of Cornell's first football heroes, lost his life in one of those glens when he dived headlong after his pet dog.

Cornell always has been noted for its remarkable running backs. One of the first, Win Osgood, the Red Grange of the 1890s, met a dramatic death in Cuba heading the Insurrectionists against Spain. It was typical of Osgood, a natural leader, that he should expose himself fearlessly to enemy fire seated astride a white horse. Witnesses testified that his body remained upright in the saddle for several seconds after a Mauser bullet pierced his skull.

Except for Dartmouth, the town of Hanover, New Hampshire, wouldn't even be on the map. The school was founded in 1769 as an Indian institution by Reverend Eleazar Wheelock, who according to song was "a very pious man; he went into the wilderness to teach the In-di-an, with a Gradus ad Parnassum, a Bible and a drum, and 500 gallons of New England rum." Naturally, the Indians fled.

Dartmouth lies tucked away in the vale of Tempe, near the Connecticut River and just on the fringe of the broad-A belt ("gaad your figah with vigah"). Remotely stationed, it is not much on the fringe of anything else, save the White Mountains. With its 4,000 undergraduates, it is one of the smallest colleges in the Ivy League. The school is noted for its beautiful campus, with white, black-shuttered dormitories facing the village green precisely as they did when Daniel Webster made his memorable speech to Congress, starting: "Dartmouth is a small college, but there are those who love her." When General Dwight D. Eisenhower was president of Columbia, he once made a speech at Dartmouth. Nobody remembers what he said, but everybody recalls one remark he made on a tour of the Dartmouth campus: "This is just what I've always thought a college should look like."

Of the eight Ivy League schools, Dartmouth is farthest north. It often snows there in October. Accordingly, some years ago there was no objection when members of the Dartmouth senior class decided to build a giant bonfire at a football rally on the eve of the Harvard game. As college seniors have done before, and will do again, they left the details up to the freshman class. The kids were told to tear down an abandoned barn at the edge of town and haul it in as firewood. On a dark night in rural New Hampshire, however, one barn looks very much like any other. The freshmen ripped up a new one by mistake, and, although it made a heck of a fire, the university could not balance the budget that year after paying off the furious farmer.

Over the years, Big Green freshmen, called Pea Green, have built the Dartmouth pregame bonfires out of hen coops, shanties, and poles, but the best are laid with railroad ties. The disappearance of American railroads could very well end this bonfire ritual, however. Even now, in Avis trucks, freshman scouting parties must forage into Maine and Canada for fuel.

Several years ago, Bob Oates, of the *Los Angeles Times*, traveled clear across the country to see for himself what a Dartmouth pregame bonfire celebration was all about. The Pea Green had found wood enough to keep the fire going all night. "The ties had been stacked as high as a two-story building before the blaze was lit by four Dartmouth seniors holding red highway flares," Oates recalled. "When the top half of the flaming structure collapsed into the middle, it looked like a settler's log cabin fired by the Indians. It's hard to say what effect a thing like this had on the football players—the team was introduced at the pep rally and, a few hours later, played well against a better team—but the effect on others was profound. The pyromaniacal urges of hundreds were doubtlessly assuaged for another year. Half the crowd was still there at midnight, four hours after the fire started, some celebrating with wine or beer, a few with booze. At 1:30 A.M., a Hanover father instructed his three children, the oldest about 12: 'One more walk around the fire and then we go.' "

Hanover's rural atmosphere is ancient, it is relaxed, and it is filled with disdain for Harvard and Yale ("those grundy schools grind out scholarships like hamburger"). Athletic events serve to keep the boys and girls out of mischief. Nearly 75 percent of the student body participates in some organized athletics. Wholesomeness fairly screams at you. At football games, some Dartmouth cheerleaders have been known to go barefoot and wear nothing but red war paint on their upper torsos, whooping it up on the sidelines with a jug marked XXX as a joke. "In 20 degrees, brother, it's no joke," said one ex-cheerleader. "It's blackberry brandy, and it stands between you and pneumonia."

Ken Rosenfield, Dartmouth's head cheerleader in

*What the well-dressed Yale football varsity wore in 1876. Back row, l. to r.: Clark, C. C. Camp, W. C. Camp, Hatch, Wurts, Taylor. Second row: Downer, Walker, Captain Gene Baker, Bigelow, Thompson. Front row: Davis, Morse.*

*If Walter Camp had not contributed anything else to football, his reputation would still be secure for introducing the scrimmage to the game, perhaps the greatest single invention in any sport. This is how Camp looked in 1879.*

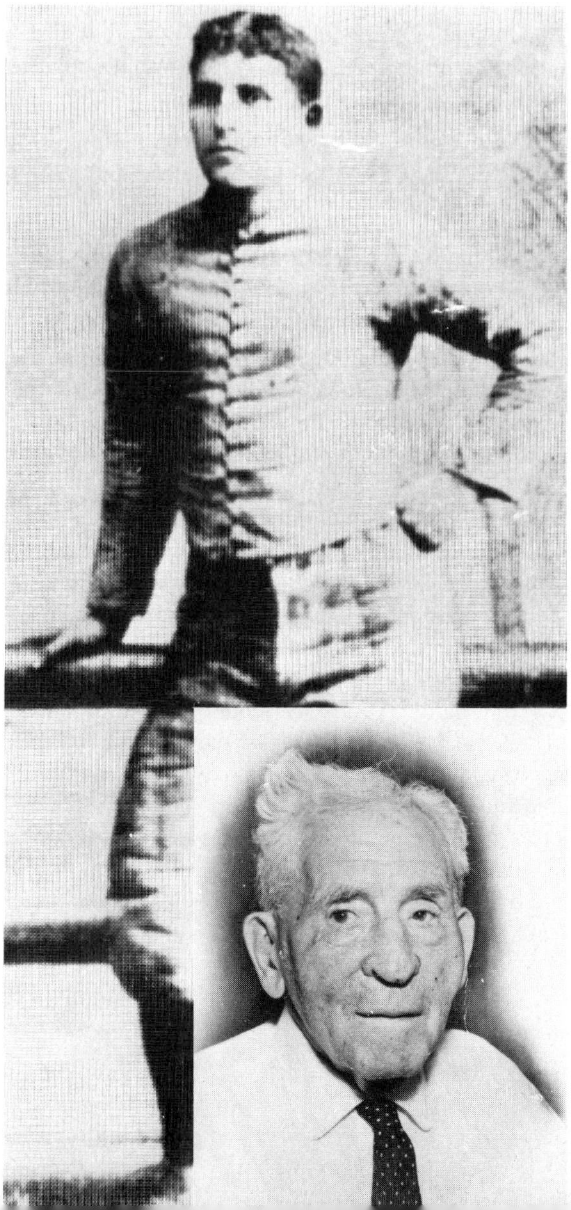

*Amos Alonzo Stagg was a 27-year-old divinity student when he played end on the famous Yale eleven of 1888. The closeup shows the way he looked at age 99. He lived to 105.*

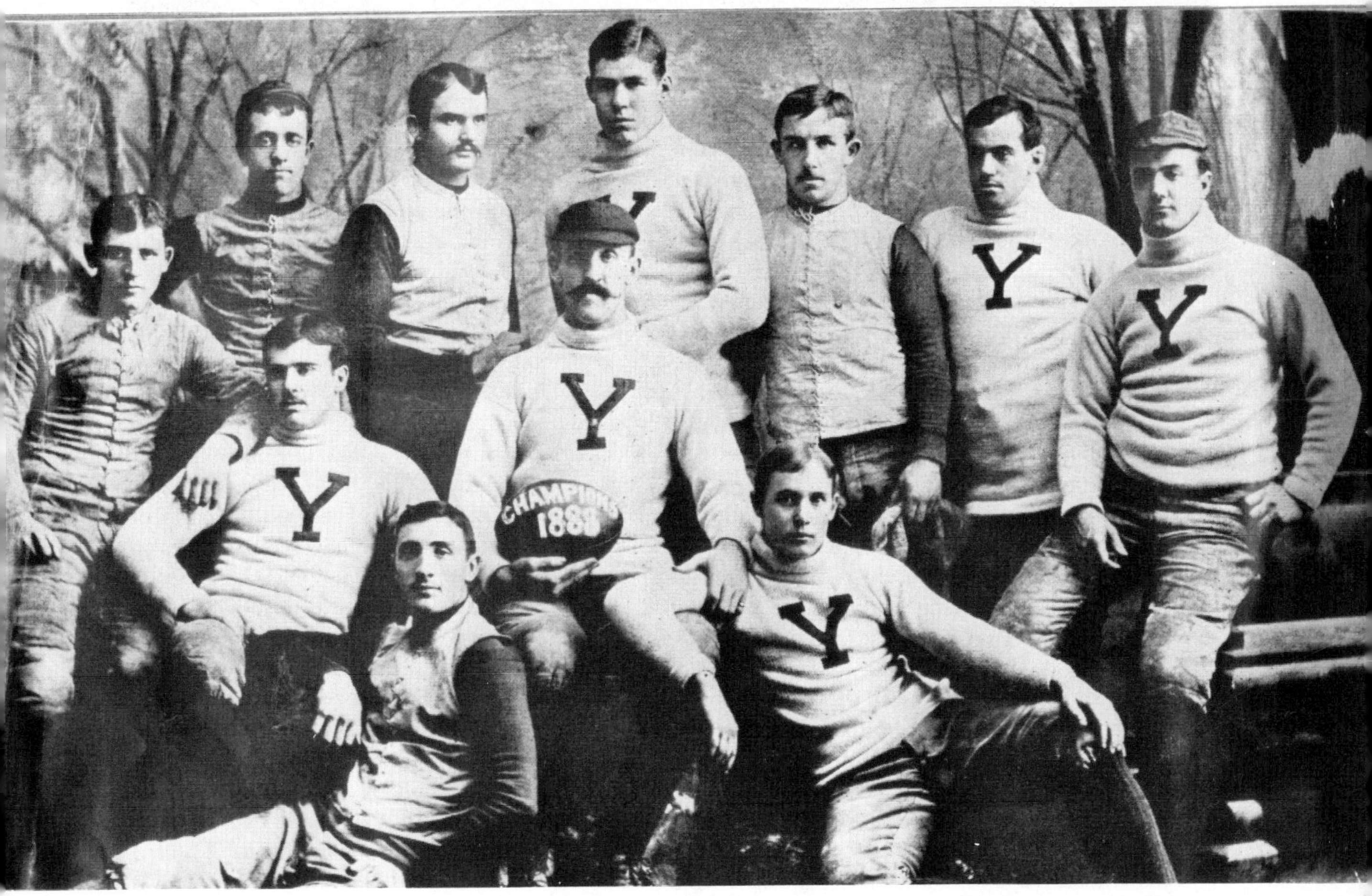


*The famous Yale eleven of 1888 won 14 straight games, scoring a total of 704 points to 0. Back row, l. to r.: Stagg, Rhodes, Woodruff, Heffelfinger, Gill, Wallace, Bull. Front row: McClung, Wurtenberg, Captain "Pa" Corbin, Graves.*

*Two big reasons why Yale flew through 13 straight victories and scored 470 points to 0 in 1891 were All-Americans Pudge Heffelfinger, left, and Captain Thomas Lee (Bum) McClung, later Secretary of the Treasury.*

1975, believed that the football spirit at Hanover was more intense and traditional than anywhere else in the Ivy League. "Why," he said, "I met this Harvard guy after a game with us and asked him if he'd been to the game that afternoon and he said, 'Not really.' Well, now what does *that* mean? At least at Dartmouth we know when we've been to a game. I'll bet 90 percent of Dartmouth men know the words of the alma mater. In the evening, groups of guys go from one fraternity to another singing it. They sing it in Thayer Hall, where the entire student body eats, and one table will stand up and begin singing, and everyone stops eating. The whole place just vibrates with spirit."

From Hanover to Cambridge is a scenic motor ride through the foothills of the White Mountains. Nowhere do you get such a sense of brooding tranquility as you do while walking across the Harvard Yard (pronounced "yaad" in good old Cambridge). Other colleges have campuses, but Harvard and Virginia are distinctive. Down at Charlottesville, the terraced enclosure laid out by Thomas Jefferson is known as the "Lawn," while up at Harvard, the university grounds were called the "Yaad" long before the colonists revolted against King George.

Established in 1636, some 16 years after the Pilgrims landed at Plymouth, Harvard is the oldest college in America. It was named after John Harvard, a young Puritan minister from Charlestown. While Dartmouth, Princeton, and Cornell have the space to expand indefinitely, landlocked Harvard is a prisoner of the city around it. The result is an urban old-world campus—that is, a group of inward-looking buildings surrounding a court. The school buildings edging Harvard's massive Yard back onto busy city streets. Predominantly colonial, these structures are a buffer between the world and a quiet inner preserve.

Priorities at Harvard have vastly changed since the frenzied days of the fabled Percy Haughton, who, according to legend, once throttled a bulldog to death to pep up his Harvards before the 1908 game against the Yales. In those years, tickets were at such a premium that eventually Harvard, in an effort to thwart the scalpers, originated its so-called Black List, whereby ticket privileges would be denied any undergraduate or alumnus who could be proved guilty of having sold any of his allotment at a profit. Harvard also had its "personal use" clause, which compelled an applicant to agree in writing that he, personally, would occupy one of his two seats. And even then there weren't enough tickets to go around. One year, in fact, the Harvard and Yale Athletic Associations had to refund more than a quarter of a million dollars to applicants whom they could not accommodate.

But it was fun—such wonderful damn fun; like the year the *Lampoon*, the Harvard humor magazine, came out with a cartoon showing the entire Yale backfield sprinting horror-stricken from the field as some heckler yelled, "Skull & Bones," the idea being, of course, that any member of that sacrosanct secret society had to leave the premises if an outsider so much as breathed the name of the lodge. But apparently there weren't any flies on the Bones either, because on the eve of the Yale-Harvard game one year, four of its members kidnapped three *Lampoon* editors, who had gone to New Haven to sell an issue carrying an article that purported to give the straight dope on all the Skull & Bones mumbo-jumbo. But that's The Game for you—anything for a laugh, like kidnapping Handsome Dan, Yale's bulldog mascot, or, in retaliation, sneaking into the Harvard Yard the night before The Game and applying several coats of blue paint to the statue of John Harvard outside University Hall.

For 90 years, every Yale captain has stood against a fragment of the famous old Yale fence, hands on the top rail and foot on the middle, and thus had his official picture taken. Longer years ago, Yale classes used to stand in small, dressed-up groups against the fence for their pictures. The fence then stood at the Chapel Street edge of the campus where Bingham and Vanderbilt Halls were later built. Seniors posed against it until 1889 when it was pulled down. Ten years before, in a particularly furious class rush, part of the fence was demolished. Someone at Pach Brothers, New Haven photographers, rescued a piece of the fence and Pach Brothers blessed him ever after for the foresight which gave that concern a monopoly on pictures of Yale captains. In 1929, there was consternation at Yale when the fence was stolen. Pach Brothers called in the police, said it valued the fence at $10,000. The *Lampoon*, after having posed its janitor up against it in sacrilegious mockery of Yale's captains, then returned the fence.

All this Ivy League spirit is still there, of course, but on a much lower key. In 1974, Harvard, with a fine team that tied Yale for the conference Championship, traveled up to Dartmouth, but hardly anyone bothered to follow them. Of the 5,500 tickets reserved for Harvard fans, 1,200 were returned. "The Harvard band accompanied the team," remembers author George Plimpton, himself a Harvard man, "and it played 'Fair Harvard' nervously under the Dartmouth dormitory windows, the tuba players turning to see if there was anything moving up behind them."

Harvard's pep rallies ceased in the 1960s when the football players began to worry about how they would be received at these affairs. In 1962, John Yovicsin, the Harvard coach, climbed the steps of the Hemenway Gym in Cambridge and, pleased with the number of Harvard men in front of him, began with a pleasantry, saying he had always heard about Harvard indifference, whereupon he was interrupted by such a long and sustained cheer for Harvard indifference that he could barely continue his speech.

I remember a conversation I had with a Harvard law student on my last trip to Cambridge. "I go to all the games," he said, "but it's hard to make generalizations about football interest at Harvard. Compared with high school or a Big Ten school, there's a wide range of attitude. The thing that surprised me when I first came here is that anybody cared about football."

Another urban old-world campus is Yale. On the streets of New Haven, it is divided into a number of individual colleges resembling Gothic castles, although instead of a moat, each has a large green patio in the middle. Some of these patios, or courts, run to the size of a football field, surrounded on all four sides by multistory college buildings.

Some of my most vivid recollections of football trips to Yale center around Mory's, that quaint little tavern that has been identified with the Elis since the old Brick Row era. There the walls are hung with photographs of all of Yale's famous teams and athletes; there the knife-whittled tables are frescoed with the initials of countless undergraduates; there the green punch flows at nightfall when the Whiffenpoofs gather to sing their familiar song. In the little rooms upstairs, football coaches have been made and unmade and football strategy has been mapped. From the wall, Pa Corbin, captain of the storied 1888 Yales, looks down with his handlebar mustache, his canvas jacket, and that glint of eagles in his eyes. A baseball cap sits jauntily on his head. It was by tugging and twisting at this cap that Pa flashed the first signals ever used in football.

It was also in that tiny room above Mory's that Frank Hinkey, the Yale coach in 1914, was coaxed against his better judgment into unveiling his secret rugby attack against a then almost unknown college from the Midwest named Notre Dame.

Old Pennsylvania, founded by Ben Franklin in 1740, was the colossus of the Ivy schools in 1904 and 1908, when the Red and Blue shared the National Championship, and turned out highly representative teams in the 1920s, 1940s, and parts of the 1950s, as well as the great "Guards Back" squads of the 1890s. For many years, Franklin Field's double-deck stadium, with its 60,546 seats, was the second largest money-maker in America, surpassed only by Michigan's awesome drawing power. Penn sits right in the middle of Philadelphia, which, unlike some major metropolitan areas, is a football-smart city. Where some large population centers do not know the difference between a double reverse and a dive tackle, the burghers of Philly always have been red-hot football fans and can cover a tablecloth with X's and O's like any chart maker. They demand good football, and the Quakers, with their liberal athletic policy, gave it to them year after year.

The open end of Franklin Field is flanked by musty old Weightman Hall, redolent of Penn football memories. A reporter who was able to find his way through that labyrinth of passageways to mild-mannered Coach George Munger's third-floor office in the old days really belonged to the cult. George took a lot of abuse from rabid Red and Blue grads. But he always seemed to weather the storm and fit into the Main Line picture. Next to the Ohio State and Syracuse Monday morning quarterbacks, those Quaker alumni of earlier days were the toughest a coach had to deal with. Following a Penn defeat by Cornell one season, they hired an airplane, with a "Goodbye, George" streamer, and flew it back and forth over Franklin Field. George was unperturbed. He went right on doing his duty as always.

George Munger was the eternal sophomore. He dressed in a regulation Penn uniform for every game and hovered solicitously over his players like a mother hen, wearing an expression of a frightened rabbit.

Chuck Bednarik, Coach Munger's most illustrious graduate, went from Penn to star for 14 fearsome years with the Philadelphia Eagles. He was bitter when Penn decided to de-emphasize football and join the Ivy League in 1954.

"I was an alumnus at the height of my football career with the Eagles, and it was just embarrassing

*This photograph, circa 1891, shows the kind of hole that Pudge Heffelfinger—head down, fist clenched, and charging—customarily opened in the opposing line.*

*One of Yale's most famous early teams—the boys of 1891. Captain Bum McClung, middle row, is holding the ball. To his right is Pudge Heffelfinger. At the extreme left of the group is the hardest tackler of the pre-1900s, Frank Hinkey.*

*The clerical clown, left, was the Harvard mascot of the Gaslight Era. Right, a high-pressure pennant salesman, vintage 1890.*

*A sideline scene at old Yale Field in the Gay Nineties version of tailgating.*

to wander in there and watch Penn lose 10 games in a row before those tiny crowds—8,000 people in the same place where the smallest crowd I ever played in front of was 56,000," Bednarik said. "But then I began to analyze it. The Ivy League degree is the greatest, it's unreal. There are so many football factories. That is where you can go if you really want to try to play football professionally. But I'll tell you something. Recently, things have begun to pick up around here."

It was a particularly cruel wrench for Penn to de-emphasize its football program, since its teams had kept company with the strongest football powers in America. Its sports program went through such a total reversal that in 1967 a commission took a look and decided that because of de-emphasis the school's athletic programs were in danger of disappearing altogether; the won-loss percentage of Penn teams was under .500. Since then, there has been a shift upward. Committees were organized, more money was allotted for hiring good coaches, athletic facilities were improved; all within the Ivy League code, but successful enough to raise the won-loss percentage of Quaker teams above .700. From 1972 to 1974, Penn had three winning football seasons in a row; it had only two others in the previous 20 years.

Each season, sports information directors at colleges and universities are paid to attract media attention to their school's football team, which in turn will encourage ticket sales. For places like Columbus, Ohio, and Lincoln, Nebraska, easy. But for losers? Meet innovative Kevin DeMarrais, who beats the publicity drums for Columbia. In his first nine football seasons at Morningside Heights in New York City , the Lions were losers for eight. So DeMarrais popped up with several hints to help other losing sports information directors to survive: (1) Play as many games as possible on the road and (2) an interesting angle can obscure the facts. "If you have a 5′ 6″ left-handed Chinese quarterback, nobody cares if he can throw or not," DeMarrais observed. "It used to be okay when Columbia lost a lot because New York had plenty of winners; nobody even noticed the Lions. But recently the Giants and Jets have failed as miserably as we have."

DeMarrais felt that things were looking up for 1977. Honest. "So you're seeing the light at the end of the tunnel?" he was asked.

"Right," he replied. "Hopefully it won't be the headlights of an oncoming truck."

In June 1976, Columbia coach Bill Campbell became a bridegroom. Later, he was asked how he liked married life.

"Fine," he said.

"How's your football team?"

"Married life is better."

Columbia celebrated its 100th year of football in 1970. One of the highlights of the centennial was to pick an all-time eleven. This involved sending out ballots to every living varsity "C" winner in the school's history. A total of 3,500 forms were dispatched. One of the top vote-getters was Walter Koppisch, an All-American halfback in 1924. All-American Bill Swiacki, the 1947 flash at end, was also on almost every Light Blue ballot; so was Bruce Gehrke, who played the other end of the Lions' wonderful team that year and went along with Swiacki to the New York Giants. Among the all-time Columbia backs in the voting were Sid Luckman, Lou Kusserow, Paul Governali, Gene Rossides, Marty Domres, and Tom Haggerty. The interior line, which never produced a bona fide All-American, offered the widest diversity. The darkest of dark horses was Al Ginepra, a 200-pound tackle who started on the 1954 team that went 1-8. Ginepra? Ben Spinelli remembered him. Ben played end for Princeton and later was an eastern college football official. "I'll never forget Ginepra," Spinelli said. "He was probably the meanest Ivy League player in history."

Inexplicably, there were very few votes for the 1915 Lions, the only undefeated Columbia team of record. The star was Howard Miller, who still holds the Light Blue field goal record (7) for a season. In a game against Lawrence Tech, he kicked four goals, and that record still stands. *The memory dims and the ardor dulls.*

Time marches on. A few summers ago, Mike Yeager, Columbia's 1975 cocaptain, and his roommate, linebacker Ray Rahamin, were sprinting up the steps of Baker Field, the Lions' antiquated stadium on the northern tip of Manhattan, when Rahamin suddenly drove one leg up to the knee through a rotten plank. Yeager was awestruck. "He just about fell *into* the stadium," Mike recalled. Columbia football was at rock bottom. But then Columbia began rebuilding: a new coaching staff, new players, a general stirring of optimism. After one of the team's rare touchdowns that season, a wearied Columbia voice drifted across near-deserted Baker Field: "All right, alumni, it's turned around. Time to bring out your checkbooks."

Founded in 1764 at Warren, Rhode Island, as Rhode Island College, the nation's seventh and New England's third oldest college, the school moved to Providence in 1770, and changed its name to Brown University, after Nicholas Brown, one of its main contributors. "It was not an accident that Brown University was founded under the leadership of the Baptists," wrote W.C. Bronson, a Brown historian. "During four decades of the eighteenth century, no fewer than 12 colleges were established. Most of these institutions were controlled by religious bodies: Harvard and Yale by the Congregationalists; the College of New Jersey (Princeton) by the Presbyterians; the University of Pennsylvania, King's College (Columbia), and William and Mary College by the Episcopalians; Rutgers College by the Reformed Dutch Church. It was natural that the Baptists also should desire a college of their own."

Over the years, Brown has maintained a strong tradition of dedication to both undergraduate (5,300) and graduate (1,425) education in the humanities, arts, and sciences. Today it has a 1-to-10 faculty-student ratio and offers its undergraduates opportunities to study with first-rate faculty who also teach at the graduate level. In 1974, the school accepted the first freshman class into its new seven-year medical program to become the first full-fledged medical school in the state.

When the Ivy League's Great Football De-emphasis came in 1956, the action seemed paradoxical to many Brown supporters, since the Bruins had been part of the very font of football dating back to 1878, had produced the towering names (John Heisman, Tuss McLaughry, Fritz Pollard, Eddie Robinson, Bill Sprackling, Wallace Wade, and Rip Engle); the unforgettable "Iron Men" eleven of 1926, the only unconquered team in Brown history; the 1915 team, participants in the 1916 Rose Bowl, the first squad from the East to play in the Pasadena New Year's Day classic; the championship teams of 1916, 1918, 1926, and 1932. Now all of this proud history was shunted aside, with the quality of football at Providence withering to such a degree that in the next 19 years of the Ivy League's official existence, the Bruins suffered through 13 losing seasons and finished last in the conference standings no fewer than 10 times. Athletes who wore the Brown and White went through the double shock of attending a college that for the better part of two decades had been the doormat of the Ivy League and found themselves in an environment that best could be described as academic, liberated, and somewhat antijock.

*The 174 career points scored by All-America halfback Dave Fultz in the mid-1890s remain an all-time high at Brown. He later played major league baseball, 1898–1905, with the Phillies, Orioles, Athletics, and Yankees, and had a .275 lifetime batting average as an outfielder-infielder.*

Dick Gerken, 6′2″, 210-pound, All-Ivy defensive end at Cornell in the mid-1960s and a history major who went on to earn a law degree at the University of Connecticut, remembers how everybody looked down on Brown football teams. "We looked at them as the Have-nots of the Ivies," he said. "We always regarded the Brown game as an opportunity to win one and stick it to 'em—and, besides, who the hell wants to go to school in Providence! Contempt, sure. The same went for Columbia. It was a fellow New York State school, but plagued with the curse of New York City. I always felt that if you were going to go to school in New York—well, Fordham and St. John's were *the* places to go, not Columbia. I remember they had to bus the players all the way up to Baker's 'dust bowl' for practice. That's got to be the poorest football stadium in the Ivy League. Then there's Columbia's losing tradition! So who the devil wants to go to Columbia? Another negative vote against the Light Blue was those powder blue suits they wore. Can you imagine running around in full view of the public in one of those pansy suits? And that damned song their cheerleaders sang: *'C-O-L-U-M-B-I-A . . . Who owns New York?'* Tra-la-la. Just awful.

"Cornell? I always felt somewhat defensive about Cornell. It's just as fine a school as any in the league. I have some warm spots for Ithaca, some cold ones, too. Cornell, I know, was viewed by the other Ivies as the cow college, the ag school, a bunch of farmers from upstate New York, a hotel administration school, a 'gut' school, easy to get through, which was not true. Opponents would chide us by saying we settled for Cornell because we couldn't get into Harvard, Yale, Princeton, or Dartmouth. Bunk!

"Tell a Dartmouth man that he didn't belong with the Big Three and he'd tell you to go soak your head. Well, the last time I played at Memorial Field in Hanover, there were ticket-takers but no ushers. The hot dog and soft drink vendors were children 8 to 12. And the water boy was a girl. The stadium holds only 21,416. But I must confess, Dartmouth does turn out great football teams, which, after all, is what your book is all about.

"My memories of Dartmouth are that the Green had great spirit, great football tradition. But it was located up in backwoods country and was totally male-oriented. I remember they'd come down out of the northwoods in their green jackets, proud as peacocks, and we loved nothing more than to knock their blocks off on the football field. I always sized up Dartmouth this way—quite frankly, I'd have loved playing for them, but I really wouldn't have wanted to go to school there because I preferred a coeducational school, even if the three-to-one ratio of coeds at Cornell was not precisely pinup types. At Hanover, the guys had to travel two hours to find a girl, and who needed that? I wanted to enjoy college life—I didn't sign up for a monastery.

"What can you say about Pennsylvania? No one ever talks about Pennsylvania. Why, outsiders even confuse the Quakers for the Nittany Lions of Penn State, at the other end of the state. But University of Pennsylvania, a private school in Philadelphia, is a super school academically, with a marvelous graduate business school and an excellent law school. Penn and Cornell have a lot in common in that they are both coeducational with fine academic traditions.

"Unfortunately, I missed out on those grand old slam-bang football classics between Penn and Cornell, because this ancient rivalry had pretty much petered out by the time I got to Ithaca. As a matter of fact, I played in the last of those Penn-Cornell Thanksgiving Day traditionals at Franklin Field. The game drew only 10,500.

"Harvard—now there's a school I'd have enjoyed; America's oldest college, with its famous Yaad where General George Washington's troops were quartered. A simply superb university. You had to feel a fantastic pleasure anytime you beat Harvard. They were always well coached, neatly attired in their trim Crimson uniforms—what a contrast to the Columbia Lions in their ragtag baby blue suits! It was always a special thrill to play in Harvard Stadium. You could almost feel the ghosts of Charlie Brickley, Eddie Casey, Percy Haughton, Eddie Mahan, and the like hovering over the field.

"As for Princeton, they were the prep school boys. We always regarded them as even more elitist than Harvard and Yale. What satisfaction it would have been to beat them. I say 'would have been' because we never defeated the Tigers while I was at Cornell. Princeton was still using the single wing, and Coach Dick Colman always seemed to show up with a million halfbacks. The sky rained Princeton tailbacks. We'd travel down to Palmer Stadium—what a magnificent field to play on, well-kept, well-manicured—and Old Nassau bore a startling resemblance to our own campus, with those marvelous old brick buildings crawling with ivy and history. Princeton had the most loyal, loud-mouthed Old Grads of all the Ivy League, dressed on game day in their orange and black ties, tweed sport jackets, clinging to their cowbells and thirsting for blood. I remember hearing about Pinky Baker, a member of Princeton's class of 1922. He was a superfan. He went to all the Princeton practices, I heard, including the freshmen's. He even carried a cowbell to lacrosse games. Whenever we played at Palmer Stadium, the whole place seemed to be packed with Pinky Bakers, they made so much noise.

"Last, but not least, was Yale. In many ways, the Elis were the most obnoxious, the most conceited in the conference. *There was no school but Yale!* Oh, how we took dead aim on the Bulldogs. The fact that I grew up in their backyard eliminated any possibility of going to school in New Haven. Like so many young guys, I wanted to get away from home, to stretch my wings, when I graduated from Rippowam High School, so Yale was out and Cornell was in. Quite a few athletes from Connecticut crossed the state line to Ithaca, which was why the Yale game always had special meaning for us each season."

From such incendiary comments do ancient football rivalries live on.

When you think of Ivy League football, you also think of Colgate, a nonmember but long united by a common bond of academic standards, social prestige, historical background, and "old tie" traditions. One is particularly reminded of Coach Andy Kerr, whose 1932 Colgate varsity was undefeated, untied, unscored on—and uninvited to the Rose Bowl. Andy was the arch-apostle of the lateral pass. In fact, he was the first coach to stress the downfield lateral, a rugby caper that revolutionized offense. It was a much more sophisticated offense than Colgate played in the old days. One of the Red Raiders' more successful scoring maneuvers against Cornell back in the Stone Age was called the "dust formation" play. Dust formation? Never heard of it. How did it work?

"Well," explained an old-timer, "the quarterback yelled 'dust formation,' and this fellow got back and when the ball was hiked to him, all the linemen threw dust in the opponents' eyes. The play was good for a lot of touchdowns."

"Was there any way to defense against it?"

"Yes."

"How?"

"Pray for rain."

# *Football the Summa Cum Laude Way*

Ask an Ivy League supporter about the caliber of football played in the conference and the conversation gets somewhat defensive, with assurances that it is good football, that Dartmouth and Yale and Harvard in their peak years could certainly perform respectably against Ohio State or Nebraska or Alabama or anybody else, and that Ivy football, after all, is played by *students.*

"In many ways, the Ivy League is still football at its best," Chet LaRoche said recently. "It's still amateur *college* football."

Opinions of the Ivies are as varied as football formations.

"Ivy teams have two things going for them that make them fun to watch," said John O. Field of Chestnut Hill, Massachusetts. "First, a solid corps of scholar-athletes from all over the country, providing at least strong first team units, and, second, some of the most innovative and able coaches at the college level. To cite one example, Joe Restic and his assistants at Harvard produce teams that play highly sophisticated, wide-open football on both sides of the line. Cynics will insist that the Ivy League is bush. In a way, they are right. Other conferences and teams are better. But the Ivy game is unabashedly (and proudly) amateur, in contrast to the semipro orientation of the 'big time.' "

Whit Hillyer, of Evanston, Illinois, said he was a trifle tired of this holier-than-thou Ivy brainwashing, the constant harping on hoary age and tradition. "Just for openers," he said, "Cornell was founded in 1865, its first president, Dr. Andrew White, having previously served as a professor of history at the University of Michigan. Re the simon-pure Ivy recruiting, don't let those Old Grads put you on. The Big Ten certainly has overemphasized football, but the Ivy League regularly takes fine high school players from many areas. The caliber of Ivy gridders is shown by such pros as Mike Pyle, Ed Marinaro, Calvin Hill, Dick Jauron, the luckless Pat McInally, and, earlier, Chuck Bednarik. Let Ivy Leaguers remember that a jock usually is a jock anywhere—except, perhaps at MIT and the University of Chicago."

For the first 50 years, Ivy League teams played the best football in America, until the superiority started moving westward and southward. Now, of course, there isn't the frenzy of the football scene at the eight schools that you will find at Alabama, Oklahoma, or Ohio State. Several years ago, for instance, the Harvard-Dartmouth freshman game had to be delayed two hours while 31 members of the Harvard squad took an economics test in a Dartmouth classroom. The examination had been scheduled for 1 p.m. by the Cambridge profs, who made only one concession, moving it up to Hanover so the game would not have to be canceled.

In 1974, Harvard's best defensive back, Mike Page, traveled with the team as usual down to New York for the Columbia game, but he didn't play. He was excused to take the law board examinations.

Other Ivy League students were equally ambivalent. On the morning after the big freshman game—three hours before the Harvard-Dartmouth varsity game—50 or 60 Dartmouth underclassmen were still hitting the books in Baker Library. Yet, under questioning most said that they intended to make the opening kickoff, or at least much of the game. And that may define intercollegiate football, Ivy-style. It isn't the biggest thing on campus, but, like match classes and rock concerts, it has a place. It belongs.

In terms of intrinsic football interest, however, it could be said that Ivy teams put on the best show in the country. Knowledgeable coaches never disparage the abilities of an Ivy League team. John Pont, who coached Yale before moving on to Indiana and Northwestern, feels that of the 22 starters on the average Ivy League team, five to seven could move into starting positions on a Big Ten team. "The difference is with the other people," he said. "A football power like Alabama or Nebraska or Oklahoma can play 50 people in a game without losing much potential. But that's certainly not the case in the Ivy League."

No longer is it a surprise when an Ivy League player turns up in the professional ranks. A few years ago, the appearance of one was greeted by considerable joshing and a certain amount of squinting, especially on the part of the veterans, as if something odd, and perhaps dainty, had appeared on the practice field. "Is that seven-man football you play back there at Cornell?" Ed Marinaro was asked when he first joined the Minnesota Vikings. "Or is it touch?"

Dick Jauron, who went from Yale to the Detroit Lions, remembered how everyone seemed a little bit bigger, faster, and stronger than he believed possible. "The football field seemed to shrink," he said. "The people on it took up so much more room. Of course, that's the impression no matter where you've come from. It's just more noticeable if you've come from the Ivy League."

Calvin Hill, who graduated from Yale and starred for Dallas before jumping to the now-defunct World Football League's (WFL) Hawaii team and then the Washington Redskins, remembers that his biggest surprise going into the pros was how much time he suddenly had to concentrate on football. "It seemed such a luxury," he said. "At Yale you had two hours of football, and that was all, and then you had to start thinking whether the Civil War was inevitable, because that was what you were going to be quizzed on in a classroom. But for many others in pro ball, going to camp was no surprise at all, because in their college there was nothing else but football. That's very sad. They can't believe that 100 percent of the Ivy League college teams actually graduate."

Halfback Hill makes an interesting point. Critics of college football have for years complained that too many players fail to complete their education. For example, according to a survey of 1975 professional teams by Richard Coleman of Los Angeles, only 30 of 135 Big Eight players in professional football had received degrees. Colorado and Oklahoma State were the worst Big Eight schools in this respect; only three of the 34 pro players from those two universities had graduated. And no major conference, outside the Ivies, could claim that even half its players in 1976 pro ball had completed their college studies. But there were exceptions. The University of California had 12 players in pro football, and 10 of them had graduated. Boston College had nine graduates among its 11 pros. Standing alone at the top of the academic heap was Notre Dame. There were 24 Irish in pro football at the time of the survey—and everyone of them had his degree.

What Ed Marinaro found most depressing is what happens to players who come out of the Big Ten or the Big Eight, where football influences everything, and then don't make it in the pros. "It's a terrible blow to their egos because they can't adjust," he said. "They don't know anything else."

When I was writing the book *Big Ten Football*, I stopped off at Minneapolis and talked to Otis Dypwick, for 31 years sports information director at the University of Minnesota. After all those years, he had soured on Big Ten football. "It's no longer a team game," he told me. "Now they play only for themselves. They're not here for a degree. They are here only to get ready for the NFL. Their college is nothing but football."

In 1949, before the Ivy League ban on participation in postseason all-star games, Harvard's Howie Houston played for the East in the annual Shrine game in San Francisco. "I remember that my teammates asked me what I got to play football at Harvard—room, board, tuition, books, part-time job, pin money, car, and such," he said. "I don't think they believed me when I said I didn't get anything—and I'm sure they didn't believe me when I added that I had to pay a fee in order to participate in athletics."

Many athletes who eventually enrolled at Harvard were subject to pressure from big-time schools. Many colleges were openly bidding for players. "A great many of us felt that the so-called big-time schools were exploiting the player," said

Dick Clasby, one of Harvard's greatest backs. "That's the reason we came to Harvard. I don't know anyone who regrets the decision."

Another example of a big-time college prospect preferring the low-key Ivy League was lineman Carl Barasich, 6′4″, 255 pounds, Princeton's All-Ivy offensive tackle in 1972. Co-winner of the John P. Poe Memorial Trophy, Carl was drafted in the 11th round by the Cleveland Browns after graduation and played swing tackle for three years. The first Ivy Leaguer ever to play for the Browns, he appeared in 42 straight games before being picked up by the Seattle Seahawks in the 1976 expansion draft. "I loved Ivy League football," Carl said. "There was no pressure. We were able to concentrate on our studies. At football factories like Ohio State, Nebraska, and Southern Cal, it's do or die. It was more fun at Princeton, where the game had a savor all its own. A game at Palmer Stadium was more than just a game and a score, it was a pilgrimage and a picnic, too, filled with the color of autumn and the noise of Princeton's highly polished brass band. Ah, those wonderful station wagon tailgate lunches along the shores of Lake Carnegie, where reminiscing crowds gathered hours before the game, and then followed the band to cheer the team."

It is testimony to their sangfroid that Ivy Leaguers don't give a damn what the nonamateurs think about the mutually exclusive brand of football they play in those Edwardian stadiums on those colonial campuses. While pigskin Philistines may protest that the Ivies are merely bush, the cloistered scholar-athletes will suggest in rebuttal that it is not so much how you play the game as how it comes out. Or something like that.

The Ivies limit their schedule to only nine games, seven of which they play against each other. They eschew spring football, and they do not demand of their players that they devote hours better spent absorbing Hegelian dialectic to reviewing game films or committing playbooks by rote. What they mainly offer is close, spirited competition, flavored occasionally by the performances of a sprinkling of genuine All-America candidates. Ivy Leaguers proved long ago that they can make it as pros. It is only the Ivy philosophy that confines them.

"There are some very good athletes in this league," said Coach Harry Gamble of Penn, a doctor of education, "but if they had to put in the practice time the big-time football schools require, they wouldn't survive academically. Our players are highly respected by the faculty on campus because they are carrying the full academic load and participating in football besides. That requires a good deal of character."

Bob Blackman, who went from Dartmouth to Illinois, says that he once had 16 high school valedictorians turned away at Dartmouth. "Contacts are many in the Ivy League, but admissions are few," he testified. "The schools always have been sympathetic to the needs of the football coach, but so are they sympathetic to piccolo players and other campus necessities." Blackman recalls that when he was at Hanover it was not at all unusual the week before a big game for some of the players to miss afternoon practices because of labs. "I know coaches who complain about not having had all their boys together for all the practices before a big game," he said. "Well, ours were *never* together at Dartmouth."

This coaching disadvantage was not restricted to Dartmouth. Carm Cozza had to live with similar frustrations at New Haven. The old Yale coach once had a big tackle named Matt Jordan. Matt was a farm boy from out in Minnesota, one of 11 kids, and there were nights when he didn't climb down off his tractor until 10 o'clock. Matt had muscles like a weightlifter, immensely strong. It was a good thing he was. "There was one night when Matt, after a hard workout on the practice field, studied until 1 A.M., got up again at 4 A.M. to check his lab experiments on the mating of fruit flies, went to my office to study game films until after 9 A.M., then went off to class, and then football practice again."

Willie Bogan, a tall, fast safetyman whose authentic credentials impressed pro scouts mightily in 1970, considered the Dartmouth football program as secondary when he was in school there. "We weren't forced to play or stay on the team," he said. "It was a matter of your own choice. Of course, I never tried to quit, either."

When it came to outside interests, few could equal those of Yale quarterback Joe Massey. As a freshman, Massey chose to sing in the glee club rather than play football. But then his voice changed in 1970, and he guided the Yale offense through a 7-2-0 season.

Take an Ivy League boy out of the library or the laboratory or the glee club and he will prove as testy an antagonist as any brute from the wheatfields. "We took the game as seriously as anyone," emphasized 1973 Harvard captain Dave St. Pierre, who pursued a demanding premedical course while in school. "We practiced just as hard when we were out there and we played just as hard. We didn't enroll in the Ivy League to escape competition."

The difference may be that the Ivy Leaguer will actually *enjoy* the game more, and for the simple reason that he is playing it for fun, not necessarily to fulfill the provisions of an athletic scholarship or to serve an apprenticeship before being called up to the National Football League.

"The time we gave to football was our own," said 1973 Harvard quarterback Jim Stoeckel, a Rhodes scholarship candidate who was nearly as brilliant on the field as in the classroom.

"I think there is more genuine dedication in the Ivy League because the boys are on the field by choice," added Penn's coach Gamble. "They don't have to play football for fear of losing a scholarship. They just want to play. I'm not saying that isn't true elsewhere, but whereas you might get 90 percent dedication out of a squad in a big-time football school, here you get 100 percent."

Harvard coach Joe Restic, who came down to Cambridge from the Hamilton Tiger-Cats, whom he coached to a division championship in the Canadian Football League in 1970, is a gaunt, tough-looking ex-pro player who seems to be the antithesis of an Ivy League mentor. But he has a master's degree in education, is an accomplished teacher, and feels keenly his responsibilities to the young savants in his charge. And he is not in the least frustrated as a football technician. His teams have run out of as many as 16 different offensive sets, including the spreads favored by the pros and the veers and wishbones now so fashionable among the major league collegians. Still, he has never lost sight of the forest.

"I want football to be an experience for these boys, not a life," he said. "I know that at Harvard I am coaching youngsters who will someday be leaders. If I can help them along the way, I've done my job."

Restic is a most generous coach. One season he awarded 54 varsity letters. To some, all of this may smack of the sort of holier-than-thou superciliousness they have come to expect from the Ivies. And yet even in these amoral times it seems to work. Purity is not always tedious.

# *Storming Those Ivy Gates*

When the American Football Coaches Association holds its annual conference, the Ivy League coaches are often left standing off by themselves. The other coaches think of them as men beset with grave problems and better left alone. They cannot imagine a college coach in these modern times unable to entice a fleet prospective All-American with the sort of athletic scholarships that have become almost routine lures elsewhere.

The Ivy schools offer scholarships only on the basis of an academically qualified student's need. It costs about $6,000 a year on the average to go to one of the Ivy League colleges. If a student applies for a scholarship, his parents must reveal their financial souls by filling out what is called a Parents Confidential Statement form, which is fed into a computer at Princeton, New Jersey, to determine how large a grant the student will get. Even if he gets a scholarship, an Ivy League student must earn about $1,500 on his own by waiting on tables in the dining halls, working in the library, and such. Dick Kazmaier, now president of the National Football Foundation and Hall of Fame and one of the most eulogized names in Princeton history, waited on tables and drove a laundry truck to supplement his scholarship, as a for instance. And since a year at Princeton in 1951 cost a minimum of $1,700, Dick also had to work every summer to get more money for school.

Bill Campbell, the Columbia coach, testified that he lost several hot prospects in 1976 because they could not afford *not* to accept an athletic scholarship from one of the colleges where football is top priority. He lost others because they wanted to play in front of 70,000 fans each Saturday afternoon. When they are offered a full football grant to go to a place where the focus is sharply on the game, it is simply too difficult to justify turning it down. An Ivy League coach, on the other hand, can show his prospect his campus, show him what the educational advantages are, and the future possibilities—and it's just plain frustrating because he knows the picture that the recruit is probably toting around in his head.

The difference between Ivy League football and Big Ten football, for example, is that in most of the Big Ten schools the admissions department takes what the athletic department gives them, whereas in the Ivy League the athletic department does what it can with what the admissions people provide.

"At Michigan State," grinned former Spartan coach Duffy Daugherty, "football scholarships are also based on need—how much does the coach need him?"

Swift-footed end Pat McInally, the first All-American from Harvard (1974) since 1941 when Chub Peabody, a 185-pound guard, was selected, sat down with a pencil and figured out that a National Collegiate Athletic Association (NCAA) football scholarship was worth 60 cents an hour to its recipients, which in most cases committed them to little else than playing football. He bristled with figures that supported his despair at the imbalance he felt existed between football and education at most NCAA colleges. "It's awful," he said. "The priorities are all wrong. Without being too sanctimonious, at college I never liked being singled out as a football player, but as someone who played football."

Cornell's Dick Gerken felt much the same way. "It wasn't hard establishing my priorities at school," the now Chicago attorney said. "I once figured out that it was costing my family $10 an hour to keep me in Cornell. I couldn't afford *not* to hit the books."

The recruiting of big-time college football prospects is usually a tedious and debilitating business, one that reduces many head coaches to clipboard-toting Willy Lomans. Proof that it need not be that way is provided by D. Keith Mano, a self-described "camp follower" of Columbia football. Mano became a big-time recruiter by association when he shadowed Penn State coach Joe Paterno several years ago. "There's really no comparison between the kind of kids Paterno recruits and the ones who wind up at Columbia," Mano said.

Mano's dedication to Columbia football put him in a very select group in 1974, since the Lions (2-7) drew an average of only 4,835 fans per game. In an attempt to buoy Columbia's football fortunes, Mano has logged countless hours scouring high school fields near his Blooming Grove, New York, home for good players interested in going to his alma mater. Since the Ivy League awards scholarships only on the basis of need, Mano faces a dilemma involving players of middle-class backgrounds never encountered by Coach Paterno. "To play football for Columbia, a kid either has to be very rich and very intelligent, which is rare, or very intelligent and very poor, which is also rare," said Mano. But the quest goes on.

As an undergraduate Mano never set foot in Baker Field. His involvement with the Lions' football program evolved from an incident in the spring of 1968, when he returned to Columbia to protest the takeover of the school's administration building by radicals. One day he found himself watching the demonstrators throw pickle jars at a building. They were trying to put them through the windows, but because most liberals seem to lack the necessary motor skills to throw straight, the jars kept shattering against the walls. Suddenly a squad of New York police arrived, mistook Mano for a demonstrator and hustled him off to jail. He had borrowed a jacket from a friend right before the cops came, and in the confusion he lost track of him. Later, Mano and his friend arranged to meet at a Harvard-Columbia game so Mano could return the jacket. He has been a Columbia football groupie ever since.

When Mano, a novelist, is not working on a book or helping to operate the family cement business, he is often composing reports for Bill Campbell, the Columbia coach. Sometimes he will spend as much as a week writing a 20-page assessment of kids in his area, stuff so complicated that even Coach Campbell has trouble understanding it. "Keith doesn't live in a great area for football talent," said Campbell. "Still he embellishes every scouting report with incredible detail. He's been a real help to us, but to be quite honest, I don't exactly know where he came from. He just appeared one day."

° ° °

Traditionally, Ivy League schools are thought of as bastions to be stormed by ambitious students, and so in a way they still are. But the view from within is quite different. In the admissions offices, the language suggests a corporation with a product to sell. In the parlance of Madison Avenue, they talk about "our market" and "our yield." They are competing for honor students. And the number of first-rate students to choose from is smaller than you might think. "You just don't walk up and enroll at Yale," said Bob Hall, who was director of athletics at New Haven in the early 1950s. "When I was there, I recall, only 950 freshmen were selected out of every 4,000 applicants. We made no concessions to athletes. If there was anything left of a promising halfback after he completed the scholastic plugging, the coaches could have it. At Yale, the coaches always sat at the second table. They got what was left after everybody else was through with the boys."

In the years since Hall was at Yale, Scholastic Aptitude Test scores have dropped nationally. Of more than one million high school seniors who take the standard examinations annually, only 15,000 score in the upper range in the verbal section, which is between 700 and 800. Academically, these students constitute much of the Ivy League's desirable "market." At Brown, for example, the average verbal S.A.T. is 630, down from 680. At Harvard, the average is down to 674.

But the undergraduate population is also determined by a more homely consideration than intelligence. There is the question of whether a student can afford to go to an Ivy League school. More than 65 percent of the Brown students pay, as they say, "the full fare," or $6,460 annually. The university estimates that the average income for all families with students at Brown, including those receiving aid, is more than $30,000. For the majority who are not on scholarship, a reasonable guess puts the average income closer to $50,000.

The dominant style at Brown is modesty about whatever privileges life has given one. Talking with Matthew Wald, a Brown *Daily Herald* editor in 1976, about financial aid, he was asked if he himself was on scholarship. "No," he said. "My dad got a promotion a while ago and that made it easier for me to come here."

"Oh? What does he do?"

"He's president of NBC News."

Although the Columbia student body of the 1960s may have projected a radical image on the public mind's eye, in its heart the institution was not intrinsically different from what it ever was, nor is it still. Columbia remains a select Ivy League school dedicated to educating an elite. The question that prospective students in the 1970s ask themselves is "How do you get in?" Despite the cost ($6,450 a year), some 1,400 of 3,500 applicants were accepted for 1976–77. Compared with 20 percent of Harvard's admittees, 47 percent of Columbia's decided to go somewhere else, in many cases another Ivy League college, leaving a freshman class of 700. How did the 1,400 get chosen? More pointedly, who made it, who didn't, and why?

Essentially, seven men are responsible for deciding who gets into Columbia. They are the admissions staff, the smallest in the Ivy League. Brown's is the next smallest with 11, and Harvard has 22 admissions people. Although Columbia faculty, alumni, and undergraduates all enter into the procedures at various points, the admissions staff ultimately makes the crucial decisions about individual candidates. All seven are Columbia graduates. Two have had parochial school affiliations, three were school athletes, five majored or did graduate work in English, four have teaching experience. Their mandate is: "We are looking for students who care about ideas, books, scientific discoveries. We are holding the line on standards that apparently other schools have abandoned."

Applicants to Columbia—as well as the rest of the Ivies—are subject to very rigorous examinations. Say, for example, that you were an excellent football player in high school and you want to go to Columbia. You have sent in your application data, containing an application form, a self-descriptive essay, a photograph, financial aid information, a transcript of high school grades, two Standard Aptitude Test scores (indicating verbal and quantitative skills), achievement test scores (indicating proficiency in specific academic subjects), comments by interviewers, recommendations from teachers and others. A member of the admissions staff has written a summary recommendation for you and assigned you three scores between 5 and 1; a score for academic talent, non-academic talent (including strength of character), and an overall score. He has sent all this material on to at least one other admissions officer, undergraduate, faculty member, or staff interviewer for an additional opinion.

In making a decision about you, the admissions committee is influenced by several factors. Do you meet the academic standards? A stiff required freshman curriculum, including two blockbuster courses in contemporary civilization and the humanities, demand that they select candidates with well-developed conceptual and writing skills. And because the cost structure, necessitating increased student subsidies, places a considerable strain on Columbia's resources (49 percent of 1975's entering freshmen received aid), they are forced to view no-aid candidates or those eligible for state aid more favorably.

Somewhere among all these factors, the collective personality, experience, and outlook of the decision-makers also operates.

As the admissions committee reviews your data, you are given two ratings: one (A, A-, B+ or B), indicating your attractiveness to Columbia, is also used by the financial aid people to guide them in making up aid packages; the other (all-around, Columbia connection; talent, sports; and so on) would ultimately yield a character profile of you.

How do you stack up? Well, you are the fourth of five children from a working-class family in Ohio. You were recruited by a preparatory school as a quarterback and won all-state honors. Many colleges attempted to recruit you. However, you want eventually to attend medical school, and you are convinced that only Harvard's or Columbia's pre-med programs will successfully prepare you. Thus, you enrolled in yet another prep school for a year of postgraduate study. Your record in the two competitive preparatory programs is mediocre. If rejected by Columbia, you will probably attend a state college where pre-med study is less competitive, and where your football contributions might recommend you to a state university medical school.

"Truthfully, at a state school, the pressure of the football program would never allow him to fulfill his pre-med requirements," a member of the Columbia admissions committee points out to the rest of the screening staff. "He'll have a better chance at medical school from here, where he will be able to concentrate on his studies and still be able to play football."

"Do we want to set a pattern by taking a kid this marginal this early?" another member asks.

The majority vote yes. Verdict: Admit. B+. Talent: Football.

Another prime football prospect—let's call him Jess Smith—is not so fortunate. He received marginal rejection scores from two committee members. In his postgraduate year at his prep school in New England, he ranked in the top half of his class while taking a light load. His S.A.T. scores are 530 and 600. In his essay, he wrote: "At present my leanings are toward a mathematical concentration within the scope of business . . . Auto mechanics is my most recent outside interest." The movie *Walking Tall* was a favorite film. Most important of all, he stood six-feet-tall and tipped the scales at 240.

"He should be slow," wrote the second reader.

"You know, this one will be brought up again later by the football coaches," a committeeman said.

Jess Smith: "Reject."

In the spring of 1965, the Yale athletic department sent questionnaires to the parents of all prospective freshman athletes. One candidate was Calvin Hill, of Riverdale Country Day School in the Bronx.

"As a small boy," replied his father, "Calvin was always interested in reading and collecting books and keeping himself physically fit, eating the right foods and exercising daily."

"Why does he want to come to Yale?"

"Because we feel it is one of the finest universities in the U.S.A."

It is not known how much Yale knew about the Hills, but the answer was perfect. Verdict: Admit. Actually, from the standpoint of Coach Carmen Cozza, the factors that weighed most heavily in Calvin's favor were that he stood 6-3, weighed over 200, ran the 40-yard dash in 4.4, and was two-time New York City All-Metropolitan in both football and basketball. The fact that he had the candlepower behind the horsepower that moved the football was pure bonus.

Recently, I asked Jack DeGange, director of sports information at Dartmouth, what percentage of Big Green football players graduate. Jack said that of those who complete four years of competition—and in any program this is probably 25 to 30 percent of those who start out as freshman team members—the figure at Dartmouth is 98 to 99 percent. "I discussed this with Coach Jake Crouthamel," DeGange said, "and he can't think of anyone who hasn't been competing into his senior year and hasn't received his degree. As for the screening of frosh football candidates, they are regarded just like any other freshman at Dartmouth. The decision on admission rests with the Office of Admissions. The goal of the Admissions Office is to develop a frosh class that has the range of interests and diversification that meets the needs of the total community of Dartmouth College. There is input from the teachers, coaches, and so forth at the secondary level, and at Dartmouth—and through the Ivy League—there is additional input that generates from interviews by admissions officers or alumni enrollment workers in all areas of the country, as well as, in the case of athletes, the input from coaches. All information is reviewed and weighed as a package. Although the Ivy League indeed does recruit, the difference is that a candidate must *want* to come to an Ivy institution, because in the total scheme it will cost him or her money for an education. Even if a student gets full financial aid, a part of that will be in the form of loans and campus jobs."

Although Ivy League teams are no longer candidates for the National Championship, there is a great deal to be said for their approach to the game. By and large, Ivy League teams have always played spirited, ultraintelligent football, and there is a perfectly reasonable argument that, year in and year out, their brand of football is the most consistently entertaining, amateur or professional, played anywhere in the country. To be honest, their matches are all that a fan could ask for—unpredictable, frequently high scoring, nearly always close, and rare manifestations of that tired adage that "on any given Saturday. . . ."

Pat McInally, the Harvard All-American end who was drafted by the Cincinnati Bengals, is a great Ivy booster. "I'll tell you one thing about the Ivy League," he said. "It's the most *competitive* conference in the country. In the Big Ten or the Pacific Eight, for example, it always works out that during the year only one or two good competitive games are played, Michigan-Ohio State and USC-UCLA. The rest are often walkovers for one team or another. But in the Ivy League, you can be assured that each team will have four or five games on its schedule that will go down to the wire."

To illustrate his point, McInally had only to mention the 1976 Harvard-Cornell game. The unbeaten Cantabs, victors over Columbia, Massachusetts, and Boston U., were heavy favorites over the winless Big Red. The game was played at Cambridge, and the teams had to contend with gusty winds, heavy rains, and turf turned to muck. In fact, the winds were so strong that they caused the goalposts at the open end of the field to sway. The oddest turn of events came when Dave Johnson, the Cornell punter, unable to kick because of an errant center snap, sped 75 yards for the only touchdown of the game. Final score: Cornell 9, Harvard 3.

It figured.

# *The Stage Is Set*

In 1869, there was a good road between Nassau Hall and New Brunswick, just 20 New Jersey miles to the north, and perhaps that explains it. In any case, one afternoon 25 students from Old Nassau (the name was not changed to Princeton until 1896) ran onto a field with a similar number of undergraduates from Rutgers, and they all appeared to go berserk. What occurred that day had some of the elements of rugger, bearbaiting, and Indian massacre—all over the possession of an improperly shaped ball. Later, there was an old cowboy named Ike from west Texas whose version of what football was all about has become a classic.

"They's a bunch of fellers in funny rig out on this here field," Ike explained to fellow cowpokes back on the ranch. "An' they's a guy in a cook's outfit totin' a pig bladder tha's been blowed up and kivvered all around with cowhide. Well, these fellers all spreads out over the field and the cook puts the bladder on the ground and then one feller comes a-runnin' and kicks that bladder a helluva kick, clean up in the air. When it comes down they put it on the ground again. Then one great big feller walks up to the bladder and bends over like as if he's gonna pick it up. He hardly no mor'n gits his hands on it when a little feller comes creepin' up behind him, all bent over, and this little feller gits closer and all of a sudden the little feller bites that big feller right square on the butt and it turns into the gol-dangest fight you ever saw in yore life!"

Improbable as it seemed, fall Saturday afternoons in the United States were done for. So was the era of good feeling between Old Nassau and Rutgers.

Of course, it took more minds than just those at the two New Jersey schools to develop college football into the slightly paranoid religion it has become—a game watched by paying millions who worship a Heisman winner one season and fire his jolly old coach the next. Harvard and Yale had much to do with its early sophistication. Without them we might never had had the scoring we know, the snapback, 11 men to a side, or tailgate picnics outside the stadium before a game.

Specifically, Knute Rockne was once asked where his highly maneuverable Notre Dame shift came from. "Yale," he confessed. "All football comes from Yale." The game was born and brought up at Yale. Yale men carried it to all parts of the country. From 1872 through 1909, Yale was almost invariably the Big Three (Yale, Harvard, Princeton), Eastern, and National champions. As football spread and it was no longer possible for any one team, or one section, to dominate, Yale, on occasion, continued to come up with standout teams: 1916, 1923, 1924, 1927, 1931, 1936, 1937, 1944, and 1946.

When former Notre Dame star Harry Mehre was coaching at Georgia, he said, "I'd rather beat any team in the country than Yale. For to me and most of us, Yale means American football." Michigan's Fielding Yost echoed the Mehre sentiments. "Walter Camp and Yale *are* football," Hurry-Up said. "Yale was the first to have the true feel of the game, a game which means spirit, body contact, and team play, all the finest elements of competition. Of course, many others have come along since, but it was Yale that set the earlier pace."

In the 18 seasons from 1883 to 1900, Yale lost only 9 games (6 to Princeton, 2 to Harvard, and 1 to Columbia), while winning 197. Three of its teams (1888, 1891, and 1892), held all opponents scoreless, while running up a total of 1,617 points, one team (1886) yielded only a field goal, and another (1883) a lone safety. Seven perfect seasons and four marred only by ties. For sustained excellence over an entire generation, Yale stood unmatched, but its perennial challenger, Princeton, fashioned quite a record of its own. The Tigers won 175 of 191 games, including three perfect seasons and four marred only by a tie. Their only nemesis was Yale—10 wins to 6 and 2 ties—and nearly always the meeting between the two teams marked the final game of the year for both. In that era anyway, Yale-Princeton was The Game, not Yale-Harvard.

To those who watch and study college football as closely as they do their checkbooks and who devote a great deal of time to genuflecting before its shrines, the name of Walter Chauncey Camp can hardly be avoided when the subject of its early development is raised. Walter Camp belongs to American history as the "Father of Football," the great architect of the game. His credentials are imposing: As a Yale undergraduate, he played football for seven years, 1876–1882, was captain for three years, and Yale's first head coach, 1888–1892.

The son of a school principal, Camp stood 6-feet-tall and weighed 157 pounds when he enrolled at Yale in 1876 as a 17-year-old freshman. Despite his callow youth, he was good enough to make Captain-elect Gene Baker's varsity. Walter was fiercely attracted to the running-tackling game. The length of the field between goal lines was 110 yards, not 100 as it is now. That made longer runs possible. There were no 5-yard stripelines running across the field, no linesmen, and no line sticks. The referee kept track of distance just by dropping a handkerchief where he estimated the ball was last in action. The players of both sides would slyly try to move the handkerchief while some teammate engaged the referee in a discussion of the rules to distract him.

There was none of this platoon business. Players had to go both ways. The teams carried only four substitutes, even though they sometimes scheduled games two or three days in succession. There were 45 minutes to a half, not 30 as now, and the old game had not yet been chopped up into quarters. Football was truly a game for iron men. Once the game was under way, a player could not leave unless he was hurt, but a team soon learned how to avoid that rule—the captain simply whispered to one of his teammates, "Get your arm hurt, or something," whenever he wanted to bring in a fresh player. Once, when John W. Heisman was playing for Penn in 1888, his captain turned to him between scrimmages and ordered, "Get your neck broke, Heisman!"

Those early-day teams wore jerseys and shorts of wide variety. They wore no helmets or pads, however. A man who dared to turn up in homemade armor was considered a sissy. Long hair was the only head protection they had, and as part of the preseason preparatory program they would begin letting their hair grow in June. Some of the players, particularly the medical and divinity students, also let their beards grow, earning the nickname "gorillas."

There was also a shortage of sweaters back in football's Stone Age, so they all wore snug-fitting canvas jackets over their game jerseys—hence the appellation, "canvasbacks." Tackling was ragged; a wild, haphazard-clutching, above-the-waist sort of tackling. When rival runners wore loose garments, they were frequently stopped by a tackler grabbing a handful of clothing. Some players wore pants or jackets of black horsehair, so when a pursuer made a fumbling grab at a runner, he lost his fingernails.

There were often arguments over the referee's decisions. The entire team took part, too, so that half of the time the officials scarcely knew who was captain. Every player was allowed to argue and blow off steam as much as he pleased with the other side, prompting Stephen Leacock, an Englishman, to observe: "The Americans are a queer people, they can't play football. They try to, but they can't. They turn football into a *fight*." One of the biggest problems was the fact that there was no neutral zone between the two scrimmage lines. There was only an imaginary scrimmage line drawn through the center of the ball. Naturally, the rush line players of both teams were constantly striving to crowd this imaginary hairline to get the jump on each other. This is what caused all the trouble between the players and game officials. There were so many charges and countercharges, so much pushing and wrestling, that it often took the quarterback a full minute to get the ball back in play.

The smell of blood was so strong that once

during the Dartmouth-Colgate game, Coach Jack Ingersoll of the Red Raiders shouted at his players, "Remember, you're not out there just to mess up the play—you're supposed to *kill* somebody!"

Colgate always played hard, rough football against its foes from the Ivy group. It was not always artistic, but there was blood. Against Yale one time, a Colgate end was banged up and had to leave the game. R. H. Tibbals, who seldom got to play, was hurried in to substitute. Tibbals grabbed what passed for a head guard, started onto the field, then suddenly pivoted and returned to the sideline.

"Whaza matter, Tibbals?" shouted Coach Buck O'Neill. "Get back out there!"

"Uh, Coach," stammered Tibbals, "where in hell does the end play?"

Pudge Heffelfinger, who later played for Walter Camp at Yale, once told me that his roughest game was the 1889 Harvard contest played at old Hampden Park in Springfield, Massachusetts. Springfield? Why not New Haven or Cambridge? "In those days the Big Three games were played on neutral grounds," Pudge explained. "We played the Princeton game at the Polo Ground in New York, about halfway from each campus. As for Springfield, it was about 75 miles from New Haven and 100 miles from Boston, which made it a good spot for Harvard and Yale to meet. From 1889 to 1894 the games were played there. Bleachers seating 15,000 were put up especially for the game, and there was always a full house.

"Another thing about Springfield," continued Heffelfinger, "was that it was a big railroad junction for New England. That's how the railroad station was wrecked one night. The Williams College team and its rooters used to change cars at Springfield going to and from Yale for the annual game. Yale used to slaughter them. All the football there was of any class in those days was played in the Big Three. But this particular year the Williams rooters were wild with delight on the way back from New Haven. Yale won by the usual 50 or 100 points—but, by gum, Williams had *scored*. Williams had actually scored a touchdown on mighty Yale. Well, sir, the Williams crowd was so exuberant on the way back, it just about tore down the Springfield railroad depot. It was a public benefit at that. Springfield needed a new one.

"But getting back to the Yale-Harvard game, I could still rattle off the lineups of both teams right now if I had to. I can still see those Traffords in their Harvard uniforms, and what uniforms they had in those days. Arthur Cumnock was the Harvard captain and Charley Gill filled the same honor for us. Lonny Stagg played right end. I remember that after the game there was a woodcut caricature in one of the Springfield papers of Lon handing one of the Harvard chaps a terrific wallop on the head. The caption read, 'Stagg's Ministerial Uppercut,' referring to the fact that Lonny was a 27-year-old divinity student. It was some bloodbath. We went out there and murdered one another for 60 minutes, and after the game we all agreed that there had been no slugging by either side. Sure. The slaughter had been so fierce it was a wonder any of us came out alive. One of the Harvards suffered a broken collarbone, and a Yale teammate had one eye nearly blinded. Practically all of us were bleeding from cuts or from kicks or smashes. Another one of our players was unconscious for five hours afterward in a Springfield hospital. I don't remember now exactly who it was, but I can still see him being carried off the field, dead to the world. They just dumped him in a pile of blankets, covered him up, and then turned to look at the game again. A bit later, just out of curiosity, one of our subs went over and lifted the blankets apart and looked in. There he was, still unconscious—and nobody was paying any attention to him! They were too absorbed in the game. So the sub covered him up again and went to have another look at the game himself.

"Oh, yes, Yale won the game, 6-0. It was Bum McClung, later Secretary of the U.S. Treasury, who scored the touchdown and kicked the goal. In those days a touchdown counted for four points, a conversion two, and you had to kick the goal from a point in front of where the touchdown had gone over the line. We had scored our touchdown over at one side of the field, and I'm telling you that William Tell couldn't have shot an arrow through the goalposts from that angle, but Bum McClung made it just the same."

° ° °

First as a player and then as a coach, Walter Camp loved the intellectual side of football, the strategy. Even at 19, he was gently autocratic, purposeful, confident of his ability to handle any situation. He seldom failed to control the team completely. He wasn't a prig. He just wanted to win. He maintained austere training. Violations by others he found difficult to tolerate. His only losing game as a Yale player, a defeat by Princeton at Hoboken in 1878, he blamed on derelictions of four upperclassmen. "The Blue went back to New Haven with a very salutary lesson on the evil of neglecting the laws of training," he recalled afterward.

Camp was quite regal, all right, yet it was not on the playing field, but in the early rules conventions, that he established himself as the "Father of American Football" and Yale its fountainhead. He attended his first rules meeting in 1878 at Springfield, and from then until his death in 1925, he was a member of every football committee. At the conference of 1878, he followed the precedent of Gene Baker and recommended 11 players instead of 15. The proposal was rejected. He tried again the following year and again was turned down.

Camp's long fight to reduce the number of players to 11 was finally rewarded in 1880. Also, the size of the playing field was chopped down from 140 yards by 70 yards to 110 yards by 53 yards. The field was marked crosswise, 25 yards from each goal. The kickoff was from the center of the field.

One other important change was that rugby scrummage became scrimmage, and the quarterback made his appearance with a new method of putting the ball in play. Instead of the ball being tossed in between two packs of rushers, or forwards, who sought to heel it out—kick it backward to one of the halfbacks with the heel—as was common in rugby "scrum," the procedure of a scrimmage was adopted for putting the ball in play. The new rule read: "A scrimmage takes place when the holder of the ball puts it on the ground before him and puts it in play while on side, either by kicking the ball or by snapping it back with the foot. The man who first receives the ball from the snapback shall be called the quarterback and shall not rush forward with the ball under penalty of foul."

The introduction of the scrimmage established the principle of possession of the ball, a very vital point that, more than anything else, differentiates rugby from American football.

"Walter Camp's scrimmage plan gave the ball into the possession of the center, and he alone could put it into play with a snapback," remarked John Heisman later. "This control of the ball made it possible for the offensive team to plan plays in advance, and the use of signals by the quarterback made for better team play."

With the reduction of the number of players from 15 to 11, Harvard, Princeton, and Yale set about aligning them. The Harvard strategy was to station seven men on the line, three at halfback, and one at fullback. The three halfs alternated at quarterback. Princeton, on the other hand, deployed six men up front, one at quarter, two at half, and two at fullback. It was Yale, however, that fashioned the best solution to the problem: a seven-man line, a quarterback, two halfbacks, and one fullback.

"Now the familiar names of the line positions arose," wrote Parke Davis, football historian of the era. "The first man in the line originally was called the 'end rush,' a heritage from our rugby comrades in England. The genius of young America at first designated the second man in the line as the 'next to end,' the third man in the line as 'next to center,' and the center, of course, as the center. It quickly was noticed, however, that the 'next to end' made more tackles than any other man in the line, and so he quickly came to be known as the 'tackler,' a name later changed to tackle. Similarly, with the snapping back of the ball by the center with his foot, it was noticed that the 'next to center' guarded the center by bracing the latter; therefore, the 'next to center' came to be called the guard.

"Another feature of the early game was the system of officials, these consisting of an umpire for each side, with a referee to decide disagreements between the umpires. The two umpires discharged their duties like an opposing pair of football lawyers. In fact, they frequently were selected more for their argumentative abilities than for their knowledge of the game."

By 1880, football no longer was the exclusive property of the Big Three. Starting in 1877, Washington and Lee and Virginia Military Institute (VMI) were the first to play the game in the South; Michigan and Racine became the first to take it up in the Midwest, in 1878; and by 1881, Stevens, Tufts, City College of New York (CCNY), Wesleyan, Pennsylvania, Trinity, Brown, Amherst, Pennsylvania Military College, Dartmouth, and Williams were playing the game. That year also, Michigan sent its team east to play Harvard, Princeton, and Yale. "The trip brought gratifying results," reported the Michigan correspondent. "Although losing to Yale and Harvard on successive days, the Wolverines earned a forfeit when they showed up willing to play Harvard again on the third day."

In 1882, another far-reaching development arrived in the structure of football. Until then, unless a team lost the ball on a fumble, there was no way for the other side to gain control of the ball. If pushed back to their own goal line, the team with the ball merely made a voluntary safety, which counted nothing against them. The ball was then taken back out to the 25-yard line, and they started over again. Rules makers, headed by Camp, finally solved the problem by saying that henceforth "a team in three trials or downs would either have to gain 5 yards or lose 10 or else surrender the ball to the opponents." This change gave boost to the development of a real offense, and it put the white lines across the field.

Now football started to grow. From the West, such schools as Minnesota, Purdue, Indiana, and Notre Dame entered the football roll call. The evolution from English rugby into the game as we know it today was well under way, with the running game forging ahead of the kicking and the system of downs installed on a field marked off as a gridiron. Gridiron? When Walter Camp proposed his 5-yards-in-three-downs legislation in 1882, delegates to the convention asked him how he was going to be able to tell when 5 yards had been made.

"We shall have to rule off the field," Walter replied, "with horizontal chalked lines every 5 yards."

"Gracious!" exploded Ned Peace, the Princeton representative. "The field will look like a gridiron!"

"Precisely," Walter said.

And so a new expression was born. In the future, college teams would play their football on the *gridiron*.

Walter Camp was thus the man responsible for putting through the system of downs and yards to gain. It was also Camp who devised the use of signals, at first sentences, then letters, and finally numbers. Michigan used signals when it played Yale at New Haven in 1881, and it is suspected that the Eli coach got the idea from the Wolverines.

In 1883, Camp introduced the numerical scoring system to football, with points awarded for goals, touchdowns, and safeties. The original values given to the scoring plays were safety, 1 point; touchdown, 2 points; goal from a try, 4 points; goal from the field, 5 points.

A year later, the point system was changed. The touchdown now counted 4 points; the goal after touchdown, 2 points; and the safety, 2 points. That same year the umpires were abolished, and the referee was assigned to work the game alone.

The reaction following the various rules changes was a healthy one, and football rapidly grew in popular favor across America. Now other colleges entered the lists, among them Navy, Cornell, Fordham, Lehigh, Lafayette, Bucknell, Penn State, MIT, Union, Dickinson, Swarthmore, Haverford, Johns Hopkins, Virginia, Southern California (USC), California, and Washington.

The first football game to capture national attention—to play a part in transforming football from a privileged Eastern pastime to a national preoccupation—was Yale vs. Princeton in 1879. Walter Camp, then a senior, was the captain. One of the Yale forwards was a young sophomore from Highland Military Academy in Worcester, Massachusetts, who was seldom seen on the campus without a sketch pad, drawing school scenes, cartoons, self-portraits. They were lively, often amusing. The boy's family, well-to-do conservative folk, regarded the sketches indulgently. They regarded almost everything he did in the same manner. Opposition came from his Uncle Lamartine, who was "opposed to having any men artists in the family." The uncle wanted the boy to have a political career.

Originally, the young man planned to go to Cornell and become a journalist who illustrated his stories. Instead, in the fall of 1878, he wound up at Yale, where the newly formed art department put him to work in a basement classroom copying a plaster cast of a faun. The boy's first published drawing appeared in *The Yale Courant*, November 2, 1878. It depicted a battered player in his room, bandaged leg propped on a table amid bottles of liniment, saying, "The doctor says I'll be all right by Thanksgiving, and that's all I care for now."

Early in the 1879 Yale-Princeton game, the sophomore forward was buried in a midfield pileup for at least 10 minutes, during which the ball did not move 10 feet in either direction. In those days the lines met in mass-collision plays, power and weight assaults, in which yardage—or inchage—was slowly ground out. In an illustration in *Harper's Weekly*, the boy's earnest, honest face is clearly visible in a pyramid of struggling players near the Princeton goal. The *Harper's* artist had plenty of time to get his likeness: the Princeton line held for another 10 straining minutes without giving up more than two feet. The game ended in a 0-0 tie, and the boy came out of it a hero—or one of the lesser heroes, for Walter Camp was the star.

The boy's name? Maybe you've heard of him. Frederic Remington, a phenomenon in the history of American painting. Ninety-four years after he left Yale for Montana, one of his artifacts sold for $175,000, a record for Western art.

# *Walter Camp on Football*

Back in the Gaslight Era of the handlebar moustache, slick-parted hair, high-buttoned jacket, and tall stiff collar—back when football players wore one-piece leather suits, did not throw forward passes, and ran with the dazzling speed of tree trunks—the game, like the wars of that age, was a fierce struggle of youthful courage and strength waged over small pieces of ground. Force drove headlong against force. Gains came in feet and often just in inches. The players were trained to block on offense, tackle on defense, and to give and take it all the time. The idea was simple enough: Sock it to them until something gave. It was a game that hurt, a game of primitive pads slapped against unguarded faces, of two stalwarts charging point-blank into an opponent and knocking him to his knees, and of crashing blocks as a wave of interference rolled a man out of the play. It was a brutal game played by tough young men.

Inevitably, the tales of American football's violence reached the Old World, and one German correspondent commented: "The football tournament between the teams of Harvard and Yale . . . had terrible results. It turned into an awful butchery. Of 22 participants, seven were so severely injured that they had to be carried from the field in a dying condition. One player had his back broken, another lost an eye, a third lost a leg. Both teams appeared upon the field with a crowd of ambulances, surgeons, and nurses. Many ladies fainted at the awful cries of the injured players. The indignation of the spectators was powerful, but they were so terrorized that they were afraid to leave the field."

Although this description was an exaggeration, the "Hampden Park Blood Bath of 1894" did cause Yale and Harvard to break off football relations for the next two years to lick their wounds.

In those days, it was fairly easy to recognize the best team and the best players every season. Somebody like Caspar Whitney in *Harper's Weekly* or J. Parmly Paret in *Outing* looked at the records of Yale, Harvard, Princeton, and Penn, quickly deciphered which one had out-groped Columbia Law School by the biggest margin, and boldly proclaimed them the mythical National Champion. Nobody argued about it, preoccupied as most people were with striking for decent wages and wondering why it was taking so long for Henry Ford to invent his Tin Lizzie. Nobody even cared. You told a man that your college was number one and all the response you got was, "That's nice, but, excuse me, I've got to go invent the radio."

Despite the indifference, there was progress. The first All-American football team was named in 1889 and turned up in either a late 1889 or early 1890 issue of *The Week's Sport*, a New York periodical. The team chosen was: Arthur Cumnock, Harvard, and Amos Alonzo Stagg, Yale, ends; Hector W. Cowan, Princeton, and Charles O. Gill, Yale, tackles; John Cranston, Harvard, and William W. Heffelfinger, Yale, guards; William J. George, Princeton, center; Edgar Allan Poe (grandnephew of the poet), Princeton, quarterback; James T. Lee, Harvard, and Roscoe H. Channing, Jr., Princeton, halfbacks; and Knowlton (Snake) Ames, Princeton, fullback.

There are riddles aplenty as to who originated the idea of selecting an All-American football team, but the strong probabilities are these: Either Caspar Whitney, reigning sportswriter of the Gaslight Era and manager of *The Week's Sport*, or Walter Camp, or both in concert, hit upon the idea of picking a mythical All-America college football team. "Most probably," wrote Tim Cohane in his delightful *The Yale Football Story* in 1951, "the idea originated with Whitney and he came to Camp with it." Pudge Heffelfinger told me that the credit belongs to Caspar Whitney. "It was Whitney's idea," Pudge said matter-of-factly. "Camp got it from him."

° ° °

Princeton had a fine eleven in 1889, with such stars as Cowan at tackle, George at center, and Poe, Channing, and Ames in the backfield. House Janeway was a stalwart at guard. Monte Cash was Cowan's running mate at tackle. Monte had played at Pennsylvania in 1888. Then he retired to Wyoming, but the Tigers wired him to come east again. He showed up at Old Nassau with a deck of monte cards and two six-shooters. To a faculty committee, which sought to impress upon him that flunking out of school would be a disgrace, Monte replied, "It may be in the East, but we don't think much of a little thing like that out West."

At left end for Princeton was Ben (Sport) Donnelly, one of Pudge Heffelfinger's favorite characters. "Sport was the only player I ever knew who could slug you and at the same time keep his eye on the ball," Pudge said. "His idea of humor was to punch you in the nose and then yell, 'Hey, Mr. Referee!' The ref usually looked around just in time to see Sport take a return punch on the jaw. Naturally, you were tossed out of the game, while Sport chuckled to himself."

° ° °

Listening to old-timers talking to today's generation, it becomes evident that although today's game is far more sophisticated and the players much bigger and swifter, the coaching philosophy of the generations is not all that far apart.

Talk to Princeton's Bob Casciola and he will tell you: "There are many reasons why a college boy plays football. It's not just the old traditional things—to please the alumni or to please the fans in the stadium. Some play because they're turned off by other college activities. Some are looking for competition—a way to measure themselves which they haven't found in the classroom. Others are looking for some discipline. A coach has to understand that when a boy leaves the field he will have other interests. He may not hurt inside as much after a defeat. You cannot expect a 38-year-old coach and a 20-year-old boy to have much in common. But they must have respect for each other. If you understand that, then the players will accept what you ask of them on the playing field."

Talk to Woody Hayes of Ohio State and you learn that he sees his job as a part of American civilization, and a *damn important part*. "I see football as being just so much above everything else," he will say. Talk to him some more and he might take you on a side trip back to the Battle of Salamis, where the Greeks beat the tail off the Persians. When Woody discusses football, he speaks a lot in terms of history and war. "To me," he says, "football is a microcosmic reflection of the ideals, emotions, strategies, pitfalls, and problems of a society. Now go back to the Battle of Salamis. Now doesn't that take in so many of the things you see in football? Fear, determination, backs to the wall, home field advantage—all those things you see in a football game. And that Battle of Salamis wasn't for the National Championship, it was for the *World* Championship. If you study your history, the Battle of Salamis decided the fate of democracy, because if the Persians had won, the Greeks would have been sucked into the abyss of Oriental despotism."

In Hayes's scheme of things, life imitates football. One minute he talks about the split T formation. Another minute he talks about Thucydides. Then Nathaniel Hawthorne . . . now goal line defenses . . . then the Battle of Midway . . . now the breakdown of respect for authority . . . then the complexities of recruiting football flesh . . . now the French Revolution . . . then the double-team block.

"Now the double-team block, of course, is the story of your First World War, very simply," he'll say. "Germany was caught in the double-team block, between the pressure from the Allies from the West—France and England—and then the pressure from the Russians in the East . . ."

Of course.

To Chuck Knox, a successful modern coach in the pros, football is not quite so complex. His personality, his philosophy, and his thinking are probably closer in character to what Walter Camp had in mind when Camp started fooling around with the strategy of the game nearly a century ago.

"I try to keep things simple and sensible," Knox explained. "I don't think it takes hours to explain something simple like taking the snap from center. I have also cut out many of our agility drills. If a man isn't agile, he has no business playing football. I don't like the idea of players lying on their backs, flopping around, doing what are supposed to be agility drills. I have never seen a play that started with an athlete on his back. There is no great mystery to being a successful coach. First you get the players. Then you teach them pride. Then you keep everything simple and efficient. That is the only answer.

"There is so much overbloated nonsense in coaching today that the essentials are ignored. I used to go to coaching schools and listen to my colleagues talk for hours on the center-quarterback exchange. They turned matters that were relatively simple into what sounded like the battle plan for World War Three. There are just two things that keep you going in this business—pride and conditioning. And pride shows up every day in practice, not just on weekends. It is a matter of instilling self-motivation in your players."

° ° °

If Walter Camp, who died in 1925, were alive, and you asked him for his impression of the way his century-old recipe has grown, he would probably argue the point. "What do you mean grown?" he would want to know. "In some form or another, we did just about everything that is done in football today. Of course, we didn't forward pass because it was against the rules. We had laterals, but they weren't used much. Our system of defense and offense was fundamentally the same as it is today. Except for refinements and a closer attention to details, due to these much larger coaching staffs, it's basically the same game. And all this talk about systems is a lot of twaddle."

A good many football games have been played at Yale since Camp entered the university as a town boy in 1876. More than any other man, he fashioned the game into the framework on which modern football is built. As the author of the very first book ever published on the subject (1891), Camp had some very definite ideas as to what football was all about. The following is the way his fundamentals came out at that time.

"It is impossible to overrate the importance of the quarterback. He is, under the captain, the director of the game. With the exception of one or two uncommon and rare plays, there is not one of any kind, his side having the ball, in which it does not pass through his hands. He must be, above all the qualifications of brains and agility usually attributed to that position, of a hopeful or sanguine disposition. He must have confidence in his centre himself, and, most of all, in the man to whom he passes the ball. He should always believe that the play will be a success. The coach can choose no more helpful course during the first few days than that of persuading his quarterback to repose confidence in his men. Many promising halfbacks are ruined by the quarter. There is nothing that makes halfbacks fumble so badly, get into such awkward positions, start so slowly, and withal play so half-heartedly, as the feeling that the quarter does not think much of them, does not trust them, or believe in their abilities. Every halfback can tell the same story—how he is nerved up by the confidence of that quarterback, and what an inspiration it is to good work to see that confident look in the eye of the man who is about to pass to him. But not alone in the work of the halfback does it make a great difference, but in that of the quarterback himself. When he lacks confidence in his man, his passing is unsteady and erratic as well as slow.

"In practice, great stress should be laid on quick handling and sharp passing of the ball. A quarterback can slow up in a game if advisable, but he can never do any faster work than that which he does in practice without throwing his men completely out. In order to make the play rapid, a quarterback must be figuratively tied to the centre's coat, or rather jacket, tails. As soon as the centre reaches the ball after a down, he should know that the quarterback is with him. Usually there is an understood signal between them, which not only shows the centre that the quarterback is on hand, but also when he is ready to receive the ball. One of the most common of these signals has been placing the hand upon the centre's leg or back. A pinch lets him know when to snap the ball. One of the best methods is for the quarterback to put his hand upon the centre and keep it there until he is ready for the ball, then take it off and let the centre snap the ball, not instantly, but at his convenience. Should the quarterback suddenly decide to stop the play, he puts his hand upon the centre again at once, and until it is once more removed the snapback understands that the quarter is not ready to have the ball come. Almost any amount of variation can be made in the signal of the quarter to his centre; but in arranging this it should be constantly borne in mind that the signal should not be such as to give the opponents the exact instant of the play, because it gives them too close an idea of the moment when they may start.

"The speed of a quarter's work depends upon his ability to take the ball close to the snapback and in proper position for a pass. . . . In giving the ball to a passing runner, it should be held free and clear of the quarter's body and slightly tilted, so that it can be taken against the body, and without the use of both hands for more than an instant, because the runner must almost immediately have use for his arm in going into the line. When the ball is to be passed any considerable distance, it should be taken so that the end is well placed against the hand of the quarter, while the ball itself lies against the forearm, the wrist being bent sharply. In receiving the ball, the right hand, or the hand with which the throw is made, should be placed upon the end of the ball, while the other hand stops its progress, and should be placed as nearly upon the opposite end of the ball as convenient.

"The quarterback must bear in mind the fact that, in order of importance, his duties are, first, to secure the ball, no matter how; second, to convey it to his own man, no matter whether in good form or not. He must never pass the ball if he has fumbled it, unless he has a perfectly clear field in which to do it. When he does pass, he should follow the ball after letting it go; in fact, he should be almost on the run as the ball leaves his hand. No matter whether the ball is caught or not, he is then ready to lend assistance; whereas if he stands still after his pass, he is of no use to the rest of the play. When the play is a run, he can do excellent work in interfering; and when the play is a kick, he can take any opponent who breaks through, and thus aid the halfback in protecting the kicker.

"When lining up, the quarterback should take a quick glance, not directly at the player who is to get the handoff, but covering the general position of all the men. In doing this he locates the recipient without making it apparent to the opponents which man is to receive the ball. Any amount of disguise may be practiced in the way of taking a last glance at the wrong man, or calling out to someone who does not figure in the play.

"When the opponents have the ball, the quarterback makes an extra man in or near the forward line, and, as a rule, he can by his shrewdness make it very uncomfortable for any point in the line which he chooses to assail. No law can govern his tactics in this respect, but he should be a law unto himself, and show by his cleverness that he is more valuable than any man in the line whose position is fixed.

"Today the teams which meet to decide the championship are brought up to the execution of at least 25 different plays, each of which is called for by a certain distinct signal of its own.

"The first signals given were *word signals;* that is, a word or a sentence called out so that the entire team might hear it and understand whether a kick or a run was to be made. Then, when signals became more general, *sign signals*—that is, some motion of the hand or arm to indicate the play—were brought in and became for a time more popular than the word signals, particularly upon those fields where the fans pressed too close to the sidelines, and their enthusiastic cheering at times interfered with hearing word signals. Of late years numerical combinations have become most popular, and as the crowd is kept at such a distance from the sidelines as to make it possible for teams to hear those signals, they have proven highly satisfactory. The numerical system, while it can be readily understood by the side giving the signal, because they know the key, is far more difficult for the opponents to solve than either the old word signals or signs.

"The question as to who should give the signals is still a disputed one, although the general opinion is that the quarterback should perform this duty. Some prefer having the captain direct the play. Of course, all is settled if the captain is himself a quarterback. The important fact to be remembered in selecting a system of signals is that it is far more demoralizing to confuse your own team than to mystify your opponents. A captain, or quarterback, must therefore choose such a set of signals as he can be sure of making his own team comprehend without difficulty and without mistake. When he is sure of that, he can think how far it is possible for him to disguise these from his opponents. The good teams devise *two* sets of signals. Considering the way the game is played today, I advise two sets.

"Early in the season, it is just as well to start the team off with only two or three signals, adding more as the season progresses. If, for instance, the captain or coach decides to make use of a numerical system, they can begin with three signals, something like this: one-two-three, to indicate that the ball is to be passed to the right halfback on a run around left end; four-five-six, that the left half will try to run around the right end; and seven-eight-nine, that the back will kick. In practice, the scrubs will probably 'get on' to these signals in short order and will make it hot at the ends for the halfback, but this will be the best kind of practice in team-work and will do no harm. After a day or two of this, it will be time to make changes in the combination of numbers, not only with an idea of deceiving the scrubs, but also to quicken the wits of the varsity side.

"Taking the same signals as a basis, the first, or signal for the right halfback to try on the left end, was one-two-three—the sum of these numbers is six. Take that, then, as the key to this signal, and any numbers the sum of which equals six will be a signal for this play. For example, three-three, or four-two, or two-three-one—any of these would serve to designate this play. Similarly, as the signal for the left half at the right end was four-five-six, or a total of 15, any numbers which added make 15—as six-six-three, or seven-eight, or five-four-six—would be interpreted in this way. Finally, the signal for a kick having been seven-eight-nine, or a sum of 24, any numbers aggregating that total would answer equally well.

"A few days of this practice will fit the men for any further developments upon the same lines and accustom them to listening and thinking at the same time. The greatest difficulty experienced by both captains and coaches since the signals and plays became so complicated has been to teach green players not to stop playing while they listen to and think out a signal. By the end of the season players are so accustomed to the signals that all this hesitation disappears, and the signal is so familiar as to amount to a description of the play in so many words.

"No matter what method of signaling is used, there is one important feature to be regarded, and that is, some means of altering the play after a signal has been given. This is, of course, a very simple thing, and the usual plan is to have some word which means that the signal already given is to be considered void, and a new signal will be given in its place. There should also be some way of advising the team of a change from one set of signals to another, should such a move become necessary. It is very unwise not to be prepared for such an emergency, because if a captain is obliged to have time called and personally advise his team one by one of such a change, the opponents are quite sure to see it and to gain confidence from the fact that they have been clever enough to make such a move necessary.

"An athlete is only as good as his body, so attention must be given to diet. I tell my boys to train by what I call the 'Common-Sense System.' Rise at six, bathe, take about two ounces (a small cup) of coffee with milk, this is really a stimulating soup. Then light exercise, chiefly devoted to lungs, a little rest, a breakfast of meat, bread, or oatmeal, vegetables, with no coffee, an hour's rest. Then the heaviest exercise of the day. This is contrary to rule, but I believe the heaviest exercise should be taken before the heaviest meal, a rest before dinner. This meal, if breakfast is taken at seven or eight A.M., should be at one or two P.M., not leaving a longer interval than five hours between meals. At dinner, again meat, vegetables, bread, perhaps a half-pint of malt liquor, no sweets. Then a longer rest, exercise till five P.M. Supper light—bread, milk, perhaps an egg. Half an hour later a cup of tea, and bed at nine P.M."

Play ball!

In 1888, Yale actually had *two* coaches—Camp and his earnest young bride, Allie, sister of Professor William Graham Sumner, the renowned Yale lecturer of sociology. Allie Camp was her husband's eyes.

"They were newlyweds, and Walter was sales manager in the New York office of the New Haven Clock Company," Pudge Heffelfinger once told me. "His superiors wouldn't let him attend our afternoon practices, so he sent his wife to stand in for him. I can still see her pacing up and down the sideline, taking notes of our scrimmages. Walter kept in touch with our progress by reading her notebook. Then, several nights a week some of us on the team would go over to the Camps' home in New Haven for a review of strategy.

"Allie Camp could spot the good points and the weaknesses in each man's play. Her woman's intuition helped Walter suggest the right man for the right position to the team captain. Remember, in those pioneer days at Yale, the head coach made no decision without first consulting the captain."

For much of the next 20 years, Walter Camp dictated Yale's football policies. He had no formal position as Yale coach, he received no pay, but his was the voice of final authority.

The Yale graduate coaching system, as Camp began to develop it in 1888, provided for a head field coach, usually the captain from the previous year. He was appointed by the new captain and worked with him under Camp. Other Old Blues came back to assist. As the big games with Princeton and Harvard neared, Camp stayed in the background, quietly manipulating. He was an excellent organizer. He anticipated the trends of the game; in fact, his power in the old rules conventions enabled him to steer trends. An Old Blue all the way, he took pains to see that Yale did not get the worst of it. He made the schedules and was the business manager who directed the saving of the moneys that were to contribute richly at a later date to the construction of Yale Bowl. His office at the Clock Company served in a very real sense as the headquarters of Yale athletics.

Beyond Yale, Camp's work on the rules committee, his writings, his officiating, his All-America selections made him the reigning football figure during the years 1888 to 1925.

It was in 1891 that Camp took the game on the road. He went west to coach Stanford, while Lee McClung signed on at the University of California. The game between those Old Blues ended in a scoreless tie that fall. The next year, Pudge Heffelfinger coached the California Bears and another former Eli, Pop Bliss, led the Stanford Cardinals. Stanford, 6-0.

The men whom Camp taught at Yale went out to teach the game all over the country. Oddly enough, the only three Yale men who became great coaches of the modern game earned their reputations away from New Haven: Amos Alonzo Stagg at the University of Chicago, Dr. Henry Williams at Minnesota, and Howard Jones at Iowa and Southern California. All three were originators. What Stagg didn't invent, Pop Warner did. Henry Williams was responsible for the Minnesota shift, the daddy of all hike maneuvers. Howard Jones introduced the three-blocker-one-ball-carrier method of backfield play.

Today, one wonders what would have become of all our Saturdays and Sundays had Walter Camp pursued his original ambition to become a doctor. In 1883, he flunked anatomy and surgery in his senior class medical examinations at Yale. When friends asked him why he was quitting medicine, he said, "I can't bear the sight of *blood!*"

This from the architect of modern football.

# *Heffelfinger and His Playmates*

He played in another civilization, or on another planet perhaps. Pudge Heffelfinger was not of this time nor of the place in which he died. He could not possibly have existed outside of romantic fiction. But he did. The newspaper morgues are full of his football adventures. They seem remarkably unreal because no modern athlete fits the style.

Time treated Pudge decently. Both Walter Camp and Grantland Rice said that he was the greatest college football guard who ever lived. He was still playing football nine days before his 66th birthday. All told, he played the game for 50 years. Yes, 50 years! Think of it. They had to strip him of his jersey, helmet, and cleats before he finally retired. He actually played his last game in a business suit, a borrowed headguard, and street shoes—against college players from the Big Ten young enough to be his grandsons.

They wouldn't stop talking about him, those Old Blues he met at Yale Bowl, at dinners, at social clubs. They rambled on and on about times that were long gone. They didn't want him to grow old. He did, and it never bothered him.

To Pudge, football was something of a religion. He got so much out of the game as a Yale undergraduate that it just logically had to mean more to him than to most of his contemporaries. Perhaps this was why he put such a high value on it. It was as if he had probed deeper and closer to its real meaning. In 1953, while I was collaborating with him on *This Was Football,* I often heard him say: "A game that can keep you young and vibrant and all steamed up is a precious thing."

Because of the oft-told story about the charity game he played in when he was in his fifties, and because he was such a big man (and from Minnesota too), the casual reader might understandingly have pictured him as a Paul Bunyan with a varsity Y on his chest. Actually, Pudge was more a brain man than a muscle man, and football must always remember him for his revolutionary concepts of line play, a much more revealing and significant measure of the man than the simple physical culture fact that he had the good sense to keep his body in shape long after his college days were over.

The late Joe Williams, famous sports columnist of the New York *World-Telegram & Sun* and originator of the Scripps-Howard Coach-of-the-Year Award, always tried to have Pudge as one of the honored guests at the annual dinner. Joe once told me that he had a delightful memory of the year (1950) they saluted Charlie Caldwell of Princeton in Dallas, Texas. Pudge sat with Amos Alonzo Stagg, another enduring and imposing Yale landmark. They had been classmates under The Elms at New Haven and played varsity football together. Joe sensed the evening had not been a complete social success for Pudge, and, somewhat abashed, Pudge presently admitted this was so.

"You know how much I think of Lonnie Stagg," Pudge told Williams. "One of the finest men God ever put breath in. And I guess the finest coach football ever had. But there are times when he goes too far."

Joe laughed as he recalled the incident.

"Turned out Stagg was enthusiastic about the subtle brush block as it is practiced in the T," Joe said. "Had it been anybody else but the intensely serious Stagg, there would have been reason to suspect a gag. In any case, nothing could have been devised that would have distressed Pudge more."

Nevertheless, Pudge could scarcely have been labeled a professional old-timer, and certainly he was not a biased traditionalist. A large part of football history was written by the Big Three. Yet Pudge thought it beyond argument that the best football in later years was played in the Big Ten. Although he was named at guard on every all-time, All-America team ever selected, he came to regard such selections as sheer nonsense. And although he went back to the Poes, Coys, Thorpes, Brickleys, and others, the best backfield he ever saw was that of Red Blaik's 1946 Army team, which spotlighted Doc Blanchard and Glenn Davis. As a matter of fact, Pudge Heffelfinger was tenaciously old-fashioned about only one proposition, namely, that line play was not exactly an ideal calling for the faint-hearted.

The late Grantland Rice once had a weekly radio broadcast in New York sponsored by Cities Service. On the Friday, November 17, 1939, show, he featured Pudge. This is an excerpt from that script:

> *Rice:* As old Bill Shakespeare said, "Cowards die many times before their death. The valiant only taste of death but once." Now I have a big treat for you—the greatest football player that ever lived—the greatest football player on Walter Camp's first All-America team in 1889—and still a great football player at the age of 66, only a few years ago, when he played for charity—think that one over—Pudge Heffelfinger of Yale.
>
> *Pudge:* Who ever said football was a rough game, Grant? I played it for 50 years. I know I was better at 45 than I was at 20. But I'll have to admit I slowed down a little when I was 66. Not much . . . but a little. All I can say is that I started out at Yale 52 years ago and would like one more shot before I turn in my cleats.
>
> *Rice:* Just one final toast, Ladies and Gentlemen:
> As we look them over in the big corral,
> As the years march by,
> As they rise and fall,
> Here's to Big Pudge,
> My pick and my pal,
> The greatest Roman of them all.

At the start of this chapter, I wondered aloud whether I'd be able to conjure up again all the memories of Pudge's Yale football career and somehow reconstruct the highlights so as to preserve everything of that era worth preserving. There were moments when I felt that what I needed was to be able to press a magic button and see a vision of Pudge and his teammates as they really were. I know there are no magic buttons. The nearest approach to them, I think, are the nostalgic conversations I had with Pudge during the years from 1948 to 1954.

"Sitting here in an easy chair, looking back on my 50 years as an active football player, I find that the games you lose are the games you can't forget," Pudge's voice comes down the years. "Victories are forgotten in the whirligig of time, but defeats get under your skin and stick in your memory. At least, that's the way it is with me. I hate to lose, always did, still do. Fortunately, it was my luck to be associated with winning teams, both in my college days at Yale and in my 40 years of football barnstorming, but the few beatings we suffered remain vividly stamped in my mind. Those are the games I play over again and again when I doze off at night. Take that 1890 licking we got from Harvard in my junior year, for instance. That was the only game we lost to the Johnnies while I was at New Haven, yet it still burns me up. One play in particular rankles. It's a perpetual nightmare!

"The score was 12 to 0 against us that afternoon when we got going and shoved Bum McClung over for a touchdown after a long march. A few minutes later I ran interference from guard for Ben Morison on an end run that went 40 yards. He was loose with me ahead of him and two Harvard tacklers closing in—Bernie Trafford in front of us and Dudley Dean behind. Which Harvard man should I take out? It was one of those tough, split-second decisions to make while running full tilt—a snap choice. Well, I guessed wrong. I chose Dean, who was coming up fast from the rear, and trusted that Morison could dodge Trafford. Ben couldn't. Trafford nailed him, and we were licked. Gosh, I play that one over in my dreams many a night, and I always take out Trafford—in my sleep! Funny thing, how such a trivial incident from the long ago gnaws at you for the rest of your life. Billy Rhodes, our captain, was so heartbroken over that defeat he never would look at another Harvard-Yale game. Years later he would pace the lobby of the old Massassoit House in Springfield with a ticket in his pocket while the game was going on! We took defeat hard in those days. Perhaps we thought there was a divine law against Yale losing at football. We lost only two games in my four years there. Princeton trimmed us in 1889 when Hector Cowan and Snake Ames wore the Orange and Black. It was my first defeat, and I felt as though I were marked for life with a branding iron. I didn't want to show my face on the campus. I recall sneaking upstairs to my room, locking the door, and keeping silent when friends shouted for me. It sounds damn silly now, but kids were like that in those days."

Football was a primitive mixture of soccer and rugby when Pudge began playing it as a schoolboy of 15 on the Minneapolis sandlots in 1883. Even before entering Central High School, he used to read about the Yale, Harvard, and Princeton games in *Spalding's Guide*. Armed with this rudimentary knowledge, he undertook to organize a team at Central High and teach the game to his schoolmates.

Even in the 1880s, Minneapolis had a large Yale alumni body. Naturally, Pudge heard a lot of Yale talk from the older men, and one of them, Harlow Gale, persuaded Pudge to try the Yale exams. First, however, he had the foresight to tutor Pudge all summer, and he did such a good job that Pudge got in without conditions.

Pudge had never been away from home alone in his life, so you can imagine his excitement when he left Minneapolis that September morning in 1888 and headed east. The train ride from New York to New Haven took three hours alone in those days, and it seemed three days to him.

Pudge got a break when he reported for football at old Yale field where the baseball diamond later sprawled. A Minneapolis friend had tipped off Kid Wallace, freshman coach and varsity end, that Pudge was a crack running halfback. Wallace kept an eye on him and gave him a chance on the freshman team.

Then came a second stroke of luck. Pa Corbin, the varsity captain, happened to be watching freshman practice when Pudge caught a low punt off his shoestrings and ran through all the opposing team except "Tot" Harvey. They were playing 15-man sides to give the ball carriers more experience in dodging, and Pudge got the impression that the sky was raining tacklers.

"Luck plus ability spells success," Pudge recalled to me. "If Pa Corbin hadn't chanced to see that run I might have spent all season on the frosh squad. Freshman were eligible for the varsity then [as they are in most Ivy League sports]. Moreover, the Yale captain outranked the coach and could pick his own team and decide what plays to use. The coach, in this case Walter Camp, was really just an adviser."

Pa Corbin's fame had spread to the Midwest. His long, lean face and handlebar moustache gave him a majestic air and made him look much older than his 24 years. His word was law on Yale field in 1888. A tall, raw-boned New Englander, he was strict but fair. He rowed on the crew, and nothing got by those octopus arms. Pa never swore. His most violent epithet was "you big cow."

After Pudge's long punt return in the frosh scrimmage, Pa sent word that he wanted to talk to him.

"Nice run," Pa grunted. "Ever play in the line?"

"No," Pudge replied.

"Well, come over to the varsity field with me," Pa said. "Let's see what you can do at guard. You're big and fast. We need linemen more than backs—fellows who can move around a bit."

Pudge's heart beat a tattoo as he walked at Pa's side over to the big field. "Have you any nickname?" Pa wanted to know.

"No," Pudge lied, remembering that his conservative father back in Minneapolis disliked his school nickname of "Pudge" and had told him not to use it at Yale.

"Fine," Pa said, "we'll call you Heff. Your real name is too long."

So Heff it was, and as Heff he made the Yale varsity line his first day out. During his college career, he never once played in the backfield where his prep school reputation had been made.

The older players gave yearlings a rough initiation in those days to find out whether they could take it. Pudge took plenty that first afternoon with the varsity, particularly from Bert Hanson, who played opposite him in the scrimmage and alternately kicked his shins and cracked his knuckles. Pa Corbin would vary this punishment occasionally by rasping the sleeve of his canvas jacket across Pudge's nose until it was raw. Meanwhile, they watched Pudge's expression to see how he was reacting.

"Let's see if he's got any guts," Kid Wallace shouted. Whereupon they gave Pudge the ball and sent three men down to crack him simultaneously like a pack of hounds after a rabbit. One tackler took him high around the neck, another hit him in the belly, and the third went for his hips.

Somehow, Pudge came through the ordeal all

right, and they seemed satisfied with everything except his tackling.

"You're too good-natured, Heff," Ray Tompkins warned him. "You've got to be mean if you want to play on this team, and you must bang 'em down hard when you tackle. This is no parlor game. Forget you've got any friends on the scrubs!"

Pudge took the advice and got rough.

"You've got to play football for all there's in it or somebody who hits harder will send you off on a stretcher," Pudge told me, recalling the scene. "We never wasted time tackling the dummy. Our workouts stressed live tackling, man against man in the open field. In my opinion, this is what made us such deadly tacklers. You can't learn how to nail a flesh-and-blood moving target by tackling a straw-stuffed dummy! In 1888, we scrimmaged for one solid hour every afternoon, except on Wednesday and Saturday, when we played games with outside teams. I used to lose four or five pounds in scrimmage. Game days seemed like a vacation to us. On Sunday we took six-mile hikes across country! Knute Rockne once said that football was 60 percent leg drive and 30 percent fight. We had both.

"Throughout my college career we had about 500 students watching practice each afternoon. We felt that the student body was behind us, and the students felt that they were part of the team. During practice they yelled at you and called you a bum when they met you after the workout, if you missed a tackle or a block. They kept us on our toes with their criticism, because it hurt our pride to hear the campus talking about our mistakes."

Pa Corbin's 1888 team ranks near the top in Yale's football history. It ran up 698 points to 0 for its opponents.

"Giants? Don't make me laugh," Pudge said. "I was the heaviest man on the team at 190 pounds. Lon Stagg, then better known as a pitcher than as an end rush, weighed a mere 157 pounds. We were strong, durable, hard as nails, and fast. Nothing lumbering or ponderous about that bunch. George Woodruff and I flanked Pa Corbin in the middle of the line. Woodruff was a picturesque character. He wore a coonskin cap and sported a set of whiskers when he first came to Yale from a Pennsylvania Dutch homestead. Life on the farms had so developed his muscles that he broke all strength test records at New Haven. Fast for his weight, Woodruff used to carry the ball most of the time until he hurt his knee badly in 1887. In his senior year he didn't run with the ball at all. I envied Woodruff's whiskers and vainly tried to sprout some of my own.

"Alonzo Stagg, whose name became synonymous with football at the University of Chicago, was a 27-year-old divinity school student when he played end on Corbin's team. For all his Biblical precepts, Stagg had a way of pulling foxy tricks. He thought two plays ahead of the other fellow. After the college season was over each fall, he organized a barnstorming team called the Christian Workers of Springfield, Massachusetts. One of his pet trick plays—the Dead Man Hoax—smacked of chicanery. When the ball was snapped, Stagg's whole team ran toward the left flank as though for an end run, except the chap who took the pass from center. This fellow flopped down on his belly with the ball concealed beneath him, and played dead. When the enemy players rushed over to stop the fake end sweep, the 'corpse' would leap to his feet and run like hell. They made a lot of touchdowns on this rather un-Christian play.

"Kid Wallace, who played the opposite end from Stagg at Yale, was a good-natured hellion who kept us laughing and relaxed by his rowdy antics. He was a gentleman to the manner born, but took keen delight in pretending to be a roughneck of the pier-20 type. Football was just an excuse for swapping punches as far as Kid was concerned, but his witty retorts turned away wrath. He could sock you and laugh it off with a wisecrack. A grim, serious gang like ours needed comic relief. The Kid supplied it.

"Lee McClung, a freshman like myself, was a spirited southerner with a puzzling hip shift and a scissors stride that baffled tacklers. 'Hold the fort, McClung is coming!' became a famous catch phrase before Lee was through at Yale. He was the first back to start as though on an end run, pivot sharply, and then cut in through tackle.

"Billy Bull, our fullback, was the best kicker of the period. He punted on the run with either foot like a rugby player, and his dropkicks often scored from 40 yards out. We used the punt as an offensive weapon to get position on the field. Billy could nick the coffin corner with his oblique, rolling kicks aimed away from the safety man. His motto was 'Kick 'em where they ain't.' He could kick through a slit two feet wide.

"Dock Wurtenberg, a peppy little guy, was our quarterback. Under the old code, he had to handle the ball on every play, but he didn't call signals. Numerical signals weren't invented until 1889. Pa Corbin used signs to let us know what play he wanted. When he yanked on his cap visor, for instance, that meant a kick. Any move of his left hand implied a play in that direction. Pa signaled a plunge over guard by tugging at his belt and an end run by touching his shoe lace. Oddly enough, our opponents never got wise.

"Shoving and hauling the runner was allowed, but tackling below the knees was illegal. I'm afraid our hands often slipped, but referees were charitable and mostly looked the other way. Laurie Bliss, our substitute back, used to hitch on to my belt and let me tow him through the line.

"One of the oddest plays I ever saw was concocted by Columbia. They called it the 'hurdle' play and tough Harold Weekes was the central figure. It was his specialty, poor fellow. Weekes would get the ball some 5 yards behind his front line, which was all pinched in tight, and he'd get off to a running start, and using the back of his center, a fellow named 'Bessy' Bruce, he'd go off like a diver from a springboard, trying to launch himself into orbit. His ends would come around and push him if he was in danger of toppling back. It was like trying to scale a mountain sometimes if the opposition bunched up on him. Well, in the Princeton game one time, the Tigers came up with a defense against Weekes. They got a guy named Dana Kafer and they hurdled him the same time that Weekes was coming over the top. They met in midflight, and both were carried off in pieces.

"In those days, Princeton was Yale's climax foe—the season's big objective. This match was played on Thanksgiving Day at the old Polo Grounds, 110th Street near Broadway [New York City]. Later on, the game was moved uptown to Manhattan Field, next to where the modern New York Giants played their home games [until 1976]. Yale headquarters in New York City was the Fifth Avenue Hotel at 23rd Street. On game day the lobby was always filled with hero worshippers and the tally-ho was draped with Yale Blue bunting and drawn by six horses on which we rode from the hotel up Fifth Avenue, through Central Park to the football grounds. We all sat on top of the stage and waved at the pretty girls who flirted with us, or jeered at the Princeton rooters when they gave us the Bronx cheer.

"On that ride in 1888 the horses got away from our driver, and we hit a hansom cab in Central Park. 'Hey, youse guys!' bellowed the disgusted cabbie, 'ain't you got enough trouble with Princeton today without looking for more?'

"While riding up Fifth Avenue, Pa Corbin warned us about Princeton's V trick—a V-shaped wedge of men which had smashed every defense it had met. Pa looked plenty worried. That Tiger wedge was a terrible thing to face. It simply murdered the men up front. The man at the apex of the V put the ball in play and the runner was screened by the phalanx. We met the lead man by socking him in the jaw with the heel of our hands, but they rolled over us just the same. Then I got an idea. Why not fight fire with fire and crash the wedge head-on in midair? They'd throw you off the field for brutality if you tried anything like that today, but nobody penalized me though Princeton protested pretty vigorously. As the wedge formed, I backed away to get a running start, put on full steam ahead, took off like a broad jumper, knees doubled up, and crashed full tilt against the chest of the chap leading the V. The impact of my 190 pounds shooting through the air like a projectile caused the wedge to shiver and collapse.

"Hector Cowan was furious. 'Hey, you big moose, you're going to kill somebody!' he yelled at me. Cowan was a chunky, deep-chested fellow, built like a smokehouse. He had the strongest shoulders and arms I've ever been up against, and his stubby legs drove like pistons when he carried the ball. He could carry a couple of tacklers on his back, yet he was plenty fast in the open. 'I'll quit it if you stop using that V wedge!' I shouted back at Hector. Naturally they wouldn't make the bargain. They foxed me by ducking low and warding off my dive with upflung arms. Luck was with me though on one critical play when I spotted a gap in the V and went through to nail Snake Ames for a big loss. That spoiled a Princeton scoring opportunity.

"Neither team made a touchdown in this knockdown and drag-out scrap as those tough lines played each other to a standstill, but we finally won, 10-0, on Billy Bull's dropkicks. I can see him now booting the first field goal with blood streaming down his face from a head cut. We wore no helmets or harness—just soft-quilted pads on shoulders and elbows. Bull's second field goal was kicked from a sharp angle on the 37-yard line with barely a minute left to play. He stood like a statue while the Tigers rushed him. But he kept his head down and his eyes rooted on the ball. The kick was perfect.

"In my junior year at Yale we again lost just one game. This time it was Harvard's turn to beat us. They had never won from us previously under modern scoring rules.

"We had been ordered to scowl at our Harvard opponents and act tough, but Francis Barbour burst out laughing when he saw his old Exeter roommate John Cranston across the scrimmage line. They had a great time kidding each other.

"Still and all, this Cranston was no laughing matter for us. Lewis, our substitute center, couldn't handle him alone. This spoiled our running guard play because I didn't dare drop out of line while Cranston was on the rampage. To make things worse, Ham Wallis, our tackle, couldn't keep Harvard's Ma Newell from crashing through. Newell weighed only 166 pounds, but he had the leg drive of a mule and the heart of a lion, a stubby, thickset chap, with unbreakable willpower. They called him 'Ma' because he mothered lonely freshmen and stood up for the weaklings. Whoever wrote 'the gentlest are the bravest' might have had Newell in mind. He was an amateur naturalist and spent Sunday mornings walking through the woods with his chums, observing and explaining. Men like Ma Newell make a college education mean something. He was killed by a locomotive a few years later while on track-walking duty for the Boston and Maine railroad.

"All through the game Captain Arthur Cumnock of Harvard kept kidding Captain Rhodes of Yale. 'It's a beautiful day, Bill,' he'd say. This got on Rhodes's nerves. Along about 4 o'clock he didn't think so much of the day. Cumnock was a born leader. He had coached his own team for two seasons, had made them do conditioning exercises both winter and summer, and had set his heart to beating Yale. Well, they did it, thanks to two long runs that caught us napping. First, Jimmy Lee, Harvard's fast little halfback, scooped up a fumble and raced 40 yards around John Hartwell's end for a touchdown. Worse luck, we didn't have the dead ball rule then. Hardly had we recovered from this shock than Dudley Dean, the Harvard quarterback, squeezed through a narrow slit at center, stole the ball from Francis Barbour's hands, and dashed 50 yards for the clincher. This stunt of Dean's revolutionized secondary defense tactics. Previously, we had played our backs about 20 feet behind the line on defense; after that we stationed them within six feet of the line.

"We ended our 1890 season by walloping Princeton at Eastern Park, Brooklyn, 32–0. Bum McClung had a field day by scoring four touchdowns. He was money in the bank. That figured—he went on to serve as Secretary of the U.S. Treasury!"

Starting his senior year in 1891, Pudge could hardly believe that it was to be his last season in a Blue jersey. Yale had an extraordinary team that fall, even stronger, in Pudge's opinion, than Pa Corbin's 1888 steamroller. Captain McClung had the sort of personality that would wake the dead.

The superbly equipped Yales flew through a 13-game schedule unhampered that season, minimizing the pressure by scoring a total of 478 points to 0. This was 220 points fewer than Corbin's total, but McClung's troops had a scrawny, sunken-eyed, deathly pale little hellcat at end named Frank Hinkey, and this fact alone would have made them the stronger of the two teams.

Hinkey was a football freak. He weighed only 152 pounds and looked anemic, but his nervous energy was such that he could manhandle giants double his size. From the waist down he had the build of a featherweight, from the waist up a heavyweight. He had muscles like iron, yet was flexible and elastic. "He folded up like an accordion when he tackled his man," Heffelfinger said. "I don't blame Harvard and Princeton runners for being afraid of him. Hinkey whipsawed them to the ground with such bone-cracking ferocity that they were left gasping for breath. To be perfectly honest, we were scared of him ourselves when his lips narrowed to a hard, thin line and his deep-set eyes glowed like live coals."

Foster Sanford, center rush on that Yale eleven, once told of breaking into a hotel room to rescue a man who had incurred Hinkey's wrath. Pulling Hinkey from the bully who had provoked the row, and who was getting more than he had bargained for, the 200-pound Sanford picked his little teammate up bodily and hurled him into a far corner of the room.

Hinkey lay huddled up for a moment, gazing at Sanford with those lambent eyes. Then he spoke. "Sanford," he said, "that was the greatest sensation I've ever experienced. Try it again!"

In Yale archives you will find an action photograph of Hinkey stalking his man, jowls protruding, teeth gritted, eyes dilated. It is not a pleasant picture. Better than a volume of words it tells why ordinarily courageous rivals made a verbal agreement with Hinkey not to whipsaw them over his shoulder if they cried "down."

Tough as a marlin spike despite his deceptively frail appearance, Hinkey never took "time out" in four years of that bruising, old-style football when 5 yards were often purchased at the price of fractured ribs and broken legs. This immunity to injury bred in him an intolerance for men of less rugged fiber. Never having had to leave a game himself, he had no sympathy for those who walked off the field on two feet before the final whistle shrilled. He was a stoic under punishment, setting a Spartan example to his mates.

Seated in the grandstand a year or so after he graduated from Yale, Hinkey could not conceal his disdain at seeing the Yale captain, punch-drunk from contact with a powerful Harvard line, totter to the sidelines at the coach's insistence.

"Why is he leaving the field?" Hinkey growled. "He can still stand!"

Much of Hinkey's uncanny skill as a player was lost on the spectators, sitting snugly up in the stands. It took his own teammates—and his adversaries—to appreciate his wizardry properly.

"One day," Heffelfinger recalled, "there was this old-time Harvard player who visited one of our practices, and he asked one of our fellows to point out some of the Yale stars to him. The Harvard grad was properly impressed by the size and broad shoulders of some of us. Finally, he asked, 'Where's this Frank Hinkey I hear so much talk about?' Well, sir, he couldn't conceal his surprise when he saw Hinkey—scrawny, with sunken cheeks, haunted, deep-set eyes, and a slender, almost fragile body, a consumptive pallor, and hands too big for the rest of him. You wouldn't have turned in the street to look at him. The Harvard old-timer exploded. 'What!' he cried. 'Harvard frightened by that little shrimp? I'm ashamed of my college!' Our visitor, of course, had never faced Hinkey when the light of battle glowed in those brooding eyes."

Shep Homans, who starred at fullback for Princeton in 1891–92, once told what it was like to play across from Hinkey.

"He tackled like a fiend," Homans said. "Johnny Poe, our halfback, and I had a play around end and I remember we never got past Hinkey at any time. He came low and hard, with arms outstretched, and the next thing we knew he was past the interference, grabbed you low, and stopped you flat in your tracks or threw you backward."

Hinkey had an undeserved reputation as a dirty player. Partisans could not understand how such a scrawny, frail-looking athlete could crucify 200-pound opponents unless he resorted to illegal measures.

"It just didn't seem logical, I know," Heffelfinger said, "yet, as a matter of fact, Hinkey never did an unfair thing on the football field in his life. He was a clean player, though granted a ferocious one. He scorned the dirty stuff—heeling, elbowing, kneeing—that was openly taught in those hard-bitten days. Yet, because of the terror of his tackling, he usually got the blame for any tough stuff pulled. A typical case in point was the infamous Springfield incident, which precipitated a two-year break between Yale and Harvard. Harvard players accused Hinkey of deliberately attempting to cripple Edgar Wrightington. Oh, sure, a Hinkey was responsible for the Harvard halfback's broken collar bone, but it wasn't Frank Hinkey, nor was the injury purposely inflicted. Frank's brother Louis accidentally struck Wrightington with his knee while trying to prevent Wrightington from squirming away. Frank wasn't within 15 yards of the play, but he accepted the blame nevertheless to shield his kid brother from undeserved censure. That was typical of Frank Hinkey."

*Frank Hinkey, the all-time football freak, weighed only 154 pounds and looked anemic, but he earned the reputation as the game's hardest tackler of his era.*

Frank Hinkey was a smoldering volcano of suppressed emotions. In football's savage body contact—that atavistic throwback to the bludgeoning battles of the Stone Age—he found emotional release. Shy, introspective, and moody, Hinkey earned the nickname of "Silent Frank." He had few friends in college, no intimate comrades. Off the field he was reticent, gruff, preoccupied, quiet, and given to brooding spells.

"He seldom spoke, and he never laughed at our training table jokes," Heffelfinger said. "He took out his repressions on the football field. The nervous reaction hit him *after* the season was over, and he suffered from fits of depression.

"As my teammate, though, he was something. He had a nose for the ball. He wasn't particularly fast, but he anticipated plays intuitively and bobbed up time and again at the crucial moment to recover fumbles. It was uncanny the way he was always in the right spot. He had football instinct. I often heard Walter Camp say, 'Hinkey drifts through interference like a disembodied spirit to nail the runner.' He was all football. Why, he lugged a football around with him on the campus and even took it along to the lecture room until some professor made him quit.

"Hinkey was a fixture at end from the day he first reported on Yale field as a freshman from Tonawanda High School by way of Andover. Josh Hartwell, later an eminent New York surgeon, played the opposite end for us on the 1891 team. He and I rowed on the Yale crew, and let me tell you football is a sissy sport compared to rowing a four-mile race. I always ran off the field full of pep after a 60-minute game, but my legs shook as though with palsy at the end of the New London boat race. Before we had pulled two miles I was praying for the race to end. In football I was always sorry to hear the final whistle. Rowing seemed drudgery to me. I couldn't have pulled 10 strokes at the age of 54 when I played practically a whole football game."

Next to Hinkey, George Foster Sanford was Yale's most fascinating recruit in 1891. A 10-second sprinter, "Sandy" talked a good game and then went out and delivered. His braggadocio made him unpopular with the conservative element, but Pudge said he liked the kid's spirit.

"Sandy's middle name should have been Ego," Pudge said. "When he first reported to us as a raw freshman off the Hopkins Grammar School sandlots, he shouted, 'I'm your center—I'll lick any man you send against me!' He did, too."

Sanford became Yale's stormy petrel in later years. "There is no king but Dodo!" he exclaimed at a football conference in New Haven in 1909. "When I walk out of this room, I'll take Yale's offensive line play with me."

This threat was prompted by a disagreement between Walter Camp and Sanford on line tactics. Sandy felt that Camp had been weaned away from the old Yale creed by misguided advisers. Tact wasn't Sandy's forte. He called a spade a spade, doubled and redoubled. His failure to resolve his differences with Camp cost him his coaching job.

"How well I recall the day Sandy got the varsity job at center for keeps," Pudge said. "We were playing Penn and couldn't decide whether Phil Stillman or Sanford should start. As acting captain, I hit upon the idea of letting each of them play half the game and then getting Bill Adams, the Pennsylvania center, to tell me which was the harder man to handle. So after the game Adams told me, 'Stillman is a very good center, but where in hell did you dig up that wild guy Sanford? He murdered me!' That settled it in my mind, though some of the Whitney Avenue bigshots called Sanford a 'New Haven townie' and wanted to keep him off the team. Sandy showed them—he went on to become one of New York's biggest insurance operators."

As a coach after graduation, Sanford specialized in keying up his players to a fighting frenzy on game days. He did a thorough job on Charley Chadwick for the 1897 Princeton game. Chadwick, a rawboned, blond-haired giant, was one of those easygoing, good-natured chaps who didn't know his own strength. In practice, he often let the scrubs shove him around. He seemed sluggish and phlegmatic. Just before the Princeton game, he was demoted to the reserves. On the morning of the contest, Sanford took Chadwick aside. "Charley," he said, "I've learned that Princeton thinks you're yellow. They plan to go through your position. Some of our Yale coaches think the only solution is to bench you, but I still have faith in you. If I start you today, how will you play?"

"I'll play like hell!" roared Chadwick, suddenly galvanized. "Just let me at 'em!" His demotion to the scrubs had obviously pricked his pride.

But Sandy took no chances. On the first play of the game, he told the Yale center to slap Chadwick's face. The instructions were obeyed. Chadwick, thinking a Princeton man was giving him the business, went berserk. He played like a wild man, ripping the Tiger line to shreds. Back on the Yale bench, Coach Sanford chuckled to himself. His psychology had worked.

"Locker room psychology has changed since the nineties," Heffelfinger confessed. "Modern coaches seldom resort to fight talks of the old blood-and-thunder type. They've learned that nervous, high-strung kids need toning down rather than keying up. Knute Rockne, most frequently identified with emotional, fiery exhortations, ironically was the one who pioneered this trend to subtle quiet methods. He once told me, 'Pudge, kids can stand just so much keying up before flying off the handle.' Knute recalled that in his playing days at Notre Dame he got an overdose of heroics from an assistant coach named Longman, who used to roar at the Irish, 'Are you going to lie down like a bunch of yellow curs or are you going to fight like men?' Rock said they were impressed at first, but as they grew older that speech lost its stimulating jolt."

In his senior year, 1891, Heffelfinger and the Elis got revenge on Harvard, whitewashing the Cantabs at Springfield, 10-0. In this game, a Harvard man gave Hinkey an uppercut under the jaw. Pointing to the aggressor, Hinkey growled, "My friend, if you hit me that hard again you will break your hand!" It was typical of Hinkey not to hint that he himself feared man or devil.

Pudge's last college game saw Yale whip Princeton, 19-0.

"I'm prejudiced, of course, but I think this 1891 Yale team could have beaten Clinton Frank's 1937 Yale outfit," Pudge said. "We blocked better, had a big edge in line play, and were every bit as fast. Anyway, as I walked off the field following my last game for Yale, a friend grabbed me by the arm and said: 'Heff, you old war horse, how does it feel to be through with football forever?' If I had had John Paul Jones's knack for coining epigrams, I would have replied: 'Me quit football? Why I've only begun to play!' That would have been the truth, too."

A lot of people forget that Pudge Heffelfinger was the first professional football player in history. In 1892, he pocketed $500 to play a game in Pittsburgh. "Until then," he told me, "they usually paid us off with silver pocket watches."

° ° °

Pudge, of course, was not the only star of that period. There were other legendary figures too. How they would stack up with today's All-Americans is questionable, but in their day their fame was undaunted.

*One of the famous Poes who played football at Princeton was quarterback Edgar A. Poe, grandnephew of the renowned poet and captain of the 1889–90 Tigers.*

There was, for example, Arthur Poe, the best of football's most famous family, the Poes of Princeton. Their father, John Prentiss Poe, a nephew of the poet, was graduated from Princeton in 1854 and sent his six sons there, all football players. Arthur, Edgar Allan, and John were All-Americans. They were small men, but tough, indomitable, spirited. The Poe that Ivy Leaguers never will forget was Arthur, a 150-pound end. In the first half of the 1898 Yale game, he picked up a Yale fumble near his own goal line and raced 95 yards for a touchdown, the only score of the game. Yale never heard the end of it. Little Arthur's sensational run was enough to make Old Blues swear!

There were other stars too: William Henry Lewis, an Amherst transfer who played center for

Harvard—handsome, moustachioed, only 170 pounds, two-time All-American, the first black to be so honored; Bill Reid, twice associated with undefeated Harvard football teams, 1898–99, the first Harvard man to score two touchdowns against Yale in one game (1898), and leader of a successful fight against revolt in the ranks among Harvard administrators to eliminate football; Alex Moffat, Princeton 1881–83, football's first great kicker, who invented the spiral punt and thereby changed the whole science of punting; Wild Bill Hickok, Yale's famous All-American guard in 1893–94 and captain of the unbeaten '94 Elis; William (Big Bill) Edwards, Princeton's 260-pound All-American guard and captain of the 1899 championship eleven that beat Yale twice in a row for the first time; Charley Brewer, All-American back in 1892, '93, and '95, who led Harvard to 48 victories in 54 games with his ball carrying; quarterback Clinton Wyckoff, the first Cornell man to make All-American (1895); Charles (Buck) Wharton, Pennsylvania's 6'1", 235-

*Knowlton L. (Snake) Ames, Princeton's 1889 All-America fullback, who bears a striking resemblance to modern singer Robert Goulet, got his nickname because he was a slippery-type runner, clever at spinning, changing direction, and faking the tackler.*

*Inducted into the National Football Hall of Fame in 1970, Cornell's Clinton Wyckoff was All-America quarterback in 1895.*

pound All-American guard in 1895, who knocked blockers and tacklers out of his way like a Paul Bunyan wading through the north woods and who led the Quakers to 52 victories in 56 games between 1893 and '96; three-time All-American guard Arthur Wheeler, who had the distinction at Princeton of never playing against Harvard—the famous series was cancelled while he was in school, 1890–95; Samuel (Brink) Thorne, All-American halfback and Yale captain in 1895, who helped the Elis amass a total of 1,137 points to 63 for opponents in 42 games; tall, blond, broad-shouldered and lean-hipped Winchester (Win) Osgood, an all-time Cornell (1891–92) and Penn (1893–94) backfield flash, who led the Big Red to a 17-4 record and then transferred to the Quakers and carried them to a 24-3 record, including the National Championship in 1894; Marshall (Ma) Newell, the first of Harvard's great linemen, first-team All-American tackle 1891–93; John Henry Minds, a tackle, end, and offensive guard on Coach George Woodruff's famous "guards back" formation, who also doubled as halfback and fullback and captained Pennsylvania in 1897, a team that won 51 of 52 games stretching back to 1894; Phil King, Princeton's 5′6″, 190-pound All-American, whose slick ball handling impressed Caspar Whitney so much that Whitney picked him at quarterback on the 1891 and 1893 All-American selections, and at halfback in 1892; All-American tackle A.R.T. (Doc) Hillebrand, a star of the 1896–99 Princeton teams that won 43 of 47 games, shared the national title with Harvard and Michigan in 1898 and won it outright the next year; Charles Gelbert, called the "Miracle Man" because he weighed only 160 pounds, yet played both guard and end, positions generally reserved for behemoths, All-American on Penn's 1894 eleven that won 12 straight games and outscored opponents 366 to 20; Gordon F. (Skim) Brown, a tall, stern-jawed, lion-eyed guard on the 1897–1900 Yale teams, and one of only three men in history who have made the All-America first team four times (Frank Hinkey and Penn's Trux Hare were the others); Charley Daly, 5′7″, 150 pounds, an excellent quarterback, ball handler, and punt returner, who played in only one losing game at Harvard (a 28-0 defeat by Yale in the finale of his senior year) while being named on Walter Camp's All-America first teams 1898–99, before going on to West Point, where he was saluted as "the greatest football player Army has yet seen."

Last, but by no means least, was T. Truxton Hare, who at 6′1″ and 198 pounds played 60 minutes at guard in every game (55) for Pennsylvania from 1897 through 1900. While making the All-America team four times, Hare led the Quakers to an overall 48-5-2 record and was a big reason why opponents were held scoreless 33 times.

When the nation's football authorities sat down in 1969—college football's centennial—and picked an all-time, all-star eleven comprised of the finest players of The First Fifty Years, they named Hare and Heffelfinger as guards. And many years after they had both retired from the game, Pudge wrote: "My old friend, Trux Hare, will always stand out in my mind as the greatest of Penn linemen. No one could put him on his back."

With few exceptions, these men still stand among the most illustrious football players in the history of their schools. They were so transcendent in their prowess, skill, and spirit as to convince historians that they truly belong to the ages.

# *Storied Rivalries, Towering Names, 1900–20*

On the early edge of the century, football went right on being a mighty rough pastime. Injuries were frequent and severe. It was a brawling game.

"Football!" snorted John L. Sullivan, the heavyweight champion (1882–92). "There's *murder* in that game. Prizefighting doesn't compare in roughness or danger with football. In the ring, at least you know what you're doing. You know what your opponent is trying to do. He's right there in front of you. There's only one of him. But in football—there's 11 guys trying to do you in!"

In 1900, kickers dominated the scoring. The players wore very little protective armor. I once asked Pudge Heffelfinger what he wore on his head to keep his brains from rattling around. "None of that sissy stuff for me," he replied. "I just let my hair grow long and pulled it through a turtleneck sweater." The few helmets around were made of hard, padded leather with leather earflaps, and they fit like a skullcap. The fullback sometimes was the only man to wear one.

Razzle-dazzle of a sort was used more frequently, with the quarterback faking a pitchout to one man, then flicking it over that receiver's head to the runner beyond; or halfbacks would crisscross, as in a modern reverse, and one would hand the ball to the other before he hit the scrimmage line. Every play into the line meant an enormous pileup, with ends, quarterback, and halfbacks on the offense all huffing and puffing to shove the ball carrier that extra inch, and the entire defensive line, plus most of the backfield, storming in to stem the tide. Often the defensive quarterback alone would remain between the runner and the goal—and the ball carrier was not whistled "down" until he surrendered.

Columbia had a pet play called the "flying hurdle." It starred a square-rigged, 210-pound projectile named Harold Weekes, a three-time All-American halfback. Weekes would get the ball some 5 yards behind his front line, which was all pinched in tight. Then he would get a running start and, using the stooped-over shoulders of his teammates Wild Bill Morley and C. Berrien, he would go off like a diver from a springboard, as though launching himself into space, and catapult headfirst across the scrimmage line. He landed on his feet like a cat and was off to the races. This was the same Harold Hathaway Weekes, self-effacing scion of an old Knickerbocker family, who had won the 1899 Yale game on a 55-yard gallop for the first Lions' victory over the Blue since 1873.

It was inevitable for Finley Peter Dunne to take a crack at football violence. For many years he wrote the most popular and most quoted newspaper column in America. Born and brought up in Chicago, he created Mr. Martin Dooley, the saloonkeeper-philosopher of Archey Road, who in his wonderful Irish dialect commented with wit and wisdom on national issues and milder phenomena, including football. In 1901, Dunne turned Mr. Dooley loose on the bloodshed in college football:

> Ye see, whin 'tis done by la-ads that wurruks at it, an'

has no other occupation, it's futball; an', whin it is done in fun an' be way of a joke, it's disordherly conduct, assault an' battery an' rite . . . Down town it's futball; out here it's the Irish killin' each other. Down town th' spectators sees it f'r a dollar apiece; out here it costs the spectator ne'er a cint, but th' players has to pay tin dollars an' costs.

could help us out if the sacrifice for her was not too great. We would certainly appreciate such a favor on her part.

You know how badly we need the game if it is possible. Would the first Saturday of November be a possibility?

I wrote Mr. Gordon Brown, captain of your team,

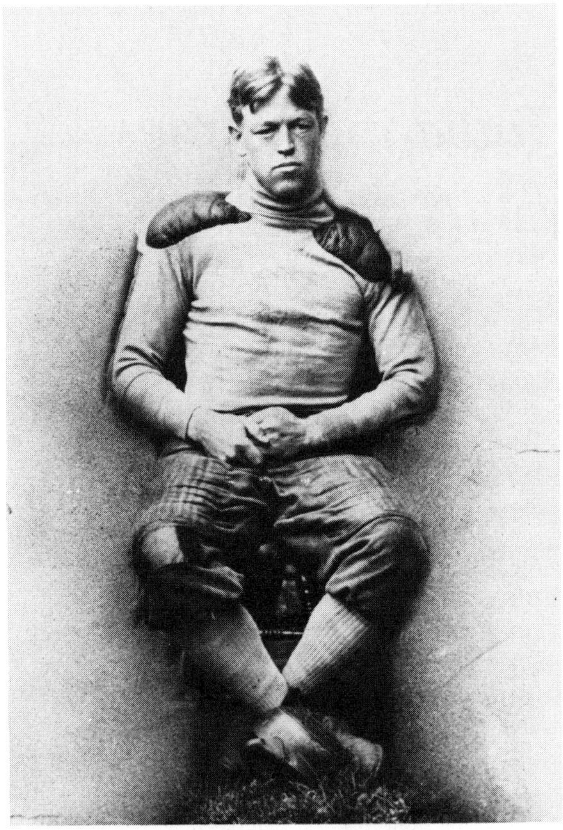

*Two All-America halfbacks who made Columbia football click at the turn of the century were William Morley, left, and Harold Weekes, both in the National Football Hall of Fame.*

Yale re-established itself at the top of American college football during the first 10 years of the new century. Six of those years, Yale was Eastern Champion with an automatically strong claim also on national honors. Even to play the Elis was to advance one's football standing.

Take the case of Navy. In the summer of 1900, a professor at Annapolis, Paul J. Dashiell, who had officiated Yale-Harvard games and was on friendly terms with Walter Camp, wrote Camp:

Dear Walter:

Would it not be possible for Yale to play the Navy cadets here next fall? It is not such a long trip and Yale who said he would speak to you about it.

Harvard and Yale have made West Point what she is—can't you help us, too? There would be no trouble about guarantees. With best regards, I am,

Sincerely yours,

Paul J. Dashiell.

Captain Gordon Brown's 1900 Yales earned the appropriate name of "The Team of the Century." They won 12 games in a row, including big victories over Princeton (29-5) and Harvard (28-0). They ran up a total of 336 points to 10. Against the

Cantabs, they gained 555 yards on the ground, almost unheard of even today in major football competition. They had excellent personnel. Seven of the team made Camp's All-America: guard Brown, center Beau Olcott, tackles Ralph Bloomer and George Stillman, quarterback Bill Fincke, right halfback George Chadwick, and fullback Perry Hale. Ends Charlie Gould and Sherman Coy and guard Dick Sheldon made the second team. The lone remaining member of the Blue varsity, halfback Al Sharpe, was named on Camp's third team. Thus, every one of the 11 starters made either first, second, or third team All-America.

In their first seven games of 1900, Yale held opponents scoreless. The eighth game on the schedule was against Columbia at the Polo Grounds. The Bulldogs sought revenge on the Lions for beating them in 1899, 5-0. The Yale line was braced to stop Harold Weekes.

When the Yale team arrived at the Polo Grounds the day of the game, it got a shock. Although the weather had been unseasonably hot and dry, leaving burned grass and baked ground on gridirons all over the East, the field at the Polo Grounds resembled a Paleozoic marsh. It developed later that Foster Sanford, Yale '92, who coached Columbia, had enlisted the aid of all nearby fire departments. The firemen, big supporters of the Lions, had attached their hoses to available fireplugs and flooded the field. Coach Sanford, of course, had prepared his players for muddy going with wooden cleats. On the other hand, Yale's cleats were designed for a hard field and now were totally impractical.

Resourcefulness was not lacking in Malcolm McBride, the Yale coach. He marched out of the Polo Grounds and went in search of a shoe store, where he bought two dozen pairs of shoes in assorted styles and sizes. Then he rushed the shoes to a carpenter.

"I want you to nail wooden mudsuckers onto the bottoms of these," he said.

"It will take me an hour," said the carpenter.

"All right," McBride said, "but you get them to me at the Polo Grounds as soon as you can."

At game time, the shoes with the wooden mudsuckers had not yet arrived. For the first half, things were not so good for Yale. Harold Weekes repeated his feat of 1899, getting loose on a 50-yard touchdown run. The conversion was missed. Columbia led, 5-0, at the half. The Blue could not maneuver in the mud.

Fortunately, the carpenter showed up with an armful of mudsucker shoes at half time. The players fought for them. Perry Hale, the pile-driving fullback, drew a beautiful pair of patent leathers.

Despite the footwear, Perry did all right for old Yale. He scored one touchdown; Gordon Brown scored the other. After each score, Perry, in his patent leathers, kicked the conversion goal. Yale won, 12-5.

On October 12, 1901, Navy got its wish. Yale traveled down to Annapolis and blasted the Midshipmen, 24-0. The Naval Academy did not renew the series for 34 years. Future Rear Admiral Emory S. Land, who broke his collarbone in the game, recalled years later: "The one thing I remember about that contest is that John Rogers, our left tackle, suddenly called, 'Time, time, I've lost my tooth!' Time was called while both teams searched for the tooth and found it."

Yale came up to the Harvard game that November undefeated in 24 games. The Crimson had a string of 11 going. Coached by William T. Reid, Jr., they were flying high. The colorful Reid, an All-American baseball catcher at Harvard the previous spring, was already becoming something of a legend around Cambridge. His arrival as a freshman in 1897 coincided with the beginning of Harvard's first serious challenge of the Yale football colossus. Harvard had beaten Yale only twice before, in 1876 and in 1890. Reid had been a fullback on Coach Guy Murchie's powerful frosh eleven, which drubbed Yale's Bullpups, 34-0, and the Pennsylvania frosh, 52-0. Bill was steady on defense, a punter of high, whirling, hard-to-handle spirals, and a glue-fingered line plunger and runner with the flat feet that helps make a good cutback man.

Quarterback Charlie Daly liked to call on Reid when the situation was smoky, and that's what he did twice at Yale Field in 1898, although Bill was only a sophomore. Both times Reid charged into the end zone, and became the first Harvard player ever to score two touchdowns on Yale in one game. That 17-0 victory completed Harvard's first undefeated season (11-0) since 1890.

A sprained ankle in the 16-0 victory over Penn kept Reid, as a junior, out of the 1899 Yale game at old Soldiers Field until the last 15 minutes. Then two of his whirling spirals forced Yale fumbles, and Harvard got a good enough field position after the second one to try a field goal. The try was no good, and the game ended, 0-0.

Bill Reid suffered a severe tendon pull in his right leg in his senior season, and he confined his

1900 football to serving as head cheerleader. So, as freshman or varsity man, he never played in a losing football game against Yale.

In those days, the captain-elect picked the coach, and the 1901 Harvard captain, Dave Campbell, a smart, spirited All-American end who was generally recognized as the greatest defensive wingman of his generation, picked Reid. From the beginning, Bill demonstrated superior aptitude as organizer, fundamentalist, and psychologist.

When Captain Campbell hurt a knee before the 1901 Yale game, Reid succeeded in keeping it a secret from the New Haven espionage corps. Practice was held in private, and Campbell worked out but avoided contact. When his Harvard teammates were about to leave the field after practice, however, and expose themselves to public view, Campbell's mates poured water over his head to simulate perspiration. To further befog Blue spies, Ed Bowditch, the other end, faked a limp and carefully arranged a piece of gauze to leak casually out of his stocking near the knee.

Campbell and Bowditch played the entire 70 minutes of the Yale game—football was then split into two 35-minute halves—and so did Crawford Blagden, that spirited left tackle who had postponed for weeks the removal of a recalcitrant appendix. Oliver Cutts, Harvard's right tackle, carried the ball 20 times on the sainted tackle-back play, and seldom failed to puncture the Yale line.

Meanwhile, Coach Reid walked the sidelines in a light felt hat, and sometimes with a cane, too, for instant identification by his quarterbacks in moments of crisis. He had four signals: more line plays, more end runs, more punting, and field goal.

The 22-0 shellacking in 1901 was the worst a Yale team had ever received. Harvard's 12-0 record included victories over Army, Carlisle, Brown, Penn, and Dartmouth. Campbell's team outscored its opponents, 254-54, and took its place at the top alongside Arthur Cumnock's 1890 team and Ben Dibblee's 1898 eleven, coached by Cam Forbes, another earlier Harvard football man who was ahead of his time.

In the next three years, 1902–04, however, Harvard football descended, losing to Yale, 23-0, 16-0, and 12-0, and in 1905 Reid, who had departed after 1901, was called back as coach. He inherited a morale problem from a system that selected the team less on the basis of talent than correctness of club credentials. Reid soon drove home the message that he wanted a winner, and that's what he got.

*Two Warners from Cornell are in the National Football Hall of Fame. The most famous, of course, is Glenn Scobey (Pop) Warner; the other is his younger brother, William, above, All-America guard in 1901–02.*

While Harvard was getting itself on the winning track, Yale, Princeton, and Penn fought fiercely for the right to call themselves Eastern Champions. The Elis were on top in 1902, were replaced by Princeton in 1903. Yale and Penn shared the top in 1904–05, as did Princeton with the Bulldogs in 1906. Yale held the throne by itself in 1907, followed by Harvard again in '08, and then it was Yale, with a 10-0-0 record, once more in '09.

Ironically, Yale, which had so dominated the East in the first decade of the century, was unable to finish first at any time during the next 10 years.

Princeton and Harvard beat all opponents in 1902 except Yale. Aside from the 12 points they

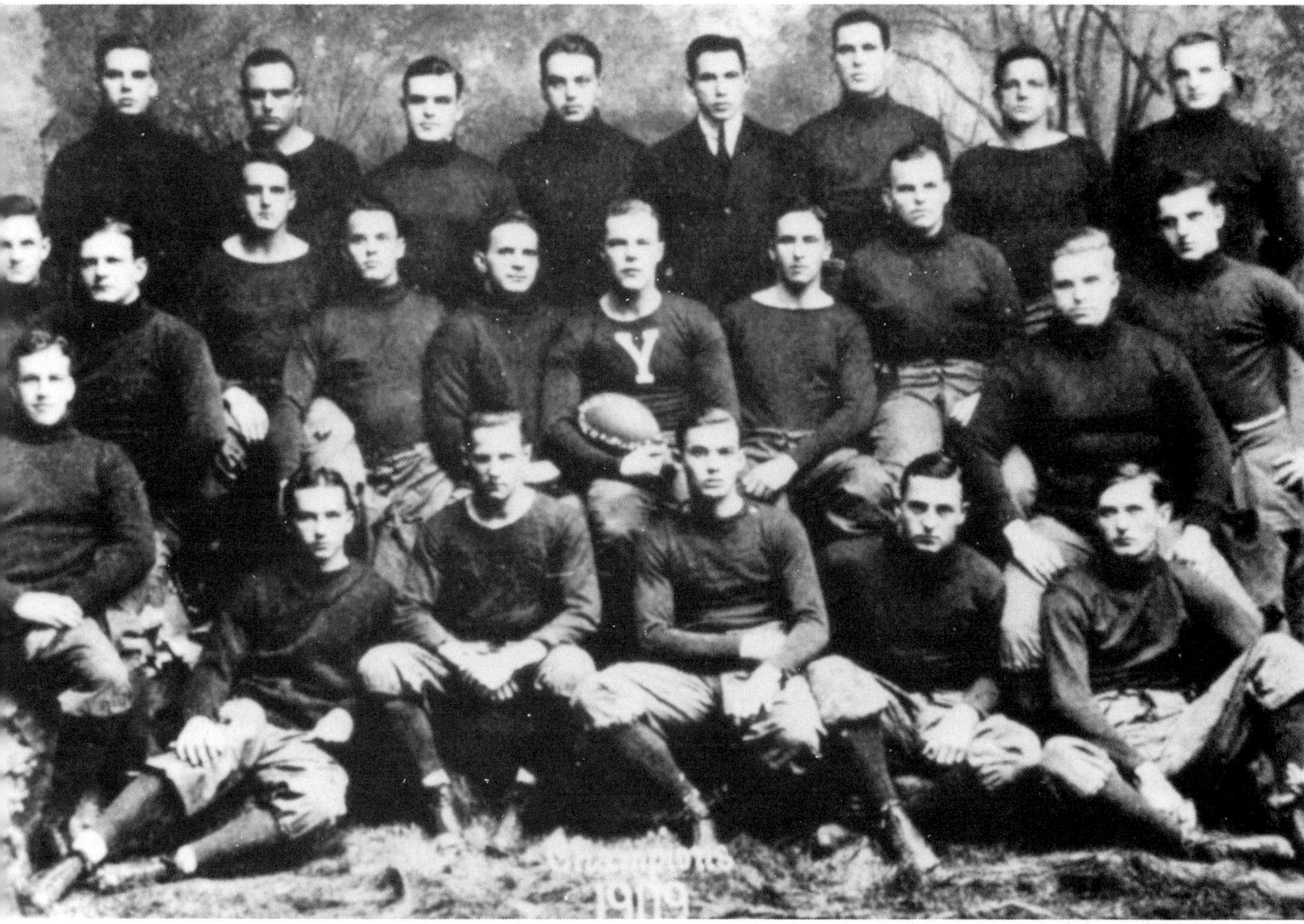


*Captain Ted Coy's 1909 Yale champions were undefeated in 10 games, scoring a total of 209 points while shutting out all their opponents. Back row, 1. to r.: Paul, Savage, Hobbs, Andrus, White, Brown, Field, Spencer. Second row: Francis, Goebel, Murphy, Logan, Daly, Captain Coy, Philbin, Corey, Conney, Naedele. Front row: Lilley, Holt, Johnson, Howe, Kilpatrick, Vaughan.*

*Yale's 1909 coaches, captain, and trainer, l to r.: Henry Wheaton, head coach Howard Jones (the Blue's first paid coach at $2,500 a year), Captain Ted Coy, and famous trainer Johnny Mack.*

yielded to the Elis, the Tigers allowed only five points all season. John DeWitt's field goal kicking was a big factor in the team's success. Against Cornell, he scored on 55- and 45-yard kicks, against Yale on a 50-yarder, and against Columbia on a 45-yard kick.

Experts rated the 1902 Yales as one of the school's finest teams. Its "Irish" line was termed by Frank Hinkey as "the best ever seen on any field." It was comprised of ends Tom Shevlin, a freshman, and Chuck Rafferty; tackles Jim Hogan and Ralph Kinney, a sophomore; guards Ned Glass and George Goss; and Henry Holt, center. Shevlin, Hogan, Kinney, Glass, and Holt were all named on the All-America team with Captain George Chadwick and Foster Rockwell of the backfield.

"Many judges rate Chadwick's 1902 eleven as even stronger than Gordon Brown's 1900 bunch," wrote George Trevor in the *New York Sun* years later. "Certainly it was superior on a man-to-man basis. Holt, a mountain of a man, fed the ball like an automatic stoker to his backs. He made only two poor snaps all season. Unhappily, one of them allowed West Point to get an undeserved tie."

Trevor was really sold on the 1902 Elis. In the poetic style of the journalists of his day, Ned Glass was "a rawboned wolfhound type, 6 feet, 4 inches tall, with the lean, hollow-cheeked aspect of Abe Lincoln, the rail-splitter." Jim Hogan was a "barrel-chested, ox-necked, gorilla-armed tackle, who cried like a child from sheer Celtic emotion when things went wrong." Ralph Kinney was "tall as a pine tree," and Tom Shevlin was "built like a Sandow, fast and agile enough to star on the track team."

Tom Shevlin had a very high opinion of himself. It was his boast that no man had ever gained a yard around his end. "Watch me," he used to tell his fellow Elis. "See—you box the tackle off this way—you get rid of the interferer this way—and then—if you're a Tom Shevlin—you also get the man with the ball."

For all his swashbuckling bravado, Shevlin was respected. He could usually back up his boasts. One afternoon he called Mike Murphy, Yale's noted trainer and father confessor to the athletes, aside during practice on Yale Field. "What's on your mind, Tom?" Murphy wanted to know.

"Mike," Tom said, "I've often heard you talk of that guy Hinkey. Tell me about him—was he as big as I am?"

"Why, no, Tom. Hinkey was just a little chap, weighed 50 pounds less than you, and wasn't nearly as tall."

Shevlin inflated his chest like a pouter pigeon. "Well, was this Hinkey as strong as I am?"

"Nothing like as strong, Tom." Murphy emphasized his words. "You're a hammer thrower, an' you broke the college strength test record."

Big Tom was obviously pleased. "Could he run as fast as me?"

"Hell, no. Why, you're a track man. He couldn't stay within five yards of you in the hundred. Hinkey was no speed boy."

"I thought so!" Shevlin's voice showed self-satisfaction. "Now, tell me one more thing. How do I compare with him as a football player?"

Old Mike smiled. "Do you really want me to tell you the truth?"

"Sure thing," Tom urged, frowning a bit.

"Well, then"—Mike bit off each word as an ax shears yellow pine—"Frank Hinkey could have made you look like the change from a counterfeit nickel!"

° ° °

With Captain John Dewitt taking his place alongside Princeton's greatest linemen, Nassau trimmed a heavily favored Yale eleven in 1903 that included Hogan, Shevlin, Kinney, Rafferty, Farmer, and Bloomer. The Princeton strong boy was the workhorse of the 11-0-0 National Champions. On the same team with him were such stars as halfback Dana Kafer, tackle Jim Cooney, ends Howard Henry and Ralph Davis, and guard Herb Dillon.

Unquestionably, DeWitt, a dropkicking specialist, had his finest hour in the 1903 Yale game. The National Championship was at stake. The Elis were unbeaten in 10 games and had scored 290 points to 15. Princeton's offense-defense stood at 248-0.

The game was played at New Haven. Yale got off fast, leading 6-0. It then drove down the field once more, but the Tigers held on the 26-yard line. Ledyard Mitchell, the Yale place-kicker, dropped back for a field goal attempt. It was to be the turning point of the game. The left side of the Princeton line poured through on Mitchell's kicking foot. DeWitt, playing his last college game, charged from right guard and scooped up the ball on the dead run. With the aid of two good peelback blocks by Davis and Henry, DeWitt broke into the clear and ran 70 yards for a touchdown. He also dropkicked the extra point to tie the score.

After that, the Tigers gradually wore down the Elis. With time for only several more plays, DeWitt got ready to attempt a 5-point place kick from the Yale 53-yard line. He rushed forward and put all his weight into the ball. Like a homing pigeon, it went spinning end over end for 53 yards, cleanly splitting the uprights high above the crossbar. For John DeWitt, All-American, it was his 11th point of the game. Final score: Princeton 11, Yale 6—a glorious way for the Princeton strong boy to close out his college career.

There was no Harvard on the 1903 Princeton schedule because the two schools were not on speaking terms, but the Tigers had the satisfaction of walloping Dartmouth and Yale, both of whom defeated the Cantabs.

° ° °

Pennsylvania's 1904 eleven is ranked by some as the best of all the early Red and Blue teams. It was coached by Dr. Carl Williams, who was captain of the 1895 Quakers and had succeeded George Woodruff, a Yale man, as head coach in 1902.

Unbeaten in 12 games, the 1904 Quakers rolled over such Ivy opponents as Brown, 6-0; Columbia, 16-0; Harvard, 11-0; and Cornell, 34-0. Bob Torrey was captain of the team, which had three members on Walter Camp's All-America first team that year, two on the second team, and two on the third. Penn lined up with Wharton Sinkler and Garfield Weede at the ends, Otis Lamson and T. A. Butkiewicz at tackles, guards Gus Ziegler and Frank Piekarski, and Captain Torrey at center. The backfield had Vince Stevenson at quarterback, Marshall Reynolds and Ed Greene at the half, and Andy Smith, who was to win greater fame as coach of California's "wonder teams," at fullback.

Twenty-seven years later, George Trevor wrote in the *New York Sun:* "If I were compelled to pick the greatest of all Penn elevens, I would name Captain Torrey's 1904 juggernaut. A stonewall on defense, allowing its opponents one paltry field goal, Torrey's team packed the hardest punch in Pennsylvania history. Despite the strength of the opposition, no rival crossed Penn's goal in 1904. They couldn't dent the line. Rough-and-tumble Bob Torrey, a born scrapper, originated the roving style of center play. He was the first center to play loose behind the line on defense. In the backfield, Vincent Stevenson had no equal at quarterback. A hard-bitten, merciless driver whose tongue stung like a scorpion, he electrified players and spectators by his blood-chilling flying hurdles. He would leap high in the air when cornered, legs lashing out sideways like scythes. Harold Weekes of Columbia was the first exponent of the flying hurdle, but he employed it to scale the line of scrimmage, whereas Stevenson's breathtaking leaps were executed on the dead run in the open field." It was Stevenson's ability to jump over a line of opposing players that led to the rules committee's legislation against hurdling.

Penn had another unbeaten team in 1905 under Carl Williams, but was held to a 6-6 tie by Lafayette. The tie broke Penn's 20-game winning streak.

Keeping pace with Penn in 1905 was Yale. The Elis had their first perfect season since 1900, winning all 10 games. They gave up only one field goal (a change in scoring rules made a field goal count 4 points instead of 5) to Princeton. The fabulous Tom Shevlin was captain of the team at end and was named on Camp's All-America for the third time. The quarterback was Tad Jones, one of Yale's most glamorous names, who was All-America 1906–07; and his brother Howard, who was to achieve huge success as coach at Yale, Iowa, and Southern California, also played on all three Eli teams.

The 1906 and 1907 Yale elevens also were unbeaten, although each was tied once while winning nine games. Princeton played the Bulldogs to a scoreless tie in 1906, and Army did the same in '07. The Tigers gave Yale a terrible scare in 1907. Trailing at half time, 10-0, the Blue rallied and managed to pound out a 12-to-10 victory. The hero of the contest was Ted Coy, whose crushing, destroying, devastating line plunging pounded ahead for two touchdowns in the second half against a pack of fighting Tigers who battled desperately for every inch they yielded. With tears streaming down his cheeks, Tad Jones sobbed out the signals—signals for the grim Coy to carry the ball—Coy, Coy, always Coy, and he did not fail.

Ted Coy, big and powerful at 6 feet and 195 pounds, was everything that Yale football enthusiasts felt an Eli gridiron hero should look like. His boyish face with the snub nose, the leonine shock of blond hair, and the white sweatband around his head gave him the appearance of a genuine Frank Merriwell come to life. When he went to work against opponents, he did not fail the Merriwell image.

Football has known relatively few great fullbacks, and Coy certainly was one of them. During his three varsity seasons, 1907–09, he played in only one losing game, a 4-0 loss to Harvard in 1908 at New Haven. He ran with high knee action, hammering speed, and fluid motion. He punted a long ball, could dropkick off his instep, was an accurate passer when called upon, and tackled and blocked with bone-jarring ferocity. Durable? He never was known to ask for a time out. Most of all, he was a runner, driving up the middle, smashing inside or outside tackle, or fanning out around end. He was a superb "pressure" player. Coy led Yale to come-from-behind victories time after time. He was so much the "hero of the Blue" that Yale alumni still spoke of him in awe many years after he graduated. Coy made Camp's All-America in 1908, and the following year he was elected Yale captain.

In 1909, Coy beat Harvard with two field goals. A great kidder, no sooner had the ball left his foot on those dropkicks than he turned to Bill Langford, the referee, and kept up a constant chatter while the ball was still in the air.

"Mr. Langford," he asked, "did you ever see a prettier kick than that one? Don't tell me you aren't going to give me a goal?"

Coy had a habit of kicking the ball so high that you couldn't be sure whether or not it crossed the bar inside the uprights. He took four shots at the goalposts that afternoon, and Langford gave him credit for two goals. Coy was not happy, and he protested to Langford.

"What's biting you, Coy?" snapped Langford. "Here I give you 50 percent of your field goal tries, and I'm not sure even now whether any of them actually went across. Boy, you're lucky and you don't know it."

That silenced Captain Coy.

Coy punted on first down consistently that day because an injury prevented him from running with the ball. John Kilpatrick, later the president of Madison Square Garden, played left end and soon was exhausted covering those towering 60-yard kicks. Finally he turned to big Ham Andrus, who was playing guard, and asked him to take a turn going down under Coy's punts. Andrus was a stolid chap who seldom spoke and then only to grunt "be gosh." He looked at Kilpatrick perturbedly and blurted, "Be gosh, whoever heard of a guard going down under a kick?" Kilpatrick had a persuasive Irish way with him, however, and Andrus reluctantly agreed to chase the next punt. Ham was fast despite his heft, and he got down in time to spill O'Flaherty, the Harvard safety man.

"Great stuff, Ham," cried Kilpatrick. "We've found a new end by accident."

Andrus gave Kilpatrick a withering look. "Be gosh!" he grunted. "I'm through." And he was.

The 1908 Yale game stands out so vividly in Harvard memories because Vic Kennard ended a long sequence of Crimson defeats with a terrific dropkick. Vic had spent the entire previous summer practicing dropkicks across an improvised goal rigged up on a farm in Maine. Bob Nourse, the varsity center, worked out with him. Together they hatched a plot.

"If I'm sent in to try a field goal in the Yale game," Kennard said, "snap the ball to me the instant I raise my right toe. Don't wait for a signal from the quarterback. We'll fool everyone."

Percy Haughton, in his first season as Harvard coach, had a profound contempt for field goal kicking.

"It's a chicken way to score," he said.

But Kennard kept hammering away at his special play, and when Harvard bogged down on the Yale 15-yard line, he caught Haughton's eye.

"Let me try it now," Vic begged.

Finally, Percy said, "All right, go ahead."

The ruse worked precisely as Kennard had long planned. With Vic standing like a statue behind the big Harvard line, even Haughton was taken by surprise when he dropkicked that 4-point goal while both lines were still standing erect, waiting for the signal that never came.

"Several years afterward," Kennard recalled, "Ted Coy told me that the Yale players never knew I had even kicked the ball till they saw it sailing above their heads. Naturally, Nourse and I felt darned good. Not the least of our boyish elation sprang from having slipped a fast one over on Old Eagle Eye himself, Percy Haughton."

It was Coach Haughton who originated Harvard's long line of sleight-of-hand quarterbacks, who never carried the ball themselves but slipped it slickly to another back with the adroitness of a pickpocket. He stumbled on this baffling now-you-see-it-now-you-don't magic quite by accident.

During the summer of 1908, Haughton was fooling around on the beach at Nantasket with his pet Newfoundland dog. He noticed that when he faked to throw the ball in one direction, then suddenly tossed it to the opposite side, he tricked the animal into falling for the bluff.

"Humph," grunted Percy, "if I can fool this

sonofabitch, maybe I can fool those Yale bums!"

From this grew Haughton's hidden ball offense, actually the harbinger of the spinner cycle series, later developed to perfection by such successful coaches as Hugo Bezdek and Dick Harlow.

Of course, one of football coaching's all-time innovators had already carved himself quite a reputation by this time. I am talking about Glenn Scobey (Pop) Warner, head coach at Cornell in 1897–98 and again in 1904–06. In five years of coaching at Ithaca, Pop's record was 36-13-3. His Cornell teams averaged 24 points per game and held opponents to only 4 per contest.

Although historians credit Amos Alonzo Stagg, the old Yale end, with numerous coaching firsts, Pop Warner also fashioned many devices. He was the first football coach to dummy-scrimmage; he introduced the practice of numbering plays; he was the first to teach the spiral punt and one of the first to advocate the spiral pass; in 1897, his fabulous Carlisle Indians wore football's first headgear; he was the first to use the football huddle; he invented the double wingback formation, with the line unbalanced for more blocking force. Mousetrap plays, the screen pass, the rolling block, the naked reverse, hidden ball plays, series plays, the unbalanced line and backfield all came out of Pop Warner's head. As early as 1908, he was giving courses in football by mail.

"You cannot play two kinds of football at once, dirty and good," he cautioned his players. "There is no system of play that substitutes for knocking an opponent down. When you hit, hit hard. You play the way you practice. Practice the right way and you will react the right way in a game."

Coach Warner's double wingback was just what it said: One halfback lined up a little behind and outside the left end and the other posted himself in the same manner near the right end. The quarterback and fullback deployed behind the center, either one taking the snap to start the play. The line was unbalanced left or right in a 4-2 split, with two tackles or two guards lined up shoulder to shoulder on the strong side.

From this, Warner used a bewildering set of spins, reverses, double reverses, fake reverses, runs from fake passes, and passes from fake runs. Eventually, like all formations, the double wing was caught up with by the defenses, which crashed their ends and drilled their other linemen not to go for the fakes.

Of all early innovators, it seems safe enough to say that Pop was topped by only one man—Stagg. Stagg himself said that Warner was more responsible than any other man in the enactment of rules that improved football.

"Glenn was never very active *on* the rules committee," Stagg said. "But we'd make a rule and Glenn would think up a way to get around it within the rules, and we'd have to meet his challenge. He kept us on our toes, I can tell you."

By this time, of course, the forward pass had become an important weapon in football's arsenal. Following the heavy player casualty list of 1905 and the demand by President Theodore Roosevelt for a more open and less brutal game, the football rules committee got together the next year and legalized the pass. The lawmakers also outlawed

*After one day of fundamentals and scrimmaging, Glenn Scobey (Pop) Warner was named first string guard at Cornell in 1892, played for three years, and then went on to devote a lifetime to coaching the game, molding it into its present image, and developing some of the greatest players ever known.*

hurdling and ruled that linemen could not line up in the backfield on the offense unless they were 5 yards or more behind the line.

It was not the forward pass that opened up the game, however, for there were only a few players in the East who could even spiral the ball. What really began to cut down on football carnage was the establishment of a "neutral zone" to restrain players of the opposing rush lines from getting any closer together, before play began, than the length of the football. The old rule permitted opposing linemen to line up head to head, or chest to chest, and invariably there was much man-to-man scuffling before the ball was snapped. This led to the lust and bloodshed and slugging that had made the game so attractive to spectators. It also had led to long delays in the game, while the referee tried to pry the combatants apart.

When the pass was first legalized, it was handicapped by severe restrictions. For example, the ball could be thrown forward only when the passer was at least 5 yards, laterally, from the center of the scrimmage line. The field was marked off with longitudinal lines to help the officials enforce this rule. Once the ball had been touched by a receiver, a forward pass, like a kick, could be recovered by either side. If it went out of bounds, it was awarded to the opponent at the point where it crossed the boundary. If it was caught behind the goal line, it became a touchback and entitled the defending team to a free kick-out from the goal.

Another 1906 rules change lengthened the yards-to-go in three downs to 10, rather than 5, and this actually inhibited the pass, which might completely "waste" a down. The quarterback kick was still relied on by many teams, some of whom had quarterbacks who could boot the ball as accurately as they could pass. Still, the forward pass gradually gained favor, and by 1908 most of the colleges were working on pass plays of their own.

Backfield men, on a pass as on a kick, would usually devote themselves to protecting the passer —although they might take a short toss if the passer could not see an end in the clear. Linemen did not immediately learn to yield a yard or two of ground to give the passer more time. It was still deemed traitorous to let an enemy tackler across the line without knocking him down.

The resemblance between the forward pass and the punt was further stressed by the frequent use of the out-of-bounds pass on last down. Like the old coffin-corner kick, this could immobilize a team near its own goal line, for the ball went over to the opponent on the spot where it crossed the sideline.

In 1910, the rules committee finally repealed many of the restrictions on the pass and put a final end to mass play by insisting that linemen could not line up in the backfield on offense at any time. It also made illegal the pushing and pulling of the ball carrier, which had often turned him into a human football and had made for an enormous crash of bone and muscle at the point of impact on a line play. The rules makers also granted an extra down in which to make 10 yards, and this provided the quarterback with a fine chance to pass before he was forced to kick. Now the third down became the standard passing down.

This opening of the offense also prompted some opening of the defense. The center now began to play "soft"—that is, to hesitate or even withdraw a step or two when the ball was snapped, to guard against deception. Soon he became a "roving center," who was ready to shift his force to whatever spot at which the enemy attack was aimed.

Bob Zuppke, the great Illinois coach, said that the first time he ever saw an overhead spiral pass used was in the Penn-Michigan game of 1908.

"Andy Smith, who later launched those 'wonder teams' at Berkeley, played in the Penn backfield that day," Zup recalled. "Hurry-Up Yost, the Michigan coach, had his forward passers throwing an overhand spiral but without gripping the ball. That same year, Pop Warner's Indians from Carlisle threw underhand spirals.

"In the early days of the pass, the ball had to be thrown so that it crossed the scrimmage line at least 5 yards on either side of the center. In that game against Pennsylvania, Yost's team used a lateral to one side, followed by a forward pass downfield.

"Not long after the pass was made legal, an amendment was made to the rules providing that a forward pass could not be made for a distance of more than 20 yards. How did the officials judge whether or not the ball traveled more than 20 yards? They put a stick down 20 yards ahead of the ball before each play."

° ° °

The tale stands tall and mad. Percy Haughton, before his first game against Yale as Harvard coach, in the dressing room at old Yale Field in 1908, was supposed to have led in a live, healthy bulldog and strangled it in front of his players. "There," seethed Percy, flinging aside the poor dead animal. "That's what I want you to do to those Yale bastards out there this afternoon."

In the figurative sense, however, Percy Duncan Haughton, out of Staten Island, New York, Groton, and Harvard, did indeed throttle the Yale Bulldog. Under Haughton, Harvard's first paid coach, the Crimson replaced the Elis as the dominant football power of America. From 1908 through 1916, the Crimson enjoyed its heroic age on the gridiron.

Haughton, who had first showed promise as a head coach at Cornell in 1899 and 1900, turned out nine Harvard teams which won 71, lost seven, tied five. From 1911 to the fifth game of the 1915 season, the Cantabs rolled 33 games in a row without defeat. Before Haughton, Harvard had beaten Yale only four times in 28 games. Under Haughton, Harvard beat Yale five times, was tied twice, lost twice.

The 1912–13 Haughton teams had perfect 9-0-0 records. The 1908, 1910, and 1914 teams were unbeaten but tied. The 1914 Harvards, tied by Penn State and Brown, whipped Yale, 36-0, in the Yale Bowl inaugural, and that team that day was rated by many Crimson supporters as the finest that ever played for Haughton.

In the opinion, however, of the late Lothrop (Lo) Withington, captain and right tackle of the 1910 eleven, and later a line coach under Haughton, Percy did his finest job with his 1908 Harvard team. That was a patchwork bunch with little depth and only one outstanding player, tackle Hamilton Fish. Yet it won nine and missed a perfect season by a 6-6 tie with Navy. In upsetting Yale at New Haven, 4-0, Harvard handed the Blue its first defeat in 43 games and gained Harvard's first victory over the Bulldogs in seven years.

Hamilton Fish, a 6′4″, 225-pound tackle and captain of Harvard's 1908 National Champions, told me that the team had brains as well as brawn.

"For some reason," he recalled, "Hooks Burr, our All-America guard, Mort Newhall, and I decided to take a course in the Harvard Divinity School called Church History Since The Reformation. The class was made up of 20 regular divinity students—and the three of us from the football team. Teaching the course was Dr. George Moore, an able and eloquent clergyman. In his lectures, he showed a strong predilection toward missionary life in China. I, therefore, decided to write my main thesis on why I wanted to become a missionary in China. The result was that Dr. Moore gave me an A in the course. Burr and Newhall got the same. None of the regular divinity students did better than a B. I tell that story because too often the critics of football claim that the I.Q. of football players is below the class average. Nuts! Consider these facts: From our 1908 Harvard champions came three prominent lawyers, three highly successful private bankers, one member of Congress (myself), one coal magnate, one prominent doctor, and our best halfback became chairman of the Portland, Oregon, Chamber of Commerce. Furthermore, Charlie Crowley, our fine sophomore end, was kicked out of Harvard for failing to understand Harvard culture. When the Dean challenged his grades, Charlie hit the roof. He finished telling the Dean off by calling him an s.o.b. So Charlie got the heave-ho and wound up playing end at Notre Dame for three years with Knute Rockne. He later became head football coach at Columbia.

"Under Percy Haughton, we didn't lose a game in 1908. I can tell you, though, that we were terribly worried about Jim Thorpe and his un-

*Hamilton Fish, now in his eighties and the last surviving member of Walter Cam's all-time, All-America eleven, is pictured here as a 6′4″ tackle on the national cochampionship Harvard team.*

beaten Carlisle team. The week before we played them they rolled over Syracuse, and the Syracuse coach was furious with Pop Warner, the Carlisle coach. He insisted that Pop had taken advantage of him by sewing half-leather, football-shaped pads on the elbows of the jerseys of his halfbacks and ends, making it almost impossible to tell who had the ball. The Syracuse coach was so mad he tipped us off in advance as to what Warner was up to, but we couldn't find anything in the rules preventing it.

"On the day of the game, here came the Carlisle players out on the field with those half-leather pads on their elbows. Percy Haughton was ready for them. Since we were the home team and had to supply the game ball, Percy had it painted crimson—to match our Harvard jerseys. Pop Warner knew when he had met his match. 'Well,' he said, 'Percy Haughton has outsmarted us,' and he sent his backs and ends inside to change their jerseys. Then we went to work and gave Carlisle its only defeat of the year, 17-0.

"As a Harvard tackle, with our ends playing a yard back of the scrimmage line, Haughton had me catching the passes in 1908, which was legal in those days. I took quite a beating, too, because the defensive backs were allowed to tackle you and knock you down *before* the ball even got to you. Well, I became so trained in concentrating on the ball and catching it that I just ignored the slashing and pounding I got. Take the 1908 Dartmouth game, for example. On this one play I went downfield on a long pass and was nailed on the 5-yard line before the ball got to me. But I never took my eyes off the ball and managed to pull it in while on my knees. The next day the papers were calling it a miracle catch. Actually, the only miraculous thing about it was that it was a well-thrown pass, and catching it was fairly routine. It won the game for Harvard and, I understand, a lot of Dartmouth money changed hands. Two years later, the rule was changed to protect the pass catcher.

"The Big Game for us in 1908, of course, was the November 21st Yale contest at New Haven. With the National Championship at stake, tickets were hard to find. Even the players and coaches were limited to a certain quota. Ticket prices suddenly zoomed. Jimmy Walker, who later became mayor of New York, managed to scrape up three, I recall. The extra two tickets were for Al Smith and Bob Wagner, a state senator. When they arrived at the game, Al Smith asked Jimmy for his ticket, saying that he wanted to linger outside the gate for five minutes and finish his cigar. Jimmy told him, 'No you don't, Al, you're coming in with me. If I give you the ticket, you will just stay out here and scalp it for $50!' In those days, Al Smith was as poor as a church mouse and could have used the dough a lot more than a good seat on the 50-yard line."

For years, Captain Fish fretted under published newspaper articles that he led the tandem that resulted in the accidental death of Ici Byrne, Army's fiery left tackle. The contest was played at West Point, October 30, 1909. Harvard concentrated on "barnyard football," hitting at one point in the line, with all available massed power either pulling or pushing the ball carrier.

"Here is what really happened that day," Ham told me. "A few plays before the fatal accident, I had shifted over to the opposite side of the line and didn't even come in contact with Byrne. He broke his neck tackling Dodo Minot, our low-slung fullback. As a matter of fact, I had noticed that Ici was weakening, and I sent a message to the Army bench suggesting that Captain Byrne was physically unfit to continue. That brought the Army trainer rushing onto the field to examine him, but Ici, as game as they come, refused to leave the field. Had he been playing today, a coach would have made him take a rest."

They carried Ici Byrne off to the hospital where he died later that night. He regained consciousness long enough to ask, "Did we win?"

The chief surgeon lied like an officer and a gentleman.

"You stopped them, son," he said.

Many years later, on the wall of Red Blaik's office at West Point, hung a photograph of Cadet Ici Byrne. The caption was grim.

"Killed in action," it read.

° ° °

Those who played for Percy Haughton confessed he was hard to play for. They concurred that his intense, sometimes brutal, approach to football could be traced to his utter dedication to the job and his conviction that he would get it done only if he were the undiluted martinet.

"Some of the guys on the team hated him," testified All-America Eddie Mahan, a member of Harvard's great 1914 backfield. "I hated him, at first. But later I got to like him and found him a good friend. He was a born aristocrat, yet he could be very rough. During the first six weeks of the season he was a tyrant, cursed, and manhandled players. After this period of rugged work was over, he would turn around and become very affable. He was an excellent teacher and never wasted words. He was able to make men play when they were very tired. He was always trying to prove that you could play 20 percent better than you thought you could when tired. His plan for every game was to wear the other fellow down for three quarters and then win in the last quarter."

Haughton's cardinal rule was: No Harvard man *walks* onto the field, he has to be *running*. To avoid injuries, he enforced the touch-tag system during practice. He also had a *thing* about football writers and old stars haunting his practice field, and he had them barred from daily sessions. A major in the chemical warfare service in World War I, there was much of the military in his brand of coaching. "Football is a miniature war game played under somewhat more civilized rules of conduct, in which the team becomes the military force of the school or university it represents," he once wrote. "Most of the combat principles of the Field Service Regulations of the U.S. Army are applicable to the modern game of football."

Haughton's Harvard dynasty tended to overshadow his contributions to football. He was the first coach to set up a modern-style staff, with special assistants for line, backfield, ends, kicking, and passing; the first to chart his practice sessions down to the minute; the first to employ a modern scouting system. He was truly a student of the game. He never hesitated to take what was good from other systems, styles of play, or ideas. He recognized the greatness of Camp and the Yale system based on sound fundamentals and superior line play. He did not hesitate to borrow deception from Warner, discipline from the army, power of Pennsylvania's guards back, nor the passing skills displayed by any opponent.

Haughton's great disappointment was Harvard's 8-0 loss to Yale in 1909. Ted Coy's championship eleven was held to two first downs in the game, but Harvard fumbles of Coy's high punts and two deep kicks following these fumbles turned the tide. The battle of the two great lines has seldom been equalled in college football, with Yale men Kilpatrick, Hobbs, Andrus, Cooney, Goebel, Lilly, and Savage facing Browne, Fish, Fisher, the Withington brothers—Paul and Lothrop—McKay, and Bud Smith for Harvard. Old-timers insisted for years that there never were two better college lines facing each other.

There were eight All-America players on the field in the 1909 Yale-Harvard game, six from Yale and two from Harvard. It was Yale's only victory over Haughton until 1916.

The 1910 Harvard eleven, captained by Lothrop Withington, won eight and played a scoreless tie with Yale. Cornell was the only team to score on it.

Brown was another strong team in the East in 1910. It had one of the best quarterbacks of the year, as well as of 1909 and 1911, in Earl Sprackling. In the words of George Trevor, he was an "eye-dazzler in an open field, a flashy punt handler, and a bull's-eye passer. He could also dropkick field goals from nearly midfield under pressure."

Jay Barry, the Brown historian, points out that the 5′9″, 150-pound Sprackling could beat you at least seven different ways: "An excellent runner, he was a constant threat from scrimmage in running back punts and kickoffs. He was a dependable field goal kicker, a solid defensive man, a smart field general, and a stirring leader."

Running the team was one of Sprack's trademarks. He was a fiery driver, a bit acid when things went wrong, but a real pepper pot. He often ran with the ball tucked under one arm and with the other at the backs of his blockers, telling them what to do. He was one of the first players in the country to use the forward pass with any consistency and success. Most passers in those days had to palm and scale the big, oval-shaped ball, but Sprack could hit the mark with it. He threw it like a baseball, with plenty of wrist action, and his receivers had no trouble catching it.

A runner who relied largely on speed, Sprackling wore as little heavy equipment as possible. He seldom wore a helmet, shoulder pads, or hip pads. Yet he never seemed to get hurt.

Sprackling's most famous play was his 110-yard kickoff return for a touchdown in Brown's upset of Carlisle, 21-8, at New York's old Polo Grounds in 1909. The same two teams met at Providence in 1910 in a showdown between Sprackling and Jim Thorpe. Sprack matched Injun Jim run for run and kick for kick, keeping the spectators on edge. Thorpe ran out of steam before Sprack did. Final score: Brown 15, Carlisle 6.

But Sprackling's greatest hour came in Brown's sensational 21-0 victory over Yale three weeks later. That was the Bruin's first win over Yale in 30 years and 17 games. For his part, Sprack merely

*William Earl Sprackling, 150-pound quarterback, was the only three-time All-America in Brown history (1909–10–11). One of the game's most successful pioneers with the forward pass, he ran brilliantly, kicked field goals, and called signals.*

kicked three field goals—a fourth was nullified by a penalty—and he completed five of six passes for 180 yards and a touchdown, and he gained 36 yards in nine carries, returned 13 punts for 150 yards, and five kickoffs for 90 yards. All told, he accounted for 456 of the 608 yards that Brown gained that day. Walter Camp watched the game from the stands and afterward called Sprackling "the best quarterback in America." For the record, Brown's accumlative won-lost-tied figures during Sprackling's four varsity seasons was 26-11-3. Most All-America selectors named him on their first teams in 1909–10–11.

° ° °

They were not on the schedules of Yale and Harvard and Princeton, but the Penn Quakers had some of their finest teams during the years 1907–10, when they accumulated a 38-3-4 record. The 1908 eleven was unbeaten. Sol Metzger, captain of the 1903 Quakers, was the head coach, and All-American fullback Bill Hollenback was the captain. Penn gave Michigan a 29-0 licking in '08—a Wolverine team, incidentally, that included the Hall of Fame Germany Shulz at center. After the game, Hurry-Up Yost, the Michigan coach, rattled a few nerves around Cambridge by telling sports writers that "Penn deserves being rated over Harvard as the nation's top team."

In addition to Hollenback, Penn end Hunter Scarlett was also chosen on Camp's All-America first team. The other members of the Pennsylvania eleven were Harry Braddock, end; Dexter Draper and Fred Gaston, tackles; Bob Lamberton and George Deitrick, guards; Bill Marks, center; Albert Miller and Chuck Keinath, alternating quarterbacks; and Jack Means and John Manier, halfbacks.

The great Jim Thorpe was once asked to name the toughest opponent he ever played against in college.

"Who else?" Thorpe said. "Bill Hollenback of Penn. I played against him only once, but that was enough. Every time we had the ball and I tried to break through the line, Bill was there to stop me. He really jarred me. I did the same to him when he carried the ball. He stood 6′3″ and weighed 210 and was a hard man to bring down. Our personal duel lasted 60 minutes. The final score ended 6-6, and we both spent a week in the hospital recuperating."

Among the other strong teams of the era was the 1908 Cornell eleven, which won seven games and tied Amos Alonzo Stagg's Chicago team before losing to Penn, 17-0.

° ° °

There were several important changes in the rules. In 1910, the game was divided into four periods of 15 minutes each; seven men were required on the offensive line of scrimmage when the ball was put in play; and pushing, pulling, and interlocking interference were abolished, ending the mass momentum plays. Restrictions against the forward pass continued to loosen up, and a field goal now counted 3 points instead of 4. A player taken out of a game could go back in the next quarter, and the checkerboard appearance of the field changed to a gridiron again.

In 1911, Harvard lost two games by a total of 5 points. It was beaten by an outstanding Princeton eleven, 8-6, and by the Carlisle Indians, 18-15. The Cantabs were three deep in every position and were heavy favorites. But Carlisle was deepest where it counted most. It had Jim Thorpe. When the Crimson moved to a 6-0 lead, Jim kicked a 23-yard field goal and a 43-yard field goal to tie the score. Then he booted a 37-yarder to send little Carlisle ahead.

Back stormed aroused Harvard in the second half for a quick touchdown. Then the Crimson added a field goal.

"Give me that ball," growled Thorpe. They gave him the ball. He battered and slashed his way 70 yards through all those All-America stars for the tying touchdown. Minutes from the end of the game Carlisle was far from pay dirt on last down.

"I'll kick one," Jim said.

"But you've already kicked three," he was told.

"Then I'll kick another," he insisted.

He did. It was a 43-yarder for an unbelievable 18-15 Carlisle victory—and Thorpe scored all the points.

The defeat by the Indians was the last Harvard was to know until it fell before Chuck Barrett's mighty Cornell champions four years later.

° ° °

Measured solely by the paucity of certified stars in its 1911 lineup, Princeton did not figure to run away and hide from anyone. But they had spirit and were fanatical about proving the prognosticators wrong. Bill Roper, who had coached the Tigers during the years 1906–08, was out of football in 1909, but now was back again and had his sights on a Big Three title. He had his players believing in miracles. "He's convinced us that if we wear Orange and Black colors and the other team doesn't, we've got 'em licked," remarked one Princetonian.

Bill Roper came from the school of great, romantic football coaches. Where others were big on tricky systems and won-lost records, he capitalized on locker room oratory, come-from-behind victories, and heart-stopping upsets. Even loyal Princeton men agree that Roper, who had played on Nassau's championship team in 1899, was no inventive genius of football science. His credo seemed to be that he had neither the time nor the inclination to mull over new trends and formations. He was no master of detail. He left the intricacies to his assistants. And yet few coaches could fire up a team mentally better than the Princeton coach. He was Mr. Inspiration. He could make his athletes play far over their heads.

During a game, Roper was unpredictable. Opponents did not know what ran through his mind. The unexpected had come to be expected so often that no one knew what to expect. He teemed with nervous energy. His mind was packed with action and ideas. He changed his mind frequently, but he was always very definite about his final decisions.

The most famous slogan in Princeton sports history—The team that won't be beat, can't be beat—for years was commonly credited to Roper. Wrong.

"The author of that line undoubtedly was Johnny Poe, third of Princeton's six football-playing brothers and a member of the 1895 class," testifies Bill Stryker, former director of sports information at Princeton. "Harvard and Princeton faced each other on November 7, 1896, up at Cambridge. The Orange and Black was captained by Garrett Cochran, a Walter Camp All-American end in 1897, while Johnny Poe served as a member of the alumni coaching committee charged with aiding the captain in directing the team. This is how the story really goes. The words are those of Cochran.

"'Johnny Poe was behind the door when fear went by. Everyone knows of his wonderful courage. I remember that in the Harvard game of '96 at Cambridge near the end of the first half, two of our best men, Ad Kelly and Sport Armstrong, were seriously hurt, which disorganized the team. Poe, with his true Princeton spirit, sent this message to each man on the team: *If you won't be beat, you can't be beat!* This worked a miracle. It put iron in each man's soul, and never from that point did Harvard gain a yard, and for four succeeding years Princeton's battle cry was: If you won't be beat, you can't be beat!' "

Princeton lived up to Poe's battle cry in 1911. Although tied by Lehigh and Navy, the Tigers won eight games, lost none. They edged Yale, 6-3, skimmed by Harvard, 8-6, and got by Dartmouth by the thin margin of a field goal, 3-0. It was a typical Bill Roper season. Defensive strength and opportunism spelled the difference. Yale, for example, might have won except for a break. Art Howe kicked a field goal to put the Elis ahead, but in the second quarter, Sam White, the Princeton end, scooped up a Yale fumble on wet, slippery Yale Field and ran 50 yards for a touchdown. That was Nassau's first victory over the Blue since 1903. Against Harvard, White grabbed a blocked kick and ran 95 yards across the goal line. Later, White tackled Henry Gardner, who had just run back to retrieve a Tiger punt, and knocked him across the goal line for a safety to win the game.

In the victory over Yale, Princeton did not make a first down, but it was so strong on defense and so vigilant to make the most of its breaks that it more than made up for its weak offense. The Orange and Black had a special incentive for beating Yale. The year before it had lost to the Blue, 5-3. The Harvard game was the first meeting of the teams since 1896.

° ° °

The year 1912 was the year that the "golden era" really set in for Harvard. For the next three years and part of a fourth, the Cantabs would remain invincible. Yale, held scoreless in 1910 and 1911, managed to scrape up only 5 points to Harvard's 71 during the next three versions of The Game.

With changes in the rules—a fourth down had been added in 1910 in which to make 10 yards, the playing field was shortened from 110 yards to 100 yards, and a touchdown counted 6 instead of 5—and an all-around back like All-American Percy Wendell, the Harvard attack was devastating Saturday after Saturday as it piled up a total of 176 points against 22 on the way to a 9-0-0 record. Brown was smashed, 30-10; Princeton fell, 16-6; and Yale crumpled, 20-0.

"Harvard possessed a remarkable collection of individual players, mostly sophomores," wrote Howell Stevens in the *Harvard A.A. News*. "Among them was sure-footed sophomore Charley Brickley, dependable Wally Trumbull, rock-ribbed Stan Pennock, slashing Tack Hardwick, and Peebo Gardner, whirling dervish on the attack and a buzz saw at cutting down opposing ball carriers in the secondary defense. Brickley was an arch wrecker. Against a Princeton eleven that scored 322 points—35 points per game average—he split the Nassau goalposts three times, twice with dropkicks and once with a prodigious placement boot of 47 yards. After this knockout blow, the Tigers slumped noticeably."

In the Yale game, Harvard scored 10 points in the first quarter on a touchdown, the first against the Elis in 11 years, and a field goal by Brickley. Bob Storer made the TD after recovering a fumble of a Sam Felton punt, induced by Hardwick's vicious tackle. Hardwick then kicked the conversion.

Soon after, still in the first period, Brickley dropkicked a field goal from the 33. That provided the Cantabs with a 10-point lead—plenty. But they got 10 more in the second half. Brickley ran 18 yards for a touchdown after recovering a fumble. Hardwick again kicked the extra point. Then Brickley added another field goal, this time from the 17 after he had intercepted a Yale pass. That made the final score, 20-0.

Brickley's two field goals in the Yale game brought his total for the season to 12.

° ° °

The one-sided Harvard victory was the straw that broke the camel's back at New Haven. The Old Blues were restless, and demanded action. It was agreed that something should be done. But what? Walter Camp, in a final effort to regain control, wrote a letter to Ray Tompkins. It was apparent that Camp was hurt because Coach Arthur Howe and Captain Jesse Spalding had ignored his counsel.

"The newspapers have arranged it all," wrote Camp. "They insist Yale's coaching system must go, that a regular paid coach like Haughton must be secured. We defeated Harvard year after year with monotonous regularity, then because a captain and a young head coach will have no help, we play two ties and then get a beating, all the past is at once forgotten. We must imitate our rivals!"

Henry Ketcham, captain-elect for 1913 and an All-American center, called a meeting of all available former Yale captains and coaches at the new Hotel Taft. Camp had a preliminary meeting with Ketcham. This became known to Jack Owsley, successful coach of the undefeated 1905 Yale eleven and a man with stout convictions. At the Taft meeting, Owsley criticized Camp for the earlier meeting with Ketcham.

Robert W. Watson, captain of the undefeated 1880 team, jumped to his feet and exclaimed, "Anything that Walter Camp does is all right with me!"

"Who the hell are you?" inquired Owsley.

A mild argument broke out before order was restored. Out of the rhubarb came a graduate committee with Camp on it, but he was minus his old power.

In a letter to me in 1976, Henry Ketcham, in his eighties, recalled the details:

"In the year of my captaincy, I appointed Howard Jones, Yale '08, as the first paid coach at Yale. Prior to 1913 it had always been the practice at New Haven for the captain of the preceding year to come back the following fall and coach the team. Harvard had hired Percy Haughton as a paid professional coach several years before—and had beaten us more often than we them—and I felt it was time for Yale to hire a head coach too. So we signed Howard Jones for $2,500 a year. In 1909, Howard had received $3,000 expense money to coach us, but 1913 was the first time Yale had ever put a coach on salary. Since Coach Coy's undefeated team in '09, Howard had coached at Ohio State in 1910, turning out an unbeaten though thrice-tied team, and had been among the Old Blues who returned to help out on Yale Field in 1911 and '12."

It was with the undefeated, untied, and unscored through 1909 Elis that Jones first showed his coaching aptitude and his appreciation that the worst mistake a coach can make is to get caught without material. The 1909 Yales were so good that nobody ever got beyond the Eli 28-yard line.

As a coach, Jones emphasized position play to his linemen: "Lick a man and hold your position. You have a spot about a yard or two either side of you to see that nobody gets through. No matter who winds up with the ball, they won't go anywhere if you guard your own small territory and don't get faked out, trying to find where the ball is."

Jones was a fundamentalist and a conservative; some thought him an archconservative. More than 60 percent of his team's total practice time was involved with purely fundamental blocking and tackling positions. He gave everything his personal attention. It was not unusual to find him down on the ground in practice showing his players how to block, following every play on the dead run, and acting as though he were still playing end. He just could not relax and let his aides do the heavy work. He thought football all his waking hours, including many in which he should have been asleep. He liked to put the names of players on gambling chips and move them about, devising formations, plays, and defenses.

Jones was so preoccupied that he often lost himself going home nights, misplaced socks and keys, forgot his appointments, and usually had to be asked a question a second or third time. His strongest language was "gol-dang" and "ye-gods" and "pshaw." Despite his austere exterior, he was an inwardly sensitive person, and by the end of each season he suffered from tension. Nervous smoking of cigarettes was his only vice. Otherwise he lived the spartan life he preached to his players. He never took a drink.

Jones would hardly ever pat a player on the back coming off the field, but after the game he would go around the dressing room and talk one by one to those who had seen action, thank them for a good effort, and look into possible injuries. He did not believe in coddling hurts and bruises, however. "When a player is hurt," he said, "he should say so, but not until then. *Nothing* is more harmful to the morale of the squad while scrimmaging than the agonizing cry of an injured man. A good rule to follow is to keep still until one is sure he's hurt, and then not yell the information from the housetops, but to report quietly to the physician in charge."

Although he was often harsh with his players, he bred in them a good team spirit. He liked to hear music in the locker room. "I like to hear the players singing songs after a hard practice and while dressing," he said. "I know then that most of the men will leave in good spirits, that they will have forgotten the unpleasant, unimportant occurrences of the practice by the time they are dressed."

Still very young, still far from the full development of the coaching powers he would achieve later at Iowa and Southern California, the Howard Jones of 1913 couldn't do much to arrest the downward curve of Yale football. The Blue was beaten by Colgate, 16-6, and held to scoreless ties by Maine and Washington and Jefferson going into the Princeton game. The Tigers had smashed Fordham, 69-0; Bucknell, 28-6; Syracuse, 13-0; Rutgers, 14-3; and Holy Cross, 54-0. Their only losses were to Dartmouth, 6-0, and Harvard, 3-0.

Yale was 5-2-2. The Tigers, 5-2-0, were 6-point favorites. But Yale got a 3-3 tie, with Otis Guernsey's 30-yard field goal matching a 43-yarder by Captain Hobey Baker. Baker saved Princeton in the fourth quarter when he dragged down Foggy Ainsworth, the Yale halfback, on the Nassau 6, after Foggy had slipped around end for 58 yards.

Yale had come up with a new chant at the Brown game (Yale 17, Brown 0) and planned to sing it at Harvard in the season's finale on November 22. It began "Good night, poor Harvard," and ended "Harvard, good night!" As it turned out, the Yale fans found little cause to sing anything at Cambridge. This was hinted during practice by a bit of Haughton psychology. Percy had an assistant manager place footballs Indian file at 10-yard intervals, beginning on the 20 and continuing past midfield. Brickley, who could place-kick as slickly as he could dropkick, began at the 20, and booted one after another squarely through the uprights.

In the game itself, Brickley was just as accurate. He dropkicked field goals from the 35-, 38-, 32-, and 24-yard lines and a placement from the 40, tying the intercollegiate record of five field goals in one game. He also missed two placements, one from the 44, the other from the 50. In the last quarter, Otis Guernsey kicked one for Yale from the 38 and the Bulldogs picked up two more points on a safety. Final score: Brickley 15, Yale 5, marking Harvard's first victory over Yale at Harvard Stadium. Previously, the Blue had won four and tied one there.

This was the second week in a row that Brickley's right toe smashed precedence. Against Princeton in the mud, his 19-yard dropkick won the game, 3-0, for the Cantabs' first victory ever at Princeton.

Howard Jones spent only one season at Yale. In 1914, he was gone. Nelson (Bud) Talbott was elected Yale captain, and Frank Hinkey, who ever since his graduation in 1895 had been a part of the school's graduate coaching system, was signed to a three-year contract as head coach. It was felt that he had the rounded experience to cope with Haughton.

As a coach, however, Hinkey never approached his stature as a player. He was imaginative offensively but too unconcerned with fundamentals.

For Frank Hinkey, everything that came after his athletic career at Yale was an anticlimax. He had crowded so much of his nervous energy into college football that he had all too little left for the daily grind of life. His repressed, pent-up personality was not adjusted to the human relationships associated with business. He lived too much in the past.

So when Hinkey was called back to Yale as head football coach, the welter of minute details devolving upon the coach aggravated his tendency to brood. He grew morose and irascible.

As Yale captain of the 1893–94 elevens, Hinkey had been worshipped by his teammates. He made a great leader. His teammates would have jumped off West Rock if he had given the order. But while leadership was his birthright, he had no knack of imparting his vast knowledge of the game to others. He lacked the patience to teach raw novices football technique from the ground up. He expected too much from them, took it for granted that they would acquire the knack of blocking, tackling, interfering, and use of hands instinctively—as he himself had done. Consequently, Hinkey neglected to school his players in the fundamentals. He concentrated all his energies upon attack. Thus, his team was an unbalanced product—all attack, no defense. It could score touchdowns, no denying that, but opponents could make them even faster.

As an offensive strategist, Hinkey was 10 years ahead of his time. He foresaw possibilities in the lateral pass that were not realized until many years later. The tactical patterns of Hinkey's rugby toss attack were more advanced, more shrewdly conceived than the lateral pass plays later in vogue.

Everybody around New Haven was talking championship as the 1914 Yales moved easily past Maine, Wesleyan, Virginia, and Lehigh. The fifth game of the season at Yale Field, October 27, was with a new opponent, Notre Dame. The East was still talking about Notre Dame's stunning 35-13, Dorais-to-Rockne victory at Army the year before. The Fighting Irish carried a 27-game winning streak against the Elis, and a lot of Chicago money was betting on the tiny Indiana school to make it 28.

Notre Dame's potent passing combination of Dorais-to-Rockne was graduated, but it still had Ray Eichenlaub, the big All-American fullback, to pulverize the Yale line. And Rockne by now was serving as Coach Jess Harper's assistant. Years later, in his autobiography, Rockne described what happened in the 1914 Yale-Notre Dame contest:

"I sat on the side line at New Haven that Saturday afternoon and saw a good Yale team captained by Bud Talbott, with a crack halfback named Harry Legore leading the attack. They made Notre Dame look like a high school squad. They lateral-passed Notre Dame out of the park and knocked our ears down to the tune of 28 to 0—the most valuable lesson Notre Dame ever had in football. It taught us never to be cocksure. Modern football at Notre Dame can be dated from that game, as we made vital use of every lesson we learned. On the following Monday, Jess Harper put in Stagg's backfield shift with my idea of flexing or shuttling the ends, which was the beginning of what is known in football today as the Notre Dame system."

Coach Hinkey had been coaxed against his better judgment into unveiling his secret rugby attack against Notre Dame. He had planned originally to save it for Princeton and Harvard, but the Yale alumni out in the Midwest, alarmed at rumors about how tough the Irish were, demanded action. "We don't want to get licked by a little cow college," they screamed. "Use your secret weapons, Hinkey." So Hinkey gave in to pressure. Notre Dame had never before faced a rugby-type offense, and repeatedly tackled the wrong man. Four times the Yale backs exploited their rugby tactics to score long-range touchdowns as the boys from South Bend groped in vain for the runner. Rockne was disgusted. He blamed his team's defeat on a collective case of "swelled head" caused by too much newspaper publicity.

"I know what was wrong with you guys," chortled Rockne on the homeward-bound train. "You forgot to bring your scrapbooks to the game. Yale didn't realize how good you really were!"

The victory over Notre Dame was sweet, but Hinkey had tipped his hand to Harvard scouts. They had discovered that the secret to stopping the rugby attack was to knock the middle man out of the play.

Although the 1914 Harvards were tied by both Brown (0-0) and Penn State (13-13), there were those who ranked them as the greatest of all the early Harvard elevens. The spark and workhorse of the backfield was Eddie Mahan, an All-American fullback for the third straight season. He could do it all—run, kick, pass, block, and tackle. Opponents were frustrated by his agile leg movements, coffin-corner punts, and pinpoint passing. He was one of the Harvard backfield's genuine adornments. He was asked one time how he ran so well, how he sidestepped so many tacklers. "I simply give them the foot, right or left, and then take it away," Eddie said. Mahan was one of the few star runners who did not care very much for an interference. He much preferred picking his own way up or down the field.

To help prepare his defense against Yale's lateral attack, Percy Haughton invited Frank (Shag) Shaughnessey down from Montreal to Cambridge. Shag, a star at Notre Dame early in the century, had coached at McGill University and won two consecutive dominion college championships in rugby. So Shag showed Percy the defense needed to negate Yale's lateral passing game: a defensive end smashing in on the middle man in the lateral trio and a fast-covering secondary.

Haughton brought Harvard to its peak for the November 21st New Haven visit. After the Penn State tie, they successfully turned back a good Michigan team, 7-0, blasted Princeton, 20-0, and fought Brown to a scoreless tie.

Yale's only loss was to the Generals of Washington and Jefferson, 13-7. Yale bounced back with victories over Colgate, 49-7, Brown, 14-6, and Princeton, 19-14. The Brown game, incidentally, was the last ever played at old Yale Field.

Haughton had a special reason for wanting to beat the Bulldogs at New Haven. Eleven years before, the Blue had celebrated its first game in the new Harvard Stadium with a 16-0 victory, and that was an old score Percy wanted to wipe out.

The 1914 Yale-Harvard game served as the inaugural for the new Yale Bowl, then the largest of

*Harvard spoiled Yale Bowl's grand opening, November 21, 1914, by trouncing the Elis, 36-0. Filled to capacity (70,874), this was at the time the largest crowd ever to witness a football game in America.*

modern amphitheaters, and 71,000 spectators sat agog in it. Some 300,000 cubic yards of earth had been excavated and 20,000 cubic yards of concrete slabs had been laid directly upon the leveled tiers of earth, with one million pounds of steel reinforcement for the concrete. The field was 27 feet below ground level. The top of the bank forming the outside of the Bowl was nine feet above the ground. There were 30 tunnels, 7 feet wide and 8 feet high, for spectators to enter and leave, and two more tunnels, 10 feet wide by 8 feet high, for the athletes to get to and from the field.

When Harvard deployed widely across the field in the first play of the game, the huge crowd was seeing what was very probably the first use of the five-man defensive line. The defense worked fairly well. Yet Yale once reached the Harvard 4-yard line on forward passes, only to lose the ball on a fumble. Jeff Coolidge, the Crimson end, picked up the ball and raced 98 yards for a touchdown. With Mahan spearheading the way, Harvard had already scored twice before Coolidge's run, and at the end it was 36-0, Yale's worst beating through that time.

"Yale," needled the Sunday newspapers, "supplied the Bowl, but Harvard had the punch."

In all departments that day, Harvard was awesome.

Looking back over 1912–14, Yale had not done all that badly. The Blue had lost only five games out of a total of 28—but three of them had been to Harvard, and none of those had been close.

Archibald MacLeish was a member of the 1913–14 Yale squad, the same MacLeish who went on to become a Boylston Professor at Harvard, poet, essayist, dramatist, Librarian of Congress, State Department official and Assistant Secretary of State, decorated Commander of the French Legion of Honor in World War I, and three-time winner of the Pulitzer Prize. At Yale, he belonged to a literary group with Stephen Vincent Benet and Thornton Wilder, and distinguished himself as Phi Beta Kappa and 1915 class poet.

"Yes, it is historically true that I played football at Yale," MacLeish said. "It is historically true that I won my freshman numerals. It is even historically true that I won my Y—as an all-purpose, all-position substitute on a series of Yale teams which never beat Harvard. But to say I was a star would be palpable fraud. I have only one glorious memory of those four years and its setting is not Soldiers Field in Cambridge but the bar of the long-vanished Tremont Hotel in Boston. We—we being the Yale freshman team of the fall of 1911—had just held the best Harvard freshman team in a generation (Brickley, Bradlee, Hardwick, Coolidge, Logan) to a nothing-to-nothing tie in a downpour of helpful rain, and we were relaxing, not without noise, when the coach of that famous Harvard frosh team approached us, looked us over, focused on me (he had had a drink or two himself), and announced in the voice of an indignant beagle sighting a fox that I was, without question, the dirtiest little *sonofabitch* of a center ever to visit Cambridge, Massachusetts. It was heady praise. But unhappily I didn't deserve that honor, either. I was little but not *that* little."

Another literary light who came out of Yale was George Trevor, the Rembrandt of American sportwriters. His was a style that touched on pure poetry. He described Ted Coy as "a leonine figure, with a pug nose and a shock of yellow hair like a Gloucester fisher girl." Red Grange, in the language of George, was a "tall, greyhound of a boy, with hair the color of a Turner sunset, the rhythm of a Pavlova, and two speeds—fast and faster." Frank Hinkey was a "living flame—a disembodied spirit who sifted through interference to nail the man with the ball."

Once, while we were collaborating on a book in 1949 shortly before his death, I asked George, who came from a Harvard family, why he violated family tradition and enrolled at Yale. The football editor of the old *New York Sun* grinned.

"I had been reared in a Harvard family and dutifully clutched a Crimson pennant during those disastrous years when the Cantabs seldom beat Yale," George explained. "But I wanted to ride with a winner, and I stunned my family by announcing that I was going to Yale, the big power in the East in those days. My parents were properly shocked. They finally abandoned me for an academic infidel."

The upshot was sublime irony. Scarcely had George enrolled at New Haven than Percy Haughton pulled his famous switch and jumped to Harvard, after being inactive for eight years, and began organizing his unbeatable Harvard teams.

"Never during my undergraduate career did I see Yale beat Harvard in football," George confessed.

As a Yale man, George Trevor's urge to become a writer was sharpened in Professor Johnny Berdan's famous Daily Themes course. In this excruciating form of mental torture, the student was handed a blank pad and told to write 500 words in 15 minutes on any topic the professor chose to chalk on the blackboard. He loved to "mousetrap" his classes. One of his pet teasers was titled "Green Thought In A Green Shade." Try to make something of that!

Despite his ineptitude in math and physics, George contrived to stay in Yale by earning a flock of high marks in English. Those daily themes were later stowed away in his parents' attic, where his younger brother, Henry, eventually made use of them. Henry went to Harvard and starred in math but flunked in English. Arthur Stanwood Pier, the noted writer of boys' books, was giving the Harvard course in theme writing in those days, and he allowed his pupils to do their work out of class on any topic they themselves selected.

After a dismal record at Christmas time, Henry went home for vacation. One day he happened to come upon brother George's themes while rummaging through the attic. Thereupon began his amazing metamorphosis as a writer. From failing marks his grades suddenly zoomed to A's and B's. Professor Pier was extremely pleased with his happy turnabout, and at the end of the semester he made a little speech to the class.

"Gentlemen," he said, earnestly, "you hear it said that writing is an instinctive art that cannot be taught, but right here in this class we have living proof to the contrary. When Henry Trevor started, he couldn't write a lick, but after completing my course his improvement has been incredible. Today he is a polished writer."

"That's one for the book," George told me. "A Harvard man going through school on *Yale* themes!"

° ° °

In 1915, Cornell had its first undefeated, untied football team in history, and the individual feats and names of its members were legendary. The stars of the team were Charley Barrett, who was to the Big Red what Eddie Mahan was to Harvard; Gib Cool, 165-pound center and team leader; Fritz Shiverick, a punter and dropkicker par excellence; Murray Shelton, an end whose work in the big games earned him a place on Camp's All-America. Coached by Dr. Albert Sharpe, a former Yale star in his fourth season at Cornell, no one on the team topped 200 pounds, but they clicked beautifully as a unit and had great confidence in their ability to put points on the scoreboard. In nine games, they ran up 287 points against 50, including victories over Harvard, 10-0; Michigan, 34-7; and Pennsylvania, 24-9.

Talking about the team many years later, Sharpe recalled the Harvard game, in which Barrett scored the only touchdown of the afternoon and then was knocked out and had to leave the field. Both teams went into the game undefeated, the Eastern Championship was at stake, and Cornell wanted it badly. With Barrett on the bench, it was now up to the leadership of Cool, the punting and dropkicking of Shiverick, and the tackling of ends Murray Shelton and Paul Eckley.

"As I recollect," Dr. Sharpe said, "we had the ball on our own 15-yard line, and Shiverick punted

*Charley Barrett, Cornell's All-America quarterback 1914–15, captained the Big Red's national champions in 1915. Sports writers of the day described him as "a true triple-threater—a tremendous runner, superior kicker, and a good passer."*

over the heads of Mahan and Wilcox, and the ball rolled out of bounds on the Harvard 13. They never were able to cross midfield after that."

The game was decided early. Four minutes into the action, Harvard got the ball on its own 20, and Mahan fumbled. Shelton recovered the ball on the 25, from where Barrett punched it across the goal six plays later and then added the extra point. Shortly after, Mahan and Barrett met in a head-on collision. Barrett was knocked unconscious. He recovered during half time, but was too shaken to go back into the game.

Gib Cool took over the direction of the team and held the Big Red together. The Cornell defense kept Mahan in check on his sweeps, and Shiverick matched him punt for punt in a fantastic kicking duel. On one occasion Mahan's punt sailed over the safety's head and rolled dead on the Cornell 3. Standing in his end zone and in the face of a bitter wind, Shiverick got off a low spiral that rolled well up the field, and Cornell was out of danger.

"Time and again Shiverick kicked Cornell out of trouble," said Allison Danzig, who joined the *New York Times* sports staff in 1922, a year after playing for Gil Dobie at Cornell. "In the third quarter, Shiverick booted his 38-yard field goal to cement the victory. Four times in the game Harvard blocked a kick, but to no avail. Shiverick recovered three."

Charley Barrett would have given the austere Amos Alonzo Stagg a case of heebie-jeebies. Like the fabled George Gipp at Notre Dame four years later, Barrett had a fine scorn for training rules, yet so great was his natural ability that he was named All-American at quarterback three times. Sportswriters described him as a "tremendous runner, superior kicker, and a good passer." Thirty years after his premature death in 1924, the result of World War I wounds, Charley was still being named by Grantland Rice on his all-time all-star first team. "When you've looked at so many hundreds of college backs for 50 years, the picture is bound to become confused," Granny said. "But Chuck Barrett belongs high on any list. He was a brilliant, hard-running back who put everything he had into every play."

Pennsylvania players had so much respect for the Cornell star both as an athlete and as a sportsman that they joined together after his death and erected a tablet to his memory on Franklin Field.

"Against Penn in 1915," Danzig recalled, "Cornell had the roughest sort of going. Bert Bell, Lud Wray, and Heinie Miller were members of the Red and Blue, and when Penn led at 9-0, it appeared that the old Franklin Field jinx was at work again. It was 9-7 going into the last quarter and Cornell's season seemed ruined, so inspired was the play of the Penn line. Then Barrett went berserk. He raced 40 yards around end for a touchdown, 25 yards for another, and kicked a field goal. He had also scored the first touchdown for the Red, and so he scored every one of Cornell's points in the 24-9 victory."

Although Cornell, Columbia (5-0-0), Harvard (8-1-0), Dartmouth (7-1-1), and Princeton (6-2-0) all had superior records in 1915, Brown, with losses to Amherst (7-0), Syracuse (6-0), and Harvard (16-7), was invited by the Tournament of Roses Committee to play Washington State at Pasadena in the first Rose Bowl game since the 1902 Michigan-

Stanford meeting. On the positive side, the Bruins did outscore their opponents that season, 167-32, and defeated Rhode Island, 38-0; Williams, 33-0; Vermont, 46-0; Yale 3-0; and Carlisle, 39-3.

Setting the pace for Coach Edward North Robinson's Bruins was flashy Fritz Pollard. Fritz stood 5′ 8″, weighed 150 pounds, and came from Chicago's Lane Technical High School. He was a hip-swiveling halfback who ran so close to the ground that tacklers would actually slide over him. Speed? He won the intercollegiate hurdles championship in 1916–17. Walter Camp called him "one of the greatest runners I have ever seen" after watching Fritz score twice against Yale (21-6) and twice against Harvard (21-0) on successive Saturdays in 1916 to lead Brown to upset victories. The win over Harvard was the first time the Bruins had ever toppled the Cantabs in football.

But in that Brown-Washington State game in the Rose Bowl, it came up mud in Pasadena, and Pollard and his teammates were unable to move the ball. Washington State won, 14-0.

Forty years later, journalist Jimmy Jemail, a halfback on that Brown eleven, tracked down some of the Cougars and Bruins who had played in the first of the modern Rose Bowl series. "How have you changed in the 40 years since playing in the 1916 Rose Bowl?" he asked them. Here were some of the answers:

"Little, other than adding 40 years," replied Benton M. Bangs, the Washington State halfback. "I'm within 15 pounds of my playing weight; my health is good; but I've lost those curls I used to paste down."

Another Cougar halfback, Marine Colonel (ret.) Leroy B. Hanley, questioned the question. "Changed?" he asked. "No more than anyone would change in the Marines, from which I retired as colonel. Living quietly in Berkeley, California now. Getting older but not old."

Businessman Basil B. Doane, the Washington State fullback, said the toughest teams he had faced in the 40 years since the Rose Bowl game were old age and health. "When I met up with them," he

*The first East team ever to play in the Rose Bowl was this 1915 Brown eleven, which outscored nine opponents, 167–32, during the regular season. At Pasadena, however, Washington State held the Bruins scoreless and won, 14-0. Brown's starting lineup: right end Josh Weeks, right tackle Mark Farnum, right guard Wallace Wade, center Ken Sprague, left guard Edgar J. Spike, left tackle Ray Ward, left end John Butler. In the backfield, l. to r.: quarterback Clair Purdy, right halfback Buff Andrews, fullback Harold Saxton, and All-America and Hall of Fame left halfback Fritz Pollard.*

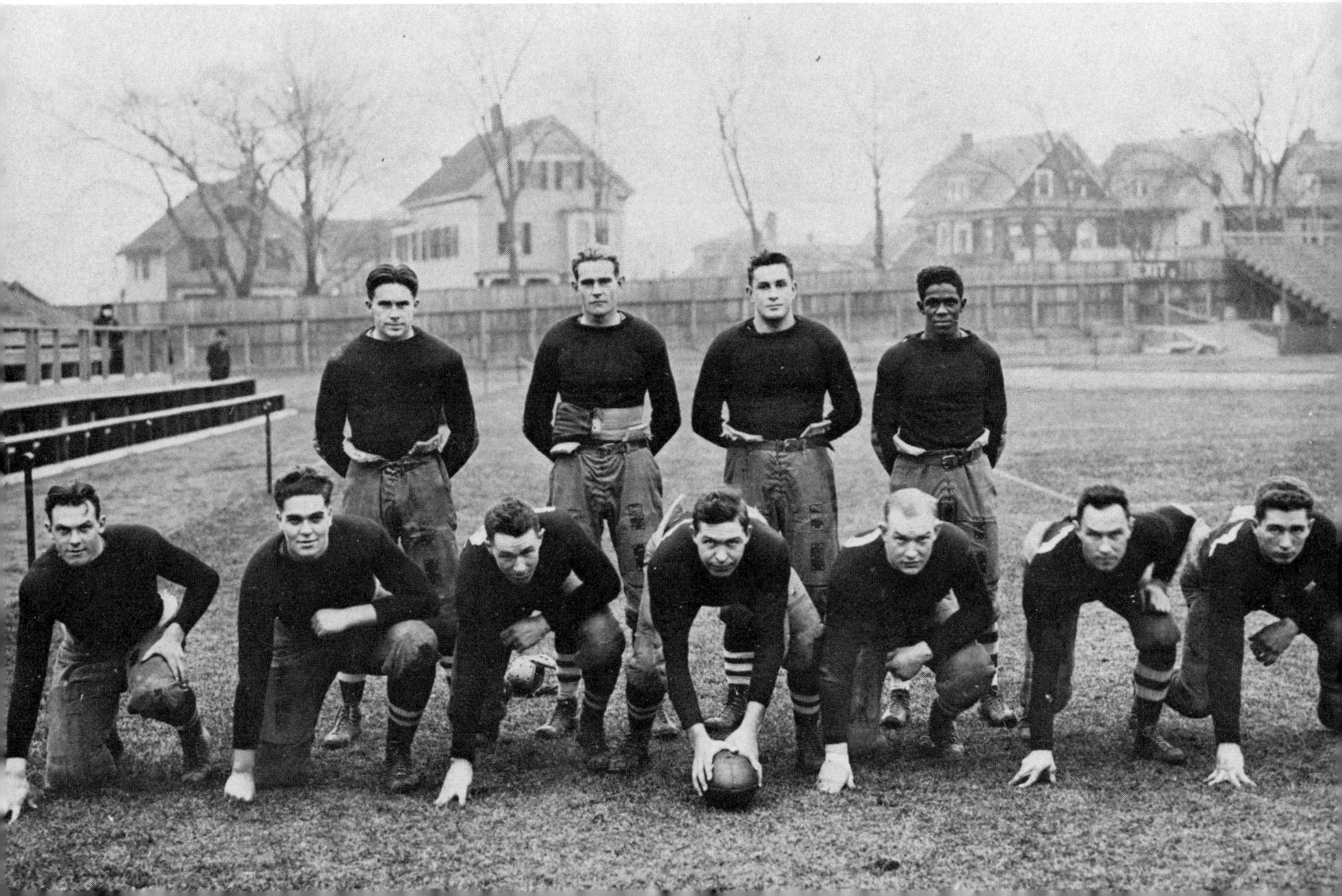

said, "the gridiron training I got in teamwork and determination served me well."

Silas E. Stites, who went from playing guard for W.S.C. to electrical engineer in Stockton, California, said, "I played at 170 pounds, and fully enjoyed the competitive spirit. I have a few wrinkles, but the same spirit made me a sports fan for 40 years."

Asa V. Clark, a state senator who had been a tackle for Washington State, felt he had grown less impetuous over the years. "I'm far more tolerant and now realize that the other fellow knows something, too," he said. "I know the world is not the rosy apple it looked in 1916."

Halfback Ralph Boone, a Glendale, California, realtor, believed he had changed very little since Washington State. He still had the same head of hair, still the same weight. "But that car in the center lane, cutting in and out, isn't mine," he added. "I'm on the right stretching my future as far as I can."

It was pretty much the same story on the Brown side. "In 1916, I weighed 155," Fritz Pollard said. "Today I weigh 215, have weighed up to 230. I worked my way through college pressing clothes. Today, I earn $20,000 a year."

*Coach Thomas Albert Dwight (T.A.D.) Jones of Yale.*

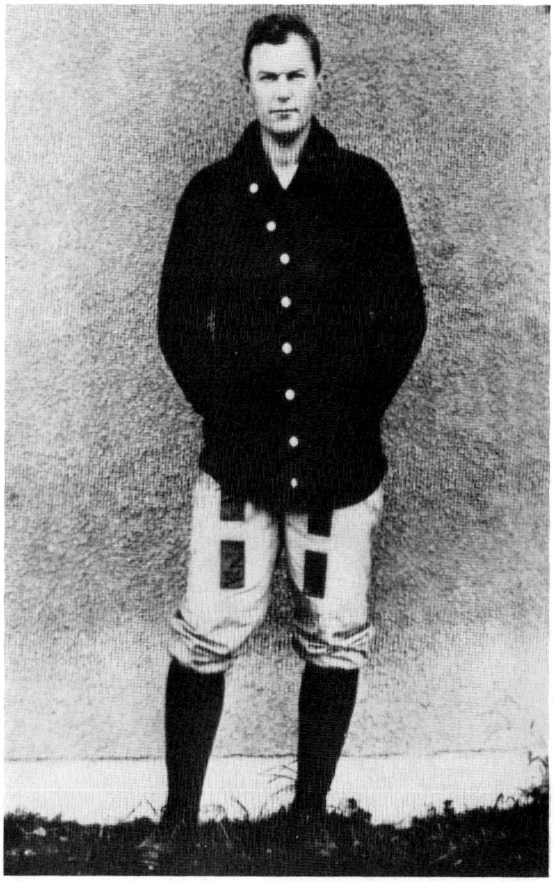

Dr. Edgar Staff, a Providence Health Department official, weighed the same as he did when he was a guard for the 1916 Bruins, but now it was differently distributed. "It isn't the same kind of weight," he said. "Football is still my top interest. I belong to the local gridiron club."

Irving Fraser, the Brown halfback, said that a year with the Seabees, after he was 50, left its notches. "In college," he said, "I could walk away with 300 pounds. Today I can barely lift 100."

The captain of the team, halfback H. P. Andrews, said that the physical change was obvious. "Forty years have slowed me down," replied the Attleboro, Massachusetts, jewelry executive, "but have left me more philosophic, more considerate of the other guy and his problems."

Now a New Bedford, Massachusetts, physician, Dr. J. H. Weeks had been hobbled by old football injuries since playing end at Brown. "A football knee plus an unsuccessful spinal fusion have restricted my activities and added great weight," he said. "I gave up golf, but my sports interest is high."

Andy Hillhouse, the Bruin halfback, could see very little change in himself. The broad grin was still there, and the hair. "The girls still look my way, but now I don't look back," he said. "That's a change. The motor runs good but knocks a bit at high speed."

*The flesh quails, and the ardor dulls.*

° ° °

Fritz Pollard was the first black to make Walter Camp's All-America first team. He was a unanimous selection in 1916, the spark that led Brown to eight victories in nine games while outscoring opponents, 254 to 37. The only loss was to Colgate, 28-0.

In 1916, Yale brought in a new head coach in the person of Thomas Albert Dwight (Tad) Jones, brother of Howard. Tad stood for Yale, the true spirit of the Old Blues, and the finest traditions of college football. He graduated from Yale in 1908, was assistant backfield coach that fall, and head coach at Syracuse in 1909–10. Then he was head coach at his old prep school, Exeter, in 1913–15.

Except for the 21-6 loss to Brown, Yale won all

*Chet LaRoche, Yale quarterback in 1916, went on to become a founder and chairman of the National Football Foundation and Hall of Fame.*

its games in that first season under Tad. The 6-3 triumph over Harvard was the first Yale victory over the Crimson in seven seasons, and the touchdown by Joe Neville was the first the Blue scored in The Game since 1907.

Tad Jones was an intense traditionalist. When he returned to Yale, he set about solidifying traditions and mending fences. One of his first moves was to invite back a number of Old Blues to help out. But the real coaching was done by the appointed staff of assistants. Dr. Arthur (Butch) Brides was the line coach, Clarence Alcott tutored the ends, and Dr. Billy Bull handled the kickers. Tad also quietly set about the task of bringing Mr. Football himself, Walter Camp, back into the picture. Although Camp had remained active as the accepted arbiter of the All-America team, editor of the football guide, and a member of the rules committee, his influence on Yale football was low key during the Frank Hinkey regime. But, admittedly, he had missed the practice sessions and the strategy councils.

Chet LaRoche, a quarterback on Captain Clinton Rutherford (Cupid) Black's team, recalls making a long run in practice one afternoon.

"Immediately, I became aware of the two most luminous and gleaming eyes I have ever seen in a man's face," Chet said. "I was almost paralyzed when I realized that Walter Camp was looking at me and speaking to me. It was like being addressed by a god. He showed me a certain way to shift my weight while running that he felt would be useful to me. I was dazed by the look in his eyes, but I had just sense enough to remember what he had shown me and to profit by it."

The 1916 Bulldogs were no rolling ball of butcher knives, but they were a good team, the best since Coy's day. The ends were George Moseley and Charlie Comerford. Artemus (Di) Gates and Mac Baldridge manned the tackles. Black and Larry Fox were guards. Tim Callahan played center. LaRoche and Shorty Smith alternated at quarter, Joe Neville and Harry Legore were at halfbacks, and Emile Jacques at fullback.

In the opening victory over Carnegie Tech, 25-0, Yale numbered its players for the first time. Henry Ketcham, 1913 captain and center, was astonished. He was totally opposed to players wearing numbers on their jerseys. Yale was one of the last colleges in the country to go without numerals, and Ketcham preferred tradition.

"My contention was that the game was being played by college boys and that it was purely a college game, not for the press or the public," he said. "In reading my scrapbook of this period, it is amusing now to read the caustic comments of the sports writers of the period. And I think, in light of what developed later, I was probably wrong to make such a fuss."

With each victory, the 1916 Elis gained converts and confidence as they kept finding new ways to outwit the opposition. Virginia, Lehigh, Virginia Tech, Washington and Jefferson, and Colgate were all sacked. The 61-3 margin over Virginia was the highest Yale score since the 67-0 win over Tufts back in 1894.

The low spot of the Yale 1916 season came against Brown. It was not a good afternoon for the Blue. The Bruins gave them more than they could handle. Brown played as if King Kong was in the backfield. There was no player that huge, of course, but there was All-American halfback Fritz Pollard.

Yale led at half time, 6-0, on the strength of Jim Braden's two dropkicks. Then in the second half, Pollard ran wild. He savaged the tackles, skirted the ends, and flew through the Yale secondary as if the defenders were paralyzed. His most brilliant effort on the way to a total of 184 yards was when he ran one of Legore's punts 60 yards for a touchdown, dodging Yale tacklers and using his blockers skillfully. The final score was Brown 21, Yale 6.

The game at Princeton a week later was regarded as a toss-up. The Tigers had lost only to Harvard, 3-0. Shorty Smith, who had been starting at quarterback while LaRoche nursed a sore leg, came up with a bad throat, and Tad Jones told Chet he would have to fill the breach.

With the ball in Yale's possession on its own 30-yard line, no score, and time running out in the first half, LaRoche picks up the story:

"Third down, four to go," Chet recalled. "We rush, no gain. Now it's fourth and four. We line up in kick formation. Everybody figures punt, but I suddenly change signals and call for a quarterback run inside their right tackle. Captain Black stands up, comes back, and says to me, 'Are you crazy? Kick that ball!' And I say, 'Get back and shut up!' Harry Legore, in punt formation, stood back poised to kick. Now he was mad too. I looked over at our bench and I could feel the commotion coming from the coaches. They seemed to be saying, 'Take him out! He's nuts! '

"Quickly I restored order on the field and called my own signal again. With Princeton expecting a punt, the ball is passed to me and I cut to the left inside their right tackle. We make four yards, and now it's first down and I call for the punt formation again. This time Legore, free of the fourth-down pressure which always bothered him—and which I knew about but our coaches didn't—lofts a tremendous kick downfield and it rolls dead on their 2-yard line. The Yale stands go crazy. Princeton is stunned. The Tigers spent the rest of the first half trying to get out of trouble. There was no score after 30 minutes of play, and we go to the locker room. The place is buzzing. Tad Jones is laying for me. He's surrounded by his assistants and all the volunteer coaches. There's Foster Rockwell and Pudge Heffelfinger and Tom Shevlin, a bundle of fire. 'They insist I take you out,' Tad says to me. 'You got away with it, but they say you're crazy. Why did you ever do such a thing?' I had the perfect answer. 'Why, Tad,' I said, 'I did what they told me to do. They said the Princeton right tackle *always* floated way to the outside when there was a punt, so I felt sure I could make it. And, anyway, Foster Rockwell told me to upset them, mix them up, do something crazy.' That settled it. Now the coaching staff beamed. Everybody took credit for the way the play fooled Princeton. Tad said, 'All right, Chet, you stay right in there in the second half.' So I stayed in the game and we went to town."

At the beginning of the second half, Moseley ran the kickoff back to the Princeton 15. Three plays netted only five yards, so Jim Braden sent over a dropkick to put Yale ahead, 3 to 0.

Early in the fourth quarter, Legore punted into the Nassau end zone. Princeton then fumbled on its 20, and Captain Black, who was everywhere, fell on the ball. Joe Neville completed a pass to Legore and Harry was dragged down on the 3. LaRoche had been meeting the test well, handling Princeton's punts expertly and running the team with sure judgment. The Tigers were still disturbed by the way he ran the ball on fourth down in the second quarter and got away with it. Now Chet took the ball himself and smashed to the 1. On the next play, Legore piled over. Comerford kicked the point, to make it 10-0, and 10-0 it stayed.

But The Game was still ahead. Harvard had lost to Tufts and Brown—Pollard had driven the Crimson crazy too. There was no Mahan, Brickley, or Hardwick in the Harvard backfield, but there was Eddie Casey, an elusive and swift sophomore halfback who ran with the ball as if the crash wall on the other side of the line was made of cardboard.

The Yales knew all about Casey. He came from Exeter, the same prep school as Cupe Black and some of the other Elis. Before the season opened, Cupe had invited Eddie down to New Haven and had thrown a little party for him at Morey's. Captain Black had heard a lot about Percy Haughton psychology. He was determined to hand some of it back to the Harvards on a platter of beef.

Black had rehearsed his fellow Elis in a little act for Casey's benefit, with the idea of showing Eddie what sort of a hard-boiled gang of cavemen wore the Blue. When the waiter asked, "How will you have your steak, Mr. Callahan?" it was Tim's cue to growl, "Raw and ruddy, please." When the question was repeated to Captain Black, the redoubtable Cupe sang out, "Bring mine running with gore!" Finally the waiter got around to Casey, who was sitting meekly in a corner, his gentle eyes registering awe. Eddie was a good actor. "And how will you have your streak, Mr. Casey?" the waiter wanted to know.

"Don't bother to do any carving," Casey told him. "Just run that steer in here and I'll take a cut at him as he goes by!"

Casey, Yale knew, was not the only danger. Haughton would have the Cantabs at their peak for Yale. Tad and Black kept the Blue driving. Spirit was high. The Old Blues came back to help, including Heffelfinger. On Wednesday, Pudge had his storied scrimmage with Cupe Black and Mac Baldridge. One of the witnesses was George Trevor.

"That was my first glimpse of Pudge," George told me. "He had come back to New Haven to show the Yale line some tricks about position play. He was then 48 years old, but he didn't bother to even put on helmet or pads. He told me afterward that he had to show the men he was still tough or else they wouldn't have paid any attention to him. He threw them around as though they had been sacks of wheat from the flour mills of his native Minneapolis."

Mac Baldridge picked up the story: "As far as we were concerned, it was supposed to be just dummy scrimmage, but Pudge meant business. We were wearing no pads, and he roared through us standing erect and telling us this was the way to do it. Cupe Black was playing guard next to me, and we got plenty sick and tired of this treatment. We secretly decided we would hit Pudge low and high the next time he charged us. Our blocking was so effective that it flipped his 280 pounds up in the air, and he came down with his right elbow on my side, breaking two ribs. You should have heard Johnny Mack, our trainer, howl."

When Baldridge went down with the rib injury, Tad Jones blew his whistle and stopped the mayhem. "Heff," he said, "it's time you took a rest. You're not as young as you used to be."

The old war-horse snorted.

"You're afraid I'll wreck your team," Pudge muttered. "This is a sissy game they play today!"

Mac Baldridge, his two broken ribs taped so tightly he could hardly breathe, played 60 minutes against Harvard. Before the game, Tad Jones addressed the team. He didn't talk very long.

"If any of you boys believe in the hereafter," he said, "you will know that Tom Shevlin is pacing up and down across the river, smoking that big black cigar, and asking the boys to go out there and do it once again for papa."

Tad let that sink in for a moment, then he added his now famous line about playing against Harvard—"Never again in your whole life will you do anything so important."

When Tad had finished, everybody in the room was intense with a desire to tear the Cantabs to pieces.

"Taken literally," Chet LaRoche told me 60 years later, "it *does* sound silly. But all of us in that room knew what Tad meant—not the way they kid about it today. When he told us it was going to be the most important thing we'd ever do in our lives, he meant he was counting on our guts, determination, unrealized resources of spirit, never admitting defeat, and all the courage in us—courage beyond anything we had ever summoned up before. *Harvard had to be beaten.* Corny, I suppose so, but none of us laughed. His message came through loud and clear: What kind of men were we going to be? Here was the test."

For a while, it looked like the same old story. Casey picked up 15 yards on two carries. Ralph Horween, the Harvard fullback, got off two long punts, one for 75 yards. Before the first quarter ended, LaRoche fumbled and Harvard recovered on the Yale 28.

"After I fumbled that first punt," Chet told me, "Bill Robinson, the Harvard quarterback, promptly dropkicked a field goal from the 30, although Charlie Comerford almost blocked it with a flying leap. My teammates were downcast. We had vowed we would not hand Harvard the game by our own errors. But here it was again, the same old story. The line was playing a fine game, but we were making mistakes in the backfield. I felt I was losing control. What to do? The team had lost confidence in me. I was a villain. They really turned against me.

"In the second quarter, Legore got off a tremendous punt to Harvard's 28. Then, on the next play, Casey bolted loose at our left side, slipped down the sidelines, shot into the clear, and was off on what appeared to be a 72-yard touchdown run. But the play was called back. Dave Fultz, the umpire, penalized Harvard for holding.

"We missed two field goals, one by Neville and one by Comerford, but Comerford's proved to be the turning point of the game. I had made a fair catch on the Harvard 40. I sensed my teammates needed something to restore their confidence. So I gambled on a field goal, even at 40 yards away. My reasoning was that if the team could score quickly, match Harvard's three points, it would be a big psychological lift. I looked at Comerford. 'You try it, Charlie,' I said. Charlie shook his head. 'Not me,' he said. 'I haven't place-kicked all year.' I reminded him he had been a good place-kicker at Exeter. 'You can do it, Charlie,' I told him. Reluctantly, he agreed. He actually got the necessary distance. The ball hit the right upright, then rolled to the outside instead of the inside. But the effect on my teammates was the same as if we had tied the score. Comerford had demonstrated that we could get the 3 points back quickly. I felt the players come back to me once more. I was in charge again."

Soon after, Yale began a drive from midfield. The Blue hammered to a first down on the Harvard 40. Legore picked up four yards outside Harvard's left tackle, but he fumbled the ball. Di Gates, Yale's left tackle, who was running interference, saved the situation by scooping up the ball and racing to the 12-yard line before he was forced out of bounds.

Legore then hit the line for four more. Neville added another four. Jacques carried to the two for a first down. Harvard dug in desperately. Yale had not scored a touchdown on them since Coy did it in 1907. On the next play, Legore got only a yard, and then Neville was stopped at the line. Legore tried another smash at the middle. When the pile was untangled, the ball was still a foot from the end zone. Captain Black called time out. The west side of Yale Bowl was shouting, "Touchdown, Yale!"

"Listen to that!" Cupe told his teammates. "It has been a long time since we have given our fans something to shout about against Harvard. What are you guys going to do about it?"

With Charlie Comerford leading the way, Neville pulverized the middle and fell into the end zone. A wild roar from the Yale side of the stands greeted the touchdown—the first points the Elis had ever scored on Harvard in the Bowl. The conversion was missed. In a minute the half was over, but Yale had the lead now, 6-3.

In the second half, Yale defended its slim lead tenaciously. The Elis even engineered a march down to the Harvard 7, but there the drive stalled. Near the end of the game, Harvard's Jeff Coolidge caught a 30-yard pass. For an instant he seemed to be in the clear, but Legore saved the day for Yale by bringing him down on the Eli 35.

Then it was over, and you could hear the chant of the Undertaker Song come welling up out of the Yale stands: "No hope for Harvard." For the first time in seven years, the Bulldogs were champions of the Big Three. Black and Moseley made Camp's All-America first team. Gates and Legore were on the second selection. Comerford and Larry Fox also won considerable attention.

Many years later, Joe Williams, sports columnist of the New York *World-Telegram & Sun,* referred to the 1916 Yale eleven as one of the greatest in the Blue's history. Tad Jones saw the article and told Joe he was wrong.

"That 1916 team could scarcely be rated among Yale's all-time best," Tad said with commendable honesty. "Now, if you had called it one of the most *courageous* Yale teams of all time, you would have been completely correct."

It was very evident that the 1916 Elis were one of Tad's favorite groups. For years, the members of that team met at a dinner in New York City, once every decade. Perhaps Tad was so very fond of them because they were the first Yale eleven he ever coached as head coach. The year before he took charge, the Yales were pretty bad. They were beaten by Virginia, Washington and Jefferson, Col-

*The 1916 Yale Bulldogs, one of Tad Jones's finest teams, lost only to Rose Bowl-bound Brown in nine games, shut out four opponents. Back row, l. to r.: Braden, Galt, Olsen, Taft, Hutchinson. Second row: Chet LaRoche (later chairman of the National Football Foundation and Hall of Fame), Jacques, Fox, Baldrige, Gates, Captain Black, Legore, Moseley, Comerford, Callahan. Front row: Church, Neville, Carey.*

gate, Brown, and Harvard. Actually, they were massacred by Harvard, 41-0. They just did beat Lehigh, 7-6. But the following year, the first season Tad was in charge, they beat everybody but Brown.

"And I want to tell you fellows here and now," Tad told the members at the team dinner many years later, "you didn't lose that Brown game—I lost it for you." This was news even to the Old Blues themselves. So Tad asked them to recall what he had said in the dressing room between halves of the Brown game. None of them could.

"Well, if you don't remember I'll tell you," he said. "We had Brown beaten, 6-0, at the half, and I told you fellows to take it easy in the second half, to save yourselves for Princeton and Harvard, which we were to meet on the following Saturdays. I broke up your concentration and your intensity of spirit. I asked you to let down, and you did. As we all know now, it was a costly mistake."

Mac Baldridge, by this time a congressman from Omaha, raised a point of order.

"Tad," he said, "if you don't mind my saying so, a fellow by the name of Fritz Pollard had a lot to do with what you call our letdown that afternoon. All he did was run for three touchdowns. I don't think any of us has laid a hand on him yet."

Tad shuddered. "Please don't mention Pollard. I can still see him racing across the goal line. I wouldn't be surprised if he wasn't just about the best ball carrier any of us ever saw."

The Yales of 1916 were only the second from New Haven to beat a Harvard team coached by Percy Haughton. The victory came after six straight winless years of frustration in The Game. Tad Jones told a revealing story behind the 6-3 score.

"The advance preparation was something, I'll tell you," he said. "In those days, Percy used to equip his linemen with skin-tight gloves of hard leather, which reached well up the forearm. Pur-

*Pennsylvania's 7-2-1 record in 1916, including big wins over Penn State, Michigan, and Cornell, earned the Quakers a Rose Bowl invitation to play Oregon on January 1, 1917. The Oregon Ducks won, 14-0. Bob Folwell was the Penn coach.*

portedly this was to protect the linemen's hands and wrists, and I suppose it did. But the effect on the opposing linemen was not at all pleasant. To be frank about it, the effect was like being hit by a pair of brass knucks.

"Well, the day before the game, I called on Percy and told him I had ordered a similar set of gloves for the Yale linemen—which was the truth—and that if he insisted on using the leather coverings, I was going to use them too.

" 'Why, if you feel we shouldn't use the gloves,' answered Percy, 'we just won't use them. I never knew you had the slightest objection.'

"I assured him we had a very positive objection, and so the equipment was discarded by both sides."

When Tad told that story at the last reunion of the 1916 Yale team, Larry Fox, the lawyer who played a major role in the reorganization of Universal Pictures, nudged Tim Callahan, the All-American center, and chuckled.

"I notice Tad isn't telling anything about that plaster of paris cast I wore on my right hand all during the game," Larry said. "I was supposed to have had a bad hand, but there wasn't anything wrong with it, and when I hit one of those Harvards, he'd drop like a ton of bricks."

"You don't think you're telling us anything new about that cast, do you?" roared Tim Callahan.

That was enough to make Joe Williams gasp in shocked amazement. "I mean," Joe said later, "the revelation that the Harvards once went in for leather thongs and at least one of the Yales molded his fist in plaster of paris with mayhem aforethought. Didn't those gentlemen have any reverence for the dear old ivy that crawled along the sacred walls?"

° ° °

At the end of the 1916 season, Percy Haughton left Harvard to concentrate on his duties as head of a syndicate that had bought the Boston Braves of the National Baseball League. On New Year's Day, 1917, Pennsylvania lost to Oregon, 14-0, in the Rose Bowl. The Penn roster included quarterback Bert Bell, later commissioner of the National Football League; right tackle Lou Little, who went on to coaching fame at Columbia; and Heinie Miller, who became president of the National Boxing Association.

To anyone with even the most rudimentary knowledge of football, it was easy to see why Pennsylvania was the best of the Ivies in 1917. Coach Bob Folwell had most of his varsity back from the Rose Bowl eleven, and it proceeded to make the handicappers appear as genuine experts in the very first game, a 73-10 pulverizing of Albright. Except for losses to Georgia Tech and Pitts-

*Edward Lawrence (Eddie) Casey, a Walter Camp All-America halfback in 1919, was the spark of the undefeated Harvard team that beat Oregon, 7-6, in the Rose Bowl on New Year's Day, 1920. Eddie was later brought back to Cambridge for a spell as head football coach. In four seasons (1931–34), his record was 20-11-1.*

burgh, the Red and Blue won the rest of its games. The last six were shutouts, and included victories over Dartmouth, Michigan, Carlisle, and Cornell.

While Penn went along on a football-as-usual policy that year, Yale, Harvard, and Princeton played only "informal" schedules. As the war sounds from Europe grew ever louder, the talk of football at home waned. The boys were going off to war. By fall, only one Yale letterman was left in school, for example—Charlie Galt, tackle. There were not enough players to field a formal varsity. So a freshman team of R.O.T.C. members played a five-game schedule, defeating Harvard and Penn freshmen, Exeter and Andover, and losing to Princeton freshmen. Tad Jones coached the Yale frosh briefly, then went to Seattle to work in a shipbuilding program. The Yale varsity schedule in 1917 consisted of victories over Loomis Institute, New Haven Naval Base, and Trinity.

In 1918, there was no football at all. America was at war.

Formal varsity football was renewed in 1919, with considerable success at Harvard. Percy Haughton served as a major in chemical warfare during World War I, and in 1919 he was too busy in the bond business to go back to coaching. Bob Fisher was named to succeed him. This was the same Bob Fisher who had played guard and cap-

*Clarence W. (Doc) Spears had the perfect profile to be nicknamed "Fats," but he brought a winning tradition to Dartmouth both as a player and coach. At 245 pounds, he was a first team All-America guard in 1915, when the Green won 16 out of 18 games; then he coached the varsity (1917–21) and rolled up a 20-9-1 record.*

tained the 1911 Crimson. In his first season as head coach, Fisher did amazingly well. His Harvards rendered eight opponents *hors de combat,* were tied by Princeton, 10-10, and beat Oregon in the Rose Bowl, 7-6. The fact that a total of only 19 points were scored against the defense explains how ruinous Harvard tacklers were to tendons, skulls, joints, and bones.

Dartmouth (6-1-1) was another strong postwar power in the East. The Big Green's only loss was a 7-6 heartbreaker to Brown in the last game of the season. This was the third year at Hanover for Coach Doc Spears, and he was fast becoming a legend. An All-America guard at Dartmouth in 1914 and '15, he thought of football primarily as a game of condition and contact. "Doc was a cruel man at practice," recalled a former Dartmouth player. "This came from his own fierce play at Dartmouth. He was so good, such a furious competitor that he could never fully understand why the average player couldn't put out more than he had in him to put out. Socially, he was just the opposite. He was the most cordial person you would want to know. His circle of closest friends included some of the jolliest stay-out-late people in town."

Doc stood 5′ 7″ and in fighting trim weighed about 236. He had the face of a cherub and the body of a gorilla. He was the driving, crack-down type of coach. He would have been too tough on the field today for most athletes. But he was a warm man with his players at Dartmouth, except at practice. The good players loved him, the rest did not.

Probably the strongest lineman ever to play for Doc at Dartmouth was Gus Sonnenberg, who later won the professional heavyweight wrestling title. Gus cost the Dartmouth Athletic Association lots of money in 1919 by ripping hotel radiators from the floor, just one of his playful habits. Together with Wild Bill Cunningham, Swede Youngstrom, and Cuddy Murphy, he formed the tough quartet of postwar football at Hanover, forcing Spears to make two separate pregame speeches to the team. Doc would chase his four bad guys out of the dressing room and deliver a sentimental address to the rest of the varsity: "Men of Dartmouth, your mothers and sweethearts are looking down on you today. . . ." Then he would dismiss the rest of the squad and call in Sonnenberg and his buddies. "As for you bums," roared Doc, "if I catch you loafing out there today, I'll kick your asses off the field! "

The only other blemish on the Dartmouth record in 1919 was a 7-7 tie with Colgate. The Red Raiders were coached by Larry Bankart—a Dartmouth man! Lovers of mythology claim that fullback Hank Gillo, in a sadistic state of mind, slashed through the Dartmouth defenders with such force to score for Colgate that he sheared off one of the goalposts and was knocked unconscious when the crossbar fell on his head.

# *The Golden Age: The 1920s*

It has been called the era of wonderful nonsense, and nowhere was the hysteria more boisterous or the screaming louder than in college football during the third decade of the twentieth century. Throwing off its bush league trappings, the game suddenly erupted as big business and lavish entertainment. It was no longer just a college game. Now it was a national industry. Graduate managers intrigued and fought for lucrative games and places on the schedules of the teams with the big drawing power—Army, Notre Dame, Illinois, Michigan, California—and politicians pulled wires to bring the Army-Navy game to Chicago. New York received play-by-play accounts of games in the Far West, and Yale and Harvard were followed as eagerly in Atlanta, Dallas, and Seattle as in New Haven and Cambridge. For three months the nation went stark mad over college football.

In New England, the game became one vast, magnificent fall pageant as it dressed itself in spangles and tinsel, and came a-swinging into the campus stadiums on a white steed behind the booming ballyhoo band; a game played in crisp, zippy air that held the smell of burning leaves; a carnival of pretty coeds and fur-coated, well-dressed men, of marching bands in scarlet capes, evolutions in the grandstand, yellow footballs in the air, running and diving figures, gold in the fields and on the trees and in the pocket. A Yale-Harvard game at New Haven brought $300,000; Notre Dame playing Southern California in Chicago resulted in close to $500,000.

This was the "Golden Age" of college football, and the times produced their share of vital, vibrant performers. Journalists had a field day. Pioneer sportswriters had stimulated interest in football, and the men who followed put a glittering polish on the tradition they inherited. The temper of the expansive times called for garish embellishment, and the boys laid on the superlatives and breathless adjectives with a trowel.

Stanley Frank, a star sports chronicler of later years, looked back on the sports pages of the Golden Age and came to the conclusion that too many of the stories were overwritten, stridently and strenuously. "By present-day standards," he said, "the color was glaring, the straining for effect was self-conscious, the round-eyed wonder was juvenile, and a competent copyreader could perform a major operation on the superfluity of words. Yet these were the stories that were considered very hot stuff, and it is significant that every news story ran on page 1 of the newspaper."

With the notable exceptions of a few, sportswriters of the twenties brought an attitude to their work that was not generally apparent in other sections of the papers. They sat down at their typewriters prepared to invest the event they were covering with the epic grandeur of the Creation.

That attitude was best expressed in a scene concerning Laurence Stallings, who was hired by a newspaper to do a trained seal act for Red Grange's first appearance in the East, against Pennsylvania at Franklin Field in 1925. Stallings had written the realistic, hard-boiled "What Price Glory?", an enormously successful Broadway play, and had seen the carnage of World War I. Grange had a super afternoon for himself against the Quakers, and as soon as the game was over, the boys in the press box took the wraps off their typewriters and went to work to preserve the event for posterity.

Stallings, going through the agony pains of composition, paced up and down the press box for an hour. He tore at his hair, clutched at his brow and breast, and uttered hoarse, hollow groans of despair. One of the colleagues who had completed his story asked Stallings what in the world was the matter.

The blood-and-thunder historian threw out his arms in a gesture of bleak frustration.

"I can't write it!" Stallings cried. "The story's too big for me!"

° ° °

Even though Ivy football was still largely a private affair, turnstiles buzzed with activity. The annual raffle for any game of importance often allotted so many tickets to Old Grads that not all the underclassmen who wished to see the game could be accommodated. Fans journeyed to their chosen battlefields by auto; thousands arrived in private trains, often with dining cars and almost always with parlor cars. The Sunday after Yale or Princeton had played at Harvard, the New Haven Railroad ran a second section of the Merchants Limited from Boston to New York—eight parlor cars, two dining cars, these offering Cape Cod oysters on the shell.

Egged on by the freewheeling literary styles of such popular and widely read greats of the pressbox as Ring Lardner, Damon Runyon, Westbrook Pegler, and Heywood Broun, an influx of a new form of spectator began showing up at Ivy football games. It was soon possible to notice a new cast of characters—of men who heretofore had come into view only as the padrones of after-hours establishments and of secret distilleries and breweries, of men familiar to police blotters by such colorful handles as "Sam the Gonoph" and "Gyp Louie" and "Dumb Dan" and "Little Hutch" and "Hot Horse Harry." The Ivies had gone public in a quite special fashion. It was, in truth, the "Damon Runyon era" brought to life.

Always a sports nut, Damon Runyon was hired by the old *New York American* in 1911, and he quickly established himself as a sports and feature writer, a ranking that gave him all the pleasure, prestige, and profit he wanted. Like Ring Lardner, Runyon found sports a fertile field for plot and dialogue in later years after he obeyed a long-standing impulse and turned to fiction. But whereas Lardner used baseball players for his source material, Runyon exploited the horse players, hustlers, hangers-on, and hoodlums of Broadway. His characterizations of guys and dolls and his unusual turns of expression, a shrewd blend of underworld and sport slang seasoned with precise five-dollar words that made for an effect at once pithy and incongruous, stamped him as the most refreshing stylist in the short-story field.

On one of his forages into sports literature, Runyon once imagined himself in New Haven for a Yale-Harvard football game. What he was doing there he did not know, because, as he said, "I am not such a guy as you will expect to find in New Haven at any time, and especially on the day of a large football game between the Harvards and the Yales."

With him in this fictional account was Sam the Gonoph, the Broadway ticket hustler, and all his best peddlers, including Gyp Louie, Nubbsy Taylor, Benny Southstreet, and old Liverlips. It seems they were sitting right in the middle of the Harvard cheering section, which was making a gosh-awful racket, what with yelling and singing and one thing and another, because it seems the game was going on when they arrived and the Harvards were shoving the Yales around more than somewhat. There was this little doll who had attached herself to the Runyon coterie and she hadn't even settled in her seat before she was letting everybody know she was in favor of the Yales by yelling, "Hold 'em, Yale!"

"Well, finally the game is over," Runyon fictionalized, "and I do not remember much about it, although afterwards I hear that our little doll's brother, John, plays substitute for the Yales very good. But it seems that the Harvards win, and our little doll is very sad indeed about this, and is sitting there looking over the field, which is now covered with guys dancing around as if they all suddenly go daffy, and it seems they are all Harvards, because there is really no reason for the Yales to do any dancing. All of a sudden our little doll looks toward one end of the field, and says as follows: 'Oh, they are going to take our goalposts! Do not let them take our posts!' "

Well, in the language of Runyon, the little doll said come on, and she jumped to her feet and ran down the aisle and out onto the field—and smack into the crowd around the goalposts. Naturally the Runyons followed her. Sam the Gonoph, not wanting any trouble with the Harvards, tried to speak nicely to the young men who were tugging at the goalposts, saying as follows: "Listen, our little doll here does not wish you to take these posts." Well, maybe they did not hear Sam's words in all the confusion, or if they did hear them they did not wish to pay any attention to them, for one of the Harvards mashed Sam's derby hat down over his eyes and another smacked old Liverlips on the left ear, while Gyp Louie and Nubbsy Taylor and Benny Southstreet were also shoved around quite a bit.

"All right," Sam the Gonoph said, as soon as he could pull his hat off his eyes, "all right, gentlemen, if you wish to play this way. Now, boys, let them have it!"

So Sam the Gonoph and Nubbsy Taylor and Gyp Louie and Benny Southstreet and old Liverlips began letting the Harvards have it, and what they let them have it with was not only their dukes, because the Runyons were by no means suckers when it came to hand-to-hand combat, but they all carried something in their pockets to put in their dukes in case of a fight, such as a dollar's worth of nickels rolled up tight.

Soon the ground around them was covered with Harvards, and it seemed that some Elis were also mixed up with them, being Elis who thought Sam the Gonoph and his gang were other Elis defending the goalposts and wanting to help out. Of course, Sam the Gonoph and his guys could not tell the Elis from the Cantabs, and did not have time to ask which was which, so they just let everybody have it who came along.

Pretty soon the Harvards were knocking down Sam the Gonoph, then they started knocking down Nubbsy Taylor, and by and by they were knocking down Benny Southstreet and Gyp Louie and old Liverlips, and it was so much fun that the Harvards forgot all about the goalposts. Of course, as fast as Sam the Gonoph and his guys hit the ground they got right up, but the Harvards were too many for them, and they were getting an awful shellacking when the nine-foot guy who flattened Runyon, and who was knocking down Sam the Gonoph so often he was becoming a great nuisance to Sam, sang out: "Listen, these are game guys, even if they do go to Yale. Let us cease knocking them down and give them a cheer."

So the Harvards knocked down Sam the Gonoph and Nubbsy Taylor and Gyp Louie and Benny Southstreet and old Liverlips just once more, and then all the Harvards put their heads together and shouted rah-rah-rah, very loud, and went away, leaving the Yale goalposts still standing.

Well, Runyon said in this fiction that he did not see Sam the Gonoph or Nubbsy Taylor or Benny Southstreet or Gyp Louie or Liverlips again for nearly a year, not until the next fall. One Friday he got to thinking that there it was the day before The Game, Yale vs. Harvard, in Boston. He figured it was a great chance for him to join up with Sam the Gonoph again and hustle tickets for The Game, and he knew Sam would be leaving for Boston at midnight with his crew. So he hurried over to Grand Central and, sure enough, who should come along, busting through the crowd in the station, but Sam the Gonoph, Nubbsy Taylor, Benny Southstreet, Gyp Louie, and old Liverlips.

"Well, Sam," Runyon said, as he rushed along with them, "here I am ready to hustle duckets for you again, and I hope and trust we do a nice business."

"Duckets! " Sam the Gonoph said. "We are not hustling duckets for this game, although you can go with us and welcome. We are going to Boston to root for the Yales to kick the slats out of the Harvards."

"Hold 'em, Yale!" old Liverlips said, as he pushed his way through the crowd. Then he and Nubbsy and Benny and the whole bunch went trotting through the gate to catch their train. They were all wearing blue feathers in their hats with a little white Y on the feathers, such as college guys always wore at football games in the twenties. Moreover, Sam the Gonoph was carrying a Yale pennant.

*Them wuz the days!*

° ° °

No other period in the history of this country has ever called forth so many aliases. The Roaring Twenties. The Golden Twenties. The Dry Decade. The Era of Excess. The Jazz Age. The Era of Wonderful Nonsense. It was the last big spree, marking a national rite of passage, a maudlin farewell to the innocence and hope of a childhood now irrevocably gone. And it was more than just a coincidence that when this age found its poet, F. Scott Fitzgerald would write longingly of the pads worn for a day on football battlefields of Princeton.

An age in quest of heroes looked to the gridiron, and found Rockne and Gipp, the Galloping Ghost and the Four Horsemen, Wrong-Way Riegels, Friedman and Oosterbaan, Wonder Teams, Divine Teams, Praying Colonels, the Team of Destiny, Ramblers and Nomads, Nagurski and Nevers, Kaw and Pfann, Red Cagle and Little Boy Blue. America went stark mad over them all. What a world! What a country! What a sport!

Football itself now bore only a faint resemblance to the game that the Old Grads had played. With linemen rigidly separated by the neutral zone, both sides crouched low, with the attackers poised to drive their shoulders into the defenders, and the latter ready to belt the attackers about the head with open hands, or submarine under their knees to nail the ball carrier.

It was still legal to wallop an opposing lineman almost anywhere about the body with the open hand.

Seven men were now required in the line of scrimmage. This made it difficult to gather the momentum needed to hit the defenders at full force, or with concentrated power. As a consequence, ends and tackles sometimes ran with the ball. On a given signal, the end, say, would suddenly pivot out of the line and into the backfield and take a hand-off.

The forward pass continued to grow in stature. The ball was far more frequently in the air, and the passer was allowed to throw it as far as he could. It was no longer ruled a free ball if it fell to the ground. The offense did not lose possession if the ball dropped out of bounds or was caught behind the goal line. Nor could a potential receiver any longer be hit, without penalty, before he got his hands on a thrown ball.

The game was opening up all the time. There were fake passes, delayed passes, razzle-dazzle end-around plays, tackle-around plays, fake hand-offs of every sort, and even a quick kick exploding out of a running formation. Field goals were kicked chiefly by dropkick, although there were fine place-kickers too.

There was no unlimited substitution. After coming out of a game, a player could not go back in during the same half.

Until 1925, it was not uncommon for two teams to play an entire game with only one football. The ball was expensive—and, more than that, it was a trophy to be fought for and carried home by the victors. If it landed in the stands or a mud puddle, it had to be recovered and dried off and put in play again. A wet field meant a sodden, slippery, and heavy ball, almost impossible to kick, dangerous to throw, and frustrating to hold on to.

° ° °

One of the big stories of the early twenties was mighty Harvard's defeat in 1921 at the hands of tiny Centre College at Cambridge. Once in a blue moon a small college team crashes the big time briefly and then fades off into obscurity again. Centre College had a colorful coach named Charley Moran, one of those jacks-of-all-jobs who doubled in brass as coach, trainer, equipment man, and father confessor to his players. He had once been a National League umpire and former football coach of the Texas Aggies. A stern taskmaster, a smart teacher, and a fundamentalist with a flair for the sensational, Uncle Charley was hired by Centre's Robert L. (Chief) Myers at a salary of $700 a season in 1917 to coach the football team. Centre had very little money for football, so Coach Moran doubled as a cobbler to keep the football shoes in shape. Blacks, recruited from the city jail, served as masseurs at 35 cents an hour. Each player had one uniform.

The language around the team was very definitely Texas drawl. Chief Myers had once taught and coached at Fort Worth's North Side High, and when he took a coaching job at Centre in 1916 he wired his old Fort Worth gang to "get on your mules and come to Kentucky." Eight of them came, including rugged, pug-nosed Alvin (Bo) McMillin, 170 pounds of star-quality quarterback. Chief Myers told them: "Bo, you're going to be an All-American. Weaver, you'll be an All-American center, and Matty, you'll be an All-American end, even if you are too skinny." He promised his Texas kids that as director of the Centre football program he would get them games with the big Eastern schools, that they would win the Southern and the National championships. "He talked like that all the time, and we believed it," Bo McMillin recalled later. "Funny thing, almost all of it came true, too."

Bo McMillin was the spiritual leader of the team. Standing on a table in the locker room one day, he warned his teammates, "If I see anybody break training rules, I'm going to whip him then and there."

In 1917, Centre shocked the football world by beating Kentucky, 3-0, on McMillin's field goal, the first and last one he ever tried. Coach Moran eschewed his usual pregame fight talk that day and gruffly asked one of the players to pray. Bob Mathias, who later became president of a Chicago bank, spoke up: "Damn it all, let me pray." After that, the pregame prayer idea stuck. Never again did the Colonels go into a game without first offering a solemn moment of prayer. A clever publicity man, Chief Myers pinned the nickname "Praying Colonels" upon his Kentucky pupils. Syndicated columnist Grantland Rice widely circulated the phrase.

By 1919, Centre was playing a big league schedule. It whipped Indiana and a strong West Virginia eleven, which had trounced Princeton. The victory over West Virginia put Centre on the football map. Eddie Mahan, the old Harvard star, subsequently scouted the Praying Colonels and recommended that his alma mater schedule Centre.

In 1920, the eager country boys were not equal to Harvard, losing 14-31. After the game, Arnold Horween, the Crimson captain, offered the ball to Captain McMillin. "No thanks," said Bo, near tears. "We'll be back next year to take it home with us."

Chief Myers agreed. If possible, he was even more anxious than Bo to get another crack at mighty Harvard. "I would smoke a cigar under a gasoline shower to see you beat Harvard," he told the Centre players.

On the way up to Cambridge in 1921, the Centre squad stopped over at the Hotel Vanderbilt in New York City for a night. While checking in, Uncle Charley Moran happened to spot Grantland Rice entering the lobby. Turning to his startled players, he muttered, "Down on your knees quick, you sonsofbitches, here comes Grantland Rice!"

At Cambridge, the Centre players were entertained lavishly by the Harvard reception committee. This round of banquets and theatre parties worried Uncle Charley. He feared his boys from the Blue Grass might lose their fighting edge. Just before game time, he called his players together and said: "I know you guys have been royally entertained by these Harvard chaps, but just remember one thing when you go on that field today. Everyone of those bums votes the straight *Republican* ticket! "

Harvard, undefeated in 25 games, had another powerful eleven. The 1921 Crimson had won five straight before being held to a 20-20 tie by Penn State a week before the Centre game. Princeton was coming up on the Harvard schedule the week afterward, and the Cantabs obviously were looking ahead to the Tigers. It was an ideal spot for an upset. Complacently, the pro-Harvard Boston newspapers announced: "Centre College, a school with only 254 students, promises to provide a sensational incident in the stadium this Saturday, but the game hardly will be more than an incident."

In the Centre dressing room before the game, a red-faced Charley Moran, half snarling and half yelling, delivered a fight talk. Then A. B. (Happy) Chandler, a Kentuckian who was then studying law at Harvard and who later became baseball commissioner, stood up and sang "Dear Old Southland," and there wasn't a dry eye in the room. After that, everyone knelt for a brief prayer. Then the players trotted out before 43,000, most of whom wore the colors of Harvard, except for a bloc of M.I.T. students who served as a self-appointed cheering section for the visitors.

Centre's tactical plan was to play it close to the vest. They played defense, concentrated on bone-smashing tackles, and waited for a break. Harvard, meanwhile, moved the ball. Twice quarterback Charlie Buell tried a field goal. Red Roberts, the big tackle, smashed through to block the first kick from the 11-yard line. The second dropkick, from the 29 where Harvard had recovered a McMillin fumble, was short. At half time the score stood 0-0.

Inside the Centre dressing room, Uncle Charley was uncommonly quiet and cautious. He warned Captain Armstrong about the flat pass, Buell to Clark Macomber, that had gained 10 yards in the first half. Armstrong nodded, said nothing. He already had noticed that Macomber's eyes revealed the direction of the coming plays—an observation that enabled him to intercept two passes in the second half. McMillin and his teammates returned to the field confident but not cocky.

"After that solid first half," McMillin recalled years later, "we went back onto the field convinced we could win. Our opportunity came soon after the start of the third quarter, when a rules infraction cost Harvard 15 yards. That put us on the Harvard 32-yard line. While Tiny Maxwell, the referee, was marching off the 15-yard penalty, I said to myself, 'Here is where I make a little speech.' And purposely shouting loud enough for the Harvard boys to hear, I said, 'Here's the break we've been waiting for, boys, here is where we can win this football game.' I looked to the sidelines. Uncle Charley's foot was on the water bucket. That was a prearranged signal for me to call the payoff play. I then turned to the guys in the huddle and said, 'Boys, everybody block a little better than you know how and I will take her all the way home.' "

Kubale centered the ball to Bo, who ran to his right, then cut inside the Harvard left end. Meanwhile, Roberts bowled over the linebacker, and James, Armstrong, and Gordy executed key blocks. Once past the line, Bo veered back sharply to the left, picked up Roberts, who leveled the safety man, and scored standing up. Harvard rushed its best players into the game and fought savagely to score, but Centre's defense, tutored by Line Coach Claude (Tiny) Thornhill, fought back just as viciously and held. Finally, in the absence of sophisticated timing devices, Referee Tiny Maxwell stepped in, grabbed the ball, and handed it to Captain Armstrong. The game was over.

Down in Danville, Kentucky, home of the Praying Colonels, there was dancing in the streets and victory bonfires lasting a week. The legend "C 6, H 0" was smeared on sidewalks, fences, store fronts, telephone poles, mailboxes, cars, and the town water tower. Not even cattle were safe. Some of the college boys painted "C 6, H 0" on the hides of a dozen milk cows and chased them, frightened and bawling, through Danville's usually peaceful business district.

Tiny Maxwell, who refereed the Harvard-Centre game, was one of the most colorful football officials the East has ever known. He weighed 300 pounds and stuttered like a chilled tin lizzie on a winter morning. He had a natural sense of humor, which extracted him from many a jam. His nimble repartee saved him from embarrassment in the 1921 Harvard-Yale game. The teams were well matched and neither could make a first down until Malcolm Aldrich got the bright idea of hiding behind Tiny's generous bulk. Using Maxwell as a buffer, Aldrich dodged first on one side and then the other until he finally broke loose on a 30-yard run. Tiny's aplomb was not upset one bit. As the players were unraveling themselves, he blew his whistle and shouted: "Ta-ta-ta-time out, ba-ba-boys, while I get my bla-bla-blue jersey! "

An irate player once called Maxwell a robber in the heat of play. Tiny's whistle shrilled.

"Ya-ya-ya-you look like a nice ka-ka-kid," he blurted, "and I am sure your ma-ma-mother would not want you to a-a-associate with r-r-obbers. Out of the g-g-game! "

° ° °

Prominent in Eastern football circles at this time was John William Heisman, for whom the Heisman Trophy is named. The old Brown (1887–89) and Penn (1890–91) lineman coached at Pennsylvania in 1920–22, compiling an overall 16-10-2 record. Next to Stagg, Warner, and Camp, Heisman was one of the leading football innovators of the day. Among other inventions, he originated the hidden ball play; was the first to place his quarterback at safety on defense; introduced the center snap; dreamed up the scoreboard listing downs, yardage, and so on; originated the "hike" or "hep" vocal signal for starting play, the "double pass," interference on end runs, the spin buck, and the Heisman shift; led the fight to divide games into quarters instead of halves; and was in the forefront in the legalization of the forward pass in 1906.

A Shakespearean actor during the off-season, Heisman had a natural sense of pomp and drama. He spoke in exaggerated stage English to his football players: "Thrust your projections into their cavities, grasping them about the knees, and depriving them of their means of propulsion. They must come to earth, locomotion being denied them." He referred to a football as "a prolate spheroid in which the outer leather casing is drawn tightly over a somewhat smaller rubber tubing."

Despite these Macbethian overtones, Coach Heisman possessed a rare instinct for football. On offense, his basic rules made sense: Try end runs on first or second downs; never order two end runs in succession; don't try an end run when the ball is less than 25 yards from your goal, unless from punt formation; divide the work so as not to wear out any one ball carrier; when you find a weak spot, hammer it; when a substitute goes into the game for the opponents, test him immediately and find out what he is good for; never pass inside your own 30-yard line—and the best passing down is the third; punt on first down if close to your own goal; when in doubt, punt anyway, anywhere; don't have your punter run with the ball on the down preceding the one on which he will probably have to kick; call signals in a peppy, confident tone.

John Heisman broke down football into these percentages: talent, 25 percent; aggressiveness, 20 percent; mentality, 20 percent; speed, 20 percent; and weight, 15 percent. His philosophy was that "a coach should be masterful and commanding, even

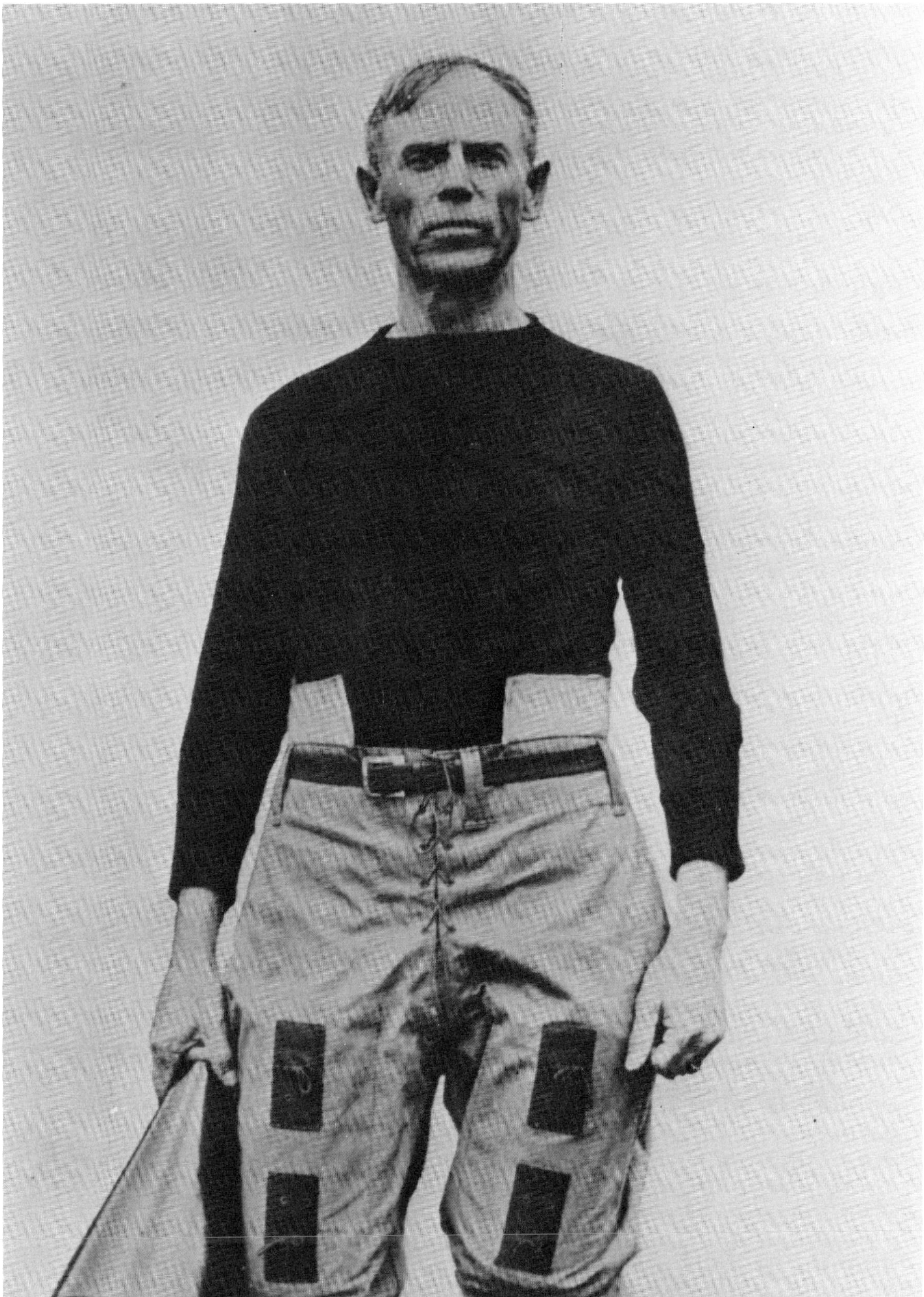

*John W. Heisman, in whose honor the trophy is named, returned to his alma mater, Pennsylvania, in 1920 as head coach.*

dictatorial. He has no time to say 'please' or 'mister,' and he must occasionally be severe, arbitrary, something of a czar."

Heisman was 66 and preparing to write the history of football when he died of bronchial pneumonia in 1936.

° ° °

The king of the hill during the years 1921, '22, and '23 was Cornell. Under Gloomy Gil Dobie, the Big Red surged to the Ivy League peak for the second time in its history. Dobie's psychological approach was the same at Ithaca as it had been at Seattle, where he had coached the Washington Huskies for nine seasons (1908–16) and compiled an unbelievable 58-0-3 record. He seemed to take a sadistic delight in disparaging the ability of his players. But he could get away with it at Cornell because he had such natural stars as Eddie Kaw, the superior mud horse; Sunny Sundstrom, the jovial tackle; George Pfann, who seemed to run on his knees; and Swede Hanson, the whipcord lineman who led the offense's dreaded off-tackle play.

Dobie built the off-tackle maneuver based on metronomic precision. The blocking back took so many steps in this direction, the center hung the ball in an exact spot in the air from where the ball carrier picked it off, and the running guard swung out of the line at just the right moment. Every move was charted. The play functioned like clockwork and was rehearsed for hours at a stretch.

Disregarding his gruff manner and simulated brutality, Dobie was worshipped by Kaw and Pfann and their teammates. They did not complain about his eccentricities. In 1921, for example, after Cornell had walloped Dartmouth, 59-7, spectators were astonished to see the Big Red varsity practicing and scrimmaging after the game. When Dobie was asked how come, he curtly replied, "Those bums didn't expect to get away with *that* performance, did they?"

At the end of the 1923 season, Allison Danzig, the *New York Times* correspondent who had played for Dobie at Cornell, rushed into the Big Red dressing room and shook Dobie's hand vigorously. Cornell had just beaten Penn, 14-7, to wrap up its third straight undefeated season—24 victories in a row.

"Congratulations on another championship," Danzig told him. Gloomy Gil stared coldly at his former pupil.

"If this is a championship team," he replied glumly, "then the human race must be degenerating! "

A shrewd Scotsman, Dobie was one of the first to realize that a coach's job depends upon the whims of the Old Grads. Thus, by predicting the worst, he could make himself appear to be something of a miracle man if his team happened to win; if it lost that was only what should have been expected.

"A football coach can only wind up two ways," he often said, "dead or a failure."

The greatest player ever coached by Dobie was George Pfann. The Marion, Ohio, native was an excellent quarterback and runner, with heavy legs that gave him power, speed, and shiftiness. He possessed that ideal combination of brains and brawn sought by all football coaches. After making the All-America team in 1923, he went on to Oxford as a Rhodes scholar and earned a law degree.

*Lanky, dour Gilmour (Gloomy Gil) Dobie was the arch apostle of Schopenhauer in his incurable pessimism in both victory and defeat. Despite his negative personality, three successive Cornell elevens won every game in 1921–22–23.*

QUARTETTE OF CORNELL'S GREAT BACKFIELD STARS

CAPT. EDGAR KAW, HALFBACK

CHARLES CASSIDY, FULLBACK

GEORGE PFANN, QUARTERBACK

FLOYD RAMSAY, HALFBACK

*The all-conquering 1922 Cornell backfield.*

Eddie Kaw, who scored five touchdowns against Penn in 1921, despite rain and mud at Franklin Field, for a 41-0 victory, was even shiftier than Pfann, although not as powerful. Together they gave Cornell a terrific one-two punch; the team ran up an incredible 1,022 points in 24 games against only 81 for opponents. Even the ordinarily Gloomy Gil had found something to smile about.

Despite his dour outlook and dire forecasts, his hostility to press representatives who wanted to watch his team work out (practice was always secret), and the relentlessness with which he scrimmaged his players, Dobie could be a friendly, sociable companion when the season ended, an entertaining, uninhibited conversationalist with a glass of brew in his hand. He was a man of learning, with a law degree, highly intelligent, an inveterate reader, and a shrewd investor in the stock market.

Dobie's, however, was not one of the great inventive minds of football. He contributed little that was new, as was true of Knute Rockne. But he was a superb teacher and drillmaster who could prepare a team letter-perfect as few others could. He was a perfectionist who might spend an entire afternoon on a single play to achieve the precise execution he demanded, and his teams exemplified a mechanical perfection probably never excelled on the gridiron. There was little of the fancy or tricky in the brand of football his teams played. Power and flawless execution of the fundamentals of blocking and tackling assignments were the factors of his success. His teams were primarily running machines, resorting to the pass only occasionally and seldom inside their own 35-yard line. The off-tackle play was Dobie's bread-and-butter operation. Meticulously executed with split-second timing and every man letter-perfect in playing his part, it brought so much power to bear that it was said that Dobie's teams could have warned their opponents of what was coming at them and they still could not have stopped them.

When Dobie went to Cornell in 1920, the Big Red had beaten Pennsylvania, its chief rival, only four times since 1893. No wonder they hailed him as something of a genius after his 1921-'22-'23 elevens beat the Quakers by scores of 41-0, 9-0, and 14-7.

Aside from insistence on flawless execution of fundamentals and careful attention to detail, George Pfann once remarked that the factors which made Dobie an outstanding coach were (1) his ability to select a team, (2) his ability to keep a team in top condition mentally and physically, (3) obtaining an extremely high degree of coordinated team play, and (4) getting the best performance of which they were capable out of the team.

"Dobie's whole theory of offensive football was power with timing, mixed with just enough passing and deception to keep the secondary from moving immediately toward the ball carrier, thereby keeping the defense sufficiently off balance to give his power plays a chance to develop," Pfann said. "Backs were instructed and trained to go for three yards on a play, and anything more than that was just so much gravy.

"He believed that in order for a team to really become a team, it must play together constantly, particularly on offense. Consequently, once he had his first team picked in the fall—and the first three weeks were a survival fight to let him pick the best 11 men—no one except Dobie could touch the team. He kept it intact, as far as possible, and he alone worked with its offense, adjusting backfield positions to fit the individual characteristics of the backs so that the entire team would charge as a unit.

"On defense he placed his men in positions which allowed for the least possible gamble. He never permitted two defensive linemen playing alongside each other to be spaced so that both could be doubled-teamed. He liked a seven-man line and a box defense and relied on rushing the passer to take care of the extra eligible receiver. His line was taught to play the cup defense, and he worked constantly to develop a fast, aggressive charge on the part of the line."

° ° °

After leaving Old Nassau in 1911, the spirit and old-fashioned psychology of Bill Roper returned to Princeton after World War I and produced one of the school's most famous legends—1922's "Team of Destiny."

"I guess we were surely that," Charlie Caldwell, a wingback on the team, told me in 1955. "We were strong defensively and won on Ken Smith's kicking and the breaks. Each Saturday the oddsmakers picked us on the short end, and we'd win, even though we lacked an attack. We had no blocking, no passing, no real ground game. Some of our plays were made up even in the huddle. We played a 7-1-2-1 defense all the time and I was the linebacker. On offense, I played wingback, but we

never ran reverses. I carried the ball once all season and had more playing time than anyone else on the varsity. Coach Roper felt that football was 90 percent fight and all the rest was 10 percent. He was a master psychologist. He would use anything to advantage. His attack consisted of the best plays taken from other teams. West Virginia, for example, beat us in 1919, and after the game, Roper kept Ira Rodgers, the star of the Mountaineers, at Princeton for the rest of the weekend teaching us the West Virginia spread, which was new that season. Roper used the spread in 1920 to tie Harvard (14-14) and beat Yale (20-0)."

Roper's Team of Destiny actually was only a so-so bunch; still it rolled up a total of 127 points against 34 while smashing through an eight-game schedule unbeaten. The Tigers simply refused to lose. Three of their victories were gained by the slim margin of a field goal or last-second touchdown.

The 1922 personnel included Herb Treat, All-American, and Harlan F. (Pink) Baker, tackles; Howard (Howdy) Gray and Saxby Tillson, ends; Captain Melville Dickenson and Barr Snively, guards; Oliver Alford, center; Johnny Gorman,

*W. W. (Bill) Roper's 17-year record at Princeton was 89-28-16.*

*Princeton's 1922 "Team of Destiny."*

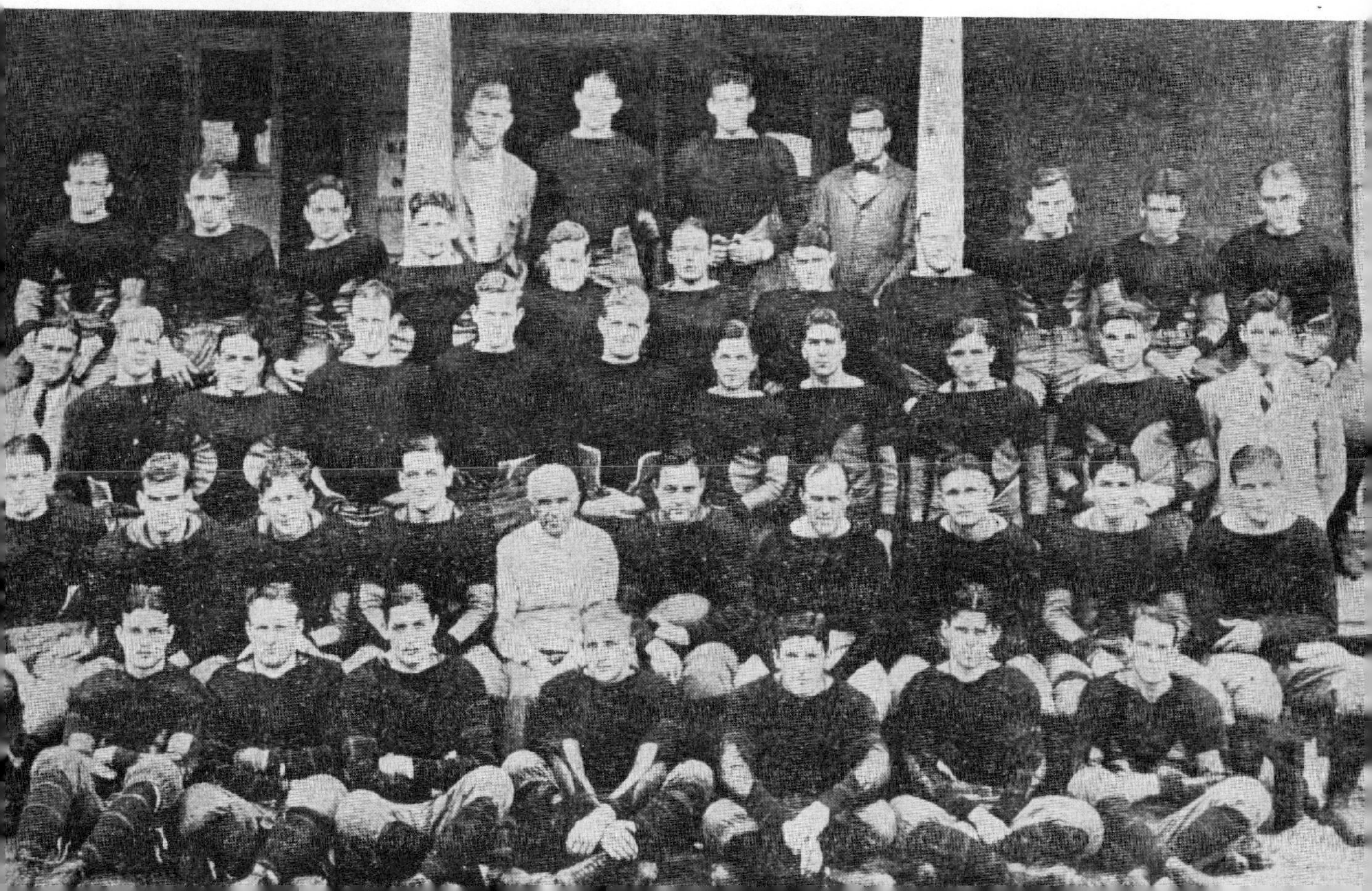

quarterback; Charlie Caldwell and Harry Crum, halfbacks; and Jack Cleaves, fullback.

When Amos Alonzo Stagg, the Chicago coach, and Bill Roper, representing a combined gridiron experience of more than a half-century, once united in picking the Princeton-Chicago game of 1922 as the most dramatic of their long careers, historians of the day were inclined to string along with them.

The contest marked the first time in history that a Princeton football team had ever played in the Midwest, and they were 3-to-1 underdogs in the betting. Stagg, as much a part of the University of Chicago as the maroon he himself had chosen for the college color, had fashioned a stone-cracking steamroller that hit an enemy line with the force of the Theban phalanx. Wise old Epaminondas of history would have grinned to see his tactical method transplanted from the battlefield of Leuctra to the modern football gridiron in America.

Princeton grads from every midwestern city and black-earth farm flocked to the Midway that afternoon, prepared to tear their lungs out in a lost cause. They came praying for a miracle, but fully expecting to see the burgundy-jerseyed giants go like a steamroller over Bill Roper's cagey eleven. They had read in the Eastern papers that Princeton had one of its traditionally alert teams, a resourceful, versatile bunch of opportunists, quick to cash a fumble at the touchdown bank.

"The City Gray," famed in Chicago battle songs, looked like a Brobdignagian anthill as game time drew near. "I could have sold 200,000 tickets if the stadium had been big enough," moaned the Chicago ticket director as he shook his head to pleas from intimate friends and influential politicians. Stagg Field, with its inadequate 40,000 seats, had been sold out weeks in advance. Not even standing room could be bought for what midwesterners were convinced would be a Waterloo for the once Napoleonic East. The whole Midwest was out to show this member of the so-called Big Three that the glory of Princeton, Yale, and Harvard was one with Nineveh and Tyre.

The Princeton players were perhaps the only persons at Stagg Field who did not anticipate being sacrificed to make a Chicago holiday. Bill Roper, a disciple of suggestion, had fed his pupils recurrent doses of psychology. Earlier that season, as they ate their meals in the Nassau Field House, they stared at placards proclaiming: "A team that won't be beat can't be beat" and "We are going to win every game on our schedule."

Self-sacrifice for a common cause was the predominant note in Princeton's string of long-shot victories. Just before the Tigers took the field at Chicago, Roper told Emery, his regular fullback, that he and his coaching staff had decided to replace him with Caldwell.

"I think Caldwell is the better man to start," replied the keenly disappointed Emery. "He's been going better than I have." This putting of the team ahead of personal desire was typical of the 1922 Princeton elelven.

As they spread out over Stagg Field, a gridiron hallowed by the churning cleats of Eckersall, Steffen, Heston, Hirschberger, O'Dea, McGovern, Stevenson, and other legendary heroes, the Tiger players commented on the springy, lush-looking quality of the smooth turf. It was as perfect as a putting green, a novelty to Eastern players accustomed to skinned or thinly covered gridirons. "Gee, Ken, we should be able to run on this," Jack Cleaves said to Ken Smith.

During the first quarter, Princeton was weak in spots, brilliant at intervals, but lacking in driving power and a sustained defense. The ponderous Maroon backs battered and tore the Tiger line to shreds. Princeton fought back stubbornly, but to no avail.

"The game had no more than begun when it dawned on us that we had never faced a forward line quite like Stagg's phalanx," Bill Roper said later. "It was massive and yet mobile. Against it the initial assaults of our backs were futile. We gained very little ground, while the powerful Chicago backs, when they swung into action, moved as one man, with our line reeling before them. John Thomas, with his brother Harry and Jim Pyott, ripped our line wide open and charged 60 yards in the first quarter for a touchdown. They found our tackles easy marks.

"In the second period, Chicago struck swiftly at us again and again—and always with the same result. Again they scored—but so did we. We got our first touchdown on a long, beautiful pass followed by four straight thrusts at the line.

"The Maroon backs smashed and hammered their way through our defenses for a third touchdown in the third quarter. And for the third straight time, the try for extra point was missed. But who cared? Nobody at that moment, but those three failures to convert were soon to spell the difference between an unsatisfying tie and a heart-breaking defeat for Chicago."

The teams changed sides for the last period. Leading now, 18-7, Chicago punted deep to little Johnny Gorman, who caught the ball in the shadow of his own goal posts and, whirling quickly, made a daring lateral pass to Jack Cleaves, who was posted wide. The referee ruled that the ball had been thrown forward. Princeton was penalized 15 yards back to its own 2-yard line. Conservative playbook strategy called for Princeton to punt out from behind its goal line. But there were barely 12 minutes to play, and it was time for drastic, shoot-from-the-hip remedies. Swaggering, insolent Johnny Gorman was a chap to stake everything on one throw of the dice.

"Kick formation, Cleaves back! " barked Gorman in the huddle.

Watching anxiously from the sideline, Coach Roper saw Gorman pause and whisper something in Cleaves's ear as the Tigers broke out of the huddle.

"I remembered that Gorman and Cleaves had been teammates at Mercersburg, and they were noted for improvising plays under pressure and for concocting schemes that weren't in our playbook," Roper said later. "Knowing this, and seeing no chance for us in straight football, I hoped when they lined up they were going to try something out of the ordinary."

Cleaves dropped back as if to punt. "Block that punt! " chanted Chicago's cheering section. Sensing another touchdown, the Maroon forwards tried desperately to smother Cleaves. They stormed through blindly, arms flailing. Faking the punt, Cleaves pivoted instead to his right and arched a long pass toward the east sideline to the flying Gorman. Johnny picked the ball out of the dank Lake Michigan air with his fingertips and darted to midfield before the Chicago safety man nailed him. There was nothing gentle about that tackle. Gorman had to be carried off the field.

The Princeton march stalled at the Maroon 42 and the Tigers were forced to kick, but on the very next play Chicago's substitute center made a crazy snap to Zorn. The ball struck Zorn's shoulder and landed straight in the arms of Howard Gray, Princeton's alert end. Gray never broke his stride. Clutching the ball, he raced into the Chicago end zone. The try for point was good, and now Princeton trailed by only four points, 18–14. The clock showed six minutes to play.

That unexpected touchdown charged up the Tigers. Suddenly the Princeton backs, hitherto impotent on attack, became dazzling dervishes, unstoppable berserkers.

A shrewdly masked pass completed Chicago's discomfiture, placing the ball on the Maroon 7-yard line. Then Chicago braced. Three Princeton lunges left the ball still 3 yards short of the goal.

Over on the Princeton bench, things were stirring. Burly Crum, nicknamed "Maud" because of his mulelike "kick" on close plunges, pleaded with Roper to put him into the game.

"Fourth down—three yards to go—only two minutes to play! Coach, I can score that touchdown, put me in! *Please.*"

Roper had a hunch. "All right, go in," he told Crum.

Crum went—and he didn't stop going until he had knifed over Chicago's goal for the go-ahead touchdown. The try split the uprights: Princeton 21, Chicago 18.

That's what the scoreboard read, but the Maroons did not intend it to be final. They went to the air. In those last 120 seconds, the air was full of footballs, and every one of them came to rest in maroon-jerseyed arms. It was just what Stagg had been waiting for. At half time, he had begged his quarterback to use the pass more. "They have tightened up their line defense. Throw the ball," he told his quarterback. Now, with the seconds ticking away, with defeat mocking them, his men finally took to the air.

That flurry of Chicago passes devoured distance. Strohmeier caught the final toss on Princeton's 6-yard stripe. Thirty seconds to play—and the Chicago strategy switched back to its line-hammering tactics again. *Whang!* 2 yards inside tackle. *Biff!* 2 yards through center. Again came the thud of colliding bodies, and only 1 yard separated the ball from the last chalk mark. Fourth down—a yard to go—a second to play!

Lonny Stagg was gritting his teeth. Bill Roper turned his eyes away from the field. Behind the big Maroon line, John Thomas crouched for the plunge that meant victory or defeat. His sweat-stained face was haggard, the corners of his mouth were drawn down in a Lon Chaney scowl. Facing him, Princeton's bedraggled forwards dug their cleats into the turf. Wingate, the peppery Tiger quarterback, stormed up and down behind his linemen, slapping one on the back, kicking another, exhorting them to hold. From the stadium above came a staccato babel, moaning, "Hurry, Chicago!"

High up in the east stand a grizzled Princeton grad, between nips from a generous flask, had been shouting maudlin advice to the Princeton quarterback all afternoon. The old boy had yelled himself hoarse, telling the Tigers what formations to use, to whom to give the ball, and how to stop Chicago's massplays. Now, in this extremity, he surrendered the wheel. Taking an extra long swig of bourbon, he summoned what was left of his voice and bellowed: "Boys, I've done the best I can for you. You'll have to use your own judgment now!"

Princeton's judgment was as good as Chicago's was bad. Still you would hardly call it judgment, for every Tiger knew intuitively that Chicago would stake its last throw of the dice on a straight center buck.

Those solid, striped legs massed for the charge. The Nassau secondaries, disregarding their exposed flanks, converged toward the middle, blanketing the Maroon wave.

For a heart-sickening second it seemed as if Thomas's leather helmet projected across the line. Then he collapsed in a welter of black and orange—a few scant inches short of the whitewashed goal line.

Nobody heard the whistle, so deafening was the roar of the crowd. The final score: Princeton 21, Chicago 18. So it stands in history.

Had Amos Alonzo Stagg been a man of less integrity, that Tiger goal-line stand might have had a different ending. During the previous winter, as a member of the rules committee, Stagg sponsored legislation to prevent the transmission of information from the bench to the playing field by a substitute. Fritz Crisler, who was his assistant coach at Chicago, pleaded with Stagg to send his son, a substitute quarterback, into the game with orders to pass.

"With Princeton massed to stop Thomas," cried Fritz, "the end zone is wide open. Your son will be the hero of the game."

Coach Stagg only shook his head.

"No," he said, "I have to live with my conscience. Let the kids work it out by themselves."

° ° °

Coming off their Team of Destiny season, Roper let Knute Rockne talk him into a two-game series in 1923–24, both games played at Palmer Stadium. Roper may have realized that he was overmatched, but he never had been one to blanch at odds. Notre Dame won the two games, 25-2 and 12-0.

On the first visit, the *Princetonian* ran an interview with Rockne, who said that it was a great honor for Notre Dame to play in historic Palmer Stadium and that he was sure his players would benefit from their contacts with Princeton men. He was right. One of the Princeton halfbacks, Charlie Caldwell, who was to become a Hall of Fame coach himself two decades later, said that his education in football began that day. "I realized that there was much more to this game than I had

*Forced to come from behind, underdog Princeton, on its first venture into the Midwest, scored two touchdowns in the last quarter to defeat Coach Amos Alonzo Stagg's University of Chicago juggernaut, 21-18. Here, Princeton back Bob Beattie rips through the Chicago line for 15 yards.*

thought," he said later. "We were being finessed. Every time I was about to do something, I was being nudged or pushed away."

On the next visit to Princeton, Rockne added a new twist to pregame pep talks. Ailing with phlebitis, he was pushed into the Notre Dame locker room in a wheelchair and didn't feel up to delivering his customary fight talk. Luckily, the visitors' dressing room was right next to Princeton's.

Just as Rockne opened his mouth to speak, the dynamic tones of Bill Roper began filtering through the flimsy doors that separated the two teams. Rockne winked at his four scourges, Elmer Layden, Don Miller, Harry Stuhldreher, and Jimmy Crowley.

"They tell me that this Roper is a terrific orator," Rock said, turning to the rest of the team. "Now you fellas just lay on the floor and listen to him while I save my voice. Maybe you'll learn something."

° ° °

Percy Haughton, out of coaching since 1916, returned to the game in 1923 as head coach at Columbia. The announcement of his appointment drew broad speculation. A sample, from the Cincinnati *Times-Star:*

> It was with a shock that the athletic world read that Percy Haughton is to resume coaching, and not with his alma mater, Harvard. This next season he is to coach Columbia, which is making a frantic effort to develop athletics so that its importance in football and other sports may be in approximate proportion to the number of its student body. So now the biggest university of the biggest city in the world is prepared to pay the biggest salary to the football coach with the biggest reputation.
>
> Columbia may be put back on the football map by Percy Haughton. But somehow there is a suspicion that the potentialities of the event are greater than the realities will prove. Haughton is being taken from an environment that helped to make his greatness. Those great victories were even more Harvard victories than Haughton victories. And Haughton in those days was working for the university that he had played for. At Columbia he will have the students to draw from. But will he have the *spirit* to draw from? And at Cambridge he gave Harvard something that Harvard could not buy. Can Columbia buy it?

In a similar vein of skepticism, the New Haven *Journal-Courier* remarked: "We hope to learn how it came about that Percy could be induced to desert his own college colors and transfer his genius to a field of instruction hostile to the pride of Harvard. The capture of Haughton by Columbia does awaken interesting speculation upon the subject of modern collegiate sports."

Aware of the charges that he was guilty of "deserting" Harvard, Haughton felt it necessary to explain his action to the New York *Tribune:*

"I have wanted to get back into football for some time. When Columbia first approached me, I could not see my way clear to take the job. But now I have so arranged my affairs so that I can give the necessary time. The splendid caliber and spirit of Columbia graduates and committees with whom I have come in contact have greatly impressed me, as has the Columbia athletic organization, which is quite similar to Harvard's, with a committee on each branch of athletics and one big committee supervising them all.

"Owing to the fact that football was abolished at Columbia for 10 years, beginning in 1905, naturally it was felt that no Columbia graduate was qualified for the coaching position, there was no football background, no one who had grown into the position, nothing like existing conditions up at Harvard. It really is a new game to Columbia.

"It is my hope to give Columbia the groundwork for a system that, if successful, can be perpetuated by Columbia graduates. I feel greatly complimented to have been given the job."

The *Tribune* estimated that Columbia had agreed to pay Haughton upward of $20,000 per season. It was a multiyear contract to afford Percy time enough to establish a winning program.

Unfortunately, Haughton hardly got started. His record at Morningside Heights was 8-5-1 in a season and a half, but then, on October 27, 1924, he suffered a fatal heart attack. He was only 48. Death came just hours before the Penn game. His last words were: "Tell the squad I'm proud of them."

Paul Withington coached the Lions for the rest of the season and wound up with a respectable 5-3-1 record.

° ° °

The Yale team most Old Blues and football fans regard as the greatest in Eli gridiron history is the team of 1923. The Big Blue Team. Bill Mallory's team. Yale was lucky to have a football captain like Mallory. Modest, yet aggressive on the field, he possessed rare qualities that made him an inspirational leader both in and out of football. Beyond his

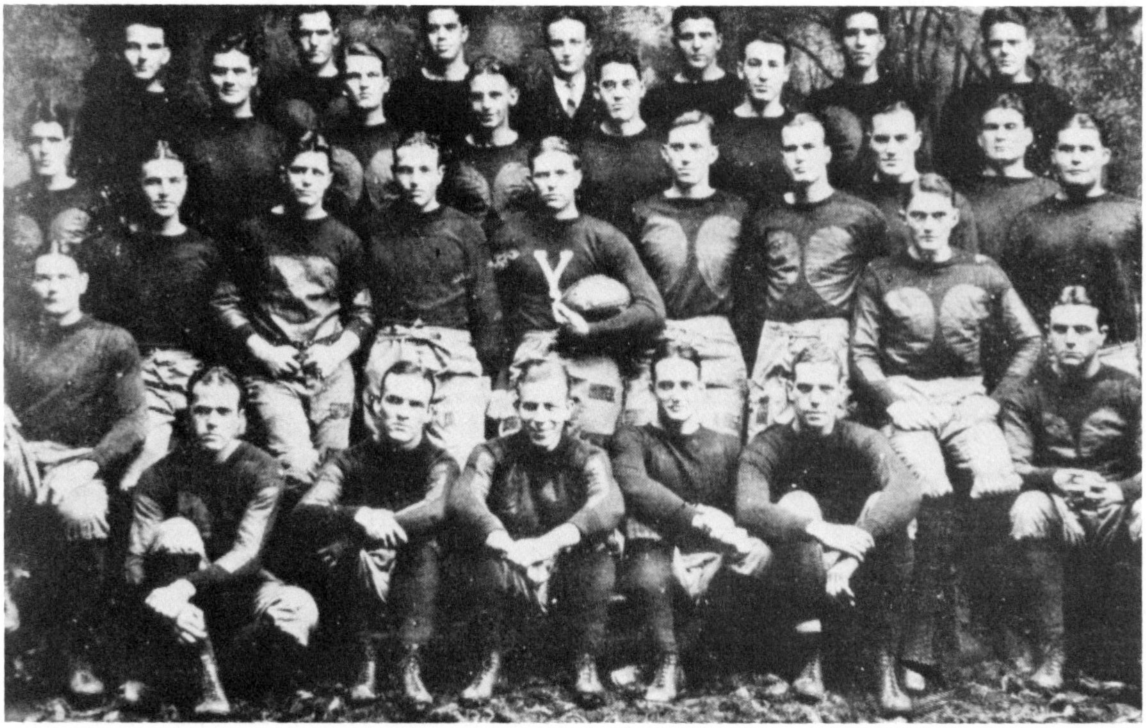

*1923 Yale champions. Back row, l. to r.: Bingham, Pond, Esselstyn, Schoonmaker, Butterworth, Hart, Eckart. Third row: Greene, Deaver, Bench, O'Hearn, Landis. Second row: Cottle, Blair, Neidlinger, Lovejoy, Captain Bill Mallory, Luman, Richeson, Milstead, Hubbard, Pillsbury. Front row: Diller, Haas, Murphy, Neale, Lincoln, Miller, Stevens, Hulman.*

football and hockey skills, he was also a member of Skull and Bones and was voted the outstanding man in his graduating class. Mallory backed up the Yale line, was a crushing, deadly blocker, and a pile-driving fullback with the ball. Walter Camp thought so much of him that he named Mallory fullback and captain on the official 1923 All-America first team.

Coached by Tad Jones, the Big Blue Team included four transfers: Century Milstead from Wabash; Mal Stevens from Washburn; Lyle Richeson from Tulane; and Widdy Neale (Greasy's kid brother), who reached New Haven by way of West Virginia and Marietta. Yale had powerful frosh teams in 1920 and '21, and by the time the '23 season arrived the varsity was bursting with talent and experience. Milstead and Ted Blair probably were the best pair of tackles the Blue ever knew at one time. Milstead, Stevens, Richeson, Neale, and Blair were only five of a great squad. The class of '24 contributed several stars, too: Captain Mallory, fullback; Newell Neidlinger, halfback; and Tex Diller, left guard.

Although Mallory, Century Milstead (he got his unusual first name from being born on January 1, 1900), center Win Lovejoy, quarterback Lyle Richeson, and halfback Mal Stevens (who worked for a New Haven undertaker to earn money for school) each received All-America recognition from Walter Camp, the Big Blue Team of '23 was not necessarily a team of one star or a handful of stars so much as a team of many stars, extending down through much of the second string, many of whom won honorable mention from Camp.

"Our team was well balanced, with excellent reserve material," testified Dr. Mal Stevens some years ago. Halfback Stevens graduated with honors from Yale, then entered medical school and made a name for himself in gynecology and obstetrics. "Milstead, Diller, Eckart, Miller, and Lovejoy were superb operatives, flanked by Dick Luman, tall, rangy, and rough, and by Hulman, fast (a track man) and good offensively and defensively, as well as Bingham to back him up, or vice versa. They gave Yale a line which made defense a pleasure for the backfield.

"In using a single wing attack, a short punt, a spread, and a deep punt formation, we were equipped with a running, passing, and kicking offense from all of these formations. A great deal of credit must be given to Lovejoy, the center, whose passing was the best I have ever seen and aided the timing of the team tremendously. He passed a wet or dry ball perfectly.

"We usually played a seven-man line, overshifting a half or a full man to the strength. This allowed our tackles to be wide enough to operate on the outside shoulder of the offensive end or the wingback. Milstead and Blair were murder when released in this fashion. Our line became a six-man line against passes as we dropped our weak side end back into the flat or back into a short zone, rushing the passer sharply with our overshifted guard, tackle, and strong end. We would criss-cross our end and tackle to block punts, and felt that with our good defense a blocked punt would win a game for us, as Blair did against Army. We were drilled constantly by Coach Jones and his two excellent assistants, Charley Comerford and Myron Fuller, on protection for our passer and especially for our punter. I do not remember having a punt blocked while I was kicking at Yale.

"We were a very alert team. We recovered 23 of 27 fumbles by our opponents. The team had a certain *anticipation.*

"Our team had the receivers and passers and worked on our passing consistently in practice, so I really feel we could have set all kinds of records at that time in passing. Another reason for our success was that we all, with the possible exception of O'Hearn and Neale, loved to block and tackle. We loved scrimmages almost as much as a game.

"But above all else, our team all liked and respected each other. It was my first experience playing on a team which had two or three millionaires, and I was amazed, coming from Kansas as I did, to find that their feelings toward contact and their love of football were the same as mine or Milstead's, which had been tempered in a little more primitive fire. The team had spirit, confidence, a good sense of humor, a genuine liking for each other, a feeling that football was a game but one to be played to win, and a feeling that we could lick any other college team in the country. Combined, those are pretty hard factors to beat."

The Big Blue capitalized on all its talent and power to smother North Carolina, 53-0, in the opening game; rack up Georgia, 40-0, in its first visit to the Yale Bowl; club Bucknell, 29-14; and then beat Brown, 21-0, in a game that drew 50,000 to New Haven.

The next week, Army came to the Bowl, and the 80,000 ticket-holders who were there saw the most spectacular game yet played in the 10-year-old stadium. The Cadets had lost to a strong Notre Dame eleven, 13-0 (the Four Horsemen's junior year), but were regarded as one of the top teams in the East. They had Ed Garbisch, a dead-eye kicker and all-around star at center, excellent backs in George Smythe and Bill Wood, and strong, rugged personnel elsewhere.

Army scored first on a 15-yard field goal by Garbisch. Not long after, Blair pounced on a fumble behind the Army goal line for a touchdown, Widdy Neale converted, and now the Bulldogs led, 7-3. Then Smythe ran a punt back 75 yards to put the Cadets ahead again. On the play, Garbisch blocked three would-be tacklers, and kicked the extra point. Army left the field at half time, 10-7.

In the second half, the Big Blue came to life and greatness. Lining up frequently in a spread, they ran and passed the Cadets dizzy. When Army attempted to get back into the game with its own passes, they were intercepted, five in all, by the alert Yale backs. Toward the end, the contest was developing into a rout. The final score was 31-10. Yale made 323 yards rushing, averaging over 4 yards a crack. The Blue completed 7 out of 11 passes for 63 yards.

The Big Blue now looked forward eagerly to Princeton and Harvard. First, however, was a date with Maryland, coached by Harry C. Byrd, later its president. The only scar on an otherwise unblemished Terrapin record was a 3-0 loss to Penn. In spite of Maryland's formidable credentials, Tad Jones and most of his staff traveled down to Princeton, where they watched the Tigers lose to Harvard, 5-0, and left the Yale varsity in charge of end coach Charlie Comerford.

Maryland, sharp and hot, mixed runs and passes and scored two touchdowns before the Yales knew what hit them. The Big Blue looked at the scoreboard, saw it was 14-0 against, and finally got down to work. With Widdy Neale, Richeson, Mallory, and Ducky Pond grinding out the yards, the Bulldogs scored a touchdown (Neale) and booted a field goal (Mallory) to draw within four points of the visitors.

The turning point in the contest came when Mal Stevens ran a punt back 50 yards to the Maryland 2. He scored on the next play to put the Elis ahead, 16-14. That's the way the game ended. The Terrapins got close enough in the last quarter to try a field goal, and barely missed.

For the Princeton game, 78,000 loaded the Bowl, and they saw the Big Blue give the Tigers the worst hiding by a Yale team in 33 years. The score was 27 to 0. Richeson, Lovejoy, Mallory, Luman, Milstead, Blair, Eckart, and Diller were brilliant in freezing off the men of Nassau.

Now came Harvard, who, under Coach Robert T. Fisher, was not having one of its better seasons. Its 4-2-1 record included a 6-6 tie with Middlebury and losses to Dartmouth (16-0) and Brown (20-7).

"Forget their poor record," Tad Jones cautioned his players. "If you need incentive, just remember Yale has won only once from Harvard in the last nine games. What's more, the school has scored only one touchdown on Harvard in 13 years."

Ten hours before the game at Cambridge, it began to rain tumultuously. It was, as somebody said, "0-0 weather." Despite the conditions, 55,000 showed up. The weather made it almost impossible to play good football. Yale fumbled 11 times, recovered 10 times. Harvard fumbled 14 times, recovered 10. The game developed into a punting duel. Yale punted 28 times, Harvard 26. The players became so basted with mud and goo that Blue and Crimson jerseys became indistinguishable.

Yale scored first, just before the first quarter ended, when Ducky Pond scooped up a fumbled punt by Marion Cheek, the Harvard left halfback, on the Yale 32-yard line and raced 68 yards for a touchdown. On his way through the quagmire, Ducky was seen to look back over his shoulder at a small, mud-splattered little figure, Yale or Harvard, he couldn't tell which, giving pursuit. Then the little figure waved at Pond reassuringly. It was Widdy Neale. Ducky ran into the end zone and touched the ball down. Mallory then gave the ball a good kick to make the score, 7-0.

That would have been enough. But in the second half Mallory put on a most remarkable kicking demonstration. On fourth down in the third period, he kicked a 24-yard field goal from out of the hold of Richeson to make the score, 10-0.

Still in the third quarter, left end Ted Hart, subbing for Shep Bingham, recovered a Crimson fumble on the Harvard 29. Richeson knelt again, took a soggy pass from center Lovejoy, set it down in the mud, and once again Mallory's powerful right leg banged the ball up and over the crossbar. That made it 13-0, the final score.

The drought was over. The mad celebration was underway. Several thousand Yale fans, slipping and sliding, snake-danced around Harvard Stadium. "Good night, poor Harvard," they sang. "Harvard, good night!"

Both Yale and Cornell, boasting 8-0-0 records, claimed the National Championship in 1923. The two teams were not scheduling each other in those days. They would not meet on the gridiron until 1936.

° ° °

Ring Lardner, poet laureate of athletes of the twenties and the most famous literary figure the craft of sportswriting yet has produced, was popular for his uncanny ear for dialogue, which enabled him to capture the humor, pathos, vanity, and distortion in athletes' speech.

"Lardner's writings are a mine of authentic Americana, his service to etymology incomparable," H. L. Mencken wrote years ago. "He reports the common speech not only with humor but with the utmost accuracy."

In 1919, Lardner had left the *Chicago Tribune* and gone to New York to do a weekly piece for a newspaper syndicate. The theater bug had bitten him violently and he confessed he wanted to be near Broadway, the nerve center of show business. He moved his family to Great Neck and soon discovered Yale football. In 1923, at the invitation of the editor of the Yale football program, he consented to write a short piece for the magazine. The result was typical Lardner:

> "Great Neck, N.Y., Nov. 15—Well friends, I may as well come right to the pt. and announce that this here is a appeal to the better nature of Yale men and I feel sure that they aint nobody that reads this appeal but what they will realize that I am justified in making this appeal.
>
> Well to begin at the beginning we will half to go back 3 yrs. to the fall of 1920 and they was a alleged football game played in N.Y. city that yr. between the Army vs. the Navy at what is laughingly called the Polo Grounds and after the game I was one of several 100 people that was invited to take tea at the apt. of H. B. Swope the editor of the N. Y. World and a prominent aluminum of Harvard university which 2 or 3 of us got together and nicknamed the Crimson. Well after 4 or 5 cups of Mr. Swope's imported tea I could not say no to nobody and it was at this junction that I was introduced to one Carlos F. Stoddard of New Haven a graduate of Yale and I made the remark that it looked like Princeton, or the Tiger as we call them,

would have quite a football team the following yr. or 1921. So Mr. Stoddard says he would bet me the sum of $100.00 and no hundreds dollars that Yale would win from the Tiger in 1921. So left the matter drop right there and did not think no more about it till a yr. later when I was down in Washington, D.C., overlooking what somebody jokingly dubbed the disarmament conference and I picked up a used Sunday paper and seen a statement that Yale had win from the Tiger. When I got back to N.Y. I made inquirys amongst personal friends and they all said the same thing namely that Yale had win from the Tiger. A few days later I recd. a letter from this Mr. Stoddard in which he just as much as said that I owed him $100.00 and no hundreds dollars so I paid same but asked him for a chance to get even which he says all right he would bet me the same amt. that Yale would beat Harvard in 1922. That is now a matter of history and I says now that we are even leave us stay even but he says no, he would bet me the same amt. on Yale vs. both Princeton and Harvard in 1923.

Now friends I have got 4 children besides their mother to say nothing about a mortgage which every 6 mos. I half to pay interest on same and people is always dropping into the house acting like they was thirsty and I belong to a couple golf clubs that posts your name and makes a sucker out of you if you dont pay the house charges on the 15 of the mo. and one thing and another so that all and all it is a struggle to make both ends meet the other without supporting nobody named Stoddard that has got a business of his own in New Haven and doing pretty good from all I hear.

So I was just wondering if some of you right minded Yale men that has got influence with Coach Jones and the athaletic assn. would mind asking them how about putting on a post-season benefit game between old Eli and say Notre Dame or Wesleyan or somebody and all they take in over $200.00 why they can keep it or give it to the Red Cross or even Mr. Stoddard himself or what not and I would guarantee that this game would get plenty of advertising and would even go as far as to personly act as referee, umpire, field judge and head linesman and may the best team win.

I hope this appeal will be recd. in the same spirit in which it is made and if so will do all I can to help old Eli towards a victory vs. the Tiger and dear old Tommy Harvard.

Yrs. truly

Ring Lardner

° ° °

The big event of Ivy Group football in 1925 was Red Grange's only appearance in the East as a college player. It came in the next to last game of his senior season, against Penn in Franklin Field, October 31.

The previous year, Penn, with a 9-1-1 record, had been considered the champion of the East, ahead of Dartmouth (7-0-1) and Yale (6-0-2). Coming to the Illinois contest, the Quakers beat Brown, Yale, and Chicago, among others, and, although Grange's exploits in the Midwest had been widely reported for two years in Eastern newspapers, most of the 65,000 spectators and the Eastern sportswriters—Grantland Rice, Damon Runyon, George Trevor, and Joe Williams, among them—came to be convinced. Twenty-four hours of rain and snow on a field covered only by straw left the players lining up in mud for the opening kickoff.

Penn kicked off and, on the third play, the first time he carried the ball, Grange went 55 yards to his first touchdown. On the next kickoff he went 55 yards again, to the Penn 25-yard line, and Illinois worked it over from there. In the second quarter Grange twisted 12 yards for another touchdown, and in the third period he scored for the last time, running 20 yards. Illinois won, 24-2, Grange having carried 363 yards in 36 tries in scoring three touchdowns and setting up another.

Two days after the game, when the train carrying the Illinois team arrived back in Champaign, there were 20,000 students, faculty members, and townspeople at the station. Once before, Bob Zuppke, the Illini coach, had had another player impersonate Grange in a float parade in Columbus, Ohio. On still another occasion Grange had swapped coat and hat with a substitute to avoid a crowd. This time he attempted to sneak out of the last car, but he was recognized and carried two miles to his fraternity house.

"Do you remember your feelings during those two miles?" Bill Heinz asked Grange years afterward.

"I remember I was embarrassed," Grange said. "You wish people could understand that it takes 11 men to make a football team. Unless they've played it I guess they'll never understand it, but I've never been impressed by individual performances in football, my own or anyone else's."

° ° °

By the mid-twenties, football in America had changed. Powerful teams had developed everywhere, not only in the East but in every section of

*The unforgettable passing star of Dartmouth's 1925 National Champions (8-0-0) was Andrew J. (Swede) Oberlander. His long completions to Sage and Tully broke up many an Ivy game. Here he hits George Tully with a touchdown pass on the way to a 32-9 victory over Harvard in game five of the 1925 season.*

the country. Dartmouth had lost only one game in 1923 and was not to lose another until 1926. Yale-Dartmouth games in the Bowl were to sustain such a high, wild dramatic tempo, that the relationship, next to Harvard and Princeton, was to prove the most attractive on the Eli schedule. The tempo for the series was clearly established in 1924 before 50,000 spectators.

Except for an error by its quarterback, Dartmouth would have won the game in the Bowl. Quixotic Eddie Dooley, a tremendous forward passer and kicker, was at the Big Green helm. Dartmouth had the ball on the Yale 1-yard line, fourth down, late in the last period. The second hand on the game clock ticked away. In the huddle, Dooley called for halfback Red Hall to take the ball on a hand-off over tackle.

"A gaping hole opened up in front of me," Hall said afterward, "but as I reached for the ball Dooley never handed it to me. I rushed into the end zone empty-handed!"

At the last instant, Dooley had decided to keep the ball himself. He was smothered by Win Lovejoy 6 inches from the goal. Dartmouth had to settle for a 14-14 tie, and a 7-0-1 record for the season.

Dooley was succeeded at Dartmouth by an even more spectacular passer, Andrew J. (Swede) Oberlander, whose long tosses to Heinie Sage and George Tully in 1925 earned him a niche in the National Football Hall of Fame. His secret timing was to whisper to himself: "Ten thousand Swedes jumped out of the weeds at the Battle of Copenhagen." After reciting the jingle, he would let the ball fly, confident that his receivers would be downfield by then. Actually, Oberlander threw such a long ball that he could have recited the Gettysburg Address and still hit his target.

The Big Green machine of '25 was devastating. It logged a total of 340 points against 29 to win eight straight games and the National Championship. The high spot of the season was its 62-13 pulverizing of Cornell at Hanover, November 17. Allison Danzig was stunned. As an old Cornell man himself, he wrote in *The New York Times:* "It was the greatest disaster to hit a Cornell football team since Gilmour Dobie took over. A superlative Dartmouth eleven, playing with the sky as the limit, buried Cornell with one of the most devastating forward-passing attacks ever witnessed in American football."

No result of the 1925 season, reported Danzig, came as so startling a surprise. After all, Cornell had not lost a game all season and boasted one of the most powerful lines in the country. Opening up in the first few minutes of play, Dartmouth filled the air with passes and Cornell's weakness was known immediately. Two touchdowns were scored before the first period was very old, both on 22-

yard heaves by Oberlander to Sage and Myles Lane.

Before the final whistle had blown, the Big Green had scored four times more through the air on two passes of 50 yards apiece, one of 54, and another of 25. A seventh touchdown came as a result of an intercepted pass, Starrett picking the ball out of the air and returning it 25 yards into the end zone.

Only one of Dartmouth's nine touchdowns was made by rushing the ball. Following a kickoff, Lane ran 20 yards to midfield and Oberlander, playing perhaps the greatest game of his career, slipped around Cornell's right end on the next play and raced 50 yards for the score. The one other running touchdown came as a result of a fumble by Vic Butterfield. Captain Nathan Parker recovered for coach Jesse Hawley's men on Cornell's 11-yard line and, with the aid of a 5-yard penalty, Dartmouth carried the ball over.

Thus did Dartmouth revenge the 59-7 savaging its team suffered at the hands of Cornell in 1921.

"Oberlander, playing his last year for Dartmouth, was the outstanding star of the game," wrote Danzig. "His mighty sweeps around the ends, his beautiful kicking, his capable interference, and, most of all, his passing were all of All-America caliber. He threw almost every pass until he went out of the game, and what an ovation he received from the Dartmouth stands as he ran in across the field, headguard in hand, and his face grimy and wet! There was not a player on the Dartmouth team whose work could not be praised. Tully's remarkable feat of making eight dropkicks in as many attempts for points after touchdown, the splendid work of both Captain Parker and Carl Diehl in the line, the generalship of Bob MacPhail, the downfield work of Sage and Tully, both in receiving passes and in covering punts, and the running of Lane were all conspicuous. Lane, Oberlander, and Tully fattened their scoring averages for the season. Lane made three touchdowns and Oberlander and Tully two each. Lane made all of his touchdowns on passes from Oberlander, the last one for 50 yards, which put Dartmouth further ahead at 42 to 13 at the end of the first half."

Both the 1924 and '25 Dartmouth elevens featured brains in their starting lineups. All 11 starters on those two teams either then or later made Phi

*Dartmouth's undefeated National Champions, 1925.*

*At 65, Walter Camp was still Mister Football. He was also still the supreme arbiter of the All-America, editor of the* Guide, *and his "daily dozen" exercises for health had made him famous. On the night of March 13, 1925, he died in his sleep in a New York hotel room while attending a football rules convention.*

*Edward North Robinson served three separate terms as head football coach at Brown (1898–1925), and won 140 games against 82 losses and 12 ties at a time when eastern football was undisputedly the nation's best. The "Father of Brown Football" was elected to the National Football Hall of Fame in 1955.*

*Quarterback Dan Caulkins scores against Yale to lead Princeton to a 10-7 victory in 1926. The Tigers were 2-0-0 in league standings, but lost out in the title chase to 3-0-0 Brown. Note goal post on goal line in those days.*

*What the well-dressed Yale cheerleaders wore in 1926.*

*Louis Alonzo Young, who played for Penn prior to World War I, coached the Quakers 1923–29, rolling up an impressive 49-15-2 record. He is shown here with his 1929 staff, l. to r.: Kreuz, Jourdet, Young, Wray, Thomas, and Light.*

Beta Kappa.

"They had it above the shoulders," Jesse Hawley said. "We were a small school of little more than 2,000 students, and we rarely were able to compete in the power game. Every man on the 1925 squad was an outstanding student. Every coach can understand the satisfaction of dealing with men like that. They surely proved that intellect had its place in football."

Coach Hawley, a successful businessman himself, taught his players more than football. After graduation, they went on to become investors, bank directors, businessmen, and educators; one became a judge, another an automobile safety pioneer, and another a school administrator. George Champion, the left guard on the 1925 team, worked his way up to chairman of the board of directors of the Chase Manhattan Bank, and center Willard Sprague was the president of the International Harvester Credit Corporation. Charles Starrett, a reserve fullback who intercepted a pass and ran it back for a touchdown in the '25 Cornell game, wound up as the "Durango Kid" in the movies, and end George Tully became a successful urologist in Worcester, Massachusetts.

Swede Oberlander said he supposed that by modern standards the 1925 Big Green eleven was not a very large team physically, but, perhaps with the exception of 150-pound Heinie Sage, it was fairly rugged.

"But if we didn't carry much weight, we did have good speed," he said. "With so many plays requiring the guards to pull out, there was not too much difference between the speed of the line and the backfield. We had a lot of self-confidence, but only on one occasion did this ever threaten our perfect record. That was before the Brown game in 1925. We were fortunate enough to squeak through, winning on two blocked punts, 14-0. It was the dedication game at Providence for the new stadium.

"Our running game was based on the off-tackle play. We started from the T and shifted into the single wing, right or left. We used plays starting from the T without shifting, on a fast signal. The good old dive-tackle play was a tough one to stop. The quarterback did not hand it off, but shoveled it out almost in one continuous motion from the center.

"Our passing game was primarily one of short passes, although most everyone remembers us as a team throwing long passes. The short passes were pretty simple plays, aimed at getting the end or wingback one stride beyond the defensive back on a fast break to his inside or outside. I played right half, and so on the shift to the left I threw going to my left, but not on a running pass. I made a complete pivot. We threw our big passes from punt formation. I believe we used the punt formation for running plays a little more frequently than is done today. It seems to me that terrific power is easily generated and some deception can be worked in via spinners.

"I would have to say that Jesse Hawley, Dartmouth class of '09, wasn't exactly the buddy-buddy type. He was strict, stood for no horseplay on the field. He taught precisely and made the details pay off. In preparing us for a game, he never tried to overstimulate us, but was cool, calm, and collected. If he felt it would help his pregame psychology, he'd even appear cold, mad, determined.

"The one game we lost, to Cornell in 1923, we went into the contest with a poor attitude. Our stands were being dedicated to the Dartmouth men who lost their lives in World War I. They had us in tears and kneeling in prayer before the game. As a result, we never got our feet on the ground until we were licked."

° ° °

For 39 years no college coach was more respected and admired than DeOrmond (Tuss) McLaughry. He first came into prominence as a coach at Amherst after a brilliant playing career at Michigan State and Westminster College, won national fame with his "Iron Men" at Brown in 1926, and was head coach at Dartmouth from 1941 through 1954, except for the time he served in World War II. But he was best known for his Iron Men and for the triple wing formation.

Brown's Iron Men sailed undefeated through 10 games in 1926; only a 10-10 tie with Colgate in the last contest of the season marred their record. One member of the squad made Collier's All-America eleven—Orland Smith, right guard. Here's how that happened.

Grantland Rice, who selected the 1926 All-America, phoned Coach McLaughry at the end of the season and said he felt that the Iron Men deserved a place on the Collier's team.

"Who's it going to be?" Granny wanted to know.

"I can't make a choice," Tuss said, honestly. "It is a toss-up between three seniors, either left end

Hal Broda, right guard Orland Smith, or halfback Dave Mishel. Captain Broda could play end on any team in the country. There isn't a better pass catcher, and he's tough on defense. As for Mishel, he can pass with the best of them—including Benny Friedman. His passing to Red Randall and Broda is one of the big factors in our offense. Then there's Smitty, Orland Smith. A tough guy. There is a tiger in his heart. When he hits you, he hurts you. He goes for the jugular vein."

"Well," Granny replied, "I've got to put Vic Hanson of Syracuse and Bennie Oosterbaan of Michigan at my end positions. I've just got to do it. And I've got Moon Baker of Northwestern and Mort Kaer of Southern California for my halfbacks. They're all set. But I've got a guard spot open."

Orland Smith played offensive guard and defensive tackle for Brown. He was the biggest man on the team at 225, and he could pull out of guard on running plays better than any man McLaughry ever coached. When he hit a linebacker, he killed him. So, Grantland Rice put Smith on his All-America eleven in 1926.

"That just goes to show how political all these so-called All-America teams are," McLaughry said in 1956, "although with the thousands of men playing the game on gridirons all over the country that's the way it has to be."

In addition to Smith, Broda, Mishel, and Randall, the Iron Men consisted of left tackle Ed Kevorkian, left guard Lou Farber, center Charlie Considine, right tackle Paul Hodge, right end Thurston Towle, halfback Ed Lawrence, and fullback Al Cornsweet. The teams they defeated in '26 were Rhode Island, 14-0; Colby, 35-0; Lehigh, 32-0; Bates, 27-14; Yale, 7-0; Dartmouth, 10-0; Norwich, 27-0; Harvard, 21-0; and New Hampshire, 40-12.

The Iron Men did not start playing 60-minute football as a unit until the Yale game. McLaughry had substituted quite freely in the first four games. As a matter of fact, he had planned to substitute at several positions at New Haven, but when Brown scored and controlled the tempo of the game, he stayed with his starters. It was not until midway through the final quarter that he realized his starters had gone all the way. In those days a team could sit on a 7-0 lead, and Tuss just let his 11 starters stay in the battle and do the job.

"When we went to Dartmouth the next week and the same 11 men played all the way again as we won, 10-0, the sportswriters started calling us the 'Iron Men,' " McLaughry said. "This was okay

*Beside being the only undefeated Brown team in history, the 1926 Bruins earned even greater fame as the "Eleven Iron Men." The starters played 60 minutes without relief on consecutive weeks against Yale and Dartmouth, and well into the fourth quarter against Harvard. The team was ranked among the top 10 nationally. The lineup, front row, l. to r.: Thurston Towle, Paul Hodge, Orland Smith, Charlie Considine, Lou Farber, Ed Kevorkian, Captain Hal Broda. Backfield: Captain Al Cornsweet, Dave Mishel, Ed Lawrence, Red Randall.*

with me because I think it gave my men a morale boost."

Two weeks after beating Dartmouth, Brown played Harvard, and the Iron Men were in all but the last five minutes. In the tie with Colgate, only one substitute was used.

That 1926 Brown eleven ran from single- and double-wing formations behind a balanced line. The Bruins capitalized on their power plays and the bull's-eye passes, short and long, from Mishel to Broda and Randall. On defense they lined up in a 7-2-2 to negate any aerial fireworks, including those of Dartmouth quarterback Eddie Dooley.

McLaughry was not only a fundamentalist but an imaginative innovator. From 1928–32, he developed a triple-wing offense. To do this he took the tailback from deep double wing and put him outside the opposite end on a double-reverse play, which hit that side. This maneuver was largely responsible for Brown's 16-13 victory over Colgate in 1928, a year that saw the Bruins (8-1-0) lose only to Yale, 32-14.

Tuss McLaughry coached at Brown for 15 seasons (1926–40). Nine of those seasons were winning ones.

° ° °

Early in September of 1927, Tad Jones shocked Old Blues by announcing his resignation as Yale football coach, to take effect at the end of the season. Then he went to work and developed one of the strongest and shiniest of all Eli teams.

The 1927 Yales are remembered chiefly for the dramatic and extraordinary circumstances of their victory over undefeated Princeton, 14-6 (preceded by the disbarment of star back Bruce Caldwell, one of Yale's all-time best), achieved through a fantastic fourth-down, defeat-cheating pass from Johnny Hoben to Dwight Fishwick after the game appeared hopelessly lost. But it was a team that had much more than glamour. It had lasting merit, based largely on a rock-ribbed line and tenacity. Otherwise, it never would have whipped one of the best Army teams of the era, 10-6. Despite the running, passing, blocking, and tackling of All-American Red Cagle, the Bulldogs were the only ones to nip the Cadets in '27.

"This 1927 Yale team was not the equal of the 1923 Elis," Allison Danzig observed. "It did not have the wealth of backs, though in Bruce Caldwell, until he was disqualified because he had played two games as a freshman substitute at Brown and was ineligible under the transfer clause of the Big Three agreement, it boasted a greater all-round performer than the 1923 champions had."

*Popular D. O. (Tuss) McLaughry coached at Brown during the years 1926–40, then succeeded Red Blaik at Dartmouth.*

The most exciting runner in Yale Bowl for that Army-Yale game was a well-groomed drunk, possibly a one-time halfback. He swooped down out of the Yale seats between halves and entertained the crowd by running up and down the gridiron with his hat under his arm as a football. Several dozen

New Haven police gave chase and tried to trap him. They finally caught him only after he threw himself exhaustedly on a pile of hay that had been used to cover the field during the week.

Yale lost only one game in 1927, to Georgia, 14-10, at New Haven—Bulldog vs. Bulldog. But the Bulldog from the North outgained the Bulldog from the South by a wide margin. Time and again Yale had scoring chances, but fumbles and Georgia's stubborn defense stopped the Blue, once a yard away from a touchdown, another time on the 8-yard line.

When Yale defeated Harvard, 14-0, for Tad Jones's valedictory, following the sensational victory over Princeton, George Carens in the *Boston Transcript* quoted Chuck Pratt, the Harvard captain, as saying: "In the nine years that Tad Jones has coached, no Yale man has ever performed an unsportsmanlike act in the games with Harvard. It was a pleasure to think that he has closed out his fine career with a team that was a credit to him and Yale."

Tad Jones's successor was his backfield assistant, Dr. Mal Stevens, almost unique among football coaches. Bob Zuppke, celebrated Illinois coach, accomplished painter, and philosopher, once told him, "You'll never be a great coach. You have too kind a face."

In Mal Stevens, the compulsion to help people had been driving him almost from the time he was a small boy. He wanted to be a doctor. He became a leading bone specialist and was also a front-rank worker in the war against polio. Few people knew about it, because he did not talk of it, but he did many surgeries for charity.

Coach Stevens found it difficult to tell a Yale team, as his predecessor had told them, that to play football against Harvard was the most important thing in their lives. Not that he didn't work hard to beat the Cantabs. It was just that he felt the game should be kept in its proper perspective; that, to him, straightening the twisted bones of some small boy offered richer rewards. Maybe the boy would never play football in Yale Bowl or Harvard Stadium, but if he could just play, that was the thing.

Stevens was the doctor first, the football coach afterward. Graduated from the college in 1925, he entered Yale Medical School that fall and was graduated in 1929. He became an instructor in surgery, gynecology, and obstetrics at the school and later an assistant professor of orthopedics. In 1936, he began his private practice in New Haven and in New York.

He became backfield assistant to Tad Jones in 1924 and continued in that capacity for the next three years. His teaching ability and personality made him a natural to succeed Tad after the 1927 season, and on March 1, 1928, he was hired as head coach for a term of three years. The salary was $8,000 per season, then the Yale-Harvard-Princeton limit.

Like Tad Jones before him, Mal found that the down curves in Yale's football chart overemotionalized the Old Blues. Phone calls, letters, and telegrams piled in on him at times, some of the less temperate offering free advice on how to jump off the Brooklyn Bridge. One self-appointed group signed its wires, "The Committee of Ten." Another, "The Committee of Fifty." After a 15-0 loss

*Mal Stevens served as Tad Jones' backfield assistant for three years, 1924–27, and was named Yale's head coach in 1928.*

to Georgia in 1929, they wired Stevens, "You are the worst coach Yale has ever had." After Yale blasted Princeton, 13-0, the same season, they wired, "You are the finest coach Yale has ever had."

While Pennsylvania (8-1-0), Brown (8-1-0) and Princeton (5-1-2) fielded the best teams of the Ivy Group in 1928, Stevens settled for a 4-4-0 record in his first season as Yale's head coach. In 1929, he was much more optimistic as he welcomed a better than average crop of sophomore candidates to the varsity. He was especially interested in one halfback, just a little fellow, 5′7″ and 144 pounds, but built like a heavyweight from the hips down. His name was Albert James Booth, Jr., a native of New Haven and the son of a foreman in the Winchester firearms factory.

Albie Booth wasn't exceptionally fast, but he was shifty. He could suddenly stop on a dime and veer the other way. He could sidestep, shift speeds, pivot, spin. He was slippery, combat-smart, and drove tacklers to frustration.

His ball carrying was only one of his skills. He could dropkick from midfield, bang the ball over the goal line on kickoffs, and coffin-corner punt with the best of them. He was not a great passer, but he was a good one, a threat. Defensively, he was sure-handed, reliable. When opponents deliberately ganged up on him in an obvious attempt to remove him prematurely from the game, he was never heard to complain.

Football provided Booth the perfect arena to parade his natural abilities. Saturday after Saturday, great thousands packed Yale Bowl in anticipation of what Little Albie, the most crowd-pleasing of all Yale football players, was going to do when he got his hands on that ball. Little Albie. The

*Walter Opekun breaks loose for 97 yards at Franklin Field in 1928 to spark Penn to a 49-0 victory over Cornell in the season's finale. The only team to beat the Quakers that year was Navy, 6-0.*

Mighty Mite. Number 48. The Mighty Atom. Little Boy Blue.

"The most popular football heroes are the escape artists," wrote Tim Cohane years ago. "And so when a little fellow like Albie Booth repeatedly escaped, frustrated, and defeated the giants and dragons of the gridiron, when, like some diminutive Ivanhoe, he entered the lists and rattled his lance against the shields of the mighty in tournament, then the thrill for the spectator was increased manifold. The underprivileged watched Booth and became rich. The meek saw him, and in their minds turned on and slew their own private bullies."

Zippy performances as a sophomore in early games with Vermont and Brown won Albie some attention, but it was against Army that his fame skyrocketed nationally. Army was coming to Yale Bowl, where Red Cagle had run wild in 1928 to beat the Elis, 18-6. Cagle in a 20-20 tie at Harvard the week before had flashed all his old, striking open-field skills as runner and passer. Booth, everybody agreed, was a terrific sophomore, but it was asking too much to expect him to match the experienced West Point star, twice All-America. Still, 80,000 packed the Bowl to see what would happen.

Army got off to a 13-0 lead. Cagle intercepted a pass and ran it back 55 yards for a touchdown. Army converted. Then fullback Johnny Murrell ran 27 yards off tackle for another touchdown. After that, Stevens pulled the blankets off Albie and sent him in. Presto—instant hero!

With the Black Knights 13 points ahead, Little Albie put on one of the greatest one-man performances ever seen in the Bowl. Over the next three periods, he scored all of his team's points to lead them to a come-from-behind 21-13 upset victory. He carried the ball 33 times for a net gain of 223 yards. He punted, he called all the plays, he dropkicked the extra points, he smashed through Army's defense for two touchdowns, and he ran back a 70-yard punt for the winning score. When he walked off the field late in the fourth quarter, 80,000 people rose and gave him the biggest ovation in the history of Yale Bowl. "Little Boy Blue" was born that day. His name sang out over the wires to every outpost of the country and beyond, and it became a byword. The newsreels of the game, reaching out to theaters everywhere, showed millions of people who never had been near New Haven the magic of this new hero of the gridiron.

The torrents of fan mail annoyed Little Albie. A lot of letters were from girls. He had no interest in girls except Marion Noble, whom he later married. So he turned over all those letters to his Yale friends, who impersonated him on dates all over Connecticut.

The year 1929 also introduced Yale to football south of the Mason-Dixon Line, when the Bulldogs went on an ill-fated argosy to the little town of Athens, Georgia, to help the University of Georgia dedicate its new bowl, Sanford Stadium. It was also Old Eli's way of saluting the oldest state-chartered college in America, whose football teams had visited Yale Bowl six consecutive seasons. Yale led in the series, 5 wins to 1. The game attracted national attention.

On the strength of an 89-0 shellacking of Vermont in its opening game, Yale was favored to defeat Georgia. Never did a more overconfident bunch of players set forth on a football trip as that 1929 Yale team headed for its downfall in the Cotton Belt.

The little town of Athens, with its magnolia trees and its antebellum college buildings, seemed to symbolize the Old South. Bright red Confederate battle flags fluttered from every window as the Yale Special pulled into the station. Gay flares burned in the streets that night as the Georgia band paraded playing "Dixie."

Taking a stroll that first evening, Mal Stevens bumped into Red Leathers, Georgia's large guard.

"What do you fellows think of Saturday's game?" Stevens asked him cordially.

"Ah dunno, coach," drawled Leathers, "but ah sure hope ol' Joejah is proud of me."

Stevens rushed back to the hotel, where his complacent Yale players were quartered, and broke the unsettling news.

"Fellahs," he said, "you're in for an awful trimming. These guys don't know that the Civil War is over."

Coach Stevens called the turn. Under a tropical sun, with the temperature in the 90s, Georgia's inspired team dedicated its brand new stadium with a smashing 15-0 victory over the shocked Elis. A barefoot boy from the red-clay hills of Georgia took personal charge of Albie Booth that afternoon. Catfish Smith, a tall, brawny end, spent a delightful time in the Yale backfield sitting on Little Albie's neck. After one particularly vicious tackle, Albie sprang to his feet. "Look here, Smith, there are some things that don't go in this game!" he snapped.

"I know it," Catfish said. "And one of 'em is

Albie Booth."

Catfish Smith caught a touchdown pass and Red Leathers made "Ol' Joejah" proud of him by blocking a kick, which the irrepressible Smith converted into another score. To add to Yale's humiliation, Catfish threw Booth ignominiously into the end zone for a safety.

Down at the railroad station afterward, where the Yale Special waited, all was gloom. The electric generators went on a sympathetic strike, leaving Yale partisans to grope their way through the pitch-dark aisles of the sleeping car. Closer inspection revealed that the locomotive had jumped the track, and southern crews made vain attempts to lift it back on the rails. Finally, a New Haven railroad executive showed them how to do it. It was the only victory scored by the North that day.

In a sense, Albie Booth's saga against Army, two weeks later, did him a grave injustice. It was a standard he or no other back could have lived up to, yet it was almost expected of him for the remainder of his college football career. But even though he was a marked man, he continued to be outstanding. At times, he touched off fireworks of the Army game brilliance, but the Army game, October 26, 1929, was to remain forever his masterpiece.

° ° °

One of the most unique personalities connected with the Ivy schools in the 1920s was Roy Mills, a Mount Vernon, New York, lawyer whose abiding hobby was teaching young men from Yale, Penn, Dartmouth, and Princeton how to kick a football. He spent most of his adult life teaching them the art of controlled kicking—and without accepting any payment except traveling expenses.

They say "the law is a jealous mistress," but Mills, who inherited a fine practice from his father,

*The 1929 Penn-Columbia game was a case of force driving headlong against force. Gains came in feet and often just in inches. But the Quakers chopped out enough inches to win, 20-0.*

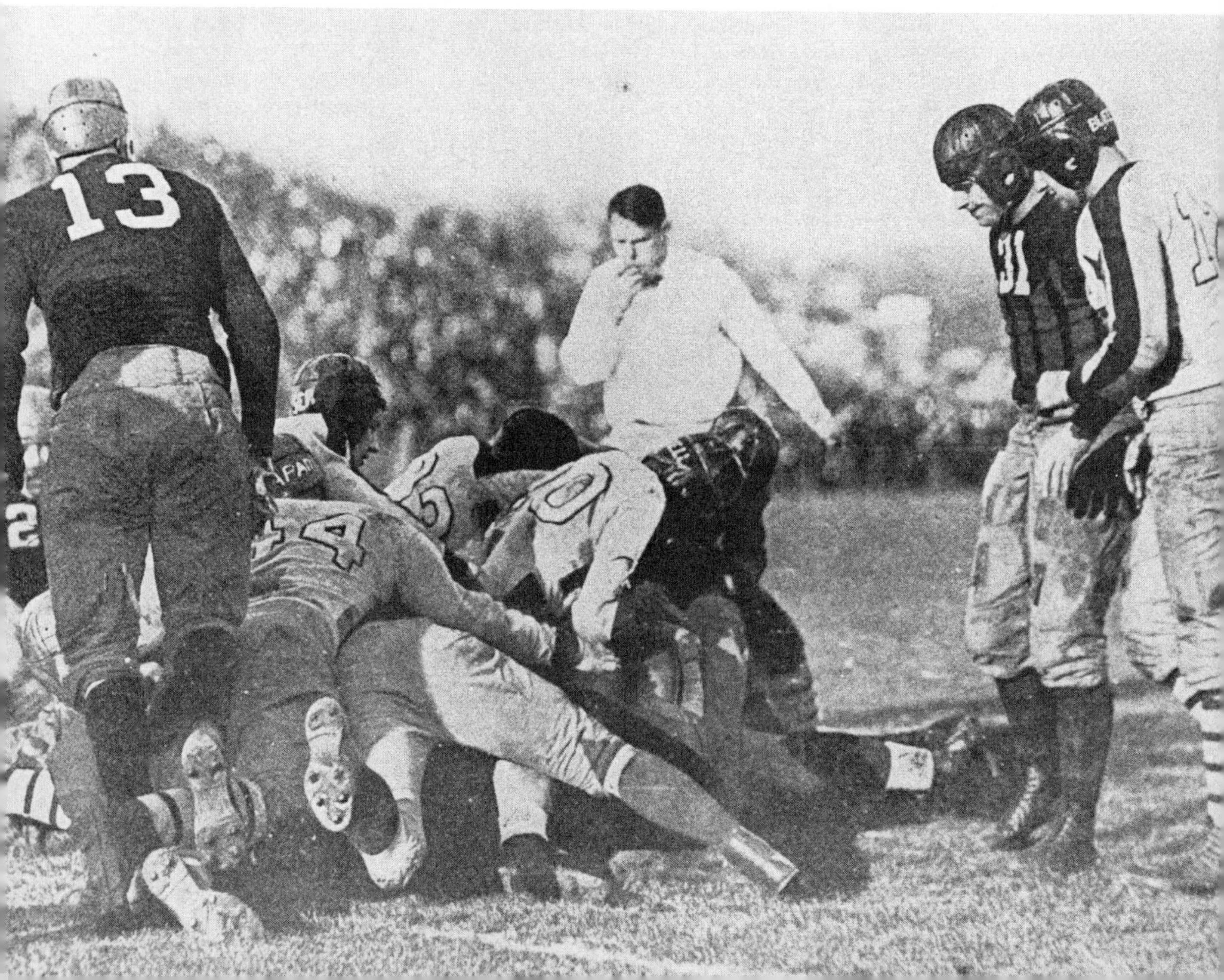

a noted judge, did not waste much time on Blackstone. He never played varsity football himself in college, because he left Princeton to get married.

Roy was a gray-haired, round-faced man who puffed away at his briar pipe as he booted the ball into the coffin corner. "Kick 'em where they ain't" was his axiom. He scorned high soaring punts that could be run back by the safety. "Always kick away from the receiver," he would tell his pupils. "Boot a low, scudding, 35-yard kick that will hit the ground and roll another 35 yards, winding up out of bounds. What good is an Albie Booth if he can't get his mitts on the ball?"

Mills had a hard time converting coaches to his oblique kicking creed. Mostly they were sold on the old cloud-scraping type of punt. Roy's technique called for the ball to be carried in the hand right down to the kicking foot on a punt—never dropped on the foot. His angled kicks revolutionized football strategy. He used to come on the field with a handful of red flags, which he planted on the sidelines near the coffin corners as targets for his students to aim at. He never bothered to put on cleats, but wearing ordinary street shoes he would split the sidelines unerringly.

"As a field goal kicker, Mills was a wizard," George Trevor told me. "Nobody else had such control of a dropkick. It was not uncommon to see him stand on the corner of the goal line and curve the ball at right angles through the goalposts—unbelievable, yes, but true, because I saw him do it. In winter, he would stand on a basketball court and dropkick baskets from midfloor. The guy was uncanny."

"Dropkicking is a lost art today," Mills once observed. "But in my opinion it is the most reliable method for booting extra points. For one thing, it eliminates the ball holder, and thus reduces the chance of human error. The fellow on his knees can be used as a blocker. Properly taught, the dropkick is faster than the place-kick and there is less chance of it being blocked."

While coaching kickers at Mississippi one fall, an unprecedented snowstorm covered the field lightly. The players were aghast. They had never seen snow before and suggested that practice be called off.

"Boys," Mills told them, "have you ever heard of a college up north called Dartmouth?"

The players nodded.

"Well," Roy continued, "they wouldn't think of playing football up there unless there was at least two inches of this white stuff on the ground."

Practice was resumed.

Although a loyal Princetonian, Mills had a hand in Yale's astounding upset of the Tigers in 1934. It was Roy who coached Stan Fuller, the Yale punter, how to kick the ball out of Garry LeVan's reach. All afternoon Fuller's grass-cutters tantalized Princeton's shifty safetyman. He couldn't run back kicks when he was chasing a rolling ball. In Roy's words: "Oblique kicking reduced LeVan to the level of a third-stringer."

Mills always said that the three greatest dropkickers of all time were Chicago's Walter Eckersall, Harvard's Charley Brickley, and Pat O'Dea of Wisconsin. Midwesterners will never forget Eckersall's five field goals against Illinois in 1905. Brickley matched that performance against Yale in 1913. Before the game, Charley struck fear into Eli hearts by giving an awesome demonstration of dropkicking. He started on the 10-yard line and, retreating 10 yards at a clip, booted field goals all the way back to midfield. Then he turned in the opposite direction and repeated the stunt without a single miss.

"After my second field goal," Brickley said afterward, "some overeager Yale lineman scratched my eye. Few people realized that I was half blind when I booted the last three. I couldn't actually see the goalposts, so I aimed where I thought the crossbar was."

For years, Roy Mills ate his heart out because his alma mater failed to call on his services. When Fritz Crisler was hired to coach Princeton in 1932, Roy's hopes rose, but Crisler turned out to be like his predecessors; he scoffed at corner kicking and ignored Mills. Not until Crisler went to Michigan did Princeton finally invite Roy to come over to Nassau and serve as kicking tutor.

Roy had long been suffering from recurring heart attacks, but his face lighted up when the telegram came from Tad Wieman, who succeeded Crisler as the Tigers' head coach. Mills spent the happiest afternoon of his life teaching the Princeton kickers in Palmer Stadium. It was a hot September day and Roy gave it that little bit extra. He was visibly tired when he trudged to the locker room. Mills had hardly peeled off his jersey when the fatal attack hit him. As his daughter, Helen, said later: "This is the way my father would have wanted to go—with his kicking boots on in the Princeton locker room."

# The Pre-World War II Years

In the 1930s, college football was played against a somber background of massive unemployment, bank holidays, and the inevitability of another world war. There was a sense of sad expectancy all around. A lot of people only walked through the motions. Living was like watching a film you had every reason to expect was new—only to realize you had seen it all before.

In Europe, the last surviving dynasties were falling, nations collapsing, politics changing, and dictators ranting. Once again the armies of traditional enemies were marching side by side as allies. Germany had started to gobble up Austria and Czechoslovakia; the day was not far off when she would join with Soviet Russia, who had already swept across the tiny Baltic countries of Estonia, Latvia, and Lithuania, to devour Poland.

Along the western redoubt of the European continent, Belgium, the Netherlands, and Denmark braced for the holocaust that was yet to come, while a self-deluded France huddled behind the Maginot Line.

Now when the Ivies met on the gridiron, you knew damned well that those husky young men would some day be tooling platoons in combat, and that the lovely, fresh young coeds who cheered them on would be the female pawns of World War II.

But college football marched on.

Now, however, the extravagant treatment football had received during the 1920s began to vanish during the next 10 years. For the first time, the men who ran our colleges were suggesting that some of Saturday's heroes had feet, as well as heads, of clay, and that the purity of college football was not so lily-white after all. Restraint brought mature objectivity and critical examination of methods and motives.

Dr. James R. Angell, president of Yale, was one of the first academicians at the national level who believed that college football had grown too commercialized. In 1930, he said, "It is no secret. Not long ago one of the leading sportswriters wrote: 'There is more proselytizing and subsidizing and actual payment for football talent than the game has ever known. Winning teams mean cash to pay for big overheads. Losing teams mean deficits. A crack halfback, or a star running guard, or an able forward passer, today can mean from $10,000 to $20,000 in a season's receipts. Coaches are soliciting high school and prep school stars. They are not only offering scholarships—but something well beyond this. College football has become big business—today in college football it is the crowds—the winners—the receipts—that count above everything else in 70 percent of all institutions.'

"If such a statement be true, it is a humiliating circumstance, but I am obliged to admit that such evidence as is in my possession leads me to think that it does not greatly exaggerate the facts. Certainly there is abundant reason to believe that the general financial stringency has markedly increased the temptation to ill-advised colleges to augment gate receipts by hiring brilliant athletes and thus incidentally to promote, as they suppose, the reputation of the institution and the loyalty of the graduates, with a hoped-for increase of student attendance as a further consequence—a hope, be it said, which has little factual basis to rest upon."

° ° °

The most successful of the Ivy Group football teams in the first half of the 1930s were Dartmouth, Cornell, Columbia, Princeton, and Brown. The era was spotlighted by the debut of a host of brilliant young coaches, and the farewell of at least one whose magic had lost its punch.

Bill Roper's last Princeton team, the ill-fated 1930 outfit, seemed to reflect his indomitable psychology to an even greater extent than some of the more successful ones. History still remembers the Tigers' last-ditch effort to pull the Yale game out of the fire that season. Trailing 7-10, Princeton marched 80 yards to the Eli 4-yard line, with Jack James and Trix Bennett alternating with the ball. Less than 6 inches were needed for a first down when Bennett lunged off tackle and was stopped under a welter of Blue jerseys. The referee later said that had Bennett been carrying the ball *horizontally* instead of vertically, he would have made the necessary distance. It was as close as that!

It was a Princeton custom in those days to have relays of black-capped freshmen ring the big bell in the tower of Nassau Hall all night after a victory over Yale. Trudging toward the train yards across the open fields flanking the Princeton campus that evening, the *New York Sun's* George Trevor could not help notice an almost eerie silence. He could *feel* that silence enveloping the countryside. It gave him the inspiration for what Grantland Rice later claimed was the best lead that George ever wrote:

". . . one sensed that the Princeton players could hear the ghostly echoes of those muted chimes; they never rang so loudly as the night they never rang at all."

Back home in Portchester, New York, while writing his Monday follow-up story for the *New York Sun*, Trevor worked himself into an emotional frenzy. He finished the piece with tears streaming down his cheeks. What was the world coming to? A Yale man weeping over a defeated Princeton team!

The Princeton situation was dark. In Bill Roper's last two years, 1929 and 1930, and Al Wittmer's one year, 1931, the total record was 4-16-2, and the last three Yale games had been lost. Something *had* to be done. The solution was to hire Herbert Orrin (Fritz) Crisler from Minnesota for $8,000 a year. Crisler learned his football at the University of Chicago under Amos Alonzo Stagg, where he had been a crack end in 1920 and 1921, and then Stagg's assistant.

Although Crisler's lifetime record is highly respectable, he never will be remembered as a football genius. He was more a salesman than a coach. The special service he performed for a university was selling renewed loyalty to the glorious destiny and traditions of the old school, and when Fritz Crisler donned his evangelical robes and really wound up, he sounded like the guy who founded the good old school and invented its cherished traditions. Above all, he did a superlative job of selling himself.

The oldest tradition in intercollegiate sports exploded in a puff of orange smoke when Crisler went to Princeton as the first nonalumnus head coach in the treasured history of the Big Three. Yale, Harvard, and Princeton since have hired outsiders, but the furor Crisler's appointment provoked was very loud indeed. Old Grads regarded it as the crowning indignity of a calamitous sequence in which Princeton had won only its opening game with Amherst in the two preceding seasons.

The new coach placated the school-tie crowd by turning on the old Crisler charm. Even the stuffed shirts conceded that the fellow comported himself as though he could have been a Princeton man. As President John G. Hibben said in announcing the appointment, "I met Mr. Crisler and was immediately impressed by his manly personality and was convinced that he would adapt himself to our life here in a wholly satisfactory manner." There were 85 Princeton alumni clubs throughout the country and Crisler visited all of them, delivering the stirring Nassau-shall-rise-again speeches his audiences wanted to hear.

The basic reasons that impelled Crisler to buck the politics and prejudices of Princeton were typical of the man.

"Princeton offered me a good deal more money than I was getting at Minnesota," Crisler explained, "but to be perfectly honest, I fell for the glamour of the Big Three. I was flattered as hell that Princeton came after me, a corn-fed yokel, to be its first nonalumnus head coach. What really clinched the decision for me, though, was the obvious fact that all business, publicity, and prestige faced east in the early thirties. Princeton football was in such a mess that it couldn't possibly get worse. It had to improve, and I would get a large share of the credit."

*Herbert O. (Fritz) Crisler in 1932 when he took over as the Princeton head coach.*

The Crisler-Princeton alumni honeymoon was beautiful while it lasted, but Fritz presently outraged the boys in the back room by advising former Tiger football heroes that their assistance would not be required in preparing the team for the Yale game. That almost broke it off.

Old Grads considered it their inalienable right to return to the campus and kibbitz the coaches the week before the Yale game; no custom was rooted deeper in the school's tradition. Annually, the old stars descended with a whoop and a holler, trying to recapture their lost youth and exhorting the kids to emulate the spirit and deeds that made up their historic legacy. In 1931, the year before Crisler arrived, there were, by actual count, 51 old-timers on the field in uniform three days before the Yale game. As someone later observed morosely, there was one old guy for each point scored by Yale in the 51-14 defeat, the most disastrous ever absorbed by Princeton up to then.

Beneath his urbanity, Crisler was a very tough-minded man who knew exactly what he wanted, and he was in the habit of getting it. His precise mind was reflected in the careful organization of his Princeton practices; he wanted no part of the hysteria and confusion engendered by the visiting firemen. He diplomatically tempered the rebuff by issuing special invitations to former varsity men for the pre-Yale workouts, which were closed to everyone else. He further indicated that he would be very happy indeed to listen to advice—off the field. Crisler beamed enthusiastically upon all suggestions, ignored them, and held favored Yale to a 7-7 tie. Overall, the Tigers were 2-2-3 in Crisler's first season at Princeton.

By 1933, Crisler no longer had to make explanations to anyone. His teams gave Princeton its most spectacular winning streak in 40 years. The 1933 outfit was unbeaten and would have gone to the Rose Bowl but for a Big Three agreement banning postseason games. Columbia, triumphant over Stanford by 7-0 in the upset of the ages at Pasadena, had been given a sound 20-0 drubbing by Princeton during the regular season. In 1934, Crisler lost only to Yale's Larry Kelley, 7-0, and in 1935 he won everything in sight.

In comparing the undefeated Princeton teams of 1933 and 1935, Crisler once wrote: "The 1933 team was largely a sophomore group, and the striking thing about it was its defensive greatness. Since it is much easier to teach defensive football, it is understandable why sophomores were able to distinguish themselves. Starting with defense as the basis, I began to build the offensive crew which culminated in the undefeated team of 1935.

"That was a great line in 1933, with Hinman at center, Bliss and Weller at the guards, Captain Lane and Ceppi at the tackles, and Lea and Fairman on the ends. The backfield of Kadlic, Constable, LeVan, and Spofford had a great scoring punch.

"The 20-0 victory over the Columbia team that went to the Rose Bowl was one of the finest clutch performances during my years at Princeton. It was a game in which every member of the team bore down. The blocking especially was of a high order.

"My impression of this team that went through 1935 largely intact was its tremendous poise and savvy. As the sophomores began to find that they could halt the other team, their confidence and poise developed and they began to acquire the know-how necessary to assimilate the fine points of attack. That left me more free of defensive worries and permitted me to place more time and emphasis upon attack. And the significant thing about these teams was their great offensive strength."

Crisler always appreciated the necessity of strong assistants, and in addition to Tad Wieman, who was responsible for much of the precision of Fritz's best teams, he had a valuable scout at Princeton in Campbell Dickson, All-American end at Chicago, Phi Beta Kappa, and former FBI sleuth. It was Dickson who spotted Columbia end Red Matal's tip-off, adopting a parallel stance when he was going out for a pass.

John A. C. (Jac) Weller, All-American Princeton guard who was tapped for the National Football Hall of Fame, attested that Crisler believed some players needed a lot of praise and others, including Weller, little or none.

"I was used to playing without a helmet," Weller recalled, "but Fritz had a rule that if anyone threw his helmet over to the bench, he came out of the game immediately. Against Dartmouth one Saturday, we had a good lead, but not a safe one, and in the fourth quarter they filled the air with passes. The helmets we had in those days interfered with vision, so I waited one play into the fourth quarter and tossed mine. It almost hit Fritz on the feet. He swore at me but left me in. As I recall, I intercepted the last one they threw without my helmet."

Jac Weller was in the middle of the 1935 Princeton-Dartmouth game that saw Palmer Stadium spilling over with 55,000, its biggest crowd in seven years. They stayed to the end despite a blizzard that turned the gridiron into a slushy skating rink and caused the 26-6 defeat of the Green to be known thereafter as "The Rape in the Snow."

That fine 1935 Princeton team put on quite a show that afternoon. Behind pistonlike blocking of a great line against a good line, the Tiger reservoir of fancy backs, despite the slippery field, drove 43, 48, 40, and 50 yards to score touchdowns.

*In his fourth season at Princeton, Fritz Crisler won his second Ivy title in three years (1933 and 1935). The Tigers were 9-0-0 both seasons. The coaching staff included, l. to r.: Earl T. Martineau, Elton E. (Tad) Wieman, Coach Crisler, Campbell Dickson, Neilson Poe.*

Before the annual Yale game, Crisler often received nocturnal phone calls from that old Princetonian, author F. Scott Fitzgerald. One of them suggested a play involving an allegory of red ants and black ants, but it did not fit into Crisler's playbook.

Fitzgerald obviously sought vicarious football adventure. He had been a second team quarterback at Newman Prep School, and when Princeton admitted him, he wired his mother: "Accepted. Send Football Pads And Shoes Immediately." A classmate later recalled Fitzgerald, 5′7″ and 138 pounds, catching punts. He stayed out for football at Princeton for three days until an ankle injury ended his career.

° ° °

In 1930, his first year at Columbia, Lou Little's Lions were swamped by Dartmouth, 52-0. Coach Little spent no time sympathizing with his players after that drubbing. He told them they now had one great objective. "For the next 12 months," he said, "you are going to be thinking about next year's Dartmouth game. Don't ever forget it." The next year, with virtually the same lineups competing, Columbia beat Dartmouth, 19-6.

The high spot of Lou Little's career at Columbia came on New Year's Day, 1934, four years after he had left Georgetown University to take over what was then considered an impossible team. Columbia's doleful record had been outstanding chiefly for the insignificance of the teams that had trampled it. Even Percy Haughton had encountered great difficulties at Columbia. In Little's first year, with only a sprinkling of really good players, the Lions won five and lost four. But for the next three years, they lost only one game a season, and Columbia men were in heaven.

At the end of the 1933 season, for reasons that forever will remain a mystery, Columbia was selected to play in the Rose Bowl against mighty Stanford. True, the Lions had lost only once to unbeaten Princeton, 20-0, but the rest of their opponents were considered fairly soft touches that fall. The press yelled bloody murder and accused Stanford of purposely choosing the weakest team it could legitimately grind into mincemeat. What happened to Stanford and the piteous protestations of sportswriters is one of football's famous stories.

One of those who knows the story best is Cliff Montgomery, quarterback of the 1933 Lions.

*When Lou Little signed his first Columbia contract in 1930, he told alumni, "I did not come here to lose." And then he went to work and guided the Lions to the 1934 Rose Bowl.*

"It had all begun when Coach Little called the team together in the dressing room at the end of the regular season and, without preliminaries, told us that we had been invited to the Rose Bowl," Montgomery recalled. "For a moment we just stood there, gaping. Then pandemonium broke loose as we pounded each other's backs, danced on the rubbing tables, and yelled like kids. None of us had seriously considered that we might be invited. Our season hadn't been too bad, but the sports experts didn't even mention us in the same breath with Stanford.

"Coach Little told us, 'Take it easy. I said we've been invited. I didn't say we were going. The Athletic Committee will decide this afternoon. Some of them feel we'd take a pretty bad beating, and there's no reason why we should let ourselves in for that.' Then Coach Little turned to me: 'Monty, as captain, I want you at that meeting to represent the team.'

"Two hours later I sat in the committee room listening to a distinguished group of Columbia educators and alumni discuss the invitation. They were all pretty negative. I began thinking about how I'd break the bad news to my teammates. Then somebody called my name: 'How do the players feel about going to Pasadena?' I looked around the room kind of angrily. 'Gentlemen,' I said, honestly, 'the team would like to go.' And I sat down. The group was silent.

"Then a tall, dignified gentleman rose. 'I'm afraid we're overlooking an important point,' he said. 'To you and me, this may be an invitation, but to the team and the student body it's a challenge. It will be difficult to explain to them that we ran from it. I think we should accept it. I think we *must.*' The man's name was Donovan. He had been the quarterback on an earlier Columbia team. Years later, the world would know him as General 'Wild Bill' Donovan, head of the wartime Office of Strategic Services. General Donovan never ran from a challenge in his life. The committee accepted his recommendation—and Columbia was in the Rose Bowl."

Prior to New Year's Day, the sportswriters out on the West Coast pulled out all the stops in their articles about Stanford. It was installed as a four-touchdown favorite over Columbia, figured by many as little better than a good high school team. Stanford, it was claimed, had the poise and finesse of a professional eleven, the nonchalance of a champion, and the healthy conceit of a team that was good—and was willing to prove it at any time.

"It's the laughingest bunch I ever saw," wrote Quentin Reynolds, the famous news correspondent. "As Coach Tiny Thornhill tells me: 'They're comedians all week in practice and football players on Saturday. They're good football players on Saturday because they're comedians all week. We save the tension for game day. There's no use leaving your game on the practice field.' Bobby Grayson is the spearhead of the team. A lot of coaches think he is the best back in the country. He is that rare combination of elusive runner and line smasher. In the open he is a whirling, untouchable will-o'-the-wisp, a carbon copy of Red Grange when the old redhead was doing his stuff for Illinois, except that actually Bobby is faster than Red ever was. When he is called on to hit the line, he has the concentrated power of an Ernie Nevers. As a matter of fact, Nevers told me, 'Grayson is the best back I've ever seen. This is a fine team, as good as any I have seen. Our Stanford teams of 1925 and 1926 were good—but, say, those of us who played on those elevens couldn't make this team.' "

The starting eleven for Stanford in the 1934 Rose Bowl were Monk Moscrip and Lyle Smith, ends; Bob (Horse) Reynolds and Claude Callaway, tackles; Bob O'Connor and Bill Corbus, guards; Wes Muller, center; Frank Alustiza, quarterback; Bob Maentz and Bones Hamilton, halfbacks; and Grayson, fullback. Reynolds, Corbus, and Grayson all were later enshrined in the National Football Hall of Fame.

Columbia started with Owen McDowell and Tony Matal, ends; Paul Jackel and Joe Richavich, tackles; Lawrence Pinckney and Stephen Dzamba, guards; Newt Wilder, center; Cliff Montgomery, Hall of Fame quarterback; Al Barabas and Ed Brominski, halfbacks; and Bill Nevel, fullback.

A week before the kickoff, a *New York Times* sportswriter named Robert F. Kelley concluded that on the basis of majority opinion, season records, and "sundry other things," the Lions from Morningside Heights would be served up as "the sacrificial lamb" in the Rose Bowl.

Few experts disagreed. On top of their loss to Princeton, the Lions had narrowly beaten Virginia, 15-6, a powerhouse that had lost to Ohio State, 75-0. Among Columbia's other victims were such "national terrors" as Lehigh and Lafayette.

Kelley had other convincing reasons for predicting a slaughter of young Lions. The "sundry other things" to which he referred were the extravagant trappings that surrounded a Rose Bowl game. Visiting teams were overpowered by the army-sized bands, the flowery floats, the flocks of starlets. So heady were these southern California revels that the befuddled New Yorkers would be beaten before they got on the field.

"Former President Hoover, a Stanford man, is expected," Kelley warned. "Rear Admiral William S. Sims, retired, is to be the grand marshal. There will be bands and bugles playing. Miss Peggy Hamilton, bearing a large bouquet, will be installed as official patroness of the Columbia team. Several motion picture quartets will sing Columbia songs, cannon will be fired, pigeons released, and various other interludes will occur during half time."

Kelley ended his column with the gloomy observation that the decline of Eastern football could be traced in part to the failure of Eastern colleges to manifest this "deeper excitement" for the game. Presumably the parlay of Hoover, the admiral, the pigeons, and Peggy Hamilton would be too much for Columbia. Besides, Stanford outweighed the

Lions 17 pounds per man and had a lineup glittering with All-Americans and future Hall of Famers.

"Perhaps if predictions for today's game are true, then the red flares of mass meetings will have to come back before the East can win again in the Rose Bowl," Kelley wrote.

What he and other Cassandras did not know was that Columbia was secretly preparing its own pregame extravaganza. It would overwhelm no one, but it would have a certain shabby charm, a crazy originality. It would be markedly appropriate for Columbia. The man responsible for the celebration was screenwriter Herman J. Mankiewicz, Columbia '17. Mankiewicz—witty, erratic, a compulsive gambler, a bad drinker, a destroyer of his own talent, a hater of Hollywood who lingered because the pay was good—and, importantly, a Columbia football fan from head to foot.

Mank's ties with Columbia ran deep. He had a sentimental and lasting affection for his alma mater and loved to talk about the place. During his youth it had been an island of peace and sanity for him. His father had earned his graduate degree there. His younger brother Joe had also graduated from Columbia. Mank had known wise professors, read great books in cool libraries. In the midst of bad debts and lost jobs, totaled cars and lawsuits, there was always the memory of Morningside Heights.

Deans and professors had been guests at the Mankiewicz house over the years. It was therefore natural when Columbia was mysteriously selected to play in the Rose Bowl that someone would hit on the idea of involving Herman (Mank) Mankiewicz. A letter was dispatched to Mank from an important alumnus. Could he arrange a proper reception for the Columbia team? Starlets for the players? A marching band, perhaps from USC? Fireworks? Louis B. Mayer? Stars like Kay Francis, Miriam Hopkins, William Powell? The mayor of Los Angeles? The governor of California? And the absolute essential: a live lion, preferably the MGM lion?

At first, Mankiewicz stored the letter on his desk under some rejected scripts. But, then, he got to thinking about it, and he said, why not? Somehow, he arranged with the Gay's Lion Farm to get a lion, and when the Columbia players left New York by train he was ready for them.

On the way west, Columbia stopped off at Tucson for a last few days of intensive practice behind locked field gates at the University of Arizona.

"If guts could do it," Cliff Montgomery told Lou Little one evening, "we'd run Stanford off the field."

But guts alone would not give the outweighed and badly overmatched Lions even a fighting chance. Since they couldn't hope to out-muscle Stanford, their only chance was to take them by surprise.

Coach Little dug into his dazzling bag of tricks and came up with what he labeled KF-79 as Columbia's little surprise bomb.

"Actually, KF-79 was nothing more than a variation of the old hidden ball trick," Montgomery recalled. "As quarterback, I was to take the pass from center, spin around, and slap it quickly into the stomach of fullback Al Barabas, a big, lumbering fellow, but surprisingly fast on his feet. Then I was to make an elaborate pretense of handing it to Ed Brominski, our tough right halfback who would smash into the line, bent over with what Stanford would think was the ball. As they ganged up on Ed, the man actually carrying the ball would drift out around end and then race for the goal line."

Used only once, in a critical moment, Coach Little believed that the play might have just enough audacity to work. So at Tucson the first team drilled KF-79 over and over. Sometimes Barabas swept by too far away for quarterback Montgomery to slip him the ball; sometimes the pass from center came too low. Again and again they ran through the maneuver until, by the time the Columbia Special pulled out of Tucson for Pasadena, Little could sense a change in his team.

"When we had first left New York," Montgomery said, years afterward, "we'd been plain scared. Only the honor of the Rose Bowl invitation kept us going. Then our play picked up—we were sharp, deft. We might not win, but we weren't scared anymore."

By some quirk, it was raining cats and dogs when the Columbia team arrived in Los Angeles. Looking at the steady downpour, Montgomery's heart sank. On a slippery, muddy field, how was he going to keep his footing on the KF-79 spin? How would Barabas hide the ball and at the same time keep from skidding across the field?

As the Columbia players and coaches stepped off the train, Herman Mankiewicz was waiting for them. Bracing himself, he walked up to Lou Little, whom he admired enormously. They shook hands. "Welcome to California, Lou," Mank said. "That's a nice bunch of fast little backs you have there."

Little jiggled his pince-nez. "Backs, hell. That's the whole damn squad."

Mankiewicz gave the rope to Little. At the other end was the sleeping beast. "Lou, you requested a lion mascot for the Rose Bowl," Mank said. "Here it is. A genuine Columbia mascot."

He then pivoted and raced for his Buick. He did not look back. For the rest of his life he wondered what happened to the lion. Perhaps the Columbia student manager relieved Little of it and donated it to a roadside zoo.

That night, Cliff Montgomery had nightmares of a wet ball slithering through his fingers and of the Stanford juggernaut crushing over his team like a steamroller.

It was still raining the next morning. In the locker room a few minutes before the Lions took the field, Coach Little appeared. Usually Lou was quick and intense, a man of dynamic energy. Now he surprised the team by practically strolling into the room. He looked the players over, rubbed his nose casually, and said: "You know, you are as ready for this game as you could ever hope to be. Don't let the rain bother you. I want you to play this game like any other football game, and you'll surprise a lot of people—some of whom are getting ready now on the other side of the field."

The Lions grabbed their helmets and ran out. The stands, which usually held about 90,000, were less than half full, but those 40,000 or so let out a deafening roar. They expected to see a rout, and they were thirsting for the spectacle.

In spite of what Little had said, it was hard for his players to think of this as just another football game. They ran through signal drill and Montgomery could see by the taut faces of his teammates that they were as nervous as he was. Had the Columbia Athletic Committee been right after all? Were they in the Rose Bowl, as one columnist had put it, "with all the boldness of boys about to enter a man's game?" Would they become the laughingstock of the country? Now, face to face with mighty Stanford, Montgomery admittedly was scared all over again.

With the kickoff, the Lions knew Stanford had earned its reputation. The team from Palo Alto was good—big, rugged, and fast. Time and again the Stanford line opened gaping holes in the Columbia defense to permit its backs to smash through for long gains. The Stanford players seemed hardly bothered by the wet field and backed the Lions deeper and deeper toward their own goal. Then suddenly the Columbia tacklers really went to work, and they had the ball.

Back and forth the teams battled on the slippery field. Once or twice, when it looked as though Columbia had a chance to strike out for the Stanford goal, the Lions fumbled and lost the ball. Then in the second quarter, Stanford drove inside Columbia's 25-yard line—only to fumble, too. "Hey," shouted Owen McDowell, the Columbia left end, "they're human after all."

A few minutes later, Cliff Montgomery got a wild idea. If surprise was his secret weapon, he would really surprise them. Rain or no rain, he would throw a pass. The ball slipped in his hand,

but he got it away. Stanford backs faded under it—and out of their midst leaped Tony Matal and snared it. Half a dozen tacklers buried the Columbia right end in a tangle of arms and legs and mud. But he hung on to the ball, and now the Lions were in possession on the Stanford 17-yard line.

This was the moment of decision—and a kind of hush fell over the stadium. As the Lions moved into the huddle, they could sense what Montgomery was going to call. "All right, gang, KF-79," Monty told them. "This time make it good!"

What few people who saw the game remember is that Columbia had tried the same play in the first quarter, but Stanford's swift safetyman had angled across the field and made a shoe-top tackle on the 12-yard line. So now when the play was called again on the 17, McDowell said to Larry Pinckney, the short-side guard: "This time you cross over and take my man, the right half. I'll go get the safetyman."

Taking a perfect pass from center, Montgomery spun as he had done so many times in practice. Al

*Good old KF-79, Lou Little's secret weapon, scores the winning touchdown against Stanford in the 1934 Rose Bowl—Al Barabas dashes around left end after a handoff from quarterback Cliff Montgomery and on into the end zone.*

Barabas was coming at him from the right. Quickly he shoved the ball into Al's stomach and completed his spin. As Ed Brominski piled by, Montgomery executed the make-believe transfer. Montgomery kept turning until he faced the line again.

In that instant before he dove in after Brominski, Montgomery saw what must remain one of the most thrilling sights of his life—the entire Stanford team in suspended animation waiting for a clue as to who had the ball. The Lions had fooled them!

If Stanford was horrified to see Al Barabas dash around end and on across the goal line for the winning touchdown, Lou Little was equally startled to find McDowell downfield smashing the safetyman. Startled and delighted, for years afterward he remembered it with a secret pleasure as great as the pleasure of victory. He always tried to teach his players to think for themselves.

In the second half, six times Columbia's squad of premeds and engineers stopped Stanford close to the Lions' goal line. Bobby Grayson banged his way over center, raced through tackle, and rushed around end for a total of 160 yards—more than all of Columbia's backs made—but he couldn't push the ball into the end zone. The Lions' hopped-up defenses, creaking and crumbling at times, managed to hang on through the rest of the contest to preserve their great 7-0 upset victory.

As the game ended with the rain still pelting down, Columbia actually was driving for a second touchdown. All told, Lou Little made only six substitutions. Of the 30 young men who made the trip to Pasadena, 17 played.

People who knew Lou Little well claimed that Rose Bowl victory demonstrated some pretty basic things about him: his fantastic drive to win, his attention to detail, and his striving for perfection.

After the Rose Bowl game, Little had his face all out of shape. He wore one of those everlasting grins as he climbed into his street clothes and prepared to leave the stadium. He had his entire family on the phone when he reached his hotel room—or, rather, his entire family of many brothers and a sister had him on the long-distance phone from Massachusetts, telling him what a great coach he was. Lou told them: "My boys were the most underrated team in America. I felt all along that Stanford was in for a rude shock, and I was right. But that Bobby Grayson, he's something else. He's the best back in the country."

A broken rib and a cracked bone in his foot testified to the battering Grayson had absorbed at the hands of the Lions. "How they smash you!" he said.

One sportswriter who covered the Rose Bowl that season was Harry Grayson, Bobby's uncle. Uncle Harry found himself in a peculiar position. As sports editor of the Eastern-based *NEA* syndicate, Harry was a New York resident and therefore, by conventional standards, a Columbia sympathizer. Yet with his nephew Bobby on the other side, it was wondered by his superiors back in Manhattan just how objective the rough-talking, hard-driving, cigar-smoking Harry could be in his reporting.

"Don't worry about me overplaying my nephew," snapped Uncle Harry. "If he doesn't run for 50 yards every time he gets the ball, I won't even mention him in my story." That gives you an inkling of how Harry felt about his brother's kid. To Harry, Bobby was a combination of Thorpe, Heffelfinger, and Grange, only better. For several years, Harry had been telling Joe Williams, sports editor of the New York *World-Telegram,* about Bobby, then in high school at Portland, Oregon, and what he would do once they turned him loose on a big-league football field. Williams suggested that Harry fetch Bobby and put him in one of the bigger Eastern universities. This amused Harry. It amused him to such a degree that he laughed out loud. To be plain about it, he roared. "Why, that would be shameful," Harry said. "My nephew would kill someone. He is much too strong to play against these frail little fellows in the East."

Harry Grayson was a ruddy-faced man, with a jutting nose, luxuriant gray hair, and outsized ears. With his massive head and roughly hewn features, he resembled a Roman senator, and when he was excited, which was most of the time, he talked in the florid and didactic manner of a southerner. If Harry wasn't the most colorful character in sports journalism, certainly he ranked close to the top. Red Smith labeled him the "sportswriter from Mars." And Joe Williams wrote of him: "Around a racetrack they'd say that Grayson is out of Greeley by Pegler."

So how did Uncle Harry accept his nephew's defeat in the Rose Bowl? Well, after the game he received a telegram from Joe Williams asking him to wire the *World-Telegram* a special feature on the contest. Actually, Joe wanted *two* pieces from Harry:

"Write me one story on the ball game and another on your nephew. I can print one and I'll enjoy reading the other, anyway."

Twenty years later, the Columbia Rose Bowl champions met in reunion to commemorate the 20th anniversary of their Pasadena epic. The team

*The Lion eleven that pulled one of the all-time upsets in Rose Bowl history—a 7-0 victory over Stanford, January 1, 1934. The Columbia starters were right end Tony Matal, right tackle Joe Richavich, right guard Stephen Dzamba, center Newt Wilder, left guard Lawrence Pinckney, left tackle Paul Jackel, left end Owen McDowell, right halfback Ed Broninski, quarterback Cliff Montgomery, fullback Bill Nevel, left halfback Al Barabas.*

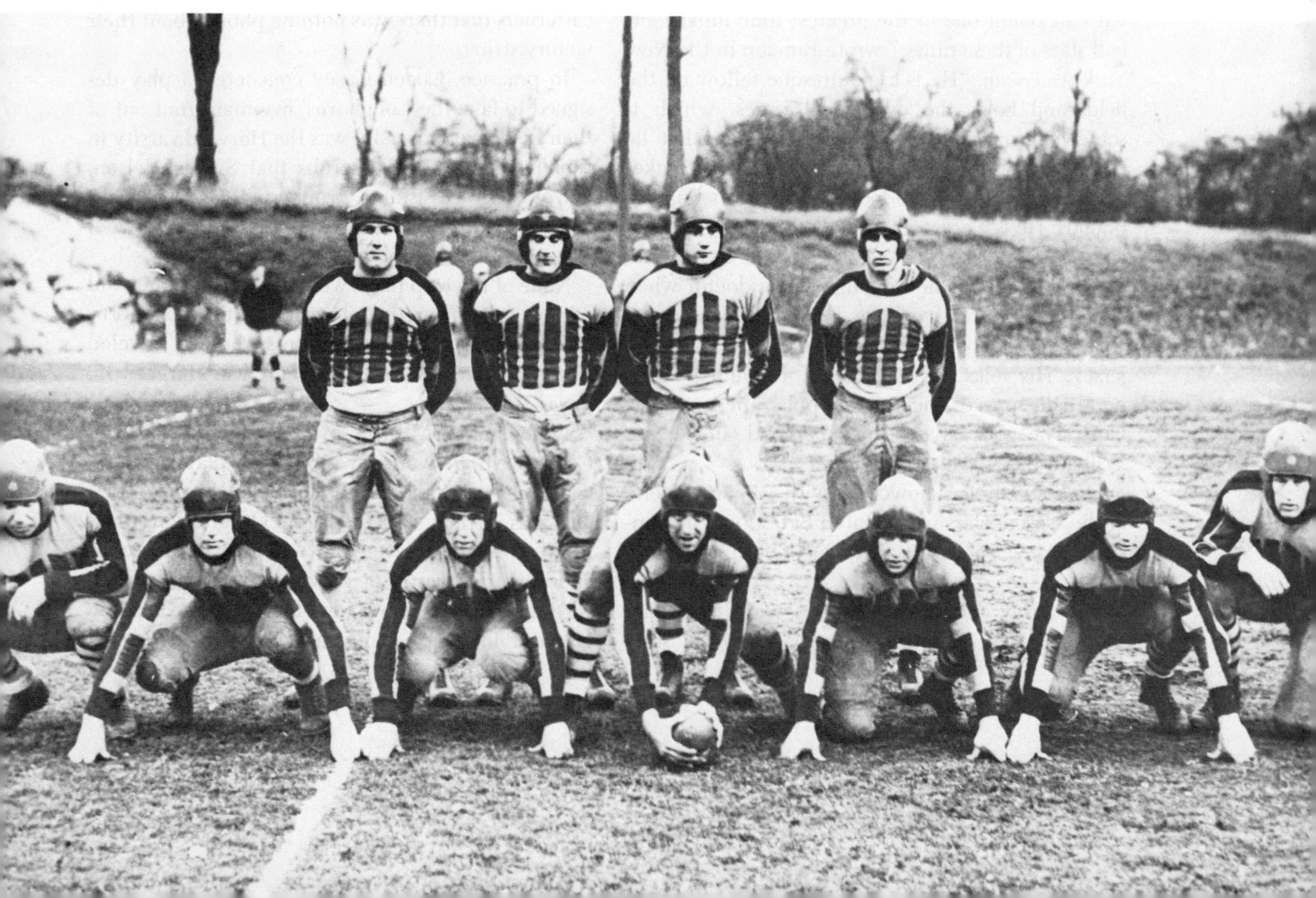

watched in tight silence as Lou Little ran off motion pictures of the game. After they had made their touchdown and the film of the second half began, Al Barabas broke the spell.

"Turn it off, Lou," he yelled. "I'm still afraid they might score!"

From 1931 through 1934, Coach Little's record at Columbia—29-4-2, .857—ranked near the top. But after 1936, except for the post-World War II seasons in 1945, '46, and '47, his Lions were almost invariably outmanned by opponents. The contrast of Lou's record up through 1936 with the two decades that followed provides ultimate proof of an ancient truism: No coach can win with silhouettes. No coach can make chicken salad out of chicken feathers.

° ° °

In 1931, Harvard had a chance for its best season in 28 years. Eddie Casey, in his first year as head coach at Cambridge, came within inches of producing the school's first undefeated and untied team since 1913. Minus the services of two-time All-American center Ben Ticknor, the one-man line who had graduated, much of the '31 Crimson's impetus was provided by All-American quarterback Barry Wood. Damon Runyon pulled out all the stops in describing Wood.

"Handsome, wealthy, and brilliant, Wood is without doubt one of the greatest individual football stars of these times," wrote Runyon in the New York *American*. "He is a picturesque fellow on the field, and holds the eye at all times, which is somewhat surprising in view of the fact that he doesn't carry the ball very often. But Wood makes you watch him. He is 6-foot-1 and weighs but 175 pounds. He is a great all-around athlete—a remarkable passer, kicker, field general—and a star student. They tell me he is going to be a doctor when he gets through with college. He is 21 years old and wears the number 52 on the back of his crimson jersey. His folks have plenty of coconuts. He is personally one of the most popular men in Harvard. The gods have been very good, indeed, to William Barry Wood, Jr."

On the way to a showdown with Yale at the end of the season, Harvard defeated Bates, New Hampshire, Army, Texas, Virginia, Dartmouth, and Holy Cross.

The Army and Texas victories were especially satisfying. The Cadets beat both Michigan State and Notre Dame that fall and were heavy favorites to roll over the Cantabs at the Point. Army operated with two powerful lines and two sets of speedy backs.

When Army scored two first-quarter touchdowns, it appeared Harvard was going to be eaten alive. Then, inexplicably, the Crimson line started breaking up the Cadet attack. On defense, Army became vulnerable, far and away the most desirable target for Harvard's trap plays, designed to open wide gaps for Jack Crickard and for Wood's bullet passes.

Early in the contest, Army had missed one of its extra-point tries, and when Harvard fought back to score two touchdowns, Wood made both conversions, one by kicking and the other when he scored on a dash around the flank after a poor pass from center. That was the difference. Harvard 14, Army 13.

Wood not only directed that pair of come-from-behind touchdowns, but late in the game he saved the day with a last-gasp tackle of an Army ball carrier who had broken into the clear and seemed on the way for the winning touchdown.

Having upset the highly favored Army, it seemed pure nonsense to expect Harvard to ready itself for a Texas eleven boasting a 15-game winning streak. The Longhorns featured a five-man defensive line that quickly put enemy backs under house arrest, and they were fanatical about proving to elite easterners that there was nothing phony about their victory string.

In practice, Coach Casey concocted a play designed to fake the Longhorns' five-man front out of their boots. So successful was the Harvard varsity in running it against the scrubs that Swede Nelson, one of Casey's assistants, prophesied, "If the Texans try that five-man line against us this Saturday, we'll run some plays all the way to Harvard Square."

None of the trap plays went that far, but they did pile up enough yardage to astonish the Longhorns and thousands of their supporters who had traveled all the way from Austin. The score was Harvard 35, Texas 7.

Following a 7-0 win over Holy Cross, Coach Casey went to work on some new plays for The Game against Albie Booth and Yale, November 21. One was a tricky kickoff return. Others were plays from a formation never shown before, to be used if and when Harvard got down within the Yale 10-yard line. On the knowledge that Yale had scouted Harvard in every game and had drilled against everything the Crimson had used previously, Casey was confident that the Elis would be confused and powerless in stopping his bag of tricks.

The once-beaten (by Georgia) Elis took dead aim on the high-riding Cantabs. Actually, Yale had three weeks of preparation after tying Dartmouth, 33-33, on October 31. On November 7, the Blue romped over St. John's of Annapolis, 52-0, in a mild workout, and on November 14, Yale had a day off.

Part of Coach Mal Stevens's strategy called for the Blue, should it have the opportunity, to begin the game by kicking off to Wood and smacking him legally but hard. The strategy almost backfired.

Yale kicked off, all right. Albie Booth kicked the ball into the north end zone, where Wood tucked it under his arm and started back upfield. At the 12-yard line, with Bulldogs bearing down all around him, he managed to hand the ball off to Jack Crickard, his left halfback. Taking advantage of the wrenching block that Bernie White, the Harvard fullback, put on Yale left end Hans Flygare, Crickard traveled clear to the Eli 7-yard line before Herty Barres, the right end, drove him out of bounds. That supreme effort by Barres probably saved the day for Yale.

The Blue line dug in and held the Crimson to four yards in the next two rushes. On third down, Crickard was stopped at the line of scrimmage, and then on fourth and three to go for the touchdown, the Yale secondaries batted down a pass from Wood to Crickard.

From behind his own goal line, Dud Parker, the Yale punter, got off the kick of his life. With the wind blowing in his face, he hoisted a spiral high up the field over the head of Crickard, the safetyman, who finally fell on the ball on the Harvard 39.

For the rest of the contest, the Cantabs were unable to get beyond the Yale 35. The inspired, spirit-numbing Yale defense, rejuvenated by the stellar play of linebackers Joe Crowley and Walt Levering, held the Harvard ball carriers to the distance of a good downwind spit. Unable to move the ball, the Crimson defense also behaved tenaciously. Twice the Blue got close. Once Booth tried a field goal and missed. As the late afternoon shadows crept across the field, a scoreless tie seemed inevitable.

Then came Yale's big opportunity. Harvard had the ball at midfield and Wood dropped back in punt formation. Tom Hawley, playing left end for Yale, smashed across the line and blocked the kick. Johnny Wilbur, left tackle, recovered the ball on the Harvard 45.

After picking up 5 yards, Albie Booth faded back and rifled a perfect diagonal pass downfield to Barres, who was finally tackled at the 12. Booth and Tommy Taylor and Booth again combined to carry the ball to the Crimson 4 on three straight cracks at the line, and now it was fourth down and three yards to go for a first down.

Pat Sullivan replaced Dud Parker at quarterback. It was the first time he ever had played in the same backfield with Booth. He was a no-nonsense, take-charge operator. He looked up at Albie in the huddle and said, "Can you kick a field goal, you little bastard?"

"Sure," Albie said.

Little Boy Blue stood back there on the 14-yard line totally unintimidated by the tense situation Sullivan had put him in. He took the pass from center, dropped the ball, and drilled it neatly over the outstretched Harvard arms and over the crossbar. That was the only scoring for the day. The game ended three minutes later with Yale 3, Harvard 0.

As the teams left the field, the "Undertaker Song" gathered doleful force in the Yale stands:

*In the local cemetery they*
*Are very, very busy with a brand new grave. . . .*

Little Boy Blue and his fellow Yales had caught up with Johnny Harvard and Barry Wood, at last.

° ° °

Colgate never has been an official member of the Ivy set, but, as pointed out earlier, the Red Raiders are united by a common bond of academic standards, social prestige, historical background, and "old-tie" traditions.

One of the most famous coaches in Eastern history was Andy Kerr, who piloted Colgate football teams during the years 1929–46. He was the first coach to stress the downfield lateral, a rugby caper that revolutionized offense.

"The public likes razzle-dazzle," Andy said, "but I use laterals mostly as whipcrackers beyond the scrimmage line—not behind it, as Frank Hinkey at Yale did. It serves to keep tacklers off balance. They don't commit themselves wholeheartedly when they suspect that their quarry may slip the ball to a confederate. However, I don't let my players go lateral-pass crazy and throw the game away. In the last analysis, there's no substitute for

*Albie Booth, 144 pounds and 5'6", will forever live in the hearts of Yale football fans as the most exciting, the most crowd-pleasing of all Eli football players. Captain of the 1931 Bulldogs, Little Boy Blue breaks loose here (A) for long gain in a 33-33 game with Dartmouth. Two weeks later he dropkicked a field goal (B) to beat Harvard, 3-0. After the season, the photographer was able to slow Booth down long enough for the traditional Yale-captain-sitting-on-fence picture (C).*

solid blocking ahead of the ball carrier."

A mathematics teacher, Andy Kerr soundly learned football as Pop Warner's assistant at Pittsburgh and Stanford. Many observers even went so far as to say that Andy taught the double wing better than Pop did.

Colgate really hit the jackpot when Kerr signed on in 1929. Kindly old Dr. George B. Cutten, a center on the 1898 Yale eleven, was then the Colgate president, and he shut his eyes obligingly as Andy went out and recruited football talent.

Andy was a quaint little hatchet-faced Scotsman who looked like a caricature of the famed figurehead on the cover of *Punch*, London's comic magazine. He lived in a white-framed house next door to the Colgate Inn fronting the green, and he kept some of his prize football prospects housed in a stable behind his home. Facing the Kerr front door was a hitching post of the boots-and-saddle era, fashioned in the form of a centaur—a man's head on a horse's body.

"When I lose a couple of games, the Old Grads want to reverse that thing," Andy often quipped.

Coach Kerr will long be remembered for his 1932 Colgate eleven—undefeated, untied, unscored on—and uninvited to the Rose Bowl. As the season progressed, Andy was always reaching for fresh motivation. First, it was not to lose, then it was not to be scored on. By the sixth game, with Penn State, he was exhorting the Raiders not to permit a first down. This caused guard Joe Hill to ask, "What in the heck will he ask us to work for in the last two games?"

Whatever it was, it worked.

Kerr picked his 1932 Colgate eleven as his best. He especially praised it for its coachability.

"I have coached football teams that were more powerful physically," he said, "but no squad ever surpassed this bunch in intelligence. They absorbed everything that they were taught and executed it in an almost perfect manner. It was not a large team, such as the ones in the previous years, but it was strong and fast, averaged about 190 pounds, and had fine precision."

Led by quarterback Charley Soleau, who handled the ball like a Houdini, the '32 Red Raiders stressed a baffling counterpart of the old shell game that flimflammed all comers. In nine straight victories, they piled up a total of 264 points to 0. The execution of the backs on reverses, double spinners, laterals, and forward passes was just about flawless.

Kerr dressed his lads in brand new game uniforms of maroon pants, maroon-trimmed white jerseys, and shining white helmets, which inspired Dexter Teed, Colgate's imaginative press agent, to dub them "the Red Raiders of the Chenango." Thus was the Colgate nickname born.

The final game of that unforgettable season, Kerr said, "was probably the most important single game in my coaching career. It was played on Thanksgiving morning against Brown in Providence, and both teams came up to it undefeated."

Brown had beaten three undefeated teams, Harvard, Holy Cross, and Columbia, as well as Yale. Colgate had easily defeated New York University, Penn State, Mississippi, and Syracuse. The Eastern Championship was definitely at stake. Colgate won, 21-0.

That year, Southern California was the host team in the Rose Bowl. A lot of people felt that Colgate's perfect record entitled it to a shot at the Trojans on New Year's Day, but the USC first choice was Michigan, undefeated and Big Ten champion. However, Western Conference policy at that time prohibited postseason games. So instead of awaiting the formal turndown from Michigan, Bill Hunter, the Southern Cal athletic director, invited Pittsburgh. The Panthers were undefeated, had beaten Notre Dame, and played scoreless ties with Ohio State and Nebraska.

That was a long, cold winter at Hamilton, New York. But it wasn't very warm in Pittsburgh either. The Panthers lost to the Trojans at Pasadena, 35 to 0.

George Werntz, Jr., who played for Andy Kerr and then served as director of admissions at Colgate, harbors fond memories of his old coach.

*Albie Booth's Harvard counterpart in 1931was All-America quarterback Barry Wood, shown here taking a pitchout. The versatile Wood ran, passed, kicked, and captained the Crimson that year to a 7-1 record, including big victories over Army and Texas.*

"As an ardent Colgate man," he told me, "I always had the highest aspirations for our poor little Baptist college—academically, socially, athletically, every way. In the early days our alumni usually went into the ministry (Harry Emerson Fosdick, Colgate 1900) or teaching. Few became tycoons to help swell the alumni fund or build attractive stadia, field houses, etcetera. There wasn't much else to do in a village of 1,500 souls, 30 miles from Utica—certainly no Athens. Football—and debating—were among the leading outlets. We enrolled some big farm boys from upstate and a few from Pennsylvania and Ohio, but proselytization was never what some of our Ivy League friends always claimed it was. As director of admissions, I knew the boys we and they were both getting, what their S.A.T. scores were. When decision time came, many (not all) of the brainier athletes went where the scholarship inducements were greater. I always regretted that more of the Ivy League teams wouldn't play us during Andy Kerr's peak years. Later, when Princeton took us on regularly, my Princeton friends would say, if we won, 'Well, I see you bought yourselves another football team this year!' If we lost, which was more often, they'd say, 'Oh, well, what can you expect from a little freshwater college in the sticks!'

"I doubt very much if Colgate will ever be able to afford the cost of a complete schedule of athletics with the Ivy League schools—hockey, basketball, track and field, and the like—but we are always grateful for the opportunities to play the colleges whose standards and traditions we respect almost as much as our own.

"I was a substitute end on the freshman team that later became famous as Kerr's 4-U team—Undefeated, Untied, Unscored-upon, and Uninvited. There were really no great stars on that squad, just a lot of hard-bitten kids in whom Andy instilled desire and to whom he taught what I still believe was the most beautiful system of football—the double wing, with double spinners and more deception and perfect timing than I have ever seen.

"As freshmen, we considered it a big honor when our squad was called to the varsity field to scrimmage Andy's team. We had a compact little guard named Jim Saydah, who one day found a slot in the varsity blocking and slipped through to nail Les Hart for a nice loss. Andy, who had been supervising the scrimmage from an elevated platform, jumped down, grabbed Saydah by the shoulders, and shouted, 'Where'd you come from, Boy?' He meant, of course, what hole in the line did Jim get through. Sticking his chest out and grinning from ear to ear, Jim replied: 'Poly Prep, Brooklyn, Sir!' That broke up the practice."

° ° °

For several years, the name of Earl Blaik was linked off and on with the head football coaching job at Yale. More than once some of his friends among the Old Blues talked to him about the possibility. Blaik never believed in a flirtation with any school unless he meant business. After the 1933 season, Yale was looking for a successor to Reggie Root. Blaik's good friend, George Trevor, practically demanded that Old Eli hire Red. On December 9, Red received a wire from George:

WITHIN A WEEK YOU MAY BE APPROACHED BY YALE. THE POSITION SEEKS THE MAN. THE YALE OF WALTER CAMP, HOGAN, SHEVLIN, AND COY LOOKS TO YOU. IT IS A MANDATE. NO MATTER WHAT YOUR INCLINATION YOU CANNOT REFUSE.

GEORGE TREVOR

Yale was not ready to break with graduate coaching, however. Raymond (Ducky) Pond, one of its fine halfbacks, coached the team from 1934 through 1940.

"If a firm offer had been made me, I can't say what my reaction would have been," Blaik said. "I think it would have been negative. I have always appreciated Yale's tremendous contributions to football as the true fountainhead of the American game; but I sensed that if the Yale coach did not have to report to a formal quarterback club, he certainly reported ultimately, if indirectly, to a lot of Old Blues, and not only at the tables down at Morey's. The truth is that at the age of 36, with eight seasons as an assistant coach behind me, I had seen enough of college football to know that a head coach's job is essentially something on which a man cannot plan a solid future. Sooner or later, too many people who know too little about football have too much to say about it. The best a coach can possibly hope for is to report directly to a college president, who has not only the authority but the character to support him so long as he justifies it. I have always considered myself extremely fortunate that I did find such a man in Ernest Martin Hopkins, president of Dartmouth College."

Ever since his undergraduate days at Hanover, President Hopkins was greatly interested in football. After the 1933 season, he decided that Dartmouth's teams should be held in greater respect by opponents, undergraduates, and alumni alike. This meant parting with old coaching friends and bring-

*The 1932 Brown varsity missed a Rose Bowl bid of the final day of the season by losing to a great Colgate team, 20-0. The Bruins went into the contest with major wins over Yale, Harvard, and Columbia. Captain of the Squad was fullback Bill Gilbane, second from left in the backfield. Quarterback Joe Buonano, third from left, was captain the following year.*

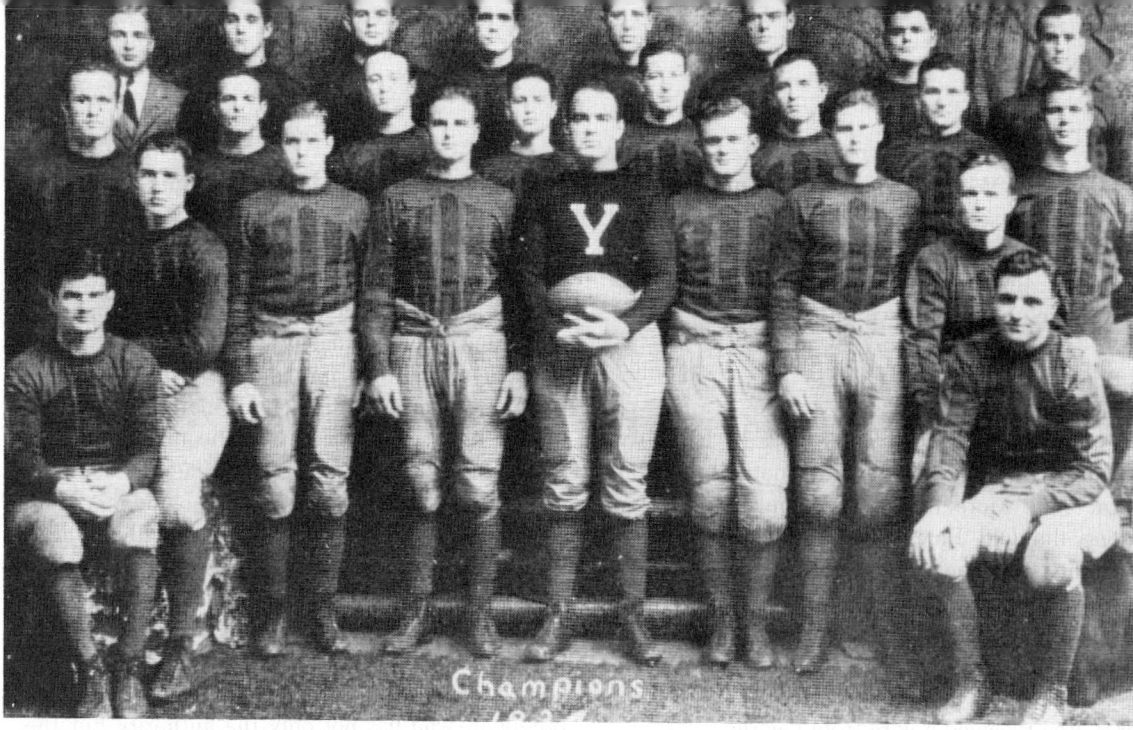


*After being upset by Columbia, 12-6, in the opening game, the 1934 Yale Bulldogs swept past Penn, Brown, Dartmouth, Princeton, and Harvard to win the Ivy League title. Back row, l. to r.: Garvan, Towle, Rankin, Wright, Strauss, Kelley, Crampton, Overall. Second row: Johnson, Davis, King, Schultz, Edmonds, Callan, T. F. Curtin, Hersey. Front row: Train, Scott, Morton, Whitehead, Captain F. C. Curtin, Grosscup, Roscoe, Fuller, DeAngelis.*

ing in new ones.

There were 126 candidates for the job. At length, the Dartmouth Athletic Council boiled down their choices to two men: Red Blaik and Dick Harlow, then coach at Western Maryland. President Hopkins made the final decision. He chose Blaik.

President Hopkins and Red talked the same language.

"Earl," President Hopkins said at their first meeting, "always remember that football is incidental to the purpose for which the player is in college." Then he added, "Let's have a winner."

Red Blaik's first visit to Hanover, in January of 1934, was attended by two feet of powdered snow, a thermometer at 12 below, and a bright sun. It was invigorating as well as inspirational. Although he was Dartmouth's first nongraduate head coach since 1899, Red and his family were welcomed by most of the Hanover community as if they were close kin of Eleazer Wheelock. They spent the first night as guests of President and Mrs. Hopkins, and after dinner Red and his new boss immediately went into a detailed discussion of the type of offense he wanted to install. It combined what he considered the strongest elements of the single wing attacks used by Army and Pittsburgh—Army's running pass, inside tackle thrust, and short reverse, and Pitt's sweep, off-tackle cutback, and deep reverse.

Red held his first meeting with his 1934 squad candidates in early February in Davis Field House. He introduced his assistant coaches as the best in America at their jobs. Then he briefly outlined the system of attack he would use as the most advanced and useful in football. And then he told them: "We'll be as successful as you men will allow us to be. If there is anybody in this room who is not ready to do some strong sacrificing, I hope we've seen him for the last time tonight. Because we're going to bring home the bacon."

Dartmouth's student aid program even then was based on a boy's all-around caliber, his personal financial situation, and a job program. It was essentially the same as that practiced by all the Ivy League schools today.

Blaik felt that his initial major problem at Dartmouth in 1934 was to replace the spirit of good fellowship, which he believed was antithetical to successful football, with the spartanism that is indispensable. He accepted the fact that there is a place for good fellowship. He also knew that good fellows are a dime a dozen, but an aggressive leader is priceless.

"The successful coach is the one who can sell the spartan approach," Red said, "the one who is able to get a willing acceptance from his men that victory or success demands a special price. The play-for-fun approach will lead the player to revolt against the coach and, eventually, even against the game itself, because play-for-fun never can lead to victory."

Once Dartmouth players understood what Red was getting at, he found them a delight to coach. They accepted discipline, sacrifice, and subordination to team effort as a necessary part of success.

The challenge that obsessed Dartmouth was to beat Yale. This was something the Green never had been able to accomplish in 17 games over 52 years. They had played nine games in Yale Bowl and, although several times favored, their best had been three ties.

Dartmouth felt there was a jinx. This was nonsense, Blaik insisted. Dartmouth had lost because in crises it had played poorly. Still, in 1934, the Green lost again to Yale because it had not stopped fighting the jinx idea.

In 1935, Blaik got his players to relax more, and their attitude changed to "Who the heck is Yale?"

On Yale's first series of downs, Jack Kenny, Dartmouth captain and center, ran over to the Eli huddle, stuck in his head, and said, "Let's have a lot of fun today, boys."

"Get the hell out of here," one of the Yales threatened, "or I'll punch you in the nose."

"The guy was dead serious too," Kenny reported to his teammates.

In the second quarter, Dartmouth took the lead on a 47-yard drive. Frank (Pop) Nairne, the right halfback, smashed over from the 9, as tackle Dave Camerer (later sports editor of *Esquire* and an author) impaled Larry Kelley, Yale's celebrated right end, on a wall-out block. John Handrahan converted. Soon after, Charlie Ewart returned a punt 65 yards for a Yale touchdown, but the extra point was missed. Dartmouth, leading 7-6, was not home free, however, until Carl Ray intercepted a desperation Eli pass on Yale's 8 and ran it in. Handrahan converted again, and the final score was 14-6. The so-called Yale jinx was ended.

Dartmouth carried an 8-0 record into their game at Princeton, but the Tigers, Fritz Crisler's strongest team at Nassau, were the favorites. They would finish the season with a sparkling 9-0-0 record, be called Eastern Champions, and earn high and well-deserved national ranking.

An overflowing sellout of 55,000, the largest Palmer Stadium crowd in seven seasons, watched Princeton overpower Dartmouth, 26-6. The contest was played in a snowstorm.

*Dartmouth coach and team captain in 1937, Earl (Red) Blaik, left, and Merrill N. Davis, Jr., right end.*

Dartmouth scored first, but behind steam-hammer blocking Princeton fought back to score on touchdown marches of 43, 48, 40, and 50 yards. After each substantial ground gainer, linebacker Jack Kenny would challenge the Tigers to "Come on through here again!" Finally, tackle Dave Camerer, an All-American, turned to Kenny and shouted, "Dammit, Jack, don't forget the sonsofbitches are coming through me before they get to you!"

In the final quarter, with the Tigers leading, 20-6, and ready to score again from the Dartmouth 2, a drunk stumbled down out of the stands, staggered through the north end zone and up to the line of scrimmage, and just as nice as you please took his three-point stance between Dave Camerer and guard Joe Handrahan.

"Kill them Princeton bastards!" he bellowed, and before the Tigers could run the ball, he lurched into their backfield, made a vain grab at fullback Pepper Constable, and fell flat on his face. The Princeton boys were not amused. Guard Jac Weller aimed a kick at him, and then the New Jersey State Police packed him off to the pokey, kicking. Today, the contest is remembered as "The Twelfth Man

Game." Nobody who played in it ever did get the man's name.

"I don't think he was a college man," Camerer said. "At least, what he yelled was, 'Kill *them* Princeton bastards.' "

Despite the loss at Princeton, the season was still a success, but it ended sourly in a 13-7 upset at Baker Field, New York, by a Columbia team that had lost four games and been tied.

The loss to Columbia raised Blaik's blood pressure.

"I thought you were a good team," he told his players. "You were beaten, badly beaten, by a great Princeton team. So what? So you couldn't forget it and carried it into this one—something a good team doesn't do. That's why I'm terribly disappointed in you!"

Coach Blaik had some fine athletes play for him at Dartmouth, but, pinned down, he will tell you that his top player there was Bob MacLeod, who reported to the varsity as a sophomore in 1936. MacLeod, out of Glen Ellyn, Illinois, played halfback for three seasons, captained the 1938 team, and was everybody's All-America. In his three seasons at Hanover, Dartmouth's records were 7-1-1, 7-0-2, and 7-2-0, for a total of 21-3-3. This included a defeatless string that comprised 19 victories and three ties. The 1936 and 1937 Green were champions of the then informal Ivy Group, and in '37 were rated number seven in the national polls. In those three years, Dartmouth never lost to Harvard, Yale, or Princeton.

Bob MacLeod excelled as runner, receiver, blocker, and on defense. As wingback in right formation of Blaik's single-wing version, he ran the deep reverse behind four blockers, the tailback and three pulling linemen. The excitement of such mass mobility made the play the most thrilling of the mid-thirties and prompted Greasy Neale, then Yale's first assistant to Coach Ducky Pond, to describe it as "that play in which the student body comes down out of the stands and gets into the interference."

Red Blaik was a man born to command. His prominent, sharply chiseled nose suggested the doer rather than the talker. Despite his nickname, he was not a redhead at all. His hair was brown with auburn undertones. A glint of red gleamed when the sun struck at a certain angle.

Blaik seldom disparaged his own players. Instead, he played up the other team and pointed out to his men the job confronting them. Yet no team coached by Red was likely to be either overconfident or lacking in self-assurance.

"Given a team solidly grounded in fundamentals and schooled in strategy," he often said, "the issue often hinges on emotional response. A team must be *up* to win."

What did he tell his Dartmouth players before they proved to themselves that they were capable of smashing the Yale Bowl jinx? "I told them that those Yale men were just a bunch of kids like they were," he said. "I pointed out that there was nothing supernatural about a big white Y on a dark blue jersey."

Blaik never went in for a lot of locker room oratory before games. There were no fiery harangues, no blood-and-thunder pep talks. He occasionally, but only occasionally, injected a sentimental note if he sensed that it wouldn't strike a false chord.

"The modern youngster is a sophisticated realist," Blaik said. "You don't dare work on his emotions with that die-for-dear-old-Rutgers stuff. He might laugh in your face. Locker room pep talks went out of style years ago. Before the Yale or Harvard or Princeton games, my Dartmouth kids needed to be calmed down rather than keyed up. Those rivalries were so hopped up that no fight talk was necessary. Instead, I tried to make the boys relax. Football is a game of the mind as well as the emotions. I wanted my players mentally keen and emotionally relaxed. Otherwise they would have tightened up under pressure. You've got to lick overconfidence."

Red Blaik was a man of axioms. He used to tell his players that there never was a champion who to himself was a good loser. "Remember," Red once told me, "there's a vast difference between a good sport and a good loser. Good fellows are a dime a dozen, I lectured my teams, but an aggressive leader is priceless. Another line I liked to use was: 'Inches make a champion, and the champion makes his own luck.' I seldom left anything to so-called luck. I maintained that it wasn't luck if the bounce of the ball went against you. If you kick it properly, it will bounce correctly. It isn't luck if a statue of liberty play fools you. If you play your position as it should be played, it won't fool you. At Dartmouth, and later at West Point, we scrimmaged our various basic offensive plays more than a hundred times apiece. Throughout the season we continued to use contact work to keep the players sharp. You don't develop good teeth by eating mush. You don't keep a blocker sharp by giving him theory and letting him go through the motions in dummy."

° ° °

Blaik's first two years at Dartmouth coincided with the last two at Cornell for Gil Dobie. By now, most of Gloomy Gil's glittering record had fallen away.

"Most of this was due to weaker material, but some of it must be charged to Gil's stubbornness," Blaik observed. "Long after it was proved impractical, he stayed with a seven-man line and a four-man box secondary on pass defense. He predicated everything on rushing the passer. But you can't always get to the passer successfully from a seven, and when you can't, you are vulnerable to the long pass. I am also convinced Gil overdid the preaching of pessimism. You may be able to tell a superior player he's not very good without hurting him, but I must doubt you help very many average players by downgrading them, privately or publicly, to themselves and others."

Dobie's record at Cornell for the 1924–33 decade was 50-23-6. But in 1934, the Big Red went 2-5, Dobie's first losing season in 28 years, and the best he could get out of seven games in 1935 was a 7-7 tie with Columbia.

While his teams were riding high, Gil's sour ways and his forecasts of gloom and doom were accepted as a brand of humor by those aboard the Cornell bandwagon. But like all coaches, he found that most football friends are transitory, and as he started to lose he heard the cry of the Old Grads. "Everybody," Dobie reminded them, "thought the box formation was pretty fair, when Kaw, Pfann, Floyd Ramsey, and Charlie Cassidy were in it."

The 1935 season evoked some acid counterstatements from Gloomy Gil. After the loss to Princeton's powerhouse, 54-0, he suggested seriously that the squad publicly absolve him of the blame. "After all," he pointed out, "I'm just the coach."

The day before the Big Red was flushed down the drain at Dartmouth, 41-6, Dobie escorted his players on a tour around Memorial Field. "You kick off here," he said sarcastically, pointing to the 40-yard line. Then he walked them over to the bench on the east side and told them, "This is where you sit when you're not playing." And, finally, he took them down to the 10-yard line. "Here," he said, "is where you'll be all afternoon with your backs to the wall."

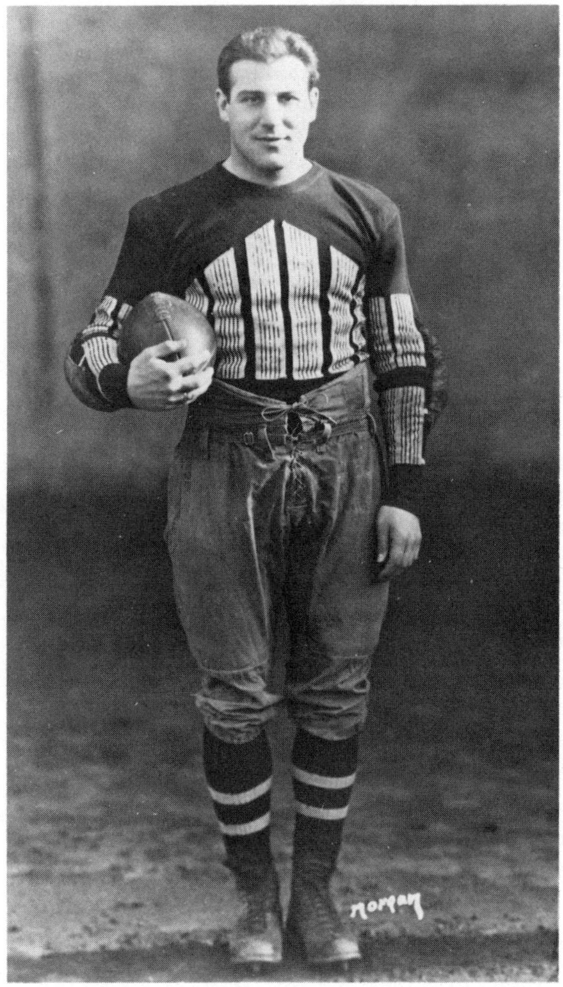


*One of the super backs in Cornell history was fullback Bart Viviano, a second team All-America in 1932.*

When Cornell bought up the rest of his two-year, $11,000 contract and replaced him with Carl Snavely, Dobie commented, "You can't win games with Phi Beta Kappas." Actually, Dobie preferred the student-athlete. He had no time for the tramp player. He himself had been a serious student and had acquired a law degree as a quarterback and an assistant under Dr. Henry L. Williams at Minnesota early in the century.

"Some people seem to have the idea that I object to a boy's coming to college to study," he said in 1935, clearing the air as to how he stood on the question of football and academics. "Let me say that I think this is the only reason a boy should come to college, and if football interferes with his studies, he should drop football."

° ° °

For 60 years, the head football coach at Harvard had been strictly Crimson. Now, in 1935, it was time for a change of policy, and Bill Bingham, the strong-minded director of athletics, was the man to make it. In early January, he called a press conference and announced that Dick Harlow was taking the place of the hero of all Harvards, Eddie Casey. Casey's four-year record at Cambridge had not been all that bad, 20-11-1. Still, the Old Grads wanted a change, and they turned to Harlow.

Dick Harlow was probably the most multisided of football coaches. A noted zoologist and botanist, he spent his summer vacations collecting rare ferns and birds' eggs. It was while hunting for eggs of the peregrine falcon that Dick tumbled from an inaccessible ledge in the Pocono Mountains and broke his leg. With spartan fortitude, he crawled six miles to the nearest highway, where he was picked up.

The gently reared type of athlete prevalent at Harvard must have posed quite a coaching problem for the rough-and-ready Harlow, but Dick adjusted his personality to the new situation and coached his players with such phrases as "Dear boy, do it my way" and "Patience, dear boy, it will come." This sort of paternal chatter aroused the scorn of cynical Stanley Woodward, the New York sports editor.

"Why don't you be yourself, Dick?" he advised Harlow privately. "Come right out and tell the world that you're not used to working with a lot of callow amateurs!"

Win or lose, Harlow held the most entertaining postgame press conferences around. He had a newspaperman's nose for news and a gift for dramatizing crucial plays. Seated in Dillon Field House, he would pick out the high spots of the game just completed and tell the reporters what really went on behind the scenes. Dick was born 20 years too soon. What a television sports analyst he would have been!

Westward bound for Michigan with a weak Harvard team in 1942, Harlow was interviewed by a group of Boston reporters at South Station just before the train pulled out.

"What are your thoughts on the eve of the trip?" one of them asked.

"Well," Dick replied, "it reminds me of the two spinsters sitting on the porch of a New Hampshire hotel one summer afternoon. As they rocked back and forth in their rocking chairs, a hen scampered across the road pursued by a rooster. Just then a truck rumbled by and the hen went up in a ball of feathers. 'Isn't that a beautiful thought?' said one old lady to the other. 'She preferred death.' Now you know how I feel about this Michigan game." Michigan 35, Harvard 7!

Harlow's spinner-cycle offense was the last word in deceptive ball handling, and in Vernon Struck he had the most baffling spin bucker of the day. Harlow called Struck "the magnificent faker," and he felt downright chagrined unless Vernon was tackled when he didn't have the ball.

In addition to his spinner-cycle, hidden-ball offense, Harlow was also noted for his deceptive faking, cross-blocking, and looping line play. He was also something of a practicing psychologist. He first invaded the realm of psychology in 1924. He was coaching at Colgate at the time and he had a friend, a pharmacist, make up some harmless sugar pills, which he took into the Colgate locker room before the opening game. Telling the assistant manager to close the doors and chase out all visitors, Dick called his players together in a circle around him.

"Men," he said, taking the bottle of pills out of his pocket, "these tablets are made from an old Indian formula that I found during my travels in Pennsylvania. They're compounded from the glands of a buffalo and will give you abnormal strength. Don't tell anybody we've got them. Now, each man take one before the game starts and we'll murder those guys."

The Colgate players flexed their muscles and threw out their chests, and then rolled over Alfred, 35-0. Harlow patted his bottle of capsules and pressed a finger against his lips. "Now don't tell anybody where you got them," he reminded his players.

The boys could hardly wait for their next "shot" the following Saturday. "Coach," they clamored, "give us those pills." They did even better this time, running up 41 points on Clarkson Tech. Then came the big trip to Lincoln, Nebraska, for a battle against the mighty Cornhuskers. One look at the hulking farm lads before the game and the easterners began to feel a bit queasy. "Double the dose, Coach," they implored Harlow. Dick doled out two pills apiece.

Apparently the pills lost their potency somewhere between Hamilton and Lincoln, because Nebraska trampled Colgate, 33-7. After the rout, the Colgate players eyed Harlow dubiously. "What went wrong with the pills today, Coach?" they wanted to know. Dick forced a laugh. "Gentlemen," he said, "those were just plain sugar pills. Football is all in the mind."

From the standpoint of victories and defeats, Harlow's Harvard teams were not eminently successful in the years preceding World War II. In the eight seasons from 1935 through 1942, his record was 29-29-7, but his teams were smart, resourceful, deceptive, and entertaining. They played in an era when finesse was appreciated as much as sheer power, when a well-conceived defense could counterbalance offensive weaknesses. And Harlow brought out the best in bright young undergraduates who recognized that what they could not achieve by brawn they could gain by guile.

"Dick Harlow was an extraordinary man," said Shaun Kelly, Jr., captain of the 1935 Harvards. "He was an innovator, a skilled strategist, whose deceptive and ingenious attack was just beginning to sink in by the end of the season. More importantly, he was a great leader of young men. He knew each of us well. He knew how to inspire us to play our best."

After four decades, Shaun Kelly still remembers the last minutes of that 1935 season. Yale was heavily favored, but the deceptive Harvard defense stymied the Bulldogs through a scoreless first half. In the third quarter, Yale turned opportunistic and forged ahead, 7-0.

"It was a lucky play," remembered Tom Bilodeau. "I made Larry Kelley an All-America on that play, too. I tipped a pass into Kelley's hands and Larry brought it back 52 yards for the touchdown."

Harvard countered with an 82-yard scoring drive in the last quarter to tie.

"With two minutes to play, the score was still 7 to 7," Shaun Kelly recalled. "We were tiring dreadfully, because most of us had played all the way on both offense and defense. Yale drove down to our 2-yard line, and then came the play I will never forget—and a play we'd practiced against the whole previous week! Al Hessberg ran around me on the short side for the winning touchdown! It still haunts me."

° ° °

Yale won a lot of games through the individual skills of Larry Kelley and Clint Frank, All-Americas and Heisman Trophy winners who have since been enshrined in the National Football Hall of Fame. Kelley's fame as a pass catcher spread from coast to coast; he was so well known that even headline writers remembered to spell his last name with two e's. About the only one to forget was Greasy Neale, aide-de-camp to head coach Ducky Pond. Greasy, a dominant personality, often got Larry's name mixed up or forgot it altogether. Because his mind was always preoccupied with football, he was not very good about names, and in getting ready for a big Harvard game one day, he wanted to be sure that Kelley was in the right place on a certain play. "Now, you, big boy!" Greasy screamed at Larry. "You be here! Hey, you, what's your name, anyhow?" It marked one of the few times that Larry, the team clown and counterwit, was stumped for a comeback.

Discipline irked Larry Kelley, and he frequently kicked over the traces. The only Yale coach he really feared was backfield coach Neale.

"My old friend Jock Sutherland at Pittsburgh wouldn't have tolerated Kelley for two minutes," Greasy said, "but how can you stay mad at a kid who goes out and wins the ball game for you Saturday after Saturday? Half the time Larry forgot to block—a cardinal sin in Jock's book. Princeton even had a play called the 'Cousin Kelley Special,' designed on the theory that Larry would chase a decoy all the way over to the opposite flank. It usually worked. Still, when the chips were down, that wild Irishman would come up with the winning play. Remember how he dribbled the ball with his foot soccer-fashion across the Navy goal and fell on it to win the game, 12-7, in 1936? They had to change the rules after that. Kelley had less tension in him than any other football player I ever saw. He would be loose as ashes at the kickoff when most athletes tighten up. His quick thinking under fire was remarkable.

"In the 1935 Harvard game," Greasy continued, "Clint Frank threw a pass which bounded off a Crimson defender's helmet. Kelley had overrun the play, but he calmly retraced his steps and caught the ball casually as it ricocheted off the headguard. Then he was off to the races. He never failed to score at least one touchdown in every Harvard and Princeton game during his Yale career. No wonder he got the big head. You should have seen the fan mail he received. Letters came in from coeds all over the country, especially from the Southwest. Those Janes would even give specifications as to measurements, color of eyes, hair, and tastes. Some even offered to lend Larry their sports cars for the

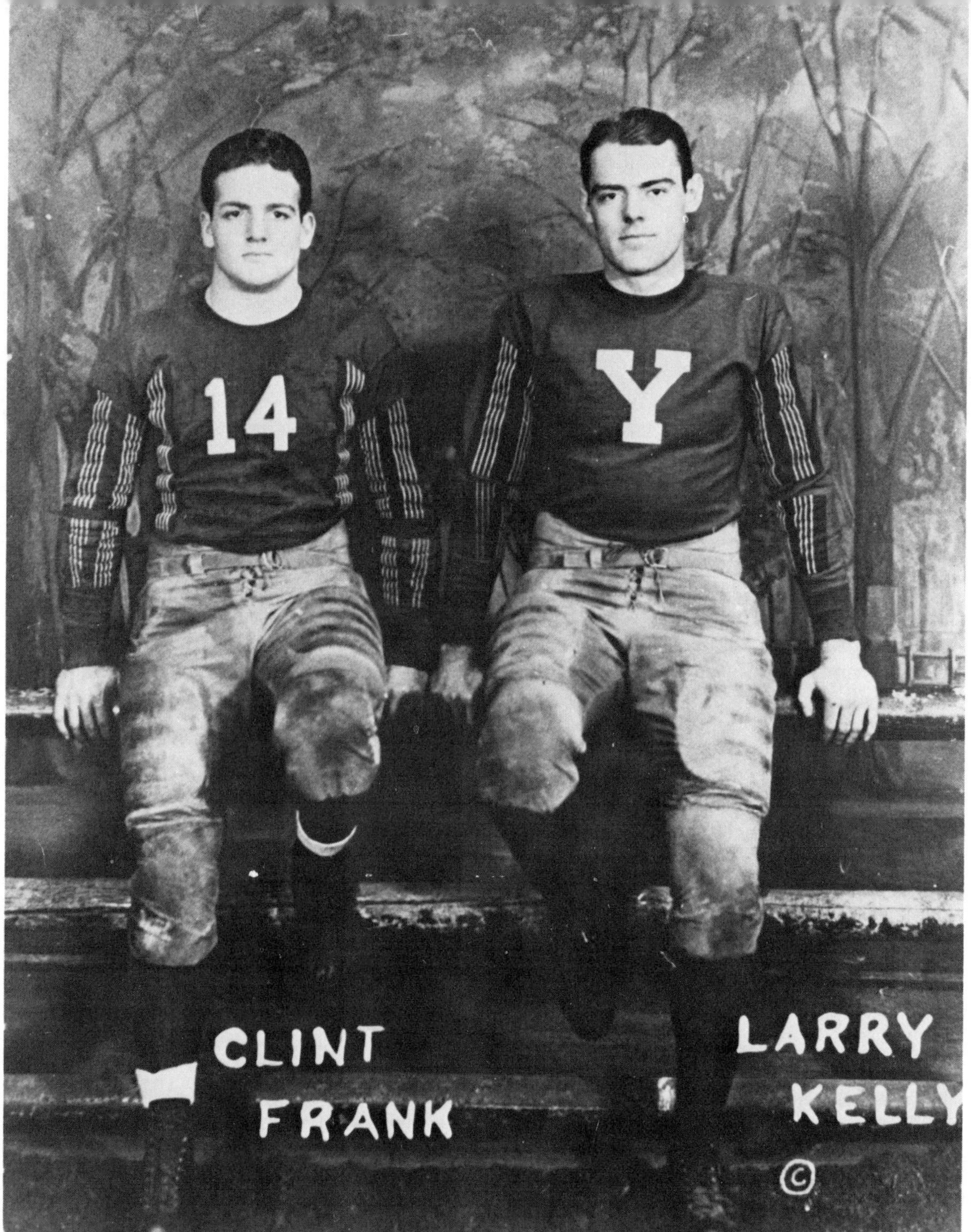


*With Larry Kelley in 1936 and Clint Frank in 1937, Yale men won the Heisman Trophy back to back. Kelley, 6′2″ and 185 pounds, is the only player in Yale-Harvard-Princeton history to score a touchdown in each of his six Big Three games. Frank, 5′10″ and 175 pounds, played in only one losing game each of his last two seasons at Yale. Both men are in the Hall of Fame.*

weekend. He used to kid me about starting a matrimonial agency."

In Fritz Crisler's opinion, the most resourceful play he ever saw in football was Kelley's spur-of-the-moment disposal of Jack White in the 1936 Yale-Princeton game. A 100-yard-dash star from Mercersberg Academy, White was the fastest man on the Princeton squad. He played safety on defense, and thus was only a stride behind Kelley when Larry gathered in a long pass labeled touchdown. Everyone in the stadium instinctively sensed that the Princeton sprinter would nail Kelley before he could cross the goal line. Then the impossible happened. Larry whirled in his tracks, ran straight backward toward his pursuer, and flattened White with a lethal straight arm. Turning again, Kelley then trotted leisurely into the end zone.

"That's what I call quick thinking under fire," Crisler said later. "Did you ever hear of a pass receiver attacking the tackler?"

Larry Kelley was one of the most popular players ever to play at Yale. He had a glib Irish wit, stage presence, and the knack of improving wisecracks on the spur of the moment. His choicest were mostly directed at Princeton, but after smearing a Harvard sweep in 1934, he tauntingly asked the Crimson quarterback, "What kind of judgment do you call that, Haley, trying Kelley's end on fourth down?"

Kelley was an opportunist, sometimes radical, more often cunning, and the result was that more disputes and arguments sprang up around the Yale captain than any single player the game had known in years. In the 1936 Navy game that Greasy Neale referred to, the Midshipmen were leading, 7-6, when a Yale punt was fumbled by the Navy's safetyman. Kelley, going down under the punt, accidentally kicked the ball and sent it rolling down close to Navy's goal, where Larry recovered it. From that point Yale scored the winning touchdown. Navy protested violently, claiming Kelley kicked the ball deliberately, but the referee allowed the play. The rule was then changed to provide that the team kicking a free ball must forfeit possession at the spot of the foul regardless of whether the act was intentional or accidental. The referee no longer needed to "read a player's thoughts."

As Yale captain and Heisman winner in 1936, there were times when the 6′2″, 185-pound Kelley's defensive strength was questioned, but the fact that Larry was placed on the opposite side from the great Clint Frank, on the weaker side of the Yale line, and always given two or three assignments to carry out, indicated that he knew what it was all about. Few knew that Kelley's job was to crash through and scatter the interference, leaving someone else to handle the runner. In addition, opponents frequently assigned two or three men to the job of covering Kelley to stop his amazing catches downfield.

For all his brilliance, Kelley had a contemporary at Yale whom most qualified judges of football flesh consider an even greater player, one of the best backs in Yale history and a member of the Hall of Fame. He was Clinton Edward Frank, who came from St. Louis, Missouri. An all-around star athlete at Evanston Township High, he enrolled at Lawrenceville Prep in New Jersey, in 1933, to finish his preparation for Yale. "I wanted to go to Yale," he said, "because I liked the school. My dad liked it, and he was paying the bills."

Frank arrived at New Haven in the fall of 1934. He stood 5′10″ and weighed 175. As a runner he was fast and strong. As a passer, he could get the ball away when surrounded and seemingly trapped. As a defensive halfback, he was a superb tackler and a sharp play diagnostician who moved all over the field. One of his specialties was breaking up the other side's passes. Highly intelligent, he ran the team from left halfback most of his junior and senior years.

Greasy Neale said the greatest backs he ever coached were Steve Van Buren and Frank. Van Buren played for him when he piloted the Philadelphia Eagles. "Steve could hit a shade harder than Clint," Greasy said, "but if I had to choose between them I might pick Frank because he was equally strong on defense. Here was a kid who gave it the old college try on every play. When we told him to freeze the ball against Harvard in 1936, with Yale leading, 14-13, and a minute to go, Frank was terrific. He was so groggy that his teammates had to prop him up on his feet after each plunge.

"Clint was a miracle on defense," Greasy continued. "I saw him play back to break up passes and still make his tackles at the line of scrimmage. He was all over the field—knocking down passes and smashing line plays, often tackling back of the line for heavy losses."

Frank picked the 1936 Princeton game as the most memorable of his college career.

"The Tigers were heavily favored and got off to a 16-0 lead in the very first quarter," he recalled. "Then, just before the half ended, we managed to push across a touchdown to make it 16-7. Early in the third quarter, our line opened a big hole for Al Hessberg and he raced 25 yards for another score. Now it was only 16-14. Soon after, we got the ball back and I spotted Kelley far downfield and hit him on the button for our third touchdown, and that put us in front, 20 to 16.

"In the last period, Princeton bounced back with a go-ahead TD and went ahead again, 23-20. Talk about seesaw, rough-and-tumble, rock-'em-sock-'em battles! With only six minutes left on the clock, we took the kickoff and started back upfield on a series of passes and runs. We moved the ball very swiftly, working against time. We finally went ahead to stay, 26-23, on a quick opener from the Princeton 12, and that was your old ball game. I remember Bill Lynch, who was barely able to walk off the field after the gun, saying to Bill John, 'I never want to be this tired again.' And Fritz Crisler, who had seen a lot of great games in his day, said it was the most exciting game he ever saw. 'If the teams could have gone on playing, it might have ended, 79-76,' he said. 'But Yale would have won.' "

A member of Yale's excellent coaching staff during the Kelley-Frank era was Jerry Ford, the ex-Michigan center who would one day find himself in the White House. He had been offered a deal to play for the Green Bay Packers in 1935—$200 a game, with a 14-game schedule and a 10-day contract cancellation provision—but when Ducky Pond, the Yale coach, asked the future president to be on his staff at New Haven, Ford saw the chance to realize two dreams at once: to stay in football and to pursue a long-nurtured aspiration for law school. Pond's offer was $2,400 for the full 12 months, as his assistant line coach, jayvee coach, and scout—and to coach the boxing team in the winter. About boxing, Ford knew absolutely nothing.

So that summer while working in his father's paint factory, Ford slipped off to the YMCA three times a week to get punched around by the Y's boxing coach. He didn't improve much, but he got good enough to fool the Yale freshmen, one of whom was Bill Proxmire, who would be in the Senate (from Wisconsin) when Ford became president.

Gerald Ford coached at Yale for six football seasons, from 1935 through 1940. His scholastic advisers were convinced that he could not handle law school and a full-time job, so they wouldn't let him try until 1938 when, with reluctance, they relented for two courses. Ford was warned that of the 125 students entering law school that year, 98 were Phi Beta Kappa. Somehow he got by, and that spring, without telling Ducky Pond, he began taking a full load of law courses.

"The Yale coaching staff was excellent," Ford said. "Greasy Neale was on it, and Ivy Williamson, who had played at Michigan before me and was my roommate one summer when I took a couple of law courses there. He was going for his master's in education. Williamson later became a winning head coach at Wisconsin. By January of 1941, I had completed my law requirements and I received my degree in June. World War II ended my football career."

° ° °

Athletics in the Big Three was on the decline in 1938, and down at Princeton Fritz Crisler, whose Tigers finished the '37 season with a mediocre 4-4 record, was getting itchy feet.

"The depression is exerting an important influence on colleges, which they are just beginning to

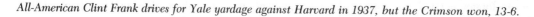

*All-American Clint Frank drives for Yale yardage against Harvard in 1937, but the Crimson won, 13-6.*

# MEN OF MICHIGAN

GERALD FORD, '35
*Center*
Grand Rapids, Michigan

*This is how former President Gerald Ford appeared in the 1932 Princeton-Michigan program as a sophomore center. The Wolverines won at Ann Arbor, 14-7. A few years later, while studying law at Yale, Ford joined the Eli coaching staff, shown here. L. to r., back row: Ford, head junior varsity coach; Marshall Wells, line; Ivan Williamson, end coach. Front row: Bill Renner, junior varsity; Ducky Pond, head coach; Earle (Greasy) Neale, chief assistant; Major Frank A. Wandle, trainer.*

feel," he said at the time. "The high tuition of privately endowed Eastern schools is turning many kids toward land-grant state institutions. There is another economic factor that will continue to react against private schools. The days of large endowments and big returns on invested capital are gone. Inheritance taxes will rise steadily, and high income taxes, cutting into money which could have sent boys to the rich social schools, will turn them to state colleges with cheap tuition. Reduced registration and endowments add up to curtailed sports activity. I think it's best to leave Princeton while my reputation is still worth something."

Crisler had special talents to sell in 1938, and Michigan wanted them urgently enough to persist in beckoning him, after two refusals, and finally to ask him what he wanted. "I thought my terms were so far out of line that they would be unacceptable," Crisler confessed later. "I haven't got over the surprise yet."

He knew there was no other candidate in the field with the qualifications that Michigan needed, and he made certain the setup was foolproof. He asked for more money than any coach ever made in the Midwest, $15,000 a year. There was to be no check on his selection of assistant coaches, and he demanded, and got, a firm hand free of Fielding H. Yost's interference in Michigan football, as well as the promise that he would be appointed athletic director when Yost reached the retirement age of 70 in 1942. Michigan accepted every condition, and Crisler signed. Succeeding him at Princeton was Tad Wieman, who had been serving as Fritz's backfield coach.

Perhaps the poorest exhibition that a Michigan football team ever gave under Crisler was its 15-13 narrow-squeak victory over a weak Yale outfit at New Haven in 1938. Late in the game, Yale was leading, 13-9, when Bob Brooks, the Eli tackle, almost blocked Regeczi's fourth-down kick from the Wolverine 15. The ball glanced off Regeczi's foot, giving Yale possession near the Michigan goal. Apparently this clinched the game, but Brooks had bumped into the Wolverine punter and the referee exacted the penalty, giving Michigan a first down, plus five yards. Michigan promptly marched 85 yards to victory. Thus did a fine individual play cost the weaker team the ball game.

During half time that afternoon,Crisler distributed paper and pencil to his sluggish Wolverines in the dressing room. A master of sarcasm, he announced: "I want all you fellows to write your alibis now, explaining how you happened to lose this ball game. Our alumni will want to know."

Ironically, Crisler will be remembered longest at Princeton for the games he lost. In 1934, for example, he talked himself out of the Yale game, which Larry Kelley won on a pass from Jim Roscoe. Crisler got so worked up during his pregame pep talk that the Tigers walked onto the field quivering in every muscle.

"Fellas," cried Fritz, "you have 60 minutes for redemption and a lifetime for regret."

The Princetonians were so worked up that they fumbled seven times in the first quarter.

"I hope the Rose Bowl has handles on it," jested Kelley.

The 11 Yales who started that game were still in there at the finish. Not a substitute was used.

One day, some years later, Crisler and Greasy Neale sat together at Toots Shor's in New York City. Fritz was still coaching out at Ann Arbor, and Greasy, by now, was the head custodian of the pro Philadelphia Eagles.

*The kickoff of the 1937 Yale-Army game in which the Bulldogs upset the Cadets, 15-7, for their first win over West Point since 1929. The game drew 50,000 to Yale Bowl.*

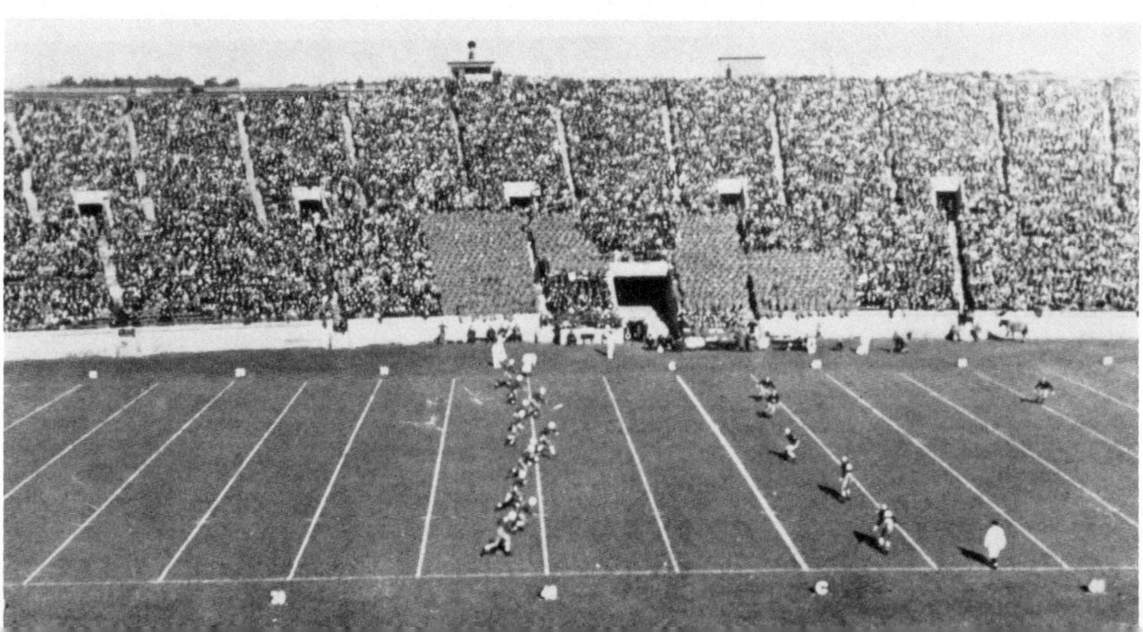

*When Number 19, Larry Kelley, went up and gathered in the football, he brought to life the precise meaning of Knute Rockne's advice to the pass receivers, "No crowbars up there today, boys!" Here the star Yale end scores the winning touchdown against Princeton in 1934.*

"Why do all these modern players fumble so much?" a reporter asked them. "In the old days the primary requisites for a football player were speed and intellect. And that still goes today."

"I wish my boys had more intellect," sighed Greasy. "One day we're having practice in pass defense and one of my backs keeps asking a lineman, 'What time does the train leave tonight? Will there be a diner on it? Is it a large diner?' A great way to learn defense, isn't it?"

"What's wrong with that?" inquired Jack Lavelle, the ponderous Notre Dame scout. "He was merely perfecting his defenses against hunger."

° ° °

Men who were playing college football in the fall of 1938 faced a singular experience; a new period of history took shape more visibly for them than for any previous college generation. In their case, the dividing line was obvious. The Munich crisis reached its climax at one o'clock on Saturday morning, October 1, 1938, when 600 gray-clad German soldiers crossed the border to begin the occupation of Czechoslovakia. In a few stunned hours the world came to the realization that war was not only threatening but imminent. In the United States, the knowledge was forcibly borne home that the nation's detachment from world affairs had ended. But for the young men who were college seniors, the drama came down to a finer point of tension. They were on the playing fields the day the crisis unfolded, and for many of them the world passed from one period to another almost between the opening kickoff and the final whistle of their football games.

Otherwise, October 1, 1938, was not unusual. In New England it was a day of unbroken sunshine that greeted the opening of the college football season. Columbia, with its All-American quarterback Sid Luckman drilling bull's-eye passes short and long, kicked the stuffing out of Yale in the Bowl, 27-14; Cornell smashed Colgate, 15-6; Dartmouth trounced Bates, 46-0; Penn defeated Lafayette, 34-6; Princeton, under new head coach Elton E. (Tad) Wieman, bombed Williams, 39-0; and Harvard lost to Brown, 20-13. Most of the Ivy Leaguers went right on following such games with gusto. "We aren't being indifferent to the world situation," said one fan. "But Great Britain, Germany, and Poland seem a long way off. Right now, we are concerned with winning football games, getting good grades, and trying to keep alive financially."

More than flawless weather attracted the crowds to Ivy League games that season. They were drawn by performers like Luckman or Robert L. Green, Jr., captain of Harvard's Big Three champions, or Jerome H. Holland, All-American end on a successful (5-1-1) Cornell team that lost only to Syracuse and was tied by Pennsylvania, or Gilbert W. Humphrey, who brought glory to Yale when he threw a touchdown pass against Navy, then beat the Midshipmen with a field goal, 9-7.

Sid Luckman was one of the first, and surely the best, of the T-formation quarterbacks. He mastered the T as though it had been invented for him, not at Columbia, but under Coach George Halas of the Chicago Bears. Luckman weighed 197 at his playing best and possessed an abundance of talent. He was a genuine student of the game, and no coach would have had to send in the plays for him.

Luckman developed one skill at Columbia that made his job with the NFL Bears more natural to him. When he played for Lou Little, he never knew much protection as a quarterback, yet he led some valiant stands against stronger opponents. Consequently, he had grown used to seeing opposing tackles and ends lumbering around in his own backfield and had become adept at darting about to escape them, always with his eyes on the watch for receivers, but picking up in his side vision the clutching hands of the enemy. Therefore, he was really skilled at scrambling, as every T-formation quarterback must be, because a stationary target to a charging lineman is like an inept matador to a mad bull.

Sid, of course, bit the dust many times—he had his nose broken often—but was far better than most of his contemporaries in dodging in and out of the pocket or taking off on a dead run to get throwing room. It became a standard joke among opponents that Luckman never had to have his football pants laundered from the start of the season to the end.

Luckman's most satisfying triumph as a collegian came on October 8, 1938, a week after beating Yale. It was the Army game, played at West Point, and the Cadets led at the half, 18-6.

Luckman went to the air in the third quarter to score the Light Blue's second touchdown. With the numbers now 18-13, Army cranked up its ground game and drove to the Columbia 9, where they missed a field goal.

Starting from their own 20, a pass from Luckman to Radvilas gained 27 yards. On the next play Luckman was smeared for a 10-yard loss, but then pitched to Siegal for 18. Seidel got three more on a plunge, and then another Luckman-to-Radvilas pass carried the Lions to the Army 19. Halfback Radvilas was knocked unconscious on the play, but he instinctively held on to the ball.

*Although he did not play the position for Lou Little at Columbia in 1938, All-America Sid Luckman went on to become professional football's first great T-formation quarterback.*

On the drive downfield, left end Siegal had been setting himself up, going down and blocking the defensive right halfback on certain plays and loafing on others. Now, with the Army right half all set up, Luckman called for Siegal's signal, a crossover pass. Siegal went down, broke to his outside, and Luckman laid the ball neatly in his arms. The play was good for 16 yards to the Army 3. With the clock showing only two minutes, Seidel powered into the end zone to put Columbia ahead to stay, 20-18.

Sitting among the crowd of 25,000 at Michie Stadium that afternoon was George Halas, owner and coach of the Chicago Bears. "Luckman had said he wasn't going to play professional football after he graduated from Columbia," Halas said. "But when I saw him with the Lions I knew I had found the quarterback I was looking for to make the T formation go. And I got him."

With Luckman around in 1939 to make it work, Halas was the man who popularized the "man-in-motion" T, which turned football upside down. The "Halas formation," as Luckman referred to it, had very little in common with the *old* T formation, which was the original football formation of the 1890s. In the modern T, Luckman kept his hand in contact with the center. He had to be an expert ball handler. In this formation he was more important than ever. It took a quarterback of Sid's developed skills to really make it function.

° ° °

George Munger, one of the youngest head coaches in college football, met Pop Warner, one of the oldest, at a football banquet in Philadelphia shortly after the close of the 1938 season. Munger had just finished his first year as head coach at Pennsylvania. The Quakers closed the season by holding a very strong Cornell eleven to a scoreless tie, and Munger knew that Warner would be interested in the details.

"Pop," George said, "I think maybe we stumbled on something new in the Cornell game. We used a different kind of a mousetrap."

Munger then went on to explain how mousetrap blocks against fast-charging Cornell linemen had been carried out by his wingback instead of the customary blocking back. The new block had worked to perfection against the Big Red.

"Smart work," Pop said. "I've always wondered why that hasn't been used much. I remember the first time we tried it. It had our opponents talking to themselves."

"How long ago was that?" Munger wanted to know.

"Oh, a long while ago," Warner said. "I think it was in 1901."

Was there anything new in the technique of football coaching? Basically, very little. One coach who did add a new dimension to coaching, however, was Carl Snavely, who piloted Cornell for nine years, starting in 1936. It's hard to think of Ithaca without picturing 101 Delaware Avenue, a pleasant brick house halfway up the hill, where the head coach traditionally lived in those years. And so it was there that the meticulous Snavely resided.

Carl Snavely was the first coach of importance to make an intensive study of football motion pictures, and he first set up a projection room in his den at Ithaca. He used to scan the action films by the hour.

"The camera reveals flaws the human eye can't see," he once explained. "Just as the doctor uses X-rays to tell us what's wrong with the body, we use movies to tell us what's wrong with our teams. I didn't know a thing about movies when I thought of the idea. At first we used 55-millimeter film. It ran too fast, we couldn't slow it down, and we couldn't reverse it because it would burn up. Then I bought my own projector, compared notes with Jock Sutherland of Pittsburgh, and the plan began to pay off. My first photographer was my wife—and she did a pretty good job of it."

The two most notable games in Snavely's long career involved Cornell in 1939 and 1940. First was the stunning upset of powerful Ohio State, 23-14, at Columbus in 1939. The heavier and highly favored Buckeyes put on two scoring drives of 86 and 72 yards, led 14-0 well into the second quarter, and looked unbeatable. It seemed as if the Western Conference observers were indeed right; the Ivy League didn't belong on the same field.

Then the contest turned sharply around. Walter (Pop) Scholl, behind perfect blocking, broke off tackle 79 yards to a touchdown. Soon after, he pitched a pass 26 yards to Swifty Bohrman, and Swifty ran another 37 to score.

"Ohio State had scouted us," Snavely said afterward, "and they were truly sorry for us. However, they were nonetheless eager for the kill. Cornell had no delusions of grandeur, but inasmuch as the game was on our schedule, we would play it and suffer the consequences. From Borhman's run on out, Hal McCullough's passing, Mort Landsberg's running, tackle Nick Drahos's field goal, and an

*Carl Snavely, the head man at Cornell.*

astonishing display of stamina on the part of all, my boys put the game on ice."

The victory remains the number one upset in Cornell's history.

Snavely, however, always maintained that his 1940 eleven, up through its first six games, was superior to 1939's; victims again included Ohio State, at Ithaca this time, 21-7. But the Cayugans were upset in their last two games, by Dartmouth, 3-0, and Penn, 22-20.

Robert J. Kane, who spent 37 years as director and dean of athletics at Cornell, remembers Snavely as an intense man.

"His whole being was dedicated to football, with time out only during the summer when he dedicated that same intensity to golf," Dean Kane said. "He was not one to get close to his players. He found personal relationships difficult. He was realistic about this. He utilized head trainer Frank J. 'Doc' Kavanagh as his intermediary with his players. They admired him, forgave him his cool detachment, his unforthcoming style. At least he was impartial in his abstractedness. In his own way, he liked and admired his players, and his intellectual approach to coaching was well suited to the kind of talent he had at Cornell, and he often said so. His players were smart and there were no prima donnas. In spite of his diffidence with them, he had an uncanny way of changing them tc positions they had not played, to new ones they became better at: Brud Holland, from fullback to end; Al Van Ranst, from tackle to center; Carl Spang, from halfback to end; Walt Matuszak, from fullback to blocking back; Mort Landsberg, from halfback to fullback. They won 18 straight games from the third game in

*Nick Drahos, All-America tackle at Cornell in 1939–40.*

*One of the genuine great backs in the late 1930s was Dartmouth's All-America halfback Bob MacLeod, shown here sweeping around Cornell's left end.*

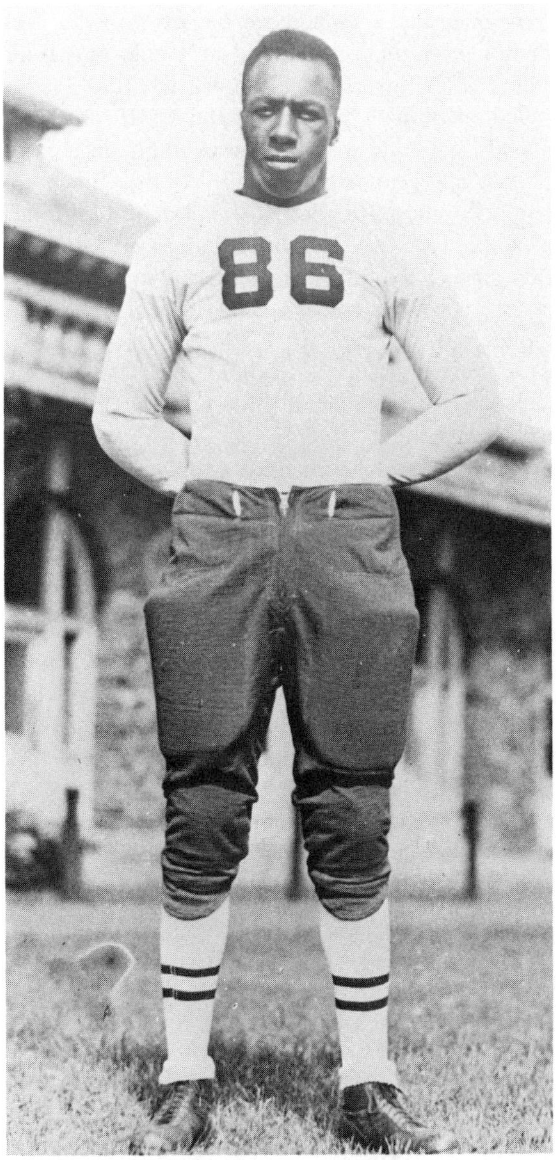


*All-America end for Cornell in 1937–38 was Jerome Heartwell (Brud) Holland, a 215-pound six-footer, who in later years went on to become ambassador to Sweden. He is also a member of the National Football Hall of Fame.*

1938 to the seventh game in 1940.

"Something not widely known is that the Rose Bowl Committee talked to Jim Lynah, the Cornell athletic director, about the possibility of the Big Red playing Southern California in the 1939 New Year's Day classic. A meeting of the Cornell Board of Physical Education and Athletics was quickly called to decide the question. It was a brief meeting. The chairman of the committee, President Edmund Ezra Day, responded to the Rose Bowl Committee, expressing thanks but regret that 'it would unduly extend the length of the season and place too much of a strain on the scholastic pursuits of the Cornell players.' There was no fanfare, no public expression of self-righteousness.

"Carl Snavely was not happy about the decision. He had a strange combination of personal reclusiveness and dogged competitiveness. In those pre-TV days, the Rose Bowl was the ultimate showcase. Carl was proud of his team and proud of his ability to prepare it for the big one. A Rose Bowl victory would have earned Cornell number one ranking in the national polls instead of number two, Carl believed."

Ben Mintz, long-time Cornell sports information director, said that the deepest memory he has of the 1939 season was the reaction out in Columbus of Cornell going out there to play the Buckeyes.

*After upsetting Ohio State in 1939, Cornell's Coach Carl Snavely and Captain Walt Matuszak plot tactics for a return match.*

"Francis Schmidt, then the coach at Ohio State, thought so lightly of Cornell that he chose to go duck hunting on Friday, the day before the game," Ben said. "Incidentally, the clinching points were accounted for by All-America tackle Nick Drahos, who kicked a 27-yard field goal. I recall quite vividly the excitement in Ithaca immediately following the game. I was an 18-year-old Cornell freshman at the time and I knew several players on the team."

An eyewitness of the Cornell-Ohio State game played at Ithaca a year later was Professor Paul M. O'Leary, a member of the Cornell faculty. With great enthusiasm, he recalled the details.

"When the Ohio State teams—three of them—rushed onto the field in ascending order in 1940 behind the 120-piece Buckeye band, all of us Ithacans shuddered," O'Leary told me. "They were massive! But Cornell licked them, 21-7. I can still see Snavely watching Jim Langhurst and Don Scott march through Cornell after the kickoff 75 yards for a touchdown. He crouched and walked, crouched and walked. He had his fine line coach Max Reed making notes. After Ohio State scored, he took out three of his defensive linemen, talked to them intensely until Cornell next went on defense, and Ohio State didn't make more than 60 yards the remainder of the game. He was really a 'grey fox' and one hell of a football coach.

"Cornell's two winning touchdowns that day were made by a sophomore substitute back, Lou Buffalino, on almost identical off-tackle runs from Ohio State's 15-yard line. Lou was what used to be called a 'whippet type' back—about 5′10″ and 170 pounds, wiry and tough. He was taking one of my courses that year. Monday morning after the game I stopped him at the end of the class and told him what a fine performance he had given on Saturday. Like many athletes (Jack Dempsey, for one), Lou had a high tenor voice. I can still hear him as he replied: 'Well, Professor, I'll tell you how it was. Coach Snavely sent me in there and said to go off tackle. I took one look at those two big Ohio State tackles and I said to myself, 'Lou, you aren't going to let either one of those guys get his hands on you or they'll kill you.' The only safe place was down in that end zone, Professor, so that's where I went!"

Professor O'Leary's exuberance for football points out that many faculty members have been known to love the game. Billy Phelps, for example. He was the famous Yale lecturer on the poet Robert Browning. Professor Phelps was a red-hot football fan too, and he treated the Yale players kindly when grades were passed out.

"Which gives you the greater kick, a perfect recitation in the classroom or a 50-yard run for a touchdown?" he was once asked.

"Well," Billy said, "I can't get too excited over a perfect recitation."

*Cornell vs. Ohio State, 1940. The camera catches McCullough pitching to Schmuck for the Big Red's third touchdown of the day and 21-7 victory over the Buckeyes.*

# *Football Survives Another War*

It is doubtful that Red Blaik will ever forget the next-to-the-last game he coached at Dartmouth. That was the 1940 Cornell contest at Hanover in which spunky Red Friesell, one of the best referees of modern times, made a wrenching blunder.

The controversy surrounding the boner tended to cloud the magnitude of the final score. Carl Snavely's juggernaut had won 18 games in a row, had ranked number four nationally in 1939, and now was gunning for the National Championship.

Dartmouth, on the other hand, had been sacked at Cornell the year before, 35-6, and had very little status.

There was no problem for Blaik to get his Indians up for the contest emotionally; they got themselves up. His job was to keep them from getting wound too tight. Physically, he had spent the week giving the team a game plan as complex and gaudy as anything designed until that time. It stressed defense and was based on forgoing an early charge and commitment, angling off in the direction of the ball, and giving up the short gain, but no more.

The Indians executed with such abandon that they put the left side of Snavely's front line out of action with injuries. In the first half, Cornell was stopped dead in its tracks. In the third quarter, they managed to move toward the Dartmouth goal, but were frustrated by an end zone interception. Then Dartmouth started downfield on the ground and set up a field goal by Bob Krieger from the Cornell 27. The kick was good, and now the Indians led, 3-0.

With only four and a half minutes to play, Cornell, on its own 48, took to the air with a ball damp from a light snow. Halfback Walt Scholl, ignoring the weather, began connecting, and his completion to right halfback Bill Murphy carried the ball to the Dartmouth 5, first down.

With the clock showing less than 60 seconds, fullback Mort Landsberg smashed to the 3. Then Scholl drove to the 1. Third and one, Landsberg was stacked up for almost no gain. The ball rested less than 2 feet from the goal line with time enough for only two more plays.

To stop the clock, Coach Snavely called for time out, and Cornell was penalized back to the 6 for delaying the game. On fourth down, Scholl's pass to Murphy in the end zone was batted down. Joe McKenney, the head linesman, picked up the ball and brought it out to the 20-yard line, first and 10 for Dartmouth. But wait! Red Friesell, confused by the scoreboard that read third down, ruled that Cornell had another down coming, fourth and goal on the 6 still. Captain Lou Young of Dartmouth protested wildly, but Friesell gave the ball back to Cornell.

Now there were only six seconds left, time for one more play. Scholl dropped back, spotted Bill Murphy in the end zone, and this time Murphy hung on to the ball. Tackle Nick Drahos converted, the game was over, and the Big Red had apparently escaped a major upset to win by the score of 7 to 3.

"Just about everybody thought that was it," Red Blaik was to recollect 30 years later. "Everybody, that is, but our players, two of the officials, and most of the writers up in the pressbox. They *knew* that Cornell had scored on a *fifth* down. That's the way the sportswriters reported it. The news of Friesell's error swept down from the pressbox, through the crowd, out onto Memorial Field, into Davis Field House, and on through Hanover like prairie fire. Students began parading, proclaiming a Dartmouth victory. They paraded throughout the weekend, every hour on the hour. One of the parades ended up in front of my house.

"When the situation was brought to the attention of Jim Lynah, the Cornell athletic director, he stated that if the officials discovered that there had been five downs, the score would go down in the record book as Dartmouth 3, Cornell 0. President Dr. Ezra Day of Cornell concurred.

"So President Hopkins of Dartmouth and I drove Referee Friesell across the Connecticut River to the White River Junction station to catch his train, and on the way Red admitted to us that he had apparently made a mistake."

The following Monday, after Cornell officials had studied the game films, which showed without doubt that there had been five downs and no evidence of a double offside, they phoned Asa Bushnell, executive secretary of the Eastern Intercollegiate Association, who then forwarded the information to Friesell.

The referee issued a statement expressing his regret. Bushnell then stated that no official had jurisdiction to change the outcome of the game and that any further action would have to come from Dartmouth or Cornell.

When this information was told to Cornell, they sent Dartmouth two wires. This one from Jim Lynah:

IN VIEW OF THE CONCLUSIONS REACHED BY THE OFFICIALS THAT THE CORNELL TOUCHDOWN WAS SCORED ON A FIFTH DOWN, CORNELL RELINQUISHES CLAIM TO THE VICTORY AND EXTENDS CONGRATULATIONS TO DARTMOUTH.

A second from Coach Snavely read:

I ACCEPT THE FINAL CONCLUSIONS OF THE OFFICIALS AND WITHOUT RESERVATION CONCEDE THE VICTORY TO DARTMOUTH WITH HEARTY CONGRATULATIONS TO YOU AND THE GALLANT DARTMOUTH TEAM.

And Dartmouth wired back to Cornell:

DARTMOUTH ACCEPTS THE VICTORY AND CONGRATULATES AND SALUTES THE CORNELL TEAM, THE HONORABLE AND HONORED OPPONENT OF HER LONGEST UNBROKEN RIVALRY.

EXTRA The Dartmouth 5¢

The Oldest College Newspaper in America

# CORNELL CONCEDES 3-0 DARTMOUTH VICTORY

## Text of Telegram

WESTERN UNION

Received at 1940 NOV 18 PM 1 34

DAV49 81 DL= PITTSBURGH PENN NOV 18 106P

LOU YOUNG=

CAPTAIN DARTMOUTH FOOTBALL TEAM

I WANT TO BE THE FIRST TO ADMIT MY VERY GRAVE ERROR ON THE EXTRA DOWN AS PROVEN BY THE MOTION PICTURES OF BOTH COLLEGES. I WANT TO APOLOGIZE TO YOU, YOUR PLAYERS, COACH BLAIK, ALL ASSISTANT COACHES, AND MR MCCARTER, I ASSUME FULL RESPONSIBILITY. I WANT TO THANK YOU ALL FOR THE VERY FAIR TREATMENT ACCORDED ME AFTER THE GAME. LOU I AM SO SORRY FOR YOU WERE SUCH A GRAND CAPTAIN AND LEADER. GIVE MY REGARDS TO PRESIDENT HOPKINS=

WM H FRIESELL JR REFEREE.

ABOVE: This telegram, apologizing for the error made in Saturday's game with Cornell, was received by Captain Lou Young at 1 p.m. today. It was the first official word to come through acknowledging that Cornell's touchdown was made on a fifth down play.

LEFT: Capt. LOU YOUNG and Coach EARL BLAIK of the Indian squad which beat Cornell 3-0 Saturday afternoon.

## Friesell Admits His Fifth Down Mistake In Wire To Young

### Snavely and Lynah Send Messages After Examination Of Chart, Movies; McCarter Formally Accepts Victory

*By Fred Begole*

Cornell, through both Director of Athletics James Lynah and Head Football Coach Carl Snavely, conceded Dartmouth Saturday's football game by a 3-0 score at 3 this afternoon. William H. McCarter, Director of the DCAC, immediately accepted.

And thus it will go down in history that a great underdog rose to the heights of football fame by defeating the number one team of the nation on November 16, 1940.

In a rapid succession of events from 2 p.m. today, the final concession rapidly took shape. At noon Capt. Lou Young received a telegram from referee W. H. (Red) Friesell admitting the official's error and extending his apologies. Directly following this wire, Mr. McCarter and Coach Earl Blaik received wires from Lynah and Snavely, respectively, accepting the conclusion of the referee and by 3, Mr. McCarter, as the official spokesman for the DCAC, accepted the concession and commented on Cornell's sportsmanship.

The full text of Friesell's wire to Young, which came from Pittsburgh, states: "I want to be the first to admit my very grave error on the extra down as proven by the motion pictures of both colleges. I want to apologize to you, your players, Coach Blaik, all assistant coaches, and Mr. McCarter. I assume full responsibility. I want to thank you all for the very fair treatment after the game. Lou, I am so sorry, for you were such a grand captain and leader. Give my regards to President Hopkins. William H. Friesell, Jr., Referee."

On receipt of Friesell's statement, Carl Snavely wired to Mr. Blaik, "I accept the final conclusions of the offi-

(Continued on page two)

The effect of the switch in the winner had a lot to do with the long range play of the college.

down Scholl threw to Murphy for the touchdown.

"I thought we had scored on the

*The front page of the November 18, 1940 edition of* The Dartmouth *tells the entire story of the incredible Cornell-Dartmouth "fifth down" game.*

On that "fifth down" play, Bill Murphy, a devout Catholic, murmured a prayer while he and his teammates lined up at the 6-yard line with only six seconds left. "Dear Lord," he confessed saying, "if you let me score this touchdown, I promise to attend mass every day for a year."

Murphy's plea was apparently granted. At any rate, he caught the pass from Scholl for what all the Cornell fans thought was the winning touchdown. They went to bed that night thinking they had won, only to tumble out the next day to hear rumors that they had lost.

Murphy didn't know what to do about his vow. He went to his Catholic chaplain at Ithaca and confessed the promise he had silently made on the last play of the game.

"Father," he wanted to know, "am I obligated to keep the promise?"

The priest weighed the matter.

"My son," he said, "this is an unusual situation. You scored the touchdown, all right, but Dartmouth was eventually declared the winner. Under the circumstances, then, I feel you are not required to fulfill that pledge. But this is the first time I ever heard of a football referee double-crossing the Lord."

For years, Red Blaik had been told by Old Grads at Dartmouth that a good part of heaven was right there in Hanover.

"Now I believe they were right," Red said. "Why, it even included the miracle of a game that was won after it was lost."

Years later, as he looked back on his long career, Red Blaik suspected that the reversal of the Cornell score was a sign that he should never leave Dartmouth to coach elsewhere.

But he did leave. On Sunday morning, December 22, 1940, he met with the new superintendent of West Point, his old friend Lieutenant General Robert L. Eichelberger, and Red told him that he had decided to accept Army's offer and become its new head football coach. Having sweated out his decision for almost a month, there was an expression of relief, but also a profound depression, on Red's face. His verdict had involved a lot of fretful soul-searching.

Colonel Charles Danielson, the West Point adjutant, said later, "I've never seen a man less happy than Blaik was the morning after he signed his new contract. He was a man in a deep fog. All of us, merely by observation, realized how much of a wrench it was for him to leave Dartmouth."

From Dartmouth, Blaik went on to great success at West Point—two National Championship teams, four undefeated teams, six Eastern Championships, unbeaten strings of 32 and 28, Coach of the Year and every other honor coaching can bestow, and the prized Gold Medal Award of the National Football Foundation and Hall of Fame.

"Just as football will remain a leading competitive sport in college athletics, so will Earl Blaik be remembered as an outstanding architect on the gridiron," General Douglas MacArthur once observed.

° ° °

Football turned a vital corner from the 1930s into the 1940s. With the new decade came a major development: a new style of offensive football called the T formation. They took the oldest formation in football, the original T, and joined it with the man in motion. This flashier, more versatile version of the old T was the brainchild of Stanford's Clark Shaughnessy and George Halas of the Chicago Bears.

This combining of the flanker and man in motion with a hard-hitting, quick-opening attack made for an offense of ever-changing structure. It put a great burden on the defense with the wide variety of its patterns. Those coaches who did not jump on the bandwagon felt compelled to add new features to their attacks for greater deception.

Although Lou Little stood by his single wing, he did come up with the cleverest and most deceptive attack he had yet worked out at Columbia by putting his tailback and fullback on a line, even with each other, and had them spin and fake to one another as well as the wingback coming around. Soon Coach Little popped up with his version of the wing T, a combination of the two.

° ° °

With the intelligent, experienced George Munger at the controls, Pennsylvania enjoyed its greatest decade in the forties. The Quakers did not lose an Ivy game in seven of those seasons; they were 38-3-2 from 1940–49 against the Ivies, and 57-21-4 overall. Outside the Ivy group, Penn played such powers as Army, Navy, Michigan, Maryland, Virginia, Penn State, and Pittsburgh.

Penn kicked off the decade winning one of the most dramatic contests in its history. This was the 1940 Cornell game in front of 80,000 at Franklin Field—the same Big Red machine that Coach Snavely picked as his greatest team, with swift 6′3″, 210-pound tackle Nick Drahos; Captain Walt Matuszak, a tremendous blocking back and signal caller; and Hal McCullough, the workhorse of the backfield who ran, passed, and kicked. And there was Mort Landsberg, the nervy, 165-pound gamester, spin-bucking like a shot and banging up the middle with punts, who came up from the junior varsity to fill a big gap at fullback when Vince Eichler was operated on and had to leave the squad for the season, as well as Bud Finneran, another recruit from the junior varsity who snared the other team's passes and seldom got any relief in feeding the ball back flawlessly from center and in backing up the line.

"Those were happy days at Cornell in 1938, '39, and '40—great boys, good teams, and thrilling games," Snavely said. "Any comments on 1940 apply also to 1939 because they were one and the same team with the exception of Whit Baker, who finished in 1939."

Professor Paul M. O'Leary of Cornell also remembers that Snavely's boys loved a good laugh to break the tension.

"In 1940," O'Leary said, "a player could not bring in a play from the bench to be run until one play had been run after he came in. But Snavely liked to sneak in plays. In those days a sub reported to an official, giving his name, position, and whom he was replacing. The Cornell players brought this information in by a written slip prepared by an assistant manager. So when Howard Dunbar, the big, tall running guard who is now an eminent orthopedic surgeon in New York, went into the game, he had this slip *and* a sequence of plays that Snavely wanted his quarterback to call. But when Dunbar reported to the referee he mistakenly gave him the *wrong* slip and promptly drew a 15-yard penalty. Snavely was fit to be tied, but the team thought it a great joke, laughing so hard and guying poor Dunbar so exuberantly that they almost drew another penalty for delay of game."

As Cornell and Pennsylvania approached their 1940 showdown, the Big Red had a slightly better won-lost record. They had beaten Ohio State, 21-7, for the second straight year, while the Quakers had lost a savage struggle to Tommy Harmon and Michigan, 14-0, but whaled the daylights out of Army, 48-0, and Yale, 50-7.

The key to the Pennsylvania attack was All-American candidate Frank Reagan, elusive and swift of foot. His open-field cuts often were executed so abruptly that they tended to escape the naked eye. Reagan had been sought by just about every major college in the East. It was learned later that Frank was recruited for Penn by a Philadelphia Catholic priest who was simply wild about football.

One of those who had tried to recruit Reagan was Jimmy Crowley at Fordham. Sleepy Jim had made a valiant effort to get Reagan. He even went down to the Philadelphia priest and argued that Reagan should attend a good Catholic institution.

"Don't tell me, Jim," said the priest with a slight smile, "that you're really interested in this boy's religious training? "

"Well, maybe not, Father," said Crowley, "but you certainly should be."

It was easy to see why Cornell had been the pregame favorite against Penn. The game was not five minutes old before the Big Red marched 80 yards in seven plays to engineer the first touchdown of the day, with Mort Landsberg plunging over. Minutes later, Bill Murphy strong-armed his way through a pack of Penn tacklers and raced 60 yards to put Cornell ahead, 13-0. There was some question that Murphy had stepped out of bounds at midfield, but films later confirmed that he had not gone over the sideline.

Bracing against a rout, Penn gathered its forces and went to work. Things started looking up when Reagan drove Cornell back to its 7 with a perfect punt. Then Snavely began to reveal his unorthodox strategy. Leading by 13 points and with their backs to the wall, Cornell chose to go to the air instead of playing it close to the vest. On the first aerial, Murphy, the intended catcher, got in the clear all alone, but the pitch missed him by a mile.

The Big Red came right back with another pass call. This time Penn was ready. Captain and center Ray Frick picked the ball out of the air on the 16 and returned it to the 10. Four cracks at the line by Reagan, and Penn had its first touchdown. He scored another just before the half ended, with tacklers draped all over him, and now it was Penn 13, Cornell 13. A field goal by quarterback Gene Davis put the Quakers ahead, 16-13, as the gun went off ending the half.

It appeared that Pennsylvania's magnificent comeback was down the drain after Cornell scored a third-quarter touchdown to take the lead again, 20-16. But the Quakers refused to give up. Rejuvenated by the realization that they were still very much in the game after 56 minutes, they went with their chief weapon, Reagan, who responded by thrusting his legs forward in a facsimile of piston rods. "It was like trying to tackle an armload of eels," a Cornell lineman said afterward.

With Reagan carrying the load, Penn slowly but steadily marched into Cornell territory. Reagan tore through, around and over tacklers, 185 pounds of speed and surprising inside power. Cornell put everybody but its equipment manager on the line in a furious attempt to stop him. But Reagan was saving his best act for last. With the ball on the Cornell 16 and the defense sparing no men trying to put him under house arrest, Reagan took the snap from center, followed his blockers over tackle, saw daylight, and suddenly flew through the secondary as if the defenders were paralyzed. It was estimated that at least seven pairs of hands touched the fleet Pennsylvania tailback, but he broke their tackles to score his third touchdown and beat Cornell, 22-20.

The victory gave Penn the best record among the Ivies (3-0-1) and an overall 6-1-1 for the season. From 1940 through 1945, the Quakers did not lose a game to an Ivy group team; as a matter of fact, they lost only three to Ivies during the entire decade, once each in 1946, 1948, and 1949. Few schools have ever dominated the Ivy League as Pennsylvania did in the forties!

° ° °

Yale had fallen on hard times. In 1940–41, the Bulldogs won only one of 11 games against Ivy competition, including an embarrassing collapse against Harvard, 28-0, in 1940. That was the same Crimson eleven (3-2-3) that tied Army (6-6), Princeton (0-0), and Penn (10-10).

In the first quarter of the Yale game, funny things started to happen in the Harvard backfield after Charlie Spreyer, the quarterback, was banged on the head running back the kickoff. For several minutes, with the bells ringing in his brain, Charlie was calling old Choate School signals from his prep school days. The Yales did not notice the difference, however, because they spent the entire afternoon trying to figure out what Harvard was doing.

Coach Dick Harlow's best prewar record (5-2-1) at Harvard was in 1941. The season included a 20-6 victory over Army only a week after the Cadets held Notre Dame to a scoreless tie. The Cantabs then battled Navy to a 0-0 deadlock in what had to be one of the greatest land battles in history—305-pound Vernon Miller of Harvard vs. 290-pound Gene Flathman of the Midshipmen.

A week after the Navy game, Harvard beat Princeton by the baseball score of 6 to 4. In a wild rainstorm, the Tigers blocked two Harvard punts for safeties and a 4-0 lead, but suddenly Harvard back Captain Francis Lee found daylight on a routine off-tackle slash and splashed 88 yards for the winning touchdown. The heart and guts of that Harvard squad, however, was Endicott "Chub" Peabody, later an able Massachusetts politician, but, from 1939 through 1941, an All-American guard of such sinew and sagacity that head coach Harlow did not demur when Peabody broke precedent by refusing to stay with the rest of the Harvards at a hotel the night before the 1941 Yale game, insisting, quite sensibly, it would seem, that he wanted to sleep in his *own* bed. The next day he showed 40,000 onlookers why he was called "Baby-Faced Assassin," as the Bulldogs were shut out, 14-0.

On December 7, 1941, the United States was again at war. A year later, many of the college athletes and their fans were overseas, and those who remained behind to keep the game alive were a mixture of servicemen, military exempts, and draft rejects. Thirty of the 40 Princeton squad members who faced Penn in 1943, for instance, were sailors or Marines enrolled in special courses on the campus; the Quakers beefed themselves up with 31 players of the same category.

What had once been a steady flow of prep stars dwindled. Ballyhoo proclaiming that 26 preparatory-school football captains would be coming to Yale ceased. The main supply line was now mostly from the high schools. The coaches simply had to make do with what they had.

During the years 1941-44, Lou Little fielded four teams that won a combined total of only eight games, while losing 25. Platoon football and tough academic standards made it difficult for Columbia to remain competitive. Losing had become a bad habit.

"Football is undergoing many changes this fall," Coach Little wrote in 1942. "Equipment is less plentiful. In the face of priorities, last year's equipment will have to do in many cases and it may become a bit threadbare before the end of the season. But who cares? Veteran players are fewer. Hundreds of players who had looked forward to their senior season when they hung up their togs last season are now in the field, flying their planes, manning machine guns, or walking the decks of the Navy's fighting craft. Spectators are not quite so plentiful in some cases. It is more difficult this season to reach the games which are played in the small, secluded college towns, which have been so easily reached by unhampered motors in other years. But these things don't matter. The game is being played and played harder, faster, perhaps even more fiercely than it has been played before. We have become an offensively minded nation. Defense bonds have become war bonds. The bombers and the ships they buy are weapons of attack, not defense. We've got to strike, not parry."

Yale hired a new football coach in 1942, Howard Harry Odell, a former assistant to Dick Harlow at Harvard and George Munger at Penn. Odell did a whale of a job at New Haven through 1947. His teams won four out of four from Harvard and four out of five from Princeton. His 1944 team, captained by Mac Whiting, played neither Harvard nor Princeton and definitely was no powerhouse, yet it won seven and tied one for Yale's first defeatless season since 1924. Odell's once-defeated and once-tied 1946 team, captained by Dick Hollingshead III, was considerably superior to the '44 team. In fact, once the Big Blue of '46 began to jell in late October, it became one of Yale's best teams ever.

Odell's six-year stay at Yale coincided with the hectic wartime seasons of 1942, '43, and '44 and the equally unpredictable postwar autumns of '45 and '46. The fluctuating conditions brought Odell both bad and good breaks in personnel.

° ° °

Pennsylvania in 1947 had its first undefeated team since Captain Bill Hollenback's 1908 championship varsity. Except for a 7-7 tie in the rain with Army, the Quakers smashed Lafayette, Dartmouth, Columbia, Navy, Princeton, Virginia, and Cornell. The numbers totaled 219 points for Penn, 35 for the opponents.

The stars of the team were Chuck Bednarik, named on most All-America teams at center; Skippy Minisi in the backfield; and All-American George Savitsky at tackle. Many of these players had come back from the war and had a background of football experience.

"In spite of what they had been through in the

*The Maxwell Award winner in 1942, and second in the Heisman balloting, was Columbia's super all-around back, Paul Governali.*

*1944 champion Yale squad, shown here, won 7, tied 1, and held eight opponents to a total of only four touchdowns. Back row, l. to r.: Coach Howie Odell, Schaffner, Kirst, Ernst, Fusilli, Morrow, Smith, Bacon. Third row: Higginbotham, Sadowski, Blanning, Penn, Ballard, Kirk, Carroll, Whitler, Montano, Collins. Second row: Lilley, Hollingshead, Loh, Walker, Captain Macauley Whiting, Smith, McCullough, Rosenberger, DeBardeleben. Front row: Gher, Hall.*

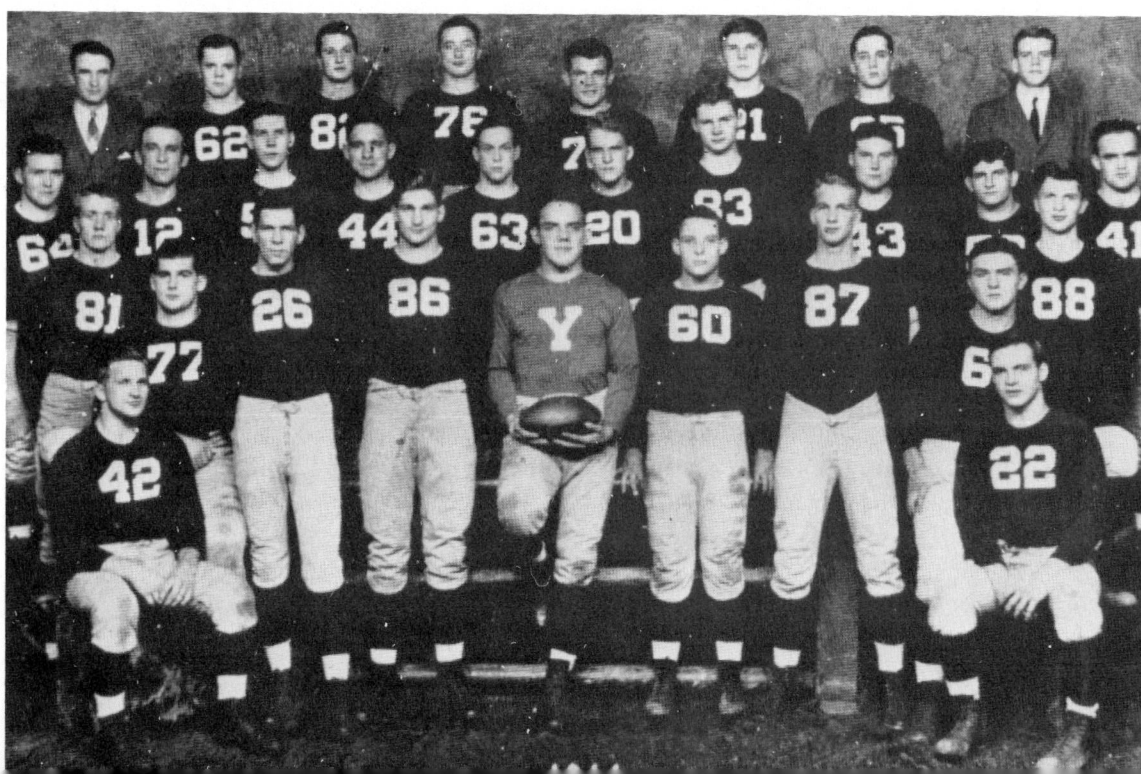

*The granddaddy of the Old Blues, Pudge Heffelfinger, was in his eighties and still visiting New Haven annually to show Yale players "how we did it under Camp." Here he demonstrates linelay for Captain Paul Walker of 1945 champion Elis.*

war," Coach George Munger said, "they trained and worked and played like young sophomores breaking in. They still had enthusiasm, that old college try."

Sergeant Chuck Bednarik flew his last mission in the spring of 1945. He came home to Bethlehem in July, an air medal, five battle stars, and five oak leaf clusters behind him. In front of him was a harvest of civilian ambitions, college and football the immediate ones.

Chuck went to see his old high school coach, Jack Butler. "I'd like to play football at a college," Chuck said.

"Fine," Butler said. "Let me call George Munger at Penn."

"Penn?" Chuck said. "Where's that?"

He found out fast. A few days later, Chuck walked into the dining room at Penn's Philadelphia campus. He was looking for Coach Munger. Munger was expecting him, but less than enthusiastically. "A center?" George had said when Butler passed along Chuck's position. "I don't need him. I've got five centers."

Munger changed his mind when Bednarik got there. There were his 17- and 18-year-old football players sitting around the table, and there came big Chuck—6-feet-2, 215 pounds, and 20 years old, of combat hardness. Munger's eyes popped when he saw him. Chuck was in.

"In" meant room and board paid by Penn and tuition courtesy of the GI Bill. It also meant an open door to glory. The top college backs of Chuck's time were Glenn Davis, Doc Blanchard, Johnny Lujack, and Doak Walker. Chuck Bednarik was the top lineman. A Penn regular four years and All-America twice, Chuck was singled out as the best college football player in the country in 1948, his senior season, when he won the Maxwell Award. George Munger was so high on him that he claimed Chuck was "capable of being All-America at any position." His bruising blocking, exciting tackling, and booming punts led the Quakers to an overall record of 24 victories in 27 games during his varsity career. Week after week, he lived in the headlines, driving the Penn backs to the bottom of the newspaper stories.

Chuck also picked up a reputation as a colorful fellow. It evolved twofold: because of the football he flung into the stands after scoring his first college touchdown and because of the unintentionally witty things he reportedly said. Once, so the story goes, Chuck looked over the menu at a college banquet and saw that the main course was filet mignon. "Holy smoke," he is said to have commented, disappointed. "We got fish! "

Penn and Army tied up in a dogfight at Franklin Field in 1948.

"We had several injuries going into the game," recalled Red Blaik. "Penn's team doctor, who had formerly held the same position with Army, came into our dressing room before the game and offered us, if needed, the services of the Penn hospital, which was near the field. His motives may have been good, but our players took his suggestion as an affront. I had the doctor shown out and informed the Cadets that Penn was planning to manhandle them."

A sellout crowd of 73,248—Army-Penn games from 1945 through 1950 averaged 71,755—saw a tremendous battle. It included a 103-yard return of a kickoff for a touchdown by Bobby Jack Stuart. Trailing 20-18, on their own 26 with three minutes to play, the Cadets went the distance in seven plays. They were on Penn's 15-yard line with only 25 seconds left when Arnold Galiffa, Army's All-

*There was happiness aplenty at Franklin Field in 1947 as Pennsylvania fought back to tie mighty Army, 7-7. Dooney, who played a whale of a game, plunges over for the Penn touchdown.*

*Masterminding Pennsylvania's undefeated campaign in 1947 was the coaching staff; l. to r.: Paul Riblett, end; Horace Hendrickson, back; George Munger, head coach; Rea Crowther, line.*

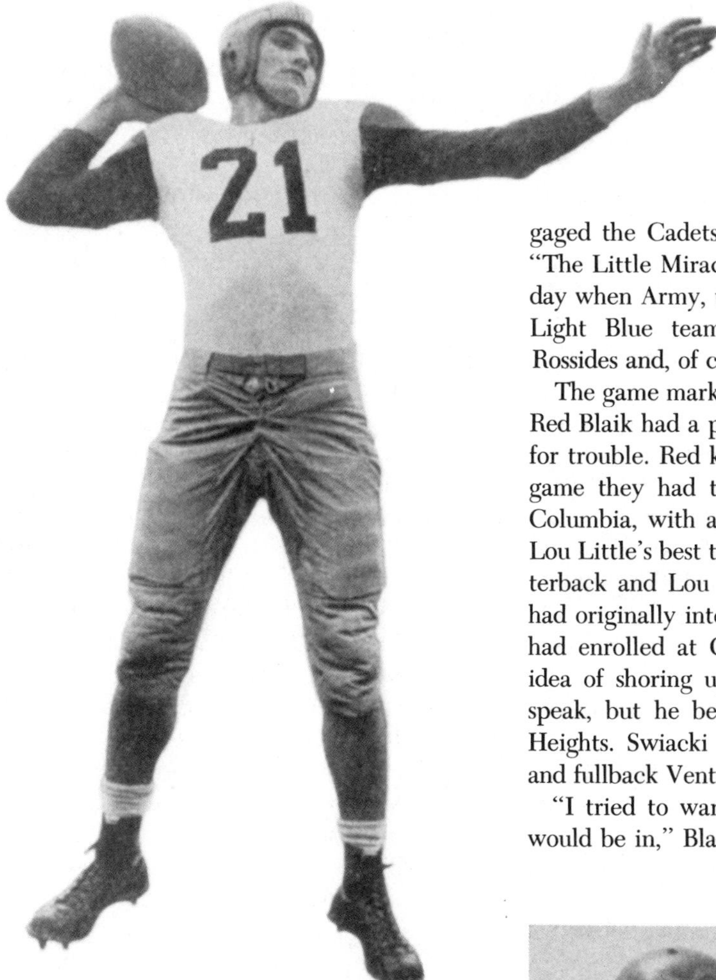

gaged the Cadets in what has since been labeled "The Little Miracle of Baker Field." That was the day when Army, unbeaten in 32 games, lost to the Light Blue team of Lou Kusserow and Gene Rossides and, of course, the great end Bill Swiacki.

The game marked Army's fifth of the season, and Red Blaik had a premonition that his boys were in for trouble. Red knew that to get by in any major game they had to be at their best at all times. Columbia, with a 6-2 record that fall, had one of Lou Little's best teams. Gene Rossides was at quarterback and Lou Kusserow at halfback. Kusserow had originally intended to go to Army. In fact, he had enrolled at Columbia for one year with the idea of shoring up his math, on lend lease so to speak, but he became enamored of Morningside Heights. Swiacki was a transfer from Holy Cross and fullback Ventan Yablonski was from Fordham.

"I tried to warn our players of the danger we would be in," Blaik said, "but I could not seem to

*Cocaptains of the 1947 Quakers were quarterback Carmen Falcone and All-America center and linebacker Chuck Bednarik.*

American quarterback, passed down the middle and Johnny Trent leaped and caught the ball in the end zone to win the game, 26-20. Later, Coach Blaik called it "one of the most splendid moments in Army football history."

The following year, Pennsylvania, accustomed to rugged football by this time, was unimpressed by undefeated Army's record or reputation, but the West Pointers, although hard pressed, won another thriller, 14-13, before 72,477. End Hal Loehlein saved the game for Army by blocking a field goal attempt.

° ° °

Penn did not have a lock on those heart-stoppers with the Point. In 1947, the Columbia Lions en-get through to them. After our Friday afternoon workout in Baker Field, I told my assistants, 'This team is not ready, and neither are you coaches.' "

In the dressing room before the kickoff, Blaik told his players, "If we don't snap out of it, we're going to get licked. I'm going to give the starting team five minutes to score. Otherwise, they'll be out of there."

Army scored after four and a half minutes and led at half time, 20-7. Rip Rowan ran 87 yards off tackle for a touchdown just before the half. As far as Coach Blaik was concerned, Rowan's run merely complicated his job of arousing his players.

"The Cadets spent most of the half time complaining about the officiating, something that occurred only one other time in my 25 years as a coach," Blaik confessed. "They were obsessed with the officiating. That's all they could talk about in the locker room. It was a most difficult thing for me to try and get them back into the game. I never did. They never really came back into the game. They didn't think it was possible to lose."

The Cadets were very ripe for a major upset, Blaik admitted.

At the end of the third quarter, Army still led, 20-7. In the fourth quarter, with the ball on the Army 28, Rossides hurled a pass down the middle into the end zone. Swiacki dove for it and the field judge called it completed.

"Careful study of our own and newsreel films the following Monday convinced us no catch was made," Blaik said. "But it was ruled a catch, and now they trailed us only 20 to 14."

Columbia had tremendous momentum going now. Blaik had sat through the game with a premonition of trouble—and now it was happening in full view of 35,000 witnesses. Army had allowed the Lions to gain control. To stop the quarterback's passes, Army shifted an extra man out of the line into the backfield. Rossides was smart enough to counter this by mixing in some runs, and the Lions marched 61 yards in six plays. Kusserow scored from the 2, Yablonski kicked the point.

More than 35,000 spectators looked up at the scoreboard in disbelief: Columbia 21, Army 20. The Cadets had not lost since 1943. For the first time all season, they had given up three touchdowns.

Time ran out, with Lou Kusserow intercepting an Army pass on his own 45-yard line. He returned it to midfield, and that was the ball game.

They called it the greatest Columbia victory since the Lions upset Stanford in the 1934 Rose Bowl.

In 1976, Red Blaik made this observation:

"Rossides was probably the headiest quarterback at Columbia any of my teams had ever met, and I'd been playing against Columbia football teams since 1932. What he did to our Army team in the last quarter was downright remarkable. We pulled a man out of the line to stop his passes, and he immediately hit us where we weren't. He mixed his plays beautifully. I'd seen all the great Columbia quarterbacks as undergraduates, but I don't think they ever had a better one than Gene Rossides."

Rossides, in victory, tied the all-time Columbia passing record with 18 completions, held jointly by Sid Luckman and Paul Governali. Kusserow, for his part, scored two touchdowns and added a game-saving interception on the last play of the game.

Recently, Rip Rowan was asked to explain why the Cadets were so terribly upset by the officiating that day. "We felt they had been somewhat unfair in some of their calls," he said. "That controversial Swiacki catch, for instance. Was it a catch or a noncatch? We thought it *wasn't* a catch. But the way Bill had been catching them all afternoon—well, the ball and Bill were there at the same time, and we knew the referee was going to give him the benefit of the doubt."

"It wasn't the calls they were making *for* Columbia, I don't mean that," added Arnold Galiffa. "What annoyed us were the calls they were making *against* us. For example, they nailed us with 15 or 16 in-motion penalties in our own backfield. I felt like I personally gained 500 yards—and got credit for only 150."

When asked in 1976 whether he actually caught the touchdown pass before it hit the turf, Bill Swiacki said, "Of course, I caught it. As I remember the play, it was a sort of out and down pattern. There was a defender between me and the ball. The ball was thrown to the inside and I had to get around him. But if you'll notice closely in the filmed rerun, my arm is *under* the ball, the ball is not under my arm. I caught passes that way many, many times, and practiced catching passes like that numerous times. What's more, the referee was right there ahead of the ball and was able to be on top of the play. He called it a legal catch."

Coach Blaik?

"I'll leave it up to the Columbia players to say," Blaik said, ending the controversy.

The Lions did not lose another game that fall. After Army, they rolled over Cornell, 22-0; Dart-

*Probably the two best backs Lou Little ever had together at Columbia were Gene Rossides, left, and Lou Kusserow.*

*Author Bill Heinz once described All-America Columbia end Bill Swiacki as one "who catches passes the way the rest of us catch common colds; he knows where he gets some, the rest he just picks up in a crowd."*

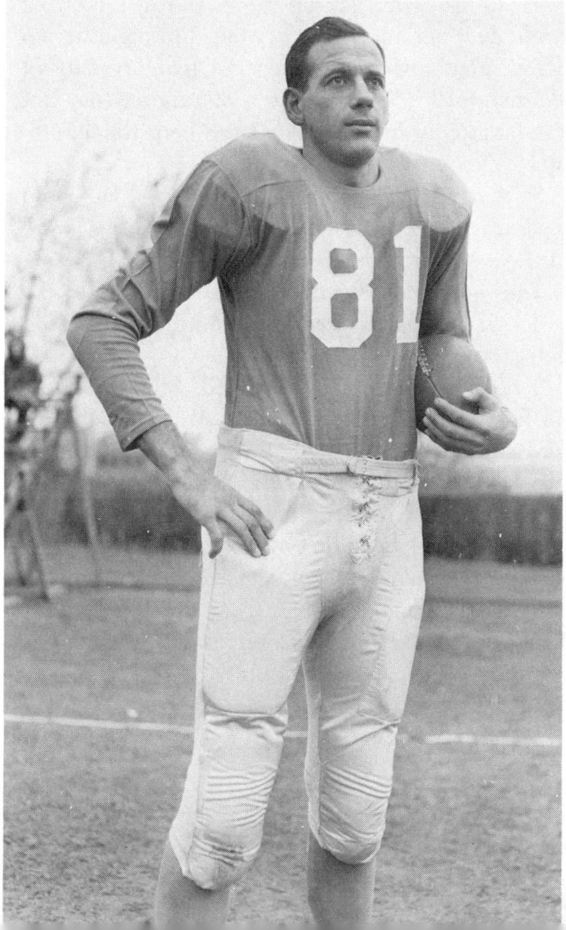

mouth, 15-0; Holy Cross, 10-0; and Syracuse, 28-8.

Lou Kusserow and Gene Rossides, probably the best two backs Lou Little ever had together, were the last to quit the locker room after helping to defeat Syracuse, 34-28, in their final game as Columbia football players in 1948, and they approached the coach together.

"Thank you," one of them said, "for everything you've done for us."

"I never did anything for you boys," Lou said, "you did everything for me."

They walked out together and Lou Little watched them go, and he had to be thinking how wonderful it was to be spending his life working with young men.

Those were the years when the Columbia University Taxi Cab Alumni, one of New York's least fashionable, most unexclusive clubs, was in its glory. They had only two qualifications for membership: the candidate could not be a graduate of Columbia, and the candidate had to pledge complete and exclusive loyalty to Lou Little and his football team. The membership included such

Broadway types as movie producer Mark Hellinger, Toots Shor, Ted Husing, Bill Corum, Quentin Reynolds, Milton Berle, Joe E. Lewis, John Garfield, Joe DiMaggio, Tom Meany of *PM*, Garry Schumacher of the New York Baseball Giants, Coach Steve Owen of the New York Football Giants, and the only English member, C. V. R. Thompson, distinguished representative of the *London Daily Express*, who lost his English accent at Baker Field during the 1947 Army-Columbia game.

There *were* those who felt that the Taxi Cab Alumni were fanatical and sometimes carried their devotion to their adopted university too far. A case in point: Ulric Calvosa, one of their oldest members, was the picture editor of *Collier's Weekly*. Each year *Collier's* picked an All-America team. It was Calvosa's job to have pictures of all likely choices available. The editor of *Collier's*, Walter Davenport, told him to hire a dozen photographers and send them around the country getting pictures of all potential stars. Calvosa said he would need only one photographer and he would have all the pictures within 24 hours.

The next day Calvosa handed Davenport 35 pictures of football players. They were fine. But Davenport was a bit puzzled because they all seemed to be wearing the same uniform. Calvosa explained that it seemed foolish to send a photographer way out to South Bend to take a picture of a guy like Johnny Lujack when you could get Gene Rossides right up at Baker Field. He said that it seemed a sinful waste of money to send lensmen to Michigan or California for pictures of those tramps when you had Kusserow and Gehrke and Swiacki and Hasselman and Yablonski right there in town.

"Why," said Calvosa, "I've saved you at least $5,000 in expenses, and there you got 35 players to choose from. I don't say all of them are of All-America caliber, but certainly 11 of them are and that's all we need—11 men. So what if they are all from Columbia? "

Walter Davenport agreed—not surprising in view of the fact that he was a charter member of the CUTCA.

One fall, Mark Hellinger was offered a job broadcasting Columbia games. This he liked. He could see the game for free from a very good seat. But it was too much to ask that Hellinger be impartial. One day Syracuse came to Baker Field with a good team. With seconds to go, Syracuse led, 13-12. But Columbia was on the Syracuse 10-yard line. The Columbia quarterback faded back to pass. He looked for a receiver and spotted one all alone in the end zone. He threw the pass.

"He's got it," Hellinger yelled into the microphone. "He's got . . . damn it all, he dropped it and there's the whistle ending the game. And those lucky bums from Syracuse beat us, 13-12."

That was a sample of Mark Hellinger's type of broadcasting. Any time a team beat Columbia, as far as the CUTCA faithful were concerned, they were "lucky bums." It could be said that the CUTCA members were not good losers.

Perhaps out of sympathy for his CUTCA followers, Lou Little put together three of his best seasons in 1945, '46, and '47, winning 21 of 27 games. But then Lou's Lions faded to 4-5 and 2-7, as Cornell (8-1-0) and Brown (7-2-0) in 1948, and then Cornell (8-1-0) and Brown (8-1-0) again in 1949, pretty much dominated their opponents as the forties wound down to the end of the decade.

° ° °

Early in the winter of 1948, Howie Odell sat talking with a newspaper friend in the Yale Club in New York.

"You know," Odell said, "Fritz Crisler has this coaching business figured out right. He came to Princeton when Princeton was down and built her up. When he saw the glory days were about over, he left Princeton and he took the Michigan job because Michigan was down and could only go up. Now, he has Michigan up there, and he's quitting while he's on top. That's what I'm figuring on doing. That's why I'm going out to University of Washington. It will be tough out there, too. But Washington is down. Maybe I can help them build up."

So that was it. Odell was leaving Yale. He could have stayed on, with a 19-7-1 record since the end of the war. But Odell was no traditionalist. Losing at Yale would have been just as hard for him to take as losing any place else. And the Yale picture did not appear bright.

To find a replacement for Odell, Athletic Director Bob Hall and such other Yale Athletic Committee members as Chet LaRoche and Ted Blair surveyed the field carefully. For a while, Lou Little was mentioned. He could have had the job, but finally decided he didn't want it. The man they took was Herman Michael Hickman, Jr., a hydrant-shaped mountain of a man from the hills of east Tennessee, who had been serving at West Point as

*Before going on to huge success at Penn State, Rip Engle served as head coach at Brown, 1944–49.*

Red Blaik's right hand from 1943 through 1947. Hickman was an excellent line coach, a solidly grounded football man. He had developed six All-America linemen at the Point.

"In the first interview I ever had with Herman," recalled Red Blaik, "to impress me with his seriousness about becoming my line coach at West Point, he said, 'Colonel, I have three loves: my wife, football, and my belly. And I don't rightfully know which I love most."

The 300-pound Hickman, prince of raconteurs, was the perfect foil for Blaik. He supplied the humor and the light touch that Red lacked. The jovial southerner could get closer to the players than the austere Blaik.

Every evening promptly at seven o'clock, Hickman had orders to report with a car at Blaik's home. Then they spent the next two hours touring the Hudson highlands, while Herman kept up a running fire of chatter to divert Red's intense mind from pressing football problems. In a way, Herman was sort of a court jester, an illusion heightened by his ample girth and prodigious appetite. Like Falstaff, Herman was a mighty trencherman, and the ascetic Blaik, who rarely touched liquor and ate sparingly, took delight in the gastronomic exploits of his affable assistant.

One morning, Herman began the day with a breakfast of orange juice and cereal, a mighty steak, a monumental ham, heaps of hashed-brown potatoes, hot hush puppies, jam, and coffee. "Actually," Herman related later, "I disregarded the cereal and jam and got right down to fundamentals—the food."

"In his first few years with us," Red Blaik recalled, "Herman's weight rose from 270 pounds to 330. I became greatly concerned about this and finally persuaded him to see a doctor. A diet was prescribed, and Herman gave it an heroic try. He lost from 25 to 30 pounds in a month. It so happened he also contracted a severe cold in the drafty highlands, and pneumonia threatened. When he recovered, Herman said with feeling, 'I love and respect Colonel Blaik, but if I am going to die, I want to die happy and not from starvation and its complications.' "

It was a sad day for Blaik when Yale lured Hickman away from West Point, not because Red couldn't find as able a line coach, but because he realized that no one else was ever again going to give him the psychic lift provided by fat Herman.

A well-rounded man in more ways than one, rotund Herman early developed a fondness for literature, especially poetry. His extraordinary memory enabled him to recite volumes of it from such favorites as Rudyard Kipling and Edgar Lee Masters. His fine voice, presence, command of English, and warm sense of humor made him a popular fixture on the platform, radio, and TV circuit.

When Herman was asked what system he was going to use at Yale, he replied: "I favor the three-platoon system. One platoon for offense, one for defense, and one to go to class."

One day Herman was diagraming some defensive maneuvers in the presence of his former college coach, Brigadier General Robert Neyland of Tennessee. He turned for Neyland's expected approval.

"Herman," Neyland said, "I guess all those defenses must be pretty good, but there is just one thing that you've got to remember: in order to be a successful head coach you must have *men* instead of X's and O's."

And Herman said, "Oh, 'tis true, 'tis true."

° ° °

Jimmy Jemail, the Inquiring Reporter for so many years on the *New York News*, once asked a black man in Harlem what, in his opinion, was the most important event ever to happen to blacks in the United States.

"You expect me to say that it was Lincoln's freeing of the slaves," the Harlem man replied, "but I'm going to fool you. In my book, it was when the Yale football team elected Levi Jackson captain of the 1949 squad. It couldn't happen—but it did!"

The son of a dining hall waiter, Levi Jackson starred at Hillhouse High School in New Haven and blossomed into a town idol. Reggie Root, head coach at Yale in 1933, was his high school mentor. Reggie testifies that the turning point in young Jackson's career came when Hillhouse played New London High School. Levi got a terrible going-over that day and asked Root to take him out of the game.

"Coach," Levi told him, "they're giving me the works because of my color. I can't take such a beating."

"Levi," Reggie replied, "your color has nothing to do with it. They're making you the target because you are our big gun and they want to get you out of there. You should have seen the roughing Yale's Mal Stevens took in 1923 when he was our meal ticket."

Reggie Root's little venture into human psychology made a changed man of Levi Jackson. He followed Reggie to Yale and never once thereafter complained about being manhandled, although he took more than his share of punishment.

*Herman Hickman, Poet Laureate of the Great Smokies.*

*Tennessean Herman Hickman in Yale Bowl with star back and captain of the 1949 Bulldogs, Levi Jackson, Yale's first black player.*

When Tennessean Hickman was appointed head coach at Yale in 1948, repercussions were feared, but Herman walked right up to halfback Jackson in the locker room and, smiling broadly, said: "Levi, I sure am glad to see you here." The rest of the story is football history.

Although the Elis lost more games than they won (8-9-0) in Hickman's first two years at Yale, they did not lose their sense of humor. Because of their lack of girth, the good-natured Herman had nicknamed his linemen "The Seven Dwarfs." One day the linemen showed up at the practice field wearing strips of adhesive tape on their chests with the names of the dwarfs printed on them, "Dopey," "Sleepy," "Bashful," and so on. Levi Jackson, who also had a keen sense of humor, wore a strip lettered "Snow White."

Yale, as Hickman found out, was an ideal place for somebody who wanted to coach, for there was lots of coaching to be done. Herman and his assistants rolled up their sleeves and went to work. Morning coaching meetings were called for 7 o'clock. The first morning, one of Hickman's assistants overslept and arrived late.

"There will be only one excuse for not being here on time," said Hickman severely, "and that's death."

Then he turned to Stu Clancy, assistant coach who doubled as an embalmer in surburban Branford, and added, "I'm not referring to *professional* death, Clancy. I mean *private.*"

Hickman was one of the few modern coaches who could get away with an old-fashioned locker room pep talk. Exhortation is no longer in vogue with members of the coaching cult. The more sophisticated breed of college athlete today would scoff at the up-and-at-em fight talks of the Bill Roper era, but Hickman was able to spout poetry without provoking snickers. Grantland Rice labeled him the "Poet Laureate of the Great Smokies." Before one Harvard-Yale game, stout Herman rallied his troops by reciting Patrick Henry's Revolutionary War speech: "I can hear the chains clanking in the streets of Boston; the Redcoats are forging them for you. . . ."

Every year Herman got the names of football players among incoming freshmen, assembled reports on their skills from their prep school coaches, and when he chanced upon a particularly choice and meaty morsel, he penciled in a special term of endearment: "Tenderloin."

"But those tenderloins," he said one day after looking the rookies over in the flesh, "they sure shrink in shipment."

"How about that kid you were talking about who could do everything but walk on water?" he was asked. "The one who was captain of all those high school teams and president of his class and won all those honors from dramatics and essays and music and everything?"

"A sad case," Herman said. "He never showed up. Died of self-esteem."

Hickman frequently quoted the classics to get his team up for a game. As his squad was about to take the field for a practice session one Friday afternoon, he suddenly raised his hand for silence. The players were tense, waiting for the formula that might enable them to defeat Harvard. And then his voice began reverberating through the dressing room:

" 'Ye call me chief,' " he declaimed, " 'and ye do well to call me chief. If ye are men, follow me! Strike down your guard, gain the mountain passes, and there do bloody work as did your sires at old Thermopylae!' " His voice impassioned now, his features grim with determination. " 'Is Sparta dead? Is the old Grecian spirit frozen in your veins, that you do crouch and cower like a belabored hound beneath his master's last? O, comrades, warriors, Thracians! If we must fight, let us fight for ourselves. If we must slaughter, let us slaughter our oppressors! If we must die, let it be under the clear sky, by the bright waters, in noble, honorable battle!' "

Then, having concluded his rendition of *Spartacus to the Gladiators,* he snapped his fingers. "Whadya say, men," he growled. "Let's go, gang. Whadya say, let's go chew up those Harvards."

Good ol' Herman Hickman.

# *Football in the Early Fifties*

For shocks and surprises, 1950 was a memorable year in college football. Notre Dame, the preseason favorite, finished with a humble 4-4-1 record. Mighty Army was derailed as Red Blaik's express-train runners were ganged by Navy's wreckers in their finale. Other elevens, such as Southern Methodist, Ohio State, and Vanderbilt, that started the season sensationally, hit the skids hard along the way.

Records fell like confetti over the nation's stadiums. Drake's Johnny Bright (total yardage gained in a season), Nebraska's Bobby Reynolds (season NCAA major college scorer), Washington's Don Heinrich (passes completed in a season), and Pennsylvania's Reds Bagnell (total yards gained in a single game) were among the pacesetters.

Of the three major unbeaten, untied college teams that emerged from regular season competition, only Princeton (9-0-0) survived New Year's Day—probably only because the Tigers kept up a traditional policy of avoiding postseason games! At any rate, the big news of the East was the dethroning of Army, which had won the Lambert Trophy five of the previous six years. Old Nassau, 5-0-0 in Ivy Group play and 9-0-0 overall, epitomized several trends of football in general: the predominance of the swift-striking offense, the rise to importance of the deceptive single wing as challenger to the T formation, and Ivy return to national prominence.

Masterfully executed plays by the quartet of Dick Kazmaier, Bill Kleinsasser (or Bob Unger), Jack Davison, and George Chandler behind a line anchored on Holland Donan and Redmond Finney made Princeton the national headliner and won for Charlie Caldwell the Coach-of-the-Year honors.

For the fourth straight year, the Tigers won the Big Three championship, burying Harvard, 63-26, and Yale, 47-12. "This is the finest Princeton eleven since 1935," wrote Allison Danzig in *The New York Times*. "In scoring its 12th successive victory since 1949, Princeton brought its point total for the season to 336. It thus excelled the modern Tiger record of 322 scored by Fritz Crisler's 1935 champions."

Against Harvard the week before, Princeton had rushed across four touchdowns in 11 minutes from the opening kickoff. Once it set sail in the Yale Bowl, in front of 59,000 heavily bundled witnesses, midway in the first period, it threatened to duplicate that furious pace, and in the space of only a few minutes whatever hopes underdog Yale entertained of winning were knocked into a cocked hat as the contest turned into a rout.

With those twin high-executioners, Dick Kazmaier and Bill Kleinsasser, going on the tear, Princeton drove 50, 63, and 54 yards for touchdowns in breathtaking succession in a total of a mere 12 plays. Kazmaier, who scored only one touchdown but passed for three others to Captain George Chandler, Kleinsasser, and end Ed Reed, was the chief artisan of the victory, gaining 147 yards along the ground and completing 8 of 10 passes for 102 more yards.

The Tiger defensive line and the backers-up also distinguished themselves, with Holland Donan, Frank Reichel, Bill Hickok, and Cliff Kurrus par-

*Fullback Bob Spears scores for Yale in 1950 victory over Fordham, 21-14. The son of Dr. Clarence (Fat) Spears could block, tackle, pick up extra yards, and he captained the Bulldogs in 1951.*

ticularly outstanding. They shut down so hard on Yale's running operations from the T, with a flanker, that the Elis could gain only 87 yards by rushing, to Princeton's 352.

In winning the Big Three title for the fourth time in a row, the Tigers tied the mark set by Percy Haughton's Crimson teams of 1912–15.

° ° °

Meanwhile, Pennsylvania was headed for a tie with Princeton in Ivy League standings, after upsetting powerful Wisconsin, 20-0, when Cornell outsplashed the Quakers in a rainstorm at Franklin Field, 13-6. Cornell, 4-2-0 against the Ivies, had another strong team, but was unable to match its 1949 record after losing to Princeton, 27-0, and Columbia, 20-19.

Kazmaier, Donan, and Finney of the Tigers all received All-America recognition in the national polls.

° ° °

The New York *Herald-Tribune* summed up the 1951 college football prospects for the East as good.

"At this preseason point," forecast the paper, "Red Blaik's powerful Army Cadets rate the top position, and Navy declared its intentions of getting back into the top bracket by whipping the Black Knights, 14-2, in last season's finale. In Ivy circles, Cornell and Pennsylvania loom as the teams to beat. . . ."

So what happened? Army finished with a 2-7 record, Navy was 2-6-1, Cornell 6-3, and Penn 5-4. For the second straight season, Princeton, which had been severely crippled by graduation losses at the outset, wound up with most of the national honors and a 9-0-0 record once more. The Tigers ranked with Tennessee, Michigan State, Maryland, Illinois, and Georgia Tech as one of the top six teams in the country. No Ivy eleven has since finished that high in the national polls.

In September, Charlie Caldwell had been faced with a vast reconstruction job. He had lost 25 of 40 lettermen—10 first-string attackers and six top defenders. Only the extraordinary Dick Kazmaier remained in the backfield. But the highly resourceful Coach Caldwell had a way of bringing stars along, and 1951 was no exception.

By now, the T craze had caught on across the country, and practically every single wing coach had switched to it. Caldwell had experimented with it too, but when the chips were down he decided that the single wing was what he knew best and was the most reliable. Based on sheer power, with two-on-one blocking in the line to force short but sure gains, Caldwell's single wing was set up like a massed infantry attack. "Let the

*Tiger great, Dick Kazmaier.*

others stampede to the T," he said. "They're giving me an advantage. They will spend so much time learning how to defense against the different forms of the T, that they'll lack the *feel* when it comes time to tackling our single wing."

The 1951 Tigers made their coach appear as a genuine expert. They opened the season by beating New York University, 54-20; Navy, 24-20; Penn, 13-7; Lafayette, 60-7; and Cornell, 53-15. Before the Brown game, I asked Caldwell what he thought of all those Monday morning quarterbacks who claimed that single wing football was antiquated when compared with the versatile modern T.

Caldwell only laughed.

"It depends upon whose single wing or T it is," he said. "The single wing I use at Princeton is a complex and elaborate system involving power, deception, perfect timing, and multiple threats from different sides. It is still geared to the power block, but the whole attack is more like an armored spearhead, which concentrates its full weight for short spurts but always threatens to go the whole distance to the goal line."

The old-style muscleman would have been totally befuddled by Caldwell's intricate offensive formations (24 in all) or the 36 spreads and shifts of the defense. Caldwell felt that agility was more important than size. During his unbeaten seasons of 1950 and 1951, for example, his biggest regular defensive lineman was 198-pound end Frank McPhee.

"Most of our heavyweights are on the jayvee," Caldwell said at the time. "A slow reactor can't play for us. What we require is, first, speed and, second, intelligence. Dumb football players can't play our game."

In the single wing, it was all specialists. A coach had to have a center who could snap the ball unerringly while upside down. He needed a quarterback who was a vicious blocker, yet fast enough

*Princeton's Charlie Caldwell.*

to stay ahead of his backs. He needed a fullback who could spin and pivot like a ballet dancer but had power to rip a line apart. Of course, the tailback was the core of the team. He had to run, pass, kick, and even block, and he had to be durable enough to stand up under game-to-game pounding. But probably the hardest man to come by was the wingback. He needed a sprinter's speed, the niftiness of a scatback, and the strength to block an end or halfback who might go 200 or 220.

To keep his Tigers nimble, Caldwell borrowed one of the tortures of the academic inquisition. Every Sunday afternoon in a darkened room in Osborn Clubhouse, the Princeton coaching staff gathered before a movie screen. The film of the last game was run off, slow motion, and every player's every play was dissected and graded by the coaching staff. Later, the players got their marks individually—and for each one a spot on next week's lineup was at stake. The grades ranged from 1 "for superb effort like a triple block," to 7 "for a bonehead play or a costly fumble." A grade of 4 was average.

The linemen were checked as meticulously as the backs. Under Caldwell's system, the unsung offensive lineman had to be almost as alert as the quarterback in diagnosing the defense. In fact, the offensive lineman was often a signal caller for his own particular area, calling for specialized blocks in cadence with the quarterback. According to Caldwell, this innovation of "line quarterbacking" insured efficient blocking for an opening and counteracted any sudden defensive shift. And since the single wing attack depended on the precision and effectiveness of two-on-one blocking, Princeton players were taught a bewildering variety, from the simple "shoulder" block to such ramifications as the cross-body, reverse cross-body, and "peelback" blocks (blocks thrown behind the runner, "peeling" them off his back so that he has room to move laterally in his downfield progress).

That kind of blocking, plus astute "line quarterbacking," ripped open holes big enough for any back, and during the glittering years of 1950–52, Princeton ball carriers scored a total of 956 points (to 250 for opponents) while winning 26 out of 27 games.

Caldwell felt that one of the single wing's biggest assets was that it lent itself to ball control. In one big 1951 game, for example, there were 137 plays. Princeton had the ball for 101.

"When our opponents came in pressing, to stop the steady attack, we went outside or passed them silly," Caldwell said. "When they drew back a little, we resumed the inside and reverse plays."

Caldwell then told why modern coaches were afraid to employ the single wing. He listed alumni displeasure and the reaction of the players, believing mistakenly that the single wing was old-fashioned. At schools where full stadiums were financially necessary, coaches were loath to institute any system that might lessen attendance because of the lack of fan-pleasing, wide-open football. A coach attributing his use of one system or the other to his material was utter nonsense, according to Caldwell.

"If you have the material for the T, you have the material for the single wing," he said.

Caldwell pointed out that passing tactics also demonstrated the difference between the two systems, and here he gave the single wing another plus.

"The T quarterback takes the ball from center, swings back faking a pitchout, and runs back farther to pass," he said. "He gets little opportunity to spot anyone except the primary receiver. On the other hand, the single wing passer is always looking forward, watching developments, and spotting secondary receivers in case the primary one is covered. He doesn't commit himself to pass until the last second, and defending backs cannot give undivided attention to potential receivers until he does. Many times the play continues as a ground attack."

Listening to Caldwell and watching his Tigers win 30 of 31 games in one streak, I wondered at the time why so many coaches were switching to the modern T with man in motion. They had modern football at its best all the while. All they had to do was embellish it, as Charlie Caldwell had.

The core of the Tigers was Richard William Kazmaier, winner of the Heisman, Maxwell, and Camp awards in 1951—the last Ivy Leaguer to win the Heisman. In retrospect, he is also a refreshing reminder, in the somewhat fetid atmosphere that has since gathered around the pseudo-amateurs of American sports, that winning football was not yet dominated by huge pro-bound players often taking snap courses at football factories. In a day when most backfields averaged 185 pounds, Kazmaier was a slender 5′11″ and 171 pounds. He was also a senior at a small university (3,000) that did not buy its football teams. At Princeton he had a scholarship, just as 42 percent of his teammates did (and 40 percent of all Princeton undergraduates). He was an above-average student majoring in psychology. He had no intention of using football as a passport to a professional athletic career.

When Princeton's 1951 varsity assembled for its first practice that fall, Dick Kazmaier was the only holdover from the 1950 offensive platoon of Princeton's 9-0-0 champions. Only five veterans were left in the defensive platoon. Coach Caldwell, like most other Princeton alumni, glumly figured that 1951 would be a "rebuilding year." Even after Princeton rolled impressively over New York University, Navy, Pennsylvania, and Lafayette, Caldwell was still stubbornly insisting: "This team hasn't the authority of last year's."

But after Princeton's 53-15 drubbing of Cornell, even cautious Caldwell had to admit that it looked as if he were heading for another perfect season and another Lambert Trophy. In a spectacular one-man show, Kazmaier ripped through the undefeated Cornell line, averaging 7 yards a crack, completed a phenomenal 15 out of 17 passes, and personally accounted for 360 yards gained—70 percent of Princeton's total and more, by half as much again, than the entire Cornell backfield. Cornell's veteran coach, Lefty James, said after the game, with the disarming candor of the squashed: "The greatest back I've ever seen." And Allison Danzig, reporting in *The New York Times,* called Kazmaier's performance "one of the greatest passing exhibitions ever seen on any gridiron since the introduction of the pass in 1906."

Against Harvard two weeks later, the score was 6-6 and the first half had only three minutes left. Princeton had the ball on Harvard's 31-yard line, fourth down, nine to go. As the Orange and Black huddle broke up, the Tigers trotted into their single wing formation. The quarterback barked, the ball shot back from the center. The slim tailback with number 42 on his jersey took the pass waist high; with practiced ease he threw a screen pass. It was good for a first down on the Harvard 10. On the next play, pivoting as precisely as a ballet dancer, he ran—he didn't seem to be running very fast—toward the right sideline. Harvard tacklers closed in. Just before they were on him, and with hardly a break in his stride, Number 42 cocked his right arm and threw. A Princeton end, running toward the goal line—he didn't seem to be going very fast either—caught the ball on the 1. The fullback bucked it over. Princeton 12, Harvard 6. In the 70 seconds of playing time before the half was over, Princeton scored again, this time on an intercepted Harvard pass.

On the Princeton side of the stadium the megaphones bellowed. As the half ended, the Princeton stands rose, applauding. They were mostly applauding Number 42—halfback Dick Kazmaier. Before the afternoon was over, they had even more cause to cheer. Thanks mainly to Kazmaier's passing (for 222 yards, 12 out of 16 completed, for three touchdowns), Harvard went down to its worst defeat ever inflicted by a Princeton team, 54 to 13. Princeton had broken its old record of 19 straight games and stretched the nation's longest winning streak to 20.

Kazmaier, who came from Maumee, Ohio, hardly looked the part of a triple-threat halfback. Off the football field, he was undistinguished and indistinguishable from hundreds of other Princeton undergraduates with their crewcuts and carefully sloppy clothes. He did not feel that he had to die for dear old Princeton. A serious 20-year-old, he rated his interests in this order: friends, studies, football. He played the game because he liked it, a view that would have been considered heretical by old Bill Roper, who once exploded: "The people who think football is a game are crazy. Football is *war!*" Whatever Coach Roper chose to call it, Kazmaier played it exceptionally well because, starting with a good share of natural ability, he also had a burning zeal to excel, which made him a meticulous attender to details. At practice he wanted to know the reason for every split-second step in every play; once he was convinced, he practiced until he had it muscle perfect.

On the practice field, under the orange-and-black helmet that added a grimness to his features, Kazmaier showed more of the fussiness of the perfectionist than the jet-flaming drive of a great halfback. But the flame was building up; it appeared on Saturdays. On the first play from scrimmage he was so tense that quarterback George Stevens had standing instructions not to let him handle the ball (a ground rule that wily Coach Caldwell was always capable of breaking against an unwary opponent). Once the warm-up of the first play was over, Kazmaier took off. Poised in his tailback spot, he provided the explosive charge that made the Princeton attack the fearsome weapon it was. The defending team was never quite sure what Kazmaier was going to do: run, pass, or quick-kick. He was effective at all three. His running had no pounding power, no blinding speed. But a trail of sprawling, frustrated tacklers attested to a swivel-hipped shiftiness, a ball-bearing glide that enabled him to change pace or direction without losing stride.

"He runs 'light,' with a nice forward lean," said Judd Timm, the Princeton backfield coach, an ex-trackman at Illinois. "If he wants to slow down to pick up a blocker, he just straightens up a bit."

When the opposing defense tightened to stop the running attack, Kazmaier was even more dangerous. He was a sharpshooting passer, and he had the rare ability of throwing on the dead run. His jump passes—that is, short gainers—were thrown "hard," of necessity; he had to get them off fast. The deeper ones, depending on the situation, were sometimes floaters. His biggest asset was accuracy.

"Kaz always hit 'em on the back of the head," said admiring Coach Caldwell.

Kazmaier's kicking was also a source of satisfaction to Caldwell. "We have boys who can kick the ball farther—though Kaz can boot it 60 yards—but none so dependable. We want high, accurate kicks so our tacklers can get underneath the ball." And here again Kazmaier got them off fast, and had to; for "protection" time he was allowed only one and a half seconds.

On Caldwell's run-pass option play, Kazmaier's triple talents came into full use. That was the key play on which the success of the Princeton attack depended. Kazmaier started to run laterally as the ball was snapped. He took the pass from center while three possible receivers started downfield, each to different depths. A fourth receiver, the end on the weak side, kept the safetyman decoyed. The deep man was, of course, the primary target. But if all four receivers were blanketed, Kazmaier could just tuck the ball under his arm and take off through the thinly spread defense, while his receivers turned into downfield blockers. In explaining the simple beauty of the play, Caldwell said: "The defense just can't cope with both the pass and the threat of the run, but only a player like Kazmaier makes it as unstoppable as it is."

Kazmaier was the first to acknowledge his debt to his Princeton teammates. In addition to a hard-charging line, he was also blessed with half a dozen agile, sure-fingered pass receivers like quarterback Stevens, ends Len Lyons and McPhee, one of the few who played on both the offensive and defensive platoons and himself All-American. And one of the big reasons for Princeton's undefeated status in 1950 and 1951 was the defensive platoon, "quarterbacked" by Captain Dave Hickok.

"They are the players," said Caldwell, "who let us get our hands on that ball."

Kazmaier's attitude toward his teammates who played defense was deferential and slightly superstitious. When the defense was making a stand deep in its own territory against Harvard, Kazmaier watched from the bench with his helmet off, so as not to put the "whammy" on them. He himself made no more than two or three tackles during his entire varsity career. Caldwell felt that he was too valuable a property to risk on that jarring job. But he got his share of lumps and bumps by enduring a series of smashing tackles and pile-ons whenever he ran, also getting knocked flat when he passed or kicked. The big white 42 on Kazmaier's chest and back marked the number one target for every opposing player.

After a rugged game against Brown in 1951—a game Kazmaier won, 12-0, with touchdown sprints of 13 and 61 yards on a field piebald with mud and snow—trainer Eddie Zanfrini gave Caldwell the casualty report, ending with: "My gosh, Kaz is black and blue all over." But Dick was durable. In three years of varsity competition, he missed only one sequence of plays (two minutes) when he was needed. That time he was knocked cold.

With Kazmaier and the others, Princeton looked very good in 1950 and 1951, winning the Lambert Trophy—but how good was it? Like the other members of the Ivy group, it played mostly only Eastern teams. The $64,000 question was, how would Princeton stack up against the powerful Big Ten in the Midwest or the giants of the West Coast? A 1951 Associated Press poll of sportwriters ranked Princeton fourth, behind Tennessee, Illinois, and Maryland, and ahead of Michigan State and Southern California. Many observers, looking at what happened in mid-November to two of Princeton's earlier victims (Cornell, which beat Michigan, 20-7, and Penn, which held Wisconsin to 16-7), felt that undefeated Princeton deserved to be ranked even higher. Coach Caldwell, 1950's Coach of the Year, took the middle, or Caldwell, view. He believed that his team on any given Saturday could have held its own with any team in the nation. But meeting power teams week after week would have been another matter. Princeton was a small college, with a small squad—and only one Kazmaier.

"Our schedule is easy, hard—easy, hard," Caldwell pointed out realistically. "In the Big Ten, for example, it's boom! boom! boom! We haven't the depth to stand that."

Princeton, like most of the Ivy Group, was short of football material for the simple reason that it was not a competitive bidder in the football market. Under a Big Three agreement, Harvard, Yale, and Princeton exchanged information on all their varsity football players. Competitive bidding in the form of scholarship offers was frowned on. Each athlete had to fill out a form showing the source of his finances; if any extracurricular subsidy cropped up, the player in question was declared ineligible. Kazmaier was a good example of how well the system worked.

Princeton's 1951 director of admissions once recalled his first meeting with Kazmaier: "Dick had been recommended as an all-around high school athlete, and I didn't know what to think when I first saw that peanut (155 pounds) walk in. I remember writing on his card after the interview: 'Probably not big enough for college athletics.' But we were glad to have him. We were interested in him for other reasons."

Princeton's director of student aid later explained that the kind of boy they wanted was the one who was going to run the Community Chest in his hometown some day. "We want him to be in the top 8 percent of his class, to be class president, editor of the school paper," he said.

Kazmaier fit the pattern. His high school grades were mostly A's, and he had been president of his class and of Hi-Y. He got his scholarship, a $400 grant, which fell $200 short of Princeton's tuition fee in 1948, his freshman year. He lost it for one term (in 1950) because his grades slipped during football season.

Even though Princeton was slow to appreciate him as an athlete, Dick had been a five-letter man at Maumee High School in Ohio. He quarterbacked the football team, was shortstop on the baseball team, high scorer on the basketball team (23 points a game), fastest man on the track team (10.3 seconds for the 100-yard dash), number two man on the golf team (middle 80s). Although he never made an all-state team, his athletic versatility did not pass unnoticed. In fact, 23 colleges approached him with offers.

Kazmaier was originally steered to Princeton by an alert alumnus, a Toledo lawyer named Gilmore Flues (1926). Flues, watching Dick play in a losing football game, was impressed by the way the youngster "instinctively did the right thing."

To get into Princeton, Dick had to pass the college board exams. To stay there, he had to do odd jobs around the campus (waiting on tables, driving laundry trucks) to supplement his scholarship. And since a year at Princeton cost a minimum of $1,700 in those days, he had to work every summer to get more money.

Kazmaier went out for freshman football, of course. But as a 155-pound freshman substitute, he got lost in the shuffle until the final game, when he earned a starting role.

In spring practice, when Caldwell first got a good look at him, he figured that Dick was too light for varsity football. Not until the 1949 Rutgers game, Kazmaier's sophomore year, did he demonstrate that he was tough enough to stand the pounding.

"From then on," Caldwell recalled later, "I knew we had something special."

Harland (Pinky) Baker, rabid member of Princeton's class of 1922, cannot even now rid his mind of the Dartmouth-Princeton game played during hurricane Flora in 1950. Princeton won, 13-7, as Kazmaier ran for two touchdowns to assure himself All-America recognition. The day will always be remembered in Ivy circles as "the day of the big wind." It was no weather for football. When kicking against the wind, the ball would soar vertically and be blown backward, often for a loss of yardage. Punting with the wind, the ball would sail 60 or 70 yards downfield.

"There were only 100 Princeton men watching that day and 10 or 12 Dartmouth people across the way," Pinky Baker recalled. "I watched the game peeking out from behind a concrete ramp, couldn't even face the wind. I was wearing these big wading boots that I use for goose and duck shooting and I wore a sou'wester. The wind just *sang* down the field, just god-awful. It was impossible to punt the ball because it came right back in your face. So it was better to run on fourth down against the wind no matter where you were on the field. They almost called the game off, but Dartmouth came all that way and the championship was at stake. Princeton needed a victory to edge out Penn for the title. I remember that wind picked up Kazmaier when he crossed the goal line, and it carried him clear into the cement stands at the end of the stadium—just ripped him up against the stone. Oh, I can't get that game out of my mind. I'll tell you something. There were so few people there it was like they were playing it all for me . . . just for my benefit."

# THE DAY OF THE HURRICANE

**Things went from bad . . .**

**To worse**

*Proof of what Princeton and Dartmouth fans mean when they talk about November 13, 1950—"The Day of the Hurricane." The Tigers won, 13-7, and Dick Kazmaier ran—it was no weather for football.*

Charley Dey, who was the Dartmouth right end and place-kicker, was amazed that the game was even played. "When we left the hotel in Trenton that morning, the wind had blown out the plate glass downstairs and trees were down everywhere," he said. "During the game our equipment trunks were afloat on the track behind our bench."

"There were pools of water an inch deep all over the field," added Jack Davison, who played fullback that day for Princeton. "The officials had to hold the ball and hand it to the center when he was ready to snap it. If they set it down it would float away."

While Pinky Baker was braving the storm in Palmer Stadium, I was covering the Harvard-Yale game in Cambridge for the *NEA* syndicate. Sitting alongside me in the pressbox was George Trevor, of the New York *World-Telegram & Sun.* Cambridge was fortunate to escape the deluge that wiped out so many Eastern games that November 25th, but it did not escape the 60-mile-per-hour northeast gale that howled through the ancient stadium. The concrete columns seemed to rock.

George had lost his left eye in an accident as a small child, and now the vision in his right eye had been damaged by what the medics call a retinal hemorrhage. He had difficulty recognizing faces except at close range, and writing his stories in longhand became a painful ordeal.

When the teams trotted onto the field at the start of the game, George turned to me and asked, "What's Harvard wearing *blue* jerseys for? "

"Have you gone blind? " I asked him. "Those shirts look the same old crimson to me."

It wasn't until George glanced across the stadium and saw what he believed was a white H on a *blue* background on the big Harvard flag flying over its rooting section, that the plain truth hit him. He was half blind and color blind. Blue and crimson appeared the same to him.

Ironically, George's last story as a New York newspaperman was never filed. The telegraph operator could not make contact with the *World-Telegram & Sun* down in New York. A cloudburst, it developed, had washed out the paper's composing room and no stories could be set in type. This report eased George's mind somewhat, but for a while he fumed and carried on as only a reporter can when he has trouble getting through to his editor.

George's satisfaction over Yale's hard-earned 14-6 victory was tempered by the fact that a peculiar feeling of weakness gripped him. It was all he could do to struggle down the stone steps of the stadium tower. Ahead of us lay a long walk to Harvard Square in the teeth of that cold-edged wind. Somehow George managed to battle the gale until we reached Larz Andersen Bridge across the Charles River. Then his legs suddenly turned to sawdust. Bent double, he leaned over the parapet, his heart pounding furiously. We realized he could go no farther.

From out of the crowd a friendly hand reached to steady George's other arm. The face was the face of a stranger to George's blurred vision, but the voice was that of Robert Hall, Yale's director of athletics and an old friend.

"What's the matter, George? You don't look so good," Bob said.

"I think it's my heart," George said, painfully. "It's going a mile a minute. I feel dizzy."

Somehow in that welter of 30,000 people surging across the bridge, Bob worked a miracle for George. He got a taxicab.

As George was being helped into the cab, Bob remarked, "I gather that no self-respecting Yale man wants to be found dead at Harvard."

For the first time that afternoon, George smiled. The taxi took him to South Station, and once aboard the Yale Special with his old classmate, Dr. Seabury, the team physician, he relaxed, feeling reassured. Seabury told him, "We've got to get you to a heart specialist." And so began a week of cardiographs, fluoroscopes, and stethoscope tests, with the doctors muttering about mitral and semiluna valves. Finally the verdict arrived.

The doctor said, "I'm laying down the law, George. No more stadium climbing, subway riding, and fighting deadlines for you, my good man."

"Hell, Doc, does that mean I'm through covering Ivy League football?"

The doctor nodded.

And so ended the brilliant career of George Trevor, the Rembrandt of Ivy League writers. One thing that made him unique was that he was the only sportswriter of note who wrote his copy in longhand. I still have some of his Ivy League scribblings in my files. Early in his career he had convinced himself that he could not make his thoughts flow smoothly on a typewriter. He hated mechanical gadgets. This aversion to typewriters was a mistake, of course, as he later discovered; few metropolitan newspapers would be as patient as the *Sun* in assigning a special linotype operator to set up longhand copy. Equipped with soft lead pencils, George managed to keep abreast of the hunt-and-peck typists in the pressbox, but the strain on eyes, fingers, and nerves took its toll in time. That was doing it the hard way.

Trevor's favorite Kazmaier story—one of George's own inventions—involved Princeton's 47-12 annihilation of Yale, which had lost only to Cornell and Dartmouth, in 1950.

"Herman Hickman stayed awake nights dreaming up a shuttling defense to stop Kaz," George said. "After the kickoff, he instructed his defensive quarterback, Chuck Masters, to give 'em 79, where the Yale defense looped to the inside. Kazmaier promptly dashed around the flank for a Princeton touchdown. With Yale in possession of the ball after the kickoff, Masters, sitting next to Hickman on the bench, asked: 'What should I do next time, Coach?' Hickman stared at him and said, 'Try 78, where our defense spreads to the outside.' Bam! Jack Davison, the powerful Princeton fullback, bulleted through the middle for another Nassau score. This time, when young Masters returned to the bench, he said: 'What can we do now, Coach?' Hickman put his palms together in a pose of prayer. 'Now,' he said, 'repeat after me: *Our Father, who art in Heaven. . . .*' "

On his way to the Heisman Trophy in 1951, Kazmaier was brilliant. Of 57 Princeton plays that started with a pass from center against Cornell, Dick handled the ball 43 times, running himself, passing, handing off, or punting once. He completed 15 of 17 passes for 236 yards and three touchdowns, and scored twice himself to make the score, 53-15. He also led the Tigers to big victories over Harvard, 54-13, Yale, 27-0, and Dartmouth, 13-0, to stretch their string to 21 straight. The wins over Harvard and Yale marked Old Nassau's fifth consecutive Big Three title, breaking the record of four in a row that Percy Haughton's Harvard elevens made in 1912–15.

° ° °

During the years 1949–51, Harvard football managed to amass the poorest record of any major university. In one stretch it won only 2 of its 17 games. To make matters worse, in its previous 10 games against its traditional rivals, Yale and Princeton, Harvard went down to defeat no less than eight times. By reputation, Harvard men were supposed to behave with "studied indifference," and the chronic ineptness of their team gave them an excellent chance to exhibit that trait. During the 1949 Yale game, after the Elis had racked up their third quick touchdown on the way to a 29-6 win, a group of students in the deactivated Harvard cheering section held aloft a banner that proclaimed, "Who Gives A Damn! " Oklahoma was never like that.

On the morning of the 1950 Princeton game, the *Crimson*, Harvard's undergraduate daily paper, faced the impending debacle with courage and humor. "Two powerful elevens will take the field in Princeton's Palmer Stadium this afternoon," the *Crimson* declared. "In a few minutes they will be joined by Harvard's football players."

In its attitude of noble resignation to harsh reality—and Caldwell's two-platoon system—the *Crimson* spoke for all Harvard undergraduates and alumni who had the stamina to follow their football team. Autumn Saturdays would have been scarcely tolerable for them had it not been for the Harvard band, which usually went undefeated against all comers. It was unanimously acclaimed the best college band in the East, if not in the entire country. Frustrated by the ineptness of their football team, Harvard rooters had come to enshrine the band as their pride and joy, the symbol of their superiority. It finally reached the point where Harvard men, on being asked how the game came out, replied exuberantly, "Came out fine. The band was never better. The glockenspiel section turned in far and away its finest performance of the season."

In 1950, in return for trampling over Harvard, 49-0, Army was treated to "Substitutions Unlimited," a brilliant parody by the Crimson band on the two-platoon system favored by Coach Red Blaik. While an announcer described the movements over the public address system, the band split up into two teams. One half, the A team, performed on the field. The B team remained silently behind on the bench. The Harvard "coach"—band conductor Mal Holmes—first sent in a few substitute clarinets and flutes, then relieved the tired trumpet section with fresh replacements who had been warming up on the sidelines. Several measures later, the A team trotted off the field and the B, or defensive, team went in en masse, heavily muscled with tubas. The high point of the satire was reached when eight bandsmen raced onto the gridiron and, arranging themselves across the 50-yard stripe, removed their white gloves with great aplomb. Like all big-time teams that had specialists who went into the game for one specific play only, the Harvard band, the announcer explained, had *its* specialists, too. "Not one of these men can play more than two notes and some of them can play only one, but these men are the best performers in the country on their particular notes."

Sounding like Knute Rockne before a big game, conductor Holmes sized up his band's prospects before the Army game.

"Except for the erraticness of our drum roll," he said, "we're in pretty good shape. We have a veteran tuba section, and coupled with the largest number of baritone saxes the freshman class has ever fed us, this gives us the sturdiest 'bottom' since 1947. Pretty fair 'top' too—all the melody instrument sections more than adequate. But our drum roll is the shakiest we've had in years, and when you consider the unusual marching block formation we use, you can see why the whole band lacks the punch we like to have. After the Columbia game, we called a special section rehearsal for the drummers, drilling them to a metronome set at 135 beats a minute until the beat permeated right into their pores. I know our student body is counting on us to shoot the works against Army, and we won't let them down. We'll be ready."

The strength of the Harvard band was that its members did not behave like Harvard men at all. En route by bus from Cambridge to New Jersey for the 1953 Princeton game, the band arrived in New Haven at 12:30 on Saturday morning. After directing the buses down dark and deserted High Street, the band assembled on the Old Campus and serenaded the sleeping Yale men with a short but noisy medley of Harvard songs. This impromptu gesture was greeted by a torrent of bags of water being dropped on their heads from the windows of adjacent dormitories.

Earlier that season, the Harvard bandsmen arrived at Cornell on the morning of the Cornell-Harvard game after an all-night bus ride. At the drill rehearsal they were dead on their feet. Nothing they did went right. Mal Holmes called for a break and pulled out a copy of that morning's *Cornell Sun* and read them a long, glowing article about how good the Cornell band was and what magic they were going to perform at half time that afternoon. There was one line about the Harvard band, the last line: "The Harvard band is also expected to appear." Holmes read it with appropriate Rockne sarcasm and then dropped the paper to the ground with a dramatic flourish. His band members let out a wild cheer of defiance. Their tiredness vanished immediately. How did they perform that afternoon?

"We blew their brains out," trumpeted one brass player.

The Harvard band's reputation as King of the

Ivies was unrivaled. In contrast, the Yale football team went up to Dartmouth one time. The trip from New Haven to Hanover was considered too far for the band to go. So the Elis sent just their bandleader, and at half time the public address announcer came on: "The Yale band presents *The Face of God!* "And just this one guy went out and stood there in the middle of the field with his face turned up to the sky.

Oh, those Ivy League bands. Many people went to the games on Saturday afternoons simply to watch their antics. Once the Brown University marchers startled a Princeton crowd in Palmer Stadium with a half time offering, complete with graphic formations, entitled "Salute to the Human Reproductive System."

Let's hear it now for the glockenspiel!

° ° °

During much of 1951, various practices and malpractices in intercollegiate football commanded widespread attention. By the spring of 1952, the agreement among the Ivies was revised by the additions of an emphasis on presidential control of athletic policy, the requirement that each team play every other team in the group at least once every five years, the abolition of spring practice, and a ban on participation in all-star and bowl games.

Absence of spring practice by the Ivies added to the difficulties of football appraisers, but consensus seemed to favor Pennsylvania and Princeton as the two top teams (in spite of Princeton's loss of Kazmaier), with Cornell close on their heels. Charlie Caldwell still had double-duty end Frank McPhee, guard Brad Glass, fullback Homer Smith, and 22 other lettermen returning, and Dick Frye was looked upon as a likely prospect for Kazmaier's replacement. Down in Philadelphia, Penn had suffered heavy graduation losses, but had a good number of standouts around which to formulate its title hopes, including such stars as Ed Bell, Bob Evans, Bill Deuber, Glenn Adams, Chet Cornog, Gerry Robinson, and Joe Varaitis. Dartmouth, Yale, and Harvard were the dark horses. Herman Hickman was gone from New Haven. He had waited until August to make his announcement. The new coach was Jordan Olivar, one of Hickman's assistants who had previously served as head coach at Villanova and Loyola.

"There were only 11 practice sessions before our first game against Connecticut," Olivar recalled. "That didn't leave us much time to get ready. We had 101 candidates out for opening practice. I didn't know much about any of them."

He soon learned about them, and what he saw brought smiles to the Olivar features. There was quarterback Ed Molloy, end Ed Woodsum, a pair of good runners in Hubert Pruett and Pete Shears, and fullback Jerry Jones. Captain Joe Mitinger and Pete Radulovic shored up the line.

A T-tactician, Coach Olivar favored the belly series, in which the quarterback faked the ball to one or two of his runners and gave it to another. It was a relatively new maneuver in 1952, at least in the detail of deployment and precision.

Coach Olivar was a tall, gracious, lantern-jawed man from Staten Island, a former teacher of history and Spanish in high school. Of all the men who had taught football at Yale, from David Schley Schaff in 1872 down through the years of Hickman, chances were that none was such a complete stranger to Yale men and Yale environs as Jordan Olivar, born Olivari. Yet to anybody who knew the man as a college player, Olivar seemed right at home at Yale.

When Olivar was the regular right tackle on a good Villanova College team, Clipper Smith, the coach, conducted noontime lectures on football theory, and once a week he gave his pupils a written examination. Grading the papers, Clipper discovered that Olivar, who had never played football in high school, always made the highest mark. Not once in a while, but every week.

"If he's the brainiest guy on my squad," Clipper reasoned, "why do I have somebody else telling him what to do?"

After that, Olivar called the plays in the huddle and Villanova was undefeated for two and a half seasons.

Following graduation, Olivar taught and coached at Radnor High, in Philadelphia's suburban Main Line section, then in Paulsboro, New Jersey, and then in Roman Catholic High in Philadelphia.

When Clipper Smith enlisted in the Marines for World War II, Villanova made tentative overtures to Olivar although it wasn't sure it would have a football squad. It was August before Naval trainees were officially allowed to play, and Olivar hustled back to the campus. He went from there to Loyola, of Los Angeles, was hired by Hickman as an assistant in 1951 after Loyola dropped football, and succeeded Herman when Hickman resigned.

Over the years, he was learning.

"Starting with what we were taught in school,"

he said, "and then learning by experience in high school and college. Experimenting, talking with other coaches, attending football clinics, swiping an idea from this opponent and another from that one—it all helps. Classroom experience is a help, too, learning how to explain a point and, above all, to demonstrate it."

"Do you learn also by doing things wrong?" he was asked.

"Oh, yes," he said. "Some of the best lessons start with a mistake. A play goes wrong but it works. You try to find out why, and maybe you've got something. Remember a Villanova play where Andy Stopper, the left halfback, would back through a hole in the line and then turn and run? That wasn't a mistake, but it started by accident. On that play Andy was supposed to turn his back to the line and hand off to one of the other backs cutting across him. After a while he said to Clipper, 'I keep backing through there and there's no resistance. Nobody hits me.' So we put in a play where he kept the ball instead of handing off, and he used to get big gains.

"I think the movies teach us most of all. At the end of a season we chart each play. Maybe we've used one 35 times. We find out that the defensive tackle stopped it five times, the linebacker made 25 tackles, and the other five were scattered around. It doesn't stand to reason that the backer-up would be the best man on the opposition in every game, so we try to see how we've been blocking him, how we can get him out of the play more successfully."

° ° °

They were calling 1952 the era of the New Deal at Penn as George Munger blended certain elements of the T formation with the single wing. Munger imported the former Ohio State and Colgate coach Paul Bixler to help him make the transition.

The Quakers beat Dartmouth, Princeton, Columbia, and Cornell to win the Ivy title; tied Notre Dame and Navy; and lost to Penn State, Georgia, and Army in outside games. Princeton popped up with an overall 8-1-0 record, followed by Yale's 7-2-0.

Although he lost to Penn, 13-7, Charlie Caldwell didn't hesitate to name Captain Frank McPhee, his 6′3″, 203-pound All-American end, as "the greatest all-around football player I have ever coached." At the end of the season, Caldwell said, "Frank can play any position of any college team and it would make very little difference whether it was offense, defense, single wing, or T."

McPhee demonstrated his versatility against Dartmouth, his final game at Princeton. In the 33-0 victory, he dropped back and threw a 53-yard pass to end Len Lyons. The Tigers' most effective striking weapon in 1952 was the "pass to McPhee." It was McPhee and "the big play by McPhee," Caldwell said, that made all of the difference to Nassau when it was necessary to swing to the attack or to stop the enemy's attack.

Yale closed out the season with a stunning 41-14 victory over Harvard. Less than two minutes remained in the first half when Dick Clasby, a waiter in the Harvard Faculty Club, rushed into the end zone to make the score read: Yale, 20; Harvard, 7. For a moment an illusion existed that perhaps this 69th renewal of The Game might develop into a contest. One minute later, the illusion was dispelled in three plays. Yale swept down the field for its fourth touchdown and an unassailable lead of 20 points.

Thereafter, this ancient and holy New England ritual became a rabbit hunt in which the Yales clubbed their quarry with scandalous cruelty, scoring so easily that even the Eli student manager got into the act.

When the score reached 40 to 7, Yale lined up to try for an extra point, with Ed Molloy crouching to tee the ball for Bob Parcells' place-kick, catching the snapback from center. Molloy sprang to his feet, ducked around to his right, picked out a blue shirt in the end zone, and threw at it.

The ball was caught for the 41st point by a little guy wearing No. 99. He was convoyed from the field by a raucous raft of playmates and when he reached the sideline other Yales swarmed off the bench, hoisted him to their shoulders, pummeled and buffeted him.

There was no No. 99 in the program. An emissary from the press box learned at the Yale bench that the stranger was Charles Yeager, of Buffalo, a 5′5″, 138-pound crew-cut senior whose ordinary duties were limited to counting headgear and checking equipment trunks.

At the very beginning of the season, Yeager, no shrinking violet, filled out the necessary papers to make himself eligible for varsity football. And then during varsity practice, when he wasn't needed, he would get someone, anyone, to pass the ball to him along the sideline. He practiced catching passes all season. It wasn't until the day before the Harvard game, however, that he got to practice with the first team. Coach Olivar told him that if Yale got far enough ahead of Harvard, he might use a special play that Yeager had been polishing all season. But on the day of The Game at Cambridge, Chuck did not suit up. He wore his civilian clothes as he always did.

"Sure," Yeager said later. "I had to manage. You can't manage in a football uniform."

But then, at half time, the coach came to Chuck and told him to put on his armor. Chuck changed into a uniform, and when the second half started, there he was, sitting on the bench right with all the other Yales, all dressed up and ready for the call.

Late in the last quarter, Yale scored its sixth touchdown of the day to make the score 40-14. Coach Olivar looked down the bench and called, "Okay, Chuck, this is what you've been waiting for. Go in there and work your play."

His blue eyes twinkling and his slight body shaking with excitement, Chuck Yeager was no longer an inconspicuous football manager. He stood up in his brand new, spotlessly clean uniform, jammed his brand new helmet on his blond head, and tore onto the field. All the Harvards figured that Bob Parcells was going to kick the extra point, just the way he always did. Ed Molloy always held the ball for him, and Yeager went in as the right end. Who looked at right ends on an extra point routine play? On the snap of the ball, Yeager slipped inconspicuously into the end zone, and waited. Sure enough, Molloy, instead of letting Parcells kick the ball, picked it up suddenly and ran with it over to near where Yeager was standing. Then he tossed it to him. It traveled only about seven yards, but Yeager caught it to make the final score: Yale 41, Harvard 14.

"It was a perfect pass," Chuck said afterward. "I grabbed it and ran as fast as I could."

"But what did you run for? You were already in the end zone."

"I had to get out of there so I wouldn't get hit," he said. "Do you think I wanted to get killed?"

The only football Yeager had ever played before was in grammar school back home in Buffalo, and later at Milford Academy, where he played six-man football in the ninth grade. But never in his wildest dreams did he ever think he would score a point in a Yale-Harvard game.

Yeager said it had all started as a gag. Jerry Neri, the Yale backfield coach, had seen him practicing pass catching. Jerry was the one who told him to fill out eligibility papers so he could play if ever the opportunity came up. But Chuck never thought it would.

On Wednesday before The Game, Yeager was given a uniform with a 99 on the jersey. But no one got around to putting his name on the squad list, so nobody in the stands knew who he was after he scored the point.

After the game, Coach Olivar was asked, "When did you decide all this?"

"Oh, the other day," Olivar replied. "I'd noticed all season that Chuck was catching passes whenever he could get anyone to throw them to him. I'll bet he has caught more passes in practice than all of our ends put together. I told him yesterday we'd use the play if the right moment came. So when we ran up that big lead in the first half, I told him to suit up between the halves. Then, just before we scored that last touchdown, I said, 'If we go over, you go in for your play.' We went over a minute or so later, so I sent him in."

Which was how tiny Chuck Yeager became the only Yale football manager who ever scored a point against Harvard.

"Long after we remember that Michigan State and Notre Dame and Tennessee were perhaps the three best college teams of 1952," wrote one reporter, "we'll remember the bizarre and hilarious spectacle of a little man who never played varsity football before being sent in to score Yale's 41st point against Harvard."

It had been a bit of clean boyish fun calculated to remind 38,114 witnesses that football is after all merely a game for the amusement of innocent lads.

## 1953

After nearly a decade of two-platooning and superspecialization, the year 1953 saw a return to one-platoon football, although in a somewhat modified form, giving rise to a new group of conference champions across the land, before and after the changeover.

Football fans seemed to enjoy watching the players prove that they could block as well as tackle, or vice versa, and if there was any deterioration in the quality of play it was not visible to the untutored eye. As a matter of fact, the season was notable for its number of close, exciting games and there were a gratifying number of upsets. Over the full course of the season, however, the strong teams established their strengths and the weak fell by the wayside. Despite fears to the contrary, the rules change did not seriously upset the natural balance of power.

In the Ivy Group, Princeton, which lost only to Penn in 1952 after winning 24 straight games over four seasons, shaped up on paper as probably the best of the eight teams and a leading candidate for the Lambert Trophy. The expectation was that Charlie Caldwell's high-geared, single wing machine, powered by Homer Smith, would pick up where it left off in 1952, when it won its last six games and captured the Big Three title for the sixth straight year. Other key players were John Henn, center; George Kovatch, tackle; Harvey Mathis, end. Royce Flippin, a touted sophomore tailback, also figured prominently in the picture.

They were saying before the season started that if Pennsylvania could have traded its high-voltage intersectional schedule for an Ivy program, George Munger's team probably would have led the league again. Unfortunately, the Quakers met only Cornell and, even with a splendid squad that included backs Joe Varaitis, Walt Hynoski, George Bosseler, and tackle Jack Shanafelt, found themselves in too deep against a string of powerful foes benefitting from spring practice: California, Ohio State, Michigan, Notre Dame, and Army. However, they did manage to beat Vanderbilt, Penn State, and Navy, and tied Cornell, the Ivy Champion. At the end of the season, Coach Munger, who was 82-42-10 since 1938 at Penn, announced his retirement. Speaking at an alumni dinner in New Jersey, Munger said: "I was called a Boy Scout coach. Well, if being close to my players, my team, and my school means that I was a Boy Scout, then that's what I was, and I'm proud of it."

After one of its poorest seasons in years, Cornell's fortunes improved sharply in 1953. The Big Red was much smoother in the split-T routines that were introduced the year before, and Coach Lefty James was able to count on a couple of gifted sophs, backs Billy DeGraaf and Dick Meade, to give the attack a lift. The veterans of the squad were fullback Guy Bedrossian, end Tom Rooney, tackle Bill George, and guard Len Oniskey. On its way to an overall 4-3-2 season, Cornell beat Colgate, Princeton, Columbia and Dartmouth, tied Yale and Penn, and lost to Rice, Navy, and Syracuse.

There were a lot of red faces around New England after both Yale and Harvard finished ahead of preseason favorite Princeton in the final 1953 standings. The so-called experts had envisaged nothing but gloom in Cambridge and New Haven in their September previews. Graduation had virtually wiped out the offensive unit of the Cantabs from 1952, and Coach Lloyd Jordan, who had been hired in 1950 after 18 years at Amherst to restore Harvard football to respectability, had to rebuild almost from scratch. His big rallying point was the highly talented tailback, Dick Clasby, who in '52 led Harvard to its first victory over Dartmouth in six years. There was also the superb passer, Carroll Lowenstein, back from Korea, and fullback John Culver and center Tom Coolidge. Lowenstein and Clasby were great friends, great competitors. At one time they had something like 43 mentions in the Harvard record book. In the 1953 Davidson game, for example, Lowenstein established one of his records by completing six of nine passes for *five* touchdowns. Clasby was hurt in the first quarter of that game, but he got back to the team in time to collaborate with John Culver in a 13-0 triumph over the Elis at Yale Bowl in front of 65,000.

Except for 6-0 losses to both Columbia and Princeton, Harvard missed a perfect season by only two touchdowns. It was 3-2-0 in the Ivy and 6-2-0 overall.

Hot on the heels of the Crimson was Yale (3-2-1 and 5-2-2), which took another long step forward on its way back under its own Jordan—Jordan Olivar. At the heart of its comeback was Ed Molloy, the team's crack passer, and Captain Pete Fortunato, a star linebacker. When Molloy was injured in preseason practice, Jim Lopez stepped into his shoes at quarterback.

"Lopez was thrown into the water and had to sink or swim," remarked Charley Loftus, the Yale sports information director. "Against Brown (13-0 Yale), he was using the dog paddle. Against Connecticut (32-0 Yale), he used the Australian crawl."

## 1954

Almost everyone had something to say about intercollegiate football in 1954. Broadly speaking, you could find two extreme attitudes in most of the authorities. Those who were "pro" football praised it out of all proportion to its actual merits. Those who were "anti" were quite blind to the values it offered.

Among those on the side of intercollegiate football was Notre Dame's Reverend Theodore M. Hesburgh, president of the most famous football university in the nation. He made it clear, however, that he favored football only as long as it was conducted within its proper dimensions.

"The fundamental difference between intercollegiate football and professional football is that in college the players are supposed to be students first and foremost," he said. "This does not mean that they should all be Phi Beta Kappas or physics majors, but neither should they be subnormal students majoring in ping-pong. Once this fundamental principle is accepted, three equally obvious conclusions follow as the day the night. First, any boy who has demonstrated during his high school days that he is quite incapable of doing collegiate work should not be admitted to college, even though he may have been an all-state high school fullback. Secondly, once a qualified student who also happens to be a good athlete is admitted to college, he should follow the same academic courses, with the same academic requirements, as the other students. Presumably he is in college for the same reason as the others: to get a good education for life and to earn a degree in four years. This means, in practice, no fresh air courses, no special academic arrangements for athletes. Thirdly, the athlete should enjoy the same student life in college as the other students. He should not be treated as prime beef, should not be given special housing and disciplinary arrangements, made a demigod on a special allowance who is above and beyond the regimen that is found to be educationally best for all the students of any given school. In this connection, I am reminded of the animal who is enthroned and crowned with great ceremony at the annual Puck Fair in Ireland. It happens to be a goat."

Robert A. Hall, former athletic director at Yale, one day gave me 15 ways to de-emphasize college football without hurting it in the least. Among his proposals were: (1) The abolition of athletic scholarships, (2) the elimination of organized practice out of season, and (3) no more postseason games between college teams.

The movement against "pressure football" at the presidential level definitely was under way.

"The superstructure of college athletics may be full of termites at this time," Bob Hall told me, "but the base is sound. All the colleges have to do is get back on an athletics-for-all policy and quit wasting football receipts on athletic scholarships and the like. Sure, innumerable boys who had athletic scholarships became fine, upstanding citizens, but a free ride because the boy is a superior performer in a game puts the emphasis where it very definitely should not be. This stuff about helping a poor boy is a lot of bunk. If a boy wants an education badly enough, he can find a way to get it. Countless young men have done it."

In 1954, the old Pacific Coast Conference (now the PAC-8) advocated ending out-of-season football practice. Bob Hall said he could go along with that. "But why," he asked, "doesn't the Far West go a step further and put an end to New Year's Day Bowl games between college teams? I grant you that postseason games serve worthy community and charitable purposes, but I object to coaches being rated according to how many teams they have put in a Bowl. Why, a coach's prestige depends entirely on his ability to land his team in a Bowl. To accomplish this, he has to recruit, and that costs money. Then he simply has to get to a Bowl to pay the bill."

The Ivies' Great De-emphasis actually began in 1954—the decision of the eight universities to relegate football (and athletics in general) to a status subservient to what was supposed to be the business of their institutions, namely to educate their students. Athletic scholarships would continue to be banned, spring practice ended permanently, the number of coaches limited, a complete round-robin football schedule starting in 1956, a ban on postseason games and all-star play, regulations governed by a strict code—steps that seemed to many paradoxical, since the Ivies had been the very font of college football, had produced the storied rivalries dating back to the 1870s, the magic names, the towering legends, the literary heroes, a whole flapper generation that identified with Eastern football, the coonskin coat and the flask and all the attendant rituals and ceremonials of those New England autumn afternoons. Now all of this brilliant history and panoply was being de-emphasized by eight men who signed what they called the "Presidents' Agreement": Henry M. Wriston, Brown; Grayson Kirk, Columbia; Deane W. Malott, Cornell; John S. Dickey, Dartmouth; Nathan M. Pusey, Harvard; Gaylord P. Harnwell, Pennsylvania; Harold W. Dodds, Princeton; and A. Whitney Griswold, Yale.

That spring, while the rest of the country's football powers indulged in their annual exercises, the Ivy coaches, headed by Lou Little, dean of the masterminds, got together in a round-table discussion at Cornell.

"Nothing official on the agenda," Lou explained.

"We just want to explore our mutual problems now that we are formally organized."

There were no indications that the ban on spring practice, one of the Ivy coaches' chief problems, would ever be rescinded.

"On the contrary," Coach Little pointed out, "the idea is gaining new converts steadily."

Many observers hoped that the Ivy League's adoption of this more balanced concept of football would be as important to the progress of the game, and perhaps to its future elsewhere, as what the eight colleges provided at its genesis.

In any event, this Ivy action provoked mixed feelings among other college leaders across the country. For example, when Major General Gar H. Davidson, Superintendent of the U. S. Military Academy at West Point, was asked if he thought other schools would follow the lead of the Ivies and de-emphasize football, he said no. "I don't think the Ivy League's approach to the problem is realistic," he said flatly. "This approach hasn't stopped recruiting of football players. If anything, recruiting becomes more important to these colleges because it's a great honor to win the Ivy League championship and a true test of ability."

Rear Admiral William R. Smedberg III, Superintendent of the U. S. Naval Academy at Annapolis, said he planned no changes in policy. "While continuing to require high academic standing," he said, "we will continue the present emphasis on football because it teaches team effort—which is so important in the Navy, aboard ship and in the air. We feel that this is more important than any attempt at de-emphasis."

Dr. C. E. Brehm, President of the University of Tennessee, approved of football de-emphasis. "What I think the Ivy League has done is reappraise the value of football in its relation to the educational system. There is a definite relationship, but football can get out of hand without proper academic controls. There is a happy compromise which many colleges have found."

Dr. Roscoe L. West, President of State Teachers College at Trenton, New Jersey, wasn't sure the Ivy formula would catch on. "That all depends on the results of the Ivy League's experiment," he said. "Many smaller colleges have already de-emphasized. College football will survive—not because it is played by great teams like Oklahoma but because it is played at hundreds of smaller colleges throughout the country."

Biggie Munn, Director of Athletics at Michigan State, was emphatically opposed to de-emphasis.

"We need more athletic competition in America, not less," he said. "Why is it that 40 per cent of our boys can't pass Army physicals? It is more important to stress athletics than to de-emphasize. We have a great football team at Michigan State, but we also have 140 touch football teams."

Secretary of the Navy Charles S. Thomas believed that there eventually would be a balance between complete de-emphasis and semi-pro college football. "I do not think any group wants complete de-emphasis, not even the Ivy League," he said. "If players were not paid, most of the abuses would immediately disappear."

And so the Great Debate roared on.

° ° °

In its second season of two-way play after a long spell of two-platoon specialization, college football produced a satisfactory quota of thrills, upsets, and glowing performances. Fans, players, and most coaches were thankful that there were no rule changes worth mentioning.

There was a new national sports magazine on the stands that year, *Sports Illustrated,* a Time-Life publication. Its resident football genius was old Mr. Pumpkin Face himself, Herman Hickman. In his September preview of the Ivies, the former Yale coach wrote:

"Yale has a hard core of veterans supplemented by the finest sophomores in Yale's proud history. Sophomore Dennis McGill is the finest outside runner since Al Hessberg of the mid-1930s. Dean Loucks, another neophyte, is a brilliant adjunct at quarterback. Jim Armstrong is a dependable senior halfback, while Captain Thorne Shugart heads a line that has size and quality. . . . Cornell has the wherewithal to cop the Ivy title, headed by a dangerous returning backfield in Dick Meade, Dick Jackson, Bill DeGraaf, and Guy Bedrossian. Powerful Len Oniskey is one of the East's best defensive tackles and practically stands alone in the front line; a strong big team with outside strength that should progress with the season. . . . Brown is very impressive. Pete Kohut's passing and generalship is magnificent, and Archie Williams at halfback has speed to spare. Jim McGuinness has few superiors at tackle in the East. This should be the Bruins' best year since 1949. . . . The fall of Princeton last season from national greatness is still inexplicable. Charlie Caldwell's single wing ranks with the best.

Few tailbacks surpass Royce Flippin. Though the Tiger defense is still a question mark, they could win the title."

Hickman held out only slim hopes for the chances of Harvard ("a disappointing season"), Penn ("the schedule is awesome"), Columbia ("short on material"), and Dartmouth ("the line is doubtful from end to end").

In three years of high school football at White Plains, New York, where he was coached by his father, and as a freshman at Yale in 1953, Dean Loucks, the promising sophomore quarterback, had never played in a losing game. The way the 1954 Yales started out, with victories over Connecticut, Brown, Columbia, and Cornell, it appeared his record might be kept intact. Then, on October 23 at Yale Bowl, undefeated and untied Colgate arrived with a sophomore quarterback of its own. He was 19-year-old Guy Martin.

Martin was the whole story for Colgate. Entering in the second period after Dick Lalla, All-East star, had faded, he passed and ran his team to a 7-0 lead.

Yale took the second-half kickoff, moved 95 yards on 15 running plays to tie the score. Then, with the third period almost gone, Martin picked the Red Raiders up again and carried them to a second touchdown, which fullback Ed Whitehair scored on a 6-yard buck. Martin's conversion attempt hit an upright and bounced back—no good.

It was Yale that drove for the final score and had a final chance to win. With less than two minutes left, the Elis brought in veteran passer Bob Brink to tie the score, 13-13. But it was only fitting that this game, full of parallels throughout, should end on the same note as Colgate. The place-kick by Vern Loucks went up a little to the right and banged against the upright, falling back on the field—no good.

In the Ivy Group, it still looked like Yale, which sported a 3-0 record in league competition. The Big Green of Dartmouth, after a meager beginning with losses to Navy (7-42), Army (6-60) and Colgate (7-13), opened its five-game group slate with a 13-7 win over Harvard, before losing to Yale by the same score the following week.

Unbeaten Yale was just beginning to look like the real thing, when Army traveled over from West Point to play them. This was the first time in 11 years that the Black Knights had played in Yale Bowl. After the cribbing scandals and resultant expulsions, Army had scheduled games with Yale for '54 and '55. Red Blaik had hopes that these games could be the first steps in restoring what had been an old, profitable, and enjoyable rivalry. Obviously the crowd hoped the same. There were a sellout 73,000 there, the largest Bowl turnout in 25 years.

The Cadets were favored, of course, but it was thought that Yale would make a battle of it.

"They have the personnel to do it," Coach Blaik conceded before the game. But Blaik also recognized that the Ivy ban on spring practice was now in its third year. "They have consequently devaluated the importance of football in the minds of their players," pointed out Blaik.

This was very evident to him in the Yale game.

"On our first play from scrimmage," he recalled, "Bell broke over Yale's left guard on a lightning dive-tackle hand-off from Vann, veered by their linebacker in almost the same motion, and raced 61 yards down the sidelines for a touchdown. Yale never recovered, and we went on to bury them, 48-7. It was the highest score in our series with Yale and the second highest ever made against a Yale team."

Blaik sat through that Yale game with a 103-degree fever. "A heavy bronchial cold had been knifing at me for over a week," Red remembered. "When I returned to the Academy immediately after the game, it was discovered I had pneumonia and I was ordered into the post hospital. As a consequence, when we played at Penn the following week, for the first and only time in my 25 seasons as a head coach, I was not with the team and not by choice. I had missed Army games to scout Notre Dame against Navy in 1944, '45, and '46, but that *had been* by choice. In my absence, Bobby Dobbs handled the Cadets for me and did well. We won, 35-0. Bell scored twice and contributed runs of 32 and 37 yards. Pete Vann threw two touchdown passes to Hollender. Penn was caught in the switches. Their schedule had been overloaded according to the blueprints of the 'Victory for Honor' program of Harold Stassen, Penn president, and Coach Steve Sebo did not have the troops to handle it. The worst thing that can ever happen to any football coach is to get caught without material."

The Ivy race tightened up considerably after Princeton upset Yale, 21-14, in Yale Bowl. This provided the final week's play with special drama. A Yale loss to Harvard, coupled with a Cornell victory over Penn, would deadlock the Elis and the Big Red in the final standings, 4-2 apiece. Cornell had lost its first four games, but now was on a four-game win streak. Yale was on a two-game losing string.

A crowd of 40,000 packed Harvard Stadium to the roof. Yale was first to get on the scoreboard when Matt Botsford, Harvard's sophomore back, intercepted a pass 2 yards from his own goal, stumbling over it to give Yale a safety. Later, Botsford was hurt on a Yale touchdown play that put the Blue ahead, 9-0.

Taking over for the injured Botsford was Jim Joslin, another sophomore. He considered himself lucky to be there. At the end of his freshman year he had thought of going back to Minneapolis to stay. Harvard's rigid study requirements were bothering him. He conquered that, but now he had another problem—a tendency to fumble. In a brief second quarter appearance, he was smothered for a 12-yard loss.

Now Botsford was out and Joslin was in, and in three plays he fumbled, hit an official with an attempted pass, and missed a touchdown by heaving the ball over the receiver's head. By this time goat horns were sprouting under Joslin's helmet. But after Harvard fumbled once more and recovered on the Yale 20, Joslin's horns disappeared. In just two plays he got to the 1-yeard line, setting up Tony Gianelly's touchdown buck, and thereafter, when Harvard got the ball back, Joslin was a slashing saber cutting through the right side of the Yale line. He brought the ball quickly to the Yale 39, where he handed off to Frank White, who threw a running pass to Bob Cochran, who set the Harvard stands mad by juggling the ball from the 16-yard line to the 8 before he finally gained control and scored the touchdown that gave Harvard a 13-9 victory and the Big Three title for the first time since 1941. (Coincidentally, they had beaten Princeton by almost the same score, 14-9.)

After The Game, Yale Captain Thorne Shugart said in the locker room: "That number 43 did it. I don't know his name, but he was great."

The name, of course, was J-o-s-l-i-n. James Joslin of Minneapolis. His flaming performance, which had lighted New England's drab November sky, merely cost Yale full possession of the Ivy Championship. Cornell had rolled over Penn, 20-6, to earn a share of the title.

## 1955

Proponents of the two-platoon game claimed that the rule makers had chased the good little man out of college football.

"One-platoon rules have forced a return to the big man, the 220-pound lineman who can withstand the pounding of two-way football," agonized Biggie Munn, athletic director of Michigan State. "The average guard or tackle just cannot absorb the punishment of both offensive and defensive play and retain the quickness which earned him a place in the platoon game. We're headed back to a college game reserved for a comparative few big men of exceptional physical qualities. And good big men are hard to find. The good little high school player is losing his chance to play college football. The finest days of my coaching life at Michigan State came when we developed the platoon system to a degree that allowed the use of small linemen. It was a pleasure to watch 175-pound guards and tackles play big-college football by using speed, quickness, and desire to overcome the natural advantages of the 220-pound opponent. We are headed back to slow-motion football. There is only time to teach the rudiments of offense and defense. More than ever, the school with the big horses will dominate. Raw physical ability will be the premium in a game of simple offense and defense. In contrast, two-platoon football was an intriguing game of new ideas and developments. It was a game of imagination—more new ideas were developed in the two-platoon days than during any like period in the history of the game. If the present trend prevails, I fear that the fans will in time be forced to look to professional football for new ideas, for action, for the 'big game.' "

Despite Munn's outraged cry against the one platoon, there was only one important rule change in 1955: a player, provided he started the quarter, could re-enter the game once during the same quarter. This was a slight concession to the free substitution addicts. The old rule allowed a player to re-enter the game in the same quarter *only* in the last four-minute segments of the second and fourth periods.

Offensively, the split T still dominated the field, with the regular or Bear T next in popularity. The variations used, however, made any resemblances to the originals purely coincidental. Quite a few of the major powers used the so-called multiple offense, shifting from an unbalanced (four men on one side of the center, two on the other) single wing to a T or split T.

Defensively, the swing was to a box type of defense, which was basically a 5-4-2, devised primarily to use against the split T. The scheme was so well masked that only the coach himself could tell the formation of the moment, and most of the time *he* didn't know until he studied the pictures the next day. Sometimes the team lined up with nine men on the line of scrimmage when the ball was ready for play, but *mentally* four of them were ready to leap back into the secondary as linebackers. With all that going on, it was better not to try to figure out the defensive alignments at all.

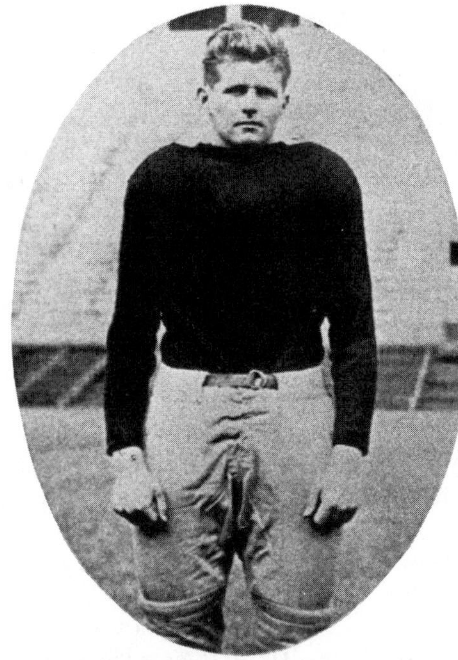

° ° °

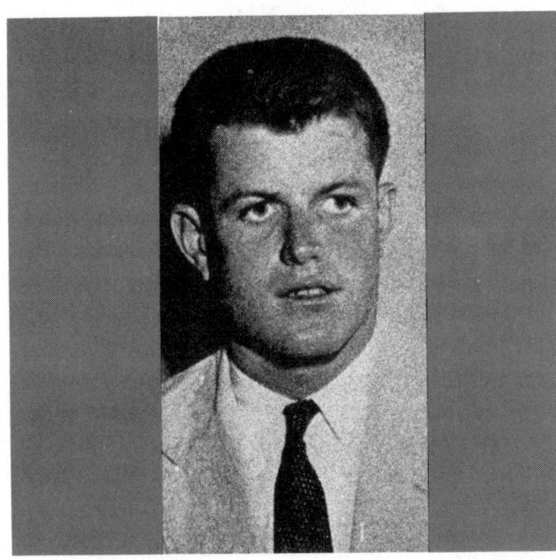

*The Kennedy brothers, Joe and Edward, as they were pictured in Harvard football programs 17 years apart. Joe, the oldest of the Kennedy sons, played for the Cantabs in 1938. Edward scored Harvard's only touchdown in a 21-7 loss to Yale in 1955.*

College football had one of its greatest seasons in 1955. The performance highlight was Oklahoma's extension of a victory string that reached 30 games with the sensational 20-6 stomping of previously unbeaten Maryland in the Orange Bowl. The Sooners injected a new dimension into football with their colorful "fast break" attack. Blitzing their opponents by sprinting out of the huddle and launching their plays with a breathless rush, Bud Wilkinson's mighty men were unanimously named the nation's number one team.

In the locker rooms at Oklahoma, huge red and white placards pounded home the words, "Play Like A Champion." Yet if a boy didn't want to play at all, that was his privilege too. Sounding much like A. Whitney Griswold, the Yale president who believed college football had forgotten its main purpose, Coach Wilkinson said: "I don't see any reason why a boy should feel he has to be a football player, if it's against his personality. He'd be better off in some other line of endeavor. A lot of kids participate in football because their girl thinks it's nice or their parents want them to, but there's a tremendous number of young men who are blessed with an abundance of physical energy and truly combative spirit. They have to relieve themselves of that pressure and test their minds and bodies. Football fulfills that demand for total effort and teaches them fair play, discipline, teamwork, and loyalty.

"I am totally of the opinion that because football is a morale game," Wilkinson continued, "because it is primarily a game of the heart, I believe you must first find a boy of character, a boy who first must be a good enough college student to do college work without undue difficulty, and to be able to graduate from college. If he doesn't have that much academic ability, he doesn't belong in college, that's all there is to it. I believe college athletics are for college students. Most people don't believe coaches feel that way. But they do."

The 1955 Elis looked like the class team of the Ivies after four straight wins, including Brown, Columbia, and Cornell. Their line was large and rugged, from flankmen Paul Lopata and Vernon Loucks on in. Junior Dean Loucks and sophomore Dick Winterbauer staged a real battle for first-string quarterback. Dennis McGill did an outstanding job at halfback against Columbia, and Al Ward was a powerhouse at the other half.

The best-balanced team in the league, however, was Princeton. The Tigers, winners of five of their first six games, operated behind Coach Charlie Caldwell's single wing offense that was smooth and difficult for the opposition's defense. Tackle Mike Bowman led an improving line, and Royce Flippin, handicapped by a broken right wrist for part of 1954, had returned to top form after his injuries and was being hailed as "the outstanding single wing tailback in the country."

Cornell and Dartmouth were the only other first division contenders. The Big Red's backs were the best in the Ivy League, with halfbacks Dick Jackson and Dick Meade and quarterback Bill DeGraaf heading the list. The paper-thin line was led by Stan Intihar. Up at Hanover, the new coach was Bob Blackman, who had some problems as Dartmouth lost heartbreakers to Colgate, Holy Cross, and Brown early in the season. Passing was the forte, with Bill Beagle doing the pitching, but the running and defensive play were ragged.

After losing to Colgate, 0-7, and beating Dartmouth, 20-0, Yale pulled one of the biggest upsets of the year, if not the decade. The Elis beat Army, 14-12, at Yale Bowl. The contest was played in heavy rain, but Coach Red Blaik did not blame the loss on the weather. "We were even sloppier than the rain and mud," he said after the game. "We fumbled repeatedly, giving Yale one opportunity after another, and they finally capitalized. The grandstand quarterbacks gave me hell."

The Black Knights got some revenge the following week by blasting Penn, 40-0.

The Ivy League Championship came down to the game between Yale and Princeton, November 12, at Palmer Stadium. Two days before the game, Winterbauer became ill and missed the game. Loucks had to carry the load alone.

Yale, the favorite, made the odds makers look good in the first quarter, even though it failed to put any numbers on the scoreboard. Alfred Ward got into the end zone on a long run, but the play was wiped out by a Yale penalty. Minutes later, Princeton recovered a Loucks fumble as he was crossing the goal line.

*Bob Blackman served Dartmouth with tremendous success from 1955 through 1970, before going to Illinois of the Big Ten in 1971. He returned to the Ivies six years later, this time as head coach at Cornell.*

The opportunistic Tigers pounced on another Yale fumble in the third quarter and turned it into a touchdown, with Flippin carrying the ball. They scored again later on an intercepted pass. Final score: Princeton 13, Yale 0.

Thus, Princeton won the final championship of what for so long had been known as the Ivy Group. As the eight schools prepared to put into effect fully in 1956 a policy of isolationism, causing a virtual schedule ban against the strong Eastern independents, there was much debate and conjecture by outsiders as to whether the Ivies were going the right route.

"Ivy League football is not going to be what it used to be," predicted Herman Hickman. "Maybe the once-great rulers have grown weary of winning or have become too civilized. Whatever it is, in the past 25 years the old-line colleges of the Ivy Group, except for sporadic outbursts, have not ranked favorably with other sections in the game. This decline in Ivy football culminated with the decision to give up spring practice."

The presidents of the Ivy eight had no apologies for their Great De-emphasis decision.

"The main purpose of an educational institution is education," explained Dr. Griswold. "The main purposes of organized athletics are recreation and exercise. Both of these are essential to good work in education as in every other calling. Neither is a substitute for such work, much less its equal or its master. This suggests a line of demarcation, a watershed, on one side of which organized athletics serve the cause of education while on the other they hurt it; and it further suggests that it is the duty of each educational institution to draw that line and defend it. This, after all, is asking no more of educational institutions than the Pure Food and Drug Act requires of the manufacturers of those products or, for that matter, than a major league manager might ask of his players if they kept skipping batting practice to study history.

"From the standpoint of athletics as well as education, the fact has logical consequences. The aspiration of most American colleges has been to achieve the standing if not the shape and size of universities, and the aspiration of most American universities has been to do full justice to that status. In its original and proper meaning, the word university signifies standards—the highest standards of integrity and quality pertaining to their activities anywhere in society. Any trifling with those standards, however slight or for whatever expedient reason, is a contradiction in terms.

"Since these standards can apply to everything a university does, they apply to athletics as well as to education. The application of the standards to college and university athletics was twofold. In the first place, they were to be *amateur* athletics, a principle early laid down by the colleges and periodically reaffirmed by their presidents, governing boards, athletic directors, coaches, and team captains, as well as by their various rules committees and intercollegiate associations. The principle was first and last a players' concept. It said nothing about the entertainment of spectators or the raising of college revenue, and it expressly forbade participation for financial or any other material remuneration.

"The second standard is succinctly stated in the preamble to the revised Ivy Group Agreement of 1954 for organized athletic programs: In the total life of the campus, emphasis upon intercollegiate competition must be kept in harmony with the essential educational purposes of the institution."

The Yale president felt that most colleges had been seduced away from the original idea of amateur athletics. The culprits, he said, were the spectators themselves. Was he exaggerating the evil? He did not think so.

"Standards that should be pure have been compromised and corrupted," he said, "and this is common knowlege among our college students and their faculties. Deliberate departures from principle of this sort cannot fail to damage the reputation of an institution consecrated to truth and excellence by its very charter. The double standard as applied to education and athletics has already caused woeful moral and intellectual confusion in the minds of young men who found themselves subjected to such policies, not to mention cynicism and disgust in the minds and hearts of their fellow students. This is meager fare from higher education, scarcely worth its salt on any pretext. It is hardly consistent with the mottoes of light and truth emblazoned in the arms of our colleges. It is disillusioning and damaging to their good name and to the integrity of their profession."

Dr. Griswold wondered if these defects were not mitigated by the educational redemption of young men who would not otherwise have gone to college. Possibly in individual cases, he said.

"Yet these can be matched by wholesale departures from college upon the close of their last football season by athletes who had absorbed so little of the college's essential purposes and held its educational opportunities in such low esteem that they did not care to complete their courses and graduate," he pointed out. "And by other cases, probably more numerous, of bizarre studies that enabled their pursuers to qualify for football but are slim collateral for claims of educational redemption."

Griswold blamed spectator pressure for the separation of academic authority from academic responsibility. "It was the spectators who drove the wedge, not football," he said. "And the spectators are we ourselves, as a nation, as college alumni, and as sports lovers. What we have done we can undo.

"I happen to belong to a group of colleges among which these things are happening," Dr. Griswold said. "These are not unrepresentative institutions. Most of them have run the whole gamut of experiences in football. All, including Yale, have plenty of unfinished business on their hands that must take precedence over any claims to perfection. Yet all have set their course in this direction, as charted in the Ivy Group Agreement. I can think of no better fate for amateur athletics and higher education than that the members of the Ivy Group live up to those provisions and prove by so doing their universal practicability. To assist them in this they may count on strong allies from education. They will draw inner strength from thriving intramural programs, and their task will be lightened by the continued progress of professional athletics. But their strongest ally now as always will be the courage of their own convictions."

# *De-emphasis in Earnest*

## 1956

In 1951, Charley Loftus, Yale's director of sports information, was asked by the New York *Herald-Tribune's* Red Smith how come Douglas Clyde (Peahead) Walker, a fairly famous head coach, had forsaken his position as top dog at Wake Forest College to take a subordinate post as assistant to plump Herman Hickman at Yale. The union of the 41-year-old Herman and the 51-year-old Peahead was, in the truest possible sense, a wedding of the arts. As Herman was a poet, so Peahead was a philosopher.

There was that time down yonder in the Little Smokies when the two old friends were loafing through a holiday at Herman's retreat in Fincastle, Virginia, just the two of them sittin' and thinkin' and spittin' in the crick. Herman, the poet, gestured toward the gray cabin of some neighbors and remarked that they sure were amiable folk.

Peahead Walker, the philosopher, agreed.

"Too poor to paint," he yawned, "and too proud to whitewash."

And so when Loftus, the prosaic type as opposed to the poetic, was asked how come Yale was raiding the Blue Ridge country for its football staff, he answered readily: "It's part of our de-emphasis program."

"De-emphasis?"

"We," Loftus explained patiently, "are de-emphasizing the faculty."

Now, in 1956, the Ivies were officially de-emphasizing football. For the first time in its history, the Ivy League was no longer just a way of life. It was a football reality. More important, the hard-core Big Three (Yale, Harvard, Princeton) had restored "full rights and privileges" to Pennsylvania. The Quakers were blackballed in 1946 by Ivy schools for going big time in a very un-Ivy way. For the next 10 years, Penn paid penance, conducting a victory-with-honor campaign wherein the Red and Blue stacked a squad of honor students week after week against such hordes as Duke, California, Navy, Penn State, Notre Dame, Wisconsin, and Army. Suffice to report, Pennsylvania was 0-18 in a most highly unsuccessful campaign through 1954 and '55.

Now the round-robin schedule was beginning in full, with each team playing the seven others every season. The schedule was limited to nine games, with Harvard playing only eight, thus precluding very much outside competition.

In 1956, the inaugural year, Yale seemed equipped to sweep through its schedule. With 33 lettermen returning and only two members of the first two teams lost by graduation, some experts forecast in their preseason analysis that "the Elis could well be one of the top teams of the nation." Among those who were so high on Yale was its old coach, Herman Hickman.

"On the strength of last year's record and light graduation losses," Herman said, "Yale must be picked as one of the best squads in the country. On my recent tour when Yale was mentioned as a possibility on the 'Eleven Elevens,' I was asked if I was really serious. I am. The Bulldogs are well fortified at quarterback with Dean Loucks and Dick Winterbauer; Dennis McGill is the best running back in modern Yale history. Although Gene Coker was lost at fullback by a recent injury, two replacements are strong. The ends are the best in a decade in size, ability, and depth. The middle of the line has some problems, but barring injury at the halfback position, Yale should take it all."

Coach Jordan Olivar was especially optimistic.

"We are anticipating a real finished and polished performance from our first team," he said. "The boys will be playing together as a unit for tl fourth year in a row, including an undefeated freshman season. Everyone is talking about an undefeated season. We realize that these are very few and far between. But teams with the potential of this year's are, by the same token, also very few and far between. Because of our experience, we should not lose games by mistakes. If we do lose, it will be because opponents have won on their own merit."

On paper, Cornell looked like the best bet to thwart Yale's bid for the first *official* Ivy League title. The Big Red had the best backfield in the conference. The big weakness during the previous two years at Cornell was in the line, but there was good experience and size returning.

Although they won only three games in 1955, Dartmouth showed tremendous improvement under the first year tutelage of Coach Bob Blackman. All the losses, with the exception of the 20-0 Yale game, were by a touchdown or less. The big line and fast backs of the undefeated '55 freshman team were expected to turn some of those close losses into wins and make the Big Green a contender.

Princeton had just three regulars returning from

*The list of Ivy League football coaches at the time the conference began formal round-robin play in 1956 reads like a Coaches* Who's Who. *From left: Lou Little, Columbia; Lloyd Jordan, Harvard; Jordan Olivar, Yale; George (Lefty) James, Cornell; Steve Sebo, Pennsylvania; Bob Blackman, Dartmouth; Alva Kelley, Brown; and Charley Caldwell, Princeton.*

*This is what the Ivy eight fight over—the Ivy League football trophy, originally a gift from one of the classes at the University of Pennsylvania in the 1920s.*

the 1955 championship team, and of those only quarterback John Sapoch remained of the starting backfield. However, Charlie Caldwell was high on sophomore tailback Fred Tiley, a 195-pounder from Lansford, Pennsylvania. The Tigers would again move out of Caldwell's streamlined single wing. Their buck-lateral series was considered one of the most spectacular offensive sequences in modern football, and that, combined with one of the best defensive lines in the Ivy League, warned conference foes not to count out the Caldwell team.

The only other first division contender was expected to be Pennsylvania. True, the Red and Blue had lost 18 straight games, but 38 talented sophomores vowed to end the two-year victory famine. Despite 16 lettermen returning, Coach Steve Sebo hoped to be starting most of his sophs by midseason, or as soon as they could pick up the intricacies of varsity football.

Technically speaking, college football across the nation was little different from that of the year before. The amended rules provided for only two changes of importance: rubber footballs could be used by those who liked the idea, and teams that got free timeouts in 1955 by ripping their own breakaway jerseys had to suffer a regular timeout to re-equip a player on the field.

The atmosphere in which Ivy League football was played and the attitude with which it was received varied widely from school to school. At Harvard, for example, it was received more casually by students than ever before—not that they didn't enjoy the games or didn't go to them. "We just don't think of football as a ritualistic orgy," said one Harvard underclassman. "You know, Mark Twain once gave a humorous lecture in Boston and was horrified at the soberness of his audience. Afterward an old lady went up to him and said, 'Mr. Twain, I enjoyed that so much that I had all I could do to keep from laughing.' Maybe we feel a little that way about football."

But, for all that, the Ivies would go on setting much of the social tone of football. There would be station wagon picnics with martinis before games as usual, the custom of setting up a big tent for student-graduate lunches at out-of-town games, just as elegant as they were when F. Scott Fitzgerald was at Princeton and Cole Porter at Yale. And there was sure to be the Old Grad, drink in hand, hurrying toward the stadium in his raccoon coat, perhaps the same one he had worn to the Harvard-Yale game since he was a student; the late-night bonfires at Hanover; bladder-ball games at New Haven; a Columbia mascot that looked more suited for combat than the team; and all those straw-hatted bandsmen downing a couple of kegs of beer before doing their thing at half time. Ah, the rituals of Ivy League football. No matter the outcome on the playing field, the real fun was simply in being there.

For the first four weeks of the season, Yale followed form, rolling over Connecticut, Brown, Columbia, and Cornell. And for the second year in a row Colgate spoiled the Elis perfect record. Yale outgained Colgate 244 yards to 150 rushing and pumped out 19 first downs to Colgate's 10, but Colgate won, 14-6. Except for two momentary defensive lapses—a pass interception for a 78-yard touchdown run and later a 14-yard touchdown pass—Yale owned the game. Early in the first quarter, the Blue marched in short, methodical bursts to Colgate's 22-yard line, and a touchdown seemed inevitable. But, as quarterback Dean Loucks delayed too long on a short jump pass over the line, someone jarred his arm. The ball wobbled a few yards into the hands of Al Jamison, the Colgate end, who ran to the midfield stripe and, just as he was tackled, lateraled to halfback Walter Betts, who continued on for the touchdown.

The second half was more of a ball game as each team scored once. First it was Yale's turn, and their season-long inability to capture the elusive point-after-touchdown hardly seemed important as they demonstrated it to the crowd of 38,236. But, when Colgate scored again and converted successfully, Yale needed two touchdowns to go in front, and time was running out. With less than eight minutes remaining, Yale took possession and reverted to its plodding ground movement, even though it was obvious to the most naive football fan that daring, fast-scoring plays were needed to erase the eight-point deficit. Dean Loucks was apparently the only one in Yale Bowl who was not watching the clock, and he wasted five of those valuable minutes bringing the ball in slow stops to the Colgate 15, where he lost possession on a fumble.

After the game, Colgate Coach Hal Lahar drawled in a soft southern accent, "It was the breaks. We got the breaks, Yale didn't." He looked a little sheepish about his team's big upset.

Although the Colgate loss did not affect Ivy League standings—Yale and Princeton were still tied for the lead with 3-0 records—the Tigers were now considered the new favorite on the strength of their 28-20 win over Colgate a week earlier.

"The only other apparent threat to the conference crown is Harvard (3-1), which in recent years has grown November muscles and used them in knocking over either Yale or Princeton or both," wrote Don Parker of *Sports Illustrated.* "It could happen again this year, too."

But it didn't happen. Jordan Olivar regrouped his troops and finished the season in a flourish, with lopsided wins over Dartmouth, 19-0; Penn, 40-7; Princeton, 42-20; and Harvard, 42-14.

Perhaps the Harvard student body did not think of The Game as "a ritualistic orgy," but 38,240 (including 1,000 standees) fans did, and they were willing to brave the wintry New England blasts to watch the rites. Many of them filled Harvard's venerable Soldiers' Field to see a Yale team lauded as possibly as good as any in two or three decades—on the days when it was in the mood to play. Although injuries had sidelined several Elis, seven of the first string were seniors, and the starting backfield of Dean Loucks, Dennis McGill, Al Ward, and Steve Ackerman was rated favorably with any starting quartet in the country.

Probably because their football careers were ending, these exceptional football players were in the mood to play one of their finest games against Harvard. Seven minutes after the kickoff, McGill scored for the first time, and the touchdown parade was on its way. In the second quarter, McGill took a pitchout from Loucks and ran 78 yards to score again. Not to be outdone, Ward, the other halfback, took a Harvard kickoff two minutes later and ran it back 79 yards for a third touchdown. Although Harvard, as it always will against Yale, played the kind of football from time to time that might have beaten anyone, it was only too obvious that November 24 was Yale's day. Harvard's seven-man line, with the secondary rigidly anchored on its flanks, could not hope to arrest an attack with the versatility, power, and speed of Yale's. Perhaps no college team could have on the farewell appearance of the great Yale seniors.

° ° °

The 1956 season also marked the farewell appearances of two coaches, Charlie Caldwell and Lou Little. Before another year rolled around, Caldwell was stricken by cancer and gave up the coaching reins to Dick Colman. On November 1, 1957, the day before the Dartmouth game, Caldwell died.

Lou Little was probably the most envied man in his "profession," not because of his record, which on the surface was not distinguished, but because of his university, which was. The pressure to win at all costs that makes many coaches' lives a hell on earth simply did not exist for Columbia Lou.

A good sample of the kind of support Little got came in 1953 after a so-so season of four wins and five losses. Robert Harron, assistant to President Grayson Kirk at Columbia, was approached in the Columbia Club by an aging football enthusiast who shook his head sadly. "Pretty bad season," he said.

"We'll do better next year," Harron told him.

"We'd better," the Old Grad said grimly. "If we don't, Lou Little's liable to leave us for another school."

With that kind of support, it would have been easy for most men to forget they ever had other ambitions. Not Lou Little. He still wished, at the age of 63, that he had had enough sense to follow his original intention of studying medicine and becoming a country doctor.

"Coaching," he said in his final year, "is something I wouldn't recommend to anyone. I tell my boys that if they're smart enough to get into Columbia, they have no business going into professional football or coaching. They ought to aim at something more productive and worthwhile, like medicine, law, or engineering."

Little did a great deal more than simply lecture to his boys. He exerted pressure in strong doses with the result that more than half of a typical year's squad actually wound up in graduate or professional study of some kind. He was particularly proud of his players who became doctors. It was a sort of compensation for his own lapse.

But while Columbia Lou preached that the primary purpose of any college should be academic development, he did not underrate football and other competitive sports. "I think every college undergraduate should participate in some form of competitive activity," he said at the time of his retirement. "It's just not right for a student to go to college and not give something in return in the way of campus participation and leadership."

Part of the reason for the lack of pressure on Little was the fact that he was regarded at Columbia as a teacher rather than just a football coach. "He's the university's best teacher," Dean Herbert Hawkes, a colleague, once said. "Some of the best teaching at Columbia is being carried on each afternoon down at the football field by Lou Little." When the distinguished Hawkes pinned that accolade on Coach Little, he was not referring to Lou's gift for inducting the young into the mysteries of the football "belly" series. Rather, he was thinking of the goals Lou always had in mind when he said, "I want men who will knock the other fellow's brains out, then help him up and brush him off." The dean was thinking of what so many boys had in mind when, after playing their last game for the Lions, they told the coach: "Thank you, Mr. Little, for teaching us so much more than football."

"An athlete at Columbia has to be a student first," Lou often said approvingly. "If he wants to go out for football or some other sport, he may, but only if he meets all the scholastic requirements. There are no 'snap' courses and no athletic scholarships."

For all the academic talk, however, the desire to win was probably as strong in Little as in any man who ever coached. He disagreed passionately with the practitioners of sport who believed in teaching athletes to lose gracefully, and he thought a man who did not mind losing a fool. "I want my boys to hate losing," he'd say, "hate it enough to force themselves to work harder to win." And Columbia players did.

Not even the discerning Little could measure the influence he exerted through his "Squad Letters," which he wrote every month and mimeographed and mailed to the hundreds who played football for Columbia after he assumed charge in 1930.

To be a taskmaster who could lead and a martinet who inspired loyalty rather than resentment was a rare art. That was Lou Little.

One year a former Columbia player fell ill with leukemia, and Lou, in his periodic letter to football grads, asked for financial aid for the man. But Lou made one stipulation: He wanted it plainly understood that he would be the only one to give more than $5. (He contributed a whole lot more.)

Sports pages and alumni, as a rule, rank football coaches according to the number of games their teams win. Not Columbia. The heads of Columbia regarded the Lions stunning 21-20 victory over heavily favored Army in 1947 as far less significant than the fact that Lou's boys flunked only four of 335 academic subjects that year.

It was the late Grantland Rice who said that a coach's won-and-loss record had little to do with the affection and respect for him. "I've learned more from a coach talking with him after a *losing* game than I ever did in discussing the play that won for him," Granny said.

Coach Little remarked on this one night after Columbia had lost a midseason game. Granny walked into the Columbia dressing room after the loss and found Lou alone. "Granny," Lou said with a laugh, "why is it that you always show up after we lose, but I seldom see you when we win one?"

"It's this way, Lou," Granny explained. "After you've won, I've got to buck a subway rush even to get a glimpse of you. But on days like this—well, it gives us a chance to get together for a nice chat. That I like."

Lou Little was employed for 27 years as head football coach at Columbia. During that time his Lions were seldom out-thought and never out-fought. He had only five winning seasons—1940, '45, '46, '47, and '51—but along the way he developed some exceptional athletes.

"I must confess," Lou said several years ago, "that I greatly miss coaching, particularly on Saturdays. I guess what I miss most is that old game excitement. It gets you. However, it pleases me greatly as I continuously hear from my former players. Practically all are doing well, indeed, in their life's chosen vocations. I like to think I helped in a small way."

Many years ago, the beloved Professor William Lyon Phelps, famous teacher and critic of English Literature at Yale, wrote: "The football coaches are a fine body of men who are expert teachers. They have unrivaled opportunities for a good influence on character and temperament. Most of them certainly deserve our respect and admiration. And we must remember nowadays, with the relaxation of discipline, that the only part of college life where discipline is maintained is in major sports."

Lou Little lived up to that philosophy in every way.

## 1957

College football, with its one-platoon rule restoring warmth and personality to the game, continued its resurgence in 1957. The crowds grew bigger, the game better. Since the days of the flying wedge, the emphasis had shifted more and more from brute force to finesse and subtlety. Plays now deceived not only the defense but the millions of people who hoped for a glimpse of the ball and seldom got one. Still, the result of perfect execution of the fluid, violent patterns of football was the long run, the long pass, or a combination. A pass, thrown well and far and on target, created a lovely clean line against the autumn sky, and the reaching quick moment when the ball and the receiver came together was a thrilling one. The long "bomb" played a vital role in deciding the 1957 Ivy League Championship.

This marked the second year of formal competition and round-robin play in the Ivies, and it was getting pretty hard to judge the caliber of play of the eight teams as a whole because of the lack of an intersectional schedule.

Princeton, with its finest group of sophomores in a long time, was picked in early September as the finest all-around team and best bet to win the conference title. Dick Colman, the new coach, had inherited from Caldwell one of the strongest backfields in several years, centered around tailback Tom Morris and fullback Fred Tiley. Morris accounted for almost one-third of Princeton's total gains in 1956, while Tiley averaged 4.4 yards per carry. Captain John Sapoch, as single wing quarterback, rarely carried the ball and was used mainly for blocking. He did, however, handle the ball on all buck-lateral and keep plays, either running, pitching out, or passing. Two brilliant sophomore backs were Dan Sachs, hailed as the best prospect since Royce Flippin, and Dick George, a left-handed wingback.

Princeton's chief opposition came from Yale and Dartmouth. The Elis, one of the outstanding teams in the country in 1956, started the season with veterans in only three positions, end, quarterback, and guard. The rest of the starters were inexperienced squadmen and rising sophomores. Dick Winterbauer, who alternated with Dean Loucks for two years, was the best quarterback in the league. As for Dartmouth, it sorely needed a good quarterback at the outset to handle Coach Bob Blackman's V formation. Blackman found him in sophomore Bill Gundy. "We may not go all the way," Blackman said at the start of the season, "but we'll come up with some surprises. We expect to make trouble for all comers."

Harvard had a new coach, John Yovicsin, and a new system (balanced T), and the changeover from Lloyd Jordan's single wing to a balanced T had to be accomplished in a brief three weeks, since the Ivy League frowned on spring practice. Although Coach Yovicsin left Gettysburg with fine references as a teacher of football, it was stretching his abilities to almost superhuman proportions to expect him to come up with a winner his first season. He did not (3-5-0), but the time was not far off when he would have to be reckoned with.

Up at Morningside Heights, Columbia also had a new coach and a new basic offense. As Lou Little's successor, Aldo (Buff) Donelli inherited only nine lettermen (six of them starters) and memories of Claude Benham, the great little passer who was the key to the Lions' attack. Coach Donelli brought with him the wing T, but the Light Blue (1-8-0) was unable to equal even its 3-6 record of 1956.

Princeton lived up to its advance notices. Except for a 10-12 loss to Colgate, the Tigers got by Rutgers, Columbia, Penn, Cornell, Brown, and Harvard, and were 5-0 in the league coming up to the Yale game. The Bulldogs had lost to Brown and Penn and were tied by Dartmouth, which was 4-0-1 in conference play.

The Ivy League's eighth Saturday of competition was quite a day. The Big Green barely squeezed past Cornell, 20-19, while Yale surprised the favored Princeton Tiger by completing 15 out of 20 passes for 234 yards and a 20-13 upset. Yale end Mike Cavallon caught three touchdown receptions to drop Princeton back to second place in the standings, a half-game behind unbeaten Dartmouth. Now everything hinged on the showdown of the season between Dartmouth and Princeton at Palmer Stadium, and the Orange, rebounding from the previous week's galling upset loss to Yale, hustled through snow and mud for a conclusive 34-14 victory to win the Ivy Championship. Danny Sachs, the sophomore tailback, his bad ankles notwithstanding, had his hand in four Tiger touchdowns. One was on a superb 60-yard punt return; another followed a pass interception.

While the Orange and Black smeared the Green, Yale handed Harvard its worst scrubbing in the 82-year history of The Game. The Elis really laid it on the helpless Cantabs, 54-0. Quarterback Dick Winterbauer took up where he left off at Princeton the week before by completing 9 of 12 passes, three for touchdowns. The last of these set a Yale career record of 20 touchdown passes.

## 1958

College football had one of its more intriguing seasons in 1958. It was marked by the first change in scoring values since 1912: the award of two points for conversions by running or passing. Nationally, it was also a year enriched by Army's introduction of the "lonely end" attack and by Louisiana State's employment of a novel three-platoon system in which a two-way "White" team was supported by offensive and defensive units dubbed "Go" team and "Chinese Bandits."

It was a year that saw the breakup of the Pacific Coast Conference, the cancellation of the PCC-Big Ten Rose Bowl pact, and the early rise of the Air Force Academy to major status.

Going into 1958, college football was divided over the rules change, but initial opposition dwindled as it became apparent that the new scoring could spice an otherwise dull play and generally enliven matters. The result was that the season had many competitive highlights.

In what one preseason forecaster called "the still-lively Ivy League," Princeton was favored to repeat its championship—and perhaps even capture the Lambert Trophy—despite threatening noises out of Dartmouth, Pennsylvania, and Yale. Coach Dick Colman had just about everything he wanted in the way of players, but he admittedly needed a solution to the number one guessing game of 1958—whether to kick for one point after the touchdown or to run or pass for two points. "I'm going to invest in an applause meter," he said before the first game of the year. "Whenever we score a touchdown, I'll ask for a display of fan sentiment. The fans will decide, and I will be off the hook."

Up at Hanover, Bob Blackman, in his fourth season as coach of the Big Green, felt that his program was a year behind schedule. In 1957, he told a reporter, "Every place I've ever gone to coach, the team was at rock bottom. But I've always been fortunate in having a championship by the third year." Now he was in his fourth term and still no title. Maybe this would be the year. After all, he did have a history of rising up out of the depths. When he came down with polio at the age of 19, he went a couple of months without being able to swallow, much less walk. Now he was jogging with only a slight limp and swallowed enough to rank as one of the roundest-faced coaches in the nation. When he took over the head coaching job at Monrovia, California, High School in 1946, the team had not won in two years, attendance averaged something under 200, and the bleachers had been condemned. Within three years he had taken Monrovia to a 10-1 season and a final game turnout of 15,000.

From Monrovia, Blackman went on to achieve the same sort of thing at Pasadena City College and the University of Denver.

Last year had been the most successful season in 20 years at Dartmouth, but now the team was faced with a major rebuilding problem. Five of that first team were gone and 14 in all had graduated from the team that lost only the Ivy League title game on the last day of last season. When the players reported to preseason practice, Coach Blackman said he especially missed Captain Joe Palermo, Dartmouth's first All-American in 20 years, pass-catching Dave Moss, and quarterback Dave Bradley. Key holdovers in the line were Captain Al Krutsch at guard, tackle Dave Bathrick, and end Scott Palmer. Other line spots would have to be manned by reserves or former members of a weak freshman team, which had won only once in a six-game schedule. Quarterbacking would be handled by Bill Gundy, the East's leading punter, who had been Bradley's understudy. Rounding out the backfield were fullback Brian Hepburn and halfbacks Jim Burke and John Crouthamel. Yes, the Big Green would be strong—but would it be strong enough?

Cornell was 3-6 in 1957, but, according to the dope sheet, the Big Red would be a greatly improved team in 1958, particularly on defense. Lettermen were back at all line positions, and Coach Lefty James's only problem was that he was short on experienced halfbacks. His chief loss in the backfield was Bob McAniff, the Ivy League's leading rusher in 1957. Now James counted on lettermen Terry Wilson and John Webster to carry the load. Other ball carriers were Captain Bob Hazzard and Phil Taylor, with speed to burn. The team's top scorer in 1957, Tom Skypeck, stood 6′2″, weighed 190 pounds, and was a powerful runner as a T quarterback. "The Big Red could finish a strong second," predicted the dopesters.

When the Princeton Tigers devoured all but Colgate and Yale en route to their first championship of the Ivy League round robin, it was the third straight year that they had scratched out a 7 and 2 record. But now Coach Colman was confronted with rebuilding a line and replacing blocking back John Sapoch. Fullback Fred Tiley, tailback Dan Sachs, and wingback Mike Ippolito gave the Tigers plenty of offensive punch. Tiley led the team with 52 points and 592 yards rushing in 1957; number two man was Sachs with 48 points and a 6.0 rushing average.

The original Big Three of the Ivies had one of their most miserable opening days in many a year. Princeton was unable to contain Billy Austin, talented Rutgers halfback who had a hand in all four touchdowns, and the Tigers lost, 28-0. Harvard, rated as the most improved team in the league and a dark horse contender, found itself a 6-3 upset victim after Buffalo's hustling Nick Bottini blocked a punt and recovered in the end zone. And Yale? The Bulldogs managed to escape the fate of Princeton and Harvard, but just by the barest of margins as a 79-yard sprint by Herb Hallas and Art LaVallie's two-point conversion edged Connecticut, 8-6. The graduation loss of quarterback Dick Winterbauer, the Ivy League's top passer in 1957 with 14 TD passes, was very evident. Now Coach Jordan Olivar was reduced to having to experiment with untried sophomores at the position. Unless a quarterback could be found, Yale definitely was in trouble for the rest of the year.

Despite a thin sophomore crop, it was stated before the season opened that the Bruins of Brown "could be Ivy League spoilers." Coach Al Kelley had one of the conference's top linemen in his center and captain, Don Warburton, a fine quarterback and passer in Frank Finney, and a promising fullback in Paul Choquette. On October 4, Brown traded touchdowns all afternoon with Yale, but the Bruins had the last word, scoring twice in the final quarter to beat the Elis, 35-29. Choquette's power lunges and Finney's sleight of hand kept Yale off balance, while Nick Pannes, Finney's sub, came up with the clincher, a 7-yard pass to Jack Cronin in the final minutes.

In other Ivy League games that weekend, Princeton opened the defense of its title by stomping all over Columbia, 43-8; contender Dartmouth held off Penn, 13-12; and Cornell, greatly improved over the year before, outscored Harvard, 21-14.

Badly battered in 10 straight losses over two seasons, Coach Buff Donelli plainly said that he expected his Columbia Lions to break out of their rut any game now. "We'll get better," he said, "because we can't get any worse." And so in their only victory of the year, the Lions finally emerged from the depths to upset Yale, 13-0, after guard Gene Appel found himself in possession of an errant Eli pass and carried it back 65 yards for a touchdown.

Meanwhile, Brown, toying with dreams of Ivy League supremacy after victories over Columbia and Yale, was shocked into reality by a hard-hitting, rugged-defending Dartmouth team, which held the Bruin backs to a mere 52 yards and struck swiftly and smartly from its V formation for a 20-0 triumph. At Philadelphia, Princeton spent most of a sunny, windy afternoon trying to overhaul Penn, finally succeeding when fullback Fred Tiley smashed over from the 1-yard line in the closing minutes to put the Tigers ahead, 20-14. John L. Sullivan, the Tigers' sophomore tailback, took over when Dan Sachs was taken off with a back injury, and Sullivan sparked Princeton to three touchdowns before he, too, limped off.

Harvard, cheerless in its first two games, uncovered Charlie Ravenel, a slick little sophomore quarterback, who led the Cantabs to a 20-0 win over favored Lehigh.

Cornell was supposed to be greatly improved on defense, but the Big Red forgot to follow the script in its third game of the year as Syracuse dipped down into its fourth and fifth strings in an attempt to hold down the final score, 55-0. The following week, Cornell found life back among the Ivies a little more tolerable. Holding off a surprisingly weak Yale, 12-7, the Big Red joined Princeton and Dartmouth, both active in nonleague games, at the top of the Ivies. Elsewhere, improving Harvard latched on to four Columbia fumbles and turned three of them into touchdowns under the guiding hand of Charlie Ravenel to win, 26-0; Penn edged Brown, 21-20, when the Bruins, gambling for the works after their third touchdown, failed to make a two-point conversion; Princeton, which seemed to have an abundance of able tailbacks, found two more in Hugh Scott and Ray Empson, who led the Tigers to an easy 40-13 triumph over Colgate; and Dartmouth, in over its head for the first time, gave it a good try against Holy Cross, losing 14-8 when Johnny Esposito grabbed a blocked field goal attempt and sprinted 81 yards for the tie breaker.

While Cornell (3-0) ran over Princeton, 34-8, to gain undisputed first place in the league standings, Harvard pulled one of the major upsets of the year, a 16-8 victory over Dartmouth. The loss dropped the Big Green into a second-place tie with Princeton.

John Yovicsin considered the win over Dartmouth a milestone in the annals of modern football at Cambridge. "It finally convinced our players that we could beat the good teams in the league," he said. Dartmouth was undone by its own guile and the alert play of end Hank Keohane, who, with five minutes remaining, intercepted a screen pass off a fake kick at the Green 16. Three plays later, Chet Boulris bulled into the end zone to break an 8-8 tie.

The 1958 season, Coach Yovicsin said, taught him a very obvious lesson about Harvard football. "I found out," he explained, "that Harvard players can dream up the weirdest ways to lose football games. I also learned that they can win games no one else believes they have a ghost of a chance to

*Dartmouth won the Ivy League football trophy for the first time in 1958. The young man instrumental in bringing it to Hanover was quarterback Bill Gundy, shown here with Coach Bob Blackman.*

*Leading rusher and All-Ivy halfback on Dartmouth's championship team in 1958 was Jake Crouthamel, who found a big hole against Cornell as the Green won, 32-15. He succeeded Bob Blackman in 1971 and coached Dartmouth to three straight Ivy titles.*

win."

For two-thirds of the season, Cornell's dream of a championship held up. Then came losses to Brown (8-12) and Dartmouth (15-32), leaving Dartmouth and Princeton to fight it out for the title on the last day of the season. The Big Green and the Tigers went at it for 60 bruising minutes as if the very fate of the world depended upon the outcome. And indeed it did—the Ivy League world. For when the last cheer pealed across Palmer Stadium, it was Dartmouth that wore the Ivy League crown, but not until Princeton tailbacks Dan Sachs and Hugh Scott, running and passing the Tigers to a 12-6 lead, had worried the Green nearly to death.

Dartmouth struck back on the accurate pitching (9 for 14) of quarterback Bill Gundy, the steady hammering of halfback John Crouthamel, a provoking figure most of the day, and crunching line play to wear down the Tigers and make off with a 21-12 victory.

Harvard and Yale, with nothing more at stake than The Game, bumbled and fumbled their way through most of a lackluster first half until nervy quarterback Ravenel, a mighty mite whose enthusiasm inspired his teammates, picked up the Cantabs and made them play decent football. Rolling out on option plays, thrusting and darting through and around the Eli forwards, Ravenel lugged Harvard all the way to the 7-yard line, from where he scored on the last play of the second quarter.

In the second half, Ravenel lit the fuse for scoring runs of 20 and 17 yards by Chet Boulris and Larry Repcher. With the gates wide open, Albie Cullen went over from the 2-yard line to complete a 28-0 rout of the de-fanged Bulldogs, who finished the league schedule still looking for their first win.

The quote of the year honors, however, went to Buff Donelli (1958 record, W 1, L 8), when a visitor asked his permission to watch a practice session. "We've got nothing to hide," Donelli said. "I wish we did."

## 1959

Acutely aware of professional football's growing appeal, the collegians widened their goalposts in 1959 from 18′6″ to 23′4″ to encourage field goal kicking. The major college place-kickers responded by booting the unprecedented total of 192 field goals of 380 tried, including a 52-yarder by Texas A. & M.'s Randy Sims, the longest by a collegian since 1941.

Another amendment to the college rules legalized a "wild card" substitution. This allowed each team to send in one player without penalty whenever the clock was stopped. It gave the college game greater scope for specialization and made it easier to pass instructions to quarterbacks and defensive signal callers.

Two other developments marked the 1959 season. The colleges lost some of their most illustrious coaches during the winter and spring. Red Blaik stepped down at West Point in favor of Dale Hall. Eddie Erdelatz resigned at Annapolis and was succeeded by Wayne Hardin. Joe Kuharich took over from Terry Brennan at Notre Dame. John McLaughry now was in charge at Brown, Bump Elliott at Michigan, and Alva Kelley at Colgate.

The other new factor was a meeting at the Netherland-Hilton Hotel in Cincinnati, where the country's independent football giants, bedeviled by competition from the pros, talked about an adventure in togetherness, a jet-flown nationwide conference of their own. As outlined, the conference would consist of 12 schools divided into East and West divisions. In the East would be Army, Navy, Notre Dame, Pittsburgh, Syracuse, and Penn State; the West would be Southern California, UCLA, California, Washington, Air Force Academy, and perhaps Stanford. Each team would play four games in its own division and one in the other. Due to scheduling difficulties—most major colleges are scheduled three or four years ahead—conference play could not begin before 1964 or 1965 and would involve only football.

The toughest problems for these independents had to do with athletic scholarships, recruiting, and academic requirements. "Some of the California schools could not live under the restrictions of the eastern colleges," said Captain Slade Cutter, the outspoken representative from the Naval Academy. "Nor could we live under some of their rules. All of the colleges involved, however, have high academic requirements, and it is not impossible to develop a comfortable framework for the conference as a whole."

The dissolution of the nine-member Pacific Coast Conference would clear the way for the creation of the proposed new "airplane" conference. The proposed league was in direct challenge to the thesis of former President Robert M. Hutchins of the University of Chicago, the tireless old opponent of college football who was responsible for Chicago dropping the game in 1939. For years Dr. Hutchins's advice to other college presidents had been: "Give it (football) up and let the pros have it." In his sternest manner, he constantly told the country that college football could never be as good, as entertaining, and as solvent as the professional game. The theme was familiar. Hutchins had been preaching it since 1954.

"The real hope lies in the slow but steady progress of professional football," he said. "Not enough people will pay enough money to support big-time intercollegiate football in the style to which it has become accustomed when for the same price they can see real professionals, their minds unconfused by thoughts of education, play the game with true professional polish. When professional football has reached this point, we shall be able to disentangle sport and higher education. Students can play—or not play—as they wish, their friends may attend and applaud if they like. But *students* will come to college to study. Alumni will believe that this is something a normal, red-blooded young American can properly do. This happened at Chicago."

In the midst of all the controversy, the Ivy League, the very cradle of football, went right along minding its own business. Without trying to convince outsiders that the glory days were returning, its teams continued playing heavily de-emphasized football and belting the blazes out of one another within conference boundaries. The primary educational responsibilities continued to be stressed; athletic recruiting and practice sessions would go on being curtailed. With the exception of the Yale Bowl, which seated 70,896, there were no huge stadiums to be filled each weekend. Harvard went so far as to remove 17,000 end-zone seats and reduce the capacity of its stadium—the first big one in America—to 38,114.

It was left to non-Ivy John P. Curley, director of athletic facilities at nearby Boston College, to sum up what was going on in New England football. "Let's face it," he said in 1959, "football in this corner of the country is very provincial. We get a good share of the local talent, but we don't draw athletes much beyond the New England-New York area. Neither do the other schools, except Harvard, Yale, Princeton and Dartmouth, which have a greater geographical representation. The reason is simple. We want the good boys, but their marks must be good too. Many fine players apply, but you'd be surprised at the number who have to be turned down. Their grades just aren't good enough to meet our standards. The high school football in New England is as good as any. This is one of the hottest recruiting sections in the country. That is obvious when the Big Ten and southern schools come in every year and siphon off a lot of good boys."

Strange as it might have seemed to observers west of the Appalachians, where the Ivy League game was regarded as little more than intramural in some quarters, Ivy League football and hard-nosed football were not mutually exclusive terms. Harvard's John Yovicsin, for example, was considered a teacher of the hard-nosed school, and he was a man who felt that some of the most competitive football in the country was played—without benefit of spring practice—right in the Ivy League. Each Saturday Ivy opponents came jaw to jaw on relatively equal terms.

"This year," Yovicsin said in 1959, "the league is stronger from top to bottom than at any time since it became a formal competitive conference."

Look too, said Ivy fans, at the diversity of offenses emerging from hallowed Ivy halls. Dartmouth had one of the game's cleverest strategists in Coach Bob Blackman, originator of the V formation. Yovicsin himself featured a T with flankers. Lefty James was coming out with a spread at Cornell. Penn used a multiple offense. Princeton stuck with the old reliable single wing. New Coach John McLaughry taught what he called the "side-saddle T" at Brown.

Down at Penn, Coach Steve Sebo had his work cut out for him. Just 10 of 32 lettermen graduated from his 4-5-0 team of 1958, but only three returnees—ends Barney Berlinger and Jon Greenawalt and center Ron Champion—could be relied on for top-flight service up front when Sebo counted noses in September. Directing the wing T traffic was Larry Purdy, who was encouraged by the Quaker coaching staff to junk some of his conservatism for a little more daring. Dave Coffin, sporting a 5.1-yard ball-carrying average, was the fleetest man in the Ivy League. The betting was that Penn would have its first winning team since 1951.

Pennsylvania's revitalization program seemed ready to pay off. Its backs generated enough drive to score consistently, and the linemen pulled out fast enough to provide the necessary interference as the Quakers mowed down Lafayette, 26-0; Dartmouth, 13-0, despite Coach Blackman's vaunted V with single and double slots, men in motion, balanced and unbalanced lines; Princeton, 18-0, one of the preseason favorites to win the Ivy title; and Brown, with number two league rusher Paul Choquette, 36-9. Then Penn, celebrating its 99th year in football, went outside the conference to play Navy to a 22-22 tie. Next, the Red and Blue suffered its first letdown of the season as gambling Charlie Ravenel brought joy to Harvard hearts, 12-0. Penn got back on the winning track with victories over Yale, 28-12, and Columbia, 24-6.

The championship was on the line when the Quakers kicked off to Cornell in the final game of the season. Early in the third quarter, Coach Sebo, hanged in effigy so many times that he winced every time he passed a clothesline, had some terrifying moments when his Penn team trailed the Big Red, 13-0. But sub quarterback George Koval, a dashing young man with an accurate throwing arm, and halfback Fred Doelling, a fearsome All-Ivy runner, bailed out the bumbling Quakers, leading them to a 28-13 victory and Penn's first Ivy League title. Doelling spread the defenders with wide sweeps around the ends and Koval filled the empty holes with three TD passes.

In spite of Penn's 7-1-1 record, the school's best since 1947, the wolves kept after Sebo's scalp, whose overall stats were now 18-35-1 in six seasons. Win or lose, the loudest rumor going into the Cornell game was that John Stiegman of Rutgers was going to replace Sebo in 1960. The rumor was true. Steve Sebo had coached his last game at Pennsylvania. But, saving the best for last, the parting mentor at least took the Ivy crown with him.

Before the last Old Grad's shout had faded to a hoarse whisper, Charlie Ravenel had a field day at the expense of Yale in The Game. The little quarterback convinced one and all that his name actually was Charlie Ravenel, not Charlie Brown. Harvard opponents soaked in that name, Ravenel, and thought, "Gee, look at the southern boy dealing out those plays like a riverboat gambler dealing faro. I mean, with a name like that, he might have a derringer up his sleeve."

All right, so Ravenel was from Charleston, the name was real. The thing was, if there were many more Charlie the Gamblers people were likely to start thinking that the bright boys down on Madison Avenue were handling Ivy League football. Because what Ravenel did to the Yale Bulldogs in the final Harvard-Yale game of the decade shouldn't have happened to a canine. The Crimson showed plenty of pep as their backs repeatedly tore through the Yale line, and in one 12-minute span scored 27 points on the way to a 35-6 roasting. When quarterback Ravenel was not dominating play, halfback Chet Boulris was, gaining 95 yards rushing, connecting on an 85-yard pass play and scoring once. It was Harvard's first winning season in five years, and the fans savored every minute of The Game by waving their handkerchiefs and exploding crimson and yellow smoke bombs.

Bob Blackman knew it would not be easy winning a second consecutive Ivy League title at Dartmouth, but the Big Green, with 15 of 29 lettermen from 1958 to build around, almost had it again. Trailing Penn in the standings only by a half-game, they kept their slim title hopes flickering with a 12-7 victory over Princeton on the final day. With 56 seconds to go, quarterback Bill Gundy hit halfback Alan Rozycki with a pass on the Tiger 5-yard line. Rozycki slithered past several tacklers and into the end zone for the winning score.

For the second time in three years, a tie had cost Dartmouth a share of the conference crown.

# *The Wide-Open Sixties*

## 1960

The big football news for the 1960 season was that the game was still a game, a bit more technical, perhaps, than it was in the 1950s. The players were more specialized, they seemed to be less individualistic, and they were, particularly if they played quarterback, packed full of data, formulas, and nomenclature. But it was still, all in all, much the same exciting contest.

The season's only significant rules change was the adoption of a liberal substitution rule, permitting players to enter and leave games almost at will. Specifically, each team was allowed to make one free substitution between successive downs, even when the game clock was running. For most coaches this meant either or both of two things: They could use one of their players as a messenger to take in signals before each play, and/or they could alternate passing quarterbacks with defensive or running quarterbacks.

It was not just an accident that the coaches were thinking in terms of quarterbacks. For the first time, good quarterbacks were coming out of high schools and prep schools in quantity. Where passers were once rare, almost every team now had at least one, and some had two and three. They knew what to do with the ball, and they knew how to direct a team. So, to get the most out of their quarterbacks and to open up the game, a number of coaches were turning to the wing T. What they liked most about it was its versatility. It permitted a team to use a power offense from a tight wing T, and it also allowed the team to split a back or end wide. Either variation could be employed without having to change basic blocking patterns and assignments. Some coaches were going in for the slot wing T, which split one end wide and put a halfback in the slot between that end and tackle. Others were adopting a multiple offense, which combined fragments of the T, wing T, or split T. Regardless of what you called the offenses, 1960 was to be a season of a lot of splits, flankers, lonely ends, and spreads.

To defend against all this wide-open style of play—the wing T, for example—coaches began turning to something called the three-deep defense. Eight men, rather than nine, were placed fairly close to the line. Three players were stationed deep to pick up the three receivers who could go down for the long passes from the wing T.

The players in 1960 were bigger than ever. Members of the first All-America squad in 1889 averaged 162 pounds and just under 5 feet 10. Seventy-one years later, the average was 208 pounds and 6 feet 1¼ inches.

There were also other things to look for in 1960. More and more teams were resorting to unbalanced lines and the man in motion. The goalposts, widened in 1959, invited more field goals. Punting was being emphasized and improved. The two-point try after touchdown was well received by fans.

There were more college men trying out for positions than ever before. This was because the number of high school players was steadily increasing, while the number of college teams remained relatively stable. The added competition and the fact that many of the boys wanted to go into pro ball after college had them all working harder. As a result they were better players, as a group, than they used to be.

° ° °

In the preseason polls, Harvard was the choice to lead the Ivy League, which appeared to have its best top-to-bottom balance in years. The key to the Crimson's attack was quarterback Charlie Ravenel. He couldn't pass (he completed only 34 of 87 in 1959), he wasn't fast, and he was small, but something remarkable always seemed to happen when he got his hands on the ball. Justly admired as a gambler, Ravenel was expected to take more chances than usual to make up for departed halfbacks Chet Boulris and Albie Cullen and fullback Sam Halaby. But Ravenel did have an experienced two-deep interior line ahead of him as he displayed his favorite rollouts from the flanker T. The best of the linemen were 210-pound tackles Eric Nelson and Bob Pillsbury and guards Terry Lenzner and Bill Swinford. And if those weren't enough, there was sophomore halfback Hobie Armstrong, a swift, deceptive 195-pounder, who could take some of the creases out of Coach John Yovicsin's brow.

Yale was expected to lead the pursuit after Harvard. The Elis had a solid, hard-hitting first team returning. Despite this, Coach Jordan Olivar had to rest his hopes on a sparkling sophomore crop, the best Yale had had in many years. Of the holdovers, quarterback Tom Singleton, adept on rollouts from the split T and a proved passer and punter, was the most talented. There were also halfbacks Lou Miller and Ken Wolfe, the team's leading pass receiver, and fullback Bob Blanchard, all of whom had shown they could move the ball. All-Ivy center Mike Pyle, a bruising linebacker and blocker, was flanked by guards Ben Balme and Paul Bursiek, and converted center Hardy Wills. They gave Yale a large, dependable middle. Still, it was going to be up to the sophomores—and there were some good ones, especially fullback Dave Weinstein, end Dillon Hoey, and tackles Stan Riveles and Dave Mawicke.

Pennsylvania, the 1959 champion, and Cornell were also touted. The Quakers had won the crown, but Coach Sebo had been fired. John Stiegman moved over from Rutgers and was installing his single wing. Fortunately, Sebo left behind some good football players. The fast backs of 1959 were gone, but George Koval, who threw a football a country mile and in '59 had excelled at quarterback in the wing T, was now the tailback. Connie DeSantis, a superior blocker as a guard, was moved to quarterback to clear the way for Koval, wingback Peter Shantz, and fullback Ed Shaw. End Jon Greenawalt, an alert defender, was still around, and All-Ivy tackle Bruce Cummings was the best of the interior linemen.

Coach Lefty James, the dean of Ivy League coaches, was beginning his 14th year with 18 lettermen at Cornell, a group of big, competent sophomores and a good chance for the title. Hoping to make his slot T more productive, Lefty planned to employ the slotback, formerly a blocker, as a runner and pass receiver. To take better advantage of the beefed-up offense, quarterback Marcy Tino, a darting open-field runner, was moved to fullback, and junior Tony Pascal, a superior runner, took over for John Beggs (switched to end) in the slot. Southpaw passer Dave McKelvey was the quarterback and swift George Telesh the left halfback. Interior line strength was good, with Bernie Iliff and John Hanley at tackles, Captain Warren Sundstrom and Dave Thomas at guards, and Dick Lipinski at center.

Dartmouth and Princeton, down from previous peaks, were expected to finish in the second division with Columbia and Brown. "However," one preseason poll reported, "Columbia could be the surprise of the Ivy League." The Lions had not had a winning season since 1951. But with 20 returning lettermen providing seasoned campaigners for every position, even Coach Donelli was cautiously optimistic and mildly hopeful of getting even with Ivy League rivals who had whomped him 18 times in the previous three years. All depended upon quarterback Tom Vasell, who showed lots of potential but often jittered as a sophomore passer in Donelli's intricate wing T.

That's the way the teams lined up in September. Ten weeks later, Yale proved clearly it was the toast of the Ivy League. On the final Saturday of play, only Harvard stood between the Blue and an unbeaten season. The game was played at Cambridge, and Yale, the very first time it got the ball, shot halfback Ken Wolfe through the Harvard right-tackle hole for 41 yards and a touchdown. The Elis added another score when end John Hutcherson alertly picked off one of Ravenel's passes and ran it back 48 yards. There was more—a

33 -yard field goal by Gordon Kaake, a short burst by fullback Bob Blanchard, and two deft scoring passes by second-string quarterback Bill Leckonby—before the limping Ravenel gimped over for Harvard's only touchdown to bring the final score to 39-6, Yale's biggest margin of victory over Harvard in history. All the while, the bruising Yale line, led by tackle Mike Pyle, guard Ben Balme, and center Howard Will, handled the Crimson with ease. When it was over, the Elis had their first unbeaten team since 1923 and the Ivy League title.

Among the other Ivies, Dick Colman's Princeton Tigers, not expected to do as well as in 1959 when they finished in a tie for fifth, beat Dartmouth, 7-0, for second place when tailback John Scott flung a 23-yard pass to John MacMurray with 53 seconds to play. Dartmouth tied Harvard for third place with a 4-3-0 league record.

The Ivy Leaguers closed up shop for the year on Thanksgiving Day in Philadelphia. Penn, a delighted champion in 1959, but desperately striving to avoid last place in 1960, finally found a way to make the best use of tailback George Koval's talents as a passer. Coach John Stiegman confused Cornell's defenders by shifting Koval in and out of all four backfield positions, and sent in the plays that caught the Big Red in the switches. Koval pitched touchdown passes from tailback, wingback, and fullback to defeat Cornell, 18-7.

At the end, only New Mexico (10-0) and Yale (9-0) were among the major teams in the nation that finished the season unbeaten and untied.

Coach Jordan Olivar did not hesitate to call his 1960 edition "the greatest Yale team I ever coached." In nine seasons at New Haven, Olivar had given the Bulldogs eight winning campaigns, including their first modern Ivy League Championship. The beer down at Morey's never tasted so good.

## 1961

By now, Coach Buff Donelli, whose 1960 Lions had moved from last to fifth in one year, was beginning to have a less poisonous view of the Ivy League as Columbia neared football respectability. The 1960 Lions had come within one point, an 8-7 loss to Harvard, of a first division finish. Now they were expected to climb higher—if Tom Vasell, a precise passer and deft wing T quarterback, stayed healthy. Running support for Vasell's passing would be provided by experienced halfbacks Tom Haggerty and Russ Warren and fullback Tom O'Connor. There was one serious problem in the line, namely a replacement for end Bob Federspiel, who caught 20 passes in 1960. But the interior was solid enough, with tackle Bob Asack, big, strong and mobile at 230 pounds; center Lee Black, a rangy 215-pounder; and guard Bill Campbell, a nervy little fellow who linebacked fiercely. Conclusion: All that talent was expected to give Lion supporters something to roar about.

*Yale won all its games and the Ivy League championship in 1960, and Coach Jordan Olivar won the New York Touchdown Club's Coach of the Year Award. His 11-year record at New Haven was 61-32-6.*

The preseason experts sized up the rest of the Ivies in this manner:

Harvard—After three exciting years of quarterback Charlie Ravenel and solid lines, Harvard will have to learn to live with dull mediocrity.

Pennsylvania—The defense needs some help, but strategic use of the wild card and a varied attack will put Penn in the Ivy race.

Princeton—Hugh Scott and Jack Sullivan, the talented alternating tailbacks who put the zing in 1960's single wing, are gone, along with 17 other lettermen. Thus, the Tigers are actually Tiger cubs now and will need time to learn fundamentals.

They will be passive in October, more formidable in November.

Yale—At first glance, it would appear that the Elis are in for trouble after a magnificent unbeaten season in 1960. Ten of last year's starters have departed. Despite severe losses, the Bulldogs are still tough. They might just take the Ivy title again—if Cornell doesn't beat them to it.

Cornell—The Big Red's new look includes Coach Tom Harp, a former Army assistant, the lonely end offense, and Pete Gogolak, a field goal kicker from Hungary. Last in 1960, Cornell could crawl to the top of the Ivy League—if Harp can find the linemen to match such talented backs as quarterback Dave McKelvey and halfbacks Marcy Tino and George Telesh."

Dartmouth—With every one of 1960's starters gone, it will take all of Coach Bob Blackman's considerable ingenuity—and the best of an unbeaten freshman team—to save the Indians from extinction. With only fair passing, Blackman will open up his tricky V formation by using more wide plays. But the outlook at Hanover is somber.

Brown—After two years with the sidesaddle T, Coach John McLaughry has sent it back to the stable and has resurrected the more conventional wing T instead. The accurate passing of quarterback Jack Rohrbach, who set school records for passes (156) and completions (76) last year, will keep Ivy rivals nervous, but it won't be enough to lift the Bruins out of the second division for the third year in a row.

Defending champion Yale polished off Connecticut and Brown in its first two games and was favored over Columbia, October 14, but Coach Buff Donelli set his defenses to hem in the familiar Yale roll-outs and fullback smashes up the middle, then spent an enjoyable afternoon in Yale Bowl admiring his handiwork as his aroused Lions beat the Elis 11-0. Quarterback Tom Vasell passed just often enough to confound Yale, sophomore fullback Al Butts battered away at the line until he scored, and Tom O'Connor kicked a 23-yard field goal to end Yale's victory string at 11 and very likely their chances for a second straight Ivy League Championship.

On the same Saturday, Princeton's swift tailbacks moved the Tigers to the top of the league by outrunning Penn, 9-3, while quarterback Bill King starred as Dartmouth routed Brown, 34-0. But two other Ivy Leaguers found themselves in over their heads. Cornell was no match for Navy and bowed, 31-7; Harvard's "staunch" defense fell apart as Colgate beat the Crimson, 15-0.

At midseason 1961, college football was an assured success all across America. There had been major upsets, such as Columbia's victory over Yale, there had been an abnormal number of last-minute victories and exciting plays, and college football attendance was up as much as 40 percent in some parts of the country.

Responsibility for the renewed enthusiasm for college ball rested in large measure on the more volatile nature of the game in 1961. Almost every good team had abandoned the conservative tactics of the split-T and taken a cue from the pros with split ends and slot and wingbacks and other diffusive deceits. As a result, the ball was moving as it hadn't moved in years.

The wild card substitute, who could be injected into the game between every play, was also important. Not only did this change make it possible for coaches to preserve their quarterbacks from the hazards of defensive play, but they could also send in specialists at almost anything from place-kicking to putting the evil eye on a 250-pound tackle. Mostly, however, coaches used the wild card to send in new plays. As one put it, "If the play works it's mine, if it doesn't it's the quarterback's."

Place-kicking was especially stressed in 1961. With the wider goalposts introduced in 1959, kickers were making good on 80 percent of their attempts, compared with 74.6 percent in 1960. Once again, games were being won by field goals.

After five weeks, the Ivy League continued to suffer at the hands of unimpressed outsiders. While Harvard upset Dartmouth, 21-15, and first place Princeton barely made it past seventh place Cornell, 30-25, Penn, coached by John Stiegman, formerly of Rutgers, collapsed before the Scarlet Knights, 20-6, Columbia fell to Lehigh, 14-7, Brown to Rhode Island, 12-9, and Yale to Colgate, 14-8, giving the Red Raiders a complete sweep over the Big Three.

On November 4, Yale's demise as the Ivy League Champion was almost complete. The bumbling Elis handed grateful Dartmouth an early touchdown, and the aggressive Indians methodically followed quarterback Bill King to an easy 24-8 triumph. However, even without Yale, there were enough live contenders to challenge first place Princeton, which stomped over Brown, 52-0. Columbia's Tom Haggerty dashed through Cornell for 84-, 64-, and 47-yard touchdown runs as the Lions won 35-7, and unpredictable Harvard throttled Penn's single wing, 37-6.

Although the Ivy League traditionally looked down its collective nose at postseason bowls, at least four teams went into the final two weeks playing as though an invitation were in the offing. While the surprising Columbia Lions were securing their future against Dartmouth, Harvard, defending with a tenacity seldom seen in Harvard Stadium in recent years, beat Princeton, 9-7. The Tigers' single wing, weakened by injuries to tailbacks Greg Riley and Hugh MacMillan, was reduced to ineffectual probing after a first period touchdown, and Harvard eventually turned a fumble into the winning score. Guard Ernie Zissis pounced on the loose ball, and sophomore quarterback Bill Humenuk led the Crimson on the 39-yard scoring march, bootlegging around end for the last yard with 4:45 left to play.

Going into the final Saturday of the season, Columbia rested on top of the Ivies with a 6-1-0 record. While they were finishing the year at Rutgers, Harvard, 5-1-0, still had a chance to tie the Lions for the championship with a victory over Yale at New Haven.

Not even the most loyal sons of Rutgers in the mob of 25,500 that overflowed the school's pretty little sunken stadium at New Brunswick gave the Scarlet Knights much of a chance after Columbia took a 19-7 lead late in the third quarter. But, fired up by Dave Brody's 58-yard kickoff return, the Knights attacked the weary Lions so relentlessly that they scored four times in the last period to finish unbeaten for the first time in 93 years. Bill Speranza's 10-yard pass to Lee Curley got Rutgers back in the ball game, his 1-yard plunge put them even at 19-19. Steve Simms crunched over from the 3-yard line, Pierce Frauenheim scored on a 30-yard pass interception, and the Scarlet Knights won, 32-19.

While Columbia was getting its lumps at New Brunswick, Harvard was trading a few with Yale, where The Game almost erupted into a battle royal. The Crimson gratefully turned three Eli misplays into touchdowns, scored another on a pass, and licked the hapless Yales, 27-0. Harvard thus tied Columbia for the Ivy League title, as Dartmouth spoiled Princeton's hopes of making it a three-way knot by beating the Tigers, 24-6.

## 1962

It took Coach Buff Donelli five long years to build a winner at Columbia and just a couple of hours to graduate it. Tom Haggerty, Russ Warren, and Tom Vasell, who gained more than a mile from scrimmage and accounted for 21 touchdowns, were gone. Only two starters remained—guard Tony Day and fullback Tom O'Connor. Donelli was counting on Archie Roberts, Jr., to pick up the slack. Archie was a gifted sophomore quarterback, who, they said, passed like a pro, ran like a halfback, and boomed his punts 60 yards. Unfortunately, the Lions had suffered too many casualties on defense to avoid a return to mediocrity.

At Cornell, Coach Tom Harp's first year was hardly a joyous one. His best backs turned up with sore legs and his lonely end attack was so lonely it often seemed desolate. Only quarterback Gary Wood, a slick option runner, looked good. A determined defense and Wood's brilliance might hold off some teams in 1962, but this wouldn't be enough to go all the way.

Over at Princeton, the woods were full of Tigers. Four deep in precious tailbacks and secure everywhere else, Coach Dick Colman's only real concern was how to make the most use of his riches. A lot of forecasters had their money riding on the Tigers.

Like most Ivy League coaches, Harvard's John Yovicsin could rarely anticipate what fall would bring. But this year he had a fairly good idea, and he wasn't altogether happy. Graduation tore apart the fine line that helped the Crimson to a share of the Ivy Championship in 1961. Tackle Ed Smith was the only regular left. Happily, there was distinction in the backfield, and Harvard would have a good offense, led by quarterbacks Mike Bassett and Bill Humenuk, along with All-Ivy fullback Bill Grana and right half Bill Taylor.

Leaky lines and lack of offense were expected to keep Yale, Penn, and Brown penned up in the lower depths of the league for another year.

This was to be the year of the Big D and B—Dartmouth and Blackman. In an era of football trickery, there were few who possessed more ingenuity than Bob Blackman. He delighted in jabbing his opponents off balance with a seemingly endless variety of stunting defenses, and he hornswoggled them with the V formation, a multiplicity of split ends, slots, and wingbacks, and men in motion. His one shortcoming, generally, was material. This year, however, he had it. The ends, Mike Nyquist and Charlie Greer, were alert defenders, while center Don McKinnon, a bruising 215-pounder, and tackles Bill Blumenschein and Dale Runge, just as big, lent tautness to the interior line. The hub of the attack was quarterback Bill King, 1961's Ivy League total offense leader, who was equally proficient at throwing the ball or running the roll-out. King got plenty of help from junior halfbacks Tom Spangenberg and Dave Lawson.

It took only three weeks for Columbia, defending co-champions, to learn the hard facts of life. Despite the abundant talents of sophomore quarterback Archie Roberts, who passed and ran superbly most of the time, the Lions were no match for Princeton. The Tigers, with the kind of depth that wins titles, sent 18 tailbacks, wingbacks, and fullbacks, six in each position, charging inside and outside the weary and inadequate Columbia defenders, and Princeton won easily, 33-0. Meanwhile, Harvard fell behind Cornell, then tried to scramble back, but a last-play field goal failed by a foot and the Crimson lost, 14-12. Dartmouth smothered Penn with a withering defense and whipped the helpless Quakers, 17-0, while Yale needed a pair of 33-yard field goals by Wally Grant to earn a 6-6 tie with improved Brown.

After beating Penn, there was no stopping Dartmouth. The Big Green rolled over Brown (41-0), Holy Cross (10-0), Harvard (24-6), Yale (9-0), and Cornell (28-21), leading up to the final game against Princeton. Long proud of their defense, which had shut out five teams, the Indians went into the Princeton game still brooding over the fact that Cornell had scored 21 points against them. And before they closed the hatches, the Tigers put 27 points on the scoreboard. But where the defense failed, the Dartmouth offense was superb. It did not fluster on the attack; it had a coolness of execution and an almost professional surety of accomplishment. At Princeton, the Indians survived an inspired challenge and won an exciting game, 38-27. It was not an artistic success for Coach Blackman, for he taught defense as well as offense, but for Dartmouth, the somewhat inscrutable backwoods member of the Ivies, it was a climax to a season that brought the Indians their first unbeaten, untied team since 1925, a warming achievement for the Hanover winter ahead.

Blackman had his first real success with the three-platoon system in 1962 (this was his biggest, deepest squad), but in serious scrapes—as against Cornell and Princeton—the system gave way to some rather frantic scrambling. It was at those times that quarterback Billy King, linebacker Don McKinnon, and halfback Tom Spangenberg were sacred members. King, from Richmond, Virginia, was a special delight to the purists because he got no scholarship help; his father, a Dartmouth grad, was president of the Virginia Bar Association. More

*Columbia's Buff Donelli, left, and Harvard's John Yovicsin shared the Ivy crown in 1961, but Dartmouth's Bob Blackman took the title back to Hanover in 1962.*

important to Dartmouth football, King was the best quarterback in the league, better than Gary Wood of Cornell, better than Archie Roberts of Columbia. He set six Ivy records. He captained the Indians, he ran, he passed, he blocked, he kicked, he made speeches at banquets in compelling southernese ("Lord sakes, we bettah win Sattaday") and charmed his elders with his courtliness.

King used himself freely, especially near the goal (13 touchdowns in 1962), and was positively audacious on third and fourth downs. In the last game of the season, he had uncanny success against Princeton: a 24-yard pass on fourth down to set up one touchdown, a 19-yard third-down pass to keep a touchdown drive going, a 23-yard third-down pass to set up a touchdown in the third quarter. But the most audacious was in the fourth quarter, third and nine on the Dartmouth 13 and an aroused Princeton trailing, 27-31. Blackman called for a quick kick into the wind. Spangenberg, a junior, suggested in the huddle that the wind might hurt him. "Why not run?" he said. At the line of scrimmage, King checked off the quick kick, called a pitchout, and Spangenberg ran 29 yards to the Dartmouth 42. Minutes later he scored the clinching touchdown.

*Powerful reasons why Dartmouth was 9-0-0 in 1962 were All-America center Don McKinnon, and Captain-quarterback Bill King, shown with Coach Blackman.*

McKinnon was the best lineman on the field, by press box vote, in every Dartmouth game. Like King, he was a prelaw student. A Yale back, asked to comment on McKinnon after the game, said, "I really couldn't say. He hit me on the first play and I was still groggy under the shower two hours later."

From 1955 through 1962, Blackman's only losing season at Dartmouth was his first, 3-6. Since 1956, when the Ivy League formalized and began round-robin play, his Big Green elevens won 36 and lost 11 for the best record in the league.

A native Iowan, the 43-year-old Blackman had the round face and chronic smile of a gingerbread man. He was short and stocky and walked—or more often, trotted and ran—with a slight limp from polio, which ended his football playing after his freshman year at Southern California. As a coach, he was an iconoclast, an innovator, a tactful administrator and diplomat, a stickler for detail and conditioning, and an untiring worker. He celebrated a stirring 15-14 victory over Cornell in 1961 by working six straight hours alone in his room on defenses for Princeton.

When Blackman went to Dartmouth in 1955, he understood and quickly accepted the Ivy code—no spring practice, no scholarships, stiff entrance requirements—and learned to live within the rules.

"If I were in another league," he said in 1962, "I'd want to play it their way—spring practice, scholarships, the works. But here in the Ivies it's different. It may sound corny, but you grow to appreciate the caliber of boy you get under this system."

The football team annually achieved grades

higher than the school academic average, and Blackman testified that he had 100 percent graduation of his varsity players.

Blackman was a remarkably complete coach whose teams were as imaginative and daring and sound defensively as they were offensively, giving up only 57 points in 1962. Cornell's Tom Harp said Dartmouth was more difficult to prepare for than anybody, Navy included. Blackman geared to do complex things in a simple manner; his offense ran the same plays from a variety of formations, including his own creation, the V, in which the fullback lined up on the quarterback's heel, between the guard and tackle, to act as a blocking back in the fashion of the single wing. It was a power formation especially effective for short yardage. Blackman made quick, subtle changes on defense to confuse the eye. "What looks like a standard 5-3 may in reality be something else," he said.

By now, Bob Blackman found he could amuse his friends back west with true stories about coaching Ivy football. "I am consistently amazed, as I am pleased, by the things that happen," he once said. "A few years ago I had a valuable player come in before an important Yale game and ask to be taken off the traveling roster. 'I can't make the trip,' he said. I asked him why, and he said, 'I've got to study.' They'll never believe that in the Big Ten."

It was Dartmouth's experience, however, and Yale's and Harvard's and Princeton's as well, that Bob Blackman was a man to be believed—and reckoned with.

## 1963

Tactics in the East were turning a corner. Ben Schwartzwalder of Syracuse said, "We've reached the end of the wide stuff, and now the thinking is that we have to move some folks out of the way in the line in order to move the ball. The success of the Green Bay Packers has clearly demonstrated that this is still the way to play the game. And we're going to see more action passes these next few years. The drop-back pass writes the defense too long a letter too soon."

John Yovicsin went even further. The Harvard coach saw the T-formation, with its power end run and double-teaming in the off-tackle hole, borrowing more and more from the old-fashioned single wing.

"We have very few original thinkers in the game today," Yovicsin pointed out. "Men like Greasy Neale, with his 5-4 defense, Steve Owen, with his 6-1, and Dick Harlow, with his looping linemen and spinning fullbacks, made important contributions to the game. We just don't have many coaches like that today."

With or without innovators, football in the Ivy League was going to be exciting, if not always formidable. Outside of Navy's Roger Staubach and Boston College's Jack Concannon, the two best of an unusual group of glittering quarterbacks in the East in 1963 were Columbia's Archie Roberts and Cornell's Gary Wood. Roberts, a junior, was an authentic triple threat, and although he played for Ivy League Columbia, most experts felt he could play for most any major college team in America. He was already being courted by the pros, the feeling being that the 6-foot, 185-pound Massachusetts youngster could make it as either a passer or a punter.

Gary Wood would rather run than throw. Of all of the quarterbacks in the East, he was probably the best with the ball tucked under his arm. In 1962, he ran for 889 yards, but he still managed to complete 60 of 117 passes.

In August, when the Ivy forecasters were making their annual predictions, they picked Dartmouth and Harvard as the two strongest teams. Defending champion Dartmouth, one of the nation's few unbeaten major college teams in 1962, lost Bill King and All-American center Don McKinnon, but it still had enough capable players to win again. Coach Blackman had 24 lettermen, some lively sophomores, and a new quarterback, Dana Kelly, considered by some a better passer than King. Kelly did not run as fast nor as well as King, but he did have Tom Spangenberg, the versatile halfback, and fullback Tom Parkinson for that chore.

Even with McKinnon gone, the Dartmouth line had a forbidding look. It was big and, like most Blackman-coached lines, it would be quick and stingy on defense. Few opposing backs would get away from Bill Curran, the 223-pound middle guard, and the two sturdy tackles, 255-pound Dave Stenger and 222-pound Dale Runge.

"Harvard may be able to match Dartmouth's defense, but the Crimson will have to find a way to speed up its flanker T," one forecaster wrote. "Coach Yovicsin, a stickler for pure defense, will get it from Tom Stephenson, a solid all-purpose end, tackles Neal Curtin, a 235-pounder, and Jeff Pochop, an aggressive 200-pounder, and center

Brad Stephens, who may be the best linebacker in the Ivy League."

Harvard, however, lacked speed in the backfield. Fullback Bill Grana was an exemplary inside runner, but halfbacks Scott Harshbarger and Tom Bilodeau were slow-footed. Too, quarterback Mike Bassett did not pass often enough to stir up a breeze. Much depended upon Wally Grant and Dave Poe, from an unbeaten freshman team. If they came through, it was believed that the Harvards might just be good enough to worry the life out of the Dartmouths when the two teams met in Cambridge on the fifth weekend of the season, October 26.

Oddly enough, the two Ivy League teams with the best quarterbacks were not regarded as authentic challengers. Buff Donelli expected his Lions to have more bite, but aside from Archie Roberts and Jack Strauch, a fine linebacker, the other young Lions were disturbingly mediocre. Cornell was in pretty much the same fix. It had Gary Wood and little else.

The other Ivy League schools were less pretentious than Columbia and Cornell, but they were stronger than in 1962. Princeton had its usual herd of good backs—holdover tailbacks Pete Poreitis and Hugh MacMillan, wingback Jim Rockenbach, and fullback Cosmo Iacavazzi, an awesome line smasher—but graduation hit hard at the line. Penn and Brown, weary of being pummeled year after year, hoped to do a bit of mauling of their own.

Yale, shocked but not really saddened by Jordan Olivar's sudden resignation during the winter, had a new look under Coach Johnny Pont, who was brought in from Miami of Ohio to lift the Elis out of their recent doldrums. Chet LaRoche, a member of the Yale Football Committee at the time, remembers the details leading up to Olivar's departure.

"Those were the days of Whit Griswold," Chet said. "While he could support football eloquently, he had his doubts about the place of the game in college life. Football de-emphasis was still on the move, and Yale's coach had limited tenure, authority, and prestige. For some reason never very clear to me, the Yale head coach was not invited, or even allowed, to live on campus during the off-season. Olivar thus divided his time between New Haven and California. The result was that his search for good talent, interested in Yale's values, was very limited. Recruiting was almost at a standstill.

*Quarterback Gary Wood of Cornell was the Ivy League leader in total offense and rushing in 1962–63 and led the nation in kickoff return yardage in 1963. His three-year performance established five Cornell and five Ivy records.*

"That winter, I flew out to the Coast to talk to Olivar. I told him of the situation at Yale, and about the seeming prejudice of having him there all year. I explained to him that I had talked this matter over with DeLaney Kiphuth, director of athletics, and that DeLaney appeared to approve of the idea that Olivar become a full-time resident of New Haven. So at a meeting at Morey's later, with Olivar and DeLaney both there, I explained to DeLaney that Olivar desired to be on the job year round and that he was willing to renew his contract under those conditions which we had recommended and which, I was given to understand, the university would approve.

"It was a great shock to both Olivar and me when DeLaney balked. He seemed to be questioning the proposal. Obviously, someone had been putting pressure on him. I gathered some faculty people, and also the president's staff and maybe the president himself, were afraid of football at Yale growing too big again. The upshot was that we were left, as often happens at Yale, in a fog of vague decisions. I sensed that Olivar had been approached by some of the West Coast colleges and had assurances they wanted him out there. In any event, he flatly turned down Yale's part-time offer—and there we were, without a coach once more."

Johnny Pont's pro-type offense was geared to a strong defense. He wanted possession of the ball as quickly as possible, and then he expected his team to break its backs into the clear. The idea had a nice sound to it, but Yale lacked the firepower to make it come off.

On September 28, the first week of play, Dartmouth and Harvard, the Ivy League favorites, had their troubles. Dartmouth barely beat Bucknell, 20-18. Harvard battled Massachusetts to a 0-0 tie. Meanwhile, Columbia, Princeton, and Penn looked like genuine challengers. Archie Roberts threw for three touchdowns and ran for two as Columbia thumped Brown, 41-14; fullback Cosmo Iacavazzi, bombing away for 102 yards, led Princeton to a 24-0 win over Rutgers. Penn trounced Lafayette, 47-0. Yale squeezed past Connecticut, 3-0, but Cornell lost to Colgate, 21-17.

On the second Saturday, it was a great day for the soccer-style kicking of the Gogolaks. Princeton's Charlie booted one off the side of his foot for the point that beat Columbia, 7-6, while brother Pete, who had been at it longer, kicked a 50-yard field goal and three extra points (for 31 in a row), as quarterback Gary Wood led Cornell past Lehigh, 24-0. Dartmouth, with new quarterback Dana Kelly passing infrequently but effectively for two scores, overwhelmed Penn, 28-0. Harvard beat Rutgers, 28-0, on the running and pass-catching of sophomores Wally Grant and Dave Poe. At Yale, all was truly blue as sophomore quarterback Bob Hall and Brown bumped the Elis, 12-7.

A week before Harvard and Dartmouth met in their Ivy League showdown, both teams had their troubles. Despite some first-half body English by a distinguished visiting alumnus, President John F. Kennedy, Harvard had to settle for an undistinguished 3-3 tie with Columbia. Dartmouth needed some late trickery, a pitchout, hand-back, and then a 12-yard pass from Dana Kelly to sub halfback Bob O'Brien, to edge Holy Cross, 13-8. Gary Wood's talented running and Pete Gogolak's last-minute 33-yard field goal put down Yale, 13-10, for Cornell. Led by tailback Hugh MacMillan and fullback Cosmo Iacavazzi, Princeton routed Colgate, 42-0, and Brown sophomore Bob Hall's passing and running stomped Penn, 41-13.

The fifth week, and Harvard vs. Dartmouth. . . .

Dartmouth arrived in Cambridge holding a 15-game winning streak, the longest of any major college team in the country. Ordinarily, the annual appearance of a Dartmouth team and its rooters was not the occasion for serious concern, one way or the other, around Harvard Square. Dartmouth people, in the minds of Harvard people, were fine football players, but their talk was too loud and they were a bit immature. But now the Harvards were more tolerant. For one thing, this marked the 60th anniversary of Harvard Stadium, the first concrete football hippodrome in America, and the Harvard people respected tradition, of which they had a great deal more than anyone else. For another thing, Harvard rather suspected that it might beat Dartmouth and go on to win the Ivy League Championship. Harvard had not lost a football game since it was beaten by Dartmouth in 1962, although those early season ties against Massachusetts and Columbia would sooner be forgotten.

Dartmouth appeared on the field in dazzling white uniforms with green striping. Harvard countered with the crimson it had been wearing almost since the Battle of Bunker Hill. On the first play, Mike Bassett, the Harvard quarterback, threw a pass to Ted Bracken, who, unfortunately for Bassett, was the Dartmouth guard. Several minutes later, Dana Kelly, the Dartmouth quarterback, threw a 13-yard pass to John McLean, his halfback, and with the game less than four minutes old, Dartmouth led, 7-0. All of a sudden the overflow crowd of 38,000—the first non-Yale sellout at Harvard in 32 years—lost its voice.

Again Harvard received, and on the next play fumbled and lost the ball. Suddenly the Harvard people began to wish that they were spending the balmy afternoon gardening or sailing or playing golf.

But a tall, soft-spoken quarterback from Philadelphia named Bill Humenuk changed the Harvard minds. With time running out in the first half, he took over from senior classmate Bassett at midfield and passed directly to the Dartmouth 1-yard line, where three passes fell incomplete and the clock ran out before Harvard could score.

But the first time Harvard got the ball in the second half, Humenuk was again in charge. He quickly noticed something about the Dartmouth defense: The right tackle was pinched in too tight and the right end spread too wide. Humenuk called for a slant through this gap by Scott Harshbarger, his best friend. Scott found running room behind his blockers, and after going 10 yards downfield decided to cut across to the right. It was a decision that looked unwise at first, but when the confusion of stumbling, tumbling bodies cleared, Harshbarger was well along on his way to a touchdown. The play traveled 36 yards, and John Hartranft's kick tied the score.

The Harvard people began to sniff victory. They had good reason. Following Dartmouth's early touchdown, Harvard had completely dominated the game, holding Dartmouth to a single first down and 38 yards while accumulating 172 yards and eight first downs of its own. The outstanding defensive play of ends Tom Stephenson, Frank Ulcickas, and Ken Boyda succeeded in converting the heretofore celebrated Dartmouth end sweeps into traffic jams.

Humenuk made Harvard move on the ground, using his fast backs, Grana, Wally Grant, and John Dockery, for sweeps, and Harshbarger for the power plays inside. He kept the Dartmouth defense loose with passes to Harshbarger, Boyda, and Ulcickas, the latter scoring Harvard's second touchdown late in the third quarter on a pass from the Dartmouth 24.

Midway through the fourth quarter, Humenuk took the team down to the Dartmouth 4. From there, Hartranft kicked the field goal that removed all suspense. Dartmouth did score a second touchdown at the very end of the game with the help of a questionable pass interference call against a Harvard defender in the end zone, but the final score of 17-13 made the teams look more evenly matched than they were.

Besides Stephenson and Frank Ulcickas and Ken Boyda, the linebacking of center Brad Stephens and fullback Bill Grana also played a major role in the Harvard victory. And the wide parabolas of Harry Van Oudenallen's punts kept Dartmouth uncertain and off balance.

"I think," said Harvard coach John Yovicsin after the game, "that defense is very definitely the most important part of the game, and kicking is next."

And Coach Yovicsin had both.

Before Yovicsin arrived from little Gettysburg College in Pennsylvania, Harvard had not been aware that he existed. He was now 44 years old and in his seventh year at Harvard. When coaching football, he was an unsmiling man with the lean and dedicated look of a deacon, and his teachings had clearly scraped Harvard football off the bottom of the barrel. The team had won three of the last four Big Three championships, the Ivy title in 1961, and was second to Dartmouth in 1962.

Harvard, naturally, was tickled to beat Dartmouth, 17-13, but now the Crimson was already worrying about Princeton, which had more good backs than most Ivy teams had players. The Tigers trampled Cornell, 51-14, while the rest of the Ivies flexed their muscles against nonleague foes. Archie Roberts ran and passed for four touchdowns as Columbia whipped Lehigh, 42-21. Yale battered Colgate, 31-0, and Brown ran over Rhode Island, 33-7. Even Penn won, over Rutgers, 7-6.

Perhaps because it was looking ahead to Princeton, Harvard, so impeccably precise against Dartmouth, came up fumbling and bumbling against

*Pete Gogolak, the first of the nation's soccer-style place-kickers, set a national major college record of 44 straight conversions from 1961 through 1963. The Cornell star's 50-yarder against Lehigh was the nation's longest in 1963 in a major college game.*

last place Penn in its next game and was upset, 7-2, to leave the ranks of the unbeaten. Meanwhile, Yale, beginning to shape up under Johnny Pont, upended Dartmouth, 10-6, on Chuck Mercein's extra point and 20-yard field goal. But undefeated Princeton's forces rolled on. Cosmo Iacavazzi's bullish charges (for three touchdowns) smacked Brown, 34-13. At Ithaca, Gary Wood's touchdown in the closing seconds and Bob Baker's two-point run overtook Columbia, 18-17, for Cornell.

The Ivy League Championship was kicked around as the contenders, Harvard, Princeton, and Dartmouth, huffed and puffed into the final weeks of the season. The race grew even more confused when Harvard polished off Princeton, 21-7.

A week later, Princeton (5-1) was an easy winner over Yale, 27-7, and could clinch the title in its last game by beating Dartmouth (4-2), which squeezed past Cornell, 12-7. Harvard (4-1-1) outscored Brown, 24-12, and needed a victory over Yale and a Princeton loss to win the championship. Columbia, out of the race, got its kicks from its Mr. All-Everything, Archie Roberts, who completed 12 out of 15 passes for 174 yards and three touchdowns, ran for 55 more yards and another score as Penn went down, 33-8.

The Ivy League was ready for a last-week showdown when, 24 hours before the kickoffs, the nation suddenly went into mourning over the assassination of President Kennedy. Harvard and Yale, on the eve of their 80th game, were the first to announce that they would not play. Princeton and Dartmouth, poised to meet with the championship at stake, quickly followed, and by early Friday evening every Eastern game had been either postponed or canceled.

A few colleges in other parts of the country decided to play, but at least one of them had some late misgivings. At Miami, President Henry King Sanford came to the press box only minutes before the kickoff ready to tell the waiting crowd of 57,773 that the game with Florida was not going to be played after all. He was talked out of his announcement by a member of the university's board of trustees.

Most of the November 23 games drew large crowds, although some traditional contests attracted considerably less than their usual quota. Often the games were viewed with subdued attention. In almost all cases, half-time hoopla was dispensed with. It was not a gala day for college football or anything else.

The Ivy showdown was pushed back to November 30, and all Princeton had to do, after building up a 21-7 lead over Dartmouth in the first 45 minutes, was sit on the ball and accept the championship. But the visiting Indians went after the Tigers with Dana Kelly's passes and Tom Spangenberg's runs, and they cut the margin to 21-15. Then, with 5:35 left, Princeton's Iacavazzi fumbled on the Tiger 2-yard line. Dartmouth's John McLean ran over for the touchdown, Gary Wilson kicked the extra point, and the Indians won, 22-21, to tie Princeton for the league title.

At New Haven, Harvard, which had beaten both Dartmouth and Princeton and could have won the championship by merely vanquishing underdog Yale, instead got drubbed, 20-6, by the Elis. Rounding out the Ivy schedule for the season, Cornell overpowered Penn, 17-8, as Gary Wood scored twice and Pete Gogolak kicked his 44th straight extra point (a major college record). And Columbia, thanks to Archie Roberts, managed to hold off Rutgers, 35-28.

## 1964

The NCAA Rules Committee provided the biggest college football news of 1964. Yielding at last to the repeated demands of the coaches, the committee opened the doors for free substitution, which had been barred in college football since back in 1951.

The new substitution rule permitted each team to replace any number of players during an intermission between periods and, during a period, between successive downs when the game clock was stopped. When the game clock was running, teams were allowed to send in only two substitutes between successive downs. The free substitution advocates among the coaches would have liked all restrictions removed. But platoon advocates admittedly could live with this liberalized rule, and, surely, the platoons would be marching again.

Early samplings, however, indicated that the major teams would not be organizing completely specialized offensive and defensive units right away. The trend seemed to favor the use of the three-platoon system devised by Paul Dietzel when he was at Louisiana State. This setup called for a two-way regular unit to start each quarter and play seven or eight minutes, with specialized offensive and defensive units piecing out the period on the basis of who had possession of the ball.

However the college coaches organized their personnel in 1964, they at least had won their point that they should be free to swing players in and out of the game in accordance with the demands of the situation.

Although the new free substitution rule made the coaches happy, it did not have any direct bearing on who beat whom during the season. The strong squads still had to be strong, and the weak ones still had the same old problems. But the trend all over the country in varsity football continued to be toward a leveling off of strength. The day was gone when a handful of college teams could dominate the scene. There were some 120 major-rated teams, and as it was often said, on any given day almost any one of them could beat almost any other.

The Ivy League was swarming with contenders. Take, for instance, Yale and Princeton, the favorites. What gave Yale a bright chance was Coach Johnny Pont, who was starting his second year at New Haven. A devotee of pure defense, he had 237-pound All-Ivy tackle Ab Lawrence, end Steve Lawrence (no relation), and guards Chuck Benoit and Ralph Vandersloot. The Yale halfbacks, Jim Howard and Jim Groninger, were slower than Pont liked, but his offense, grim and pounding, was not really geared to speed or passing. Instead, Pont hammered his fullbacks up the middle and his halfbacks off the tackles. Not very subtle to be sure, but extremely effective when one has 220-pound fullbacks like Chuck Mercein, Pete Cummings, and Dick Niglio to do the thumping. Tone Grant, a wispy 156-pounder who threw left-handed, and Ed McCarthy were the quarterbacks. It was the best Yale team since 1960.

Beating out Princeton, however, would not be easy. Once more, Coach Dick Colman's cup was overflowing with good single-wing tailbacks. The latest was Don McKay, a stylish runner and passer who could really make the Tigers roar when double teamed with All-Ivy fullback Cosmo Iacavazzi who scored 14 touchdowns in 1963.

Princeton also had a supply of staunch linemen, another Colman stock in trade. Guards Paul Savidge and Stas Maliszewski, quick 215-pounders who could get out to lead Princeton's sweeps, were as good as any in the Ivy League, and opponents thought twice before running at 225-pound tackle Ernie Pascarella.

Up at Dartmouth, Bob Blackman lost 18 lettermen, but he had his usual collection of hard, uncompromising types, among them center Bob Komives, guard Ted Bracken, and end Tom Clarke. They were the core of an excellent line. Much depended upon quarterback Bruce Gottschall's ability to muster an offense.

Harvard's John Yovicsin, who almost always came up with a big, strong line and a weak quarterback, had both again to start the season. Tackles Neal Curtin and Joe Jurek were 240 and 235 pounds, while guard John Hoffman was 235. They were, however, slow afoot and had some trouble getting out in front of Wally Grant and Dave Poe, the fastest halfbacks the Crimson had had in years. Grant and Poe could really step, but, like several of the more recent Harvard quarterbacks, John McClusky could not throw.

One of the darkest horses of all was Columbia, where Coach Buff Donelli entertained some hope for his young Lions. The reason, of course, was a very special senior named Archie Roberts, who did the quarterbacking and just about everything else. In 1963, he had completed 62 percent of his passes for 1,184 yards, had run for 341, and was responsible for 20 touchdowns. The pro scouts had been casing him since his sophomore year. They cooled off after Roberts said that he intended to go on to medical school. Then they started flocking around again when they heard that Archie might reconsider.

"Two or three scouts were at practically every workout," Donelli said. "Both the NFL and AFC wanted him, and when we played our last game against Brown two weeks before the 1963 draft, the Los Angeles Rams phoned from the Coast, asking Archie if he had changed his mind about playing pro football. Everyone here at Columbia was against the idea. In the long run he'll be happier as a doctor. Then the football people began to throw money around like confetti. I'm as skeptical as the next guy about athletes' salaries reported in the newspapers, but I can vouch for the authenticity of the offer Archie got from the New York Jets. It was an $80,000 package, a $40,000 bonus and a two-year contract for $40,000. He had an even better bid from the Montreal Alouettes of the Canadian League. They offered him $80,000, plus full tuition for him and his young wife, also a premed student, at the McGill Medical School."

All the Ivy Leaguers opened the 1964 season as winners, except Cornell, which tied Buffalo, 9-9.

Harvard quarterback John McCluskey, who earlier had run 82 yards for a touchdown, was so pleased when he found himself in the clear on a two-yard sweep that he threw the ball high in the air, just like the pros. Only trouble was, he was on the Massachusetts 1-yard line. The Redmen recovered the ball, but Harvard won anyway, 20-14.

Eight weeks later, Princeton, 6-0-0 in Ivy play, had the championship all sewed up as it got ready to meet Cornell (3-3-0). The big game was at Cambridge between Yale (4-1-1) and Harvard (4-2-0) in the battle for runner-up. Harvard's quick backs kept Yale hopping frantically. One of them, sophomore Bobby Leo, eventually did in the Elis, 18-14, with a 46-yard power sweep in the last quarter.

Princeton, with nothing at stake but face, had to fight desperately to maintain its unbeaten record as a tough Cornell team took liberties with the Tigers good defense. But Iacavazzi and his teammates ultimately prevailed, 17-12.

Brown, with its best Ivy League finish since 1958, treated Columbia's Archie Roberts shabbily—89 yards in losses, only 10 yards in total offense—and beat the Lions, 7-0. Down at Philadelphia, Dartmouth thrashed Penn, 27-7.

If he couldn't beat Brown, Archie Roberts could join them—the Cleveland Browns. The following winter, the NFL champions drafted Archie in the first round. "It was a six-year arrangement adding up to $100,000, with the proviso that he could devote all his time to his studies at the Western Reserve Medical School for the first two years," Buff Donelli said.

"Roberts may be too old and rusty for pro football by the time he finishes medical school," he added, "but he'll be a great team physician for the Browns."

*Leading Princeton to an undefeated season in 1964 was All-America fullback Cosmo Iacavazzi. An aeronautical engineering honor student, the team captain excelled on both offense and defense in an era when most platooners went only one way.*

## 1965

Staying abreast of college football's changing moods and trends in 1965 was difficult. Take the offenses. Just when a coach thought he had learned all the deceits of the split T, where the quarterback handed off or faked and ran, it was replaced by the simple power of the wing T, where the quarterback pitched and blocked. Then as the coach tried to get the jump on an opponent, along came the shifting T or the I formation, where the quarterback suddenly became a thrower. In 1965, most systems were yielding in popularity to something called the I slot, which was a pretty good combination of the formations immediately preceding it. It had the deception of the early T, it scattered out the defense like the I, and it provided running strength as well, for, ideally, the halfback in the slot—between the end and tackle—would be capable of blocking as splendidly as he could catch. With practically every team committed to a balance of running and passing, the I slot seemed perfect for the times.

Although for the majority of spectators, defense was the uncomplicated art of chasing people, there was a little more to it. The 5-4 was still in vogue, along with the use of a "monster," or roaming, strength-equalizing linebacker. But the split six was also growing in popularity. This was a six-man front with a curious gap in the middle and all linemen slanting in, the gap designed to lure runners into the arms of alert, nimble linebackers.

Giving in at last to the relentless pressure exerted by a majority of the college coaches, the NCAA Rules Committee lowered virtually all the remain-

*Archie Roberts, Columbia's record-breaking passer, tied with Iacavazzi in 1964 for Ivy League Player of the Year honors.*

ing barriers against free substitution. As a result, in 1965 each team could send in any number of subs between periods, after any type of a score, following a change in ball possession, and after repossession by the kicking team as the consequence of a foul or a fumble recovery. In addition, each team was permitted to send in two substitutes any time before the ball was put into play.

This change just about completed the cycle back to free substitution. During the years since 1951, the coaches had campaigned unceasingly to have the restrictions lifted, gaining tiny compromises each year until now they again had things just about the way most of them wanted them.

The rule cleared the way for unhampered two-platooning—alternating specialized offensive and defensive units. Under it, coaches had diminished fear of getting caught in the switches, which happened occasionally in 1964, when the change of possesssion and repossession clauses were not part of the rule.

Surveys indicated that practically all major teams planned to set up in two platoons. Of course, there were traditionalists who grieved at the disappearance of the two-way player, who could block as well as tackle, and sounded off against the depersonalized, push-button aspects of two-platoon football. But having the platoons march again had its rewards too. There was no disputing that specialized one-way play produced stepped-up performance and a higher grade of technical football. It also gave more people a chance to play.

Under any set of rules, however, the teams with the best players could be counted on to lead their conferences.

In the Ivy League, Princeton, undefeated in 1964 and still seething over not getting the Lambert Trophy, remained the team to beat. But both Dartmouth and Harvard were given a chance to hold the Tigers this time. What encouraged the challengers was that Princeton had suffered some severe losses, notably All-American fullback Cosmo Iacavazzi and tailback Don McKay.

Dartmouth was going after Princeton's title with one of the flashiest sets of backs that Coach Bob Blackman had ever had. Quarterback Mickey Beard, a 19-year-old junior who could run and throw (he did both for 865 yards in 1964), was the leader, assisted by Bob O'Brien and Paul Klungness, a pair of scatbacks, and Mike Urbanic, a hammering fullback. When Beard threw, which was often, his number one target was Bob MacLeod Jr., a 6-foot-4 junior who ran patterns and caught passes like a pro.

The ingenious Blackman liked nothing better than to tantalize his Ivy colleagues with a wild variety of formations, and in 1965 his Indians displayed everything from the V to the wing T, slot T, double slot, and anything else he could think of.

When the Ivy League publicists assembled the previous spring for their annual guess-together, they picked Dartmouth and Harvard to win the championship. That prompted one churlish fellow—not a Yale man either—to note, enviously, that each year the Crimson got "the best material in the league."

Harvard Coach John Yovicsin, healthy again after undergoing successful open heart surgery in April, scoffed at that. Further, he insisted that his squad had been mortally wounded by the loss of an entire line and, quite unexpectedly, half his offense.

Despite his woes, Yovicsin still had enough experienced players (16) around to form his usual demanding defense.

Cornell, despite the loss of six All-Ivy players, five of them linemen, had the defense and the backs to make a first-rate run at the championship. Yale had a new coach. Although Coach John Pont, who departed for Indiana after a sobering two years without spring practice, left behind 20 lettermen for his successor and former assistant, Carmen Cozza, they were mostly second-line reserves. There was also a coaching change at Penn. Coach John Stiegman was fired, and Bob Odell, a former Penn All-American halfback, was lured away from Bucknell to replace him. Then Penn announced it would pursue a "more aggressive alumni-supported recruitment policy." At Brown there was little to make the heart sing, and for the first time in three years Columbia had to go without Archie Roberts.

The first week of competition demonstrated that there was no sympathy for the inept in the Ivy League. Princeton hammered Rutgers, 32-6, Dartmouth clobbered New Hampshire, 56-6, Harvard beat Holy Cross, 17-7, and Penn outscored Lehigh, 20-14, but everywhere else there was big trouble. Colgate held Cornell to a scoreless tie, Lafayette surprised Columbia, 14-10, Rhode Island defeated Brown, 14-6, and Connecticut upset Yale, 13-6, the first time the Elis had been beaten by a home state rival in 87 games since 1875.

The Princeton-Rutgers contest produced an item for Ripley's Believe It Or Not: The captain and center for Rutgers was 205-pound George Peter Savidge; the captain and defensive right tackle for Princeton was 220-pound George Paul Savidge—twin brothers. As usual, the brothers' battle ended in a rather bloody standoff, but Princeton's George Paul had the help of Charles Gogolak, a 155-pound place-kicker who swiped at the ball sideways. Gogolak kicked six field goals, including one that was recorded as 52 yards but carried nearly 70. George Peter had to swallow the fourth straight loss by Rutgers to Princeton, 32-6.

Living up to preseason forecasts, Princeton rolled over team after team. They were unstoppable. First Columbia (31-0) and then Cornell (36-27), Colgate (27-0), Penn (51-0), Brown (45-27), Harvard (14-6), and Yale (31-6) were chewed up by the Tigers. Now only Dartmouth blocked Princeton's path to clear claim to the title, an unbeaten season, and number one ranking in the East. But, oh, that Big Green machine, victor over Holy Cross (27-6), Penn (24-9), Brown (35-9), Harvard (14-0), Yale (20-17), Columbia (47-0), and Cornell (28-14)!

Twenty-four hours before the showdown, the Dartmouth players were gamboling around Yankee Stadium. Practice had been sharp but short. Now the squad was congregated around home plate. They began to burlesque a baseball game, throwing a football and batting it with fists and elbows. It was good mimicry of the Harlem Globetrotters' famous act, with the plate umpire making exaggerated gestures, the pitcher taking a Goose Tatum windup, runners stealing home with wild slides, all to the accompaniment of boyish laughter.

New York sportswriters, accustomed to the detached professionalism of the New York Giants, watched the show with big-city skepticism. Finally, one of the reporters turned to Coach Blackman and asked, "Do you really think your boys are ready for Princeton tomorrow?" Smiling, Blackman replied, "I'd be disappointed if they weren't cutting up like this today. They're just having a little fun. I encourage it. It relaxes them." He might have added, "You don't monkey around with success." His winning percentage at Hanover was .747.

Working with a group of intelligent athletes who did not have to play football unless they wanted to, Blackman had molded his technique accordingly. He challenged the team's intellect with a vastly intricate and copious repertoire of plays. He spiced every practice with an aerial, tag football game, including an original scoring system compiled by a covey of student managers on blackboards. Special imaginative plays or defenses, on which orthodox coaches would have frowned, were put in for each opponent.

For the Princeton game, Blackman introduced a "human steps" kick-blocking stunt against the magnificent Charley Gogolak, a "tackle eligible" pass on offense, and a daring kickoff return. These not only excited his team's interest, but served to allay the tension brought on by this climactic meeting of unbeaten teams. And they were practical. Only the kickoff return was not used. That was junked because a key principal was injured before Dartmouth could return a kickoff.

The "human steps" play was typical of Blackman's attention to detail. The complicated maneuver was the brain child of line coach Jack Musick, a Blackman assistant since 1947. "All we need is a tall, leggy halfback who will get a running start, take two climbing steps off the backs of two crouching teammates and leap as high as he can over the Princeton line," explained Musick before the game. "But he can't be the type who'll worry about how hard he comes down."

The young man who earned the assignment was Sam Hawken, a sophomore reserve.

"I'm expendable," Sam said.

Blackman put light, ripple-soled, cross-country shoes on the flying Hawken. He put foam rubber padding on the backs of the crouching linemen. A mathematician figured the angle of approach and the play was tested all week in Dartmouth's Leverone Fieldhouse. When Hawken got so he could knock the crossbar off the pole vault standards at 14 feet, Blackman said, "Okay, we're ready."

Before the Princeton game, Hawken broke out in a cold sweat. "My gosh," he said, "for the first time in my varsity career I've got pregame jitters."

He wasn't alone. Over on the Princeton side, Coach Dick Colman confessed, "If we make mistakes, we'll lose."

In the first quarter, the Tigers drove down within field goal range. Blackman sent Hawken into the game. Princeton seemed to sense that something fishy was up. They delayed the centering count. Hawken, trained to take off at a certain interval, suddenly found himself 14 feet in the air before the ball was snapped. The upshot was that Dartmouth was penalized 5 yards for offside, its sleeper play had been exposed, and poor Sam Hawken, the human missile, suffered an elbow in the ribs from an irate Princeton lineman for his trouble.

"Actually, though, the play was not a total loss," Sam said afterward. "Gogolak was so shaken by the sight of me zooming through the air that though he stood 5 yards closer on the next play, he hurried his kick and came up short."

That wasn't Princeton's only mistake. The biggest error was allowing Mickey Beard, the Dartmouth quarterback, to cock his deadly right arm. That, plus a spate of chicanery concocted by Coach Blackman and a determined stunting defense, wrecked the Tiger 17-game winning streak, 28-14, before 45,725 at Palmer Stadium. Beard set up two touchdowns with his passes, then scored both on 1-yard sneaks. One other toss, to end Bill Calhoun, covered 79 yards and a TD. Sophomore Gene Ryzewicz, who hip-wriggled and frug-danced his way through lines, ran 12 yards for another touchdown.

When Dartmouth was not making like an un-Ivy bowl candidate, Princeton's Ron Landeck was emulating a human computer. He ran and passed for 249 yards to break Dick Kazmaier's school season record with 1,949 yards and Gary Wood's Ivy League mark with 1,646 yards—all to no avail.

"We were confident," said Coach Blackman later, "but awfully scared."

In The Game at New Haven, Harvard and Yale, after wallowing in first-half depression, came half alive. Unfortunately for the Elis, it was the Harvard half that lived. Cantabs Buzz Baker and Dave Poe picked off errant Yale passes, Harvard scored twice within three minutes, and the Crimson won, 13-0, for its fourth victory in five years over Yale.

*Dartmouth's Sam Hawken (38) mounted a human ladder in the 1965 battle of unbeaten teams at Princeton. The Big Green capped a perfect season, 28-14, and won the Lambert Trophy.*

*Mickey Bear quarterbacked Dartmouth to an undefeated season, the Ivy title, and the Lambert Trophy in 1965 and the conference tri-title (with Harvard and Princeton) in 1966.*

Brown's Bob Hall, who had broken five Ivy passing records, hurt Columbia more with his excellent running than with his throws. He scored three times as the Bruins romped, 51-7, to tie the Lions for the last place in the standings.

### 1966

Just mention Dartmouth around the Ivy League and almost everybody threw up his hands in despair. For good reason, too. The Big Green, unbeaten in 1965 and winner of the Lambert Trophy as the best college team in the East, was loaded again.

And Coach Bob Blackman was back.

There were hopes—other than at Dartmouth—that Blackman would take the bait Iowa had offered during the previous winter. He only nibbled, however, and the rest of the league would just face him again. He spent the long hot summer devising new corollaries to the bewildering assortment of offensive and defensive sets he fancied. Dartmouth opponents were likely to see still more variations of the V, T, and I, and maybe even an unexpected defense or two.

"You have to keep changing," said Blackman.

With everybody shooting at the Dartmouths, there was plenty of competition, however, and at least three teams, Princeton, Harvard, and Yale, struck the preseason guessers as dangerous. The Tigers, of course, had an added incentive. They were still smarting over last season's loss to Dartmouth. Despite the graduation of its stars—tailback Ron Landeck, kicker Charley Gogolak, and guards Stas Maliszewski and Paul Savidge—Princeton still had enough good players left to be a strong contender.

John Yovicsin moaned about the loss of 17 lettermen at Harvard, including a dozen starters from his two platoons, but Ivy Leaguers weren't listening. They were all too familiar with Yovicsin's talent for building staunch defenses.

Yale coach Carm Cozza showed the patience of a saint in his first year among the Ivies. About the only thing that kept him going during a drab 3-6-0 season was the knowledge that help was on the way from an unbeaten freshman team. Happily, it was the kind of help that could make Yale an instant challenger. Cozza would hardly wait to put the best of his new sophomores to work. The one he counted on most was Brian Dowling, a highly skilled quarterback who could run, throw, and kick. Another was halfback Calvin Hill, a big, hard-hitting runner who scored five touchdowns against the Princeton freshmen in 1965.

About all Columbia, Brown, and Penn could hope for was to stay out of the cellar. The Lions' Buff Donelli was under fierce alumni attack to resign, and Bob Hall, the Ivy League's number one passer in 1965, graduated and left Brown's offense very skimpy.

If the Ivy League had a dark horse, it was Cornell. Tom Harp was gone. The new coach was Jack Musick, former assistant to Dartmouth's Blackman. Coach Musick promised to build the Big Red attack "from varied formations that just might shake up a few opponents."

About the only thing the Ivies proved on the opening Saturday was that they were masters of the minors, if by unimpressive margins. Dartmouth, with two long touchdown runs by safety Sam Hawkens and halfback Gene Ryzewicz, held off Massachusetts, 17-7, while Princeton barely beat rallying Rutgers, 16-12, and Cornell had a time stopping tough little Buffalo, 28-21. Brown came from behind to whip Rhode Island, 40-27, and Penn had to do the same to catch Lehigh, 38-28. Harvard and Yale had the easiest days. The Crimson battered Lafayette, 30-7, and Brian Dowling threw two touchdown passes to lead Yale past Connecticut, 16-0. Only Columbia saw defeat. Colgate, very much on the way up, mangled the Lions, 38-0.

Although upset by Holy Cross, 6-7, in its next game, Dartmouth bounced back to drub Princeton, 31-13. Their worries in the Ivy League, it seemed, were still to come. Harvard, Yale, and Cornell all looked good enough in early games to test them. Unbeaten Cornell whipped Penn, 45-28. Harvard's good backs—Rick Zimmerman, Bobby Leo, Vic Gatto, and Tom Choquette—rolled over Columbia, 34-7, and Yale trounced Brown, 24-0.

Harvard got past big, tough Cornell, 21-0, and then came Dartmouth. The Harvards seethed with hostility. Part of the friction between the schools was caused by their proximity, only 120 miles apart, and the fact that a lot of Green and Crimson graduates were scattered all around Greater Boston. Part was caused by the clash of two images: the virile outdoorsman vs. the effete egghead. It bugged the Dartmouths that Harvard got so much publicity around Boston. It was the Yale game this and the Yale game that, while Dartmouth was just "that little school up in the woods of New Hampshire."

"We're trying to make the Harvards darn well think that the Dartmouth game is The Game for them, not Yale," said Mickey Beard, Dartmouth's very bright and exceptionally versatile quarterback a week before the Harvard showdown.

Ric Zimmerman, the tall, intelligent, southpaw quarterback whose poise and passing had helped Harvard to serve up the kind of well-balanced attack that had been lacking in Cambridge for some time, would not go *that* far, but he had a few ideas of his own on why Harvard wanted to beat Dartmouth.

"Those Dartmouth guys come down here to Boston in their green jackets," he said, with a slight tone of distaste. "They come to our weekend parties and they lounge around on the floor with our dates and give you the idea it would be the easiest thing in the world to take our girls away from us. The Dartmouth game is *always* a good one to win."

The record did not show how many girls the Dartmouth boys stole from Harvard, but it did show how many points the Big Green got away with during the previous two seasons. In 1964. the score was 48-0, on network television no less. In 1965, Dartmouth shut out Harvard again, 14-0. This year, with plenty of muscle back, the Big Green was picked once more to dominate the league. With only 14 lettermen returning from 1965's 5-2-2 team, Harvard looked pitiful by comparison. But on the eve of the game, Harvard surprisingly stood at the top of the NCAA charts in rushing with 333 yards per game and in scoring defense with a stingy 3.5 points a game. For the first time in recent memory, Harvard had a quarterback in Zimmerman who could move the team on the ground as well as pass effectively. It also had two fine halfbacks in Bobby Leo and a stubby, snarling 5′6″, 180-pound sophomore named Vic Gatto. The offensive line, led by Steve Diamond, a high school All-American from Miami who originally had signed a letter of intent with Georgia Tech, was very fast and provided plenty of oil for Harvard's flanker T offense. The entire defense, although not big, was as quick as the offensive unit.

Halfback Leo was perhaps the finest runner ever enrolled at Harvard, certainly in modern times. His Everett High School team in suburban Boston went undefeated in his last two years and won the Class A title. Leo scored 21 touchdowns in his senior season. A good student, he applied to Dartmouth, Harvard, Yale, and Columbia (after also visiting Michigan State, Syracuse, and Notre Dame), hit four for four, but, said Leo, "I was always thinking of Harvard." And a good thing too. In 1964 and again in 1965, he scored the winning touchdown against Yale.

On that October 22 afternoon against Dartmouth, Bobby Leo had his finest hour. He blocked and passed furiously, got away on a long 64-yard touchdown run, and gained 173 yards in 20 carries as Harvard, buoyed by the kind of resourceful vigor that it reserved only for Dartmouth, won the game, 19-14. More than 10,000 tickets were snapped up by Dartmouth grads and students, who trooped into Harvard Square in green caps, green coats, green scarves, and green ribbons bearing the words "Green Power." The Crimson backlash, in the person of Leo, was felt before the end of the first quarter. Two long Dartmouth drives ended in lost fumbles, and then, with a first and 10 on its own 36,

Harvard ended a record of scoreless frustration against Dartmouth that had stretched to almost 146 minutes. As Harvard lined up over the ball, Zimmerman observed that Dartmouth's roving linebacker, Steve Luxford, had taken his position on the left.

"I had called a sweep left with Gatto carrying," Zimmerman said, "but when I saw the rover I called a change at the line of scrimmage to a sweep right with Leo. The play needs a solid block by Gatto to work, and it got it. Their left end just disappeared."

Leo turned downfield, found his route, popped into the clear on the Dartmouth 40, and then won a desperate match race with Wynn Mabry, Dartmouth's fast, all-league defensive halfback, to score. Dartmouth finally held onto the ball long enough to move 84 yards on seven plays and scored when Beard rolled out from his 10-yard line, bounced off two tacklers, and swan-dived into the end zone over a third.

The two teams traded touchdowns in the third and fourth quarters. Then, with 9:30 left in the game and trailing 14-13, Harvard took over the ball on its own 20 after a Dartmouth punt and launched a rugged, exciting, time-consuming, 16-play, 80-yard march that produced the winning touchdown with less than two minutes to play.

Suddenly, surprising Harvard was five up with only four games to go toward its first undefeated and untied season in 53 years. "How sweet it is," cried Harvard's sturdy, 230-pound defensive tackle, Skip Sviokla, when the game, if not The Game, was over. "How sweet it is to beat the boys from the woods."

The Ivy League race was not over yet. Harvard still had to play Princeton and Yale. While the Crimson were beating Dartmouth, the Tigers, with all their good backs healthy again, trounced Penn, 30-13, but Yale lost to Cornell, 16-14, when the Big Red's Pete Larson ran back a kickoff 99 yards and Pete Zogby kicked a 20-yard field goal. Brown, also on Harvard's future list, went down ingloriously to independent Colgate, 48-7.

Princeton, behind 14-3, battled back valiantly in the second half to stop Harvard's march to an undefeated season, 18-14. Fullback Dave Martin scored twice, and then an aroused defense stopped Harvard on the 16-yard line, only inches short of a first down. That threw the Ivy lead into a four-way tie as Dartmouth drubbed Columbia, 56-14, and Cornell outscored Brown, 23-14, to join Princeton and Harvard at the top. Yale, only a game behind, beat Penn, 17-14, on Dan Begel's 29-yard field goal with just 21 seconds to go.

With one week left, the Ivy League race got down to three teams—Dartmouth, Princeton, and Harvard. Dartmouth had quarterback Mickey Beard to thank for its 32-23 victory over Cornell. With his team behind, 17-7, Beard, who had already passed for one touchdown, threw for two more and ran for another. Princeton squeezed past Yale, 13-7, on Larry Stupski's 41-yard run with a blocked punt with 3:02 to go, while Harvard whipped Brown, 24-7. There was even a bit of cheer for Columbia. The Lions beat Penn, 22-14, for their first win.

The Ivy League came down to its last Saturday in a three-way tie for first place—Harvard, Dartmouth, and Princeton—and that was just the way it ended. A triple tie for the championship.

Harvard had the pressure game to win against Yale, and came through handsomely, 17-0. While the sturdy Crimson defense held the Elis down, shifty halfback Bobby Leo plunged 1 yard for one touchdown, sprinted 52 for another, and gained 106 yards in all.

Dartmouth, too strong for game Penn, attacked

*Dick Gerken, 6'2", 210-pound defensive end at Cornell in 1966, is a practicing Chicago attorney today.*

smartly from Bob Blackman's ingenious and irritating variety of offenses for 413 yards on the ground, most of them by Pete Walton and Jim Menter. But Penn's Bill Creeden, passing for 317 yards, made it a ball game before giving in, 40-21.

Princeton, the only team to conquer Harvard, had its hands full with Cornell. Despite some fumbling and bumbling, the Big Red held the Tigers scoreless until the last quarter. Then tailback Dick Bracken led Princeton on a 51-yard march, covering the last 5 yards himself for a 7-0 victory.

In the battle for last place, Columbia and Brown struggled furiously before the Lions won the slugfest, 40-38. Tailback Jim O'Connor, with 225 yards rushing for an Ivy record and four touchdowns, was the difference.

## 1967

For the past five years the Ivy League had been divided into two camps: Dartmouth and the others. In that period the Big Green failed to win outright or share the conference championship only once—in 1964—and now they were going for five out of six.

As always, Dartmouth seemed to have lost the most by graduation and, as always, seemed to have the most coming back anyway. Coach Blackman, the Hanover magician who had won 29 of his last 35 league games, had a way of just shuffling a few players around and winning championships. This season the shuffle would be a crucial one, as halfback Gene Ryzewicz switched to quarterback and defensive back Steve Luxford moved to left half. Ryzewicz had limited ability as a passer, so Blackman retooled his multiple offense to make use of Gene's excellent running. With linebacker Norm Davis and tackle Giff Foley to steady the defense and not a sophomore in the lineup, a lot of pundits favored Dartmouth to go all the way.

But not easily. Yale had 35 lettermen, including 240-pound tackle Glenn Greenberg, who hit as hard as his father, Hank, the old baseball star, used to. However, quarterback Brian Dowling, who had a knee operation last year, and halfback Calvin Hill, who was out for part of the season, had to stay healthy for the Elis to have a good chance at the championship.

Cornell, Harvard, and Princeton would be in the thick of the race too. Harvard lacked quantity but it had quality, especially in the backfield with Ric Zimmerman, the first Crimson quarterback in years who could pass, and a characteristically uncompromising line.

Princeton's losses had been severe, but Coach Dick Colman had his usual wealth of good single-wing tailbacks plus Ellis Moore, a quick sophomore fullback.

The rest of the Ivies had problems. Among the three of them—Penn, Brown, and Columbia—they would win a total of only three league games in 1967. Brown had a new coach, Len Jardine, but the same old team.

The Ivy League opened against outsiders and met some unexpected difficulties. Princeton looked beaten when Rutgers halfback Bryant Mitchell ran 33 yards for his third touchdown to put the Scarlet ahead, 21-14, with only 2:04 to go. In the last minute, however, tailback Bob Weber threw an 11-yard pass to Bob Schoene and then caught a two-point pass from Norman MacBean to win for the Tigers, 22-21. Dartmouth also had to come from behind to beat Massachusetts, 28-10, while Yale lost to Holy Cross, 26-14. Harvard trounced Lafayette, 51-0, as quarterback Ric Zimmerman threw three touchdown passes. In other Ivy games, Columbia took Colgate, 17-14, Penn outscored Lehigh, 35-23, Cornell beat Bucknell, 23-7, and Brown lost to Rhode Island, 12-8.

Yale's loss to Holy Cross represented the largest score ever run up against the Blue in an opening game. The Bulldogs fumbled nine times, losing five of them. Twice the Crusaders cashed in on Yale fumbles in the first quarter.

The trouble with the Yales was that there was no Brian Dowling in the lineup. Prone to injury, the brilliant quarterback missed seven and a half games in 1966 and Yale was pretty ordinary. During his football career, he had bruised a kidney, chipped his backbone, torn a knee, broken a collarbone, broken his nose, and broken a hand. Because of such mishaps, he also missed the first three games of 1967 as Yale lost to Holy Cross, but then bounced back to beat Connecticut and Brown.

Dowling got his quarterback job back in time for the Columbia game—and, ah, the Elis suddenly became world beaters. He led them past Columbia, Cornell, Dartmouth, Penn, and Princeton with ease. He did it with big plays that resulted in Yale averaging 35.5 points per game, which is a lot of points against anybody, and posting a 7-1 season record coming up to The Game against Harvard. Without a great amount of exaggeration, Dowling was probably the most exciting back in the Ivies since Princeton's Dick Kazmaier. Daring and cool, he ran just fast enough to get away from tacklers, threw just well enough to complete the big ones, and had a winning electricity about him. Brian Dowling had made Yale an Eastern power again.

Despite his build of 6′2″ and 190 pounds, Dowling did not present a football player's image. He had the smooth muscles and relaxed carriage of a country club athlete, dark eyes and black, slightly curly hair, plus poise and an affable manner. He also grinned a lot. He had offers from at least 60 colleges after becoming a high school star at Cleveland's St. Ignatius. He seriously considered USC, Michigan, Ohio State, and Northwestern, and Notre Dame wanted him as badly as it wanted (and got) Terry Hanratty.

Dowling was primarily responsible for the fact that even though the Bulldogs had already won the Ivy Championship after beating Princeton, 29-7, on November 18, the Yale Bowl creaked with 68,000 fans for the Harvard game a week later. Brian did not disappoint them.

So much was expected of Dowling—so much pressure put on him—that he threw two interceptions and no completions in his first five tries. Yale managed its first touchdown drive only after Dowling finally hit on a pass to end Bruce Weinstein in the middle of a mudhole. Encouraged, Yale kept moving until halfback Jim Fisher fumbled as he crossed the goal line—plop—right into the arms of Yale end Del Marting for a touchdown.

The luck of the Elis continued in the second quarter when Dowling faded back to pass from his own 47 and got trapped. He ran left and escaped a tackler. He ran backward and pulled away from another. He ran to the right and got away from still another. Players were scattered everywhere now, a mosaic of blue, white, and red dots, bodies twisting and heads spinning. It looked like a massive exhibition of acrobatics gone wild. Dowling, still running but keeping his cool, threw the ball to Calvin Hill, who caught it and ran another 53 yards for a touchdown.

It was not the first time. "It's kind of a play," Hill said later. "Dowling gets in trouble, I wave my hand, and he throws the ball to me. We do that a lot."

Yale was soon ahead, 17-0, but then Harvard dominated play for the next 20 minutes as Ric Zimmerman, Vic Gatto, and Ray Hornblower took turns carrying the ball on drives of 80 yards, 80 more, 88, and 40, scoring three touchdowns and taking the lead.

There were now less than three minutes to play when Yale, trailing 17-20, took the kickoff and returned it to its own 23-yard line. Still Dowling remained calm. "There was plenty of time left to score," he said later. "I just knew we would score"—even though at that point he had thrown four interceptions.

Dowling moved his forces to the 34 and a first down in two plays. "Sprint right on two," he said in the huddle. He also told his end, Marting, to run as far as he could down the sideline. Dowling took the snap and sprinted right, but he stopped. He waited. He looked back to his left. Then he reared and threw that long pass right into Marting's hands, a 66-yard strike for the winning touchdown. Up in the press box, Yale publicity chief Charley Loftus ran down the aisle saying, "He got mixed up on his timing. Frank Merriwell would have waited until there were only seven seconds left."

Harvard would not quit. Back the Crimson came up the field for one last, heroic try. It ran out of steam on the Yale 10-yard line when fullback Ken O'Connell fumbled and Yale recovered. So instead of a touchdown and victory, Harvard lost the ball and The Game.

Thus, Yale had its first Ivy League Championship since 1960. It had also come up with somebody to shout about as Brian Dowling finished the season by running and passing for more than 900 yards in nine games and 13 touchdowns. Visions of Bill Mallory and Bruce Caldwell and Albie Booth and Clint Frank went dancing through the heads of Old Blues.

The big Ivy League game was in New Haven, of course, but Dartmouth salvaged some glory by beating Princeton, 17-14, on Pete Donovan's 25-yard field goal with eight seconds to play, to take second place. Cornell battered Penn, 33-14, and Brown, stirring to life under new coach Len Jardine, defeated Columbia, 14-7. For the Lions, 0-7-0 in Ivy play, there would be a new coach, Frank Navarro, stalking the sidelines in 1968.

## 1968

The most noteworthy, stimulating, and memorable college football happening in 1968 was the way the offenses overwhelmed defenses and introduced frenzy to so many games. There were more touch-

*Ivy League bands are a community unto themselves. This is the Princeton band heating up the air at Palmer Stadium, and its sector is usually the noisiest. The fans, including some of the band members' girl friends, love it.*

downs scored, more total yardage gained, more passes thrown, and more completed for more yardage than ever before. Five hundred-yard total offense figures were not uncommon, and the average number of points scored in all major college games was 42.5, breaking the old record of 38.8 set in 1951, an increase of 5.7 per game in just one year. A team with a 20-point lead was about as safe as a mule in a glue factory.

There were several reasons for the scoring splurge. Teams ran more plays—an average of 9.8 per game—partly because of the rule change that provided for a timeout after every first down, but mainly because they called plays quicker and used shorter counts. Even more of a factor was that defenses, set wider and wider to protect against spread formations, were increasingly vulnerable to running games. Sixteen backs topped the once-sacred figure of 1,000 yards running in one season.

"What was once a perfectly good defense technically," said one coach, "is no longer sound. You have to keep up with the times."

The other most surprising trend was the emergence of the sophomore quarterback. Two-platoon football and the attractive money offered by the pros had by now made a science of the advanced training of high school quarterbacks. It was not uncommon any longer for a 19-year-old quarterback to be able to read seven different defenses with poise and call audibles at the line faster than a circus pitchman could talk. And so coach after coach and team after team was flabbergasted in 1968 by what its sophomore quarterback could do or, worse yet, what the other team's sophomores could do.

The new rule calling for the clock to be stopped after every first down meant far more than the fact that games obviously would last longer. A team trailing by no more than a touchdown or field goal near the end of a game now was able to squeeze in several more plays, if it could keep a drive going by making first downs. Those long, sustained drives on the ground thus did not consume as much playing time. Best of all, a team that had used up its timeouts and was racing the clock did not have to waste a down throwing an intentional incomplete pass to halt the second hand. It could gamble on a run for a first down, since the clock would stop if the down was made. In turn, the defense now had to guard against the run—which increased the chance for a successful pass. In short, the entire last-minute strategy of the game was affected, primarily in favor of a running team.

Two other 1968 rules changes were important, although not noticed as much. The punt return rule that was tried in 1967, whereby interior linemen could not start covering until the ball was kicked, was ditched. And the numbering of players finally became specific. Backs had to wear numbers between 1 and 49, interior linemen from 59 to 79, and ends from 80 to 99.

### *The Tie*

The Ivy League belonged to Yale and Harvard in 1968. For the first time since 1909, both teams were unbeaten (8-0-0) coming up to The Game. The winner would get the conference championship and the ancient Big Three title.

Harvard versus Yale was a promoter's dream. All season, mighty Yale, ranked behind Penn State and Army as the best team in the East, and the improving Harvards had been on a collision course. The Bulldogs had not lost in 16 games; the Crimson had a streak of 8 going. Coach Cozza's team was basically offensive minded, although it surely played good defense when pressed. For the most part, however, the Elis were attackers. In eight games they had rolled up 288 points. Cozza had his backs operating from a flamboyant, well-conceived T variation that he himself had refined to include motion, shifting, and zone-wrecking passes. It was one of the most exciting offenses in the East, and a lot of smart coaches were trying to copy it.

Since midseason when Yale and Harvard started to edge up into top-level rankings in the Eastern polls, trying to rate their strengths and deficiencies had been a parlor game. You gave Yale two points for offense, Harvard one point for offense. You gave Yale speed and strength and depth, but Harvard had quickness. Yale had a good blocking line, but Harvard had a better pursuing defense. The Bulldogs had the best passing and receiving, but the Crimson could counter this with such good runners as Hornblower, Gatto, and Crim, plus two fine pass-catching ends in Varney and Kiernan. The kicking was just about even and the coaching was even, but Yale was deeper in reserves.

So who would win? For any big college football game, there are always more so-called intangibles than there are old chums who want tickets. Intangibles involve emotion, character, voodoo, tradition, and intuition. And as far as emotion went, both teams had reached a high, frenzied peak, but that was how Yale and Harvard players usually looked before The Game.

A day before the game, a friend of mine, a Yale man who had not missed a Yale-Harvard football contest in 25 years, went to the blackboard and evaluated the two teams, player by player. He had figured out a point-grading system for this, and when he was through adding point by point, he totaled the figures for each side. They came out with Yale holding a slight edge. When that happened, I told my friend he had failed to take into consideration how the two teams fared against six common foes: Columbia, Cornell, Dartmouth, Brown, Penn, and Princeton. Harvard piled up a total of 121 points against them, while holding them to 41; Yale was 208 against 90. Those numbers clearly gave Harvard the edge in defense, but Yale appeared almost twice as tough in scoring. Adding this information to his curious point-grading system, my friend stepped back from the blackboard and made the least newsworthy comment of what the editors of *Sports Illustrated* later voted as one of the 10 most exciting college football games in history: "Sir," he said, "it's going to be a helluva game."

Despite my friend's point system for determining a winner, most of the forecasters favored Yale by seven. They felt that the one-two punch of quarterback Brian Dowling and halfback Calvin Hill would be just too much for the Crimson to overcome. Inspired by the strong right arm of the fluid and mythic Dowling, who had won every football game he had finished since the seventh grade, Yale averaged 36 points a contest and ranked third in the nation in total yardage. Harvard, on the other hand, had achieved 10 fewer points each Saturday and had gained 1,133 yards less. Even Harvard supporters publicly admitted that Yale was invincible and that the Crimson was Number Two.

There was one Harvard man who wasn't quitting, however. "We've got everything to gain," John Yovicsin said before the game. "My lads aren't going to put their undefeated record on the block without putting up a fight. To beat us they must score a lot of points, because we're going to get across that goal line."

A loss at the hands of Yale was a revolting prospect in ordinary years, but now it would mean the ruin of a perfect record and the loss of the league title as well.

The stage was all set. The coaches were ready. The players were ready. With some tickets selling for $125 apiece (at least one Old Blue paid $1,000 to a scalper for a block of eight seats), The Game was a sellout, 40,280. Some 15,000 tickets had been shipped down to New Haven, where the majority were doled out at the rate of four per student. The rest went to the alumni, two per person. For three straight days, Yale ticket manager Jack Blake's phone never stopped ringing.

"They were demanding to know why they ordered six or eight and only got two," Blake recalled. "That was the first time such a thing ever happened."

Harvard did things differently. It gave out 9,000 tickets to undergraduates, the highest student ticket demand ever at Cambridge. It filled its alumni orders by starting with the oldest class. When officials got to the class of 1949, they ran out of tickets and quit. But Gordon Page, the Harvard ticket manager, had the solution. "I just avoided phone calls," he said.

The Yale Fan Academy Award went to two sophomores from New Haven. Shut out by the crush of tickets at Cambridge, they simply put on blue blazers, borrowed a trumpet and trombone, fell into step with the Yale band, and marched into Soldiers' Field.

During the first 25 minutes of play, there seemed no way that The Game was going to match the buildup. In a contest played on a dry, fast field, in sunny 41-degree weather, Brian Dowling threatened to take what was supposed to be a classic in the annals of Ivy League Championship play and turn it into a laugh-in, an embarrassment, a Harvard humiliation. Running boldly, scrambling until his receivers could work themselves clear, the Yale quarterback scored one touchdown himself and passed to Cal Hill and end Del Marting for two more to put the Blue ahead, 22-0.

With both the first half and Harvard fading, Coach Yovicsin finally, desperately, turned to his second-string quarterback, Frank Champi, and said, "Okay, you go in for George [Lalich] and try it for a while." Champi was a balding 20-year-old history major who could throw a football 85 yards with his right arm and 50 yards with his left and who was the best javelin man in Harvard history until he strained a muscle. George Lalich, the regular quarterback, had been as instrumental as anyone in bringing Harvard into the game undefeated, but his passing had soured at midseason and now it hadn't been improving against Yale. But why Frank Champi? All season he had completed exactly five passes! Even his own teammates paled when they saw him running onto the playing field. They knew he had a powerful arm, but, to be perfectly honest, they felt he was a bit too inexperienced to get them back into the ball game. He was a junior and had shown evidence of nervousness all season under pressure. ("Frankly, we were surprised to see him," confessed Harvard captain Vic Gatto later. "He hadn't played a whole lot, and confidence is something you get by playing, not by sitting on the bench. But we needed to be shaken up.")

For an opening shake, with 39 seconds left in the half, quarterback Champi flipped a nifty 15-yard touchdown pass to Bruce Freeman, a sophomore split end. A poor snap from center spoiled the attempted conversion, but six points were better than none, and 22-6 was not quite as depressing as 22-0.

At half time, Yovicsin told his players that all they had to do to win was to shut out Yale in the second half while getting two touchdowns and a field goal themselves. He said that he was sure they could do it.

"Oh, sure he was sure," growled one of the team's 22 seniors with unexpected emotion later. "Listen. Yovicsin had given up on us. All he wanted us to do was go out there and get the rest of the game over as quickly as possible. But we weren't playing for him and we weren't playing for the school. We were playing for *ourselves*. And we were the ones—the only ones—who knew we could still win."

Before the season, the majority of seniors on the Harvard team had almost walked out. They felt that they had been the "forgotten guys" on the squad. "Ever since our freshman year we'd been ignored," one of them said. "But we changed our minds about quitting after Gatto was elected captain. We decided to rally around him, to play for ourselves. We wanted to show the school, the coaches, and the experts that we were a lot better than any of them gave us credit for."

When Harvard returned to the field for the second half, George Lalich was still at quarterback. He stayed for only three plays. The three plays gained nothing, and Harvard had to punt. But Yale was now struck by a series of fumbles. It began with the punt, which Harvard recovered on the Yale 25. Once more in came Frank Champi. Harvard scored in three plays, with fullback Gus Crim getting the touchdown. The conversion made it 22-13, and the hometown crowd began to stir. Perhaps the game would turn out to be worth the price after all.

After Crim's third-quarter run cut Yale's lead to nine points, a strange thing happened. Yale had scored in 22 straight quarters, but in this one it didn't, largely because it gave up two more fumbles to Harvard.

Stung, perhaps by the ending of the long scoring streak, Brian Dowling needed just seven plays to cover 45 yards early in the fourth quarter to begin a new streak, rolling 5 yards around right end himself for the touchdown, his second of the game.

Now, from the Yale side of the field, Coach Cozza glanced up at the scoreboard: Yale 28, Harvard 13, 10:44 left to play. Cozza shrugged and told Bob Bayless, his place-kicker, to go in and kick the extra point, which he did. Following Yale's third score, Cozza had ordered a two-point conversion, which Dowling had picked up on a pass to Marting. The Yale coach figured those two points surely would put the game out of reach. After the fourth touchdown, he asked himself what difference did it make? There was no way Harvard could fight back, no way it could win. Or so Carmen Cozza told himself.

Yale's 15-point lead held up for 10 minutes, which was slightly less than it should have. With Yale rooters waving handkerchiefs and screaming across the field at the Harvards, "You're number two," Champi rallied his troops.

"When they started waving those white hankies and yelling," said Captain Gatto, "it really got to us."

Harvard drove downfield from its own 14 to the Yale 15-yard line in eight plays, aided by a 15-yard holding penalty against the Bulldogs. With only 42 seconds left on the clock, Champi threw a 15-yard scoring strike to Freeman. A Yale penalty gave Harvard two tries at the vital two-point conversion, and Crim got it the second time over left guard on a hand-off from Champi. Now the Cantabs trailed by eight points.

It was obvious to just about everyone what Harvard intended to do next. "Onside kick!" screamed its supporters. But the Yale team apparently did not believe them, for out trotted the usual kickoff return team and up front went the big lumbering blockers. So, of course, here came the onside kick, and, sure enough, Harvard's Bill Kelly wound up with the ball on the Yale 49.

With Champi running for 14 yards and getting 15 more when his face mask was grabbed, Harvard needed only five plays and 39 seconds to get down to the Yale 8-yard line. Now the clock had wound down to the last three seconds.

On the sideline, Yovicsin wondered if he could last. Behind him the Harvard fans were going mad. The whole stadium was going crazy. High above the floor of the playing field, in the press box, one sportswriter was seen putting a piece of paper into his portable, tearing it out, crumpling it up, doing the same thing over and over. He had a feeling that he couldn't go on much longer either.

Down on the field, Champi led his teammates out of the huddle. His back was wet and dark where the sweat had soaked through, his helmet shoved down tight on his head. You wondered if he was nervous out there. A lot of Harvards were seen to grab their thumbs and say a short, silent prayer for him. They were almost afraid to look.

Champi bent over the center and barked the signals. Now he scrambled back, forward, back, looking, looking for a receiver in the open. His blockers swept to the right, sucking the defenders along with them, while over on the left, in the end zone, far from any company, stood Captain Gatto, waiting for the ball. The ball rode in an arc from Champi's palm as he released his throw. Suddenly the 85th edition of The Game was reduced to a pass and a prayer. The blur of the ball assumed shape. It came to Gatto's hands and he felt the old elation and he heard the deafening noise break on the Harvard side as he hauled the ball in and hugged it to his chest for six more points.

There was bedlam. The Harvards were beside themselves. It was wonderful. It was beautiful. It was impossible. But there it was suddenly: Yale 29, Harvard 27. Time had run out and now, coming up, was the most important play of The Game. Harvard had no choice but to go for the two-point conversion. On the sideline, John Yovicsin was shouting at Champi, "All right, Frank, let's make it! Let's not die here now!" He was thinking that his players had driven all that way, 51 yards in six plays, and now there were just two more points to pick up for a tie.

"You linemen!" cried Yovicsin. "Block!"

Both teams were exhausted, drained. They had played their hearts out for 60 minutes. Now it had all come down to this one play. What an absurd ending to an absurd game. I mean, what were the odds against the chain of events that had just transpired in those last 42 seconds of play? Consider the likelihood of pass interference on the first P.A.T., providing a successful second try; a stopped clock that awards precious time to Harvard; a Yale turnover on the onside kick; a 15-yard face mask penalty on Yale that advances Harvard's ball to the 20-yard line with 20 seconds to play; and now a Champi touchdown through the air after time elapses. Utterly unlikely, but utterly the case.

"And when all is said and done," *The Harvard Crimson* had editorialized on The Game of 1913, "the better team probably will win, for failures and flukes are as much a measure of a team as splendid gains and wonderful charges. If a team fails in a crucial test, it is not the better team at that time, whatever it may have been before or after."

Back to The Game of 1968. While the grandstand quarterbacks doped out the strategy ("I see the game in mystical terms . . . a mystic creates an event by thought . . . there was a lot of thinking in those stands," Champi said recently, looking back), Yovicsin watched his players break from the huddle and walk slowly up to the line of scrimmage. Once more, he watched Champi lean over the center, hands at the ready. Frank was so tired he wasn't even nervous. The referee's whistle blew and the two lines braced themselves. Tension hung over the stadium. Everybody was standing now, hearts pounding, as they watched Champi count off his signals. A long murmur ran around the stands. You could almost hear the silent prayers of the Harvard cheer section, the pleas, encouraging the Crimson, helping it all they could. No one was sitting.

Once more, Champi dropped back to pass. Once more, he scrambled around—back, forward, back—looking for a Crimson jersey in the clear. Suddenly, there stood Pete Varney, all alone in the corner and waving his arms. Champi cocked his arm, the ball sailed, and Varney gathered it in for two more points, adding up to a preposterous 29-29 compromise.

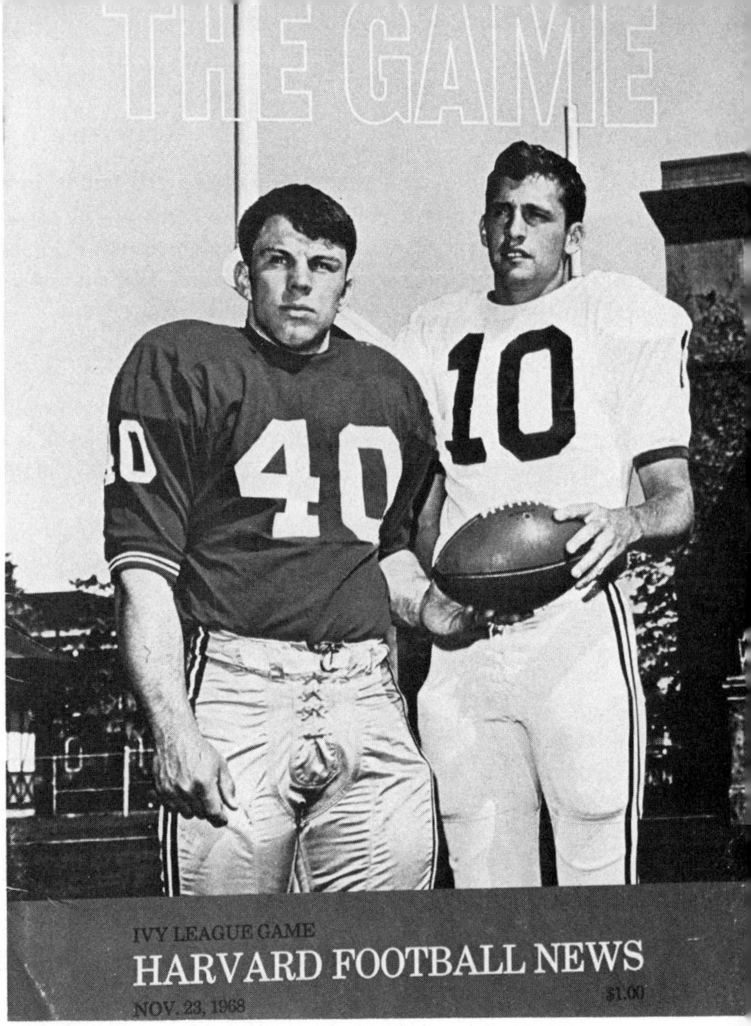


*Captains Vic Gatto, Harvard, left, and Yale's Brian Dowling posed for the cover of the* Harvard Football News *before what* Sports Illustrated *later picked as "one of the 10 most exciting college football games in history." That was the 29-29 tie at Cambridge in 1968.*

The riot was on. Champi, who after three discontented seasons of monotonous practice and Saturday subordination had finally hit the jackpot, and Varney were being squeezed to death by teammates gone crazy. Grown people carrying red banners with black H's sewn in the middle of them were doing strange dances on the seats and hugging and kissing and crying. Out on the field everybody was trying to congratulate Champi at once, shaking his hand, smothering him with bear hugs, and you could tell by the wide grin on his face that this was the supreme moment of his life. And then, all at once, you could hear the roar from down out of the stadium start and gather force, and then it rolled up and out of the arena and across old Harvard Square, and I think they heard it way up in New Hampshire and Maine and perhaps into Canada.

In the Yale dressing room, no one spoke. Fred Morris, who had played a whale of a game at center, sat on the stairs, his head cradled in his arms. He was still wearing his helmet. Silently, slowly, his teammates went about pulling off their uniforms, showered, then dressed. Still no one spoke. Finally, an Old Blue said, "You guys didn't lose. You're still undefeated. You're still the Ivy League co-champions."

"No," said giant tight end Bruce Weinstein softly, "when you've done what we just did you've lost. It's the same as a defeat. We don't feel much like champions."

*The Crimson* said much the same thing in its Monday morning headline: *Harvard Beats Yale, 29-29.* An editorial inside explained this presumption thusly:

"Rarely has justice dispensed itself with such timing. Who will remember the team that lumbered ahead to a lopsided lead in the first half? No one. Who can forget the team that cut the lead to shreds in the last 42 seconds of the game?

"For its efforts, Harvard can lay claim to more than a draw. All save the most fearless of its gambling partisans won their bets, and all save the most underhanded of the nation's newspapers (one thinks of *The Yale Daily News*) will surely see fit to play Cambridge well over New Haven in the headlines.

"A draw in name only, then. By every other reckoning, a magnificent victory."

Immediately after the game, downstairs in the Harvard locker room, Frank Champi sat amidst a wild scene of jublilation and wondered aloud where he was, if it really wasn't all a dream. It had been a very strange day for him from the time he got up, he said. "I'm an intuitive guy," he said, "and when I woke up this morning I was sort of in a dream. It felt like something great was going to happen to me. Then when I got to the stadium I still felt strange. It didn't feel like I was here but someplace else. I still don't feel like I'm here. It's all very strange."

For the rest of his life, Frank Champi would carry the memory of The Tie in a deep, private place where old love affairs are held. His heroics had nothing to do with daily life, and no one who was there will ever allow it to be so.

The severe disappointment over The Tie has diffused into a bad memory for Brian Dowling today. He is still irked when people mention his participation in "that game that Harvard beat you." Yet he, too, slips in conversation, referring to the tie as "the first time I lost at Yale." Dowling feels frustration but not guilt over the final score. He had been criticized for profligate play-calling in the fourth quarter—throwing like a wild man rather than eating up the clock. A more prudent style would have voided Harvard's comeback. But if a Yale fullback hadn't fumbled at the Harvard 14 on a Dowling screen with 3:31 remaining, Harvard would have been stymied anyhow. Dowling never touched the ball again as Champi went into his unbelievable act for 18 straight plays. It was painful for Dowling to watch from the sidelines as Harvard threatened his personal win streak and Yale's spotless season. Dowling begged Coach Cozza in vain to appoint him to the defensive backfield, whose inexperience was fast blowing the lead. The rest, of course, is history.

"I don't want to take anything from Champi," Dowling said sincerely, "but he fumbled once and his tackle ran 23 yards, and that face mask penalty wasn't any of his doing either. He didn't pull it out, his team did."

Yale coach Cozza hasn't screened the 29-29 film since 1968. He endured it once to rate the officials for the Eastern College Athletic Conference. The tie still bothers him.

"Harvard had momentum," he concedes, "but they also had help. I don't question the integrity of the game officials, but they sure as hell got caught up in the emotion of the game, and it cost us. I've had a good career at Yale though. One game doesn't make much difference. Here my guys had a great career and everybody remembers them for a tie—in a game they had no control over. But how can I say that without detracting from those Harvard kids, who were great. If we hadn't fumbled six times, we could have named our score. But I wouldn't have run it up. Our kids . . . that's what still hurts inside."

Peter Easton, Yale's affable sports information director, remembers that he was seated in the press box next to Baaron Pittenger, the Harvard press agent, and when the clock froze at 42 seconds with Yale ahead by 10 points, he reached over to give comfort to Baaron. Below them, the Old Blues on the Yale side were waving their victory hankies. Harvard was hopelessly and haplessly behind—or so Easton and most everybody else thought.

"I really had to eat crow," Peter told me. "That's the last time I've ever tried to console anybody before the final whistle."

### *The Lineups*

YALE

ENDS—Marting, Weinstein, Madden, Jim Gallagher, Robinson, Lussen, Roney

TACKLES—Bass, D. Gee, Neville, F. Gallagher, Peacock, Kleber, Livingston, Mackie, Mattas

GUARDS—Whiteman, Perkowski, Dick Williams, Puryear, Lee, Jackson

CENTERS—Morris, Pace

QUARTERBACK—Dowling

HALFBACKS—Hill, Davidson, Kropke

FULLBACK—Levin

LINEBACKERS—Bouscaren, Coe, Kell, Schmoke, Franklin, Martin, Downing, Waldman, Boyer

SAFETY—Goldsmith.

KICKING SPECIALIST—Bayless

HARVARD

ENDS —Varney, Kiernan, Gloyd, T. Smith, Hall, Cramer, Ranere, Freeman, McKinney

TACKLES—Reed, Dowd, Zebal, Berne, Kaplan, Sadler

GUARDS—Jones, Jannino, MacLean, Georges

CENTERS—Skowronski, Teske

QUARTERBACKS—Lalich, Champi

HALFBACKS—Hornblower, Gatto, Ballantyne, Reynolds

FULLBACKS—Crim, Miller

LINEBACKERS—Farneti, Emery, Ignacio, Frisbie, Neal, Ananis, Koski, Kundrat, Marino

SAFETIES—Wynne, Conway, Kelly, Martucci, Fenton, Thomas, Manny

KICKING SPECIALISTS—Singleterry, Szaro

### *Score By Periods*

| | | | | | |
|---|---|---|---|---|---|
| Yale | 7 | 15 | 0 | 7 | 29 |
| Harvard | 0 | 6 | 7 | 16 | 29 |

### *Final Statistics*

| | *Yale* | *Harvard* |
|---|---|---|
| First Downs | 19 | 17 |
| Rushing Yardage | 251 | 118 |
| Passing Yardage | 116 | 104 |
| Return Yardage | 60 | 30 |
| Passes | 13-23-1 | 8-22-0 |
| Punts | 3-36 | 8-36 |
| Fumbles Lost | 6 | 1 |
| Yards Penalized | 7 for 66 yds. | 4 for 30 yds. |
| Punt Returns | 60 yds. | 7 yds. |

° ° °

Not all the Ivy League shouting was in Cambrige on that final Saturday of the 1968 season. It was like old times in Penn's Franklin Field, with 50,188 on hand to watch the best Quaker team since 1959. It was their biggest crowd in years. Penn had lost only to Yale and Harvard.

With quarterback Bernie Zbrzeznj passing for 176 yards and fullback Gerry Santini running for 133, Penn defeated Dartmouth, 26-21. Princeton and Columbia also had some finale fun. The Tigers hammered Cornell, 41-13, as tailback Brian McCullough scored three touchdowns, while Columbia battered Brown, 46-20.

In a way it was a sad day at Columbia, for it was the swan song of Marty Domres, the brilliant quarterback who completed 30 of 54 passes for 329 yards and two touchdowns and scored twice on runs. All told, the versatile Domres set 15 Columbia and 12 Ivy League records for passes thrown and completed, passing yardage, and total offense. He also broke the NCAA mark for total offensive plays—1,132 in three years—and was headed for the pros. Frank Navarro, the Columbia coach, called Domres the "best college quarterback I've ever seen."

Another Ivy star bowing out was Calvin Hill, who one year later would be named the National Football League's Rookie of the Year—from Yale to the Dallas Cowboys in one jump. At 14, Hill had won a scholarship to the predominantly white Riverdale Boys' School in New York City. There his athletic talents bloomed. He pitched and batted over .400 for the baseball team, made an all-city basketball team with an average of 26 points per game, and was named to a high school All-America football team as quarterback. Graduating with honors, he went on to Yale, partly because they offered him a "needy student scholarship, not a football scholarship." He said he liked the idea of not having to play football if he didn't want to.

Yale fans liked it even more when Hill decided to go out for football, although his exploits were mostly overshadowed by the massive publicity Brian Dowling received. The 144 points he scored in three seasons broke Albie Booth's old Yale record of 138, but Calvin was bypassed by most of the All-America teams as well as by most of the pro scouts. No one, it seemed, was quite ready to believe that the tweedy Ivy League could produce a hard-nosed pro. No one, that is, except the Dallas Cowboys, who made him their number one draft choice. A history major at Yale and a deep thinker, Hill scored in the top 2 percent in the Cowboys' intelligence test. Sample: Asked why so many of today's professional football stars are black, Hill said he had a theory. "I think it all boils down to survival of the fittest," he said. "Think of what the African slaves were forced to endure in America to survive. Well, we black athletes are their descendants, the offspring of those who were physically and mentally tough enough to simply survive."

*A first-round pro draft choice in 1968 was Columbia's twice All-Ivy quarterback, Marty Domres.*

## 1969

As college football marked its 100th anniversary and began a new century, it may well have said goodbye forever to the fullback constantly running up the backs of his guards and tackles. It may have also bid farewell to the quick kick, field position, clawing defense—to every conservative element that once upon a time helped distinguish the game by regions and made it different from the pitch-and-catch style of the professionals.

For better or worse the collegiate game was now being played the same way over the entire country. Everybody was throwing the ball, everybody was catching it, and everybody was running with such alarming success that scoreboards had taken on the appearance of a neon sign at Times Square.

The rules makers probably hadn't intended this when they gradually resurrected free substitution and then, in 1968, added more plays per game by stopping the clock after every first down, but that is what they got. The season of 1968 had produced so much offense that even the pros looked stodgy. The average number of points scored in a game leaped to 42.4, the average total offense per game jumped to 657 yards, the average passing yardage climbed to 315.4, and the number of total-offense plays reached a peak of 150.1.

What the collegiate sport had come to could be highlighted by reviewing the scores of a few of 1968's games: Abilene Christian 50, Howard Payne 49; Ohio 60, Cincinnati 48; Wake Forest 48, North Carolina 31; Indiana 40, Baylor 36; Air Force 58, Colorado 35; Washington 35, Rice 35—and Yale 29, Harvard 29.

Just about every team had somebody trying to be a passer, it seemed, and a record 16 ball carriers, led by O. J. Simpson, gained more than 1,000 yards. The paranoia that beset coaches who thought they taught good defense was best exemplified by Frank Broyles of Arkansas, whose Razorbacks led Southern Methodist into the fourth quarter by 35 points, but barely held on to win, 35-29. "A 35-point lead just isn't safe anymore," Broyles said after the game.

Darrell Royal of Texas said there was a time when he didn't mind giving up the football because he trusted his defense. "But now," he said in 1969, "we aren't so eager to give up the ball to anybody—anywhere."

In an effort to try to keep the ball with a strong ground game, Coach Royal developed a formation in 1968, the wishbone T, that a lot of college teams were picking up in 1969. Basically, it was a straight T formation utilizing the triple option play of the quarterback, but a receiver was split wide and the fullback was moved a step closer to the line of scrimmage. So, in 1969, nearly all the major powers were expected to trot out their version of the wishbone T, just as everybody went to the I formation of John McKay at Southern California a few years before.

*After three big years at Yale, halfback Calvin Hill went to immediate stardom in the National Football League with the Dallas Cowboys in 1969.*

As the Ivies prepared to do battle, their fans were still talking about The Last 42 Seconds, the berserk 42 seconds in which undefeated Harvard scored 16 points to tie undefeated Yale, 29-29, and earn a share of the league championship. It was the fourth time in the last eight years that the title in the well-balanced Ivy League had to be split up.

The experts were all wrong about the Ivies in their preseason reports. One writer predicted: "Harvard could go seatless and defeatless again if Coach John Yovicsin can rebuild the defense and if back Richie Szaro heals. End Pete Varney, tackle Fritz Reed, halfbacks Ray Hornblower and sophomore Steve Harrison, quarterback Frank Champi, and defensemen John Cramer and Rick Frisbie put brimstone in Puritan Power.

"Yale, losing its entire backfield and all its stars, including Dowling, Calvin Hill, and Bruce Weinstein, will surrender its 17-game unbeaten streak and fall into the second division. Princeton is playing it close to the vest, but the word is that the Tigers may be giving up the single wing so that Scott MacBean and Brian McCullough can be in the backfield at the same time. If Princeton does go to the T formation, sophomore Rod Plummer could become Princeton's first black quarterback.

"Penn is the other serious contender. Quarterback Bernie Zbrzeznj, center George Joseph, and fullback Bill Sudhaus talon a hawkish offense. Dartmouth, with quarterbacks Bill Koenig and Jim Chasey, cannot be discounted. Split end Rick Furbush and defensemen Keith Cummins and Theo Jacobs provide the Cornell guns, and Brown will be more respectable. Columbia, as customary, will be a riot to watch."

Days before Princeton and Rutgers took the field to decide which of them would start football's second century with a victory, the funny stuff began. On Wednesday night 12 Princetonians removed the Little Cannon originally fired by George Washington's underdog team at the Battle of Princeton from its concrete base on the campus and buried it three feet away. They left a sign at the base reading, "Thanks Princeton, love Rutgers '72." Local Trenton papers documented the theft, and soon the story was picked up by the wire services. Rutgers students confessed to the caper, guessing one of their pranksters surely did it. When the truth was revealed, as one Princetonian put it, "Rutgers had egg all over its face."

But by 4 o'clock on Saturday afternoon, it was Princeton, not Rutgers, wearing the egg. Rich Policastro, the Rutgers quarterback, had stuck to his game plan, calling quick-opening plays that sent tailback Bruce Van Ness and fullback Steve Ferrughelli through the eight-man defensive front for long gains. He also completed 24 passes, a school record, for 260 yards. The final score, 29-0, was hardly an auspicious start to Princeton's first non-single-wing offense since 1945. "Today," said a reporter after the game, "Princeton set football back 100 years."

A week later, Harvard, stepping outside the Ivies, wore a bit of egg too. At half time, with the Crimson ahead, 10-7, the Harvard band serenaded the Boston University stands—and its team—with the "Mickey Mouse Theme." Normally that would seem like asking for trouble, but the Harvards were not worried. Weren't their heroes undefeated in 10 straight games, dating back to 1968? And wasn't their opponent funny old Boston U. from across the Charles River, the team that had yet to beat Harvard in football?

Back in the dressing room, the BU players heard the music. They got the message. And it made them fighting mad. "That's the impression everybody has of us," said Quarterback Pete Yetten, "that we play Mickey Mouse football. Let's show them that we play it another way."

That's just what they did. Yetten, who had lost his first-string job 10 days earlier, popped off the bench in the second half and threw the game-winning pass to Gary Capehart. Final score: Boston U. 13, Harvard 10. On defense, BU held Harvard to only 100 yards. After the win, the victorious players carried their coach, Larry Naviaux, off the field.

"You have a good football team," Naviaux told John Yovicsin.

"Thank you," replied the Harvard coach, "but you have a better one."

° ° °

For the second week in a row, Rich Policastro, the nation's leading percentage passer, was the nemesis of the Ivy League. In what for him was an "off" day, he completed 16 of 27, as Rutgers trounced Cornell, 21-7.

° ° °

Dartmouth, with lopsided victories over New Hampshire and Holy Cross, opened league competition by rushing for 509 yards to crush Penn, 41-0, but all was not well in the Indians' tepee. The Big Green's real Indians put the hatchet to the school mascot. "He perpetuates a romantic, naive, and unrealistic view of the American Indian," said freshman Howard Bad Hand.

There was also trouble in the Harvard camp. Quarterback Frank Champi, the hero of 1968's tie with Yale, quit the team a few days before the Columbia game because "football has lost its meaning to me," so the Crimson proceeded to score its most points ever against an Ivy opponent while demolishing the Lions, 51-0.

A week later, however, Cornell upset Harvard, 41-24, for its first win of the season as sophomore Ed Marinaro dazzled everyone with five touchdowns and 281 yards rushing on 40 carries. While all that was going on, Yale routed Columbia, 41-6, to remain unbeaten against Ivy opponents since 1966.

Dartmouth kept in the thick of things by beating Brown, 38-13, for its fourth straight victory of the year. John Short returned the opening kickoff 90 yards for a touchdown. "We didn't try anything new or different," said Bob Blackman after the game, "because we have an important game with Harvard next week and we knew their scouts would be watching."

In Philadelphia, the casualty rate among Penn quarterbacks continued to escalate. In a hard-fought 13-7 triumph over Lehigh, Phil Procacci, who had been switched from defense only after Penn's first two quarterbacks each suffered a shoulder injury, was the latest victim. He broke his jaw against Lehigh and would be out for the rest of the season. He was replaced by Terry Groome, and now everyone wondered how long he would last. After all, Groome had missed his entire freshman season because of a broken foot.

Despite a 24-10 win over Harvard for his fifth straight of the season, Dartmouth Coach Bob Blackman told the press in a postgame interview, "We were robbed." How was that again? "I don't mean on the field," he said. "I mean somebody ransacked our dressing room during the game and stole the players' rings and watches." Even before the players discovered the theft, the dressing room was like a tomb. "The team didn't react as if it had won," Blackman said. "They know they didn't play a good game."

The Harvard defense held the Big Green to 213 yards. That was less than half their average. The first-team Dartmouth defense, which had allowed just one touchdown in five games, was responsible for much of Dartmouth's scoring, as the Big G got all its points in the first 18 minutes as a result of two pass interceptions, a field goal, and a 65-yard punt return by Tom Quinn.

"You can tell by our eyes how good we are defensively," said Russ Adams, a junior defensive halfback. "You get in that defensive huddle when you're under pressure, you look around, and you see it in our eyes."

After five weeks, Yale and Princeton remained unbeaten against Ivy League opposition. Ellis Moore, the Princeton fullback, scored three times and the defense yielded only four first downs as the Tigers found Penn full of brotherly love, trouncing the Red and Blue, 42 to 0.

And Yale? "There are only two Italians I ever lost sleep over," said Bill Narzuzzi, Yale's defensive coach, after the Blue had shut out Cornell, 17-0. "The first was my wife and the other was Ed Marinaro." Cornell's sensational sophomore began the afternoon as the nation's leading rusher, but Narzuzzi's crew limited him to 30 yards. The victory extended Yale's Ivy League unbeaten string to 17 games. Columbia was less fortunate, losing to Rutgers in the last 36 seconds, 21-14.

The last two times Dartmouth traveled to the Yale Bowl, Yale had run up a total of 103 points, and after the first quarter of their 1969 game, November 1, unbeaten Dartmouth must have thought it was going to happen again. Yale led, 14-7, but then the Big Green scored three touchdowns in succession, and it was all downhill from there. Halfback Tom Quinn registered his second touchdown punt return in as many weeks (for 54 yards) and added a touchdown for good measure, as Dartmouth ended Yale's conference victory streak, 42-21. Yale did supply the leading rusher, Don Martin, a converted defensive back, who gained 137 yards and caused the NFL's leading rusher, Calvin Hill, to say that Martin should have been switched to offensive halfback in 1968. Reminded that he himself was the Yale halfback in 1968, Hill amended: "You're right. He should have been on defense."

If any Princeton diehards were unhappy that the Tigers finally junked the single wing, the 1969 edition did not leave them much room for complaint. As happy with the T (or the "cockeyed I," as they called it) as a kid with a new toy, the Tigers flattened Harvard, 51-20, to remain tied for the Ivy lead with unbeaten Dartmouth after five league games. Dartmouth kept its record clean by beating Columbia, 37-7, and was now being clustered with Penn State and West Virginia as one of the three top teams in the East.

Nobody at Princeton was happier without the single wing than quarterback Scott MacBean.

"It gave me a new life," he said. "I was about to be beaten out at tailback. Besides, the single wing is dull football. Last year, with it, we were last in America in passing."

Against Harvard, the hero was not MacBean but the Princeton captain, senior fullback Ellis Moore, who scored three touchdowns, two fewer than he got on his previous trip to Cambridge.

"Players seem to return to the scene of the crime quite often," said Jake McCandless, the Princeton coach. The Tiger defense threw Harvard halfback Ray Hornblower for a net loss of 7 yards rushing.

Both Dartmouth and Princeton were supposed to go into their November 22 game at Palmer Stadium with perfect Ivy League records, but—oops—the Tigers slipped and were upset by Yale, 17-14. Now Dartmouth needed only to beat Princeton to wrap up its unbeaten season and third Ivy title in five years. If Princeton won, however, and if Yale beat Harvard as expected, then there would be a three-way tie for the championship.

Dartmouth tuned up for Princeton by whipping Cornell, 24-7, despite Ed Marinaro's 122 yards rushing, which put the Big Red sophomore only 17 yards away from the Ivy season record. Yale's winning margin over Princeton was a 23-yard field goal by Harry Klebanoff, a 5′ 6″, 140-pound soccer-style kicker.

There were some who felt that Dartmouth was the greatest Ivy League team since those long-ago days of bowl bids. The unbeaten Big Green had routed eight opponents by 26 points a game. Now Princeton, their final obstacle, was all that stood in the way. But, ah, Princeton coach Jake McCandless, who had done graduate study in psychology, was primed. All week long he kept replaying films of the Columbia-Dartmouth game, one of the Big Green's poorer showings. Just when Dartmouth began to look human, McCandless took his boys aside and told them to throw conservatism into the ash can—attack, attack. Finally, before the Tigers went out to face Dartmouth, he stood before them and spoke just two words: "I'm proud."

The Tigers roared out of their locker room and, using outside sweeps and tough defense, stunned Dartmouth, 35-7. It was never even close as 175-pound halfback John Bjorklund, starting only his second game, scored three touchdowns. "Beating Dartmouth had become an odyssey," spoke defensive end Jim Nixon, "but we told ourselves, what have we got to lose? Let's go out and attack, and if we blow it, we really blow it."

The victory created a three-way tie for the Ivy Championship among Dartmouth, Princeton, and Yale. The only other time that had ever happened, since the Ivy League was officially formed in 1956, was in 1966, when Dartmouth, Harvard, and Princeton deadlocked with 6-1-0 Ivy records.

Yale, which had been knocked out of the honor of sole titleholder in the final 42 seconds against Harvard in 1968, seemed to be awaiting another final-second crush in '69 at Yale Bowl. Alas, the only interest at the end came from the Yale fans, who counted off the remaining 42 seconds as the Elis crawled away with a big 7-0 victory. Their defensive team held the Crimson to a mere 27 yards rushing, forced four fumbles, and let the passing get no farther than their 11.

The Bulldog score came on a third-quarter two-yard plunge by fullback Bill Primps after an 80-

yard drive inspired by quarterback Joe Massey, a junior who once quit the freshman team due to a preference for singing in the glee club.

Yale wasn't the only Ivy team to enjoy the day's outcome. Columbia upset Brown, 18-3, closing the season at 1-8 for the Lions.

For Len Jardine, the Brown coach, it had been a frustrating three seasons since he first joined the Bruins in 1967. Against Ivy League competition, his record was now 2-18-1. All those problems notwithstanding, Coach Jardine maintained his sense of humor.

"In my first game as a head coach I discovered there wasn't any chalk for my pregame discussion," he said. "I had to use my ulcer pills to write on the board."

So ended the first 100 years of football.

# The Seventies

## 1970

College football coaches were openly concerned about the "mood" of young people and how it might affect their game as a whole new decade of the sport entered the fresh season of 1970. With the transition came so many problems of a complex and sophisticated nature that some alarmists were wondering if college football would ever be the same again. A coach was now faced with a new kind of nightmare.

"All I know is, you can't talk to athletes like you once could," said Penn State's Joe Paterno. "You can't sit on 'em. They're exposed to too many things. They're too smart, too aware. If they're not convinced that self-discipline is for their own good, they're not going to perform like you want them to."

In 1969, Cornell students became vigilantes, Princeton students became politicians, and Yale students became girls. The Ivy League frenzy apparently rubbed off on the gridiron: Yale, which was supposed to fade out of contention, shared its unprecedented third straight title with Dartmouth and Princeton. And favored Harvard? It tied for fifth.

Now, in 1970, the old politics of certainty was expected to dominate Ivy football. Dartmouth, which had the best winning percentage (.745) and most titles (6) in the 14 years of play since the formal formation of the Ivy League, was a slight favorite over Princeton and Yale. The Big Green had 20 lettermen and graduates from an undefeated freshman team. They lacked depth at quarterback, but Jim Chasey was still the league's best.

At Princeton, where Coach Jake McCandless had lost 13 of 22 starters, he was forced to turn to promising sophomores, led by fullback Bill Early, who had gained 289 yards in one freshman game.

Meanwhile, at New Haven, Yale's 1969 defense, second nationally, more than acquitted the Bulldogs. Nine defensive starters returned to complement such offensive stars as quarterback Joe Massey, the one-time glee club singer, and tailback Don Martin.

Hopes were also soaring at titleless Cornell. There were 27 Big Red lettermen, among them Ed Marinaro, second leading rusher in the nation. Harvard Coach John Yovicsin opened preseason practice with the announcement that this, his 14th year at Cambridge, would be his last. He had only 17 lettermen to help him win the one game he needed for a Crimson record. Columbia, celebrating its football centennial, Penn, and Brown were destined to win only four Ivy games among them in 1970.

The battle for the conference championship came down to one game: Dartmouth vs. Yale, October 31, at Yale Bowl. Seldom in recent years had there been so much genuine cause for excitement about an Ivy League football game. With both Dartmouth (5-0) and Yale (5-0) unbeaten and rated nationally, not only in both of the wire service polls but also in the NCAA statistics, the largest crowd (60,820) to see a non-Harvard game at Yale Bowl since Army was there in 1954 assembled to watch the two teams settle "the *amateur* college

*All-Ivy offensive back and punter in 1970, Princeton's Hank Bjorklund.*

football championship of the season." Let Ohio State, Texas, Nebraska, Alabama, and Southern California make what they would out of that designation. After all, Ivy League football was played by *students.*

An example of the perspective in which the game was viewed by the players themselves was Wayne Pirmann, Dartmouth's best field goal kicker, who had to remain up in Hanover on Saturday morning to play soccer, for heaven's sake. Clearly, such behavior would never be tolerated by Woody Hayes or Bear Bryant. It fell to an eager Dartmouth grad, class of '33, to volunteer to fly Pirmann down to New Haven after the soccer match. When Pirmann finally got to Yale Bowl, he trotted onto the field near the end of the half time show to try a few warm-up kicks and was promptly pushed aside by the band. Later, however, Pirmann proved himself to have been worth the trouble by kicking a 30-yard field goal the only time he was allowed to swing his leg.

Going into the big game against Dartmouth, Yale quarterback Joe Massey had driven the Bulldogs to straight victories over Connecticut, Colgate, Brown, Columbia, and Cornell. There was a saying at Yale that the Old Grads would rather beat Harvard, the players would rather beat Princeton, and the coaches would rather beat Dartmouth, which meant that in 1969 the Yale coaches must have been especially disappointed. Dartmouth won, 42-21, and appeared headed for another Ivy title before Princeton upset them. But now the 1970 Big Green had already knocked the Tigers out of the way, 38-0, and with Pitt on the verge of being defeated by Syracuse, the winner of the Dartmouth-Yale game figured to wind up with the Lambert Trophy, awarded the best team in the East.

Unfortunately for the Yale fans, it didn't take long to establish which was the better team. Massey stuck to a plan that stubbornly insisted his two fast running backs, Dick Jauron and Don Martin, could break through between the Dartmouth tackles, despite evidence to the contrary. Meanwhile, Dartmouth quarterback Jim Chasey demonstrated great faith in his arm by continually completing deep and difficult passes at a cross-field angle, and once he rolled to his left and laid a long pass deftly over a defensive back and into the hands of a racing receiver. Dartmouth had an early touchdown called back and five times moved inside the Yale 20 without scoring, a circumstance that might have been different had Pirmann not been playing soccer.

Three of Chasey's passes were intercepted, two of them in the end zone, but Dartmouth kept rolling up yards and finally scored on a 3-yard run by Brendan O'Neill just before the half. Although there was a feeling that Dartmouth could have been leading by 40 points, Yale actually was in the game until the last three minutes, when an interception stopped a drive to give Dartmouth the game, 10-0.

Back to the tailgates and the striped tents went the crowd, and into a monster traffic jam lightened by the sound of singing voices. In the Yale locker room, Dick Jauron, who had been fifth in the nation in rushing before the Big Green smothered him, said, "It's only a game, right?"

For Ivy Leaguers, anyway, it was the biggest game of the year.

The nationally ranked Big Green continued to roll through its schedule. After Yale, they shut out Columbia, 55-0. Never before in Ivy history had there been that big a victory margin. Dartmouth was determined to have an undefeated season, and the Green kept thinking about how they had one going in 1969 until Princeton upset them on the last day, 35-7. Coming up next for Dartmouth was Cornell, which featured now the nation's leading rusher, Ed Marinaro.

Penn, meanwhile, was as flat as its homecoming festivities as Yale won, 32-22. "We had a pep rally in the ice skating rink, and hardly anybody showed up," grumbled Jim Fuddy, the Quaker captain. Maybe the homecoming loss was getting to be a Penn tradition; the school was now 2-16-1 since 1952.

Harvard, helped by three fumble recoveries and five interceptions, upset Princeton, 29-7, in the fight with Yale for second place.

The following week, Dartmouth (7-0) moved on the ground and through the air, but it wasn't moving into the Cornell end zone in the first 48 minutes of the game. The best the number 15 ranked Big Green could show was a 3-0 lead. Then, at just 3:07 of the fourth quarter, halfback John Short smashed over from the 3. Turned on now, Dartmouth punched across two more touchdowns to win its eighth straight victory, 24-0. The Dartmouth defense, ranked fourth in the nation, recorded its fifth shutout while holding Ed Marinaro to 60 yards, his lowest total of the season.

The triumph moved Dartmouth up a notch in the national polls to number 14 and first in the East. Its next opponent was Penn, and after it rolled up a 28-0 lead and then rubbed it in by recovering a perfect onside kick, Pennsylvania Coach Bob Odell said that he was so mad he couldn't see. Well, Pancho Micir, the Penn quarterback, hadn't been able to see very well all day. The Dartmouth defensemen had sworn to bury Micir, and they did. He completed only 9 of 24 passes for 97 yards and was thrown for eight losses. Dartmouth intercepted four passes, the first leading to a 4-yard touchdown by John Short. Jim Chasey, the Dartmouth quarterback, got a touchdown of his own on a 16-yard carry, then he let the Short show resume. John capped a 72-yard drive with a 34-yard pass reception, and it was Short again with a 22-yarder for the final score and the Green's sixth shutout since September 26.

"This has got to be my best team," Coach Blackman said after the game, as he sorted out all his winning years at Hanover. Winner of the 1970 Lambert Trophy, Blackman's Big Green had rolled up 311 points against 42 in nine games.

*Three-time All-Ivy halfback Dick Jauron set still-standing rushing, scoring, and total offense records at Yale in 1970–71–72.*

At Cambridge, popular John Yovicsin retired as the winningest coach in Harvard's long football history with a 78-42-5 record, exceeding even the legendary Percy Haughton. His was also the best record against Yale, and it was sustained in an emotional upset of the Elis, 14-12, in the final game of the year. Yovvy's farewell present was somewhat late in the wrapping. Behind 14-10, Yale had a first down on the Harvard 25 in the final minutes. The Crimson held, however, limiting Yale to 5 yards in four plays. A bizarre finale was still to come. With time running out, Eric Crone, Harvard's sophomore quarterback, dashed wildly around in the end zone waving the football triumphantly. Well-wishers from the Crimson side flooded the field. Suddenly, Yale's Ron Kell, in the midst of all this Harvard jubilation, tackled Crone, and officials signaled a safety. Had Kell simply walked up to Crone, offered a handshake and snatched the ball, he would have had a touchdown and the final score

*Jim Chasey, quarterback of Dartmouth's unbeaten Ivy League champions in 1970, who also won the Lambert Trophy, rolls against Harvard in a 37-14 victory.*

would have been Yale 16, Harvard 14. Oh, well, it was only a game, right? Sure.

## 1971

Bob Blackman had a genius for brutalizing the Ivy League, but never so much as in 1970 when he came up with his third undefeated Dartmouth team, his sixth Ivy title, his second Lambert Trophy, and a number 14 national ranking. He enjoyed a reputation as the Vince Lombardi of the Ivy League.

Defense or offense, Blackman's teams were formidable. The offense operated with 250 formations, and for 10 years opponents were unable to hold Dartmouth scoreless in a game. In 1970, never once did the defense allow the enemy to take over the ball beyond the opponent's 40. Statistics like those had a lot to do with Blackman's admirable 22-year record of 150-49-8, sixth in percentage and fourth in wins among active major college coaches.

But, in 1971, Dartmouth foes believed everything was going to be different. Bob Blackman had taken the head coaching job at the University of Illinois. Now the Big Green was not so big. It was barely favored over Harvard, Yale, Princeton, and Cornell. Strong offenses, weak defenses, and perhaps the best running back in the country could further confuse the Ivy picture with a mélange of high-scoring games.

The back, of course, was Cornell's spraddle-legged, rubber-kneed Ed Marinaro, who had led the nation in rushing average (158.3 yards) in 1970. On the way to becoming the first Ivy League national rushing champion of recent years, he set an Ivy season record of 1,014 yards, breaking his own mark, and surpassed Gary Wood's Cornell and Ivy career high by totaling 2,016 as a junior. His 47 carries against Princeton in 1970 were also a league record. Although not as fast as O. J. Simpson, he cut as quickly. "He cuts so sharply," said the retired John Yovicsin of Harvard, "that I had to slow my pursuit to have any chance of containing him. Otherwise he cuts back against the flow and gets away."

The preseason forecasters figured that if Marinaro and the Cornell quarterback, either junior Barrett Rosser or sophomore Mark Allen, clicked, the Big Red could be Big Trouble. It was suggested, however, that the Cornell line and defense, habitually weak, might be too vulnerable.

Jack Crouthamel, Blackman's replacement at Hanover, had lost his best backs, but runners like Brendan O'Neill, Chuck Thomas, and Alex Turner were counted on to help cool the new coach's baptism of fire. Meanwhile, Yale's Carmen Cozza told Coach Joe Restic, Harvard's replacement for Yovicsin, to expect one problem. "You have to decide which of the best quarterbacks in the Ivy League to start." He was referring to Rod Foster and Eric Crone. Harvard's real problem was in its defensive secondary.

In Philadelphia, Penn's coach Harry Gamble would have to do without Pancho Micir, the Ivy League's total-offense leader. At New Haven, Yale had good offensive linemen and ends and an excellent tailback in Dick Jauron, while Princeton's Doug Blake and Hank Bjorklund, first 1,000-yard rusher in school history, bolstered the Tiger attack.

Rounding out the 1971 Ivy focus, Columbia had its usual pass-catch combo—Don Jackson to Jesse Parks—and Brown faced another season of despair.

For the first time since 1945, seven years before most of its sophomores were even born, Columbia defeated Princeton. The game was played on the second Saturday of the season, and the 22-20 Lion victory barely survived a 32-yard field goal attempt by Princeton in the last six seconds. Defensive back Charlie Johnson had earlier rifled through to prevent a game-tying two-point conversion. The Light Blue presented the game ball to Columbia president Bill McGill who, carried away with the moment, made a somewhat un-Ivy locker room appearance.

While all that was going on, Ed Marinaro, who had grown up in New Milford, New Jersey, ruined nearby Rutgers at New Brunswick by gaining 246 yards and scoring four touchdowns as Cornell won, 31-17, and Marinaro came closer to the all-time NCAA yardage record.

The Ivies were in their third week of play when Harvard gave new coach Joe Restic his first league victory, a 21-19 thriller over Columbia. Ted DeMars switched from fullback to halfback and outgained all of the Light Blue backs put together.

On the same day, Penn had a 3-3 tie with Dartmouth in the first half, but two Big Green quarter-

*Ed Marinaro, Cornell's All-America tailback, broke 12 Ivy League records, eight NCAA career records, and six NCAA single game marks during 1969–70–71. Standing 6′2″ and weighing 210, he went on to play in the NFL. The action photo shows Marinaro starting out on a 39-yard touchdown romp as Cornell beat Columbia, 24-21, in 1971.*

backs stayed with their ground attack in the second half and wore the Quakers down, 19-3. And Ed Marinaro got 144 yards in 30 carries as Cornell beat Princeton, 19-8.

Dartmouth's 13th win in a row, the following week, was touch and go. Although it was a heavy favorite against winless Brown, which had not defeated the Big Green since 1955, Dartmouth was held scoreless after the first quarter and narrowly squeaked to a 10-7 victory.

Cornell, meanwhile, remained unbeaten with its fourth win, 21-16, over Harvard, but it wasn't secured until Steve Lahr intercepted a Crimson pass with 37 seconds remaining. Ed Marinaro, as usual, provided a big chunk of the Big Red offense with 146 yards in 32 carries, including a 15-yard touchdown run. It had been 20 years since Cornell, once the power of the East, had won its opening four games.

For the first time in six years, Yale lost to Columbia, 15-14. The upset came on a touchdown and two-point conversion with only 1:36 left to play. Bill Irish scored the TD on a 5-yard pass from Don Jackson, and Mike Jones added the two-pointer on a pass from halfback John Sefcik. Yale moved the ball effectively on the ground, but 3 of its 10 passes were intercepted.

Losers of six straight games, Princeton finally brought the streak to an end with a one-sided victory over Colgate, 35-12. The Tigers stormed to a 21-0 half-time lead and totaled 442 yards in a flashy offensive showing led by Jim Flynn, a sophomore who was making his first start of the season. Hank Bjorklund moved to within 45 yards of Dick Kazmaier's career rushing record by gaining 196 yards on 28 carries.

For the first time in the history of the modern Ivy League, Cornell found itself ranked (with Penn State and West Virginia) as one of the three best teams in the East. Ed Marinaro, the nation's leading rusher, carried 43 times, mostly off tackle, and crunched out 230 yards and three touchdowns as the undefeated Big Red walloped Yale, 31-10. At the same time, Dartmouth extended its winning streak to 14, edging Harvard, 16-13, on a 46-yard field goal by Ted Perry in the last two seconds. That same weekend, Columbia nipped Rutgers, 17-16, and Princeton stretched its win streak to two by routing Penn, 31-0.

The Big Red machine kept rolling right along. October 30, Ed Marinaro set an NCAA career rushing record and became the first major college player to top 4,000 yards as Cornell edged Columbia, 24-21. Marinaro, who gained 272 yards and scored two touchdowns, broke Steve Owens' mark of 3,867 on his second carry. The record came on carry number 750 of his 24th game, while Owens did it with 905 attempts in 30 games. It took a 37-yard field goal by John Killian in the final quarter to beat Columbia, however. The Lions' record dropped to 3-3, all its games decided by three points or less.

Columbia did a creditable job of containing Marinaro, and still he wound up with all those yards and touchdowns in 47 carries. When the game bore down to the decisive minutes, the Lions tying the score early in the last quarter, Marinaro showed his credentials to the Heisman Trophy selectors. He carried nine times in a row, 10 times in 11 plays as Cornell ground out 48 yards to set up the winning field goal. He went up the middle for 2 yards, around left end for 3. He gained 11 on a draw, got 0 up the middle, and then 6 up the middle. It was Marinaro for 8 yards on a pitchout, Marinaro up the middle for 3, Marinaro off left tackle for 8, Marinaro up the middle for 3.

"We have so much confidence in Ed," said quarterback Mark Allen after the game.

"It makes you breathe hard," Marinaro said. "In the huddle, I kept thinking, 'Let the fullback carry it this time.' When you line up for the ball to be snapped, you may feel tired, but then it's concentration. You know they're calling your number because they have faith in you. So you suck it up."

Marinaro did not have awesome speed, but he ran with gliding strides that made it appear one foot was always planted and driving and he had a quickness that gave each of his three basic running plays excellent variations. It also made him able to turn a defender's assets against him.

"You're liable to be on one side of the line in pursuit, and he'll cut back past you," said Frank Dermody, Columbia linebacker.

Marinaro's line generally tried to move the defense in whichever direction it would go. "I never know where the line is going to go," Ed said. "There's going to be a hole somewhere. It's my responsibility to find it. Some guys can't find the holes. Some guys can see the hole and can't get to it. I can find it and get to it. That's my biggest asset."

Another asset was his ability to get along with his linemen, the guys who set the blocks and watched Marinaro set the records. After the Columbia game, Ed told them, "I made you guys what you are today."

"What did you make us?" guard Randy Shayler wanted to know.

"Unsung heroes," Marinaro said.

More than 23,000 people saw the Cornell-Columbia game. It was the largest crowd at Ithaca in 20 years.

A late field goal kept Dartmouth even with Cornell in the Ivy League race. Ted Perry was at it again. He kicked a 40-yarder with 59 seconds remaining—his second last-minute winning field goal in two weeks—to beat Yale, 17-15.

In other league games, Princeton walloped Brown, 49-21, and Penn missed a two-point conversion attempt in the final three minutes to fall short of Harvard, 28-27. Don Clune caught eight passes for the Quakers, three of them for touchdowns, and totaled an Ivy record of 284 yards.

A week later, Columbia, with a 4-3 record, played its seventh game of the season in which the point margin was three points or less, this time upsetting favored and undefeated Dartmouth, 31-29, on a 34-yard field goal by Paul Kaliades with 48 seconds to go. Steve Howland plunged for two touchdowns and quarterback Don Jackson threw touchdown passes to Rick Assaf and Jess Parks to give Columbia a 28-14 lead in the third period and an apparent end to its string of heart-stoppers. But Steve Stetson, Dartmouth's reserve quarterback, threw touchdown passes of 8 yards to Rich Klupchak and 63 yards to Tyrone Byrd to lift the Big Green in front, 29-28. The lead held up until a wobbling kick by Kaliades just did clear the crossbar. It was Dartmouth's first football loss after 15 straight victories.

With Dartmouth out of the way, undefeated Cornell had first place in the conference all to itself after beating Brown, 21-7. The Bruins led, 7-6, after an 80-yard scoring drive in the third quarter. Then Ed Marinaro, who ground out 176 yards on 37 carries, scored his 16th and 17th touchdowns of the season as Cornell rallied before a home field crowd that shouted, "We're number one!" Actually, the Big Red ranked number two in the East behind Penn State (8-0).

In other games, Princeton came back from a 10-0 deficit to cut down Harvard, 21-10, and Yale beat Penn, 24-14.

In what was billed as the Ivy League's answer to the Super Bowl, Cornell traveled to Hanover, on November 13, to settle the championship with Dartmouth. A victory would give the Big Red the undisputed title. A loss would drop them into a tie. Dartmouth got right down to business, scoring two touchdowns and a field goal.

Even at half time, trailing 17-0, none of Ed Marinaro's rooters were overly worried, however. The game was Cornell's only TV appearance, right? And big Ed wanted to win the Heisman, right? And Cornell needed a victory to insure its first undisputed Ivy Championship and its first unbeaten season since 1939, right? So surely in the second half Marinaro would come roaring out with that Frank Merriwell glint in his eyes and stomp Dartmouth into a big green pulp while the boys up in the TV booth golly-gee-whizzed. That's how it just had to end, didn't it?

Well, yes and no. Marinaro did indeed bestir himself after an unspectacular first half. Early in the third quarter, Cornell scored after a blocked punt and nine straight Marinaro carries. The next time Cornell got its hands on the ball, Marinaro broke a 46-yard touchdown run, by far his biggest gainer of the day. Right then would have been a fine time for Dartmouth to holler uncle. Instead, quarterback Steve Stetson, who did not know he was going to start until several hours before the kickoff, pulled his team together and took it on a quick touchdown march for a 24-14 lead. And early in the last quarter, when Cornell had a fourth and four on the Dartmouth 22, Weymoth Crowell stopped Marinaro short of a first down. That ended Cornell's last serious threat of the day because the Big Red did not have any such thing as a catch-up offense. In the waning moments, when it should have been going for the bomb, Cornell still was running Marinaro into the line, as if it was sitting on a 10-point lead. When it was apparent that Cornell was done, a segment of the Dartmouth cheering section could not resist sticking a fork in Marinaro, serenading him with that old ditty that was number one on the college football charts, "Goodbye Heisman." Which, of course, was slightly out of tune with Marinaro's statistics: 177 yards and two touchdowns on 44 carries.

The season ended seven days later, with Cornell taking out its frustration on Pennsylvania, 41-13, to tie Dartmouth, conqueror over Princeton, 33-7, for a share of the Ivy League crown.

In the Heisman Trophy sweepstakes, Auburn's quarterback, Pat Sullivan, edged out Marinaro—a decision greeted in many Eastern quarters with pinched noses. In his three varsity seasons, Ed

Marinaro set rushing and scoring records wholesale and won every major honor with the exception of the Heisman. In the 24th game of his 27-game career, against Columbia at Ithaca, he broke the all-time career rushing mark by Oklahoma's Steve Owens of 3,867 yards by gaining 272 yards for a grand total of 4,132—the first collegian to pass the three-season 4,000 figure. He finished with a total of 4,715.

Marinaro also set an NCAA season record of 1,881 yards and a season per-game average of 174.6. Overall, he established eight NCAA career records and tied another, six NCAA single season marks, and three other NCAA records. In 1971, he won the national triple crown—rushing, all-purpose running, and scoring, each based on game average. As the holder of 12 Ivy League records, he was the first nonpasser in history to win the conference's total offense title (196.4 yards average, 1971).

While Ed Marinaro was running up all those figures, the Old Grads would buttonhole him by his locker or on the campus and ask him about George Pfann, the school's Hall of Famer. How did he think he compared with the old 1921–23 star? Ed, of course, had no answer because Pfann was a quarterback 30 years before he was even born.

"I was asked a lot about George Pfann, and I never had the slightest idea what to say," Marinaro said. "But I was always very polite about George Pfann."

At a Cornell game one day, Robert J. Kane, dean of the school's Physical Education and Athletics Department, was asked by one of the boys of the press to rate Marinaro.

"Is Ed Marinaro the best Cornell football player you ever saw?"

Now Dean Kane, whose association with Cornell football dated back some 40 years, was on the spot. Sitting with him at the time was Bart Viviano, another all-time Big Red star. He pondered the question for a moment, and glanced sidelong at Viviano, before replying. Finally, he said, "I'm not sure about that, but he's the best *Italian* player I ever saw at Cornell."

"I thought Bart was going to kill me," Dean Kane recalled later. "Now I'm very careful what I say."

Dean Kane believes it is impossible to compare football by generations. "I was too young to have seen Gil Dobie's great teams of the early twenties," he told me, "but I did see some fine Ivy League teams in the thirties and forties. I can't say which was the best of them because the style of football was so different. It's the same with players. Suffice to say, though, the Ivies have produced some authentically great ones."

Deep in this vein, Hamilton Fish is the only Harvard man on Walter Camp's all-time All-America team. Tall and powerful for his 80-odd years, he is a noted American conservative. Recently he was asked for a general observation about modern football.

"The fundamentals have always been the same," he replied thoughtfully. "The main difference is the shape of the ball. I suppose, in a way, it's an improvement. I have no objection to it. It's opened up the game."

° ° °

When a school is bogged down in defeat, year after year, there are inevitably questions about dropping football. Columbia, which had had a long losing tradition, heard that sort of talk in a 1970 student editorial. The editors presented a low key argument that Columbia begin "setting its priorities and decide what it can and cannot afford." It had pointed to football as an expensive activity "which does not serve any essential purpose of the university." Then, in 1971, the Lions went from 1-6 in the Ivy standings to 5-2 to finish third behind co-champions Cornell and Dartmouth, the school's highest finish since sharing the Ivy title with Harvard in 1961.

There was no more talk around Columbia about dropping football.

## 1972

At their January meeting, the NCAA major colleges made freshmen eligible for the varsity, and the big debate was on. The cries that freshmen wouldn't be able to help any good team—not really—were loud and far-flung. Kansas' Don Fambrough said he could not win in the tough Big Eight with very many sophomores in his lineup, so how, for crying out loud, was he going to win with freshmen? Oklahoma's Chuck Fairbanks said, "I wouldn't expect a freshman to help out in a program like ours." Nebraska's Bob Devaney said he didn't want to see a freshman unless he was Johnny Rodgers. John McKay at Southern California asked what a freshman was. Bear Bryant, the toast of

Alabama, said he didn't even like freshman coaches. And Woody Hayes didn't understand the question.

The coaches of the elite took the new freshman rule personally. They almost unanimously looked upon the legislation as a trick to damage their recruiting, a way to help out the have-nots. A good athlete would now avoid a Nebraska, for example, where there would be a lot of competition, in favor of an Oklahoma State, where he could probably earn a starting position as a rookie.

While coaches like Bob Devaney were bemoaning the freshman rule as "stupid" and "ridiculous," Ivy League coaches did not have to contend with the question of whether or not an 18-year-old was smart, strong, big, or fast enough to do anything on the football field a 19-year-old or 20-year-old could do. It was life as usual among the Ivies; freshmen were still ineligible for varsity competition in football, basketball, and crew. So what was all the shouting about?

At Hanover, they were talking championship again. They did not anticipate as much trouble as in 1971 when Ed Marinaro and Cornell gained a share of the title with them. The Dartmouth offense was banking on junior halfback Rich Klupchak, who in '71 averaged 6 yards a carry and totaled 638, the most for any sophomore in Big Green history, including Coach Jake Crouthamel. Quarterback Steve Stetson had a .583 completion rate in the league, and if he slipped below .500 he could lose his position to Tom Snickenberger, a 6′ 5″ sophomore. Again the Dartmouth defense was loaded with seniors, headed by end Fred Radke.

The most likely challengers were Columbia, if quarterback Don Jackson remained healthy, and Harvard, with a backfield of quarterback Eric Crone and halfbacks Ted DeMars and Rich Gatto. Jackson, who had had operations on both knees in his last two seasons, had All-Ivy receiver Jesse Parks as a target and linebacker Paul Kaliades to harass the enemy. Kaliades attended high school in New Jersey with Rich Glover, the middle guard who played at Nebraska. Both knew how to depress a ball carrier.

Both Penn and Yale were expected to develop as contenders in direct relation to the maturity of their sophomores. Adolph Bellizeare was the top rusher and scorer on a 4-1 Penn freshman squad, and he could relieve Don Clune, one of the nation's better receivers, of some of the offensive burden. The Yale frosh were unbeaten in six games, and Coach Carmen Cozza was counting on them to help rebuild the offensive line for halfback Dick Jauron.

If Princeton wanted to be taken seriously, it would have to solve its defensive troubles, and Cornell had to revamp its offense now that Ed Marinaro was gone, although quarterback Mark Allen was returning, as was Bob Lally, its best linebacker.

Brown, which never seemed to have much, had even less since Gary Bonner, who needed only 261 yards to become the leading rusher in the school's history, left school. That's the way the wind blew as the Ivies warmed up for 1972.

For the first five weeks, the league race showed little semblance of order as Yale, playing on the road for the first time after victories at Yale Bowl over Connecticut, Colgate, Brown, and Columbia,

*Carl Barisich, 6′4″, 255-pound All-Ivy offensive tackle in 1972 and cowinner of Princeton's coveted John P. Poe Memorial Trophy, was the first Ivy Leaguer ever to play for the Cleveland Browns. He appeared in 42 straight NFL games before being picked by the Seattle Seahawks in the 1976 expansion draft.*

suddenly ran into a red-hot Cornell and lost, 24-13. Five fumbles on the damp artificial turf of Schoellkopf Field did the Elis in. Cornell, which had lost only to Harvard, was now 4 and 1 on the season, including nonconference wins over Colgate and Rutgers.

The Ivy League leader might have emerged from the Dartmouth-Harvard game, but a 21-21 deadlock maintained the jam at the top. Fumbles hurt the Big Green too. Leading 21-14, Steve Stetson, the Dartmouth quarterback, lost the ball on his own 2-yard line and the Crimson quickly converted the gift into the tying score.

In other October 28 games, Gary Shue came off the bench to lead Penn past Princeton, 15-10, and Columbia lost outside the league to Rutgers, 6-3, two field goals by John Pesce doing the trick.

A week later, there was nothing gentlemanly about the way Yale ran the wishbone against Dartmouth. Led by Tom Doyle, a sophomore quarterback making his first start, the Bulldogs churned out 391 rushing yards against the Ivy's second-best defense to surprise the Green, 45-14. Doyle, an Indiana boy born in the shadow of Notre Dame's golden dome, woke a few echoes himself with 160 yards in 12 carries. He directed the team to three touchdowns and a field goal the first four times it had the ball, and when all of that Saturday's results were in, Yale was leading the Ivy League with a 3-1 conference record.

Penn and Columbia also managed upsets, beating Harvard and Cornell. The Quakers' first success in nine seasons against Harvard was highlighted by their biggest scoring day—38-27—since the series began in 1881. The Crimson led 14-9 at half time despite an 80-yard touchdown run by Penn's Adolph Bellizeare on the first run from scrimmage. Bellizeare, who gained 203 yards overall, added another touchdown from 37 yards out in the fourth quarter to pace a 29-point second half.

Columbia's 14-0 upset of favored Cornell was its first in 1972 league competition even though it was the third time the defense had not yielded a touchdown. Don Jackson's passes provided most of the offense. He completed 20 of 32 for 233 yards and set up the game's first touchdown late in the third quarter with four straight completions. The Light Blue defense did an excellent job of containing Cornell, which had been averaging nearly 28 points a game.

In the only Ivy contest that did not significantly affect the league standings that weekend, Princeton showed its first signs of life by thrashing Brown, 31-10, to end a four game winless streak. Brown's Tyler Chase kicked a 46-yard field goal, his 10th of the season, which pushed him past Charlie Gogolak's Ivy League career record of 16.

The Ivies were seven weeks into the season before the mad scramble for the championship began to resolve itself with Dartmouth finishing where it often did—on top. The Big Green moved back into the lead, November 11, by crushing Columbia, 38-8, while Pennsylvania was upsetting Yale, 48-30. The first of five Columbia fumbles opened the way for Dartmouth, which passed consistently against the third-ranking air defense in the country. Steve Stetson completed 16 of 24 passes for 186 yards and one touchdown. Meanwhile, Penn's fourth straight victory secured its first sweep of Harvard, Princeton, and Yale in 31 years. The Quakers, guided by Marc Mandel, their third starting quarterback in three weeks, led, 41-0, before the Elis scored.

A 37-yard field goal by John Bartges with 5:17 left gave Princeton a 10-7 win over Harvard, whose complicated, multiformation offense gained only 162 yards. Mark Allen passed for four touchdowns in the second quarter as Cornell stuffed Brown down the drain, 48-28. The Bruins also passed exceptionally well as Chip Regine tied an Ivy League record with 12 receptions, two for touchdowns.

The Ivy League Championship came down to the last week's Dartmouth-Penn and Harvard-Yale games. Dartmouth set itself up for the finale by whipping Cornell, 31-22, and Penn topped Columbia, 20-14. Penn had the tougher time, trailing 14-0 before getting untracked. Yale maintained its chance for a share of the title by blasting Princeton, 31-7, behind Dick Jauron's three touchdowns, and Rod Foster came off the bench to gain 159 yards in 13 carries and score two TDs in Harvard's 21-14 victory over Brown.

Although Philadelphians were not accustomed to winners, especially if they wore helmets and pads, more than 42,000 of them wandered into 77-year-old Franklin Field on the last Saturday of the Ivy League season to see if Penn could bag its first title in 13 years. For 20 minutes, as the Quakers took a 14-0 lead over Dartmouth, it seemed likely. Then the Big Green came alive and posted a 31-17 victory that gave *them* the championship, their fourth straight won or shared.

Dartmouth broke a 17-17 tie with a pair of fourth-quarter touchdowns 1:36 apart. The first was made possible when receiver Chuck Thomas intercepted an interception, or so it seemed. Quarterback Steve Stetson let one go from his 30, and it was headed for Penn's Tom Welsh, but as the defensive back stood waiting to catch it, Thomas swooped in from nowhere for a 35-yard completion. Six plays later Steve Webster went in from the 1 to put Dartmouth ahead.

The Quakers were still in the game until quarterback Tom Pinto ran into one of his own backs and fumbled a minute later. Dartmouth recovered, and on the next play, Rich Klupchak raced 50 yards to put the game on ice.

Dartmouth's victory shut the door on Yale, which finished second in the conference standings. The Elis ended their season with a 28-17 win over Harvard after trailing, 17-0. Dick Jauron's 74-yard run in the third quarter sparked the comeback. It was one of two touchdowns in a performance that also produced 183 yards gained on 28 carries. Jauron set two school records with 1,055 yards for the season and 2,947 for his career, both totals supplanting standards set by Levi Jackson.

Cornell continued its roller-coaster pattern of the last seven weeks of the season by beating Princeton, 22-15. Mark Allen scored twice and passed for another touchdown.

Columbia ended Len Jardine's coaching career at Brown with a 28-12 defeat. The Light Blue mounted long drives for two of their touchdowns and capitalized on a fumble and an interception for the others as they scored in every quarter. George Georges (he was so good his parents named him twice) scored three times and gained 190 yards in 35 carries for the Lions.

## 1973

By now, Old Ivy had a reputation in college football circles as "The Master of the Last Weekend," and Dartmouth its champion. In that 1972 race, for example, Yale, Penn, and Dartmouth all entered the final Saturday with a shot at the title, but when the smoke had cleared, there was Dartmouth again with its fourth straight championship.

Dartmouth rivals could take heart, however, from the fact that 31 lettermen (15 of them starters) were gone from a senior group that, including freshman games, compiled a 31-2-1 record at Hanover. The only proven stars returning were All-Ivy halfback Rich Klupchak, running back Ellis Rowe, and two-time All-Ivy defensive end Tom Csatari. Coach Jake Crouthamel was talking about starting as many as eight sophomores to fill the holes.

No wonder then that Cornell, Penn, and Yale anticipated the 1973 season with delight. Cornell possessed what would normally be considered Dartmouthian experience and balance, but would have to overcome a lack of explosiveness.

Yale and Penn had two of the league's most exciting players. Eli quarterback Tom Doyle showed heart and speed in the humiliation of Dartmouth in 1972. And Penn's Adolph (Beep Beep) Bellizeare raced for 849 yards and 11 touchdowns in his first varsity season.

Brown and Princeton both had new coaches. John Anderson had 32 lettermen and halfback Hubie Morgan, up from the undefeated freshmen, to build with at Providence, and Bob Casciola, an

*Dartmouth's all-time career rushing leader, halfback Rich Klupchak, led the Big Green to Ivy League titles in 1971–72–73.*

All-Ivy tackle in 1957, would have to come to grips with mediocrity at Princeton.

One Ivy League watcher predicted that the November 24 Cornell-Penn game would establish 1973's King of the Last Weekend.

"That is," he hedged, "unless both teams have already been *Greened.*"

Actually, the Ivy forecaster could not have been more unexpert. Dartmouth, which had won 32 of its last 36 varsity games, opened with losses to New Hampshire, Holy Cross, and Pennsylvania, before settling down to beat Brown, Harvard, and Yale. By November 3, three teams (Dartmouth, Harvard, and Penn) were tied for the league lead as they took turns beating each other. First, Penn upset the Big Green, 22-16, then the Big Green beat Harvard, 24-18, and then Harvard, going into the last third of the season, beat Penn, 34-30, in one of the most exciting games of the year. And since Yale, Brown, and Cornell were only one game in arrears at this juncture, the league championship was far, far from settled.

The Harvard-Penn game at Franklin Field was something to remember. There was enough dedication and ferocity on the field to launch a cavalry charge. Granted, there were nine fumbles, two interceptions, and one blocked punt; at least three of the touchdowns came as a direct result of turnovers; and in one sequence deep in Penn territory the two teams exchanged fumbles on successive plays before Harvard cut off the largesse by scoring. But consider also that Harvard and Penn, which had ranked one-three in the league on defense, gained 989 yards between them, setting seven team and league offensive records, and that the winning touchdown came with but 1:26 remaining in the game on a sprawling, grappling goal line catch of a Jim Stoeckel pass by Harvard end Pat McInally that would not have embarrassed Paul Warfield.

The rival quarterbacks, Stoeckel and Penn's dauntless Marty Vaughn, enjoyed truly remarkable success, Stoeckel connecting on a Harvard record 27 of 48 passes for 291 yards and a touchdown and Vaughn hitting on 18 of 31 for 303 yards and a touchdown. McInally caught 10 of Stoeckel's passes for 117 yards, and Penn's Don Clune, a legitimate professional prospect, caught 10 for 163 yards. Stoeckel's tight end, Pete Curtin, whose brown hair flowed to his shoulders, had seven catches, an extraordinarily productive day for a college man playing his position. And Penn's swift little halfback, Beep Bellizeare, gained 138 yards on only 15 carries, including one electrifying, tackle-breaking touchdown run of 67 yards. Harvard's Neal Miller, a sophomore, had 130 yards and two touchdowns.

It was the sort of now-we've-got-'em-now-we-don't contest that the Ivies dismiss as routine.

With Penn leading, 28-27, and with slightly more than three minutes left in the game, Harvard took possession of the ball on its own 37. Three plays lost three yards. Then on fourth down, Stoeckel, scrambling desperately, passed to McInally for 15 yards and a life-saving first down. Two more completions and a Miller run carried the ball to the Penn 30. With third down and three, 1:26 remaining on the clock and no timeouts left, Stoeckel faded deep as 6′ 6″ McInally circled in the end zone. The ball reached him near the goal line flag. He leaped, snatching first with one hand, then the other, and finally toppled into the end zone and out of bounds with the winning touchdown. It was one of those classic moments in football, any kind of football.

The skinny, 190-pound McInally waved his arms exuberantly in the locker room afterward. "Impossible things happen when you have faith," he said finally. "Harvard is the greatest place on earth. *Period.*"

"This," said Harvard coach Joe Restic, observing all the tumult and shouting around him, "is what it's all about."

That, as the Ivies have always insisted, and no more.

Harvard, looking ahead to its big November 24 final with Yale, had to fight for its life to beat Princeton, 19-14, and then had to overcome a 13-point disadvantage before downing surprising Brown, 35-32, to remain in a tie with Dartmouth for the league lead. At that, Harvard beat Brown only because the Bruins twice missed on placement conversions and once on a two-point pass conversion attempt.

After losing its first three games, Dartmouth came on with a big rush, making Columbia (24-6) and Cornell (17-0), the preseason Ivy favorite, its fourth and fifth straight victims. Rich Klupchak, out for three games with a shoulder separation, ran for 128 yards in the Cornell game, mostly around the corners.

Going into the final weekend, the league championship was still far from settled. Four teams remained in contention. Yale got there by first knocking off Penn, 24-21, and then Princeton, 30-13. While Dartmouth and Harvard were tied for first with 5-1 records, Penn had to wallop Columbia, 42-8, to stay in second place with the Elis at 4-2.

Dartmouth, as expected, won its fifth straight Ivy Championship and its 10th in 18 years by beating weak Princeton, 42-24. Rich Klupchak scored three touchdowns and gained 154 yards. His career mark of 1,788 bettered by 25 the 1957–59 total of Jake Crouthamel, now the Dartmouth coach.

In The Game, played at Yale Bowl, there was almost no competition at all after Yale had taken a 14-0 lead in the second quarter. Hitting with a fervor that it had shown only sporadically in its previous eight games, the Eli defense, led by uncharitable Elvin Charity, helped bury Harvard, 35-0. Yale was equally devastating on offense. Rudy Green and John Donohue took turns running around and through the Crimson, and second string Kevin Rogan passed over them. Total offense: 523 yards.

"We had tremendous consistency," said Carmen Cozza. "For the first time this year we had offense and defense."

Harvard had no one to blame but itself for the passing part of it.

"When I was in high school," said quarterback Kevin Rogan, "Harvard didn't recruit me that heavily. I got a letter or two, but Harvard acted as though it was doing me a favor. On the other hand, Yale alumni took me out to dinner and showed interest in me."

So he went to Yale, but he suffered a separated shoulder in his first frosh game and had played in only nine varsity games prior to 1973.

Except for the Yale game and the 57-0 blitzing of Columbia in the Ivy opener, every one of Harvard's Ivy League games in 1973 was a tense, exciting contest that was decided in the last few minutes of the game. End Pat McInally (56 completions, 752 yards, 7 touchdowns) and quarterback Jim Stoeckel (112 completions of 208 attempts for 1,391 yards and 11 touchdowns) combined to rewrite the Harvard record book for receiving and passing, and Stoeckel became the first Crimson player to win the Asa S. Bushnell Award as the Ivy League's best player.

Meanwhile, the usually hapless Brown Bruins, who hadn't done much on the football field since a quarterback from Brooklyn named Joe Paterno left some years before, beat Columbia, 37-14, and improved their Ivy record to 4-3, the best since 1958. First-year coach John Anderson, who had worked similar miracles at Middlebury, was riding high, but it was a sad day for Columbia coach Frank Navarro, who had already announced his departure after six years of trying to get the Lions out of the muck of failure.

It was a big day for several passers. Brown quarterback Pete Beatrice completed 18 of 26, including two for touchdowns, and down at Franklin Field in Philadelphia, Penn's Marty Vaughn threw three TD passes as the Quakers beat Cornell, 31-22, to finish in a tie for second with Yale and Harvard.

## 1974

For the first time in years, passing had become passé for many of the country's leading teams. There was mounting evidence that ground-oriented teams, especially those with veer and wishbone attacks, were more successful than those that passed frequently. In 1973, for example, the triple-option teams had a higher winning percentage, scored more points, and, interestingly, fumbled less often. Ten of the nation's 15 best rushing teams finished in the top 20, compared to just two teams, Arizona State and Kansas, with potent passing attacks. Thus, for the time being it was the runners, not the quarterbacks, who were dominating college football and causing the loudest roars.

As sure as death and taxes, each football season brought the prediction that *this* was the year that Dartmouth was going to be dethroned as Ivy League Champion. But consider the record: the Big Green had won or shared the title five seasons running, grabbing it outright in 1973 after Coach Jake Crouthamel had the gall to dismiss it as a "rebuilding year."

On the debit side, however, Dartmouth had lost its three top rushers and a dozen starters in all. Most missed was Rich Klupchak, the record-breaking rusher. On the credit side, quarterback Tom Snickenberger, a rangy 6′ 5″ option passer, split end Tom Fleming, the league's leading punt returner, and All-Ivy linebacker Reggie Williams were back in uniform.

The team most likely to depose Dartmouth was Penn, largely because of a pair of players who shattered no fewer than 20 Quaker offensive records in 1973. Marty Vaughn, passing for 17 touchdowns and 1,926 yards, led the league and ranked fifth nationally in total offense. Adolph (Beep Beep)

*Walt Snickenberger, Princeton's All-America back in 1974.*

Bellizeare, the most productive runner in Penn history, was the Ivy League's top scorer and the NCAA's third leading all-purpose rusher.

Yale finished strong in 1973 with five wins in its final six games and was expected to continue its momentum with 14 regulars coming back. Among them was Rudy Green, the league's leading ground-gainer. Harvard would be satisfied with more of the same from Neal Miller, the compact fullback who rocked Dartmouth for 114 yards and Penn for 130, and Pat McInally, the 6′ 6″ split end who gathered in 56 passes to finish second nationally.

Brown, down for so long, came scrambling back under rookie coach John Anderson in '73 to equal its best Ivy record (4-3). With 12 starters returning and a bumper crop of sophomores, the Bruins appeared to be first division bound. As for Princeton, Cornell, and Columbia, they figured to fight it out in the Battle for the Bottom.

The Ivies opened the season in what was described as "a good week for the league." In eight games against outside opponents, they posted five victories and an unusual tie. Brown bombed Rhode Island, 45-15, Cornell ripped Colgate, 40-21, Yale topped Connecticut, 20-7, and Harvard beat Holy Cross, 24-14. Princeton's game with Rutgers ended in a 6-6 tie because the Tigers failed to complete a two-point conversion pass after tying the game with 22 seconds left. Why was Princeton going for two? It seems that the visiting Rutgers fans were so certain of victory that they tore down the goalposts with two minutes left. After the referee refused to wait for an extra set to be erected, Princeton had no other choice. The Tigers' coach Bob Casciola said he would not protest, but even Rutgers coach Frank Burns admitted that Princeton should have been allowed to kick for the extra point. The tie was the first in the history of the nation's oldest collegiate rivalry.

On the minus side for the Ivies that weekend, Lafayette beat Columbia, 15-0, and Dartmouth lost to Massachusetts, 14-0. The latter's victory ended a 21-game, 72-year famine against Dartmouth.

The following week, Brown's soccer-style kicker, Jose Violante, connected from 37, 47, and 49 yards, the last a school record, to give the Bruins a 9-7 lead over Pennsylvania. But then, with just 2:42 to play, Beep Beep Bellizeare, who had been held to just 45 yards in 14 carries, returned a punt 61 yards for a touchdown and a 14-9 Penn victory. Pat McInally, Harvard's fancy end, caught three TD passes from quarterback Milt Holt, each giving the Crimson the lead, but Rutgers came back each time and finally won, 24-21. The winning score, a 1-yard lunge by quarterback Bert Kosup, capped an 80-yard, 11-play drive. Meanwhile, Yale drubbed Colgate, 30-7; Princeton won its first Ivy League game in two seasons by blasting inept Columbia, 40-13; Dartmouth lost its second in a row, 14-3, to Holy Cross; and Cornell scored its first shutout in six years by routing Bucknell, 24-0.

As the season progressed, it grew more and more evident that Yale and Harvard were headed on a collision course. The Elis continued to romp, stomping Columbia (42-2), Cornell (27-3), Dartmouth (14-9), and Penn (37-12). The Harvards kept pace week after week. Behind 21-10 at the half, they came up with 29 third-period points to put down Cornell, 39-27. Then they sneaked out of Hanover with a 17-15 decision over Dartmouth, but were forced to bat down a desperate pass as the gun sounded to get past the northerners for the first time since 1968. Next, the Crimson walked all over undefeated Penn, 39-0, in a game that had been rated even before the kickoff. A rugged Harvard defense kept the supposedly explosive Quakers scoreless for the first time since 1971 as halfback Tom Winn led an assault that churned out 468 yards in total offense.

On November 16, Brown provided the upset of the year as Kevin Slattery scored a fourth quarter touchdown to down Harvard, 10-7. It marked the third straight victory by the Bruins and Harvard's first league loss. The defeat assured Yale at least a share of the league championship. Powerful running by Rudy Green and stifling defense led unbeaten Yale, the nation's least-scored-upon team, to a 19-6 victory over Princeton. Green scored twice and gained 138 yards as he and his senior teammates won for the 16th time in 17 home games.

It was just like old times as Yale and Harvard got ready to play The Game on the last Saturday of the Ivy season. Cambridge was alive with excitement. In an act reminiscent of a John O'Hara novel, 450 students, alumni, and fans from Yale chartered seven railroad cars to haul themselves and cases of booze up from New Haven to root for their undefeated, untied team. And in equally elegant counter, two of the Harvard football managers showed up for The Game attired in black ties and dinner jackets.

Tickets were impossible to find. Scalpers were so desperate they were *offering* $50 for a seat.

Several days before The Game, Yale coach Carmen Cozza voiced concern that his 1974 players would be remembered for just one thing, The Game, especially if they lost. The players themselves felt slighted that Yale was not rated in the top 20 teams nationally or even included among the top three in the East and in the running for the Lambert Trophy. After all, Yale's defense was the best in the country, holding opponents, Ivy or otherwise, to a measly 5.8 points a game. A win, a big win, over Harvard like the previous season's 35-0, would cap a perfect season, win the Ivy title, and possibly force national recognition of some sort. As if to prove his determination to end his running career with a thumping of Harvard, Eli captain Rudy Green persistently butted his head against a telephone pole in Thursday afternoon practice. And to bolster the will to win, Yale had its first pep rally in years on Thursday night before the team embarked for Cambridge.

"I'm tired of being compared to the 1968 team," summed up guard Ken Burkus. "I want them to compare future teams here to *this* team."

Meanwhile, in Cambridge, Harvard was down in the dumps after having lost to Brown. A win in The Game would make Harvard co-champion of the league, but spirits did not perk up until Wednesday. Then Pat McInally, the best receiver in Harvard history, a hopeful Rhodes scholar, and a possible NFL first-round draft choice, said, "The coaches gave us a great lift when word came out that we had a new defense." The defense was the brain work of Coach Joe Restic and assistants Larry Glueck and Carl Schuette and was devised to stop Yale's running attack by using four tackles and two ends for strength and weight in the line.

"If we're going to give Yale anything, it's the pass," Coach Restic told his players. "We have to take our chances on that. But we *must* stop the run."

By game time, Harvard spirit was bursting. The Crimson players were loose; so loose, in fact, that their looseness almost unraveled as they lost three fumbles to Yale in the first quarter, before a standing room crowd of more than 40,500. Yet, despite the breaks, Yale could score only seven points, so tough was the Harvard defense. Another negative factor working against the Yalies was the wet field. The footing was so slippery that Eli runners had difficulty cutting to the outside. Tom Doyle, the Yale quarterback, finally turned to the pass, mostly to Gary Fencik, his split end who played a whale of a game, catching 11 of Doyle's 16 completions. Doyle-to-Fencik passes moved Yale from its own 34 to the Harvard 5 in two plays, and from there Captain Rudy Green, the telephone-pole abuser, scored his second touchdown of the day, making the score, 13-0.

Then Harvard's Hawaiian quarterback, Milt Holt, began to call the wide-open passing game favored by Coach Restic from his coaching days in Canada's professional league. Yale was forced to split its coverage between McInally and tight end Peter Curtin. Alternating between the two, Holt worked Harvard downfield to first-and-goal on the Yale 3. He passed again to McInally in a crowd of Elis for Harvard's first touchdown.

With less than two minutes remaining in the half, Holt began throwing from his 24. The big play came on Harvard's version of the old flea flicker. With Harvard on the Yale 48, Holt lateraled back to McInally at the Crimson 45, and the tall end, a quarterback in high school, threw a bomb to split end Jim Curry, who was brought down on the Yale

2. With only nine seconds left in the half and with the crowd on its feet, Holt pitched to Curtin for another TD. The extra point was good, and now Harvard led, 14-13, as the two teams broke for the dressing rooms.

McInally said later that the Harvard excitement at half time was unbelievable. "It was even more powerful than after the game," he recalled. "We were really high."

Owing largely to Harvard's stacked line and some excellent punting from the all-around McInally, the home team held stubbornly to its 14-13 lead until early in the fourth quarter. Then Yale started driving toward the Harvard goal, only to stall at the 38-yard line, where a field goal by Randy Carter just made it over the crossbar. Yale 16, Harvard 14.

There was only 5:07 left in the game when Harvard got the ball on its own 10. A penalty sent the Crimson back to their 5-yard line. But then Holt began hitting McInally and halfback Steve Dart with passes, and with only 19 seconds to go they had the ball on the Yale 1. Holt took the snap from center and ran to his left looking for a receiver in the open. Everyone was covered. But neither were there any Yalies between him and the goal. Holt waltzed into the end zone, where he was mobbed by teammates and fans. The kick was good, and now Harvard was back in front, 21-16.

Because there were too many extra players in Crimson jerseys on the field, Harvard was penalized back to the 25 when lining up to kick off, but McInally was so elated by the turn of events that he boomed the football 70 yards. Yale was dead. It was worse than 1968.

After the game, a press conference was held in Dillon Field House. Carmen Cozza sat in a chair, looked at the ceiling, blew out his breath and fidgeted in silence as Restic faced the reporters. In the back of the room, Mike Buxbaum, the sports editor for the *Yale Daily News*, stood with moist eyes.

"It's like writing about my mother's funeral," he said. "I feel wasted. I'm going to ask my other two editors if they can do the page tomorrow."

Then Mike Buxbaum caught himself.

"Wait a minute," he said. "As much as I hate to say it, this is what makes the Ivy League the best to watch."

Elsewhere in the Ivy League, Penn came from behind to beat Dartmouth, 27-20, Brown concluded its second straight winning season by whipping Columbia, 28-19, and Princeton downed Cornell, 41-20, as halfback Walt Snickenberger scored four touchdowns to break Cosmo Iacavazzi's single-season Princeton touchdown mark of 14 and become the second Tiger to gain more than 1,000 yards in a season. As winner of the Asa S. Bushnell Cup, symbolic of the Ivy League's Most Valuable Player, Snickenberger made the AP's All-American third team in 1974, the first Princetonian to gain All-American recognition since 1965 when Charlie Gogolak and Stas Maliszewski were picked.

"Walt always made the big play," Coach Bob Casciola said. "He was the best runner I ever coached."

There was one game played on that last day of the 1974 Ivy League season whose score did not appear in Sunday's newspaper line results. It was played on an obscure touch football field adjacent to Harvard Stadium between the Yale and Harvard political science departments. Some considered it an even larger battle than the varsity contest scheduled a few hours later. It was, after all, a contest of philosophies as well as wills. Would the Harvard Theorists, weak on behavior but strong on vision, beat the Yale Empiricists?

One Yale behaviorist vowed his team would win because Harvard wouldn't let its graduate students play. "It's a typical example of statist thinking," he said. Both sides agreed, however, that there be at least three political science professors playing continually for each team.

The game began less on a note of aggression than containment. Yale owed an 8-6 lead to a safety, which many of the scholarly spectators mistook for a touchback. Indeed, the only record being set was for largest number of players wearing glasses.

Early in the second half, Harvard scored a go-ahead touchdown following a controversial interference penalty that set up a first down on the Yale 2-yard line. Yale captain Douglas Rae protested.

"It's easy to confuse your legitimate belief in fairness with your own self-interest," scoffed a Harvard player. "You must be consonant."

Yale rallied to win, 14-12, on an empirical plunge by Joe Morone. Not that any of the issues were settled. Some Yale players admitted Morone might have gone out of bounds before crossing the goal line.

"It's a victory for people who know how to handle the real world," insisted Joseph LaPalombara, chairmain of the Yale political science department. His counterpart, Harvard chairman James Q.

Wilson, who was sidelined when he injured his knee stepping where a dog had paused, was unmoved.

"We'll be at Yale next year," he said confidently, "if we have to pay our way down to New Haven with a slush fund."

## 1975

Brown was no longer the butt of all those old Ivy jokes. The days of paying penance were gone. Jeers had turned to cheers. In fact, as they used to say about the New York Yankees, wasn't it about time to break up the Bruins? In 1974, they had the third-best rushing defense (108 yards per game) in the country, and John Anderson had already done what

*A front and back view of pass-grabbing Pat McInally (84), 6′6″, 210-pound split end, the first All-America from Harvard (1974) since 1941 when Chub Peabody was selected.*

no other Brown coach had been able to do since 1956, '57, and '58—put successive winning seasons together.

With 18 starters returning in 1975, all Brown lacked, it seemed, was a quarterback. To fill that void it could thank Vermont for folding its team and delivering 6′ 6″ Bob Bateman, who in 1974 had passed for more than 1,800 yards. Up in the trenches, the Bruins had linebacker Paul Serrano and tackle Phil Bartlett leading the defense. And for close games, there was Jose Violante, whose two 49-yarders in 1974 pinpointed him as the finest place-kicker in the Ivy League since the Gogolaks.

Harvard fans bemoaned the loss of split end Pat McInally, their first All-American since 1941. But then, the Crimson didn't have anyone who could have thrown to him anyway. So Coach Joe Restic had to count on his running game—all he needed was someone to give the ball to 1974's leading rusher, Tommy Winn, or fullback Neal Miller.

At Princeton, where the Tigers dropped four of their last five games in '74, Coach Bob Casciola's main hopes were lodged around veteran quarterback Ron Beible, who would be trying for new Tiger passing records, and fullback Bob Reid. With 15 starters on hand, Princeton had its best title chance since 1969.

Carmen Cozza of Yale seldom got bothered when Blue fans mourned the loss of a good senior class. They were depressed in 1969 after the Calvin Hill-Brian Dowling group departed, but Cozza quickly cheered them up by winning another cochampionship. So now, just three offensive regulars were back from 1974's cochamps and—guess what?—no quarterback. But only Michigan had yielded fewer points per game, and most of the Eli defenders were returning.

Dartmouth's superb linebackers, Reggie Williams and Skip Cummins, provided an excellent defensive nucleus at Hanover, but offensive inconsistency cost the Big Green its sixth straight title in '74. The new quarterback was Mike Brait. Penn also had problems. Adolph (Beep Beep) Bellizeare was gone. But the Quakers still had Jack Wixted, the league's best returning runner.

At Ithaca, Cornell's new coach, George Seifert, neglected to bring a quarterback with him from Stanford, so All-Ivy split end Bruce Starks was bound to be lonely. As for Columbia, the Lions intended to improve on their 1-8 record, although attendance wasn't expected to be very healthy now that New York City's subway fare had gone up.

On the first weekend of play, September 27, there were a number of surprises for the Ivies as they began the 1975 season with four wins in eight nonconference games. Princeton's 10-7 victory over Rutgers was unexpected, as was Penn's 34-23 loss to Lehigh, its first in a 35-game series. More predictably, Brown bombed Rhode Island, 41-20, Yale blasted Connecticut, 35-14, and Harvard beat Holy Cross, 18-7. Other league losers were Dartmouth, 7-3, to Massachusetts, Columbia, 10-7, to Lafayette, and Cornell, 24-22, to Colgate.

The following week, Brown scored its sixth victory in a row over a two-year span—look out, Ohio State—as Bob Bateman ran for one touchdown and passed for another in a 17-8 defeat of Penn. Harvard held a 9-7 lead against Boston U. late in the game, but Peter Kessel gathered in a 45-yard pass from Greg Geiger to give the Terriers a 13-9 win. Colgate committed four turnovers against Yale, which the Elis turned into three scores and a 24-10 triumph before a sparse Yale Bowl "crowd" of 13,758. Princeton had no trouble beating Columbia, 27-7.

Brown certainly looked like a serious contender, October 11, as it ran all over Yale, 27-12, in an important game, while Harvard held off aroused Columbia, 35-30, Dartmouth tripped Pennsylvania, 19-14, and Princeton got by Cornell, 16-8.

Brown ended the first half of its season settling for a 10-10 tie with Dartmouth to slip half a game behind Harvard and Princeton in the conference race. The Crimson's attack continued to roll in a 34-13 defeat of Cornell, split end Jim Curry catching nine passes for a school-record 214 yards and one touchdown. Yale ran over Columbia, 34-7, Penn whipped Lafayette, 13-0, and Colgate shocked Princeton with a touchdown and a two-point conversion in the last 14 seconds to win, 22-21.

On October 25, Harvard gained sole possession of first place by whipping Dartmouth, 24-10, while Penn, a 10-point underdog, knocked off Princeton with a 24-20 victory. Jim Kubacki, the Harvard quarterback, threw touchdown passes of 5, 14, and 9 yards to Bob McDermott and ran for another 107 yards. Meanwhile, Yale's 55-yard, fourth-quarter drive dumped Cornell, 20-14, while Brown and Columbia each suffered nonconference setbacks, the Bruins 21-20 to Holy Cross and the Lions 41-0 to Rutgers.

With Jack Wixted, the number two all-purpose runner in college football, sidelined with injuries,

Penn lost to Harvard, 21-3, the next Saturday. By winning, Harvard remained undefeated in league competition with a 4-0 record. Brown (3-0-1) held on to second place by building up a 17-0 lead over Princeton and then battling for its life to win, 24-16. At New Haven, Yale overcame Dartmouth, 16-14, on the game's last play, Randy Carter place-kicking a 47-yard field goal, his third three-pointer of the contest. Columbia won its first game of the season as Doug Jackson matched Cornell's Tim LaBeau with three touchdowns apiece, but it was the Lions who stiffened their defenses and prevailed, 42-19.

The drama was building now. With Bob Bateman and Paul Michalko completing 25 of 42 passes for 363 yards, Brown crumpled Cornell, 45-23. That victory, coupled with Harvard's 24-20 loss to Princeton, moved the Bruins (4-0-1) to the top of the Ivy ladder. Early in the fourth quarter, with Harvard trailing the Tigers, 24-0, hundreds of Crimson fans began leaving the stadium to beat the upcoming traffic. As soon as they did, the Harvard offense got under way too. Tim Davenport, a sophomore who had played just three minutes all season at quarterback, rallied the Crimson for 20 points in seven and a half minutes before running out of magic.

That same day, Yale (4-1) tied Harvard for second place, stopping Penn, 24-14, as Don Gesicki gained 164 yards rushing. Dartmouth, which had knocked off Columbia for its 300th victory in 1937 and for its 400th in 1960, kept the sequence going with a 22-17 come-from-behind win for its 500th.

The Ivies were coming down to their last two big weekends of the season, and for the first time since 1932 there was a sellout at Brown. A pep rally, almost as rare, was also part of the scene. Causing all the hoopla was something even more uncommon, a chance for the Bruins to all but lock up their first modern Ivy League title. Alas, Harvard beat the Bruins, 45-26. Most responsible for turning Providence's joy into gloom was Jim Kubacki. The Harvard quarterback, who had missed the Princeton game because of a slight shoulder separation, completed 15 of 18 passes for 289 yards and three touchdowns.

Thus, the Ivy Championship would be settled in The Game, November 22, when Harvard played at Yale.

The Elis tied for first place by stopping Princeton, 24-13, with the help of a 97-yard scoring pass, the longest in Yale history. Halfback Don Gesicki tossed the ball and split end Gary Fencik caught it on his 35, broke two tackles, and went all the way.

Dartmouth, too, scored through the air, Mike Brait firing three touchdown passes to Tom Fleming in a 33-10 win over Cornell, but Columbia relied on the rushing of Doug Jackson, whose 194 yards and three touchdowns led to a 28-25 defeat of Penn.

After eight hard weekends of play, it all boiled down to The Game. Harvard traveled to Yale Bowl to settle the league race. As always, there were many whimsical sidelights to this classic series. Members of *The Yale Record*, the humor magazine, visited Cambridge earlier in the week, passed themselves off as Harvard students, stole a big VERITAS banner and hung it upside down in front of Yale's Sterling Library. The political science departments of the two schools had another touch football game. Yale, possibly inspired by cheers of "Clap your hands, stamp your feet/ We want blood on every cleat," prevailed, 21-0, and gained possession of a cracked teacup, more formally known as The Cooperman Cup.

Then came 1:30 P.M. and the 100th meeting of the Elis and the Crimson. Stone Phillips put Yale in front with a 5-yard run, after which came the half time festivities. Harvard has long claimed it has the world's largest drum. So Yale produced a 1-foot drum and a 10-foot drumstick.

In the third quarter, Harvard tied matters at 7-all on a 2-yard plunge by Tom (Apple Juice) Winn.

Late in the game, Jim Kubacki hit Bob McDermott for 21 yards on a fourth-and-12 pass. That put the ball on the Yale 14, and with 33 seconds left, Mike Lynch booted a 26-yard field goal that gave Harvard its first undisputed championship in the 20 years there had been, officially, an Ivy League.

Rounding out the 1975 schedule, quarterbacks led Brown, Penn, and Dartmouth to other Ivy wins. Bob Bateman scored three touchdowns and passed for two others as the Bruins bopped Columbia, 48-13, to gain sole possession of second place, their highest finish in Ivy history. Bob Graustein accounted for four touchdowns as Pennsylvania outlasted Cornell, 27-21. And Mike Brait scored once and combined with Tom Fleming on touchdown passes of 70 and 85 yards to enable the Big Green to get past Princeton, 21-16.

*Named to the* Sports Illustrated *Silver Anniversay All-America team in 1965, former Yale guard DeLaney Kiphuth served from 1954 to mid-1976 as the school's director of athletics.*

## 1976

Under a revamped schedule, every Ivy League team began the season with a league game. Yale opened on the road for the first time this century in a televised contest against Brown that was expected to have significant bearing on the Ivy race.

Going into the game, Carmen Cozza, whose Yale teams ran up a school record of 69 victories in 11 seasons, told the press that this would probably be his last year as head football coach. He was slated to succeed DeLaney Kiphuth as the school's athletic director.

"I don't think I will have time to coach football once I get going on a program to revitalize all sports at Yale," Cozza explained. "I think we were the low school in the Ivy League last year in total wins in all sports."

The Elis had an outstanding quarterback in Stone Phillips, a solid group of runners headed by John Pagliaro, and an offensive line with experience at every position. The Yale defense, however, had to rely on reinforcements from the 1975 freshman team.

Brown had graduated 13 starters, but Coach John Anderson, looking more like a prophet than a coach, believed that he had no serious weaknesses. His multiple offense had some breakaway threats and an outstanding pass catcher in Bob Farnham, but Anderson was still wondering about a replacement for graduated quarterback Bob Bateman.

The game between Yale and Brown developed into a comedy of errors: Brown, which made fewer, won, 14-6.

The outcome was supposed to hinge on how well Yale's inexperienced defense handled Brown's relatively new offensive unit, but the Bulldogs' downfall was their offense, which lost four of seven fumbles. Brown scored its first touchdown after a fumble recovery on the Yale 15. It earned its second with a 74-yard march that ended with a sparkling 33-yard broken field run on a reverse by flanker Charley Watkins.

Meanwhile, Harvard, now favored to take its third straight Ivy title, made the preseason forecasters appear as genuine experts as it showed its strength by blasting Columbia, 34-10.

Dartmouth, out of first place for two years now and Coach Jack Crouthamel feeling alumni pressure, won its first opening-day game in four years. It shut out Pennsylvania, 20-0, as its defense held the Quakers to 58 yards rushing. Princeton and Cornell almost shut out each other, but the Tigers finally pulled it out, 3-0, on Chris Howe's 23-yard fourth-quarter field goal.

For the next two Saturdays, Brown took dead aim on an undefeated season by beating Rhode Island, 3-0, and Princeton, 13-7. Harvard kept pace with victories over Massachusetts, 24-13, and Boston University, 37-14. Yale kept close with 21-10 and 21-6 triumphs over Connecticut and Lehigh, respectively.

And then, as they say, came the rude awakening for the Bruins and Crimson. On October 9, Ivy Leaguers had to contend with gusty winds, heavy rains, and turf turned to muck. Best of the mudders were Princeton, Yale, and previously winless Penn and Cornell. The Tigers, who now had a 2-1 record, went into a tie for the Ivy lead with Brown by slogging past Columbia, 9-3. Princeton halfback Mike Howard slithered for 133 yards in 37 carries in a game in which each side fumbled six times. The Elis, now 1-1 in the conference, edged Dartmouth, 18-14. And heretofore undefeated Brown and Harvard? Well, Pennsylvania, which had lost three straight, upset Brown, 7-6, when, with 1:51 left, Johnny Mason, a 5′ 9″, 172-pound human bomb, exploded 1 yard into the end zone and Tim Mazzetti added the extra point. That one point would haunt the Bruins for the rest of the season.

The winds were so strong at Harvard that they caused the goalposts at the open end of the field to sway, reminding a lot of people of the great hurricane of 1950 that whipped the East. With an excellent opportunity to take over first place, the Cantabs failed to get into the swim of things and were the shocking victims of a 9-3 upset at the hands of Cornell. The oddest turn of events came when the Big Red punter Dave Johnson, unable to kick because of an errant center snap, sped 75 yards for the game's only touchdown.

Harvard bounced back to beat Dartmouth, 17-10, and Princeton, 20-14; Brown got untracked with wins over Cornell, 28-12, and Holy Cross, 28-18; while Yale stayed in a tie for first place with impressive victories over Columbia, 37-6, and Penn, 21-6. With two-thirds of the season gone, Harvard had a 3-1 Ivy record and was tied with Yale and Brown in the race for the championship. In the Yale victory over Penn, running back John Pagliaro, whose father is a mailman, also did a lot of carrying. He tied the Yale record for rushing attempts (33) as he gained 187 yards and scored three times. Coach Cozza, who has coached the likes of Calvin Hill and Dick Jauron, said after the Penn game that Pagliaro could play for any team in the country. "I usually don't go overboard on a player, but I said it about Hill, I said it about Jauron, and now I'm saying it about Pagliaro."

On October 30, Brown and Yale parlayed late efforts into Ivy League wins to keep their title hopes alive. There was a mighty strong possibility now that the Bruins would win or share their first Ivy League football title in history.

Brown, which trailed Harvard, 7-0, in the second quarter, was forced to zipper up its defense against the Crimson's multiflex offense to rally for a 16-14 victory. And quarterback Paul Michalko perked up the Bruin aerial game with passes to Bob Farnham, who made five receptions, one a leaping grab of a 10-yard toss in the end zone.

*Harvard Stadium, the first reinforced concrete stadium built in the U.S., entered its 73rd year in 1977 as a site for college football. It once seated 57,166, but in 1951 the capacity was cut to 37,289.*

The victory over the defending Ivy League Champions was celebrated as if it were the most important in Brown football history. But it didn't come easy. It came by uphill work, and it was not assured until the last few moments after Harvard had scored a touchdown with 81 seconds to play. When Brown corralled the following short kickoff, the Bruins nailed down their best chance at an Ivy title since the formal inception of an Ivy round robin in 1956. Now Brown was tied with Yale for first place, with Harvard and Dartmouth a game back. The Big Green was next on the Brown schedule, so the Bruins still had to work before getting a piece of the Ivy crown.

While Brown was getting past Harvard, last-place Cornell gave Yale fits before succumbing, 14-6. Two short scoring plunges by Johnny Pagliaro and pass receptions by John Spagnola sent Yale to an early lead, and the Eli defense stood up for the victory. Steve Skrovan and Kurt Nondorf each stole two Cornell passes, and the Yale defense twice dramatically stopped long Big Red drives in the fourth quarter to thwart last-minute touchdown threats.

The Yale football song, "March, march on down the field," was appropriate in Yale Bowl the next Saturday as the Elis defeated Princeton, 39-7, before a crowd of 33,218, the largest in the Ivy League so far in 1976. Led once again by Johnny Pagliaro, the hip-swinging junior halfback who scored three touchdowns and set another Yale record, the Elis were ahead by 8-0, 15-0, and 29-0 at the end of the first three quarters as Princeton accomplished very little. Pagliaro's touchdowns were his 13th, 14th, and 15th of the season, the most by a Yale player in this century. Calvin Hill set the old record, 14, in 1968.

The scoreboard, the statistics, and the action on the field all told the same old tale—Yale. First downs: Yale 25, Princeton 11. Total yards gained: Yale 465, Princeton 107. Yards gained rushing: Yale 388, Princeton 29.

For Old Nassau, losing one game to Yale was not so bad. But losing 10 games in a row was indigestible. Not since 1966 had Princeton beaten Yale. Even worse, 1976's margin was the most decisive in that string of defeats and the greatest in a 103-year rivalry.

At Providence, Brown, like a hungry bear awakening after 20 years, overwhelmed Dartmouth in the first half, then held on to win, 35-21, to stay tied with Yale going into the final Saturday of play. Tasting what could be its very first Ivy League Championship, the Bruins defeated the Big Green for the first time since the eight Ivy colleges established their formal rivalry, and raised its won-lost record to 7-1. Dartmouth was the last major hurdle in Brown's path to the title.

Unleashing an uncharacteristic air attack that produced four touchdowns of 48, 40, 33, and 31 yards, Brown was leading, 35-7, when Dartmouth suddenly burst alive with two scores and threatened to get more. That's when the characteristically strong Brown defense finally made itself felt, turning back the Green on the 9-yard line and then the 11 in the final minutes to preserve the victory.

Paul Michalko, the Brown quarterback, set a school record by passing for 314 yards. His four touchdowns by air also set a Brown record. Michalko's favorite receiver, Bob Farnham, caught 12 passes for two touchdowns and set an Ivy League career mark of 107 receptions. Don Clune of Penn held the old mark of 99.

Yale now faced a nemesis—Harvard. In 1974 and '75, the Crimson beat the Blue in the last minute of each game, costing the Elis the title the first time and a tie for it the second.

Before John Anderson became the Brown coach in 1973, the Bruins didn't know about championships. They hardly knew about winning seasons, having achieved just one in the previous 14 years. But after the 1976 eleven won seven of its first eight games for Brown's best start in football in 27 years, Anderson told of a conversation he had with his seniors. "They were the first group we recruited," he said, "and I told them we were going to win a title."

Well, the title didn't come easily. Brown played Columbia at Baker Field and the combination of an inspired Light Blue team, 2-4 on the Ivy season, which was determined to be a spoiler, and a variety of Brown mistakes made certain of that. The Bruins lost the ball on a fumble at the Columbia 1-yard line, two of their passes were intercepted, and they drew several costly penalties. They trailed at half time, 17-7.

"We tried to make it hard on ourselves," Anderson said.

In the final period, however, they finally made some moves toward their half of the Ivy League title. After scoring in the third quarter, they recovered an errant Columbia pitchout and then drove 47 yards for the touchdown, which, with the conversion, put them in front for the first time, 21-17. Billy Hill twisted his way into the end zone from 1 yard out after Seth Morris had carried six times for 29 yards on the drive.

Then they sealed the victory with a 2-yard touchdown burst by Hill after he had scampered 54 yards to the Columbia 3. Final score: Brown 28, Columbia 17.

Yale didn't have it any softer. It took the Elis half the game to prove that they were better than Harvard, but at the end the Bulldogs had convinced everyone in the crowd of 42,000 at Harvard Stadium. Yale won, 21-7, and thus shared the Ivy League Championship with Brown, the only team to beat the Blue all season.

Yale's eighth and final victory in 1976 was slow to develop as Harvard had made the big play of the first half, a 74-yard run with an intercepted pass by Russ Savage, the defensive end. That touchdown, and the conversion kick by Mike Lynch, gave the Crimson a 7-0 lead that stood up until midway through the third quarter. Then the Elis, led by Johnny Pagliaro, turned on their power and put the Crimson away.

Pagliaro gained 125 yards in 25 running plays and finally turned the Harvard flanks as Yale did exactly what it intended to do, run over its old adversary. Pagliaro scored one touchdown and Mike Southworth, the big fullback, the other two as Yale ran for 286 yards and passed for only 30. Yale's big playmaker, who gained 1,003 yards in 1976 and scored 16 touchdowns to lead the Ivies in both skills, was the important figure in the scoring drives of 42, 31, and 58 yards. Pagliaro's longest run was a 34-yard dash around right end, and his best a 5-yard sprint to the end zone for a touchdown that put Yale ahead at the end of the third quarter.

For Carmen Cozza, the victory at Cambridge terminated a series of indignities and defeats his teams had suffered there. They had won only once before at Harvard Stadium in the last decade, and Cozza can never forget the 29-29 tie of 1968 or the loss in the last 10 seconds that cost Yale an undefeated season in 1974.

When it was all over, Cozza, who had guided the Elis to five Ivy League Championships in the last 12 years, suddenly decided he didn't want to be the school's athletic director after all. He had been told by Blue officials that he could not have both the football and athletic director's jobs. He would have to make a choice—football coach or athletic director. Cozza decided he liked football more than sitting behind a desk. The decision was not even close. Cozza had been looking forward to coaching Yale against Miami of Ohio, his alma mater, in 1977—and, in 1978, he was due to become president of the American Football Coaches Association.

## 1977

In February the Ivy presidents met and voted to permit their teams to play 10 games per season. But this may not happen every year. No game may be played earlier than the next-to-last Saturday in September, and the last game may not be played after the Saturday before Thanksgiving. Because of quirks in the calendar, 10-game cards will be in only seven of the next ten years. It's easy to believe that only the Ivy League presidents could have devised such a formula.

*Yale football coach Carm Cozza was picked to succeed Kiphuth as director of athletics, but after earning a share of the 1976 Ivy League championship with Brown, he decided to stay on as head mentor and leave the desk job to someone else.*

James Litvak, secretary of the Ivy League, as well as a Princeton professor of economics, said, "You'll need a differential equation to figure out your football schedule now."

In any event, Yale's coach was pleased, and he looked forward to scheduling teams like Stanford and the three service academies. But those teams have their schedules made many years in advance. He suggested, "It may be still some time before we get to play them or any 10th game."

# The Record

*A recent issue of* Harvard Football News *shows admission tickets of glorious Ivy League contests gone by.*

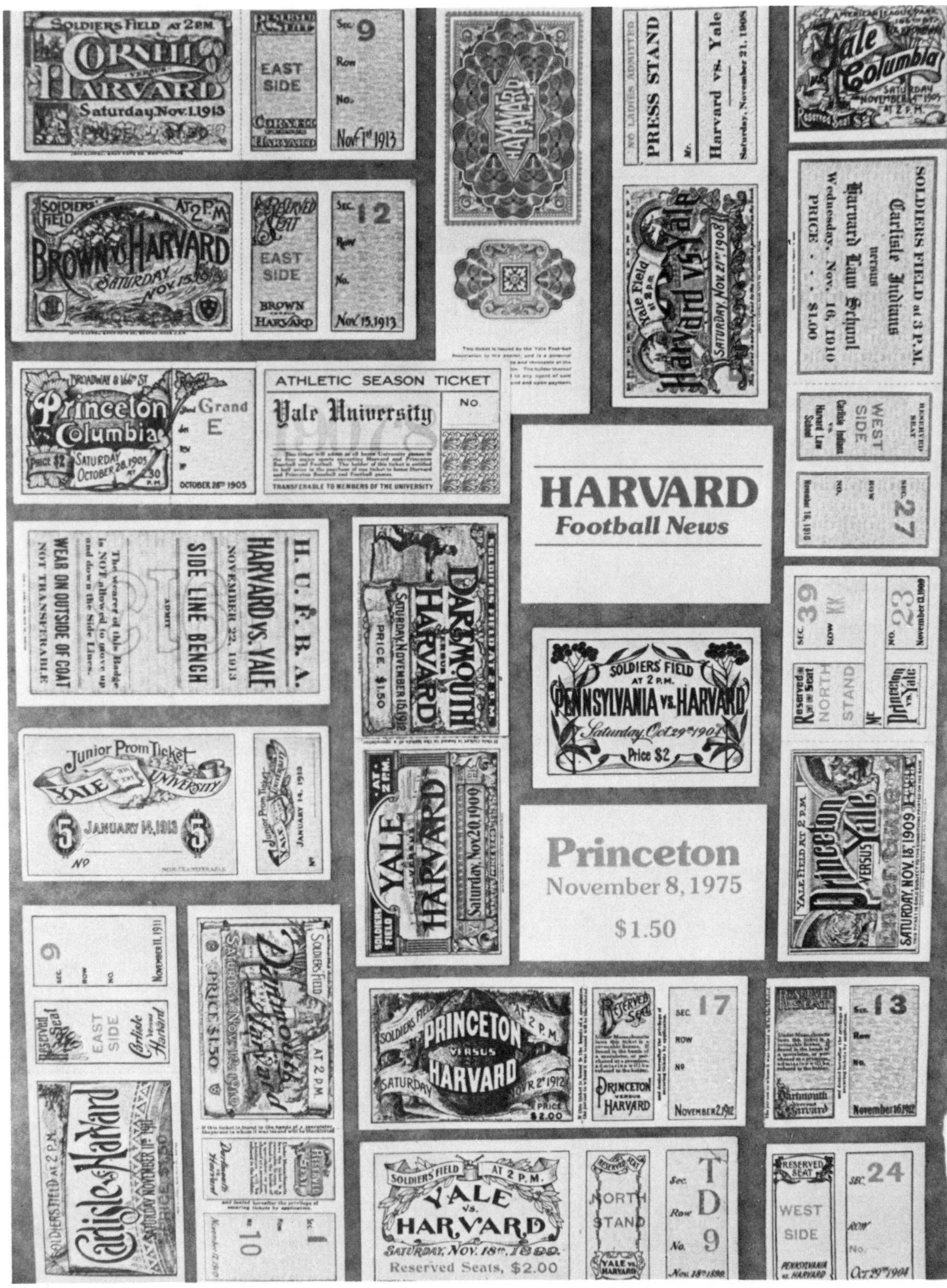

## Ivy League Players and Coaches In The National Football Hall of Fame

### Players

| | *College* | *Position* | *Years Played* | *Date of Election* |
|---|---|---|---|---|
| Aldrich, Malcolm | Yale | Halfback | 1919–21 | 1972 |
| Ames, Knowlton (Snake) | Princeton | Fullback | 1886–89 | 1969 |
| Baker, Hobey | Princeton | Back | 1911–13 | 1975 |
| Ballin, Harold | Princeton | Tackle | 1912–14 | 1973 |
| Barrett, Charles | Cornell | Quarterback | 1913–15 | 1958 |
| Bednarik, Charles | Pennsylvania | Center | 1945–48 | 1969 |
| Bomeisler, Doug | Yale | Guard | 1912 | 1972 |
| Booth, Albert (Albie) | Yale | Halfback | 1929–31 | 1966 |
| Brewer, Charles | Harvard | Halfback | 1892–94 | 1971 |
| Brooke, George | Pennsylvania | Halfback | 1894–95 | 1969 |
| Brown, Gordon | Yale | Guard | 1897–1900 | 1954 |
| Campbell, David C. | Harvard | End | 1899–1901 | 1958 |
| Casey, Edward | Harvard | Halfback | 1916–19 | 1968 |
| Cochran, Gary | Princeton | End | 1896–98 | 1971 |
| Corbin, William (Pa) | Yale | Center | 1886–88 | 1969 |
| Cowan, Hector | Princeton | Tackle | 1885–89 | 1951 |
| Coy, Edward | Yale | Fullback | 1907–09 | 1951 |
| Daly, Charles | Harvard | Quarterback | 1898–1900 | 1951 |
| DeWitt, John | Princeton | Guard | 1901–03 | 1954 |
| Edwards, William | Princeton | Tackle | 1898–99 | 1971 |
| Fish, Hamilton | Harvard | Tackle | 1907–09 | 1954 |
| Fisher, Robert | Harvard | Guard | 1909–11 | 1973 |
| Frank, Clinton | Yale | Halfback | 1935–37 | 1955 |
| Gelbert, Charles | Pennsylvania | End | 1894–96 | 1960 |
| Hardwick, Tack | Harvard | End | 1912–14 | 1954 |
| Hare, Truxton | Pennsylvania | Guard | 1897–1900 | 1951 |
| Hart, Edward | Princeton | Tackle | 1909–11 | 1954 |
| Healey, Edward | Dartmouth | Tackle | 1915–16 | 1974 |
| Heffelfinger, W.W. | Yale | Guard | 1888–91 | 1951 |
| Hickok, William | Yale | Guard | 1892–94 | 1971 |
| Hillebrand, Art (Doc) | Princeton | Tackle | 1898–99 | 1970 |
| Hinkey, Frank | Yale | End | 1891–94 | 1951 |
| Hogan, James | Yale | Tackle | 1902–04 | 1954 |
| Holland, Jerome (Brud) | Cornell | End | 1936–38 | 1965 |
| Hollenback, William | Pennsylvania | Halfback | 1906–08 | 1951 |
| Howe, Arthur | Yale | Quarterback | 1911 | 1973 |
| Kaw, Edgar L. | Cornell | Halfback | 1920–22 | 1954 |
| Kazmaier, Richard | Princeton | Halfback | 1949–51 | 1966 |
| Keck, James | Princeton | Tackle | 1920–21 | 1959 |
| Kelley, Lawrence | Yale | End | 1934–36 | 1969 |
| Ketcham, Henry | Yale | Center | 1911–13 | 1968 |
| Kilpatrick, John Reed | Yale | End | 1908–10 | 1955 |
| King, Philip | Princeton | Quarterback | 1890–93 | 1962 |
| Lane, Myles | Dartmouth | Halfback | 1925–27 | 1970 |
| Lea, Langdon | Princeton | Tackle, end | 1892–95 | 1964 |
| Lourie, Don | Princeton | Quarterback | 1919–21 | 1974 |
| Luckman, Sid | Columbia | Quarterback | 1936–38 | 1960 |
| McClung, Thomas | Yale | Halfback | 1889–91 | 1963 |
| McCormick, James | Princeton | Fullback | 1905–17 | 1954 |
| Mahan, Edward | Harvard | Fullback | 1913–15 | 1951 |
| Mallory, William | Yale | Fullback | 1921–23 | 1964 |
| Mercer, LeRoy | Pennsylvania | Fullback | 1910–12 | 1955 |
| Minds, John | Pennsylvania | Fullback | 1894–97 | 1962 |
| Moffat, Alexander | Princeton | Halfback | 1881–83 | 1971 |
| Montgomery, Cliff | Columbia | Quarterback | 1931–33 | 1963 |
| Morley, William | Columbia | Halfback | 1900–02 | 1971 |

| | *College* | *Position* | *Years Played* | *Date of Election* |
|---|---|---|---|---|
| Morton, William | Dartmouth | Quarterback | 1929–31 | 1972 |
| Newell, Marshall | Harvard | Tackle | 1890–93 | 1957 |
| Oberlander, Andrew | Dartmouth | Halfback | 1923–25 | 1954 |
| O'Hearn, Jack | Cornell | End | 1913–15 | 1972 |
| Osgood, Winchester | Cornell | Back | 1891–92 | 1970 |
| Peabody, Endicott | Harvard | Guard | 1939–41 | 1973 |
| Pennock, Stanley | Harvard | Guard | 1912–14 | 1954 |
| Pfann, George | Cornell | Quarterback | 1921–23 | 1957 |
| Poe, Arthur | Princeton | End | 1898–99 | 1969 |
| Pollard, Fritz | Brown | Halfback | 1914–16 | 1954 |
| Reid, William | Harvard | Fullback | 1898–99 | 1970 |
| Scarlett, Hunter | Pennsylvania | End | 1898 | 1970 |
| Shelton, Murray | Cornell | End | 1913–15 | 1973 |
| Shevlin, Thomas | Yale | End | 1903–05 | 1954 |
| Spears, Clarence | Dartmouth | Guard | 1914–15 | 1955 |
| Sprackling, William | Brown | Quarterback | 1908–11 | 1964 |
| Stagg, Amos Alonzo | Yale | End | 1885–89 | 1951 |
| Stevens, Marvin (Mal) | Yale | Back | 1923 | 1974 |
| Stevenson, Vincent | Pennsylvania | Quarterback | 1903–05 | 1968 |
| Thorne, Samuel | Yale | Back | 1895 | 1970 |
| Ticknor, Benjamin | Harvard | Center | 1928–30 | 1954 |
| Torrey, Robert | Pennsylvania | Center | 1902–05 | 1971 |
| Warner, William | Cornell | Guard | 1900–04 | 1971 |
| Weekes, Harold | Columbia | Halfback | 1900–02 | 1954 |
| Weller, John | Princeton | Guard | 1933–35 | 1957 |
| Wendall, Percy | Harvard | End | 1910–12 | 1972 |
| Wharton, Charles | Pennsylvania | Guard | 1893–96 | 1963 |
| Wheeler, Arthur | Princeton | Guard | 1892–94 | 1969 |
| Wyckoff, Clinton | Cornell | Quarterback | 1895–96 | 1970 |

*'P" on Hector Cowan's chest could have tood for Pirate instead of Princeton, the way he players dressed in 1888. "Hector was a hunky, deep-chested fellow, built like a mokehouse, and one of the strongest players ever faced," testified Pudge Heffelfinger.*

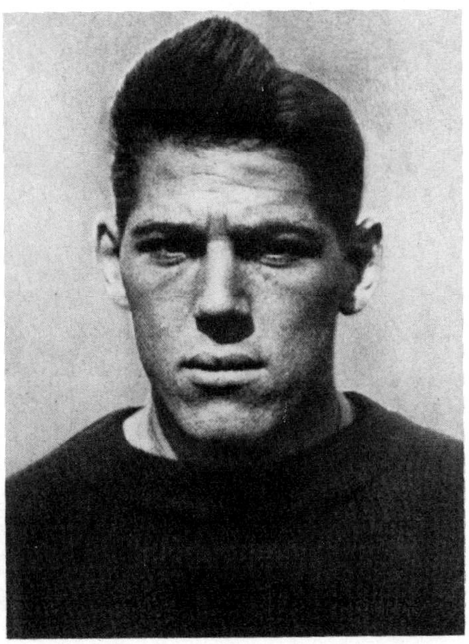

*All-America and Hall of Famer Huntington R. (Tack) Hardwick was a fine halfback as a sophomore at Harvard and later a famous end on Percy Haughton's great Crimson teams of 1912–13–14. The multisided Haughton was many things to many men, but Tack Hardwick was one of those who loved him. "Why," Tack said, "if Percy asked me to jump out of a tenth-story window, I'd do it."*

*James Stanton Keck was All-America at both tackle and guard on Princeton elevens of 1920-21, and was elected to the Hall of Fame in 1959.*

## Coaches

| | *Ivy Affiliation* | *Years* | *Date of Election* |
|---|---|---|---|
| Blaik, Earl | Dartmouth | 1934–40 | 1955 |
| Caldwell, Charles | Princeton | 1945–56 | 1961 |
| Camp, Walter | Yale | 1888–92 | 1951 |
| Cavanaugh, Frank | Dartmouth | 1911–16 | 1954 |
| Crisler, Fritz | Princeton | 1932–37 | 1954 |
| Dobie, Gilmour | Cornell | 1920–35 | 1951 |
| Engle, Rip | Brown | 1944–49 | 1973 |
| Harlow, Richard | Harvard | 1935–42 | 1954 |
| Haughton, Percy | Cornell | 1899–1900 | 1951 |
| | Harvard | 1908–16 | |
| | Columbia | 1923–24 | |
| Heisman, John | Pennsylvania | 1920–22 | 1954 |
| Jones, Howard | Yale | 1909–13 | 1951 |
| Jones, T.A.D. | Yale | 1916–27 | 1958 |
| Little, Lou | Columbia | 1930–56 | 1960 |
| McLaughry, Tuss | Brown | 1926–40 | 1962 |
| | Dartmouth | 1941–42 | |
| | | 1945–54 | |
| O'Neill, Frank | Columbia | 1920–22 | 1951 |
| Robinson, E. N. | Brown | 1898–1907 | 1955 |
| | | 1910–25 | |
| Roper, William | Princeton | 1906–08 | 1951 |
| | | 1910–11 | |
| | | 1919–30 | |
| Sanford, George | Columbia | 1899–1901 | 1971 |
| Smith, Andy | Pennsylvania | 1909–12 | 1951 |
| Snavely, Carl | Cornell | 1936–44 | 1965 |
| Warner, Glenn (Pop) | Cornell | 1897–98 | 1951 |
| Wieman, E. E. (Tad) | Princeton | 1938–42 | 1956 |
| Woodruff, George | Pennsylvania | 1892–1901 | 1963 |

## All-Ivy League Team 1956–1972

In 1973, coaches, writers, and sportscasters closely associated with Ivy League football during the first 17 years of formal league competition (1956–72), picked an all-time conference team. The first-team backfield represented more than 16,000 yards of total offense and scored 202 touchdowns, while the defensive unit included a horde of defenders who shared in over 30 shutouts during the highest scoring era in college football history.

### Offensive Team

**First Team**

| Pos | Name, College, Class |
|---|---|
| E | John Parry, Brown '65 |
| E | Don Clune, Penn '74 |
| T | Steve Diamond, Harvard '67 |
| T | Bob Asack, Columbia '62 |
| G | Ben Balme, Yale '61 |
| G | Tony Day, Columbia '61 |
| C | Mike Pyle, Yale '61 |
| QB | Archie Roberts, Columbia '65 |
| QB | Brian Dowling, Yale '69 |
| RB | Ed Marinaro, Cornell '72 |
| RB | Calvin Hill, Yale '69 |
| RB | Cosmo Iacavazzi, Princeton '65 |
| KSp | Charlie Gogolak, Princeton '66 |

**Second Team**

| Pos | Name, College, Class |
|---|---|
| E | Barney Berlinger, Penn '60 |
| E | Bruce Weinstein, Yale '69 |
| T | Kyle Gee, Yale '69 |
| T | Bob Shaunessy, Harvard '59 |
| G | Joe Palermo, Dartmouth '58 |
| G | John Owseichik, Yale '57 |
| C | Chuck Matuszak, Dartmouth '67 |
| QB | Marty Domres, Columbia '69 |
| RB | Dick Jauron, Yale '73 |
| RB | Gary Wood, Cornell '64 |
| RB | Jake Crouthamel, Dartmouth '60 |
| KSp | Pete Gogolak, Cornell '64 |

Tabulation: First Team = 2 points
Second Team = 1 point
Maximum Points = 52/26

### Defensive Team

**First Team**

| Pos | Name, College, Class |
|---|---|
| E | Jim Gallagher, Yale '71 |
| E | Ken Boyda, Harvard '66 |
| T | Tom Neville, Yale '71 |
| T | John Sponheimer, Cornell '69 |
| LB | Stas Maliszewski, Princeton '66 |
| LB | Murry Bowden, Dartmouth '71 |
| LB | Don Chiofaro, Harvard '68 |
| LB | Bob Lally, Cornell '74 |
| DB | Keith Mauney, Princeton '70 |
| DB | Gordie Rule, Dartmouth '68 |
| DB | Willie Bogan, Dartmouth '71 |
| P | Joe Randall, Brown '67 |

**Second Team**

| Pos | Name, College, Class |
|---|---|
| E | Tom Csatari, Dartmouth '74 |
| E | Walt Kozumbo, Princeton '67 |
| T | Phil Ratner, Cornell '66 |
| T | Barry Brink, Dartmouth '71 |
| LB | Gary Farneti, Harvard '71 |
| LB | Paul Kaliades, Columbia '72 |
| LB | Don McKinnon, Dartmouth '63 |
| LB | Paul Savidge, Princeton '66 |
| DB | Win Mabry, Dartmouth '67 |
| DB | Dave Ignacio, Harvard '72 |
| DB | John Tyson, Harvard '69 |
| P | Gary Singleterry, Harvard '70 |

Tabulation: First Team = 2 points
Second Team = 1 point
Maximum Points = 52/26

*Top row, l. to r.: Halfback Calvin Hill, Yale '69; Tailback Ed Marinaro, Cornell '72; Fullback Cosmo Lacavazzi, Princeton '65; Placekicker Charlie Gogolak, Princeton '66. Middle row: End John Parry, Brown '65; Quarterback Brian Dowling, Yale '69; Quarterback Archie Roberts, Columbia'65; End Don Clune, Pennsylvania '74. Bottom row: Tackle Steve Diamond, Harvard '67; Guard Ben Balme, Yale '61; Center Mike Pyle, Yale '61; Guard Tony Day, Columbia '62; Tackle Bob Asack, Columbia '62.*

*Top row, l. to r.: Halfback Gordie Rule, Dartmouth '68; Safety Willie Bogan, Dartmouth '71; Halfback Keith Mauney, Princeton '70; Punter Joe Randall, Brown '67. Middle row: Linebacker Stas Maliszewski, Princeton '66; Linebacker Murry Bowden, Dartmouth '71; Linebacker Don Chiofaro, Harvard '68; Linebacker Bob Lally, Cornell '74. Bottom row: End Jim Gallagher, Yale '71; Tackle John Sponheimer, Cornell '69; Tackle Tom Neville, Yale '71; End Ken Boyda, Harvard '66.*

## All-Time Won-Lost-Tied Records (includes 1976)

| | Won | Lost | Tied |
|---|---|---|---|
| Yale | 701 | 195 | 51 |
| Princeton | 621 | 212 | 45 |
| Harvard | 620 | 242 | 45 |
| Dartmouth | 508 | 247 | 39 |
| Pennsylvania | 608 | 332 | 39 |
| Cornell | 470 | 292 | 31 |
| Brown | 408 | 380 | 36 |
| Columbia | 293 | 362 | 38 |

## All-Time Standings

(Note: Prior to 1956, when the league was formally organized, Ivy League football was played on an informal basis. For the years 1869–1955, teams are listed alphabetically; ° represents best won-lost record against Ivy schools. Standings shown here are reprinted by permission of the Ivy League Sports Information Directors Committee.)

**1869**

| | League W | L | T | Overall W | L | T |
|---|---|---|---|---|---|---|
| Princeton | 0 | 0 | 0 | 1 | 1 | 0 |

**1870**

| | League W | L | T | Overall W | L | T |
|---|---|---|---|---|---|---|
| Brown | 0 | 0 | 0 | 0 | 1 | 0 |
| Princeton | 0 | 0 | 0 | 1 | 0 | 0 |

**1871**

No Games Played

**1872**

| | League W | L | T | Overall W | L | T |
|---|---|---|---|---|---|---|
| Columbia | 0 | 1 | 0 | 1 | 2 | 1 |
| Princeton | 0 | 0 | 0 | 1 | 0 | 0 |
| °Yale | 1 | 0 | 0 | 1 | 0 | 0 |

**1873**

| | League W | L | T | Overall W | L | T |
|---|---|---|---|---|---|---|
| Columbia | 0 | 0 | 0 | 2 | 1 | 0 |
| °Princeton | 1 | 0 | 0 | 1 | 0 | 0 |
| Yale | 0 | 1 | 0 | 2 | 1 | 0 |

**1874**

| | League W | L | T | Overall W | L | T |
|---|---|---|---|---|---|---|
| Columbia | 0 | 3 | 0 | 1 | 5 | 0 |
| Harvard | 0 | 0 | 0 | 1 | 0 | 1 |
| Princeton | 1 | 0 | 0 | 2 | 0 | 0 |
| °Yale | 2 | 0 | 0 | 3 | 0 | 0 |

**1875**

| | League W | L | T | Overall W | L | T |
|---|---|---|---|---|---|---|
| Columbia | 1 | 1 | 0 | 4 | 1 | 1 |
| °Harvard | 1 | 0 | 0 | 5 | 1 | 0 |
| °Princeton | 1 | 0 | 0 | 2 | 0 | 0 |
| Yale | 0 | 2 | 0 | 2 | 2 | 0 |

**1876**

| | League W | L | T | Overall W | L | T |
|---|---|---|---|---|---|---|
| Columbia | 0 | 2 | 0 | 1 | 3 | 0 |
| Harvard | 0 | 1 | 0 | 3 | 1 | 0 |
| Pennsylvania | 0 | 2 | 0 | 1 | 2 | 0 |
| Princeton | 3 | 1 | 0 | 3 | 1 | 0 |
| °Yale | 3 | 0 | 0 | 3 | 0 | 0 |

**1877**

| | League W | L | T | Overall W | L | T |
|---|---|---|---|---|---|---|
| Columbia | 0 | 2 | 0 | 2 | 2 | 0 |
| °Harvard | 2 | 1 | 0 | 3 | 1 | 0 |
| Princeton | 2 | 1 | 1 | 2 | 1 | 1 |
| Yale | 0 | 0 | 1 | 3 | 0 | 1 |

**1878**

| | League W | L | T | Overall W | L | T |
|---|---|---|---|---|---|---|
| Brown | 0 | 0 | 0 | 0 | 1 | 0 |
| Columbia | 0 | 0 | 1 | 0 | 0 | 1 |
| Harvard | 0 | 2 | 0 | 1 | 2 | 0 |
| Pennsylvania | 0 | 2 | 1 | 1 | 2 | 1 |
| °Princeton | 4 | 0 | 0 | 6 | 0 | 0 |
| Yale | 1 | 1 | 0 | 4 | 1 | 1 |

**1879**

| | League W | L | T | Overall W | L | T |
|---|---|---|---|---|---|---|
| Columbia | 0 | 3 | 0 | 0 | 3 | 2 |
| Harvard | 0 | 1 | 1 | 2 | 1 | 2 |
| Pennsylvania | 1 | 2 | 0 | 2 | 2 | 0 |
| °Princeton | 3 | 0 | 1 | 4 | 0 | 1 |
| Yale | 2 | 0 | 2 | 3 | 0 | 2 |

**1880**

| | League W | L | T | Overall W | L | T |
|---|---|---|---|---|---|---|
| Brown | 0 | 1 | 0 | 0 | 1 | 0 |
| Columbia | 0 | 2 | 0 | 1 | 2 | 0 |
| Harvard | 1 | 2 | 0 | 3 | 2 | 1 |
| Pennsylvania | 0 | 2 | 0 | 2 | 2 | 0 |
| Princeton | 2 | 0 | 1 | 4 | 0 | 1 |
| °Yale | 4 | 0 | 1 | 4 | 0 | 1 |

### 1881

| | League W | League L | League T | Overall W | Overall L | Overall T |
|---|---|---|---|---|---|---|
| Columbia | 1 | 3 | 0 | 3 | 3 | 1 |
| Dartmouth | 0 | 0 | 0 | 1 | 0 | 1 |
| Harvard | 2 | 1 | 1 | 5 | 1 | 2 |
| Pennsylvania | 0 | 4 | 0 | 0 | 5 | 0 |
| °Princeton | 3 | 0 | 2 | 7 | 0 | 2 |
| Yale | 2 | 0 | 1 | 5 | 0 | 1 |

### 1882

| | League W | League L | League T | Overall W | Overall L | Overall T |
|---|---|---|---|---|---|---|
| Columbia | 0 | 4 | 0 | 0 | 5 | 0 |
| Dartmouth | 0 | 1 | 0 | 1 | 1 | 0 |
| Harvard | 3 | 1 | 0 | 7 | 1 | 0 |
| Pennsylvania | 0 | 2 | 0 | 2 | 4 | 0 |
| Princeton | 4 | 2 | 0 | 7 | 2 | 0 |
| °Yale | 3 | 0 | 0 | 8 | 0 | 0 |

### 1883

| | League W | League L | League T | League PF | League PA | Overall W | Overall L | Overall T | Overall PF | Overall PA |
|---|---|---|---|---|---|---|---|---|---|---|
| Columbia | 0 | 2 | 0 | 1 | 128 | 1 | 3 | 0 | 13 | 147 |
| Dartmouth | 0 | 0 | 0 | – | – | 0 | 1 | 0 | 3 | 5 |
| Harvard | 1 | 2 | 0 | 13 | 49 | 8 | 2 | 0 | 135 | 63 |
| Pennsylvania | 1 | 2 | 0 | 41 | 44 | 6 | 2 | 1 | 204 | 67 |
| Princeton | 2 | 1 | 0 | 65 | 19 | 7 | 1 | 0 | 239 | 26 |
| °Yale | 3 | 0 | 0 | 122 | 2 | 8 | 0 | 0 | 485 | 2 |

### 1884

| | League W | League L | League T | League PF | League PA | Overall W | Overall L | Overall T | Overall PF | Overall PA |
|---|---|---|---|---|---|---|---|---|---|---|
| Columbia | 0 | 0 | 0 | – | – | 1 | 1 | 0 | 21 | 35 |
| Dartmouth | 0 | 2 | 0 | 0 | 142 | 1 | 2 | 1 | 30 | 132 |
| Harvard | 1 | 3 | 0 | 35 | 88 | 7 | 4 | 0 | 281 | 115 |
| Pennsylvania | 1 | 1 | 0 | 4 | 31 | 5 | 1 | 1 | 118 | 59 |
| °Princeton | 2 | 0 | 1 | 67 | 6 | 9 | 0 | 1 | 404 | 13 |
| °Yale | 2 | 0 | 1 | 161 | 0 | 8 | 0 | 1 | 491 | 10 |

### 1885

| | League W | League L | League T | League PF | League PA | Overall W | Overall L | Overall T | Overall PF | Overall PA |
|---|---|---|---|---|---|---|---|---|---|---|
| Pennsylvania | 0 | 4 | 0 | 25 | 266 | 8 | 5 | 0 | 354 | 343 |
| °Princeton | 4 | 0 | 0 | 219 | 25 | 9 | 0 | 0 | 637 | 25 |
| Yale | 1 | 1 | 0 | 58 | 11 | 7 | 1 | 0 | 366 | 11 |

### 1886

| | League W | League L | League T | League PF | League PA | Overall W | Overall L | Overall T | Overall PF | Overall PA |
|---|---|---|---|---|---|---|---|---|---|---|
| Brown | 0 | 0 | 0 | – | – | 1 | 1 | 0 | 76 | 10 |
| Dartmouth | 0 | 1 | 0 | 0 | 70 | 2 | 2 | 0 | 113 | 94 |
| Harvard | 2 | 2 | 0 | 102 | 41 | 12 | 2 | 0 | 765 | 41 |
| Pennsylvania | 0 | 5 | 0 | 15 | 216 | 9 | 7 | 1 | 344 | 286 |
| °Princeton | 4 | 0 | 1 | 125 | 15 | 7 | 0 | 1 | 320 | 27 |
| Yale | 2 | 0 | 1 | 104 | 4 | 9 | 0 | 1 | 687 | 4 |

### 1887

| | League W | League L | League T | League PF | League PA | Overall W | Overall L | Overall T | Overall PF | Overall PA |
|---|---|---|---|---|---|---|---|---|---|---|
| Cornell | 0 | 0 | 0 | – | – | 0 | 2 | 0 | 20 | 62 |
| Dartmouth | 0 | 1 | 0 | – | – | 3 | 1 | 1 | 189 | 28 |
| Harvard | 2 | 1 | 0 | 62 | 17 | 10 | 1 | 0 | 660 | 23 |
| Pennsylvania | 0 | 5 | 0 | 0 | 287 | 6 | 7 | 0 | 137 | 337 |
| Princeton | 3 | 2 | 0 | 205 | 24 | 7 | 2 | 0 | 430 | 24 |
| °Yale | 3 | 0 | 0 | 79 | 8 | 9 | 0 | 0 | 515 | 12 |

### 1888

| | League W | League L | League T | League PF | League PA | Overall W | Overall L | Overall T | Overall PF | Overall PA |
|---|---|---|---|---|---|---|---|---|---|---|
| Cornell | 0 | 0 | 0 | – | – | 4 | 2 | 0 | 96 | 20 |
| Dartmouth | 0 | 1 | 0 | 0 | 74 | 3 | 4 | 0 | 120 | 134 |
| Harvard | 2 | 1 | 0 | 130 | 18 | 12 | 1 | 0 | 635 | 32 |
| Pennsylvania | 0 | 6 | 0 | 0 | 243 | 9 | 7 | 0 | 278 | 296 |
| Princeton | 4 | 1 | 0 | 123 | 16 | 11 | 1 | 0 | 609 | 16 |
| °Yale | 3 | 0 | 0 | 98 | 0 | 13 | 0 | 0 | 694 | 0 |

### 1889

| | League | | | | | Overall | | | | |
|---|---|---|---|---|---|---|---|---|---|---|
| | W | L | T | PF | PA | W | L | T | PF | PA |
| Brown | 0 | 0 | 0 | – | – | 1 | 1 | 0 | 16 | 48 |
| Columbia | 0 | 4 | 0 | 0 | 177 | 2 | 7 | 2 | 54 | 298 |
| Cornell | 1 | 2 | 0 | 26 | 130 | 7 | 2 | 0 | 354 | 130 |
| Dartmouth | 0 | 1 | 0 | 0 | 38 | 7 | 1 | 0 | 239 | 72 |
| Harvard | 2 | 2 | 0 | 88 | 47 | 9 | 2 | 0 | 419 | 53 |
| Pennsylvania | 1 | 3 | 0 | 38 | 129 | 7 | 6 | 0 | 198 | 167 |
| °Princeton | 4 | 0 | 0 | 194 | 19 | 10 | 0 | 0 | 484 | 29 |
| Yale | 5 | 1 | 0 | 220 | 26 | 15 | 1 | 0 | 661 | 31 |

### 1890

| | League | | | | | Overall | | | | |
|---|---|---|---|---|---|---|---|---|---|---|
| | W | L | T | PF | PA | W | L | T | PF | PA |
| Brown | 0 | 0 | 0 | – | – | 2 | 4 | 1 | 78 | 104 |
| Columbia | 0 | 3 | 0 | 0 | 139 | 1 | 5 | 1 | 46 | 178 |
| Cornell | 1 | 1 | 0 | 36 | 77 | 8 | 4 | 0 | 342 | 134 |
| Dartmouth | 0 | 2 | 0 | 0 | 107 | 4 | 4 | 0 | 133 | 122 |
| °Harvard | 4 | 0 | 0 | 196 | 6 | 11 | 0 | 0 | 555 | 12 |
| Pennsylvania | 1 | 3 | 0 | 18 | 84 | 11 | 3 | 0 | 259 | 134 |
| Princeton | 3 | 1 | 0 | 109 | 32 | 11 | 1 | 1 | 478 | 58 |
| Yale | 2 | 1 | 0 | 98 | 12 | 13 | 1 | 0 | 486 | 18 |

### 1891

| | League | | | | | Overall | | | | |
|---|---|---|---|---|---|---|---|---|---|---|
| | W | L | T | PF | PA | W | L | T | PF | PA |
| Brown | 0 | 0 | 0 | – | – | 4 | 6 | 0 | 118 | 176 |
| Columbia | 0 | 0 | 0 | – | – | 1 | 5 | 0 | 32 | 220 |
| Cornell | 0 | 1 | 0 | 0 | 6 | 7 | 3 | 0 | 298 | 34 |
| Dartmouth | 0 | 1 | 0 | 0 | 16 | 2 | 2 | 1 | 60 | 62 |
| Harvard | 1 | 1 | 0 | 16 | 10 | 13 | 1 | 0 | 588 | 26 |
| Pennsylvania | 0 | 2 | 0 | 0 | 72 | 11 | 2 | 0 | 267 | 109 |
| Princeton | 2 | 1 | 0 | 30 | 19 | 12 | 1 | 0 | 391 | 19 |
| °Yale | 3 | 0 | 0 | 77 | 0 | 13 | 0 | 0 | 488 | 0 |

### 1892

| | League | | | | | Overall | | | | |
|---|---|---|---|---|---|---|---|---|---|---|
| | W | L | T | PF | PA | W | L | T | PF | PA |
| Brown | 0 | 0 | 0 | – | – | 4 | 5 | 1 | 60 | 86 |
| Cornell | 0 | 1 | 0 | 14 | 20 | 10 | 1 | 0 | 434 | 54 |
| Dartmouth | 0 | 1 | 0 | 0 | 48 | 5 | 3 | 0 | 102 | 146 |
| Harvard | 2 | 1 | 0 | 68 | 20 | 10 | 1 | 0 | 365 | 42 |
| Pennsylvania | 1 | 1 | 0 | 6 | 32 | 15 | 1 | 0 | 405 | 52 |
| Princeton | 0 | 2 | 0 | 4 | 18 | 12 | 2 | 0 | 433 | 18 |
| °Yale | 3 | 0 | 0 | 46 | 0 | 13 | 0 | 0 | 435 | 0 |

Note: Columbia did not play football from 1892-98.

### 1893

| | League | | | | | Overall | | | | |
|---|---|---|---|---|---|---|---|---|---|---|
| | W | L | T | PF | PA | W | L | T | PF | PA |
| Brown | 0 | 2 | 0 | 0 | 76 | 6 | 3 | 0 | 168 | 88 |
| Cornell | 0 | 3 | 0 | 0 | 130 | 4 | 6 | 1 | 110 | 172 |
| Dartmouth | 0 | 3 | 0 | 0 | 80 | 4 | 3 | 0 | 84 | 90 |
| Harvard | 5 | 1 | 0 | 170 | 10 | 12 | 1 | 0 | 418 | 15 |
| Pennsylvania | 1 | 3 | 0 | 60 | 44 | 12 | 3 | 0 | 484 | 62 |
| °Princeton | 3 | 0 | 0 | 56 | 0 | 11 | 0 | 0 | 270 | 14 |
| Yale | 4 | 1 | 0 | 66 | 12 | 10 | 1 | 0 | 330 | 12 |

### 1894

| | League | | | | | Overall | | | | |
|---|---|---|---|---|---|---|---|---|---|---|
| | W | L | T | PF | PA | W | L | T | PF | PA |
| Brown | 1 | 4 | 0 | 24 | 80 | 10 | 5 | 0 | 264 | 102 |
| Cornell | 0 | 3 | 0 | 16 | 40 | 6 | 4 | 1 | 174 | 58 |
| Dartmouth | 0 | 3 | 0 | 4 | 76 | 5 | 4 | 0 | 112 | 80 |
| Harvard | 4 | 2 | 0 | 88 | 46 | 11 | 2 | 0 | 334 | 46 |
| Pennsylvania | 3 | 0 | 0 | 36 | 4 | 12 | 0 | 0 | 304 | 20 |
| Princeton | 1 | 2 | 0 | 12 | 40 | 8 | 2 | 0 | 208 | 44 |
| °Yale | 5 | 0 | 0 | 100 | 4 | 16 | 0 | 0 | 485 | 13 |

**1895**

| | League | | | | | Overall | | | | |
|---|---|---|---|---|---|---|---|---|---|---|
| | W | L | T | PF | PA | W | L | T | PF | PA |
| Brown | 1 | 4 | 1 | 26 | 58 | 7 | 6 | 1 | 150 | 109 |
| Cornell | 1 | 3 | 0 | 8 | 81 | 3 | 4 | 1 | 28 | 91 |
| Dartmouth | 0 | 4 | 0 | 4 | 72 | 7 | 5 | 1 | 184 | 99 |
| Harvard | 3 | 2 | 0 | 73 | 35 | 8 | 2 | 1 | 179 | 35 |
| °Pennsylvania | 3 | 0 | 0 | 75 | 16 | 14 | 0 | 0 | 480 | 24 |
| Princeton | 2 | 1 | 0 | 28 | 24 | 10 | 1 | 1 | 224 | 28 |
| Yale | 4 | 0 | 1 | 88 | 16 | 13 | 0 | 2 | 316 | 38 |

**1896**

| | League | | | | | Overall | | | | |
|---|---|---|---|---|---|---|---|---|---|---|
| | W | L | T | PF | PA | W | L | T | PF | PA |
| Brown | 0 | 4 | 1 | 16 | 74 | 4 | 5 | 1 | 126 | 100 |
| Cornell | 0 | 3 | 0 | 14 | 82 | 5 | 3 | 1 | 162 | 82 |
| Dartmouth | 0 | 2 | 1 | 10 | 68 | 5 | 2 | 1 | 122 | 84 |
| Harvard | 2 | 2 | 0 | 31 | 24 | 7 | 4 | 0 | 132 | 40 |
| °Pennsylvania | 4 | 0 | 0 | 72 | 16 | 14 | 1 | 0 | 326 | 24 |
| Princeton | 3 | 0 | 0 | 73 | 6 | 10 | 0 | 1 | 299 | 12 |
| Yale | 3 | 1 | 0 | 84 | 30 | 13 | 1 | 0 | 218 | 44 |

**1897**

| | League | | | | | Overall | | | | |
|---|---|---|---|---|---|---|---|---|---|---|
| | W | L | T | PF | PA | W | L | T | PF | PA |
| Brown | 0 | 3 | 0 | 14 | 76 | 7 | 4 | 0 | 180 | 152 |
| Cornell | 0 | 3 | 0 | 5 | 38 | 5 | 3 | 1 | 133 | 42 |
| Dartmouth | 0 | 3 | 0 | 0 | 77 | 4 | 3 | 0 | 164 | 77 |
| Harvard | 3 | 1 | 1 | 61 | 20 | 10 | 1 | 1 | 233 | 20 |
| °Pennsylvania | 4 | 0 | 0 | 93 | 6 | 15 | 0 | 0 | 463 | 20 |
| Princeton | 2 | 1 | 0 | 40 | 6 | 10 | 1 | 0 | 339 | 6 |
| Yale | 2 | 0 | 1 | 24 | 14 | 9 | 0 | 2 | 170 | 35 |

**1898**

| | League | | | | | Overall | | | | |
|---|---|---|---|---|---|---|---|---|---|---|
| | W | L | T | PF | PA | W | L | T | PF | PA |
| Brown | 1 | 4 | 0 | 24 | 80 | 6 | 4 | 0 | 136 | 96 |
| Cornell | 0 | 2 | 0 | 6 | 18 | 10 | 2 | 0 | 296 | 29 |
| Dartmouth | 0 | 2 | 0 | 0 | 33 | 5 | 6 | 0 | 205 | 134 |
| °Harvard | 4 | 0 | 0 | 65 | 6 | 11 | 0 | 0 | 257 | 19 |
| Pennsylvania | 2 | 1 | 0 | 30 | 16 | 12 | 1 | 0 | 358 | 32 |
| Princeton | 3 | 0 | 0 | 35 | 0 | 11 | 0 | 1 | 266 | 5 |
| Yale | 1 | 2 | 0 | 22 | 29 | 9 | 2 | 0 | 146 | 34 |

**1899**

| | League | | | | | Overall | | | | |
|---|---|---|---|---|---|---|---|---|---|---|
| | W | L | T | PF | PA | W | L | T | PF | PA |
| Brown | 1 | 2 | 1 | 28 | 40 | 7 | 3 | 1 | 175 | 57 |
| Columbia | 2 | 2 | 0 | 27 | 40 | 8 | 3 | 0 | 196 | 85 |
| Cornell | 2 | 1 | 0 | 34 | 29 | 7 | 3 | 0 | 134 | 52 |
| Dartmouth | 0 | 4 | 0 | 5 | 61 | 2 | 7 | 0 | 70 | 99 |
| °Harvard | 3 | 0 | 1 | 38 | 0 | 10 | 0 | 1 | 210 | 10 |
| Pennsylvania | 1 | 1 | 1 | 35 | 22 | 8 | 3 | 2 | 268 | 81 |
| Princeton | 3 | 1 | 0 | 40 | 21 | 12 | 1 | 0 | 185 | 21 |
| Yale | 1 | 2 | 1 | 22 | 16 | 7 | 2 | 1 | 191 | 16 |

**1900**

| | League | | | | | Overall | | | | |
|---|---|---|---|---|---|---|---|---|---|---|
| | W | L | T | PF | PA | W | L | T | PF | PA |
| Brown | 1 | 3 | 0 | 23 | 45 | 7 | 3 | 1 | 143 | 67 |
| Columbia | 1 | 3 | 0 | 11 | 71 | 7 | 3 | 1 | 124 | 77 |
| Cornell | 2 | 1 | 0 | 35 | 33 | 10 | 2 | 0 | 167 | 55 |
| Dartmouth | 0 | 3 | 0 | 11 | 52 | 2 | 4 | 2 | 38 | 68 |
| Harvard | 3 | 1 | 0 | 52 | 39 | 10 | 1 | 0 | 205 | 44 |
| Pennsylvania | 3 | 1 | 0 | 79 | 22 | 12 | 1 | 0 | 335 | 45 |
| Princeton | 1 | 3 | 0 | 27 | 52 | 8 | 3 | 0 | 169 | 57 |
| °Yale | 4 | 0 | 0 | 86 | 10 | 12 | 0 | 0 | 336 | 10 |

### 1901

| | League W | League L | League T | League PF | League PA | Overall W | Overall L | Overall T | Overall PF | Overall PA |
|---|---|---|---|---|---|---|---|---|---|---|
| Brown | 0 | 4 | 0 | 0 | 131 | 4 | 7 | 1 | 70 | 212 |
| Columbia | 1 | 3 | 0 | 15 | 52 | 8 | 5 | 0 | 157 | 91 |
| Cornell | 2 | 1 | 0 | 53 | 14 | 11 | 1 | 0 | 333 | 14 |
| Dartmouth | 1 | 1 | 0 | 34 | 27 | 9 | 1 | 0 | 240 | 46 |
| °Harvard | 5 | 0 | 0 | 148 | 18 | 12 | 0 | 0 | 254 | 24 |
| Pennsylvania | 1 | 3 | 0 | 38 | 66 | 10 | 5 | 0 | 203 | 121 |
| Princeton | 2 | 1 | 0 | 43 | 18 | 9 | 1 | 1 | 247 | 24 |
| Yale | 2 | 1 | 0 | 22 | 27 | 11 | 1 | 1 | 251 | 37 |

### 1902

| | League W | League L | League T | League PF | League PA | Overall W | Overall L | Overall T | Overall PF | Overall PA |
|---|---|---|---|---|---|---|---|---|---|---|
| Brown | 2 | 3 | 0 | 49 | 34 | 5 | 4 | 1 | 115 | 52 |
| Columbia | 0 | 3 | 0 | 0 | 66 | 6 | 4 | 1 | 163 | 101 |
| Cornell | 0 | 2 | 0 | 11 | 22 | 8 | 3 | 0 | 324 | 38 |
| Dartmouth | 1 | 1 | 0 | 18 | 22 | 6 | 2 | 1 | 105 | 44 |
| Harvard | 3 | 1 | 0 | 33 | 29 | 11 | 1 | 0 | 184 | 46 |
| Pennsylvania | 2 | 2 | 0 | 35 | 37 | 9 | 4 | 0 | 157 | 68 |
| Princeton | 2 | 1 | 0 | 36 | 12 | 8 | 1 | 0 | 164 | 17 |
| °Yale | 3 | 0 | 0 | 45 | 5 | 11 | 0 | 1 | 286 | 22 |

### 1903

| | League W | League L | League T | League PF | League PA | Overall W | Overall L | Overall T | Overall PF | Overall PA |
|---|---|---|---|---|---|---|---|---|---|---|
| Brown | 0 | 4 | 0 | 0 | 150 | 5 | 4 | 1 | 98 | 161 |
| Columbia | 2 | 1 | 0 | 35 | 43 | 9 | 1 | 0 | 148 | 43 |
| Cornell | 0 | 3 | 0 | 12 | 103 | 6 | 3 | 1 | 120 | 103 |
| Dartmouth | 2 | 1 | 0 | 73 | 17 | 9 | 1 | 0 | 242 | 23 |
| Harvard | 2 | 2 | 0 | 46 | 37 | 9 | 3 | 0 | 150 | 59 |
| Pennsylvania | 2 | 2 | 0 | 88 | 35 | 9 | 3 | 0 | 370 | 57 |
| °Princeton | 4 | 0 | 0 | 101 | 6 | 11 | 0 | 0 | 259 | 6 |
| Yale | 2 | 1 | 0 | 47 | 11 | 11 | 1 | 0 | 312 | 26 |

### 1904

| | League W | League L | League T | League PF | League PA | Overall W | Overall L | Overall T | Overall PF | Overall PA |
|---|---|---|---|---|---|---|---|---|---|---|
| Brown | 0 | 3 | 0 | 5 | 40 | 6 | 5 | 0 | 181 | 51 |
| Columbia | 1 | 2 | 0 | 12 | 56 | 7 | 3 | 0 | 120 | 68 |
| Cornell | 0 | 3 | 0 | 12 | 64 | 7 | 3 | 0 | 226 | 92 |
| Dartmouth | 1 | 0 | 1 | 12 | 5 | 7 | 0 | 1 | 143 | 13 |
| Harvard | 0 | 2 | 1 | 0 | 23 | 7 | 2 | 1 | 119 | 28 |
| °Pennsylvania | 4 | 0 | 0 | 67 | 0 | 12 | 0 | 0 | 222 | 4 |
| Princeton | 1 | 1 | 0 | 18 | 18 | 8 | 2 | 0 | 181 | 34 |
| °Yale | 4 | 0 | 0 | 80 | 0 | 10 | 1 | 0 | 220 | 20 |

### 1905

| | League W | League L | League T | League PF | League PA | Overall W | Overall L | Overall T | Overall PF | Overall PA |
|---|---|---|---|---|---|---|---|---|---|---|
| Brown | 0 | 4 | 0 | 12 | 53 | 7 | 4 | 0 | 281 | 58 |
| Columbia | 1 | 3 | 0 | 12 | 94 | 4 | 3 | 2 | 77 | 109 |
| Cornell | 0 | 3 | 0 | 17 | 34 | 6 | 4 | 0 | 173 | 59 |
| Dartmouth | 2 | 0 | 1 | 36 | 12 | 7 | 1 | 2 | 150 | 34 |
| Harvard | 1 | 2 | 1 | 22 | 24 | 8 | 2 | 1 | 147 | 41 |
| °Pennsylvania | 4 | 0 | 0 | 49 | 17 | 12 | 0 | 1 | 259 | 33 |
| Princeton | 2 | 2 | 0 | 32 | 35 | 8 | 2 | 0 | 229 | 45 |
| °Yale | 4 | 0 | 0 | 93 | 4 | 10 | 0 | 0 | 227 | 4 |

### 1906

| | League W | League L | League T | League PF | League PA | Overall W | Overall L | Overall T | Overall PF | Overall PA |
|---|---|---|---|---|---|---|---|---|---|---|
| Brown | 1 | 3 | 0 | 28 | 28 | 6 | 3 | 0 | 113 | 32 |
| Cornell | 0 | 1 | 1 | 5 | 14 | 8 | 1 | 2 | 237 | 37 |
| Dartmouth | 0 | 3 | 0 | 9 | 87 | 6 | 3 | 1 | 72 | 87 |
| Harvard | 2 | 1 | 0 | 31 | 20 | 10 | 1 | 0 | 167 | 26 |
| Pennsylvania | 1 | 0 | 1 | 14 | 0 | 7 | 2 | 3 | 186 | 58 |
| °Princeton | 2 | 0 | 1 | 56 | 5 | 9 | 0 | 1 | 205 | 9 |
| °Yale | 2 | 0 | 1 | 11 | 0 | 9 | 0 | 1 | 144 | 6 |

Note: From 1906-14, football was banned at Columbia.

**1907**

| | League | | | | | Overall | | | | |
|---|---|---|---|---|---|---|---|---|---|---|
| | W | L | T | PF | PA | W | L | T | PF | PA |
| Brown | 0 | 3 | 0 | 5 | 39 | 7 | 3 | 0 | 166 | 50 |
| Cornell | 1 | 1 | 0 | 10 | 17 | 8 | 2 | 0 | 176 | 45 |
| Dartmouth | 1 | 0 | 0 | 22 | 0 | 8 | 0 | 1 | 150 | 10 |
| Harvard | 1 | 2 | 0 | 6 | 39 | 7 | 3 | 0 | 122 | 71 |
| Pennsylvania | 2 | 0 | 0 | 23 | 4 | 11 | 1 | 0 | 256 | 41 |
| Princeton | 0 | 2 | 0 | 15 | 18 | 7 | 2 | 0 | 282 | 23 |
| °Yale | 3 | 0 | 0 | 46 | 10 | 9 | 0 | 1 | 206 | 10 |

**1908**

| | League | | | | | Overall | | | | |
|---|---|---|---|---|---|---|---|---|---|---|
| | W | L | T | PF | PA | W | L | T | PF | PA |
| Brown | 0 | 2 | 1 | 12 | 28 | 5 | 3 | 1 | 117 | 40 |
| Cornell | 0 | 1 | 0 | 4 | 17 | 7 | 1 | 1 | 96 | 43 |
| Dartmouth | 1 | 1 | 0 | 10 | 12 | 6 | 1 | 1 | 97 | 17 |
| °Harvard | 3 | 0 | 0 | 16 | 2 | 9 | 0 | 1 | 132 | 8 |
| Pennsylvania | 2 | 0 | 0 | 29 | 4 | 11 | 0 | 1 | 215 | 18 |
| Princeton | 0 | 2 | 0 | 12 | 21 | 5 | 2 | 3 | 84 | 25 |
| Yale | 1 | 1 | 1 | 21 | 20 | 7 | 1 | 1 | 153 | 20 |

**1909**

| | League | | | | | Overall | | | | |
|---|---|---|---|---|---|---|---|---|---|---|
| | W | L | T | PF | PA | W | L | T | PF | PA |
| Brown | 0 | 3 | 0 | 5 | 47 | 7 | 3 | 0 | 102 | 58 |
| Cornell | 0 | 2 | 0 | 6 | 35 | 3 | 4 | 1 | 66 | 65 |
| Dartmouth | 0 | 1 | 1 | 9 | 18 | 5 | 1 | 2 | 89 | 18 |
| Harvard | 3 | 1 | 0 | 41 | 11 | 8 | 1 | 0 | 103 | 17 |
| Pennsylvania | 2 | 0 | 0 | 30 | 11 | 7 | 1 | 2 | 146 | 38 |
| Princeton | 0 | 1 | 1 | 6 | 23 | 6 | 2 | 1 | 101 | 50 |
| °Yale | 3 | 0 | 0 | 48 | 0 | 10 | 0 | 0 | 209 | 0 |

**1910**

| | League | | | | | Overall | | | | |
|---|---|---|---|---|---|---|---|---|---|---|
| | W | L | T | PF | PA | W | L | T | PF | PA |
| Brown | 1 | 2 | 0 | 21 | 32 | 7 | 2 | 1 | 198 | 47 |
| Cornell | 0 | 2 | 0 | 11 | 39 | 5 | 2 | 1 | 165 | 44 |
| Dartmouth | 0 | 2 | 0 | 0 | 24 | 5 | 2 | 0 | 111 | 27 |
| Harvard | 3 | 0 | 1 | 57 | 5 | 8 | 0 | 1 | 155 | 5 |
| °Pennsylvania | 2 | 0 | 0 | 32 | 6 | 9 | 1 | 1 | 184 | 14 |
| Princeton | 1 | 1 | 0 | 9 | 5 | 7 | 1 | 0 | 101 | 5 |
| Yale | 1 | 1 | 1 | 5 | 24 | 6 | 2 | 2 | 90 | 39 |

**1911**

| | League | | | | | Overall | | | | |
|---|---|---|---|---|---|---|---|---|---|---|
| | W | L | T | PF | PA | W | L | T | PF | PA |
| Brown | 1 | 2 | 0 | 12 | 35 | 7 | 3 | 1 | 187 | 53 |
| Cornell | 0 | 1 | 0 | 9 | 21 | 7 | 3 | 0 | 101 | 52 |
| Dartmouth | 0 | 2 | 0 | 3 | 8 | 8 | 2 | 0 | 137 | 22 |
| Harvard | 2 | 1 | 1 | 31 | 17 | 6 | 2 | 1 | 98 | 35 |
| Pennsylvania | 1 | 1 | 0 | 21 | 15 | 7 | 4 | 0 | 131 | 83 |
| °Princeton | 3 | 0 | 0 | 17 | 9 | 8 | 0 | 2 | 179 | 15 |
| Yale | 1 | 1 | 1 | 18 | 6 | 7 | 2 | 1 | 161 | 15 |

**1912**

| | League | | | | | Overall | | | | |
|---|---|---|---|---|---|---|---|---|---|---|
| | W | L | T | PF | PA | W | L | T | PF | PA |
| Brown | 1 | 2 | 0 | 40 | 47 | 6 | 4 | 0 | 117 | 107 |
| Cornell | 0 | 2 | 0 | 2 | 31 | 3 | 7 | 0 | 63 | 136 |
| Dartmouth | 1 | 2 | 0 | 31 | 25 | 7 | 2 | 0 | 281 | 34 |
| °Harvard | 4 | 0 | 0 | 69 | 16 | 9 | 0 | 0 | 176 | 22 |
| Pennsylvania | 1 | 1 | 0 | 14 | 32 | 7 | 4 | 0 | 201 | 106 |
| Princeton | 1 | 1 | 1 | 34 | 29 | 7 | 1 | 1 | 322 | 35 |
| Yale | 1 | 1 | 1 | 16 | 26 | 7 | 1 | 1 | 89 | 32 |

## 1913

| | League | | | | | Overall | | | | |
|---|---|---|---|---|---|---|---|---|---|---|
| | W | L | T | PF | PA | W | L | T | PF | PA |
| Brown | 0 | 3 | 0 | 0 | 82 | 4 | 5 | 0 | 70 | 111 |
| Cornell | 1 | 1 | 0 | 27 | 23 | 5 | 4 | 1 | 132 | 89 |
| Dartmouth | 2 | 0 | 0 | 40 | 21 | 7 | 1 | 0 | 218 | 79 |
| °Harvard | 4 | 0 | 0 | 78 | 11 | 9 | 0 | 0 | 225 | 21 |
| Pennsylvania | 1 | 2 | 0 | 49 | 55 | 6 | 3 | 1 | 169 | 81 |
| Princeton | 0 | 2 | 1 | 3 | 12 | 5 | 2 | 1 | 181 | 21 |
| Yale | 1 | 1 | 1 | 25 | 18 | 5 | 2 | 3 | 126 | 34 |

## 1914

| | League | | | | | Overall | | | | |
|---|---|---|---|---|---|---|---|---|---|---|
| | W | L | T | PF | PA | W | L | T | PF | PA |
| Brown | 0 | 2 | 1 | 13 | 42 | 5 | 2 | 2 | 105 | 65 |
| °Cornell | 2 | 0 | 0 | 52 | 19 | 8 | 2 | 0 | 257 | 54 |
| Dartmouth | 1 | 1 | 0 | 53 | 16 | 8 | 1 | 0 | 359 | 25 |
| Harvard | 2 | 0 | 1 | 56 | 0 | 7 | 0 | 2 | 187 | 28 |
| Pennsylvania | 0 | 2 | 0 | 12 | 65 | 4 | 4 | 1 | 89 | 121 |
| Princeton | 1 | 2 | 0 | 30 | 51 | 5 | 2 | 1 | 87 | 65 |
| Yale | 2 | 1 | 0 | 33 | 56 | 7 | 2 | 0 | 178 | 79 |

## 1915

| | League | | | | | Overall | | | | |
|---|---|---|---|---|---|---|---|---|---|---|
| | W | L | T | PF | PA | W | L | T | PF | PA |
| Brown | 1 | 1 | 0 | 10 | 16 | 5 | 4 | 1 | 166 | 46 |
| Columbia | 0 | 0 | 0 | – | – | 5 | 0 | 0 | 126 | 28 |
| °Cornell | 2 | 0 | 0 | 34 | 9 | 9 | 0 | 0 | 287 | 50 |
| Dartmouth | 1 | 1 | 0 | 14 | 33 | 7 | 1 | 1 | 196 | 40 |
| Harvard | 3 | 1 | 0 | 67 | 23 | 8 | 1 | 0 | 164 | 36 |
| Pennsylvania | 0 | 2 | 0 | 12 | 31 | 3 | 5 | 2 | 109 | 88 |
| Princeton | 1 | 2 | 0 | 43 | 30 | 6 | 2 | 0 | 136 | 33 |
| Yale | 1 | 2 | 0 | 13 | 51 | 4 | 5 | 0 | 83 | 98 |

## 1916

| | League | | | | | Overall | | | | |
|---|---|---|---|---|---|---|---|---|---|---|
| | W | L | T | PF | PA | W | L | T | PF | PA |
| °Brown | 2 | 0 | 0 | 42 | 6 | 8 | 1 | 0 | 254 | 37 |
| Columbia | 0 | 0 | 0 | – | – | 1 | 5 | 2 | 13 | 81 |
| Cornell | 0 | 2 | 0 | 3 | 46 | 6 | 2 | 0 | 165 | 73 |
| Dartmouth | 0 | 1 | 1 | 10 | 14 | 5 | 2 | 2 | 206 | 47 |
| Harvard | 2 | 2 | 0 | 29 | 27 | 7 | 3 | 0 | 187 | 34 |
| Pennsylvania | 1 | 0 | 1 | 30 | 10 | 7 | 3 | 1 | 120 | 57 |
| Princeton | 1 | 2 | 0 | 7 | 16 | 6 | 2 | 0 | 135 | 16 |
| Yale | 2 | 1 | 0 | 22 | 24 | 8 | 1 | 0 | 182 | 44 |

## 1917

| | League | | | | | Overall | | | | |
|---|---|---|---|---|---|---|---|---|---|---|
| | W | L | T | PF | PA | W | L | T | PF | PA |
| Brown | 1 | 0 | 0 | 13 | 0 | 8 | 2 | 0 | 160 | 62 |
| Columbia | 0 | 0 | 0 | – | – | 2 | 4 | 0 | 110 | 38 |
| Cornell | 0 | 1 | 0 | 0 | 37 | 3 | 6 | 0 | 78 | 146 |
| Dartmouth | 0 | 2 | 0 | 0 | 20 | 5 | 3 | 0 | 83 | 68 |
| Harvard | 0 | 0 | 0 | – | – | 3 | 1 | 3 | 75 | 14 |
| °Pennsylvania | 2 | 0 | 0 | 44 | 0 | 9 | 2 | 0 | 245 | 71 |
| Princeton | 0 | 0 | 0 | – | – | 2 | 0 | 0 | 50 | 0 |
| Yale | 0 | 0 | 0 | – | – | 3 | 0 | 0 | 47 | 0 |

## 1918

| | League | | | | | Overall | | | | |
|---|---|---|---|---|---|---|---|---|---|---|
| | W | L | T | PF | PA | W | L | T | PF | PA |
| °Brown | 2 | 0 | 0 | 34 | 3 | 2 | 3 | 0 | 48 | 98 |
| Columbia | 0 | 0 | 0 | – | – | 5 | 1 | 0 | 87 | 27 |
| Dartmouth | 0 | 2 | 0 | 0 | 49 | 3 | 3 | 0 | 78 | 83 |
| Harvard | 0 | 1 | 0 | 3 | 6 | 2 | 1 | 0 | 24 | 12 |
| Pennsylvania | 1 | 0 | 0 | 21 | 0 | 5 | 3 | 0 | 105 | 77 |
| Princeton | 0 | 0 | 0 | – | – | 3 | 0 | 0 | 61 | 7 |

Note: Cornell and Yale did not field teams in 1918.

### 1919

| | League | | | | | Overall | | | | |
|---|---|---|---|---|---|---|---|---|---|---|
| | W | L | T | PF | PA | W | L | T | PF | PA |
| Brown | 1 | 2 | 1 | 14 | 34 | 5 | 4 | 1 | 74 | 61 |
| Columbia | 0 | 0 | 1 | 7 | 7 | 2 | 4 | 3 | 48 | 107 |
| Cornell | 0 | 2 | 0 | 0 | 33 | 3 | 5 | 0 | 34 | 95 |
| Dartmouth | 2 | 1 | 0 | 35 | 26 | 6 | 1 | 1 | 141 | 53 |
| °Harvard | 2 | 0 | 1 | 27 | 13 | 9 | 0 | 1 | 229 | 19 |
| Pennsylvania | 1 | 1 | 0 | 43 | 20 | 6 | 2 | 1 | 283 | 40 |
| Princeton | 1 | 0 | 1 | 23 | 16 | 4 | 2 | 1 | 94 | 54 |
| Yale | 1 | 2 | 0 | 23 | 23 | 5 | 3 | 0 | 148 | 35 |

### 1920

| | League | | | | | Overall | | | | |
|---|---|---|---|---|---|---|---|---|---|---|
| | W | L | T | PF | PA | W | L | T | PF | PA |
| Brown | 0 | 3 | 0 | 16 | 55 | 6 | 3 | 0 | 149 | 62 |
| Columbia | 0 | 2 | 0 | 14 | 61 | 4 | 4 | 0 | 96 | 120 |
| Cornell | 1 | 2 | 0 | 37 | 49 | 6 | 2 | 0 | 231 | 68 |
| °Dartmouth | 3 | 0 | 0 | 72 | 16 | 7 | 2 | 0 | 199 | 68 |
| Harvard | 2 | 0 | 1 | 50 | 14 | 8 | 0 | 1 | 208 | 28 |
| Pennsylvania | 2 | 1 | 0 | 62 | 51 | 6 | 4 | 0 | 167 | 133 |
| Princeton | 1 | 0 | 1 | 34 | 14 | 6 | 0 | 1 | 144 | 23 |
| Yale | 1 | 2 | 0 | 14 | 39 | 5 | 3 | 0 | 137 | 67 |

### 1921

| | League | | | | | Overall | | | | |
|---|---|---|---|---|---|---|---|---|---|---|
| | W | L | T | PF | PA | W | L | T | PF | PA |
| Brown | 0 | 2 | 0 | 14 | 54 | 5 | 3 | 1 | 107 | 89 |
| Columbia | 0 | 2 | 0 | 14 | 72 | 2 | 6 | 0 | 89 | 148 |
| °Cornell | 3 | 0 | 0 | 141 | 14 | 8 | 0 | 0 | 392 | 21 |
| Dartmouth | 1 | 1 | 1 | 52 | 80 | 6 | 2 | 1 | 166 | 103 |
| Harvard | 2 | 1 | 0 | 22 | 20 | 7 | 2 | 1 | 101 | 54 |
| Pennsylvania | 0 | 1 | 1 | 14 | 55 | 4 | 3 | 2 | 164 | 135 |
| Princeton | 1 | 1 | 0 | 17 | 16 | 4 | 3 | 0 | 91 | 45 |
| Yale | 2 | 1 | 0 | 61 | 24 | 8 | 1 | 0 | 202 | 31 |

### 1922

| | League | | | | | Overall | | | | |
|---|---|---|---|---|---|---|---|---|---|---|
| | W | L | T | PF | PA | W | L | T | PF | PA |
| Brown | 1 | 2 | 0 | 3 | 27 | 6 | 2 | 1 | 92 | 47 |
| Columbia | 0 | 2 | 0 | 7 | 84 | 5 | 4 | 0 | 147 | 183 |
| °Cornell | 3 | 0 | 0 | 88 | 0 | 8 | 0 | 0 | 339 | 27 |
| Dartmouth | 2 | 2 | 0 | 38 | 42 | 6 | 3 | 0 | 111 | 55 |
| Harvard | 2 | 2 | 0 | 25 | 19 | 7 | 2 | 0 | 128 | 29 |
| Pennsylvania | 0 | 1 | 0 | 0 | 9 | 6 | 3 | 0 | 100 | 38 |
| Princeton | 2 | 0 | 0 | 13 | 3 | 8 | 0 | 0 | 127 | 34 |
| Yale | 1 | 2 | 0 | 23 | 13 | 6 | 3 | 1 | 192 | 29 |

### 1923

| | League | | | | | Overall | | | | |
|---|---|---|---|---|---|---|---|---|---|---|
| | W | L | T | PF | PA | W | L | T | PF | PA |
| Brown | 1 | 2 | 0 | 34 | 44 | 6 | 4 | 0 | 159 | 71 |
| Columbia | 0 | 3 | 0 | 13 | 85 | 4 | 4 | 1 | 68 | 107 |
| °Cornell | 3 | 0 | 0 | 81 | 14 | 8 | 0 | 0 | 320 | 33 |
| Dartmouth | 3 | 1 | 0 | 70 | 52 | 8 | 1 | 0 | 202 | 54 |
| Harvard | 1 | 3 | 0 | 12 | 49 | 4 | 3 | 1 | 75 | 55 |
| Pennsylvania | 1 | 1 | 0 | 26 | 21 | 5 | 4 | 0 | 95 | 63 |
| Princeton | 0 | 2 | 0 | 0 | 32 | 3 | 3 | 1 | 73 | 73 |
| °Yale | 3 | 0 | 0 | 61 | 0 | 8 | 0 | 0 | 230 | 38 |

### 1924

| | League | | | | | Overall | | | | |
|---|---|---|---|---|---|---|---|---|---|---|
| | W | L | T | PF | PA | W | L | T | PF | PA |
| Brown | 1 | 2 | 0 | 13 | 23 | 5 | 4 | 0 | 154 | 65 |
| Columbia | 0 | 2 | 0 | 7 | 24 | 5 | 3 | 1 | 210 | 53 |
| Cornell | 1 | 2 | 0 | 28 | 47 | 4 | 4 | 0 | 209 | 71 |
| Dartmouth | 3 | 0 | 1 | 57 | 31 | 7 | 0 | 1 | 225 | 31 |
| Harvard | 0 | 4 | 0 | 6 | 66 | 4 | 4 | 0 | 61 | 78 |
| °Pennsylvania | 2 | 0 | 0 | 30 | 7 | 9 | 1 | 1 | 203 | 31 |
| Princeton | 1 | 1 | 0 | 34 | 10 | 4 | 2 | 1 | 112 | 48 |
| Yale | 3 | 0 | 1 | 56 | 23 | 6 | 0 | 2 | 144 | 36 |

**1925**

| | League | | | | | Overall | | | | |
|---|---|---|---|---|---|---|---|---|---|---|
| | W | L | T | PF | PA | W | L | T | PF | PA |
| Brown | 0 | 4 | 0 | 7 | 46 | 5 | 4 | 1 | 215 | 80 |
| Columbia | 0 | 1 | 0 | 14 | 17 | 6 | 3 | 1 | 288 | 55 |
| Cornell | 1 | 2 | 0 | 30 | 83 | 6 | 2 | 0 | 258 | 83 |
| °Dartmouth | 3 | 0 | 0 | 108 | 22 | 8 | 0 | 0 | 340 | 29 |
| Harvard | 1 | 2 | 1 | 12 | 68 | 4 | 3 | 1 | 118 | 88 |
| °Pennsylvania | 3 | 0 | 0 | 32 | 13 | 7 | 2 | 0 | 165 | 64 |
| Princeton | 2 | 0 | 0 | 61 | 12 | 5 | 1 | 1 | 125 | 44 |
| Yale | 1 | 2 | 1 | 45 | 48 | 5 | 2 | 1 | 204 | 76 |

**1926**

| | League | | | | | Overall | | | | |
|---|---|---|---|---|---|---|---|---|---|---|
| | W | L | T | PF | PA | W | L | T | PF | PA |
| °Brown | 3 | 0 | 0 | 38 | 0 | 9 | 0 | 1 | 223 | 36 |
| Columbia | 1 | 1 | 0 | 17 | 12 | 6 | 3 | 0 | 144 | 73 |
| Cornell | 1 | 1 | 1 | 43 | 50 | 6 | 1 | 1 | 191 | 64 |
| Dartmouth | 0 | 4 | 0 | 42 | 64 | 4 | 4 | 0 | 203 | 64 |
| Harvard | 1 | 3 | 0 | 23 | 57 | 3 | 5 | 0 | 140 | 105 |
| Pennsylvania | 1 | 0 | 1 | 13 | 10 | 7 | 1 | 1 | 204 | 20 |
| Princeton | 2 | 0 | 0 | 22 | 7 | 5 | 1 | 1 | 90 | 54 |
| Yale | 2 | 2 | 0 | 33 | 31 | 4 | 4 | 0 | 103 | 79 |

**1927**

| | League | | | | | Overall | | | | |
|---|---|---|---|---|---|---|---|---|---|---|
| | W | L | T | PF | PA | W | L | T | PF | PA |
| Brown | 0 | 4 | 0 | 19 | 70 | 3 | 6 | 1 | 109 | 103 |
| Columbia | 0 | 1 | 1 | 0 | 27 | 5 | 2 | 2 | 135 | 54 |
| Cornell | 0 | 3 | 1 | 17 | 109 | 3 | 3 | 2 | 136 | 121 |
| Dartmouth | 3 | 1 | 0 | 102 | 39 | 7 | 1 | 0 | 280 | 53 |
| Harvard | 1 | 3 | 0 | 24 | 74 | 4 | 4 | 0 | 85 | 108 |
| Pennsylvania | 4 | 0 | 0 | 100 | 6 | 6 | 4 | 0 | 167 | 78 |
| Princeton | 1 | 1 | 0 | 27 | 24 | 6 | 1 | 0 | 151 | 31 |
| °Yale | 4 | 0 | 0 | 66 | 6 | 7 | 1 | 0 | 157 | 32 |

**1928**

| | League | | | | | Overall | | | | |
|---|---|---|---|---|---|---|---|---|---|---|
| | W | L | T | PF | PA | W | L | T | PF | PA |
| Brown | 1 | 1 | 0 | 28 | 32 | 8 | 1 | 0 | 167 | 72 |
| Columbia | 0 | 2 | 1 | 14 | 55 | 5 | 3 | 1 | 132 | 95 |
| Cornell | 0 | 3 | 1 | 0 | 80 | 3 | 3 | 2 | 72 | 86 |
| Dartmouth | 2 | 3 | 0 | 56 | 58 | 5 | 4 | 0 | 182 | 103 |
| Harvard | 2 | 1 | 0 | 36 | 14 | 5 | 2 | 1 | 125 | 29 |
| °Pennsylvania | 3 | 0 | 0 | 90 | 7 | 8 | 1 | 0 | 271 | 26 |
| Princeton | 2 | 0 | 0 | 15 | 2 | 5 | 1 | 2 | 143 | 29 |
| Yale | 2 | 2 | 0 | 52 | 43 | 4 | 4 | 0 | 106 | 73 |

**1929**

| | League | | | | | Overall | | | | |
|---|---|---|---|---|---|---|---|---|---|---|
| | W | L | T | PF | PA | W | L | T | PF | PA |
| Brown | 1 | 2 | 0 | 25 | 39 | 5 | 5 | 0 | 140 | 117 |
| Columbia | 0 | 3 | 0 | 6 | 66 | 4 | 5 | 0 | 160 | 111 |
| Cornell | 2 | 2 | 0 | 46 | 48 | 6 | 2 | 0 | 204 | 60 |
| Dartmouth | 4 | 1 | 0 | 111 | 43 | 7 | 2 | 0 | 305 | 56 |
| Harvard | 1 | 1 | 0 | 17 | 40 | 5 | 2 | 1 | 158 | 30 |
| °Pennsylvania | 2 | 0 | 0 | 37 | 7 | 7 | 2 | 0 | 116 | 68 |
| Princeton | 0 | 3 | 0 | 19 | 39 | 2 | 4 | 1 | 66 | 67 |
| Yale | 3 | 1 | 0 | 49 | 28 | 5 | 2 | 1 | 172 | 69 |

**1930**

| | League | | | | | Overall | | | | |
|---|---|---|---|---|---|---|---|---|---|---|
| | W | L | T | PF | PA | W | L | T | PF | PA |
| Brown | 2 | 1 | 0 | 13 | 21 | 6 | 3 | 1 | 135 | 78 |
| Columbia | 1 | 2 | 0 | 10 | 65 | 5 | 4 | 0 | 141 | 138 |
| Cornell | 2 | 2 | 0 | 45 | 43 | 6 | 2 | 0 | 273 | 63 |
| °Dartmouth | 3 | 0 | 1 | 78 | 15 | 7 | 1 | 1 | 301 | 43 |
| Harvard | 1 | 1 | 0 | 15 | 7 | 4 | 4 | 1 | 126 | 59 |
| Pennsylvania | 0 | 1 | 0 | 7 | 13 | 5 | 4 | 0 | 225 | 145 |
| Princeton | 0 | 3 | 0 | 14 | 29 | 1 | 5 | 1 | 46 | 73 |
| Yale | 2 | 1 | 1 | 31 | 20 | 5 | 2 | 2 | 196 | 58 |

**1931**

| | League | | | | | Overall | | | | |
|---|---|---|---|---|---|---|---|---|---|---|
| | W | L | T | PF | PA | W | L | T | PF | PA |
| Brown | 1 | 1 | 0 | 26 | 16 | 7 | 3 | 0 | 189 | 100 |
| Columbia | 2 | 1 | 0 | 28 | 26 | 7 | 1 | 1 | 223 | 26 |
| Cornell | 3 | 1 | 0 | 53 | 14 | 7 | 1 | 0 | 239 | 20 |
| Dartmouth | 1 | 2 | 1 | 59 | 59 | 5 | 3 | 1 | 216 | 110 |
| Harvard | 1 | 1 | 0 | 7 | 9 | 7 | 1 | 0 | 149 | 29 |
| Pennsylvania | 0 | 1 | 0 | 0 | 7 | 6 | 3 | 0 | 121 | 94 |
| Princeton | 0 | 3 | 0 | 21 | 103 | 1 | 7 | 0 | 55 | 164 |
| °Yale | 2 | 0 | 1 | 87 | 47 | 5 | 1 | 2 | 198 | 79 |

**1932**

| | League | | | | | Overall | | | | |
|---|---|---|---|---|---|---|---|---|---|---|
| | W | L | T | PF | PA | W | L | T | PF | PA |
| °Brown | 3 | 0 | 0 | 28 | 8 | 7 | 1 | 0 | 81 | 42 |
| Columbia | 2 | 1 | 0 | 32 | 14 | 7 | 1 | 1 | 199 | 32 |
| Cornell | 1 | 2 | 1 | 28 | 25 | 5 | 2 | 1 | 174 | 39 |
| Dartmouth | 0 | 4 | 0 | 20 | 51 | 4 | 4 | 0 | 156 | 51 |
| Harvard | 1 | 2 | 0 | 10 | 40 | 5 | 3 | 0 | 169 | 99 |
| Pennsylvania | 2 | 0 | 0 | 27 | 14 | 6 | 2 | 0 | 178 | 58 |
| Princeton | 0 | 1 | 2 | 14 | 27 | 2 | 2 | 3 | 96 | 41 |
| Yale | 2 | 1 | 1 | 34 | 14 | 2 | 2 | 3 | 41 | 41 |

**1933**

| | League | | | | | Overall | | | | |
|---|---|---|---|---|---|---|---|---|---|---|
| | W | L | T | PF | PA | W | L | T | PF | PA |
| Brown | 0 | 3 | 0 | 12 | 59 | 3 | 5 | 0 | 68 | 116 |
| Columbia | 1 | 1 | 0 | 9 | 26 | 8 | 1 | 0 | 179 | 45 |
| Cornell | 2 | 1 | 0 | 33 | 21 | 4 | 3 | 0 | 116 | 89 |
| Dartmouth | 1 | 3 | 1 | 34 | 42 | 4 | 4 | 1 | 128 | 87 |
| Harvard | 2 | 0 | 1 | 38 | 19 | 5 | 2 | 1 | 139 | 56 |
| Pennsylvania | 0 | 2 | 0 | 19 | 34 | 2 | 4 | 1 | 57 | 80 |
| °Princeton | 4 | 0 | 0 | 87 | 2 | 9 | 0 | 0 | 217 | 8 |
| Yale | 2 | 2 | 0 | 36 | 65 | 4 | 4 | 0 | 64 | 100 |

**1934**

| | League | | | | | Overall | | | | |
|---|---|---|---|---|---|---|---|---|---|---|
| | W | L | T | PF | PA | W | L | T | PF | PA |
| Brown | 0 | 3 | 0 | 0 | 89 | 3 | 6 | 0 | 64 | 169 |
| °Columbia | 4 | 0 | 0 | 78 | 18 | 7 | 1 | 0 | 140 | 49 |
| Cornell | 1 | 3 | 0 | 34 | 88 | 2 | 5 | 0 | 55 | 114 |
| Dartmouth | 1 | 3 | 0 | 31 | 66 | 6 | 3 | 0 | 177 | 73 |
| Harvard | 1 | 3 | 0 | 13 | 43 | 3 | 5 | 0 | 84 | 99 |
| Pennsylvania | 1 | 2 | 0 | 41 | 40 | 4 | 4 | 0 | 118 | 83 |
| Princeton | 3 | 1 | 0 | 102 | 20 | 7 | 1 | 0 | 280 | 38 |
| Yale | 5 | 1 | 0 | 85 | 20 | 5 | 3 | 0 | 104 | 54 |

**1935**

| | League | | | | | Overall | | | | |
|---|---|---|---|---|---|---|---|---|---|---|
| | W | L | T | PF | PA | W | L | T | PF | PA |
| Brown | 0 | 4 | 0 | 0 | 112 | 1 | 8 | 0 | 21 | 197 |
| Columbia | 2 | 1 | 1 | 38 | 48 | 4 | 4 | 1 | 86 | 115 |
| Cornell | 0 | 3 | 1 | 20 | 135 | 0 | 6 | 1 | 59 | 201 |
| Dartmouth | 4 | 2 | 0 | 123 | 57 | 8 | 2 | 0 | 302 | 64 |
| Harvard | 1 | 3 | 0 | 46 | 63 | 3 | 5 | 0 | 107 | 89 |
| Pennsylvania | 2 | 2 | 0 | 93 | 45 | 4 | 4 | 0 | 199 | 80 |
| °Princeton | 5 | 0 | 0 | 160 | 19 | 9 | 0 | 0 | 256 | 32 |
| Yale | 3 | 2 | 0 | 78 | 79 | 6 | 3 | 0 | 182 | 99 |

**1936**

| | League | | | | | Overall | | | | |
|---|---|---|---|---|---|---|---|---|---|---|
| | W | L | T | PF | PA | W | L | T | PF | PA |
| Brown | 0 | 4 | 0 | 12 | 124 | 3 | 7 | 0 | 76 | 234 |
| Columbia | 1 | 1 | 0 | 33 | 33 | 5 | 3 | 0 | 145 | 73 |
| Cornell | 0 | 5 | 0 | 38 | 118 | 3 | 5 | 0 | 145 | 132 |
| °Dartmouth | 5 | 0 | 1 | 124 | 46 | 7 | 1 | 1 | 238 | 53 |
| Harvard | 1 | 2 | 1 | 62 | 54 | 3 | 4 | 1 | 178 | 112 |
| Pennsylvania | 3 | 1 | 0 | 69 | 19 | 7 | 1 | 0 | 166 | 44 |
| Princeton | 1 | 2 | 2 | 101 | 73 | 4 | 2 | 2 | 145 | 80 |
| Yale | 5 | 1 | 0 | 81 | 53 | 7 | 1 | 0 | 131 | 60 |

**1937**

| | League | | | | | Overall | | | | |
|---|---|---|---|---|---|---|---|---|---|---|
| | W | L | T | PF | PA | W | L | T | PF | PA |
| Brown | 1 | 3 | 0 | 14 | 100 | 5 | 4 | 0 | 73 | 119 |
| Columbia | 1 | 3 | 0 | 32 | 54 | 2 | 5 | 2 | 102 | 100 |
| Cornell | 3 | 1 | 1 | 74 | 42 | 5 | 2 | 1 | 146 | 82 |
| °Dartmouth | 4 | 0 | 2 | 136 | 26 | 7 | 0 | 2 | 248 | 33 |
| Harvard | 3 | 1 | 0 | 83 | 39 | 5 | 2 | 1 | 158 | 46 |
| Pennsylvania | 0 | 3 | 0 | 33 | 87 | 2 | 5 | 1 | 75 | 129 |
| Princeton | 0 | 4 | 0 | 22 | 113 | 4 | 4 | 0 | 96 | 126 |
| Yale | 4 | 1 | 1 | 96 | 29 | 6 | 1 | 1 | 137 | 36 |

**1938**

| | League | | | | | Overall | | | | |
|---|---|---|---|---|---|---|---|---|---|---|
| | W | L | T | PF | PA | W | L | T | PF | PA |
| Brown | 2 | 2 | 0 | 83 | 94 | 5 | 3 | 0 | 203 | 129 |
| Columbia | 1 | 3 | 0 | 74 | 87 | 3 | 6 | 0 | 154 | 144 |
| °Cornell | 3 | 0 | 1 | 57 | 14 | 5 | 1 | 1 | 110 | 45 |
| Dartmouth | 4 | 1 | 0 | 100 | 40 | 7 | 2 | 0 | 254 | 69 |
| Harvard | 2 | 3 | 0 | 53 | 60 | 4 | 4 | 0 | 157 | 106 |
| Pennsylvania | 2 | 1 | 1 | 35 | 26 | 3 | 2 | 3 | 89 | 58 |
| Princeton | 2 | 2 | 0 | 40 | 55 | 3 | 4 | 1 | 117 | 107 |
| Yale | 1 | 5 | 0 | 47 | 113 | 2 | 6 | 0 | 69 | 135 |

**1939**

| | League | | | | | Overall | | | | |
|---|---|---|---|---|---|---|---|---|---|---|
| | W | L | T | PF | PA | W | L | T | PF | PA |
| Brown | 0 | 1 | 1 | 26 | 40 | 5 | 3 | 1 | 188 | 91 |
| Columbia | 0 | 3 | 0 | 21 | 37 | 2 | 4 | 2 | 72 | 88 |
| °Cornell | 4 | 0 | 0 | 94 | 20 | 8 | 0 | 0 | 197 | 52 |
| Dartmouth | 2 | 2 | 0 | 62 | 44 | 5 | 3 | 1 | 154 | 75 |
| Harvard | 0 | 4 | 0 | 20 | 67 | 4 | 4 | 0 | 162 | 67 |
| Pennsylvania | 2 | 1 | 0 | 28 | 33 | 4 | 4 | 0 | 70 | 98 |
| Princeton | 5 | 1 | 0 | 78 | 59 | 7 | 1 | 0 | 132 | 65 |
| Yale | 2 | 3 | 1 | 51 | 80 | 3 | 4 | 1 | 78 | 122 |

**1940**

| | League | | | | | Overall | | | | |
|---|---|---|---|---|---|---|---|---|---|---|
| | W | L | T | PF | PA | W | L | T | PF | PA |
| Brown | 1 | 2 | 1 | 12 | 36 | 6 | 3 | 1 | 124 | 94 |
| Columbia | 1 | 1 | 1 | 20 | 33 | 5 | 2 | 2 | 81 | 72 |
| Cornell | 2 | 2 | 0 | 68 | 25 | 6 | 2 | 0 | 201 | 38 |
| Dartmouth | 3 | 3 | 0 | 52 | 59 | 5 | 4 | 0 | 134 | 82 |
| Harvard | 2 | 1 | 2 | 58 | 17 | 3 | 2 | 3 | 77 | 49 |
| °Pennsylvania | 3 | 0 | 1 | 128 | 65 | 6 | 1 | 1 | 247 | 79 |
| Princeton | 2 | 1 | 1 | 52 | 62 | 5 | 2 | 1 | 119 | 112 |
| Yale | 1 | 5 | 0 | 29 | 122 | 1 | 7 | 0 | 43 | 162 |

**1941**

| | League | | | | | Overall | | | | |
|---|---|---|---|---|---|---|---|---|---|---|
| | W | L | T | PF | PA | W | L | T | PF | PA |
| Brown | 1 | 2 | 0 | 20 | 36 | 5 | 4 | 0 | 102 | 81 |
| Columbia | 3 | 1 | 0 | 57 | 25 | 3 | 5 | 0 | 81 | 103 |
| Cornell | 3 | 2 | 0 | 61 | 49 | 5 | 3 | 0 | 88 | 65 |
| Dartmouth | 2 | 2 | 0 | 46 | 53 | 5 | 4 | 0 | 146 | 104 |
| Harvard | 4 | 2 | 0 | 50 | 37 | 5 | 2 | 1 | 70 | 43 |
| °Pennsylvania | 5 | 0 | 0 | 105 | 29 | 7 | 1 | 0 | 180 | 55 |
| Princeton | 1 | 4 | 0 | 37 | 76 | 2 | 6 | 0 | 64 | 152 |
| Yale | 0 | 6 | 0 | 26 | 97 | 1 | 7 | 0 | 54 | 136 |

**1942**

| | League | | | | | Overall | | | | |
|---|---|---|---|---|---|---|---|---|---|---|
| | W | L | T | PF | PA | W | L | T | PF | PA |
| Brown | 1 | 3 | 0 | 41 | 87 | 4 | 4 | 0 | 96 | 114 |
| Columbia | 1 | 3 | 0 | 60 | 109 | 3 | 6 | 0 | 174 | 193 |
| Cornell | 2 | 2 | 0 | 54 | 74 | 3 | 5 | 1 | 95 | 148 |
| Dartmouth | 3 | 2 | 0 | 85 | 60 | 5 | 4 | 0 | 193 | 135 |
| Harvard | 2 | 3 | 0 | 38 | 54 | 2 | 6 | 1 | 52 | 123 |
| °Pennsylvania | 4 | 0 | 1 | 136 | 38 | 5 | 3 | 1 | 168 | 72 |
| Princeton | 1 | 3 | 1 | 65 | 70 | 3 | 5 | 1 | 109 | 135 |
| Yale | 4 | 2 | 0 | 77 | 64 | 5 | 3 | 0 | 116 | 83 |

## 1943

| | League | | | | | Overall | | | | |
|---|---|---|---|---|---|---|---|---|---|---|
| | W | L | T | PF | PA | W | L | T | PF | PA |
| Brown | 2 | 0 | 0 | 49 | 40 | 5 | 3 | 0 | 194 | 180 |
| Columbia | 0 | 5 | 0 | 33 | 159 | 0 | 8 | 0 | 33 | 313 |
| Cornell | 2 | 2 | 0 | 77 | 46 | 6 | 4 | 0 | 158 | 138 |
| Dartmouth | 4 | 1 | 0 | 135 | 39 | 6 | 1 | 0 | 185 | 39 |
| Harvard | 0 | 0 | 0 | — | — | 2 | 2 | 1 | 34 | 39 |
| °Pennsylvania | 5 | 0 | 0 | 148 | 36 | 6 | 2 | 1 | 248 | 88 |
| Princeton | 1 | 5 | 0 | 74 | 181 | 1 | 6 | 0 | 96 | 226 |
| Yale | 2 | 3 | 0 | 80 | 95 | 4 | 5 | 0 | 132 | 166 |

## 1944

| | League | | | | | Overall | | | | |
|---|---|---|---|---|---|---|---|---|---|---|
| | W | L | T | PF | PA | W | L | T | PF | PA |
| Brown | 1 | 2 | 0 | 25 | 27 | 3 | 4 | 1 | 132 | 150 |
| Columbia | 0 | 5 | 0 | 24 | 117 | 2 | 6 | 0 | 71 | 125 |
| Cornell | 2 | 2 | 0 | 46 | 56 | 5 | 4 | 0 | 131 | 130 |
| Dartmouth | 2 | 3 | 0 | 51 | 53 | 2 | 5 | 1 | 57 | 142 |
| Harvard | 0 | 0 | 0 | — | — | 5 | 1 | 0 | 100 | 37 |
| Pennsylvania | 3 | 0 | 0 | 75 | 13 | 5 | 3 | 0 | 165 | 149 |
| Princeton | 0 | 0 | 0 | — | — | 1 | 2 | 0 | 22 | 40 |
| °Yale | 4 | 0 | 0 | 62 | 17 | 7 | 0 | 1 | 120 | 32 |

## 1945

| | League | | | | | Overall | | | | |
|---|---|---|---|---|---|---|---|---|---|---|
| | W | L | T | PF | PA | W | L | T | PF | PA |
| Brown | 1 | 3 | 0 | 33 | 98 | 3 | 4 | 1 | 123 | 141 |
| Columbia | 5 | 1 | 0 | 148 | 84 | 8 | 1 | 0 | 251 | 105 |
| Cornell | 1 | 4 | 0 | 65 | 138 | 5 | 4 | 0 | 169 | 166 |
| Dartmouth | 0 | 4 | 1 | 26 | 72 | 1 | 6 | 1 | 40 | 119 |
| Harvard | 1 | 1 | 0 | 14 | 35 | 5 | 3 | 0 | 161 | 80 |
| °Pennsylvania | 5 | 0 | 0 | 181 | 13 | 6 | 2 | 0 | 237 | 88 |
| Princeton | 1 | 3 | 1 | 48 | 99 | 2 | 3 | 2 | 69 | 112 |
| Yale | 4 | 2 | 0 | 92 | 68 | 6 | 3 | 0 | 160 | 102 |

## 1946

| | League | | | | | Overall | | | | |
|---|---|---|---|---|---|---|---|---|---|---|
| | W | L | T | PF | PA | W | L | T | PF | PA |
| Brown | 1 | 3 | 0 | 32 | 123 | 3 | 5 | 1 | 122 | 184 |
| Columbia | 2 | 2 | 0 | 67 | 86 | 6 | 3 | 0 | 222 | 176 |
| Cornell | 3 | 1 | 1 | 73 | 46 | 5 | 3 | 1 | 135 | 115 |
| Dartmouth | 1 | 6 | 0 | 68 | 180 | 3 | 6 | 0 | 91 | 194 |
| Harvard | 3 | 1 | 0 | 76 | 46 | 7 | 2 | 0 | 214 | 65 |
| Pennsylvania | 3 | 1 | 0 | 120 | 49 | 6 | 2 | 0 | 265 | 102 |
| Princeton | 2 | 4 | 0 | 84 | 103 | 3 | 5 | 0 | 104 | 130 |
| °Yale | 4 | 1 | 1 | 165 | 52 | 7 | 1 | 1 | 272 | 72 |

## 1947

| | League | | | | | Overall | | | | |
|---|---|---|---|---|---|---|---|---|---|---|
| | W | L | T | PF | PA | W | L | T | PF | PA |
| Brown | 1 | 3 | 0 | 44 | 61 | 4 | 4 | 1 | 185 | 139 |
| Columbia | 2 | 2 | 0 | 58 | 51 | 7 | 2 | 0 | 170 | 113 |
| Cornell | 1 | 4 | 0 | 41 | 99 | 4 | 5 | 0 | 126 | 161 |
| Dartmouth | 3 | 4 | 0 | 74 | 120 | 4 | 4 | 1 | 102 | 127 |
| Harvard | 1 | 3 | 0 | 54 | 85 | 4 | 5 | 0 | 139 | 177 |
| °Pennsylvania | 4 | 0 | 0 | 113 | 21 | 7 | 0 | 1 | 219 | 35 |
| Princeton | 4 | 2 | 0 | 113 | 80 | 5 | 3 | 0 | 140 | 100 |
| Yale | 4 | 2 | 0 | 99 | 79 | 6 | 3 | 0 | 182 | 101 |

## 1948

| | League | | | | | Overall | | | | |
|---|---|---|---|---|---|---|---|---|---|---|
| | W | L | T | PF | PA | W | L | T | PF | PA |
| Brown | 1 | 2 | 0 | 55 | 78 | 7 | 2 | 0 | 242 | 103 |
| Columbia | 1 | 5 | 0 | 120 | 143 | 4 | 5 | 0 | 194 | 177 |
| °Cornell | 4 | 0 | 0 | 110 | 59 | 8 | 1 | 0 | 224 | 112 |
| Dartmouth | 4 | 2 | 0 | 153 | 108 | 6 | 2 | 0 | 213 | 130 |
| Harvard | 3 | 3 | 0 | 103 | 151 | 4 | 4 | 0 | 130 | 184 |
| Pennsylvania | 3 | 1 | 0 | 89 | 57 | 5 | 3 | 0 | 169 | 117 |
| Princeton | 3 | 3 | 0 | 123 | 120 | 4 | 4 | 0 | 184 | 156 |
| Yale | 1 | 4 | 0 | 91 | 128 | 4 | 5 | 0 | 167 | 170 |

**1949**

| | League | | | | | Overall | | | | |
|---|---|---|---|---|---|---|---|---|---|---|
| | W | L | T | PF | PA | W | L | T | PF | PA |
| Brown | 3 | 1 | 0 | 72 | 48 | 8 | 1 | 0 | 225 | 120 |
| Columbia | 1 | 5 | 0 | 49 | 172 | 2 | 7 | 0 | 82 | 276 |
| °Cornell | 5 | 1 | 0 | 185 | 77 | 8 | 1 | 0 | 284 | 111 |
| Dartmouth | 4 | 2 | 0 | 125 | 87 | 6 | 2 | 0 | 183 | 107 |
| Harvard | 0 | 6 | 0 | 67 | 164 | 1 | 8 | 0 | 103 | 276 |
| Pennsylvania | 3 | 1 | 0 | 83 | 49 | 4 | 4 | 0 | 159 | 118 |
| Princeton | 4 | 2 | 0 | 125 | 81 | 6 | 3 | 0 | 192 | 137 |
| Yale | 2 | 4 | 0 | 102 | 130 | 4 | 4 | 0 | 142 | 137 |

**1950**

| | League | | | | | Overall | | | | |
|---|---|---|---|---|---|---|---|---|---|---|
| | W | L | T | PF | PA | W | L | T | PF | PA |
| Brown | 0 | 5 | 0 | 25 | 167 | 1 | 8 | 0 | 147 | 271 |
| Columbia | 3 | 3 | 0 | 102 | 94 | 4 | 5 | 0 | 151 | 169 |
| Cornell | 4 | 2 | 0 | 91 | 60 | 7 | 2 | 0 | 170 | 85 |
| Dartmouth | 3 | 3 | 0 | 81 | 93 | 3 | 5 | 1 | 123 | 157 |
| Harvard | 1 | 5 | 0 | 67 | 173 | 1 | 7 | 0 | 74 | 248 |
| Pennsylvania | 3 | 1 | 0 | 132 | 39 | 6 | 3 | 0 | 223 | 95 |
| °Princeton | 5 | 0 | 0 | 184 | 45 | 9 | 0 | 0 | 349 | 94 |
| Yale | 3 | 3 | 0 | 82 | 93 | 6 | 3 | 0 | 142 | 120 |

**1951**

| | League | | | | | Overall | | | | |
|---|---|---|---|---|---|---|---|---|---|---|
| | W | L | T | PF | PA | W | L | T | PF | PA |
| Brown | 1 | 3 | 0 | 49 | 88 | 2 | 7 | 0 | 124 | 222 |
| Columbia | 5 | 1 | 0 | 133 | 68 | 5 | 3 | 0 | 149 | 103 |
| Cornell | 3 | 3 | 0 | 125 | 100 | 6 | 3 | 0 | 207 | 139 |
| Dartmouth | 2 | 4 | 0 | 73 | 124 | 4 | 5 | 0 | 121 | 152 |
| Harvard | 1 | 4 | 1 | 94 | 199 | 3 | 5 | 1 | 143 | 266 |
| Pennsylvania | 3 | 1 | 0 | 81 | 40 | 5 | 4 | 0 | 121 | 117 |
| °Princeton | 6 | 0 | 0 | 172 | 35 | 9 | 0 | 0 | 310 | 82 |
| Yale | 0 | 5 | 1 | 44 | 117 | 2 | 5 | 2 | 126 | 131 |

**1952**

| | League | | | | | Overall | | | | |
|---|---|---|---|---|---|---|---|---|---|---|
| | W | L | T | PF | PA | W | L | T | PF | PA |
| Brown | 1 | 3 | 0 | 28 | 102 | 2 | 7 | 0 | 89 | 220 |
| Columbia | 2 | 5 | 0 | 103 | 142 | 2 | 6 | 1 | 117 | 184 |
| Cornell | 2 | 3 | 0 | 41 | 75 | 2 | 7 | 0 | 68 | 195 |
| Dartmouth | 1 | 5 | 0 | 71 | 114 | 2 | 7 | 0 | 116 | 198 |
| Harvard | 1 | 4 | 0 | 89 | 145 | 5 | 4 | 0 | 214 | 198 |
| °Pennsylvania | 4 | 0 | 0 | 61 | 31 | 4 | 3 | 2 | 122 | 107 |
| Princeton | 6 | 1 | 0 | 188 | 55 | 8 | 1 | 0 | 297 | 74 |
| Yale | 5 | 1 | 0 | 159 | 76 | 7 | 2 | 0 | 240 | 120 |

**1953**

| | League | | | | | Overall | | | | |
|---|---|---|---|---|---|---|---|---|---|---|
| | W | L | T | PF | PA | W | L | T | PF | PA |
| Brown | 0 | 3 | 0 | 33 | 67 | 3 | 5 | 1 | 134 | 127 |
| Columbia | 2 | 3 | 0 | 70 | 79 | 4 | 5 | 0 | 124 | 153 |
| °Cornell | 3 | 0 | 2 | 88 | 65 | 4 | 3 | 2 | 128 | 152 |
| Dartmouth | 2 | 3 | 0 | 125 | 85 | 2 | 7 | 0 | 152 | 219 |
| Harvard | 3 | 2 | 0 | 60 | 46 | 6 | 2 | 0 | 146 | 78 |
| Pennsylvania | 0 | 0 | 1 | 7 | 7 | 3 | 5 | 1 | 96 | 152 |
| Princeton | 3 | 3 | 0 | 108 | 118 | 5 | 4 | 0 | 144 | 204 |
| Yale | 3 | 2 | 1 | 52 | 76 | 5 | 2 | 2 | 123 | 89 |

**1954**

| | League | | | | | Overall | | | | |
|---|---|---|---|---|---|---|---|---|---|---|
| | W | L | T | PF | PA | W | L | T | PF | PA |
| Brown | 2 | 1 | 1 | 84 | 74 | 6 | 2 | 1 | 225 | 120 |
| Columbia | 1 | 5 | 0 | 41 | 143 | 1 | 8 | 0 | 71 | 306 |
| °Cornell | 4 | 2 | 0 | 146 | 87 | 5 | 4 | 0 | 194 | 153 |
| Dartmouth | 2 | 3 | 0 | 74 | 109 | 3 | 6 | 0 | 121 | 250 |
| Harvard | 3 | 2 | 1 | 74 | 71 | 4 | 3 | 1 | 108 | 97 |
| Pennsylvania | 0 | 2 | 0 | 13 | 33 | 0 | 9 | 0 | 73 | 308 |
| Princeton | 4 | 3 | 0 | 166 | 110 | 5 | 3 | 1 | 182 | 124 |
| °Yale | 4 | 2 | 0 | 122 | 93 | 5 | 3 | 1 | 169 | 154 |

**1955**

| | League | | | | | Overall | | | | |
|---|---|---|---|---|---|---|---|---|---|---|
| | W | L | T | PF | PA | W | L | T | PF | PA |
| Brown | 2 | 4 | 0 | 67 | 81 | 2 | 7 | 0 | 86 | 139 |
| Columbia | 1 | 5 | 0 | 68 | 147 | 1 | 8 | 0 | 74 | 251 |
| Cornell | 4 | 3 | 0 | 139 | 107 | 5 | 4 | 0 | 159 | 134 |
| Dartmouth | 3 | 3 | 0 | 38 | 49 | 3 | 6 | 0 | 92 | 120 |
| Harvard | 2 | 4 | 0 | 57 | 82 | 3 | 4 | 1 | 143 | 114 |
| Pennsylvania | 0 | 2 | 0 | 7 | 46 | 0 | 9 | 0 | 34 | 270 |
| *Princeton | 6 | 1 | 0 | 92 | 44 | 7 | 2 | 0 | 139 | 66 |
| Yale | 5 | 1 | 0 | 148 | 60 | 7 | 2 | 0 | 176 | 79 |

## Formal Ivy League Play Begins

**1956**

| | League | | | | | Overall | | | | |
|---|---|---|---|---|---|---|---|---|---|---|
| | W | L | T | PF | PA | W | L | T | PF | PA |
| 1. Yale | 7 | 0 | 0 | 221 | 69 | 8 | 1 | 0 | 246 | 97 |
| 2. Princeton | 5 | 2 | 0 | 181 | 109 | 7 | 2 | 0 | 278 | 94 |
| 3. Dartmouth | 4 | 3 | 0 | 102 | 82 | 5 | 4 | 0 | 122 | 89 |
| Pennsylvania | 4 | 3 | 0 | 90 | 128 | 4 | 5 | 0 | 106 | 218 |
| 5. Brown | 3 | 4 | 0 | 77 | 87 | 5 | 4 | 0 | 124 | 94 |
| 6. Columbia | 2 | 5 | 0 | 76 | 165 | 3 | 6 | 0 | 94 | 237 |
| Harvard | 2 | 5 | 0 | 140 | 180 | 2 | 6 | 0 | 153 | 199 |
| 8. Cornell | 1 | 6 | 0 | 94 | 161 | 1 | 8 | 0 | 100 | 209 |

**1957**

| | League | | | | | Overall | | | | |
|---|---|---|---|---|---|---|---|---|---|---|
| | W | L | T | PF | PA | W | L | T | PF | PA |
| 1. Princeton | 6 | 1 | 0 | 189 | 83 | 7 | 2 | 0 | 206 | 95 |
| 2. Dartmouth | 5 | 1 | 1 | 122 | 70 | 7 | 1 | 1 | 163 | 77 |
| 3. Yale | 4 | 2 | 1 | 165 | 88 | 6 | 2 | 1 | 212 | 88 |
| 4. Brown | 3 | 4 | 0 | 100 | 111 | 5 | 4 | 0 | 154 | 118 |
| Cornell | 3 | 4 | 0 | 87 | 111 | 3 | 6 | 0 | 100 | 159 |
| Pennsylvania | 3 | 4 | 0 | 100 | 84 | 3 | 6 | 0 | 121 | 140 |
| 7. Harvard | 2 | 5 | 0 | 64 | 173 | 3 | 5 | 0 | 78 | 180 |
| 8. Columbia | 1 | 6 | 0 | 41 | 148 | 1 | 8 | 0 | 54 | 214 |

**1958**

| | League | | | | | Overall | | | | |
|---|---|---|---|---|---|---|---|---|---|---|
| | W | L | T | PF | PA | W | L | T | PF | PA |
| 1. Dartmouth | 6 | 1 | 0 | 154 | 69 | 7 | 2 | 0 | 182 | 83 |
| 2. Cornell | 5 | 2 | 0 | 134 | 80 | 6 | 3 | 0 | 147 | 135 |
| Princeton | 5 | 2 | 0 | 177 | 123 | 6 | 3 | 0 | 217 | 164 |
| 4. Brown | 4 | 3 | 0 | 136 | 128 | 6 | 3 | 0 | 211 | 140 |
| Pennsylvania | 4 | 3 | 0 | 145 | 84 | 4 | 5 | 0 | 153 | 177 |
| 6. Harvard | 3 | 4 | 0 | 126 | 93 | 4 | 5 | 0 | 149 | 99 |
| 7. Columbia | 1 | 6 | 0 | 21 | 196 | 1 | 8 | 0 | 35 | 291 |
| 8. Yale | 0 | 7 | 0 | 70 | 190 | 2 | 7 | 0 | 92 | 203 |

**1959**

| | League | | | | | Overall | | | | |
|---|---|---|---|---|---|---|---|---|---|---|
| | W | L | T | PF | PA | W | L | T | PF | PA |
| 1. Pennsylvania | 6 | 1 | 0 | 147 | 52 | 7 | 1 | 1 | 195 | 74 |
| 2. Dartmouth | 5 | 1 | 1 | 76 | 40 | 5 | 3 | 1 | 96 | 106 |
| 3. Harvard | 4 | 3 | 0 | 121 | 73 | 6 | 3 | 0 | 177 | 101 |
| Yale | 4 | 3 | 0 | 118 | 95 | 6 | 3 | 0 | 159 | 95 |
| 5. Cornell | 3 | 4 | 0 | 77 | 115 | 5 | 4 | 0 | 110 | 136 |
| Princeton | 3 | 4 | 0 | 76 | 82 | 4 | 5 | 0 | 124 | 97 |
| 7. Brown | 1 | 5 | 1 | 31 | 106 | 2 | 6 | 1 | 51 | 139 |
| 8. Columbia | 1 | 6 | 0 | 56 | 139 | 2 | 7 | 0 | 82 | 189 |

## 1960

| | League W | L | T | PF | PA | Overall W | L | T | PF | PA |
|---|---|---|---|---|---|---|---|---|---|---|
| 1. Yale | 7 | 0 | 0 | 206 | 51 | 9 | 0 | 0 | 253 | 73 |
| 2. Princeton | 6 | 1 | 0 | 188 | 94 | 7 | 2 | 0 | 232 | 133 |
| 3. Dartmouth | 4 | 3 | 0 | 83 | 51 | 5 | 4 | 0 | 98 | 66 |
| Harvard | 4 | 3 | 0 | 65 | 86 | 5 | 4 | 0 | 90 | 119 |
| 5. Columbia | 3 | 4 | 0 | 118 | 121 | 3 | 6 | 0 | 126 | 191 |
| 6. Pennsylvania | 2 | 5 | 0 | 69 | 108 | 3 | 6 | 0 | 104 | 149 |
| 7. Brown | 1 | 6 | 0 | 43 | 184 | 3 | 6 | 0 | 100 | 212 |
| Cornell | 1 | 6 | 0 | 55 | 132 | 2 | 7 | 0 | 78 | 167 |

## 1961

| | League W | L | T | PF | PA | Overall W | L | T | PF | PA |
|---|---|---|---|---|---|---|---|---|---|---|
| 1. Columbia | 6 | 1 | 0 | 214 | 71 | 6 | 3 | 0 | 240 | 117 |
| Harvard | 6 | 1 | 0 | 143 | 60 | 6 | 3 | 0 | 160 | 87 |
| 3. Dartmouth | 5 | 2 | 0 | 156 | 84 | 6 | 3 | 0 | 197 | 104 |
| Princeton | 5 | 2 | 0 | 160 | 97 | 5 | 4 | 0 | 173 | 128 |
| 5. Yale | 3 | 4 | 0 | 73 | 91 | 4 | 5 | 0 | 99 | 105 |
| 6. Cornell | 2 | 5 | 0 | 102 | 106 | 3 | 6 | 0 | 143 | 137 |
| 7. Pennsylvania | 1 | 6 | 0 | 22 | 167 | 2 | 7 | 0 | 42 | 194 |
| 8. Brown | 0 | 7 | 0 | 9 | 203 | 0 | 9 | 0 | 24 | 245 |

## 1962

| | League W | L | T | PF | PA | Overall W | L | T | PF | PA |
|---|---|---|---|---|---|---|---|---|---|---|
| 1. Dartmouth | 7 | 0 | 0 | 199 | 54 | 9 | 0 | 0 | 236 | 57 |
| 2. Harvard | 5 | 2 | 0 | 155 | 77 | 6 | 3 | 0 | 202 | 118 |
| 3. Columbia | 4 | 3 | 0 | 96 | 169 | 5 | 4 | 0 | 124 | 206 |
| Princeton | 4 | 3 | 0 | 157 | 123 | 5 | 4 | 0 | 187 | 146 |
| Cornell | 4 | 3 | 0 | 156 | 173 | 4 | 5 | 0 | 168 | 237 |
| 6. Pennsylvania | 2 | 5 | 0 | 70 | 151 | 3 | 6 | 0 | 89 | 174 |
| 7. Yale | 1 | 5 | 1 | 70 | 80 | 2 | 5 | 2 | 102 | 108 |
| 8. Brown | 0 | 6 | 1 | 98 | 174 | 1 | 6 | 2 | 116 | 188 |

## 1963

| | League W | L | T | PF | PA | Overall W | L | T | PF | PA |
|---|---|---|---|---|---|---|---|---|---|---|
| 1. Dartmouth | 5 | 2 | 0 | 142 | 68 | 7 | 2 | 0 | 175 | 94 |
| Princeton | 5 | 2 | 0 | 181 | 83 | 7 | 2 | 0 | 247 | 83 |
| 3. Harvard | 4 | 2 | 1 | 94 | 76 | 5 | 2 | 2 | 122 | 76 |
| 4. Yale | 4 | 3 | 0 | 101 | 78 | 6 | 3 | 0 | 135 | 78 |
| Cornell | 4 | 3 | 0 | 111 | 144 | 5 | 4 | 0 | 152 | 165 |
| 6. Columbia | 2 | 4 | 1 | 113 | 116 | 4 | 4 | 1 | 190 | 165 |
| 7. Brown | 2 | 5 | 0 | 124 | 161 | 3 | 5 | 0 | 157 | 168 |
| 8. Pennsylvania | 1 | 6 | 0 | 43 | 183 | 3 | 6 | 0 | 97 | 189 |

## 1964

| | League W | L | T | PF | PA | Overall W | L | T | PF | PA |
|---|---|---|---|---|---|---|---|---|---|---|
| 1. Princeton | 7 | 0 | 0 | 197 | 46 | 9 | 0 | 0 | 216 | 53 |
| 2. Harvard | 5 | 2 | 0 | 90 | 85 | 6 | 3 | 0 | 131 | 123 |
| 3. Yale | 4 | 2 | 1 | 124 | 110 | 6 | 2 | 1 | 195 | 120 |
| 4. Dartmouth | 4 | 3 | 0 | 167 | 129 | 6 | 3 | 0 | 235 | 135 |
| 5. Cornell | 3 | 4 | 0 | 184 | 122 | 3 | 5 | 1 | 196 | 137 |
| Brown | 3 | 4 | 0 | 69 | 100 | 5 | 4 | 0 | 119 | 117 |
| 7. Columbia | 1 | 5 | 1 | 89 | 142 | 2 | 6 | 1 | 145 | 194 |
| 8. Pennsylvania | 0 | 7 | 0 | 28 | 206 | 1 | 8 | 0 | 48 | 222 |

## 1965

| | League W | L | T | PF | PA | Overall W | L | T | PF | PA |
|---|---|---|---|---|---|---|---|---|---|---|
| 1. Dartmouth | 7 | 0 | 0 | 188 | 59 | 9 | 0 | 0 | 271 | 71 |
| 2. Princeton | 6 | 1 | 0 | 222 | 94 | 8 | 1 | 0 | 281 | 100 |
| 3. Harvard | 3 | 2 | 2 | 70 | 55 | 5 | 2 | 2 | 120 | 62 |
| 4. Cornell | 3 | 3 | 1 | 143 | 124 | 4 | 3 | 2 | 192 | 137 |
| 5. Yale | 3 | 4 | 0 | 78 | 118 | 3 | 6 | 0 | 84 | 138 |
| 6. Pennsylvania | 2 | 4 | 1 | 100 | 165 | 4 | 4 | 1 | 136 | 192 |
| 7. Brown | 1 | 6 | 0 | 116 | 155 | 2 | 7 | 0 | 128 | 169 |
| Columbia | 1 | 6 | 0 | 61 | 208 | 2 | 7 | 0 | 83 | 229 |

**1966**

| | League | | | | | Overall | | | | |
|---|---|---|---|---|---|---|---|---|---|---|
| | W | L | T | PF | PA | W | L | T | PF | PA |
| 1. Dartmouth | 6 | 1 | 0 | 250 | 117 | 7 | 2 | 0 | 273 | 131 |
| Harvard | 6 | 1 | 0 | 156 | 53 | 8 | 1 | 0 | 229 | 60 |
| Princeton | 6 | 1 | 0 | 119 | 84 | 7 | 2 | 0 | 135 | 103 |
| 4. Cornell | 4 | 3 | 0 | 138 | 122 | 6 | 3 | 0 | 181 | 157 |
| 5. Yale | 3 | 4 | 0 | 119 | 109 | 4 | 5 | 0 | 149 | 126 |
| 6. Columbia | 2 | 5 | 0 | 122 | 231 | 2 | 7 | 0 | 156 | 306 |
| 7. Pennsylvania | 1 | 6 | 0 | 117 | 181 | 2 | 7 | 0 | 176 | 237 |
| 8. Brown | 0 | 7 | 0 | 80 | 204 | 1 | 8 | 0 | 127 | 279 |

**1967**

| | League | | | | | Overall | | | | |
|---|---|---|---|---|---|---|---|---|---|---|
| | W | L | T | PF | PA | W | L | T | PF | PA |
| 1. Yale | 7 | 0 | 0 | 250 | 78 | 8 | 1 | 0 | 278 | 110 |
| 2. Dartmouth | 5 | 2 | 0 | 153 | 128 | 7 | 2 | 0 | 205 | 146 |
| 3. Cornell | 4 | 2 | 1 | 164 | 131 | 6 | 2 | 1 | 210 | 145 |
| 4. Harvard | 4 | 3 | 0 | 176 | 130 | 6 | 3 | 0 | 256 | 164 |
| Princeton | 4 | 3 | 0 | 183 | 141 | 6 | 3 | 0 | 233 | 162 |
| 6. Pennsylvania | 2 | 5 | 0 | 111 | 186 | 3 | 6 | 0 | 173 | 237 |
| 7. Brown | 1 | 5 | 1 | 61 | 194 | 2 | 6 | 1 | 76 | 206 |
| 8. Columbia | 0 | 7 | 0 | 68 | 178 | 2 | 7 | 0 | 109 | 205 |

**1968**

| | League | | | | | Overall | | | | |
|---|---|---|---|---|---|---|---|---|---|---|
| | W | L | T | PF | PA | W | L | T | PF | PA |
| 1. Yale | 6 | 0 | 1 | 237 | 119 | 8 | 0 | 1 | 317 | 147 |
| Harvard | 6 | 0 | 1 | 150 | 70 | 8 | 0 | 1 | 236 | 90 |
| 3. Pennsylvania | 5 | 2 | 0 | 104 | 121 | 7 | 2 | 0 | 165 | 131 |
| 4. Princeton | 4 | 3 | 0 | 207 | 115 | 4 | 5 | 0 | 228 | 149 |
| 5. Dartmouth | 3 | 4 | 0 | 168 | 154 | 4 | 5 | 0 | 206 | 183 |
| 6. Columbia | 2 | 5 | 0 | 143 | 183 | 2 | 7 | 0 | 174 | 247 |
| 7. Cornell | 1 | 6 | 0 | 96 | 147 | 3 | 6 | 0 | 130 | 170 |
| 8. Brown | 0 | 7 | 0 | 60 | 258 | 2 | 7 | 0 | 97 | 286 |

**1969**

| | League | | | | | Overall | | | | |
|---|---|---|---|---|---|---|---|---|---|---|
| | W | L | T | PF | PA | W | L | T | PF | PA |
| 1. Dartmouth | 6 | 1 | 0 | 213 | 93 | 8 | 1 | 0 | 282 | 99 |
| Yale | 6 | 1 | 0 | 151 | 88 | 7 | 2 | 0 | 206 | 127 |
| Princeton | 6 | 1 | 0 | 230 | 74 | 6 | 3 | 0 | 248 | 138 |
| 4. Cornell | 4 | 3 | 0 | 127 | 113 | 4 | 5 | 0 | 148 | 162 |
| 5. Pennsylvania | 2 | 5 | 0 | 63 | 161 | 4 | 5 | 0 | 104 | 185 |
| Harvard | 2 | 5 | 0 | 142 | 153 | 3 | 6 | 0 | 165 | 166 |
| 7. Brown | 1 | 6 | 0 | 68 | 170 | 2 | 7 | 0 | 95 | 200 |
| Columbia | 1 | 6 | 0 | 48 | 180 | 1 | 8 | 0 | 84 | 237 |

**1970**

| | League | | | | | Overall | | | | |
|---|---|---|---|---|---|---|---|---|---|---|
| | W | L | T | PF | PA | W | L | T | PF | PA |
| 1. Dartmouth | 7 | 0 | 0 | 234 | 28 | 9 | 0 | 0 | 311 | 42 |
| 2. Harvard | 5 | 2 | 0 | 160 | 151 | 7 | 2 | 0 | 227 | 157 |
| Yale | 5 | 2 | 0 | 169 | 90 | 7 | 2 | 0 | 218 | 97 |
| 4. Cornell | 4 | 3 | 0 | 135 | 164 | 6 | 3 | 0 | 193 | 185 |
| 5. Princeton | 3 | 4 | 0 | 123 | 152 | 5 | 4 | 0 | 196 | 180 |
| 6. Pennsylvania | 2 | 5 | 0 | 130 | 175 | 4 | 5 | 0 | 185 | 195 |
| 7. Columbia | 1 | 6 | 0 | 111 | 201 | 3 | 6 | 0 | 164 | 224 |
| Brown | 1 | 6 | 0 | 85 | 196 | 2 | 7 | 0 | 112 | 220 |

**1971**

| | League | | | | | Overall | | | | |
|---|---|---|---|---|---|---|---|---|---|---|
| | W | L | T | PF | PA | W | L | T | PF | PA |
| 1. Cornell | 6 | 1 | 0 | 171 | 99 | 8 | 1 | 0 | 240 | 136 |
| Dartmouth | 6 | 1 | 0 | 148 | 90 | 8 | 1 | 0 | 207 | 106 |
| 3. Columbia | 5 | 2 | 0 | 149 | 117 | 6 | 3 | 0 | 166 | 136 |
| 4. Harvard | 4 | 3 | 0 | 147 | 139 | 5 | 4 | 0 | 180 | 167 |
| 5. Princeton | 3 | 4 | 0 | 142 | 115 | 4 | 5 | 0 | 195 | 160 |
| Yale | 3 | 4 | 0 | 106 | 128 | 4 | 5 | 0 | 150 | 156 |
| 7. Pennsylvania | 1 | 6 | 0 | 77 | 176 | 2 | 7 | 0 | 120 | 207 |
| 8. Brown | 0 | 7 | 0 | 86 | 162 | 0 | 9 | 0 | 139 | 238 |

## 1972

| | League W | L | T | PF | PA | Overall W | L | T | PF | PA |
|---|---|---|---|---|---|---|---|---|---|---|
| 1. Dartmouth | 5 | 1 | 1 | 219 | 147 | 7 | 1 | 1 | 260 | 168 |
| 2. Yale | 5 | 2 | 0 | 228 | 143 | 7 | 2 | 0 | 283 | 157 |
| 3. Pennsylvania | 4 | 3 | 0 | 178 | 164 | 6 | 3 | 0 | 263 | 203 |
| Cornell | 4 | 3 | 0 | 155 | 154 | 6 | 3 | 0 | 228 | 183 |
| 5. Harvard | 3 | 3 | 1 | 146 | 144 | 4 | 4 | 1 | 198 | 186 |
| 6. Princeton | 2 | 4 | 1 | 87 | 110 | 3 | 5 | 1 | 120 | 161 |
| Columbia | 2 | 4 | 1 | 96 | 118 | 3 | 5 | 1 | 143 | 124 |
| 8. Brown | 1 | 6 | 0 | 131 | 250 | 1 | 8 | 0 | 172 | 301 |

## 1973

| | League W | L | T | PF | PA | Overall W | L | T | PF | PA |
|---|---|---|---|---|---|---|---|---|---|---|
| 1. Dartmouth | 6 | 1 | 0 | 175 | 99 | 6 | 3 | 0 | 184 | 119 |
| 2. Harvard | 5 | 2 | 0 | 184 | 150 | 7 | 2 | 0 | 224 | 157 |
| Pennsylvania | 5 | 2 | 0 | 198 | 124 | 6 | 3 | 0 | 237 | 160 |
| Yale | 5 | 2 | 0 | 176 | 95 | 6 | 3 | 0 | 213 | 140 |
| 5. Brown | 4 | 3 | 0 | 163 | 143 | 4 | 3 | 1 | 183 | 163 |
| 6. Cornell | 2 | 5 | 0 | 128 | 126 | 3 | 5 | 1 | 170 | 154 |
| 7. Columbia | 1 | 6 | 0 | 56 | 246 | 1 | 7 | 1 | 58 | 274 |
| 8. Princeton | 0 | 7 | 0 | 76 | 173 | 1 | 8 | 0 | 127 | 161 |

## 1974

| | League W | L | T | PF | PA | Overall W | L | T | PF | PA |
|---|---|---|---|---|---|---|---|---|---|---|
| 1. Yale | 6 | 1 | 0 | 176 | 53 | 8 | 1 | 0 | 229 | 67 |
| Harvard | 6 | 1 | 0 | 191 | 91 | 7 | 2 | 0 | 236 | 129 |
| 3. Pennsylvania | 4 | 2 | 1 | 122 | 154 | 6 | 2 | 1 | 187 | 179 |
| 4. Brown | 4 | 3 | 0 | 86 | 92 | 5 | 4 | 0 | 141 | 152 |
| 5. Princeton | 3 | 4 | 0 | 149 | 130 | 4 | 4 | 1 | 188 | 160 |
| Dartmouth | 3 | 4 | 0 | 100 | 87 | 3 | 6 | 0 | 103 | 115 |
| 7. Cornell | 1 | 5 | 1 | 119 | 172 | 3 | 5 | 1 | 183 | 193 |
| 8. Columbia | 0 | 7 | 0 | 43 | 210 | 1 | 8 | 0 | 81 | 258 |

## 1975

| | League W | L | T | PF | PA | Overall W | L | T | PF | PA |
|---|---|---|---|---|---|---|---|---|---|---|
| 1. Harvard | 6 | 1 | 0 | 189 | 113 | 7 | 2 | 0 | 216 | 133 |
| 2. Brown | 5 | 1 | 1 | 197 | 127 | 6 | 2 | 1 | 258 | 168 |
| 3. Yale | 5 | 2 | 0 | 137 | 99 | 7 | 2 | 0 | 196 | 123 |
| 4. Dartmouth | 4 | 2 | 1 | 129 | 107 | 5 | 3 | 1 | 160 | 121 |
| 5. Princeton | 3 | 4 | 0 | 132 | 128 | 4 | 5 | 0 | 163 | 155 |
| 6. Pennsylvania | 2 | 5 | 0 | 115 | 150 | 3 | 6 | 0 | 151 | 184 |
| Columbia | 2 | 5 | 0 | 144 | 210 | 2 | 7 | 0 | 152 | 262 |
| 8. Cornell | 0 | 7 | 0 | 108 | 217 | 1 | 8 | 0 | 151 | 247 |

## 1976

| | League W | L | T | PF | PA | Overall W | L | T | PF | PA |
|---|---|---|---|---|---|---|---|---|---|---|
| 1. Yale | 6 | 1 | 0 | 156 | 61 | 8 | 1 | 0 | 198 | 77 |
| Brown | 6 | 1 | 0 | 140 | 84 | 8 | 1 | 0 | 171 | 102 |
| 3. Dartmouth | 4 | 3 | 0 | 167 | 91 | 6 | 3 | 0 | 236 | 111 |
| Harvard | 4 | 3 | 0 | 115 | 88 | 6 | 3 | 0 | 176 | 115 |
| 5. Cornell | 2 | 5 | 0 | 75 | 131 | 2 | 7 | 0 | 109 | 177 |
| Princeton | 2 | 5 | 0 | 56 | 118 | 2 | 7 | 0 | 63 | 152 |
| Pennsylvania | 2 | 5 | 0 | 55 | 121 | 3 | 6 | 0 | 90 | 159 |
| Columbia | 2 | 5 | 0 | 99 | 169 | 3 | 6 | 0 | 137 | 247 |

## Brown University

Providence, R.I.
Established 1764
Colors: Brown and White
Nickname: Bruins

*Head Coaches*

No coaches, informal teams, 1878-1886
No teams, 1887-1888
Coached by captains, 1889-1891
Mr. Howland, 1892
William Odlin, 1893
Mr. Norton, 1894
Wallace Moyle, 1895-1897
E. N. Robinson, 1898-1901
1904-1907
1910-1925
J. A. Gammons, 1902; 1908-1909
D. S. Fultz, 1903
D. O. McLaughry, 1926-1940
J. N. Stahley, 1941-1943
C. A. (Rip) Engle, 1944-1949
G. G. Zitrides, 1950
A. E. Kelley, 1951-1958
John McLaughry, 1959-1966
Len Jardine, 1967-1972
John Anderson, 1973-

### Scores 1878-1976

**1878**
0 Amherst 4t, 1g

**1880**
0 Yale 5t, 8g

**1886**
70 Prov. H.S. 0
6 Boston U. 10

**1889**
14 Pawtucket C.C. 0
0 MIT 48
16 Tufts 0
0 Boston A.C. 16

**1890**
8 MIT 8
0 Fall River 8
14 Tufts 0
12 Boston A.C. 26
16 Trinity 20
22 Harvard Fr. 8
6 Wesleyan 34

**1891**
6 MIT 4
0 Trinity 8
18 Fall River 4
0 Andover 26
18 Bowdoin 22
6 MIT 14
18 Bowdoin 0
0 Williams 58
32 WPI 6
12 Tufts 34

**1892**
8 WPI 4
24 Fall River 0
6 Andover 4
6 MIT 30
4 Tufts 24
0 Trinity 0
6 MIT 12
0 Bowdoin 8
0 WPI 4
6 Wesleyan 0

**1893**
0 Yale 18
30 WPI 0
0 Boston A.C. 6
34 Trinity 0
10 Andover 0
0 Harvard 58
36 MIT 0
28 MIT 6
30 Tufts 6

**1894**
56 Fort Adams 0
0 Yale 28
28 Boston A.C. 0
4 Harvard 18
10 Army 0
14 Andover 0
26 Wesleyan 0
4 MIT 8
30 Tufts 0
0 Yale 12
12 Orange A.A. 10
0 Harvard 18
42 Bowdoin 0
20 Dartmouth 4
16 MIT 4

**1895**
22 Newton A.A. 0
0 Yale 4
28 Tufts 0
6 Harvard 26
14 MIT 0
22 Lehigh 4
0 Penn 12
0 Crescent A.C. 16
10 Wesleyan 5
6 Yale 6
28 MIT 0
4 Cornell 6
0 Army 26
10 Dartmouth 4

**1896**
20 WPI 0
0 Yale 18
44 Amherst 6
0 Harvard 12
16 Lehigh 0
0 Penn 16
10 Dartmouth 10
6 Yale 18
6 Army 8
24 Carlisle 12

**1897**
24 Tufts 0
44 Boston U. 0
20 Andover 4
24 Wesleyan 12
14 Yale 18
0 Harvard 18
0 Penn 40
24 Newton A.A. 0
18 Carlisle 14
0 Army 42
12 Wesleyan 4

**1898**
29 Tufts 6
19 Holy Cross 0
0 Penn 18
41 Colby 5
6 Yale 22
6 Boston College 0
0 Princeton 23
16 Newton A.A. 5
6 Harvard 17
12 Dartmouth 0

**1899**
19 Holy Cross 0
6 Tufts 0
6 Penn 6
25 Campello 0
0 Harvard 11
35 Newton A.A. 0
6 Princeton 18
38 MIT 0
18 Boston College 0
16 Dartmouth 5
6 Chicago 17

**1900**
27 Colby 0
18 Holy Cross 0
22 MIT 0
0 Penn 12
11 Chicago 6
5 Princeton 17
12 Needham 5
26 Tufts 5
6 Harvard 11
12 Dartmouth 5
6 Syracuse 6

**1901**
12 Boston College 0
16 Colby 0
0 Syracuse 20
6 Manhattan 5
0 Penn 26
0 Princeton 35
6 Holy Cross 6
0 Harvard 48
0 Homestead 34
6 Lafayette 11
24 Union 5
0 Dartmouth 22

**1902**
0 Vermont 0
5 Wesleyan 0
0 Yale 10
15 Penn 6
0 Harvard 6
5 Lafayette 6
45 Tufts 12
28 Columbia 0
11 Springfield 0
6 Dartmouth 12

**1903**
23 Colby 0
11 Wesleyan 0
0 Princeton 29
0 Penn 30
0 Harvard 29
22 Williams 0
24 Vermont 0
12 Syracuse 5
6 Springfield 6
0 Dartmouth 62

**1904**
0 Maine 6
27 Massachusetts 0
12 Wesleyan 0
0 Penn 6
0 Amherst 5
22 Bowdoin 0
33 Vermont 0
41 Tufts 0
0 Yale 22
41 Colby 0
5 Dartmouth 12

**1905**
16 New Hampshire 5
24 Massachusetts 0
42 WPI 0
70 Colby 0
34 U. Maine 0
6 Penn 8
0 Harvard 10
27 Syracuse 0
0 Yale 11
56 Vermont 0
6 Dartmouth 24

**1906**
12 New Hampshire 0
17 Wesleyan 0
17 Massachusetts 0
0 Penn 14
26 Norwich 4
5 Harvard 9
0 Yale 5
12 Vermont 0
23 Dartmouth 0

**1907**
16 New Hampshire 0
5 Massachusetts 0
24 Norwich 0
40 U. Maine 0
0 Penn 11
24 Williams 11
5 Harvard 6
0 Yale 22

36 Vermont 0
18 Amherst 0

**1908**

34 New Hampshire 0
35 Bates 4
6 Colgate 0
12 Bowdoin 0
0 Penn 12
6 Lafayette 8
2 Harvard 6
10 Yale 10
12 Vermont 0

**1909**

6 URI 0
14 Colgate 0
17 Bates 0
10 Amherst 0
5 Penn 13
0 Harvard 11
12 Massachusetts 3
0 Yale 23
17 Vermont 0
21 Carlisle 8

**1910**

31 Norwich 0
5 URI 0
0 Colgate 0
0 Penn 20
0 Harvard 12
27 Tufts 9
21 Yale 0
50 Vermont 0
49 Massachusetts 0
15 Carlisle 6

**1911**

56 New Hampshire 0
12 URI 0
26 Massachusetts 0
33 Bowdoin 0
6 Penn 0
6 Harvard 20
30 Tufts 0
0 Yale 15
6 Vermont 0
6 Trinity 6
6 Carlisle 12

**1912**

3 Colby 0
14 URI 0
6 Wesleyan 7
30 Penn 7
10 Harvard 30
12 Vermont 7
0 Yale 10
21 Lafayette 7
21 Norwich 7
0 Carlisle 32

**1913**

0 Colby 10
19 URI 0
6 Ursinus 0
0 Penn 28
26 Springfield 6
19 Vermont 0
0 Yale 17
0 Harvard 37
0 Carlisle 13

**1914**

24 Norwich 0
20 URI 0
0 Amherst 0
16 Wesleyan 0
7 Cornell 28
12 Vermont 9
6 Yale 14
0 Harvard 0
20 Carlisle 14

**1915**

38 URI 0
0 Trinity 0
0 Amherst 7
33 Williams 0
0 Syracuse 6
46 Vermont 0
3 Yale 0
7 Harvard 16
39 Carlisle 3
0 Washington State 14

**1916**

18 URI 0
42 Trinity 0
69 Amherst 0
20 Williams 0
21 Rutgers 3
42 Vermont 0
21 Yale 6
21 Harvard 0
0 Colgate 28

**1917**

27 URI 0
20 Johns Hopkins 0
27 Holy Cross 6
7 Boston College 2
7 Colgate 6
0 Syracuse 6
0 USN Reserve 35
40 Camp Devens 0
19 Colby 7
13 Dartmouth 0

**1918**

7 Camp Devens 19
0 Syracuse 53
7 League 1, Navy Yd. 23
28 Dartmouth 0
6 Harvard 3

**1919**

27 URI 0
7 Bowdoin 0
0 Colgate 14
0 Harvard 7
20 Norwich 0
0 Syracuse 13
0 Yale 14
7 Dartmouth 6
6 New Hampshire 0
7 Columbia 7

**1920**

25 URI 0
13 Amherst 0
32 U. Maine 6
14 Colgate 0
14 Springfield 0
35 Vermont 0
10 Yale 14
0 Harvard 27
6 Dartmouth 14

**1921**

6 URI 0
12 Colby 7
13 NYU 0
0 Syracuse 28
0 Springfield 0
7 Yale 45
55 St. Bonaventure 0
7 Harvard 9
7 Colgate 0

**1922**

27 URI 0
13 Colby 0
0 Syracuse 0
6 Lehigh 2
16 Boston U. 6
0 Yale 20
27 Bates 12
3 Harvard 0
0 Dartmouth 7

**1923**

34 Haverford 0
33 Colby 0
7 Wash. & Jeff. 12
20 Boston U. 3
0 Yale 21
19 St. Bonaventure 0
14 Dartmouth 16
20 Harvard 7
6 New Hampshire 0
6 Lehigh 12

**1924**

45 Colby 0
7 Chicago 19
35 Boston U. 0
3 Yale 13
3 Dartmouth 10
13 Haskell 17
7 Harvard 0
21 New Hampshire 0
20 Colgate 6

**1925**

33 URI 0
33 Colby 0
0 Penn 9
48 Bates 0
7 Yale 20
0 Dartmouth 14
42 Boston U. 6
0 Harvard 3
38 New Hampshire 14
14 Colgate 14

**1926**

14 URI 0
35 Colby 0
32 Lehigh 0
27 Bates 14
7 Yale 0
10 Dartmouth 0
27 Norwich 0
21 Harvard 0
40 UNH 12
10 Colgate 10

**1927**

27 URI 0
20 Albright 0
6 Penn 14
0 Yale 19
12 Lebanon Valley 13
0 Temple 7
7 Dartmouth 19
6 Harvard 18
31 UNH 13
0 Colgate 0

**1928**

32 WPI 0
13 Dayton 7
14 Yale 32
19 Tufts 13
6 Holy Cross 0
14 Dartmouth 0
20 UNH 0
33 URI 7
16 Colgate 13

**1929**

6 Springfield 14
14 URI 6
13 Princeton 12
6 Yale 14
0 Syracuse 6
15 Holy Cross 14
6 Dartmouth 13
66 Norwich 6
14 UNH 7
0 Colgate 32

**1930**

7 URI 0
54 WPI 0
7 Princeton 0
0 Yale 21
13 Holy Cross 0
16 Syracuse 16
32 Tufts 7
6 Columbia 0
0 UNH 7
0 Colgate 27

**1931**

22 Colby 0
18 URI 0
19 Princeton 7
33 Tufts 12
38 Lehigh 0
0 Holy Cross 33
26 Ohio Wesleyan 13
7 Columbia 9
19 UNH 13
7 Colgate 13

**1932**

19 URI 0
13 Springfield 6
7 Yale 2
11 Tufts 0
14 Harvard 0
10 Holy Cross 7
7 Columbia 6
0 Colgate 21

**1933**

26 URI 0
13 Springfield 6
6 Yale 14
7 Holy Cross 19
0 Princeton 33
10 Syracuse 7
6 Harvard 12
0 Colgate 25

**1934**

18 Boston U. 0
13 URI 0
0 Harvard 13
0 Yale 37
0 Syracuse 33
13 Springfield 7
0 Columbia 39
7 Holy Cross 20
13 Colgate 20

**1935**

7 URI 13
0 Springfield 20
0 Dartmouth 41
0 Syracuse 19
0 Harvard 33
0 Yale 20
14 Boston U. 0
0 Columbia 18
0 Colgate 33

**1936**

0 U. Conn. 27
7 URI 6
0 Harvard 28
0 Dartmouth 34
6 Penn 48
38 Tufts 7
6 Yale 14
19 Colby 6
0 Holy Cross 32
0 Colgate 32

**1937**

20 U. Conn. 0
13 URI 6
7 Harvard 34
0 Dartmouth 41
7 Columbia 6
19 Tufts 0
0 Yale 19
0 Holy Cross 7
7 Rutgers 6

**1938**

DNP Conn. State
20 Harvard 13
20 Lafayette 0
13 Dartmouth 34

40 URI 21
48 Tufts 0
14 Yale 20
12 Holy Cross 14
36 Columbia 27

**1939**
34 URI 0
20 Amherst 14
0 Colgate 10
0 Holy Cross 20
12 Princeton 26
54 Tufts 7
14 Yale 14
41 U. Conn. 0
13 Rutgers 0

**1940**
41 Wesleyan 0
20 URI 17
3 Colgate 20
26 Tufts 6
9 Holy Cross 6
6 Yale 2
13 Army 9
0 Harvard 14
6 Dartmouth 20
0 Columbia 0

**1941**
20 Wesleyan 6
6 Columbia 13
14 URI 7
28 Tufts 6
13 Lafayette 0
7 Yale 0
0 Holy Cross 13
7 Harvard 23
7 Rutgers 13

**1942**
28 URI 0
28 Columbia 21
7 Lafayette 0
13 Princeton 32
0 Yale 27
20 Holy Cross 14
0 Harvard 7
0 Colgate 13

**1943**
0 Holy Cross 20
35 Tufts 6
62 Camp Kilmer [NJ] 3
28 Princeton 20
21 Yale 20
34 Coast Guard Acad. 31
0 Army 59
14 Colgate 21

**1944**
44 Tufts 0
7 Army 59
24 Holy Cross 24
13 Dartmouth 14
0 Coast Guard Acad. 20
0 Yale 13
12 Columbia 0
32 Colgate 20

**1945**
0 Penn 50
51 Boston College 6
0 Holy Cross 25
6 Columbia 27
33 Coast Guard Acad. 6
20 Yale 7
7 Harvard 14
6 Colgate 6

**1946**
14 Canisius 6
12 Princeton 33
29 URI 0
20 Dartmouth 13
14 Boston U. 14
19 Holy Cross 21
0 Yale 49
0 Harvard 28
14 Colgate 20

**1947**
33 U. Conn. 13
7 Princeton 21
55 URI 6
10 Dartmouth 13
13 Colgate 13
20 Holy Cross 19
20 Yale 14
7 Harvard 13
20 Rutgers 27

**1948**
13 Yale 28
23 Princeton 20
33 URI 0
14 Holy Cross 6
49 U. Conn. 6
20 Rutgers 6
36 Western Res. 0
19 Harvard 30
35 Colgate 7

**1949**
28 Holy Cross 6
46 URI 0
14 Princeton 27
48 Lehigh 0
28 Western Res. 14
14 Yale 0
28 Harvard 14
16 Columbia 7
41 Colgate 26

**1950**
12 Yale 36
21 Holy Cross 41
55 URI 13
0 Princeton 34
34 Colgate 35
12 Rutgers 15
0 Penn 50
13 Harvard 14
0 Columbia 33

**1951**
14 Temple 20
14 Yale 13
20 URI 13
14 Colgate 32

*Halfback Bob Margarita established Brown's all-time single game rushing record in 1942 with 233 yards against Columbia and was second in the nation in 1941 with 531 yards on punt returns. He later was All-Pro with the Chicago Bears.*

6 Holy Cross 41
0 Princeton 12
21 Rutgers 28
21 Harvard 34
14 Columbia 29

**1952**
0 Yale 28
6 URI 7
0 Holy Cross 46
7 Rutgers 19
0 Princeton 39
21 U. Conn. 13
28 Harvard 21
0 Columbia 14
27 Colgate 33

**1953**
6 Amherst 7
0 Yale 13
13 URI 19
27 Rutgers 20
6 Holy Cross 0
13 Princeton 27
42 U. Conn. 7
20 Harvard 27
7 Colgate 7

**1954**
18 Columbia 7
24 Yale 26
35 URI 0
21 Princeton 20
14 Temple 19
34 Lehigh 6
40 Springfield 7
21 Harvard 21
18 Colgate 14

**1955**
12 Columbia 14
20 Yale 27
7 Dartmouth 0
12 Rutgers 14
7 URI 19
7 Princeton 14
7 Cornell 20
14 Harvard 6
0 Colgate 25

**1956**
20 Columbia 0
2 Yale 20
7 Dartmouth 14
7 Penn 14
27 URI 7
7 Princeton 21
13 Cornell 6
21 Harvard 12
20 Colgate 0

**1957**
20 Columbia 23
21 Yale 20
0 Dartmouth 35
20 Penn 7
21 URI 7
0 Princeton 7
6 Cornell 13
33 Harvard 6
33 Colgate 7

**1958**
22 Columbia 0
35 Yale 29
0 Dartmouth 20
20 Penn 21
47 URI 6
18 Princeton 28
12 Cornell 8
29 Harvard 22
28 Colgate 6

**1959**
6 Columbia 21
0 Yale 17
0 Dartmouth 0
9 Penn 36
6 URI 0
0 Princeton 7
0 Cornell 19

16 Harvard 6
14 Colgate 33

**1960**

0 Columbia 37
0 Yale 9
0 Dartmouth 20
7 Penn 36
36 URI 14
21 Princeton 54
7 Cornell 6
8 Harvard 22
21 Colgate 14

**1961**

0 Columbia 50
3 Yale 14
0 Dartmouth 34
0 Penn 7
9 URI 12
0 Princeton 52
0 Cornell 25
6 Harvard 21
6 Colgate 30

**1962**

6 Colgate 2
20 Columbia 22
6 Yale 6
0 Dartmouth 41
15 Penn 18
12 URI 12
12 Princeton 28
26 Cornell 28
19 Harvard 31

**1963**

14 Columbia 41
12 Yale 7
7 Dartmouth 14
41 Penn 13
33 URI 7
13 Princeton 34
25 Cornell 28
12 Harvard 24
DNP Colgate

**1964**

20 Lafayette 3
3 Penn 0
7 Yale 15
14 Dartmouth 24
30 URI 14
0 Princeton 14
31 Cornell 28
7 Harvard 19
7 Columbia 0

**1965**

6 URI 14
0 Penn 7
0 Yale 3
9 Dartmouth 35
6 Colgate 0
27 Princeton 45
21 Cornell 41
8 Harvard 17
51 Columbia 7

**1966**

40 URI 14
0 Penn 20
0 Yale 24
14 Dartmouth 49
7 Colgate 48
17 Princeton 24
14 Cornell 23
7 Harvard 24
38 Columbia 40

**1967**

8 URI 12
7 Penn 28
0 Yale 35
7 Dartmouth 41
7 Colgate 0
14 Princeton 48
14 Cornell 14
6 Harvard 21
14 Columbia 7

**1968**

10 URI 9
13 Penn 17
13 Yale 35
0 Dartmouth 48
27 Colgate 19
7 Princeton 50
0 Cornell 31
7 Harvard 31
20 Columbia 46

**1969**

21 URI 0
2 Penn 23
13 Yale 27
13 Dartmouth 38
6 Colgate 20
6 Princeton 33
7 Cornell 14
24 Harvard 17
3 Columbia 18

**1970**

21 URI 14
9 Penn 17
0 Yale 28
14 Dartmouth 42
6 Colgate 10
14 Princeton 42
21 Cornell 35
10 Harvard 17
17 Columbia 12

**1971**

21 URI 34
16 Penn 17
10 Yale 17
7 Dartmouth 10
32 Colgate 42
21 Princeton 49
7 Cornell 21
19 Harvard 24
6 Columbia 24

**1972**

24 Holy Cross 30
17 URI 21
28 Penn 20
19 Yale 53
20 Dartmouth 49
10 Princeton 31
28 Cornell 48
14 Harvard 21
12 Columbia 28

**1973**

20 URI 20
20 Penn 28
34 Yale 25
16 Dartmouth 28
7 Princeton 6
17 Cornell 7
32 Harvard 35
37 Columbia 14

**1974**

10 Holy Cross 45
45 URI 15
9 Penn 14
0 Yale 24
6 Dartmouth 7
17 Princeton 13
16 Cornell 8
10 Harvard 7
28 Columbia 19

**1975**

41 URI 20
17 Penn 8
27 Yale 12
10 Dartmouth 10
20 Holy Cross 21
24 Princeton 16
45 Cornell 23
26 Harvard 45
48 Columbia 13

**1976**

14 Yale 6
3 URI 0
13 Princeton 7
6 Penn 7
28 Cornell 12
28 Holy Cross 18
16 Harvard 14
35 Dartmouth 21
28 Columbia 17

## Columbia University

New York, New York
Established: 1754
Colors: Light Blue and White
Nickname: Lions

*Head Coaches*

George Sanford, 1899-1901
William F. Morley, 1902-1905
T. Nelson Metcalf, 1915-1918
Fred Dawson, 1919
Frank O'Neil, 1920-1922
Percy Haughton, 1923-1924
Paul Withington, 1924
Charles F. Crowley, 1925-1929
Lou Little, 1930-1956
Buff Donelli, 1957-1967
Frank Navarro, 1968-1973
Bill Campbell, 1974-

### Scores 1870–1976

**1870**
3 Rutgers 6

**1871**
No games played

**1872**
0 Rutgers 0
5 Rutgers 7
0 Yale 3
6 Stevens 0

**1873**
2 Stevens 1
4 Rutgers 5
4 Rutgers 3

**1874**
1 Rutgers 6
2 Stevens 4
4 Rutgers 1
0 Princeton 6
1 Yale 5
1 Yale 6

**1875**
1 Rutgers 1
2 Stevens 1
5 CCNY 0
2 Princeton 6
6 CCNY 0
3 Yale 2

**1876**
3 Stevens 5
0 Princeton 3
4 Stevens 0
0 Yale 2

**1877**
0 Harvard 6g, 9t
6T Rutgers 0
3T Princeton 4g, 6t

**1878**
0 Pennsylvania 0

**1879**
0 Stevens 0
0 Princeton 2g, 3t
0 Pennsylvania 1t
0 Yale 2g, 3t
0 Rutgers 0

**1880**
0 Harvard 3g, 1t
0 Yale 12g, 3t
3G, 1T Rutgers 3t

**1881**
3G, 2S Stevens 1g, 1t
0 Harvard 1g, 3t
1S Rutgers 4s
3S Princeton, 1g, 2t, 2s
6S Yale 1g
1g, 3t Rutgers 3s
2G Pennsylvania 0

**1882**
0 Princeton 8g, 3t
1T Rutgers 2g, 1t
0 Harvard 2g, 4t
0 Yale 11g, 4t
0 Princeton 3g, 1t

**1883**
12 CCNY 0
0 Stevens 19
1 Pennsylvania 35
0 Yale 93

**1884**
5 Rutgers 35
16 CCNY 0

**1885**
No games played

**1886-1888**
No teams

**1889**
0 Crescent 30
10 Lafayette 10
4 Trinity 24
0 Yale 62
6 Lehigh 51
0 Princeton 71
0 Pennsylvania 24
12 Stevens 6
22 Manhattan AC 0
0 Amherst 0
0 Cornell 20

**1890**
0 Wesleyan 4
0 Pennsylvania 18
40 Fordham 0
0 Crescent 29
0 Princeton 85
6 Rutgers 6
0 Cornell 36

**1891**
32 Berkeley 0
0 Manhattan AC 28
0 Crescent 42
0 Stevens 52
0 Trinity 54
0 Rutgers 44

**1892-1898**
No games played. Columbia had freshman teams only, 1893-1895.

NOTE: The 52-0 game of 1898 which some sources have ascribed to Columbia was actually a game between Navy and the "Columbia A.C. of Washington, D.C.," Navy winning.

**1899**
26 Rutgers 0
21 Union 0
0 Princeton 11
40 NYU 0
18 Amherst 0
5 Yale 0
46 Stevens 0
0 Cornell 29
16 Army 0
22 Dartmouth 0
0 Carlisle 45

**1900**
11 Rutgers 0
12 Wesleyan 0
0 Williams 0
0 Harvard 24
45 Stevens 0
0 Pennsylvania 30
5 Yale 12
6 Princeton 5
17 Buffalo 0
11 Navy 0
17 Carlisle 6

**1901**
0 Buffalo 5
27 Rutgers 0
5 Williams 0
0 Harvard 18
12 Hamilton 0
5 Yale 10
29 Haverford 6
10 Pennsylvania 0
18 Georgetown 0
5 Syracuse 11
0 Cornell 24
6 Navy 5
40 Carlisle 12

**1902**
43 Rutgers 0
45 Fordham 0
5 Buffalo 0
24 Swarthmore 0
35 Hamilton 0
0 Princeton 21
0 Pennsylvania 17
0 Brown 28
0 Amherst 29
5 Navy 0
6 Syracuse 6

**1903**
10 Wesleyan 0
16 Alumni 0
36 Union 0
29 Hamilton 0
5 Williams 0
5 Swarthmore 0
12 Amherst 0
18 Pennsylvania 6
0 Yale 25
17 Cornell 12

**1904**
10 Union 0
28 F & M 0
16 Wesleyan 0
31 Tufts 0
11 Williams 0
12 Swarthmore 0
0 Amherst 12
0 Pennsylvania 16
0 Yale 34
12 Cornell 6

**1905**
23 Union 0
21 Seton Hall 0
0 Wesleyan 0
11 Williams 5
10 Amherst 10
0 Princeton 12
0 Yale 53
12 Cornell 6
0 Pennsylvania 23

**1906-1914**
Football banned at Columbia

**1915**
57 St. Lawrence 0
15 Stevens 6
17 Connecticut 6
19 NYU 16
18 Wesleyan 0

**1916**
7 Hamilton 14
6 Vermont 0
0 Union 3
0 Williams 0
0 Stevens 0
0 Swarthmore 18
0 Wesleyan 40
0 NYU 6

**1917**
21 Union 0
6 Williams 9
6 Amherst 14
70 Hobart 0
0 Wesleyan 6
7 NYU 9

**1918**
7 Merritt 0
21 Amherst 7
33 Union 0
14 Wesleyan 0
12 NYU 0
0 Syracuse 20

**1919**
0 USS Arizona 0
7 Vermont 0
0 Williams 25
9 Amherst 7

12 NYU 27
0 Union 0
0 Stevens 13
13 Wesleyan 28
7 Brown 7

**1920**

21 Trinity 0
14 NYU 7
20 Amherst 7
0 Wesleyan 10
20 Williams 14
7 Swarthmore 21
7 Cornell 34
7 Pennsylvania 27

**1921**

7 Amherst 9
14 Wesleyan 3
19 NYU 0
7 Dartmouth 31
0 Williams 20
7 Cornell 41
21 Ohio U. 23
14 Colgate 21

**1922**

48 Ursinus 7
43 Amherst 6
10 Wesleyan 6
6 NYU 2
10 Williams 13
0 Cornell 56
17 Middlebury 6
7 Dartmouth 28
6 Colgate 59

**1923**

13 Ursinus 0
0 Amherst 0
12 Wesleyan 6
7 Pennsylvania 19
0 Williams 10
9 Middlebury 6
0 Cornell 35
21 NYU 0
6 Dartmouth 31

**1924**

*(Haughton died during the season of 1924 and Withington coached the team for the remainder of that year.)*

29 Haverford 3
52 St. Lawrence 0
35 Wesleyan 0
7 Pennsylvania 10
27 Williams 3
0 Cornell 14
40 NYU 0
14 Army 14
6 Syracuse 9

**1925**

59 Haverford 0
47 J. Hopkins 0
64 Wesleyan 0
0 Ohio State 9
26 Williams 0
14 Cornell 17
6 NYU 6
21 Army 7
46 Alfred 0
5 Syracuse 16

**1926**

14 Vermont 0
26 Union 0
41 Wesleyan 0
7 Ohio State 32
24 Duke 0
17 Cornell 9
13 W & M 10
0 Pennsylvania 3
2 Syracuse 19

**1927**

32 Vermont 0
28 Union 0
28 Wesleyan 0
7 Colgate 13
19 Williams 0
0 Cornell 0
7 J. Hopkins 7
0 Pennsylvania 27
14 Syracuse 7

**1928**

20 Vermont 0
27 Union 0
31 Wesleyan 7
7 Dartmouth 21
20 Williams 6
0 Cornell 0
14 J. Hopkins 13
7 Pennsylvania 34
6 Syracuse 14

**1929**

38 Middlebury 6
31 Union 0
52 Wesleyan 0
0 Dartmouth 34
33 Williams 0
6 Cornell 12
0 Colgate 33
0 Pennsylvania 20
0 Syracuse 6

**1930**

48 Middlebury 0
25 Union 0
48 Wesleyan 0
0 Dartmouth 52
3 Williams 0
10 Cornell 7
0 Colgate 54
0 Brown 6
7 Syracuse 19

**1931**

61 Middlebury 0
51 Union 0
37 Wesleyan 0
19 Dartmouth 6
19 Williams 0
0 Cornell 13
27 Virginia 0
9 Brown 7
0 Syracuse 0

**1932**

51 Middlebury 0
41 Lehigh 6
20 Princeton 7
22 Virginia 6
46 Williams 0
6 Cornell 0
7 Navy 6
6 Brown 7
0 Syracuse 0

**1933**

39 Lehigh 0
15 Virginia 6
0 Princeton 20
33 Penn State 0
9 Cornell 6
14 Navy 7
46 Lafayette 6
16 Syracuse 0
7 Stanford 0
*(Rose Bowl)*

**1934**

12 Yale 6
29 VMI 6
7 Navy 18
14 Penn State 7
14 Cornell 0
39 Brown 0
13 Pennsylvania 12
12 Syracuse 0

**1935**

12 VMI 0
20 Rutgers 6
0 Pennsylvania 34
7 Michigan 19
7 Cornell 7
2 Syracuse 14
7 Navy 28
18 Brown 0
13 Dartmouth 7

**1936**

34 Maine 0
16 Army 27
38 VMI 0
0 Michigan 13
20 Cornell 13
13 Dartmouth 20
17 Syracuse 0
7 Stanford 0

**1937**

40 Williams 6
18 Army 21
26 Pennsylvania 6
6 Brown 7
0 Cornell 14
6 Navy 13
6 Syracuse 6
0 Dartmouth 27
0 Stanford 0

**1938**

27 Yale 14
20 Army 18
0 Colgate 12
13 Pennsylvania 14
7 Cornell 23
39 Virginia 0
9 Navy 14
12 Syracuse 13
27 Brown 36

**1939**

7 Yale 10
6 Army 6
7 Princeton 14
26 VMI 7
7 Cornell 13
19 Navy 13
0 Tulane 25
0 Colgate 0

**1940**

15 Maine 0
20 Dartmouth 6
19 Georgia 13
0 Syracuse 3
0 Cornell 27
7 Wisconsin 6
0 Navy 0
20 Colgate 17
0 Brown 0

**1941**

13 Brown 6
21 Princeton 0
3 Georgia 7
0 Army 13
7 Cornell 0
16 Pennsylvania 19
0 Michigan 28
21 Colgate 30

**1942**

39 Fort Monmouth 0
34 Maine 2
21 Brown 28
6 Army 34
12 Pennsylvania 42
14 Cornell 13
26 Colgate 35
9 Navy 13
13 Dartmouth 26

**1943**

7 Princeton 26
7 Yale 20
0 Army 52
0 Pennsylvania 33
6 Cornell 33
13 Dartmouth 47
0 Navy 61
0 Colgate 41

**1944**

21 Union 0
26 Syracuse 2
10 Yale 27
0 Colgate 6
7 Cornell 25
7 Pennsylvania 35
0 Brown 12
0 Dartmouth 18

**1945**

40 Lafayette 14
32 Syracuse 0
27 Yale 13
31 Colgate 7
27 Brown 6
34 Cornell 26
7 Pennsylvania 32
32 Princeton 7
21 Dartmouth 0

**1946**

13 Rutgers 7
23 Navy 14
28 Yale 20
14 Army 48
33 Dartmouth 13
0 Cornell 12
6 Pennsylvania 41
46 Lafayette 0
59 Syracuse 21

**1947**

40 Rutgers 28
13 Navy 6
7 Yale 17
14 Pennsylvania 34
21 Army 20
22 Cornell 0
15 Dartmouth 0
10 Holy Cross 0
28 Syracuse 8

**1948**

27 Rutgers 6
24 Harvard 33
34 Yale 28
14 Pennsylvania 20
14 Princeton 16
13 Cornell 20
21 Dartmouth 26
13 Navy 0
34 Syracuse 28

**1949**

27 Amherst 7
14 Harvard 7
7 Yale 33
7 Pennsylvania 27
6 Army 63
0 Cornell 54
14 Dartmouth 38
0 Navy 28
7 Brown 16

**1950**

42 Hobart 12
28 Harvard 7
14 Yale 20
0 Pennsylvania 34
0 Army 34
20 Cornell 19
7 Dartmouth 14
7 Navy 29
33 Brown 0

**1951**

35 Harvard 0
14 Yale 0
13 Pennsylvania 28

9 Army 14
21 Cornell 20
21 Dartmouth 6
7 Navy 21
29 Brown 14

**1952**
0 Princeton 14
16 Harvard 7
28 Yale 35
17 Pennsylvania 27
14 Army 14
14 Cornell 21
14 Dartmouth 38
0 Navy 28
14 Brown 0

**1953**
14 Lehigh 7
19 Princeton 20
7 Yale 13
6 Harvard 0
7 Army 40
13 Cornell 27
25 Dartmouth 19
6 Navy 14
27 Rutgers 13

**1954**
7 Brown 18
20 Princeton 54
7 Yale 13
7 Harvard 6
12 Army 67
0 Cornell 26
0 Dartmouth 26
6 Navy 51
12 Rutgers 45

**1955**
14 Brown 12
7 Princeton 20
14 Yale 46
7 Harvard 21
0 Army 45
19 Cornell 34
7 Dartmouth 14
0 Navy 47
6 Rutgers 12

**1956**
0 Brown 20
0 Princeton 39
19 Yale 33
26 Harvard 20
0 Army 60
25 Cornell 19
0 Dartmouth 14
6 Pennsylvania 20
18 Rutgers 12

**1957**
23 Brown 20
6 Princeton 47
0 Yale 19
6 Harvard 19
6 Lehigh 40
0 Cornell 8
0 Dartmouth 7
6 Pennsylvania 28
7 Rutgers 26

**1958**
0 Brown 22
8 Princeton 43
13 Yale 0
0 Harvard 26
14 Buffalo 34
0 Cornell 25
0 Dartmouth 38
0 Pennsylvania 42
0 Rutgers 61

**1959**
21 Brown 6
0 Princeton 22
0 Yale 14
22 Harvard 38
0 Holy Cross 34
7 Cornell 34
0 Dartmouth 22
6 Pennsylvania 24
26 Rutgers 16

**1960**
37 Brown 0
0 Princeton 49
8 Yale 30
7 Harvard 8
6 Holy Cross 27
44 Cornell 6
6 Dartmouth 22
16 Pennsylvania 6
2 Rutgers 43

**1961**
50 Brown 0
20 Princeton 30
11 Yale 0
26 Harvard 14
7 Lehigh 14
35 Cornell 7
35 Dartmouth 14
37 Pennsylvania 6
19 Rutgers 32

**1962**
22 Brown 20
0 Princeton 33
14 Yale 10
14 Harvard 36
22 Lehigh 15
25 Cornell 21
0 Dartmouth 42
21 Pennsylvania 7
6 Rutgers 22

**1963**
22 Brown 14
6 Princeton 7
7 Yale 19
3 Harvard 3
42 Lehigh 21
17 Cornell 18
6 Dartmouth 47
33 Pennsylvania 8
35 Rutgers 28

**1964**
21 Colgate 14
13 Princeton 23
0 Harvard 3
9 Yale 9
35 Rutgers 38
20 Cornell 57
14 Dartmouth 31
33 Pennsylvania 12
0 Brown 7

**1965**
10 Lafayette 14
0 Princeton 31
6 Harvard 21
21 Yale 7
12 Rutgers 7
6 Cornell 20
0 Dartmouth 47
21 Pennsylvania 31
7 Brown 51

**1966**
0 Colgate 38
12 Princeton 14
7 Harvard 34
21 Yale 44
34 Rutgers 37
6 Cornell 31
14 Dartmouth 56
22 Pennsylvania 14
40 Brown 38

**1967**
17 Colgate 14
14 Princeton 28
13 Harvard 49
7 Yale 21
24 Rutgers 13
14 Cornell 27
7 Dartmouth 13
6 Pennsylvania 26
7 Brown 14

**1968**
14 Lafayette 36
16 Princeton 44
14 Harvard 21
7 Yale 28
17 Rutgers 28
34 Cornell 25
19 Dartmouth 31
7 Pennsylvania 13
46 Brown 20

**1969**
22 Lafayette 36
7 Princeton 21
0 Harvard 51
6 Yale 41
14 Rutgers 21
3 Cornell 10
7 Dartmouth 37
7 Pennsylvania 17
18 Brown 3

**1970**
23 Lafayette 9
22 Princeton 24
28 Harvard 21
15 Yale 32
30 Rutgers 14
20 Cornell 31
0 Dartmouth 55
14 Pennsylvania 21
12 Brown 17

**1971**
0 Lafayette 3
22 Princeton 20
19 Harvard 21
15 Yale 14
17 Rutgers 16
21 Cornell 24
31 Dartmouth 29
17 Pennsylvania 3
24 Brown 6

**1972**
44 Fordham 0
0 Princeton 0
18 Harvard 20
14 Yale 28
3 Rutgers 6
14 Cornell 0
8 Dartmouth 38
14 Pennsylvania 20
28 Brown 12

**1973**
0 Bucknell 0
14 Princeton 13
0 Harvard 57
0 Yale 29
2 Rutgers 28
14 Cornell 44
6 Dartmouth 24
8 Pennsylvania 42
14 Brown 37

**1974**
0 Lafayette 15
13 Princeton 40
6 Harvard 34
2 Yale 42
38 Bucknell 33
0 Cornell 24
0 Dartmouth 21
3 Pennsylvania 21
19 Brown 28

**1975**
7 Lafayette 10
7 Princeton 27
30 Harvard 35
7 Yale 34
0 Rutgers 41
42 Cornell 19
17 Dartmouth 22
28 Pennsylvania 25
13 Brown 48

**1976**
10 Harvard 34
38 Lafayette 31
14 Pennsylvania 10
3 Princeton 9
6 Yale 37
0 Rutgers 47
14 Dartmouth 34
35 Cornell 17
17 Brown 28

## Cornell University

Ithaca, New York
Established: 1865
Colors: Carnelian and White
Nickname: Big Red

*Head Coaches*

No regular coach, 1887-1893
Marshall Newell, 1894-1895
Joseph Beacham, 1896
Glenn (Pop) Warner, 1897-1898
Percy Haughton, 1899-1900
Raymond Starbuck, 1901-1902
William Warner, 1903
Glenn (Pop) Warner, 1904-1906
Henry Schoellkopf, 1907-1908
George Walder, 1909
Daniel Reed, 1910-1911
Al Sharpe, 1912-1917
No team, 1918
John Rush, 1919
Gil Dobie, 1920-1935
Carl Snavely, 1936-1944
Ed McKeever, 1945-1946
George (Lefty) James, 1947-1960
Tom Harp, 1961-1965
Jack Musick, 1966-1974
George Seifert, 1975-1976
Bob Blackman, 1977-

## Scores 1887-1976

**1887**
10 Union 24
10 Lehigh 38

**1888**
26 Palmyra 0
20 Williams 0
30 Union 0
0 Lafayette 16
20 Bucknell 0
0 Lehigh 4

**1889**
66 Bucknell 0
10 Lafayette 0
6 Yale 56
124 Rochester 0
38 Stevens Inst. 4
0 Yale 70
66 Michigan 0
20 Columbia 0
24 Lafayette 0

**1890**
98 Rochester 0
32 Union 0
8 Williams 18
0 Harvard 77
0 Amherst 18
26 Trinity 0
2 Wesleyan 4
26 Bucknell 0
20 Michigan 5
36 Columbia 0
12 Chicago U. Club 8
82 St. Johns 4

**1891**
68 Syracuse 0
0 Bucknell 4
72 Stevens Inst. 0
30 Lafayette 0
24 Lehigh 0
0 Princeton 6
58 Michigan 12
32 Detroit A.C. 0
4 Chicago U. Club 12
10 Michigan 0

**1892**
16 Syracuse A.C. 0
58 Syracuse 0
54 Bucknell 0
58 Dickinson 0
76 Lehigh 0
24 Williams 12
14 Harvard 20
44 Michigan 0
44 M.I.T. 12
16 Manhattan A.C. 0
30 Michigan 10

**1893**
50 Syracuse 0
16 Gettysburg 0
16 Penn State 0
18 Union 6
0 Princeton 46
0 Tufts 6
10 Williams 10
0 Harvard 34
0 Tufts 6
0 Lehigh 14
0 Pennsylvania 50

**1894**
39 Syracuse 0
37 Union 0
24 Lafayette 0
4 Princeton 12
12 Harvard 22
22 Michigan 0
22 Crescent A.C. 0
0 Williams 0
0 Pennsylvania 6
4 Michigan 12
10 Lehigh 6

**1895**
8 Syracuse 0
0 Penn State 0
12 Western Reserve 4
0 Lafayette 6
0 Harvard 25
0 Princeton 6
6 Brown 4
2 Pennsylvania 46

**1896**
6 Colgate 0
22 Syracuse 0
48 Western Reserve 0
18 Tufts 0
4 Harvard 13
0 Princeton 37
54 Bucknell 0
0 Williams 0
10 Pennsylvania 32

**1897**
6 Colgate 0
16 Syracuse 0
15 Tufts 0
4 Lafayette 4
0 Princeton 10
5 Harvard 24
45 Penn State 0
42 Williams 0
0 Pennsylvania 4

**1898**
28 Syracuse 0
29 Colgate 5
41 Hamilton 0
47 Trinity 0
30 Syracuse 0
23 Carlisle Indians 6
27 Buffalo 0
0 Princeton 6
6 Oberlin 0
12 Williams 0
47 Lafayette 0
6 Pennsylvania 12

**1899**
42 Colgate 0
17 Syracuse 0
12 Hamilton 0
12 Williams 0
6 Chicago 17
6 Lehigh 0
5 Princeton 0
29 Columbia 0
5 Lafayette 6
0 Pennsylvania 29

**1900**
16 Colgate 0
6 Rochester 0
6 Bucknell 0
6 Syracuse 0
16 Wash. & Jeff. 5
11 Union 0
23 Dartmouth 6
12 Princeton 0
29 Oberlin 0
0 Lafayette 17
42 Vermont 0
0 Pennsylvania 27

**1901**
17 Colgate 0
50 Rochester 0
6 Bucknell 0
39 Hamilton 0
24 Union 0
17 Carlisle Indians 0
29 Oberlin 0
6 Princeton 8
30 Lehigh 0
24 Columbia 0
68 Vermont 0
23 Pennsylvania 6

**1902**
5 Colgate 0
31 Rochester 0
42 Union 0
57 Hobart 0
37 Williams 6
6 Carlisle Indians 10
57 Oberlin 0
0 Princeton 10
50 Wash. & Jeff. 0
28 Lafayette 0
11 Pennsylvania 12

**1903**
12 Hobart 0
26 Alfred 0
11 Rochester 0
12 Colgate 0
6 Bucknell 0
41 Western Reserve 0
0 Princeton 44
0 Lehigh 0
12 Columbia 17
0 Pennsylvania 42

**1904**
17 Colgate 0
29 Rochester 6
24 Hobart 0
34 Hamilton 0
24 Bucknell 12
36 F & M 5
6 Princeton 18
50 Lehigh 5
6 Columbia 12
0 Pennsylvania 34

**1905**
5 Hamilton 0
12 Colgate 11
28 Hobart 0
24 Bucknell 0
30 Pittsburgh 0
57 Haverford 0
0 Swarthmore 14
6 Princeton 16
6 Columbia 12
5 Pennsylvania 6

**1906**
0 Colgate 0
21 Hamilton 0
25 Oberlin 5
23 Niagara 6
24 Bucknell 6
72 Bowdoin 0
5 Princeton 14
23 Pittsburgh 0
16 Holy Cross 6
28 Swarthmore 0
0 Pennsylvania 0

**1907**
23 Hamilton 0
22 Oberlin 5
47 Niagara 0
18 Colgate 0
6 Penn State 8

6 Princeton 5
18 Pittsburgh 5
14 Army 10
18 Swarthmore 0
5 Pennsylvania 12

**1908**
11 Hamilton 0
23 Oberlin 10
9 Colgate 0
9 Vermont 0
10 Penn State 4
6 Amherst 0
6 Chicago 6
18 Trinity 6
4 Pennsylvania 17

**1909**
16 R.P.I. 3
16 Oberlin 6
6 Fordham 12
16 Vermont 0
0 Williams 3
0 Harvard 18
6 Chicago 6
6 Pennsylvania 17

**1910**
50 Hobart 0
24 R.P.I. 0
0 Oberlin 0
47 St. Bonaventure 0
15 Vermont 5
5 Harvard 27
18 Chicago 0
6 Pennsylvania 12

**1911**
35 Allegheny 0
6 Colgate 0
15 Oberlin 3
0 Penn State 5
6 Wash. & Jeff. 0
9 Pittsburgh 3
15 Williams 14
6 Michigan 0
0 Chicago 6
9 Pennsylvania 21

**1912**
3 Wash. & Jeff. 0
7 Colgate 13
0 Oberlin 13
14 N.Y.U. 6
6 Penn State 29
14 Bucknell 0
10 Williams 24
0 Dartmouth 24
7 Michigan 20
2 Pennsylvania 7

**1913**
41 Ursinus 0
0 Colgate 0
37 Oberlin 12
0 Carlisle Indians 7
10 Bucknell 7
7 Pittsburgh 20
6 Harvard 23
0 Michigan 17
10 Lafayette 3
21 Pennsylvania 0

**1914**
28 Ursinus 0
3 Pittsburgh 9
3 Colgate 7
21 Carlisle Indians 0
48 Bucknell 0
28 Brown 7
48 Holy Cross 3
26 F & M 3
28 Michigan 13
24 Pennsylvania 12

**1915**
13 Gettysburg 0
34 Oberlin 7
46 Williams 6
41 Bucknell 0
10 Harvard 0
45 V.P.I. 0
34 Michigan 7
40 Wash. & Lee 21
24 Pennsylvania 9

**1916**
26 Gettysburg 0
42 Williams 0
19 Bucknell 0
0 Harvard 23
15 Carnegie Tech. 7
23 Michigan 20
37 Mass. State 0
3 Pennsylvania 23

**1917**
22 Oberlin 0
10 Williams 14
0 47th Infantry 6
0 Colgate 20
20 Bucknell 0
20 Carnegie Tech. 0
6 Michigan 42
0 Fordham 27
0 Pennsylvania 7

**1918**
NO TEAM

**1919**
9 Oberlin 0
3 Williams 0
0 Colgate 21
0 Dartmouth 9
2 Lafayette 21
20 Carnegie Tech. 0
0 Penn State 20
0 Pennsylvania 24

**1920**
13 Rochester 6
55 St. Bonaventure 7
60 Union 0
42 Colgate 6
24 Rutgers 0
3 Dartmouth 14
34 Columbia 7
0 Pennsylvania 28

**1921**
41 St. Bonaventure 0
55 Rochester 0
110 Western Reserve 0
31 Colgate 7
59 Dartmouth 7
41 Columbia 7
14 Springfield 0
41 Pennsylvania 0

**1922**
55 St. Bonaventure 6
66 Niagara 0
68 New Hampshire 7
14 Colgate 0
56 Columbia 0
23 Dartmouth 0
48 Albright 14
9 Pennsylvania 0

**1923**
41 St. Bonaventure 6
84 Susquehanna 0
28 Williams 6
34 Colgate 7
32 Dartmouth 7
35 Columbia 0
52 Johns Hopkins 0
14 Pennsylvania 7

**1924**
56 St. Bonaventure 0
27 Niagara 0
7 Williams 14
0 Rutgers 10
14 Columbia 0
91 Susquehanna 0
14 Dartmouth 27
0 Pennsylvania 20

**1925**
80 Susquehanna 0
26 Niagara 0
48 Williams 0
41 Rutgers 0
17 Columbia 14
13 Dartmouth 62
33 Canisius 0
0 Pennsylvania 7

**1926**
6 Geneva 0
28 Niagara 0
49 Williams 0
24 Michigan State 14
9 Columbia 17
41 St. Bonaventure 0
24 Dartmouth 23
10 Pennsylvania 10

**1927**
41 Clarkson 0
19 Niagara 6
53 Richmond 0
10 Princeton 21
0 Columbia 0
6 St. Bonaventure 6
7 Dartmouth 53
0 Pennsylvania 35

**1928**
20 Clarkson 0
34 Niagara 0
18 Hampden-Sidney 6
0 Princeton 3
0 Columbia 0
0 St. Bonaventure 0
0 Dartmouth 28
0 Pennsylvania 49

**1929**
60 Clarkson 0
22 Niagara 6
40 Hampden-Sidney 6
13 Princeton 7
12 Columbia 6
36 Western Reserve 0
14 Dartmouth 18
7 Pennsylvania 17

**1930**
66 Clarkson 0
61 Niagara 14
47 Hampden-Sidney 6
12 Princeton 7
7 Columbia 10
54 Hobart 0
13 Dartmouth 19
13 Pennsylvania 7

**1931**
68 Clarkson 0
37 Niagara 6
27 Richmond 0
33 Princeton 0
13 Columbia 0
54 Alfred 0
0 Dartmouth 14
7 Pennsylvania 0

**1932**
72 Buffalo 0
7 Niagara 0
27 Richmond 0
0 Princeton 0
0 Columbia 6
40 Albright 14
21 Dartmouth 6
7 Pennsylvania 13

**1933**
48 St. Lawrence 7
28 Richmond 7
0 Michigan 40
7 Syracuse 14
6 Columbia 9
7 Dartmouth 0
20 Pennsylvania 12

**1934**
14 St. Lawrence 0
0 Richmond 6
7 Syracuse 20
0 Princeton 45
0 Columbia 14
21 Dartmouth 6
13 Pennsylvania 23

**1935**
6 St. Lawrence 12
19 Western Reserve 33
14 Syracuse 21
0 Princeton 54
7 Columbia 7
6 Dartmouth 41
7 Pennsylvania 33

**1936**
74 Alfred 0
0 Yale 23
20 Syracuse 7
13 Penn State 7
13 Columbia 20
13 Princeton 41
6 Dartmouth 20
6 Pennsylvania 14

**1937**
26 Penn State 19
40 Colgate 7
20 Princeton 7
6 Syracuse 14
0 Yale 9
14 Columbia 0
6 Dartmouth 6
34 Pennsylvania 20

**1938**
15 Colgate 6
20 Harvard 0
17 Syracuse 19
21 Penn State 6
23 Columbia 7
14 Dartmouth 7
0 Pennsylvania 0

**1939**
19 Syracuse 6
20 Princeton 7
47 Penn State 0
23 Ohio State 14
13 Columbia 7
14 Colgate 12
35 Dartmouth 6
26 Pennsylvania 0

**1940**
34 Colgate 0
45 Army 0
33 Syracuse 6
21 Ohio State 7
27 Columbia 0
21 Yale 0
0 Dartmouth 3
20 Pennsylvania 22

**1941**
6 Syracuse 0
7 Harvard 0
0 Navy 14
21 Colgate 2
0 Columbia 7
21 Yale 7
33 Dartmouth 19
0 Pennsylvania 16

**1942**
20 Lafayette 16
6 Colgate 18
8 Army 28

0 Penn State 0
7 Syracuse 12
13 Columbia 14
13 Yale 7
21 Dartmouth 19
7 Pennsylvania 34

**1943**

7 Bucknell 6
27 Sampson N.T.S. 13
7 Navy 46
30 Princeton 0
20 Holy Cross 7
7 Colgate 20
33 Columbia 6
13 Penn State 0
0 Dartmouth 20
14 Pennsylvania 20

**1944**

39 Syracuse 6
26 Bucknell 0
7 Yale 16
7 Colgate 14
13 Sampson N.T.S. 6
25 Columbia 7
0 Navy 48
14 Dartmouth 13
0 Pennsylvania 20

**1945**

26 Syracuse 14
19 Bucknell 8
39 U.S. Sub Base 0
6 Princeton 14
7 Yale 18
26 Columbia 34
20 Colgate 6
20 Dartmouth 13
6 Pennsylvania 59

**1946**

21 Bucknell 0
21 Army 46
13 Colgate 9
6 Yale 6
14 Princeton 7
12 Columbia 0
7 Syracuse 14
21 Dartmouth 7
20 Pennsylvania 26

**1947**

27 Lehigh 0
0 Yale 14
27 Colgate 18
19 Navy 38
28 Princeton 21
0 Columbia 22
12 Syracuse 6
13 Dartmouth 21
0 Pennsylvania 21

**1948**

47 N.Y.U. 6
13 Navy 7
40 Harvard 6
34 Syracuse 7
6 Army 27
20 Columbia 13
14 Colgate 6
27 Dartmouth 26
23 Pennsylvania 14

**1949**

27 Niagara 0
39 Colgate 27
33 Harvard 14
48 Yale 14
14 Princeton 12
54 Columbia 0
33 Syracuse 7
7 Dartmouth 16
29 Pennsylvania 21

**1950**

27 Lafayette 0
26 Syracuse 7
28 Harvard 7
7 Yale 0
0 Princeton 27
19 Columbia 20
26 Colgate 18
24 Dartmouth 0
13 Pennsylvania 6

**1951**

21 Syracuse 14
41 Colgate 18
42 Harvard 6
27 Yale 0
15 Princeton 53
20 Columbia 21
20 Michigan 7
21 Dartmouth 13
0 Pennsylvania 7

**1952**

7 Colgate 14
7 Navy 31
6 Syracuse 26
0 Yale 13
0 Princeton 27
21 Columbia 14
7 Michigan 49
13 Dartmouth 7
7 Pennsylvania 14

**1953**

27 Colgate 7
7 Rice 28
6 Navy 26
0 Yale 0
26 Princeton 19
27 Columbia 13
0 Syracuse 26
28 Dartmouth 26
7 Pennsylvania 7

**1954**

14 Colgate 19
20 Rice 41
12 Harvard 13
21 Yale 47
27 Princeton 0
26 Columbia 0
14 Syracuse 6
40 Dartmouth 21
20 Pennsylvania 6

**1955**

14 Lehigh 6
6 Colgate 21
20 Harvard 7
6 Yale 34
20 Princeton 26
34 Columbia 19
20 Brown 7
0 Dartmouth 7
39 Pennsylvania 7

**1956**

6 Colgate 34
0 Navy 14
7 Harvard 32
7 Yale 25
21 Princeton 32
19 Columbia 25
6 Brown 13
14 Dartmouth 27
20 Pennsylvania 7

**1957**

13 Colgate 14
20 Harvard 6
0 Syracuse 34
7 Yale 18
14 Princeton 47
8 Columbia 0
13 Brown 6
19 Dartmouth 20
6 Pennsylvania 14

**1958**

13 Colgate 0
21 Harvard 14
0 Syracuse 55
12 Yale 7
34 Princeton 8
25 Columbia 0
8 Brown 12
15 Dartmouth 32
19 Pennsylvania 7

**1959**

20 Colgate 15
13 Lehigh 6
20 Harvard 16
0 Yale 23
0 Princeton 20
13 Columbia 7
19 Brown 0
12 Dartmouth 21
13 Pennsylvania 28

**1960**

8 Colgate 28
15 Bucknell 7
12 Harvard 0
6 Yale 22
18 Princeton 21
6 Columbia 44
6 Brown 7
0 Dartmouth 20
7 Pennsylvania 18

**1961**

34 Colgate 0
0 Harvard 14
7 Navy 31
0 Yale 12
25 Princeton 30
7 Columbia 35
25 Brown 0
14 Dartmouth 15
31 Pennsylvania 0

**1962**

12 Colgate 23
14 Harvard 12
0 Navy 41
8 Yale 26
35 Princeton 34
21 Columbia 25
28 Brown 26
21 Dartmouth 28
29 Pennsylvania 22

**1963**

17 Colgate 21
24 Lehigh 0
14 Harvard 21
13 Yale 10
14 Princeton 51
18 Columbia 17
28 Brown 25
7 Dartmouth 12
17 Pennsylvania 8

**1964**

9 Buffalo 9
3 Colgate 8
33 Pennsylvania 0
0 Harvard 16
21 Yale 23
57 Columbia 20
28 Brown 31
33 Dartmouth 15
12 Princeton 17

**1965**

0 Colgate 0
49 Lehigh 13
27 Princeton 36
3 Harvard 3
14 Yale 24
20 Columbia 6
41 Brown 21
0 Dartmouth 20
38 Pennsylvania 14

**1966**

28 Buffalo 21
15 Colgate 14
45 Pennsylvania 28
0 Harvard 21
16 Yale 14
31 Columbia 6
23 Brown 14
23 Dartmouth 32
0 Princeton 7

**1967**

23 Bucknell 7
23 Colgate 7
47 Princeton 13
12 Harvard 14
7 Yale 41
27 Columbia 14
14 Brown 14
24 Dartmouth 21
33 Pennsylvania 14

**1968**

17 Colgate 0
17 Rutgers 16
8 Pennsylvania 10
0 Harvard 10
13 Yale 25
25 Columbia 34
31 Brown 0
6 Dartmouth 27
13 Princeton 41

**1969**

24 Colgate 28
7 Rutgers 21
17 Princeton 24
41 Harvard 24
0 Yale 17
10 Columbia 3
14 Brown 7
7 Dartmouth 24
28 Pennsylvania 14

**1970**

17 Colgate 7
41 Lehigh 14
32 Pennsylvania 31
24 Harvard 27
7 Yale 38
31 Columbia 20
35 Brown 21
0 Dartmouth 24
6 Princeton 3

**1971**

38 Colgate 20
31 Rutgers 17
19 Princeton 8
21 Harvard 16
31 Yale 10
24 Columbia 21
21 Brown 7
14 Dartmouth 24
41 Pennsylvania 13

**1972**

37 Colgate 7
36 Rutgers 22
24 Pennsylvania 20
15 Harvard 33
24 Yale 13
0 Columbia 14
48 Brown 28
22 Dartmouth 31
22 Princeton 15

**1973**

35 Colgate 21
7 Lehigh 7
37 Princeton 6
15 Harvard 21
3 Yale 20
44 Columbia 14
7 Brown 17
0 Dartmouth 17
22 Pennsylvania 31

**1974**

| | |
|---|---|
| 40 | Colgate 21 |
| 24 | Bucknell 0 |
| 28 | Pennsylvania 28 |
| 27 | Harvard 39 |
| 3 | Yale 27 |
| 24 | Columbia 0 |
| 8 | Brown 16 |
| 9 | Dartmouth 21 |
| 20 | Princeton 41 |

**1975**

| | |
|---|---|
| 22 | Colgate 24 |
| 21 | Bucknell 6 |
| 8 | Princeton 16 |
| 13 | Harvard 34 |
| 14 | Yale 20 |
| 19 | Columbia 42 |
| 23 | Brown 45 |
| 10 | Dartmouth 33 |
| 21 | Pennsylvania 27 |

**1976**

| | |
|---|---|
| 0 | Princeton 3 |
| 20 | Colgate 25 |
| 14 | Rutgers 21 |
| 9 | Harvard 3 |
| 12 | Brown 28 |
| 0 | Dartmouth 35 |
| 6 | Yale 14 |
| 17 | Columbia 35 |
| 31 | Pennsylvania 13 |

## Dartmouth College

Hanover, New Hampshire
Established: 1769
Color: Oak Green
Nickname: Big Green

*Head Coaches*

Team captains, no coaches, 1881-1892
Wallace S. Moyle, 1893-1894
William C. Wurtenberg, 1895-1899
Frederick E. Jennings, 1900
Walter McCornack, 1901-1902
Fred Folsom, 1903-1906
John O'Connor, 1907-1908
Walter Lillard, 1909
William Randall, 1910
Frank Cavanaugh, 1911-1916
Clarence (Doc) Spears, 1917-1920
Jackson Cannell, 1921-1922, 1929-1933
Jesse Hawley, 1923-1928
Earl (Red) Blaik, 1934-1940
Tuss McLaughry, 1941-1942, 1945-1954
Earl Brown, 1943-1944
Bob Blackman, 1955-1970
John (Jake) Crouthamel, 1971-

### Scores 1881-1976

**1881**
1 Amherst 0
0 Amherst 0

**1882**
5 McGill 0
0 Harvard 53

**1883**
3 Williams 5

**1884**
0 Yale 113
0 Harvard 29
10 Tufts 10
20 Tufts 0

**1885**
No football

**1886**
11 Andover 18
11 M.I.T. 6
91 Vermont 0
0 Harvard 70

**1887**
52 Tufts 0
4 Stevens 4
15 M.I.T. 24
52 Amherst 0
66 Trinity 0

**1888**
0 Harvard 74
10 Exeter 12
4 Andover 14
30 M.I.T. 0
36 Williams 6
0 Stevens 30
40 Amherst 0

**1889**
45 Andover 4
34 Exeter 0
20 Andover 4
0 Harvard 38
60 Amherst 6
42 M.I.T. 6
20 Williams 9
18 Stevens 5

**1890**
10 Andover 5
0 Harvard 43
71 Vermont 0
0 Harvard 64
10 Andover 0
42 Bowdoin 0
0 Amherst 4
0 Williams 6

**1891**
0 Harvard 16
32 Stevens 12
14 Amherst 14
6 Williams 14
8 M.I.T. 6

**1892**
0 Harvard 48
10 Springfield 8
26 Andover 0
8 Boston A.A. 30
20 Wesleyan 8
12 Tufts 10
24 Williams 12
2 Amherst 30

**1893**
0 Harvard 16
16 Trinity 6
0 Yale 28
0 Harvard 36
20 Williams 0
14 Tufts 4
34 Amherst 0

**1894**
0 Harvard 22
0 Yale 34
12 Tufts 0
42 Bowdoin 0
14 Bowdoin 0
10 Williams 0
30 Amherst 0
4 Brown 20
0 Chicago A.C. 4

**1895**
50 Exeter 0
0 Harvard 4
10 So. Berwick 6
10 Bowdoin 10
38 Bates 0
0 Yale 26
30 M.I.T. 0
0 West Point 6
12 Boston Univ. 0
0 Yale 32
20 Amherst 0
10 Williams 5
4 Brown 10

**1896**
30 Worcester A.A. 0
0 Pennsylvania 16
0 Yale 42
28 Bowdoin 10
10 Brown 10
32 Amherst 0
10 Williams 0
12 Newton A.C. 6

**1897**
34 Exeter 0
0 Harvard 13
0 Pennsylvania 34
0 Princeton 30
54 Amherst 0
52 Williams 0
24 Newton A.C. 0

**1898**
23 Exeter 5
0 Harvard 21
35 Bowdoin 6
45 Vermont 6
5 Wesleyan 23
64 Amherst 6
10 Williams 6
0 Brown 12
5 Chicago A.C. 17
12 Cincinnati 17
6 Carlisle 17

**1899**
16 Exeter 5
37 Bowdoin 0
0 Yale 12
10 Williams 12
2 West Point 6
0 Wesleyan 11
0 Harvard 11
0 Columbia 22
5 Brown 16

**1900**
10 Exeter 0
0 Union 0
0 Yale 17
0 Vermont 0
12 Tufts 0
6 Cornell 23
5 Wesleyan 16
5 Brown 12

**1901**
51 N. H. State 0
23 Trinity 0
45 Boston College 0
22 Tufts 0
6 Williams 2
35 Bowdoin 6
29 Wesleyan 12
22 Vermont 0
12 Harvard 27
22 Brown 0

**1902**
11 Vermont 0
0 M.A.C. 0
29 Tufts 0
18 Williams 0
6 Amherst 12
12 Wesleyan 5
11 Springfield 0
6 Harvard 16
12 Brown 6

**1903**
12 M.A.C. 0
18 Holy Cross 0
36 Vermont 0
36 Union 0
17 Williams 0
0 Princeton 17
34 Wesleyan 6
18 Amherst 0
11 Harvard 0
62 Brown 0

**1904**
17 M.A.C. 0
37 Vermont 0
11 Williams 0
18 Holy Cross 4
33 Wesleyan 0
0 Harvard 0
15 Amherst 4
12 Brown 5

**1905**
34 Norwich 0
18 M.A.C. 0
12 Vermont 0
16 Holy Cross 6
10 Colgate 16
24 Williams 0
6 Princeton 0
0 Amherst 0
6 Harvard 6
24 Brown 6

**1906**
5 Norwich 0
8 Vermont 0
16 Holy Cross 0
4 Maine 0
26 M.A.C. 0
0 Williams 0
0 Princeton 42
4 Amherst 0
9 Harvard 22
0 Brown 23

**1907**
12 Norwich 0
0 Vermont 0
6 Tufts 0
10 N. H. State 0
6 M.A.C. 0
27 Maine 0
15 Amherst 10
52 Holy Cross 0
22 Harvard 0

**1908**
11 Vermont 0
23 M.A.C. 0
18 Tufts 0
0 Williams 0
18 Holy Cross 5
17 Amherst 0
10 Princeton 6
0 Harvard 6

**1909**
23 M.A.C. 0
0 Vermont 0
15 Bowdoin 0
18 Williams 0
12 Amherst 0
12 Holy Cross 0
6 Princeton 6
3 Harvard 12

**1910**
6 M.A.C. 0
18 Colby 0
33 Vermont 0
39 Williams 0
0 Princeton 6
15 Amherst 3
0 Harvard 18

**1911**
18 Norwich 3
22 M.A.C. 0
23 Bowdoin 0
12 Colby 0
6 Holy Cross 0
23 Williams 5
12 Vermont 0
18 Amherst 6
0 Princeton 3
3 Harvard 5

**1912**
26 Bates 0
41 Norwich 9
47 M.A.C. 0
55 Vermont 0
21 Williams 0
7 Princeton 22
60 Amherst 0
24 Cornell 0
0 Harvard 3

**1913**
13 M.A.C. 3
53 Colby 0
33 Vermont 7
48 Williams 6
6 Princeton 0
21 Amherst 7
34 Pennsylvania 21
10 Carlisle 35

**1914**
29 M.A.C. 6
74 Norwich 0
21 Williams 3
42 Vermont 0
12 Princeton 16
32 Amherst 0
68 Tufts 0
41 Pennsylvania 0
40 Syracuse 0

**1915**
13 M.A.C. 0
34 Maine 0
20 Tufts 7
60 Vermont 0
7 Princeton 30
26 Amherst 0
7 Pennsylvania 3
29 Bates 0
0 Syracuse 0

**1916**
33 N. H. State 0
32 Boston College 6
47 Lebanon Valley 0
62 M.A.C. 0
0 Georgetown 10
3 Princeton 7
15 Syracuse 10
7 Pennsylvania 7
7 West Virginia 7

**1917**
14 Springfield 0
32 Middlebury 6
6 West Virginia 2
21 N. H. State 6
10 Penn State 7
0 Pennsylvania 7
0 Tufts 27
0 Brown 13

**1918**
20 Norwich 0
6 Syracuse† 34
26 U.S. Marines 0
26 Middlebury† 0
0 Brown† 28
0 Pennsylvania† 21
†Student Army Training Corps

**1919**
40 Springfield 0
13 Norwich 0
27 M.A.C. 7
19 Penn State 13
9 Cornell 0
7 Colgate 7
20 Pennsylvania 19
6 Brown 7

**1920**
31 Norwich 0
7 Penn State 14
27 Holy Cross 14
0 Syracuse 10
34 Tufts 7
14 Cornell 3
44 Pennsylvania 7
14 Brown 6
28 Washington 7

**1921**
34 Norwich 3
28 Middlebury 3
24 New Hampshire 0
14 Tennessee 3
31 Columbia 7
7 Cornell 59
14 Pennsylvania 14
7 Syracuse 14
7 Georgia 0

**1922**
20 Norwich 0
19 Maine 0
21 Middlebury 0
3 Vermont 6
3 Harvard 12
10 Boston Univ. 7
0 Cornell 23
28 Columbia 7
7 Brown 0

**1923**
13 Norwich 0
6 Maine 0
24 Boston Univ. 0
27 Vermont 2
16 Harvard 0
7 Cornell 32
16 Brown 14
62 Colby 0
31 Columbia 6

**1924**
40 Norwich 0
52 McGill 0
38 Vermont 0
14 Yale 14
6 Harvard 0
10 Brown 3
38 Boston Univ. 0
27 Cornell 14

**1925**
59 Norwich 0
34 Hobart 0
50 Vermont 0
56 Maine 0
32 Harvard 9
14 Brown 0
62 Cornell 13
33 Chicago 7

**1926**
59 Norwich 0
50 Hobart 0
20 Virginia Tech 0
7 Yale 14
12 Harvard 16
0 Brown 10
32 Boston Univ. 0
23 Cornell 24

**1927**
47 Norwich 0
46 Hobart 0
38 Allegheny 7
47 Temple 7
30 Harvard 6
0 Yale 19
19 Brown 7
53 Cornell 7

**1928**
39 Norwich 6
44 Hobart 0
37 Allegheny 12
21 Columbia 7
7 Harvard 19
0 Yale 18
0 Brown 14
28 Cornell 0
6 Northwestern 27

**1929**
67 Norwich 0
68 Hobart 0
53 Allegheny 0
34 Columbia 0
34 Harvard 7
12 Yale 16
13 Brown 6
18 Cornell 14
6 Navy 13

**1930**
79 Norwich 0
20 Bates 0
74 Boston Univ. 0
52 Columbia 0
7 Harvard 2
0 Yale 0
43 Allegheny 14
19 Cornell 13
7 Stanford 14

**1931**
56 Norwich 6
61 Buffalo 0
14 Holy Cross 7
6 Columbia 19
20 Lebanon Valley 6
33 Yale 33
6 Harvard 7
14 Cornell 0
6 Stanford 32

**1932**
73 Norwich 0
32 Vermont 0
6 Lafayette 0
7 Pennsylvania 14
7 Harvard 10
0 Yale 6
25 New Hampshire 0
6 Cornell 21

**1933**
41 Norwich 0
39 Vermont 6
14 Bates 0
14 Pennsylvania 7
7 Harvard 7
13 Yale 14
0 Princeton 7
0 Cornell 7
0 Chicago 39

**1934**
39 Norwich 0
32 Vermont 0
27 Maine 0
27 Virginia 0
10 Harvard 0
2 Yale 7
21 New Hampshire 7
6 Cornell 21
13 Princeton 38

**1935**
39 Norwich 0
47 Vermont 0
59 Bates 7
41 Brown 0
14 Harvard 6
14 Yale 6
34 William & Mary 0
41 Cornell 6
6 Princeton 26
7 Columbia 13

**1936**
58 Norwich 0
56 Vermont 0
0 Holy Cross 7
34 Brown 0
26 Harvard 7
11 Yale 7
20 Columbia 13
20 Cornell 6
13 Princeton 13

**1937**
39 Bates 0
31 Amherst 7
42 Springfield 0
41 Brown 0
20 Harvard 2
9 Yale 9
33 Princeton 9
6 Cornell 6
27 Columbia 0

**1938**
46 Bates 0
51 St. Lawrence 0
22 Princeton 0
34 Brown 13
13 Harvard 7
24 Yale 6
44 Dickinson 6
7 Cornell 14
13 Stanford 23

**1939**
41 St. Lawrence 9
34 Hampden-Sydney 6
0 Navy 0
14 Lafayette 0
16 Harvard 0
33 Yale 0
7 Princeton 9
6 Cornell 35
3 Stanford 14

**1940**
35 St. Lawrence 0
21 Franklin & Marshall 23
6 Columbia 20
7 Yale 13
7 Harvard 6
26 Sewanee 0
9 Princeton 14
3 Cornell 0
20 Brown 6

**1941**
35 Norwich 0
47 Amherst 7
18 Colgate 6
0 Harvard 7
7 Yale 0
0 William & Mary 3

*William H. (Bill) Morton shows how fat the football was in 1931. Despite its size, however, the Dartmouth star was a slick magician at quarterback and made Grantland Rice's All-America second team.*

20 Princeton 13
19 Cornell 33
0 Georgia 35

**1942**

17 Holy Cross 6
58 Miami (Ohio) 7
19 Colgate 27
14 Harvard 2
7 Yale 17
14 William & Mary 35
19 Princeton 7
19 Cornell 21
26 Columbia 13

**1943**

3 Holy Cross 0
47 Coast Guard 0
6 Pennsylvania 7
20 Yale 6
47 Columbia 13
20 Cornell 0
42 Princeton 13

**1944**

6 Holy Cross 6
6 Pennsylvania 20
0 Notre Dame 64
14 Brown 13
0 Yale 6
0 Coast Guard 19
13 Cornell 14
18 Columbia 0

**1945**

6 Holy Cross 13
0 Pennsylvania 12
0 Notre Dame 34
8 Syracuse 0
0 Yale 6
13 Princeton 13
13 Cornell 20
0 Columbia 21

**1946**

3 Holy Cross 0
20 Syracuse 14
6 Pennsylvania 39
13 Brown 20
13 Columbia 33
2 Yale 33
7 Harvard 21
7 Cornell 21
20 Princeton 13

**1947**

0 Holy Cross 0
28 Syracuse 7
0 Pennsylvania 32
13 Brown 10
14 Harvard 13
14 Yale 23
0 Columbia 15
21 Cornell 13
12 Princeton 14

**1948**

13 Pennsylvania 26
19 Holy Cross 6
41 Colgate 16
14 Harvard 7
41 Yale 14
26 Columbia 21
26 Cornell 27
33 Princeton 13

**1949**

0 Pennsylvania 21
31 Holy Cross 7
27 Colgate 13
27 Harvard 13
34 Yale 13
35 Columbia 14
16 Cornell 7
13 Princeton 19

**1950**

21 Holy Cross 21
7 Michigan 27
26 Pennsylvania 42
14 Lehigh 16
27 Harvard 7
7 Yale 0
14 Columbia 7
0 Cornell 24
7 Princeton 13

**1951**

6 Fordham 14
14 Pennsylvania 39
28 Army 14
14 Syracuse 0
26 Harvard 20
14 Yale 10
6 Columbia 21
13 Cornell 21
0 Princeton 13

**1952**

9 Holy Cross 27
0 Pennsylvania 7
7 Army 37
29 Rutgers 20
19 Harvard 26
7 Yale 21
38 Columbia 14
7 Cornell 13
0 Princeton 33

**1953**

6 Holy Cross 28
7 Navy 55
0 Army 27
14 Colgate 24
14 Harvard 20
32 Yale 0
19 Columbia 25
26 Cornell 28
34 Princeton 12

**1954**

27 Holy Cross 26
7 Navy 42
6 Army 60
7 Colgate 13
13 Harvard 7
7 Yale 13
26 Columbia 0
21 Cornell 40
7 Princeton 49

**1955**

20 Colgate 21
21 Holy Cross 29
0 Brown 7
13 Lafayette 21
14 Harvard 9
0 Yale 20
14 Columbia 7
7 Cornell 0
3 Princeton 6

**1956**

13 New Hampshire 0
7 Pennsylvania 14
14 Brown 7
7 Holy Cross 7
21 Harvard 28
0 Yale 19
14 Columbia 0
27 Cornell 14
19 Princeton 0

**1957**

27 New Hampshire 0
6 Pennsylvania 3
35 Brown 0
14 Holy Cross 7
26 Harvard 0
14 Yale 14
7 Columbia 0
20 Cornell 19
14 Princeton 34

**1958**

20 Lafayette 0
13 Pennsylvania 12
20 Brown 0
8 Holy Cross 14
8 Harvard 16
22 Yale 14
38 Columbia 0
32 Cornell 15
21 Princeton 12

**1959**

8 Holy Cross 31
0 Pennsylvania 13
0 Brown 0
12 Boston College 35
9 Harvard 0
12 Yale 8
22 Columbia 0
21 Cornell 12
12 Princeton 7

**1960**

7 New Hampshire 6
15 Pennsylvania 0
20 Brown 0
8 Holy Cross 9
6 Harvard 9
0 Yale 29
22 Columbia 6
20 Cornell 0
0 Princeton 7

**1961**

28 New Hampshire 3
30 Pennsylvania 0
34 Brown 0
13 Holy Cross 17
15 Harvard 21
24 Yale 8
14 Columbia 35
15 Cornell 14
24 Princeton 6

**1962**

27 Massachusetts 3
17 Pennsylvania 0
41 Brown 0
10 Holy Cross 0
24 Harvard 6
9 Yale 0
42 Columbia 0
28 Cornell 21
38 Princeton 27

**1963**
20 Bucknell 18
28 Pennsylvania 0
14 Brown 7
13 Holy Cross 8
13 Harvard 17
6 Yale 10
47 Columbia 6
12 Cornell 7
22 Princeton 21

**1964**
40 New Hampshire 0
28 Boston Univ. 6
7 Princeton 37
24 Brown 14
48 Harvard 0
15 Yale 24
31 Columbia 14
15 Cornell 33
27 Pennsylvania 7

**1965**
56 New Hampshire 6
27 Holy Cross 6
24 Pennsylvania 19
35 Brown 9
14 Harvard 0
20 Yale 17
47 Columbia 0
20 Cornell 0
28 Princeton 14

**1966**
17 Massachusetts 7
6 Holy Cross 7
31 Princeton 13
49 Brown 14
14 Harvard 19
28 Yale 13
56 Columbia 14
32 Cornell 23
40 Pennsylvania 21

**1967**
28 Massachusetts 10
24 Holy Cross 8
23 Pennsylvania 0
41 Brown 6
23 Harvard 21
15 Yale 56
13 Columbia 7
21 Cornell 24
17 Princeton 14

**1968**
21 New Hampshire 0
17 Holy Cross 29
7 Princeton 34
48 Brown 0
7 Harvard 22
27 Yale 47
31 Columbia 19
27 Cornell 6
21 Pennsylvania 26

**1969**
31 New Hampshire 0
38 Holy Cross 6
41 Pennsylvania 0
38 Brown 13
24 Harvard 10
42 Yale 21
37 Columbia 7
24 Cornell 7
7 Princeton 35

**1970**
27 Massachusetts 0
50 Holy Cross 14
38 Princeton 0
42 Brown 14
37 Harvard 14
10 Yale 0
55 Columbia 0
24 Cornell 0
28 Pennsylvania 0

**1971**
31 Massachusetts 7
28 Holy Cross 9
19 Pennsylvania 3
10 Brown 7
16 Harvard 13
17 Yale 15
29 Columbia 31
24 Cornell 14
33 Princeton 7

**1972**
24 New Hampshire 14
17 Holy Cross 7
35 Princeton 14
49 Brown 20
21 Harvard 21
14 Yale 45
38 Columbia 8
31 Cornell 22
31 Pennsylvania 17

**1973**
9 New Hampshire 10
0 Holy Cross 10
16 Pennsylvania 22
28 Brown 16
24 Harvard 18
24 Yale 13
24 Columbia 6
17 Cornell 0
42 Princeton 24

**1974**
0 Massachusetts 14
3 Holy Cross 14
7 Princeton 7
15 Harvard 17
7 Brown 6
9 Yale 14
21 Columbia 0
21 Cornell 9
20 Pennsylvania 27

**1975**
3 Massachusetts 7
28 Holy Cross 7
19 Pennsylvania 14
10 Brown 10
10 Harvard 24
14 Yale 16
22 Columbia 17
33 Cornell 10
21 Princeton 16

**1976**
20 Pennsylvania 0
24 New Hampshire 13
45 Holy Cross 7
14 Yale 18
10 Harvard 17
35 Cornell 0
34 Columbia 14
21 Brown 35
33 Princeton 7

*With exception of two wartime years, the three head football coaches at Dartmouth during 1934–1970 were, left, Tuss McLaughry, Earl (Red) Blaik, and Bob Blackman.*

## Harvard University

Cambridge, Massachusetts
Established: 1636
Color: Crimson
Nickname: Crimson

*Head Coaches*

Coached by captains, 1874-1880
Lucius N. Littauer, 1881
Coached by captains, 1882-1884
No team, 1885
Frank A. Mason, 1886
Coached by captains, 1887-1889
George A. Stewart, George C. Adams, 1890-1892
George A. Stewart, Everett G. Lake, 1893
William A. Brooks, 1894
Robert W. Emmons, 1895
Bertram G. Waters, 1896
W. Cameron Forbes, 1897-1898
Benjamin H. Dibblee, 1899-1900
William T. Reid, 1901
John W. Farley, 1902
John S. Cranston, 1903
Edgar N. Wrightington, 1904
William T. Reid, 1905-1906
Joshua Crane, 1907
Percy D. Haughton, 1908-1916
Wingate Rollins, 1917
Pooch Donovan, 1918
Robert T. Fisher, 1919-1925
Arnold Horween, 1926-1930
Edward L. Casey, 1931-1934
Richard C. Harlow, 1935-1942
Henry N. Lamar, 1943-1944
Richard C. Harlow, 1945-1947
Arthur L. Valpey, 1948-1949
Lloyd P. Jordan, 1950-1956
John M. Yovicsin, 1957-1970
Joseph Restic, 1971-

## Scores 1874-1976

**1874**
3 McGill 0
0 McGill 0

**1874-75**
†0 McGill 0
0 Tufts 1
†Won by Harvard with 3 touchdowns

**1875-76**
1 All Canada 0
1 Tufts 0
4 Yale 0
1 All Canada 0

**1876-77**
2 All Canada 0
1 McGill 0
0 Yale 1
1 Princeton 0

**1877**
3 Tufts 0
1 McGill 0
0 Princeton 1
8 Columbia 0

**1878**
3 Amherst 0
†0 Princeton 0
0 Yale 1
†Won by Princeton with 1 touchdown

**1879**
2 Britannia 0
1 Britannia 0
0 McGill 0
0 Yale 0
0 Princeton 1

**1880**
0 Britannia 0
2 Ottawa 1
0 Montreal 0
3 Columbia 0
1 Princeton 2
0 Yale 1

**1881**
2 Montreal 0
9 Ottawa 1
2 Britannia 0
4 Michigan 0
2 Penn 0
1 Columbia 0
†0 Yale 0
0 Princeton 0
†Yale winner with 4 less safeties

**1882**
1 M.I.T. 0
3 M.I.T. 0
2 McGill 0
1 Amherst 0
53 Dartmouth 0
3 Columbia 0
†1 Princeton 1
0 Yale 1
†Won by Harvard with 1 field goal and 1 touchdown vs. 1 field goal by Princeton

**1883**
23 Wesleyan 1
4 Pennsylvania 0
14 M.I.T. 1
14 Stevens 4
18 Wesleyan 6
39 Williams 0
11 Stevens 2
7 Princeton 26
3 Michigan 0
2 Yale 23

**1884**
43 M.I.T. 5
0 Pennsylvania 4
42 M.I.T. 0
67 Trinity 0
0 Wesleyan 16
23 Williams 0
20 Ottawa 6
29 Dartmouth 0
51 Tufts 0
6 Princeton 36
0 Yale 52

**1886**
82 Tufts 0
54 M.I.T. 0
46 Tufts 0
44 Stevens 0
59 M.I.T. 0
86 Andover 0
70 Dartmouth 0
158 Exeter 0
34 Wesleyan 0
38 Graduates 0
0 Princeton 12
62 M.I.T. 0
4 Yale 29
28 Pennsylvania 0

**1887**
86 Tufts 0
68 Exeter 0
62 M.I.T. 0
52 Williams 6
98 Amherst 0
68 Tufts 0
54 Exeter 0
110 Wesleyan 0
12 Princeton 0
42 Pennsylvania 0
8 Yale 17

**1888**
70 Worc. Poly 0
18 M.I.T. 0
39 Exeter 6
34 Wesleyan 0
14 Williams 6
68 Andover 0
68 Worc. Poly 0
74 Dartmouth 0
42 M.I.T. 0
102 Amherst 0
50 Wesleyan 2
6 Princeton 18
50 Pennsylvania 0

**1889**
28 Exeter 0
28 Stevens 4
38 Dartmouth 0
62 M.I.T. 0
41 Williams 0
41 Andover 0
64 Wesleyan 0
35 Pennsylvania 0
67 Wesleyan 2
15 Princeton 41
0 Yale 6

**1890**
41 Exeter 0
43 Dartmouth 0
74 Amherst 6
38 Williams 0
64 Dartmouth 0
54 Bowdoin 0
55 Wesleyan 0
77 Cornell 0
33 Orange A. C. 0
64 Amherst 0
12 Yale 6

**1891**
16 Dartmouth 0
17 Exeter 0
18 Amherst 0
26 M.I.T. 0
26 Williams 0
76 Andover 0
39 Amherst 0
79 Bowdoin 0
34 Stagg's Team 0
124 Wesleyan 0
44 Stagg's Team 4
38 Trinity 0
51 Boston A. A. 12
0 Yale 10

**1892**
48 Dartmouth 0
62 Exeter 0
26 Amherst 0
55 Williams 0
40 Boston A. A. 0
32 Chicago A. C. 0
34 M.I.T. 0
32 Amherst 10
20 Cornell 14
16 Boston A. A. 12
0 Yale 6

**1893**
16 Dartmouth 0
54 Exeter 0
32 Amherst 0
34 M.I.T. 0
52 Williams 0
36 Dartmouth 0
6 Graduates 0
58 Brown 0
60 Andover 5
34 Cornell 0
10 Boston A. A. 0
0 Yale 6
26 Pennsylvania 4

**1894**
22 Dartmouth 0
48 Exeter 0
46 Andover 0
18 Brown 4
14 Orange A. C. 0
30 Amherst 0
32 Williams 0
22 Cornell 12
40 Boston A. A. 0
36 Chicago A. C. 0
18 Brown 0
4 Yale 12
4 Pennsylvania 18

**1895**

4 Dartmouth 0
24 Amherst 0
42 Exeter 0
4 Army 0
32 Williams 0
26 Brown 6
25 Cornell 0
4 Princeton 12
4 Michigan 0
0 Boston A. A. 0
14 Pennsylvania 17

**1896**

6 Williams 0
34 Trinity 0
18 Newton A. A. 0
28 Wesleyan 0
12 Brown 0
13 Cornell 4
5 Graduates 8
4 Carlisle 0
0 Princeton 12
6 Boston A. A. 8
6 Pennsylvania 8

**1897**

20 Williams 0
24 Bowdoin 0
13 Dartmouth 0
38 Amherst 0
10 Army 0
24 Newton A. A. 0
18 Brown 0
22 Newtowne A. C. 0
24 Cornell 5
34 Wesleyan 0
0 Yale 0
6 Pennsylvania 15

**1898**

11 Williams 0
28 Bowdoin 6
21 Dartmouth 0
53 Amherst 2
28 Army 0
22 Newtowne A. C. 0
39 Chicago A. C. 0
11 Carlisle 5
10 Pennsylvania 0
17 Brown 6
17 Yale 0

**1899**

29 Williams 0
13 Bowdoin 0
20 Wesleyan 0
41 Amherst 0
18 Army 0
29 Bates 0
11 Brown 0
22 Carlisle 10
16 Pennsylvania 0
11 Dartmouth 0
0 Yale 0

**1900**

24 Wesleyan 0
12 Williams 0
12 Bowdoin 0
18 Amherst 0
24 Columbia 0
41 Bates 0
29 Army 0
17 Carlisle 5
17 Pennsylvania 5
11 Brown 6
0 Yale 28

**1901**

16 Williams 0
12 Bowdoin 0
16 Bates 6
11 Amherst 0
18 Columbia 0
16 Wesleyan 0
6 Army 0
29 Carlisle 0
48 Brown 0
33 Pennsylvania 6
27 Dartmouth 12
22 Yale 0

**1902**

11 Williams 0
17 Bowdoin 6
23 Bates 0
6 Amherst 0
22 Maine 0
35 Wesleyan 5
14 Army 6
6 Brown 0
23 Carlisle 0
11 Pennsylvania 0
16 Dartmouth 6
0 Yale 23

**1903**

17 Williams 0
24 Bowdoin 0
6 Maine 0
23 Bates 0
0 Amherst 5
17 Wesleyan 6
5 Army 0
29 Brown 0
12 Carlisle 11
17 Pennsylvania 10
0 Dartmouth 11
0 Yale 16

**1904**

24 Williams 0
17 Bowdoin 0
23 Maine 0
11 Bates 0
4 Army 0
12 Carlisle 0
0 Pennsylvania 11
0 Dartmouth 0
28 Holy Cross 5
0 Yale 12

**1905**

12 Williams 0
16 Bowdoin 0
22 Maine 0
34 Bates 6
12 Springfield YMCA 0
6 Army 0
10 Brown 0
23 Carlisle 11
6 Pennsylvania 12
6 Dartmouth 6
0 Yale 6

**1906**

7 Williams 0
10 Bowdoin 0
17 Maine 0
27 Bates 6
21 Massachusetts 0
44 Springfield YMCA 0
5 Army 0
9 Brown 5
5 Carlisle 0
22 Dartmouth 9
0 Yale 6

**1907**

5 Bowdoin 0
30 Maine 0
33 Bates 4
18 Williams 0
6 Navy 0
9 Springfield YMCA 5
6 Brown 5
15 Carlisle 23
0 Dartmouth 22
0 Yale 12

**1908**

5 Bowdoin 0
16 Maine 0
18 Bates 0
10 Williams 0
44 Springfield YMCA 0
6 Navy 6
6 Brown 2
17 Carlisle 0
6 Dartmouth 0
4 Yale 0

**1909**

11 Bates 0
17 Bowdoin 0
8 Williams 6
17 Maine 0
11 Brown 0
9 Army 0
18 Cornell 0
12 Dartmouth 3
0 Yale 8

**1910**

22 Bates 0
32 Bowdoin 0
21 Williams 0
17 Amherst 0
12 Brown 0
6 Army 0
27 Cornell 5
18 Dartmouth 0
0 Yale 0

**1911**

15 Bates 0
8 Holy Cross 0
18 Williams 0
11 Amherst 0
20 Brown 6
6 Princeton 8
15 Carlisle 18
5 Dartmouth 3
0 Yale 0

**1912**

7 Maine 0
19 Holy Cross 0
26 Williams 3
46 Amherst 0
30 Brown 10
16 Princeton 6
9 Vanderbilt 3
3 Dartmouth 0
20 Yale 0

**1913**

34 Maine 0
14 Bates 0
23 Williams 3
47 Holy Cross 7
29 Penn State 0
23 Cornell 6
3 Princeton 0
37 Brown 0
15 Yale 5

**1914**

44 Bates 0
44 Springfield 0
10 Wash. & Jeff. 9
13 Tufts 6
13 Penn State 13
7 Michigan 0
20 Princeton 0
0 Brown 0
36 Yale 0

**1915**

39 Colby 6
7 Massachusetts 0
29 Carlisle 7
9 Virginia 0
0 Cornell 10
13 Penn State 0
10 Princeton 6
16 Brown 7
41 Yale 0

**1916**

10 Colby 0
26 Bates 0
3 Tufts 7
21 No. Carolina 0
47 Massachusetts 0
23 Cornell 0
51 Virginia 0
3 Princeton 0
0 Brown 21
3 Yale 6

**1917**

27 Dean Academy 0
35 Bump. Is. N.R. 0
13 lst Me. Hvy. Art. 0
0 Depot Brigade 0
0 Portland N. R. 0
0 Camp Devens 0
0 Newport N. R. 14

**1918**

7 Tufts 0
14 Boston College 6
3 Brown 6

**1919**

53 Bates 0
17 Boston College 0
35 Colby 0
7 Brown 0
47 Virginia 0
20 Springfield 0
10 Princeton 10
23 Tufts 0
10 Yale 3
7 Oregon 6
(Rose Bowl)

**1920**

3 Holy Cross 0
41 Maine 0
21 Valparaiso 0
38 Williams 0
31 Centre 14
24 Virginia 0
14 Princeton 14
27 Brown 0
9 Yale 0

**1921**

10 Boston Univ. 0
16 Middlebury 0
3 Holy Cross 0
19 Indiana 0
10 Georgia 7
21 Penn State 21
0 Centre 6
3 Princeton 10
9 Brown 7
10 Yale 3

**1922**

20 Middlebury 0
20 Holy Cross 0
15 Bowdoin 0
24 Centre 10
12 Dartmouth 3
24 Florida 0
3 Princeton 10
0 Brown 3
10 Yale 3

**1923**

35 Rhode Island 0
6 Middlebury 6
6 Holy Cross 0
0 Dartmouth 16
16 Tufts 0
5 Princeton 0
7 Brown 20
0 Yale 13

**1924**

14 Virginia 0
16 Middlebury 6
12 Holy Cross 6
0 Dartmouth 6
13 Boston Univ. 0
0 Princeton 34

0 Brown 7
6 Yale 19

**1925**
18 Rens. Poly 6
68 Middlebury 0
6 Holy Cross 7
9 Dartmouth 32
14 Wm. & Mary 7
0 Princeton 36
3 Brown 0
0 Yale 0

**1926**
7 Geneva 16
14 Holy Cross 19
27 Wm. & Mary 7
16 Dartmouth 12
69 Tufts 6
0 Princeton 12
0 Brown 21
7 Yale 12

**1927**
21 Vermont 3
0 Purdue 19
14 Holy Cross 6
6 Dartmouth 30
26 Indiana 6
0 Pennsylvania 24
18 Brown 6
0 Yale 14

**1928**
30 Springfield 0
20 No. Carolina 0
0 Army 15
19 Dartmouth 7
39 Lehigh 0
0 Pennsylvania 7
0 Holy Cross 0
17 Yale 0

**1929**
48 Bates 0
35 New Hampshire 0
20 Army 20
7 Dartmouth 34
14 Florida 0
12 Michigan 14
12 Holy Cross 6
10 Yale 6

**1930**
35 Vermont 0
33 Coast Guard 0
27 Springfield 0
0 Army 6
2 Dartmouth 7
13 Wm. & Mary 13
3 Michigan 6
0 Holy Cross 27
13 Yale 0

**1931**
28 Bates 0
39 New Hampshire 0
14 Army 13
35 Texas 7
19 Virginia 0
7 Dartmouth 6
7 Holy Cross 0
0 Yale 3

**1932**
66 Buffalo 0
40 New Hampshire 0
46 Penn State 13
10 Dartmouth 7
0 Brown 14
0 Army 46
7 Holy Cross 0
0 Yale 19

**1933**
33 Bates 0
34 New Hampshire 0
7 Holy Cross 10
7 Dartmouth 7
27 Lehigh 0
0 Army 27
12 Brown 6
19 Yale 6

**1934**
12 Bates 0
13 Brown 0
6 Holy Cross 26
0 Dartmouth 10
0 Princeton 19
6 Army 27
47 New Hampshire 3
0 Yale 14

**1935**
20 Springfield 0
0 Holy Cross 13
0 Army 13
6 Dartmouth 14
33 Brown 0
0 Princeton 35
41 New Hampshire 0
7 Yale 14

**1936**
38 Amherst 6
28 Brown 0
0 Army 32
7 Dartmouth 26
14 Princeton 14
65 Virginia 0
13 Navy 20
13 Yale 14

**1937**
54 Springfield 0
34 Brown 7
0 Navy 0
2 Dartmouth 20
34 Princeton 6
6 Army 7
15 Davidson 0
13 Yale 6

**1938**
13 Brown 20
0 Cornell 20
17 Army 20
7 Dartmouth 13
26 Princeton 7
47 Chicago 13
40 Virginia 13
7 Yale 0

**1939**
20 Bates 0
61 Chicago 0
7 Pennsylvania 22
0 Dartmouth 16
6 Princeton 9
15 Army 0
46 New Hampshire 0
7 Yale 20

**1940**
13 Amherst 0
0 Michigan 26
6 Army 6
6 Dartmouth 7
0 Princeton 0
10 Pennsylvania 10
14 Brown 0
28 Yale 0

**1941**
0 Pennsylvania 19
0 Cornell 7
7 Dartmouth 0
0 Navy 0
6 Princeton 4
20 Army 6
23 Brown 7
14 Yale 0

**1942**
0 N. C. Pre-Flight 13
7 Pennsylvania 19
7 Wm. & Mary 7
2 Dartmouth 14
0 Army 14
19 Princeton 14
7 Michigan 35
7 Brown 0
3 Yale 7

**1943**
7 Camp Edwards 0
0 Worc. Poly 13
14 Camp Edwards 7
7 Tufts 13
6 Boston College 6

**1944**
19 Tufts 12
43 Bates 6
13 Worc. Poly 0
13 Boston College 0
0 Melville P.T. Boat 13
12 Tufts 6

**1945**
6 Tufts 7
21 Rochester 13
7 N.L. Sub-Base 18
25 Coast Guard 0
28 Kings Point 7
14 Brown 7
60 Boston Univ. 0
0 Yale 28

**1946**
7 Connecticut 0
49 Tufts 0
13 Princeton 12
69 Coast Guard 0
13 Holy Cross 6
0 Rutgers 13
21 Dartmouth 7
28 Brown 0
14 Yale 27

**1947**
52 W. Maryland 0
19 Boston Univ. 14
0 Virginia 47
7 Holy Cross 0
13 Dartmouth 14
7 Rutgers 31
7 Princeton 33
13 Brown 7
21 Yale 31

**1948**
33 Columbia 24
6 Cornell 40
7 Army 20
7 Dartmouth 14
20 Holy Cross 13
7 Princeton 47
30 Brown 19
20 Yale 7

**1949**
0 Stanford 44
7 Columbia 14
14 Cornell 33
14 Army 54
13 Dartmouth 27
22 Holy Cross 14
13 Princeton 33
14 Brown 28
6 Yale 29

**1950**
7 Columbia 28
7 Cornell 28
0 Army 49
7 Dartmouth 27
7 Holy Cross 26
26 Princeton 63
14 Brown 13
6 Yale 14

**1951**
21 Springfield 13
6 Holy Cross 33
0 Columbia 35
6 Cornell 42
22 Army 21
20 Dartmouth 26
13 Princeton 54
34 Brown 21
21 Yale 21

**1952**
27 Springfield 7
7 Columbia 16
42 Washington U. 0
21 Colgate 20
26 Dartmouth 19
35 Davidson 26
21 Princeton 41
21 Brown 28
14 Yale 41

**1953**
16 Ohio Univ. 0
28 Colgate 26
0 Columbia 6
20 Dartmouth 14
42 Davidson 6
0 Princeton 6
27 Brown 20
13 Yale 0

**1954**
7 Massachusetts 13
13 Cornell 12
6 Columbia 7
7 Dartmouth 13
27 Ohio Univ. 13
14 Princeton 9
21 Brown 21
13 Yale 9

**1955**
60 Massachusetts 6
7 Cornell 20
21 Columbia 7
9 Dartmouth 14
26 Bucknell 26
7 Princeton 6
6 Brown 14
7 Yale 21

**1956**
13 Tufts 19
32 Cornell 7
20 Columbia 26
28 Dartmouth 21
14 Pennsylvania 28
20 Princeton 35
12 Brown 21
14 Yale 42

**1957**
6 Cornell 20
14 Ohio Univ. 7
19 Columbia 6
0 Dartmouth 26
13 Pennsylvania 6
20 Princeton 28
6 Brown 33
0 Yale 54

**1958**
3 Buffalo 6
14 Cornell 21
20 Lehigh 0
26 Columbia 0
16 Dartmouth 8
6 Pennsylvania 19
14 Princeton 16
22 Brown 29
28 Yale 0

**1959**
36 Massachusetts 22
20 Bucknell 6

16 Cornell 20
38 Columbia 22
0 Dartmouth 9
12 Pennsylvania 0
14 Princeton 0
6 Brown 16
35 Yale 6

**1960**

13 Holy Cross 6
12 Massachusetts 27
0 Cornell 12
8 Columbia 7
9 Dartmouth 6
8 Pennsylvania 0
12 Princeton 14
22 Brown 8
6 Yale 39

**1961**

17 Lehigh 22
14 Cornell 0
0 Colgate 15
14 Columbia 26
21 Dartmouth 15
37 Pennsylvania 6
9 Princeton 7
21 Brown 6
27 Yale 0

**1962**

27 Lehigh 7
12 Cornell 14
20 Holy Cross 34
36 Columbia 14
6 Dartmouth 24
36 Pennsylvania 0
20 Princeton 0
31 Brown 19
14 Yale 6

**1963**

0 Massachusetts 0
28 Rutgers 0
21 Cornell 14
3 Columbia 3
17 Dartmouth 13
2 Pennsylvania 7
21 Princeton 7
24 Brown 12
6 Yale 20

**1964**

20 Massachusetts 14
21 Bucknell 24
3 Columbia 0
16 Cornell 0
0 Dartmouth 48
34 Pennsylvania 0
0 Princeton 16
19 Brown 7
18 Yale 14

**1965**

17 Holy Cross 7
33 Tufts 0
21 Columbia 6
3 Cornell 3
0 Dartmouth 14
10 Pennsylvania 10
6 Princeton 14
17 Brown 8
13 Yale 0

**1966**

30 Lafayette 7
45 Tufts 0
34 Columbia 7
21 Cornell 0
19 Dartmouth 14
27 Pennsylvania 7
14 Princeton 18
24 Brown 7
17 Yale 0

**1967**

51 Lafayette 0
29 Boston Univ. 14
49 Columbia 13
14 Cornell 12
21 Dartmouth 23
45 Pennsylvania 7
6 Princeton 45
21 Brown 6
20 Yale 24

**1968**

27 Holy Cross 20
59 Bucknell 0
21 Columbia 14
10 Cornell 0
22 Dartmouth 7
28 Pennsylvania 6
9 Princeton 7
31 Brown 7
29 Yale 29

**1969**

13 Holy Cross 0
10 Boston University 13
51 Columbia 0
24 Cornell 41
10 Dartmouth 24
20 Pennsylvania 6
20 Princeton 51
17 Brown 24
0 Yale 7

**1970**

28 Northeastern 7
39 Rutgers 9
21 Columbia 28
27 Cornell 24
14 Dartmouth 37
38 Pennsylvania 23
29 Princeton 7
17 Brown 10
14 Yale 12

**1971**

16 Holy Cross 21
17 Northeastern 7
21 Columbia 19
16 Cornell 21
13 Dartmouth 16
28 Pennsylvania 27
10 Princeton 21
24 Brown 19
35 Yale 16

**1972**

19 Massachusetts 28
33 Boston Univ. 14
20 Columbia 18
33 Cornell 15
21 Dartmouth 21
27 Pennsylvania 38
7 Princeton 10
21 Brown 14
17 Yale 28

**1973**

24 Massachusetts 7
16 Boston Univ. 0
57 Columbia 0
21 Cornell 15
18 Dartmouth 24
34 Pennsylvania 30
19 Princeton 14
35 Brown 32
0 Yale 35

**1974**

24 Holy Cross 14
21 Rutgers 24
34 Columbia 6
39 Cornell 27
17 Dartmouth 15
39 Pennsylvania 0
34 Princeton 17
7 Brown 10
21 Yale 16

**1975**

18 Holy Cross 7
9 Boston Univ. 13
35 Columbia 30
34 Cornell 13
24 Dartmouth 10
21 Pennsylvania 3
20 Princeton 24
45 Brown 26
10 Yale 7

**1976**

34 Columbia 10
24 Massachusetts 13
37 Boston Univ. 14
3 Cornell 9
17 Dartmouth 10
20 Princeton 14
14 Brown 16
20 Pennsylvania 8
7 Yale 21

## University of Pennsylvania

Philadelphia, Pennsylvania
Established: 1740
Colors: Red and Blue
Nickname: Quakers

*Head Coaches*

No coach, 1876-1884
Frank Dole, 1885-1887
E. O. Wagenhurst, 1888-1891
George Woodruff, 1892-1901
Carl S. Williams, 1902-1907
Sol Metzger, 1908
Andy Smith, 1909-1912
George Brooke, 1913-1915
Robert F. Folwell, 1916-1919
John W. Heisman, 1920-1922
Louis A. Young, 1923-1929
Ludlow Wray, 1930
Harvey Harman, 1931-1937
George A. Munger, 1938-1953
Steve Sebo, 1954-1959
John Stiegman, 1960-1964
Bob Odell, 1965-1970
Harry Gamble, 1971-

### Scores 1876-1976

**1876**
0 Princeton 6g
4g All-Phila. 0g
0 Princeton 6g

**1878**
0 Princeton 2g, 4t
9g, 16t Swarthmore 0
1g Princeton 2g, 5t
0 Columbia 0

**1879**
0 Princeton 6g, 4t
0 Yale 3g, 3t
1t Columbia 0
7g, 1t Pa. Military 0

**1880**
5g, 6t Crescent 0g, 1t
0 Princeton 1t
3g, 5t Stevens Inst. 0
0 Yale 8g, 1t

**1881**
0 Princeton 2g, 2t
0 Harvard 2g, 2t
0 Princeton 5g, 6t
1g Rutgers 1g, 2t
0 Columbia 2g

**1882**
5g, 7t Crescent 3 safety
0 Princeton 9g, 3t
1t Rutgers 3t, 1 safety
0 Princeton 10g, 4t
2t Rutgers 1g, 2t 1s
1g, 3t Lafayette 2s

**1883**
0 Harvard 4
26 Johns Hopkins 6
44 Lafayette 4
6 Princeton 40
30 Johns Hopkins 0
35 Columbia 1
18 Rutgers 0
39 Graduates 7
6 Stevens Inst. 6

**1884**
4 Harvard 0
0 Princeton 31
21 Lafayette 0
30 Stevens Inst. 0
33 Johns Hopkins 0
16 Graduates 16
14 Wesleyan 12

**1885**
42 Graduates 0
54 Lehigh 0
68 Swarthmore 6
6 Graduates 5
0 Princeton 57
54 Lafayette 10
10 Princeton 70
30 Lafayette 22
18 Wesleyan 25
5 Yale 53
35 Lehigh 0
22 Stevens Inst. 9
10 Princeton 76

**1886**
64 Falls of Schuylkill 0
18 Tioga 0
26 Lehigh 4
4 Graduates 0
0 Princeton 30
6 All-Phila. 6
0 Lafayette 12
9 Princeton 55
14 Wesleyan 0
20 Lafayette 10
16 Haverford 4
6 Princeton 28
65 Rutgers 0
0 Yale 75
96 Vineland Col. 6
0 Lehigh 28
0 Harvard 28

**1887**
14 Graduates 6
46 Tioga 0
18 Graduates 0
0 Princeton 57
0 Princeton 42
0 Yale 50
13 Rutgers 10
0 Princeton 96
36 Haverford 0
6 Lehigh 4
0 Lafayette 20
0 Harvard 42
4 Wesleyan 10

**1888**
20 All-Phila. 6
48 Stevens Inst. 0
0 Princeton 63
0 Yale 34
44 Swarthmore 6
0 Princeton 38
12 Tioga 4
36 Lehigh 0
0 Yale 54
6 Lafayette 12
0 Princeton 4
0 Harvard 50
50 Lafayette 0
18 Wesleyan 6
24 Johns Hopkins 10
20 Navy 9

**1889**
30 All-Phila. 6
82 Swarthmore 0
4 Rutgers 0
6 Lehigh 4
4 Princeton 72
10 Yale 20
0 Harvard 35
8 Lafayette 10
24 Columbia 0
14 Rutgers 0
0 Lehigh 8
14 Lafayette 0
2 Wesleyan 10

**1890**
10 Swarthmore 0
16 Rutgers 4
20 Penn State 0
0 Princeton 18
8 Lehigh 0
18 Columbia 0
28 F. & M. 0
72 Virginia 0
34 A.C.S.N. 10
0 Princeton 6
0 Yale 60
17 Lehigh 14
16 Wesleyan 10
20 Rutgers 12

**1891**
4 All-Phila. 0
24 A.C.S.N. 0
34 Haverford 0
26 Orange A.C. 0
32 Rutgers 6
42 Lehigh 0
15 Lafayette 6
28 Trinity 5
0 Princeton 24
0 Yale 48
12 Lafayette 10
32 Lehigh 0
18 Wesleyan 10

**1892**
22 Swarthmore 0
20 Penn State 0
56 Haverford 0
32 Virginia 0
23 Crescent 0
16 Navy 0
78 Dickinson 0
34 F. & M. 0
50 Williams 0
8 Lafayette 6
12 Chicago A.C. 10
6 Princeton 4
0 Yale 28
10 Lafayette 4
4 Lehigh 0
34 Wesleyan 0

**1893**
48 F. & M. 0
74 Gettysburg 0
30 Columbia A.C. 0
20 Columbia A.C. 6
12 Georgetown 0
34 Navy 0
34 Volunteer 0
32 Lehigh 6
40 Crescent 0
18 Penn State 6
82 Lafayette 0
0 Princeton 4
6 Yale 14
50 Cornell 0
4 Harvard 26

**1894**
34 F. & M. 0
66 Swarthmore 0
22 Crescent 0
46 Georgetown 0
30 Lehigh 0
18 Crescent 10
14 Virginia 6
12 Navy 0
26 Lafayette 0
12 Princeton 0
6 Cornell 0
18 Harvard 4

**1895**
40 Swarthmore 0
40 Bucknell 0
42 F. & M. 0
32 Crescent 0
54 Lehigh 0
36 Indians 0
54 Virginia 0
30 Duquesne A.C. 0
30 Lafayette 0
12 Brown 0
12 Chicago A.C. 4
35 Penn State 4
17 Harvard 14
46 Cornell 2

**1896**
24 F. & M. 0
32 Gettysburg 0
40 Bucknell 0
8 Navy 0
16 Dartmouth 0
20 Virginia 0
34 Lehigh 0
14 Amherst 0
4 Lafayette 6
16 Brown 0
30 Dickinson 2
21 Indians 0
27 Penn State 0
8 Harvard 6
32 Cornell 10

**1897**
17 Bucknell 0
33 F. & M. 0
18 W. & J. 4
46 Lafayette 0
33 Bucknell 0
57 Gettysburg 0

58 Lehigh 0
42 Virginia 0
34 Dartmouth 0
24 Penn State 0
40 Brown 0
20 Indians 10
22 Wesleyan 0
15 Harvard 6
4 Cornell 0

**1898**
41 F. & M. 0
50 Gettysburg 0
40 Penn State 0
50 Mansfield 0
18 Brown 0
40 Virginia 0
17 Lehigh 0
32 Wesleyan 0
32 Lafayette 0
23 Chicago 11
0 Harvard 10
35 Indians 5
12 Cornell 6

**1899**
48 F. & M. 0
20 Lehigh 0
47 Bucknell 10
6 Brown 6
33 Virginia 6
5 Indians 16
17 Wesleyan 6
0 Lafayette 6
5 Chicago 5
0 Harvard 16
11 Michigan 10
47 Penn State 0
29 Cornell 0

**1900**
27 Lehigh 6
47 F. & M. 0
38 Haverford 0
35 Dickinson 0
12 Brown 0
17 Penn State 5
30 Columbia 0
41 Chicago 0
5 Harvard 17
12 Lafayette 5
16 Indians 6
28 Navy 6
27 Cornell 0

**1901**
28 Lehigh 0
6 F. & M. 0
23 Penn State 6
28 Swarthmore 0
26 Brown 0
20 Virginia 5
6 Bucknell 0
5 Navy 6
22 Gettysburg 0
11 Chicago 0
0 Columbia 10
6 Harvard 33
16 Indians 14
0 Army 24
0 Cornell 23

**1902**
12 Lehigh 0
16 F. & M. 0
17 Penn State 0
18 Haverford 5
11 Swarthmore 6
36 Gettysburg 0
6 Brown 15
6 Navy 10
6 Bucknell 5
17 Columbia 0
0 Harvard 11
0 Indians 5
12 Cornell 11

**1903**
27 Dickinson 0
17 F. & M. 0
16 Lehigh 0
58 Haverford 0
39 Penn State 0
72 Gettysburg 0
30 Brown 0
6 Columbia 18
47 Bucknell 6
10 Harvard 17
6 Indians 16
42 Cornell 0

**1904**
6 Penn State 0
6 Swarthmore 4
24 Virginia 0
34 F. & M. 0
24 Lehigh 0
21 Gettysburg 0
6 Brown 0
16 Columbia 0
11 Harvard 0
22 Lafayette 0
18 Indians 0
34 Cornell 0

**1905**
35 Lehigh 0
16 Gettysburg 6
11 Swarthmore 4
38 F. & M. 0
17 N. Carolina 0
39 Ursinus 0
8 Brown 6
6 Indians 0
6 Lafayette 6
12 Harvard 6
42 Villanova 0
23 Columbia 0
6 Cornell 5

**1906**
32 Lehigh 6
6 Gettysburg 6
11 N. Carolina 0
47 F. & M. 6
0 Swarthmore 4
31 Medico Chi 0
14 Brown 0
6 Indians 24
0 Lafayette 0
17 Michigan 0
22 Villanova 12
0 Cornell 0

**1907**
37 N. Carolina 0
16 Villanova 0
29 Bucknell 2
57 F. & M. 0
16 Swarthmore 8
23 Gettysburg 0
11 Brown 0
6 Indians 26
15 Lafayette 0
28 Penn State 0
6 Michigan 0
12 Cornell 4

**1908**
6 W. Virginia 0
30 Ursinus 0
16 Bucknell 0
11 Villanova 0
6 Penn State 0
23 Gettysburg 4
12 Brown 0
6 Indians 6
25 Carnegie T. 0
34 Lafayette 4
29 Michigan 0
17 Cornell 0

**1909**
20 Gettysburg 0
22 Ursinus 0
18 Dickinson 0
12 W. Virginia 0
13 Brown 5
3 Penn State 3
29 Indians 6
6 Lafayette 6
6 Michigan 12
17 Cornell 6

**1910**
5 Ursinus 8
18 Dickinson 0
29 Gettysburg 0
17 F. & M. 0
38 W. Virginia 0
20 Brown 0
10 Penn State 0
17 Indians 0
18 Lafayette 0
0 Michigan 0
12 Cornell 6

**1911**
5 Gettysburg 3
14 F. & M. 0
9 Ursinus 0
22 Dickinson 10
22 Villanova 0
0 Brown 6
6 Penn State 22
0 Indians 16
23 Lafayette 6
9 Michigan 11
21 Cornell 9

**1912**
35 Gettysburg 0
35 F. & M. 0
16 Dickinson 0
34 Ursinus 0
3 Swarthmore 6
7 Brown 30
3 Lafayette 7
0 Penn State 14
27 Michigan 21
34 Indians 26
7 Cornell 2

**1913**
53 Gettysburg 0
13 F. & M. 6
10 Lafayette 0
20 Swarthmore 0
28 Brown 0
7 Indians 7
17 Penn State 0
21 Dartmouth 34
0 Michigan 13
0 Cornell 21

**1914**
14 Gettysburg 0
0 F. & M. 10
0 Lafayette 0
13 Navy 6
7 Indians 0
40 Swarthmore 6
3 Michigan 34
0 Dartmouth 41
12 Cornell 24

**1915**
7 W. Virginia 0
63 Albright 0
10 F. & M. 6
3 Penn State 13
7 Navy 7
7 Pittsburgh 14
0 Lafayette 17
3 Dartmouth 7
0 Michigan 0
9 Cornell 24

**1916**
3 W. Virginia 0
27 F. & M. 0
0 Swarthmore 6
15 Penn State 0
0 Pittsburgh 20
19 Lafayette 0
7 Dartmouth 7
10 Michigan 7
16 W. Va. Wes. 0
23 Cornell 3
0 Oregon 14

**1917**
73 Albright 10
0 Georgia Tech 41
10 Swarthmore 0
20 Bucknell 6
6 Pittsburgh 14
27 Lafayette 0
23 P.M.C. 0
7 Dartmouth 0
16 Michigan 0
26 Indians 0
37 Cornell 0

**1918**
0 Marines 7
13 Navy Yard 6
12 Swarthmore 20
12 St. Joseph's 0
34 Lafayette 0
0 Pittsburgh 37
13 Swarthmore 7
21 Dartmouth 0

**1919**
16 Bucknell 0
54 P.M.C. 0
89 Delaware 0
55 Swarthmore 7
23 Lafayette 0
0 Penn State 10
19 Dartmouth 20
3 Pittsburgh 3
24 Cornell 0

**1920**
35 Delaware 0
7 Bucknell 0
21 Swarthmore 0
7 Lafayette 0
7 V.M.I. 27
7 Penn State 28
21 Pittsburgh 27
7 Dartmouth 44
27 Columbia 7
28 Cornell 0

**1921**
89 Delaware 0
20 F. & M. 0
7 Gettysburg 0
7 Swarthmore 7
21 V.M.I. 7
0 Pittsburgh 28
6 Lafayette 38
14 Dartmouth 14
0 Cornell 41

**1922**
14 F. & M. 0
27 Sewanee 0
12 Maryland 0
14 Swarthmore 0
13 Navy 7
7 Alabama 9
6 Pittsburgh 7
7 Penn State 6
0 Cornell 9

**1923**
20 F. & M. 0
0 Maryland 3
13 Swarthmore 10
19 Columbia 7
24 Centre College 0
6 Pittsburgh 0
6 Lafayette 8
0 Penn State 21
7 Cornell 14

**1924**

- 34 Ursinus 0
- 52 Drexel 0
- 26 F. & M. 0
- 25 Swarthmore 7
- 10 Columbia 7
- 27 Virginia 0
- 6 Lafayette 3
- 3 Georgetown 0
- 0 Penn State 0
- 20 Cornell 0
- 0 California 14

**1925**

- 32 Ursinus 0
- 26 Swarthmore 13
- 9 Brown 0
- 16 Yale 13
- 7 Chicago 0
- 2 Illinois 24
- 66 Haverford 0
- 0 Pittsburgh 14
- 7 Cornell 0

**1926**

- 41 F. & M. 0
- 40 Johns Hopkins 7
- 44 Swarthmore 0
- 27 Chicago 0
- 36 Williams 0
- 0 Illinois 3
- 3 Penn State 0
- 3 Columbia 0
- 10 Cornell 10

**1927**

- 8 F. & M. 0
- 33 Swarthmore 0
- 14 Brown 6
- 0 Penn State 20
- 7 Chicago 13
- 6 Navy 12
- 24 Harvard 0
- 27 Columbia 0
- 35 Cornell 0
- 13 California 27

**1928**

- 34 Ursinus 0
- 46 F. & M. 0
- 67 Swarthmore 0
- 14 Penn State 0
- 0 Navy 6
- 20 Chicago 13
- 7 Harvard 0
- 34 Columbia 7
- 49 Cornell 0

**1929**

- 14 F. & M. 7
- 20 Swarthmore 6
- 14 Virginia Tech 8
- 7 California 12
- 10 Lehigh 7
- 7 Navy 2
- 7 Penn State 19
- 20 Columbia 0
- 17 Cornell 7

**1930**

- 63 Swarthmore 0
- 40 Virginia 6
- 0 Wisconsin 27
- 40 Lehigh 0
- 21 Kansas 6
- 20 Notre Dame 60
- 34 Georgia Tech 7
- 7 Cornell 13
- 0 Navy 26

**1931**

- 32 Swarthmore 7
- 14 F. & M. 0
- 32 Lehigh 0
- 27 Wisconsin 13
- 3 Lafayette 0
- 0 Notre Dame 49
- 13 Georgia Tech 12
- 0 Cornell 7
- 0 Navy 6

**1932**

- 38 F. & M. 0
- 54 Swarthmore 0
- 14 Dartmouth 7
- 33 Lehigh 6
- 14 Navy 0
- 21 Pittsburgh 19
- 0 Ohio State 19
- 13 Cornell 7

**1933**

- 9 F. & M. 0
- 7 Dartmouth 14
- 0 Navy 13
- 16 Lafayette 7
- 7 Ohio State 20
- 6 Penn State 6
- 12 Cornell 20

**1934**

- 6 Ursinus 7
- 6 Yale 14
- 27 Rutgers 19
- 0 Navy 17
- 41 Lafayette 0
- 3 Penn State 0
- 12 Columbia 13
- 23 Cornell 13

**1935**

- 6 Princeton 7
- 20 Yale 31
- 34 Columbia 0
- 67 Lafayette 0
- 6 Michigan 16
- 0 Navy 13
- 33 Penn State 6
- 33 Cornell 7

**1936**

- 35 Lafayette 0
- 0 Yale 7
- 7 Princeton 0
- 48 Brown 6
- 16 Navy 6
- 27 Michigan 7
- 19 Penn State 12
- 14 Cornell 6

**1937**

- 28 Maryland 21
- 7 Yale 27
- 6 Columbia 26
- 0 Georgetown 0
- 14 Navy 7
- 0 Penn State 7
- 0 Michigan 7
- 20 Cornell 34

**1938**

- 34 Lafayette 6
- 21 Yale 0
- 0 Princeton 13
- 14 Columbia 13
- 0 Navy 0
- 13 Michigan 19
- 7 Penn State 7
- 0 Cornell 0

**1939**

- 6 Lafayette 0
- 6 Yale 0
- 22 Harvard 7
- 6 N. Carolina 30
- 13 Navy 6
- 0 Penn State 10
- 17 Michigan 19
- 0 Cornell 26

**1940**

- 51 Maryland 0
- 50 Yale 7
- 46 Princeton 28
- 0 Michigan 14
- 20 Navy 0
- 10 Harvard 10
- 48 Army 0
- 22 Cornell 20

**1941**

- 19 Harvard 0
- 28 Yale 13
- 23 Princeton 0
- 55 Maryland 6
- 6 Navy 13
- 19 Columbia 16
- 14 Army 7
- 16 Cornell 0

**1942**

- 6 Georgia Naval Av. Cadets 14
- 19 Harvard 7
- 35 Yale 6
- 6 Princeton 6
- 42 Columbia 12
- 19 Army 0
- 0 Navy 7
- 7 Penn State 13
- 34 Cornell 7

**1943**

- 47 Princeton 9
- 41 Yale 7
- 7 Dartmouth 6
- 74 Lakehurst 6
- 33 Columbia 0
- 13 Army 13
- 7 Navy 24
- 6 N. Carolina 9
- 20 Cornell 14

**1944**

- 18 Duke 7
- 20 Dartmouth 6
- 46 Wm. & Mary 0
- 0 Navy 26
- 19 Michigan 41
- 35 Columbia 7
- 7 Army 62
- 20 Cornell 0

**1945**

- 50 Brown 0
- 12 Dartmouth 0
- 49 N. Carolina 0
- 7 Navy 14
- 28 Princeton 0
- 32 Columbia 7
- 0 Army 61
- 59 Cornell 6

**1946**

- 66 Lafayette 0
- 39 Dartmouth 6
- 40 Virginia 0
- 32 Navy 19
- 14 Princeton 17
- 41 Columbia 6
- 7 Army 34
- 26 Cornell 20

**1947**

- 59 Lafayette 0
- 32 Dartmouth 0
- 34 Columbia 14
- 21 Navy 0
- 26 Princeton 7
- 19 Virginia 7
- 7 Army 7
- 21 Cornell 0

**1948**

- 26 Dartmouth 13
- 29 Princeton 7
- 20 Columbia 14
- 20 Navy 14
- 40 Wash. & Lee 7
- 0 Penn State 13
- 20 Army 26
- 14 Cornell 23

**1949**

- 21 Dartmouth 0
- 14 Princeton 13
- 27 Columbia 7
- 28 Navy 7
- 21 Pittsburgh 22
- 14 Virginia 26
- 13 Army 14
- 21 Cornell 29

**1950**

- 21 Virginia 7
- 7 California 14
- 42 Dartmouth 26
- 34 Columbia 0
- 30 Navy 7
- 13 Army 28
- 50 Brown 0
- 20 Wisconsin 0
- 6 Cornell 13

**1951**

- 0 California 35
- 39 Dartmouth 14
- 7 Princeton 13
- 28 Columbia 13
- 14 Navy 0
- 12 Wm. & Mary 20
- 7 Wisconsin 16
- 7 Army 6
- 7 Cornell 0

**1952**

- 7 Notre Dame 7
- 7 Dartmouth 0
- 13 Princeton 7
- 27 Columbia 17
- 7 Navy 7
- 7 Penn State 14
- 27 Georgia 34
- 13 Army 14
- 14 Cornell 7

**1953**

- 13 Vanderbilt 7
- 13 Penn State 7
- 0 California 40
- 6 Ohio State 12
- 9 Navy 6
- 14 Michigan 26
- 20 Notre Dame 28
- 14 Army 21
- 7 Cornell 7

**1954**

- 0 Duke 52
- 7 Wm. & Mary 27
- 7 Princeton 13
- 27 G. Washington 32
- 6 Navy 52
- 13 Penn State 35
- 7 Notre Dame 42
- 0 Army 35
- 6 Cornell 20

**1955**

- 0 Virginia Tech 33
- 7 California 27
- 0 Princeton 7
- 6 G. Washington 25
- 0 Navy 33
- 0 Penn State 20
- 14 Notre Dame 46
- 0 Army 40
- 7 Cornell 39

**1956**

- 0 Penn State 34
- 14 Dartmouth 7
- 0 Princeton 34
- 14 Brown 7
- 6 Navy 54
- 28 Harvard 14
- 7 Yale 40
- 20 Columbia 6
- 7 Cornell 20

IRVING MENDELSON—A lightweight for a guard but a brilliant defensive player.

CLIFFORD ENGLER—The tallest man on the squad and a dependable tackle.

BERNARD KUCZYNSKI — Only a sophomore but a regular at left end.

EDWARD ALLEN—One of the surest ground gainers at fullback and a capable forward passer.

FRANK REAGAN—One of the country's best kickers. He has scored 73 points to date.

*These photos from a 1940 Penn football program tell who the stars were as the Quakers went on to dominate the decade.*

**1957**
14 Penn State 19
3 Dartmouth 6
9 Princeton 13
7 Brown 20
7 Navy 35
6 Harvard 13
33 Yale 20
28 Columbia 6
14 Cornell 6

**1958**
0 Penn State 43
12 Dartmouth 13
14 Princeton 20
21 Brown 20
8 Navy 50
19 Harvard 6
30 Yale 6
42 Columbia 0
7 Cornell 19

**1959**
26 Lafayette 0
13 Dartmouth 0
18 Princeton 0
36 Brown 9
22 Navy 22
0 Harvard 12
28 Yale 12
24 Columbia 6
28 Cornell 13

**1960**
35 Lafayette 14
0 Dartmouth 15
0 Princeton 21
36 Brown 7
0 Navy 27
0 Harvard 8
9 Yale 34
6 Columbia 16
18 Cornell 7

**1961**
14 Lafayette 7
0 Dartmouth 30
3 Princeton 9
7 Brown 0
6 Rutgers 20
6 Harvard 37
0 Yale 23
6 Columbia 37
0 Cornell 31

**1962**
13 Lafayette 11
0 Dartmouth 17
8 Princeton 21
18 Brown 15
7 Rutgers 12
0 Harvard 36
15 Yale 12
7 Columbia 21
22 Cornell 29

**1963**
47 Lafayette 0
0 Dartmouth 28
0 Princeton 34
13 Brown 41
7 Rutgers 6
7 Harvard 2
7 Yale 28
8 Columbia 33
8 Cornell 17

**1964**
13 Lehigh 6
0 Brown 3
0 Cornell 33
7 Rutgers 10
0 Princeton 55
0 Harvard 34
9 Yale 21
12 Columbia 33
7 Dartmouth 27

**1965**
20 Lehigh 14
7 Brown 0
19 Dartmouth 24
16 Bucknell 13
0 Princeton 51
10 Harvard 10
19 Yale 21
31 Columbia 21
14 Cornell 38

**1966**
38 Lehigh 28
20 Brown 0
28 Cornell 45
21 Bucknell 28
13 Princeton 30
7 Harvard 27
14 Yale 17
14 Columbia 22
21 Dartmouth 40

**1967**
35 Lehigh 23
28 Brown 7
0 Dartmouth 23
27 Bucknell 28
14 Princeton 28
7 Harvard 45
22 Yale 44
26 Columbia 6
14 Cornell 33

**1968**
27 Bucknell 10
17 Brown 13
10 Cornell 8
34 Lehigh 0
19 Princeton 14
6 Harvard 28
13 Yale 30
13 Columbia 7
26 Dartmouth 21

**1969**
28 Bucknell 17
23 Brown 2
0 Dartmouth 41
13 Lehigh 7
0 Princeton 42
6 Harvard 20
3 Yale 21
17 Columbia 7
14 Cornell 28

**1970**
24 Lehigh 0
17 Brown 9
31 Cornell 32
31 Lafayette 20
16 Princeton 22
23 Harvard 28
22 Yale 32
21 Columbia 14
0 Dartmouth 28

**1971**
28 Lehigh 14
17 Brown 16
3 Dartmouth 19
15 Lafayette 17
0 Princeton 31
27 Harvard 28
14 Yale 24
3 Columbia 17
13 Cornell 41

**1972**
55 Lafayette 12
20 Brown 28
20 Cornell 24
30 Lehigh 27
15 Princeton 10
38 Harvard 27
47 Yale 30
20 Columbia 14
17 Dartmouth 31

**1973**
14 Lafayette 16
28 Brown 20
22 Dartmouth 16
27 Lehigh 20
24 Princeton 0
30 Harvard 34
21 Yale 24
42 Columbia 8
31 Cornell 22

**1974**
37 Lafayette 7
14 Brown 9
28 Cornell 28
28 Lehigh 18
20 Princeton 18
0 Harvard 39
12 Yale 37
21 Columbia 3
27 Dartmouth 20

**1975**
14 Dartmouth 19
23 Lehigh 34
25 Columbia 28
8 Brown 17
13 Lafayette 0
14 Yale 24
24 Princeton 20
3 Harvard 21
27 Cornell 21

**1976**
0 Dartmouth 20
20 Lehigh 24
10 Columbia 14
7 Brown 6
15 Lafayette 14
7 Yale 21
10 Princeton 9
8 Harvard 20
13 Cornell 31

## Princeton University

Princeton, New Jersey
Established: 1746
Colors: Orange and Black
Nickname: Tigers

*Head Coaches*

Player-coaches, player-alumni committees, 1869-1900
Langdon Lea, 1901
Garrett Cochran, 1902
A.R.T. Hillebrand, 1903-1905
William W. Roper, 1906-1908
James B. McCormick, 1909
William W. Roper, 1910-1911
Logan Cunningham, 1912
W. Gresham Andrews, 1913
Wilder G. Penfield, 1914
John H. Rush, 1915-1916
Keene Fitzpatrick, 1917-1918
William W. Roper, 1919-1930
Albert Wittmer, Jr., 1931
Herbert 0. (Fritz) Crisler, 1932-1937
Elton E. (Tad) Wieman, 1938-1942
Harry A. Mahnken, 1943-1944
Charles W. Caldwell, Jr., 1945-1956
Richard W. Colman, Jr., 1957-1968
J. L. McCandless, 1969-1972
Robert F. Casciola, 1973-

### Scores 1869-1976

**1869**
4g Rutgers 6g
8g Rutgers 0

**1870**
6g Rutgers 2g

**1871**
Games only with Seminary; no records kept

**1872**
4g Rutgers 1g

**1873**
3g Yale 0

**1874**
6g Columbia 0
6g Rutgers 0

**1875**
6g Columbia 2g
6g Stevens Inst. 0

**1876**
6g Pennsylvania 0
3g Columbia 0
6g Pennsylvania 0
0 Yale 2g, 2t

**1877**
1t Harvard 1g, 2t
1g, 1t Harvard 2t
4g, 1t Columbia 0
0 Yale 0

**1878**
2g, 4t Pennsylvania 0
4g, 6t Stevens Inst. 0
5g, 10t Rutgers 0
2g, 5t Pennsylvania 1g
1t Harvard 0
1g Yale 0

**1879**
6g, 4t Pennsylvania 1s
2g, 3t Columbia 0
7g, 4t Stevens Inst. 10s
1g, 7s Harvard 5s
0 Yale 0

**1880**
6g, 6t Stevens Inst. 6s
8g, 4t, 1s Rutgers 1t, 3s
1t, 3s Pennsylvania 1s
2g, 2t, 6s Harvard 1g, 1t, 4s
0 Yale 0

**1881**
3g, 5t Rutgers 11s
7g, 9t Stevens Inst. 4s
7g, 5t Pennsylvania 2s
1g, 2t, 1s Michigan 3s
4g, 6t Pennsylvania 4s
1g, 1t Rutgers 3s
1g, 2t, 1s Columbia 4s
0 Harvard 0
0 Yale 0

**1882**
5g, 4t Graduates 0
5g, 6t Rutgers 0
8g, 4t Pennsylvania 0
8g, 3t Columbia 2s
10g, 4t Pennsylvania 0
3g, 4t Rutgers 2s
1g Harvard 1g, 1t
3g, 1t Columbia 0
1g, 1s Yale 2g, 2t, 1s

**1883**
20 Rutgers 0
54 Lafayette 7
15 Stevens Inst. 5
61 Rutgers 0
39 Pennsylvania 6
24 Wesleyan 0
26 Harvard 7
0 Yale 6

**1884**
23 Rutgers 5
4 Stevens Inst. 0
22 Wesleyan 2
35 Rutgers 0
31 Pennsylvania 0
140 Lafayette 0
56 Stevens Inst. 0
57 Johns Hopkins 0
36 Harvard 6
0 Yale 0

**1885**
94 Stevens Inst. 0
76 Stevens Inst. 0
76 Pennsylvania 10
80 Pennsylvania 10
64 Columbia Law S 0
10 Johns Hopkins 0
76 Wesleyan 0
6 Yale 5
57 Pennsylvania 0

**1886**
58 Stevens Inst. 0
61 Stevens Inst. 6
30 Pennsylvania 0
55 Pennsylvania 9
28 Pennsylvania 6
12 Harvard 0
76 Wesleyan 6
0 Yale 0

**1887**
47 Lafayette 0
30 Rutgers 0
80 Lehigh 0
61 Pennsylvania 0
48 Pennsylvania 0
69 Wesleyan 0
95 Pennsylvania 0
0 Harvard 12
0 Yale 12

**1888**
65 Lehigh 0
31 Crescent A.C. 0
63 Pennsylvania 0
80 Stevens Inst. 0
80 Rutgers 0
38 Pennsylvania 0
82 Rutgers 0
108 Johns Hopkins 0
44 Wesleyan 0
4 Pennsylvania 0
18 Harvard 6
0 Yale 10

**1889**
16 Lehigh 0
16 Lehigh 4
49 Stevens Inst. 0
72 Pennsylvania 4
98 Wesleyan 0
71 Columbia 0
41 Harvard 15
54 Orange A.C. 6
10 Yale 0
57 Washington 0

**1890**
33 Frank. & Marsh. 16
27 Rutgers 0
0 Orange A.C. 0
18 Pennsylvania 0
12 Crescent A.C. 0
26 Lafayette 6
50 Lehigh 0
60 Columbia A.C. 0
115 Virginia 0
85 Columbia 0
6 Pennsylvania 0
46 Wesleyan 4
0 Yale 32

**1891**
12 Rutgers 0
18 Lehigh 0
28 Crescent A.C. 0
30 Lehigh 0
44 Frank. & Marsh. 0
24 Lafayette 0
28 New York A.C. 0
78 Manhattan A.C. 0
73 Wesleyan 0
26 Orange A.C. 0
24 Pennsylvania 0
6 Cornell 0
0 Yale 19

**1892**
30 Rutgers 0
16 Lehigh 0
40 Lafayette 0
42 Columbia A.C. 0
28 Navy 0
50 Lehigh 0
40 New York A.C. 0
42 Crescent A.C. 0
46 Manhattan A.C. 0
60 Wesleyan 0
12 Chicago A.C. 0
4 Pennsylvania 6
23 Orange A.C. 0
0 Yale 12

**1893**
20 Lafayette 0
12 Lehigh 0
26 Crescent A.C. 0
8 Lawrenceville 4
46 Cornell 0
28 Lehigh 6
76 Wesleyan 0
4 Pennsylvania 0
8 Orange A.C. 0
36 Army 4
6 Yale 0

**1894**
40 Lafayette 0
8 Lehigh 0
48 Rutgers 0
12 Virginia 0
12 Cornell 4
32 Lehigh 0
40 Volunteers 0
0 Pennsylvania 12
16 Orange A.C. 4
0 Yale 24

**1895**
38 Elizabeth A.C. 0
22 Rutgers 0
36 Virginia 0
14 Lafayette 0
38 Lawrenceville 0
10 Seminary 4
16 Lehigh 0
22 Union 0
0 Orange A.C. 0
12 Harvard 4
6 Cornell 0

10 Yale 20

**1896**
44 Rutgers 0
0 Lafayette 0
16 Lehigh 0
22 Carlisle Indians 6
11 Army 0
48 Virginia 0
39 Penn State 0
46 Lawrenceville 0
37 Cornell 0
12 Harvard 0
24 Yale 6

**1897**
43 Lehigh 0
53 Rutgers 0
28 Navy 0
34 Penn State 0
18 Carlisle Indians 0
54 Frank. & Marsh. 0
10 Cornell 0
12 Elizabeth A.C. 0
30 Dartmouth 0
57 Lafayette 0
0 Yale 6

**1898**
21 Lehigh 0
42 Stevens Inst. 0
58 Frank. & Marsh. 0
34 Lafayette 0
24 Maryland A.C. 0
30 Navy 0
6 Cornell 0
5 Penn State 0
23 Brown 0
12 Virginia 0
5 Army 5
6 Yale 0

**1899**
28 Maryland A.C. 0
5 Navy 0
12 Lafayette 0
11 Columbia 0
12 Penn State 0
23 Army 0
17 Lehigh 0
0 Cornell 5
18 Brown 6
30 North Carolina 0
12 Carlisle Indians 0
6 Wash. & Jeff. 0
11 Yale 10

**1900**
40 Stevens Inst. 0
12 Lehigh 5
26 Penn State 0
11 Baltimore Medical 0
5 Navy 0
43 Syracuse 0
5 Lafayette 0
17 Brown 5
0 Cornell 12
5 Columbia 6
5 Yale 29

**1901**
37 Villanova 0
47 Haverford 0
23 N.Y.U. 0
35 Lehigh 0
23 Dickinson 0
35 Brown 0
29 Orange A.C. 0
6 Lafayette 0
8 Cornell 6
6 Army 6
0 Yale 12

**1902**
18 Swarthmore 0
23 Lehigh 0
11 Navy 0
30 Haverford 0
23 Wash. & Jeff. 5
23 Dickinson 0
22 Columbia 0
10 Cornell 0
5 Yale 12

**1903**
34 Swarthmore 0
5 Georgetown 0
68 Gettysburg 0
29 Brown 0
12 Lehigh 0
11 Carlisle Indians 0
17 Bucknell 0
17 Dartmouth 0
44 Cornell 0
11 Lafayette 0
11 Yale 6

**1904**
12 Dickinson 0
10 Georgetown 0
39 Wesleyan 0
16 Wash. & Jeff. 0
5 Lafayette 0
9 Navy 10
60 Lehigh 0
18 Cornell 6
12 Army 6
0 Yale 12

**1905**
41 Villanova 0
23 Wash. & Jeff. 0
34 Georgetown 0
29 Lehigh 6
48 Bucknell 0
22 Lafayette 4
12 Columbia 0
0 Dartmouth 6
16 Cornell 6
4 Yale 23

**1906**
24 Villanova 0
22 Stevens Inst. 0
6 Wash. & Jeff. 0
52 Lehigh 0
5 Navy 0
32 Bucknell 4
14 Cornell 5
42 Dartmouth 0
8 Army 0
0 Yale 0

**1907**
47 Stevens Inst. 0
53 Wesleyan 0
52 Bucknell 0
45 Villanova 5
40 Wash. & Jeff. 0
5 Cornell 6
16 Carlisle Indians 0
14 Amherst 0
10 Yale 12

**1908**
18 Springfield 0
21 Stevens Inst. 0
0 Lafayette 0
6 Villanova 0
10 V.P.I. 4
17 Fordham 0
0 Syracuse 0
0 Army 0
6 Dartmouth 10
6 Yale 11

**1909**
47 Stevens Inst. 12
12 Villanova 0
3 Fordham 0
8 V.P.I. 6
20 Sewanee 0
0 Lafayette 6
5 Navy 3
6 Dartmouth 6
0 Yale 17

**1910**
18 Stevens Inst. 0
36 Villanova 0
12 N.Y.U. 0
3 Lafayette 0
6 Carlisle Indians 0
6 Dartmouth 0
17 Holy Cross 0
3 Yale 5

**1911**
37 Stevens Inst. 0
37 Rutgers 0
31 Villanova 0
6 Lehigh 6
31 Colgate 0
0 Navy 0
20 Holy Cross 0
8 Harvard 6
3 Dartmouth 0
6 Yale 3

**1912**
65 Stevens Inst. 0
41 Rutgers 6
35 Lehigh 0
31 V.P.I. 0
62 Syracuse 0
22 Dartmouth 7
6 Harvard 16
54 N.Y.U. 0
6 Yale 6

**1913**
14 Rutgers 3
69 Fordham 0
28 Bucknell 6
13 Syracuse 0
0 Dartmouth 6
54 Holy Cross 0
0 Harvard 3
3 Yale 3

**1914**
12 Rutgers 0
10 Bucknell 0
12 Syracuse 7
16 Lafayette 0
16 Dartmouth 12
7 Williams 7
0 Harvard 20
14 Yale 19

**1915**
13 Georgetown 0
10 Rutgers 0
3 Syracuse 0
40 Lafayette 3
30 Dartmouth 7
27 Williams 0
6 Harvard 10
7 Yale 13

**1916**
21 Holy Cross 0
29 North Carolina 0
3 Tufts 0
33 Lafayette 0
7 Dartmouth 3
42 Bucknell 0
0 Harvard 3
0 Yale 10

**1917**
Informal Season
7 307th F.A. (Fort Dix) 0
43 Wissahickon Barracks 0

**1918**
Informal Wartime Season
26 Navy Pay School 0
7 Govt. Aero School 0
28 Camp Upton 7

**1919**
28 Trinity 0
9 Lafayette 6
34 Rochester 0
0 Colgate 7
0 West Virginia 25
10 Harvard 10
13 Yale 6

**1920**
17 Swarthmore 6
35 Maryland 0
34 Washington & Lee 0
14 Navy 0
10 West Virginia 3
14 Harvard 14
20 Yale 0

**1921**
21 Swarthmore 7
19 Colgate 0
0 Navy 13
0 Chicago 9
34 Virginia 0
10 Harvard 3
7 Yale 13

**1922**
30 Johns Hopkins 0
5 Virginia 0
10 Colgate 0
26 Maryland 0
21 Chicago 18
22 Swarthmore 13
10 Harvard 3
3 Yale 0

**1923**
16 Johns Hopkins 7
17 Georgetown 0
2 Notre Dame 25
3 Navy 3
35 Swarthmore 6
0 Harvard 5
0 Yale 27

**1924**
40 Amherst 6
0 Lehigh 0
17 Navy 14
0 Notre Dame 12
21 Swarthmore 6
34 Harvard 0
0 Yale 10

**1925**
20 Amherst 0
15 Washington & Lee 6
10 Navy 10
0 Colgate 9
19 Swarthmore 7
36 Harvard 0
25 Yale 12

**1926**
14 Amherst 7
7 Washington & Lee 7
13 Navy 27
7 Lehigh 6
27 Swarthmore 0
12 Harvard 0
10 Yale 7

**1927**
14 Amherst 0
42 Lehigh 0
13 Washington & Lee 0
21 Cornell 10
35 William & Mary 7
20 Ohio State 0
6 Yale 14

**1928**
50 Vermont 0
0 Virginia 0

47 Lehigh 0
3 Cornell 0
6 Ohio State 6
25 Washington & Lee 12
12 Yale 2
0 Navy 9

**1929**

7 Amherst 0
12 Brown 13
7 Cornell 13
13 Navy 13
7 Chicago 15
20 Lehigh 0
0 Yale 13

**1930**

23 Amherst 0
0 Brown 7
7 Cornell 12
0 Navy 31
0 Chicago 0
9 Lehigh 13
7 Yale 10

**1931**

27 Amherst 0
7 Brown 19
0 Cornell 33
0 Navy 15
0 Michigan 21
7 Lehigh 19
0 Washington & Lee 6
14 Yale 51

**1932**

22 Amherst 0
7 Columbia 20
0 Cornell 0
0 Navy 0
7 Michigan 14
53 Lehigh 0
7 Yale 7

**1933**

40 Amherst 0
45 Williams 0
20 Columbia 0
6 Washington & Lee 0
33 Brown 0
7 Dartmouth 0
13 Navy 0
26 Rutgers 6
27 Yale 2

**1934**

75 Amherst 0
35 Williams 6
14 Washington & Lee 12
45 Cornell 0
19 Harvard 0
54 Lehigh 0
0 Yale 7
38 Dartmouth 13

**1935**

7 Pennsylvania 6
14 Williams 7
29 Rutgers 6
54 Cornell 0
26 Navy 0
35 Harvard 0
27 Lehigh 0
26 Dartmouth 6
38 Yale 7

**1936**

27 Williams 7
20 Rutgers 0
0 Pennsylvania 7
7 Navy 0
14 Harvard 14
41 Cornell 13
23 Yale 26
13 Dartmouth 13

**1937**

26 Virginia 0
7 Cornell 20
16 Chicago 7
6 Rutgers 0
6 Harvard 34
9 Dartmouth 33
0 Yale 26
26 Navy 6

**1938**

39 Williams 0
0 Dartmouth 22
13 Pennsylvania 0
13 Navy 13
7 Harvard 26
18 Rutgers 20
20 Yale 7
7 Army 19

**1939**

26 Williams 6
7 Cornell 20
14 Columbia 7
26 Brown 12
9 Harvard 6
9 Dartmouth 7
13 Yale 7
28 Navy 0

**1940**

7 Vanderbilt 6
6 Navy 12
28 Pennsylvania 46
28 Rutgers 13
0 Harvard 0
14 Dartmouth 9
10 Yale 7
26 Army 19

**1941**

20 Williams 7
0 Columbia 21
0 Pennsylvania 23
7 Vanderbilt 46
4 Harvard 6
13 Dartmouth 20
20 Yale 6
0 Navy 23

**1942**

20 Lakehurst Naval 6
7 Williams 19
10 Navy 0

*John A. C. (Jac) Weller was a stalwart in the 1933–35 Princeton line. His All-American play at guard earned him a niche in the National Football Hall of Fame.*

6 Pennsylvania 6
32 Brown 13
14 Harvard 19
7 Dartmouth 19
6 Yale 13
7 Army 40

**1943**

9 Pennsylvania 47
26 Columbia 7
0 Cornell 30
20 Brown 28
22 Villanova 45
6 Yale 27
13 Dartmouth 42

**1944**

16 Muhlenberg 6
0 Swarthmore 3
6 Atlantic City N.A.S. 31

**1945**

7 Lafayette 7
14 Cornell 6
14 Rutgers 6
0 Pennsylvania 28
13 Dartmouth 13
7 Columbia 32
14 Yale 20

**1946**

33 Brown 12
12 Harvard 13
14 Rutgers 7
7 Cornell 14
17 Pennsylvania 14
6 Virginia 20
2 Yale 30
13 Dartmouth 20

**1947**

21 Brown 7
7 Rutgers 13
20 Colgate 7
21 Cornell 28
7 Pennsylvania 26
33 Harvard 7
17 Yale 0
14 Dartmouth 12

**1948**

20 Brown 23
7 Pennsylvania 29
6 Rutgers 22
16 Columbia 14
55 Virginia 14
47 Harvard 7
20 Yale 14
13 Dartmouth 33

**1949**

26 Lafayette 14
7 Navy 28
13 Pennsylvania 14
27 Brown 14
12 Cornell 14
34 Rutgers 14
33 Harvard 13
21 Yale 13
19 Dartmouth 13

**1950**

66 Williams 0
34 Rutgers 28
20 Navy 14
34 Brown 0
27 Cornell 0
45 Colgate 7
63 Harvard 26
47 Yale 12
13 Dartmouth 7

**1951**

54 N.Y.U. 20
24 Navy 20
13 Pennsylvania 7
60 Lafayette 7
53 Cornell 15
12 Brown 0
54 Harvard 13

27 Yale 0
13 Dartmouth 0

**1952**

14 Columbia 0
61 Rutgers 19
7 Pennsylvania 13
48 Lafayette 0
27 Cornell 0
39 Brown 0
41 Harvard 21
27 Yale 21
33 Dartmouth 0

**1953**

20 Lafayette 14
20 Columbia 19
9 Rutgers 7
7 Navy 65
19 Cornell 26
27 Brown 13
6 Harvard 0
24 Yale 26
12 Dartmouth 34

**1954**

10 Rutgers 8
54 Columbia 20
13 Pennsylvania 7
20 Brown 21
0 Cornell 27
6 Colgate 6
9 Harvard 14
21 Yale 14
49 Dartmouth 7

**1955**

41 Rutgers 7
20 Columbia 7
7 Pennsylvania 0
6 Colgate 15
26 Cornell 20
14 Brown 7
6 Harvard 7
13 Yale 0
6 Dartmouth 3

**1956**

28 Rutgers 6
39 Columbia 0
34 Pennsylvania 0
28 Colgate 20
32 Cornell 21
21 Brown 7
35 Harvard 20
20 Yale 42
0 Dartmouth 19

**1957**

7 Rutgers 0
47 Columbia 6
13 Pennsylvania 9
10 Colgate 12
47 Cornell 14
7 Brown 0
28 Harvard 20
13 Yale 20
34 Dartmouth 14

**1958**

0 Rutgers 28
43 Columbia 8
20 Pennsylvania 14
40 Colgate 13
8 Cornell 34
28 Brown 18
16 Harvard 14
50 Yale 14
12 Dartmouth 21

**1959**

6 Rutgers 8
22 Columbia 0
0 Pennsylvania 18
42 Colgate 7
20 Cornell 0
7 Brown 0
0 Harvard 14
20 Yale 38
7 Dartmouth 12

**1960**

8 Rutgers 13
49 Columbia 0
21 Pennsylvania 0
36 Colgate 26
21 Cornell 18
54 Brown 21
14 Harvard 12
22 Yale 43
7 Dartmouth 0

**1961**

13 Rutgers 16
30 Columbia 20
9 Pennsylvania 3
0 Colgate 15
30 Cornell 25
52 Brown 0
7 Harvard 9
26 Yale 16
6 Dartmouth 24

**1962**

15 Rutgers 7
33 Columbia 0
21 Pennsylvania 8
15 Colgate 16
34 Cornell 35
28 Brown 12
0 Harvard 20
14 Yale 10
27 Dartmouth 38

**1963**

24 Rutgers 0
7 Columbia 6
34 Pennsylvania 0
42 Colgate 0
51 Cornell 14
34 Brown 13
7 Harvard 21
27 Yale 7
21 Dartmouth 22

**1964**

10 Rutgers 7
23 Columbia 13
37 Dartmouth 7
9 Colgate 0
55 Pennsylvania 0
14 Brown 0
16 Harvard 0
35 Yale 14
17 Cornell 12

**1965**

32 Rutgers 6
31 Columbia 0
36 Cornell 27
27 Colgate 0
51 Pennsylvania 0
45 Brown 27
14 Harvard 6
31 Yale 6
14 Dartmouth 28

**1966**

16 Rutgers 12
14 Columbia 12
13 Dartmouth 31
0 Colgate 7
30 Pennsylvania 13
24 Brown 7
18 Harvard 14
13 Yale 7
7 Cornell 0

**1967**

22 Rutgers 21
28 Columbia 14
13 Cornell 47
28 Colgate 0
28 Pennsylvania 14
48 Brown 14
45 Harvard 6
7 Yale 29
14 Dartmouth 17

**1968**

14 Rutgers 20
44 Columbia 16
34 Dartmouth 7
7 Colgate 14
14 Pennsylvania 19
50 Brown 7
7 Harvard 9
17 Yale 42
41 Cornell 13

**1969**

0 Rutgers 29
21 Columbia 7
24 Cornell 17
28 Colgate 35
42 Pennsylvania 0
33 Brown 6
51 Harvard 20
14 Yale 17
35 Dartmouth 7

**1970**

41 Rutgers 14
24 Columbia 22
0 Dartmouth 38
34 Colgate 14
22 Pennsylvania 16
45 Brown 14
7 Harvard 29
22 Yale 27
3 Cornell 6

**1971**

18 Rutgers 33
20 Columbia 22
8 Cornell 19
35 Colgate 12
31 Pennsylvania 0
49 Brown 21
21 Harvard 10
6 Yale 10
7 Dartmouth 33

**1972**

7 Rutgers 6
0 Columbia 0
14 Dartmouth 35
26 Colgate 35
10 Pennsylvania 15
31 Brown 10
10 Harvard 7
7 Yale 31
15 Cornell 22

**1973**

14 Rutgers 39
13 Columbia 14
6 Cornell 37
37 Colgate 21
0 Pennsylvania 24
6 Brown 7
14 Harvard 19
13 Yale 30
24 Dartmouth 42

**1974**

6 Rutgers 6
40 Columbia 13
14 Dartmouth 7
33 Colgate 24
18 Pennsylvania 20
13 Brown 17
17 Harvard 34
6 Yale 19
41 Cornell 20

**1975**

10 Rutgers 7
27 Columbia 7
16 Cornell 8
21 Colgate 22
20 Pennsylvania 24
16 Brown 24
24 Harvard 20
13 Yale 24
16 Dartmouth 21

**1976**

3 Cornell 0
0 Rutgers 17
7 Brown 13
9 Columbia 3
7 Colgate 17
14 Harvard 20
9 Penn 10
7 Yale 39
7 Dartmouth 33

## Yale University

New Haven, Connecticut
Established: 1701
Color: Yale Blue
Nickname: Bulldogs

*Head Coaches*

No coach, 1872-1887
Walter Camp, 1888-1892
William Rhodes, 1893-1894
John Hartwell, 1895
S. B. Thorne, 1896
F. Butterworth, 1897-1898
J. O. Rodgers, 1899
Malcolm McBride, 1900
George Stillman, 1901
Joseph Swan, 1902
G. B. Chadwick, 1903
C. D. Rafferty, 1904
J. E. Owsley, 1905
Foster Rockwell, 1906
William Knox, 1907
L. H. Biglow, 1908
Howard Jones, 1909, 1913
Edward Coy, 1910
John Field, 1911
Arthur Howe, 1912
Frank Hinkey, 1914-1915
T.A.D. Jones, 1916-1917, 1920-1927
Albert Sharpe, 1919
Marvin (Mal) Stevens, 1928-1932
Reginald Root, 1933
Raymond Pond, 1934-1940
Emerson Nelson, 1941
Howard Odell, 1942-1947
Herman Hickman, 1948-1951
Jordan Olivar, 1952-1962
John Pont, 1963-1964
Carmen Cozza, 1965-

### Scores 1872-1976

**1872**
3g Columbia 0

**1873**
3g Rutgers 1g
0 Princeton 3g
2g Eton Players 1g

**1874**
6g Rutgers 0
5g Columbia 1g
6g Columbia 1g

**1875**
4g Rutgers 1g
0 Harvard 4g, 2t
6g Wesleyan 0
2g Columbia 3g

**1876**
1g Harvard 2t
2g, 1t Princeton 0
2g, 5t Columbia 1t

**1877**
1g, 2t Tufts 0
7g,13t Trinity 0
13g, 17t Stevens Institute 0
2t, 2s Princeton 5s
Since only goals counted toward winning a game, the Princeton score was called a tied game by the referee.

**1878**
2g, 3t Amherst 0
2g Trinity 0
3g, 5t, 2s Trinity 0
1s Amherst 13s
1g, 7s Harvard 13s
2s Princeton 1g, 7s
Again, since only goals counted, the second Amherst game was a tie.

**1879**
3g, 5t Pennsylvania 0
2s Harvard 4s
5g, 3t Rutgers 7s
2g, 3t, 2s Columbia 7s
2s Princeton 4s

**1880**
13g, 5t Columbia 0
8g, 5t, 1s Brown 11s
8g, 1t Pennsylvania 0
1g, 1t, 2s Harvard 9s
5s Princeton 11s

**1881**
2g, 4t Amherst 0
2g, 2t Michigan 0
4g, 8t Amherst 0
0 Harvard 4s
1g, 1t Columbia 6s
0 Princeton 0

**1882**
9g Wesleyan 0
9g, 3t Rutgers 3s
5g, 1t Rutgers 1t
6g, 2t M.I.T. 0
9g, 1t Amherst 0
11g, 4t Columbia 0
1g, 3t Harvard 2s
2g, 1s Princeton 1g, 1s

**1883**
60 Wesleyan 0
90 Wesleyan 0
48 Stevens Institute 0
98 Rutgers 0
93 Columbia 0
64 Michigan 0
6 Princeton 0
23 Harvard 2

**1884**
31 Wesleyan 0
96 Stevens Institute 0
63 Wesleyan 0
76 Rutgers 10
113 Dartmouth 0
46 Wesleyan 0
18 Graduates 0
52 Harvard 0
0 Princeton 0

**1885**
55 Stevens Institute 0
18 Wesleyan 0
71 Wesleyan 0
51 M.I.T. 0
52 Crescent A.C. 0
53 Pennsylvania 5
5 Princeton 6
61 Wesleyan 0

**1886**
75 Wesleyan 0
62 Wesleyan 0
96 M.I.T. 0
54 Stevens Institute 0
76 Williams 0
136 Wesleyan 0
84 Crescent A.C. 0
75 Pennsylvania 0
29 Harvard 4
0 Princeton 0

**1887**
38 Wesleyan 0
106 Wesleyan 0
74 Williams 0
50 Pennsylvania 0
74 Rutgers 0
68 Crescent A.C. 0
76 Wesleyan 4
12 Princeton 0
17 Harvard 8

**1888**
76 Wesleyan 0
65 Rutgers 0
34 Pennsylvania 0
46 Wesleyan 0
39 Amherst 0
30 Williams 0
68 M.I.T. 0
69 Stevens Institute 0
58 Pennsylvania 0
28 Crescent A.C. 0
70 Amherst 0
105 Wesleyan 0
10 Princeton 0
6 Harvard 0
N.B. Yale defeated Harvard by forfeit.

**1889**
38 Wesleyan 0
63 Wesleyan 5
36 Williams 0
60 Cornell 6
42 Amherst 0
64 Trinity 0
62 Columbia 0
22 Pennsylvania 10
30 Stevens Institute 0
18 Crescent A.C. 0
70 Cornell 0
32 Amherst 0
70 Williams 0
52 Wesleyan 0
6 Harvard 0
0 Princeton 10

**1890**
8 Wesleyan 0
18 Crescent A.C. 6
34 Wesleyan 0
26 Lehigh 0
40 Trinity 0
16 Orange A.C. 0
36 Williams 0
12 Amherst 0
76 Wesleyan 0
52 Crescent A.C. 0
70 Rutgers 0
60 Pennsylvania 0
6 Harvard 12
32 Princeton 0

**1891**
28 Wesleyan 0
26 Crescent A.C. 0
36 Trinity 0
46 Williams 0
28 Springfield Y.M.C.A. 0
36 Orange A.C. 0
38 Lehigh 0
70 Crescent A.C. 0
76 Wesleyan 0
27 Amherst 0
48 Pennsylvania 0
10 Harvard 0
19 Princeton 0

**1892**
6 Wesleyan 0
28 Crescent A.C. 0
32 Williams 0
22 Manhattan A.C. 0
29 Amherst 0
58 Orange A.C. 0
50 Springfield Y.M.C.A. 0
44 Tufts 0
72 Wesleyan 0
48 New York A.C. 0
28 Pennsylvania 0
6 Harvard 0
12 Princeton 0

**1893**
18 Brown 0
16 Crescent A.C. 0
28 Dartmouth 0
52 Amherst 0
50 Orange A.C. 0
82 Williams 0
28 U.S. Military Academy 0
42 New York A.C. 0

14 Pennsylvania 6
6 Harvard 0
0 Princeton 6

**1894**

42 Trinity 0
28 Brown 0
10 Crescent A.C. 0
23 Williams 4
34 Lehigh 0
34 Dartmouth 0
24 Orange A.C. 0
23 Boston A.A. 0
12 U.S. Military Academy 5
42 Volunteer A.C. 0
12 Brown 0
67 Tufts 0
50 Lehigh 0
48 Chicago A.C. 0
12 Harvard 4
24 Princeton 0

**1895**

8 Trinity 0
4 Brown 0
26 Union 0
36 Amherst 0
8 Crescent A.C. 2
26 Dartmouth 0
24 Orange A.C. 12
54 Williams 0
0 Boston A.C. 0
32 Dartmouth 0
28 U.S. Military Academy 8
18 Carlisle 0
6 Brown 6
26 Orange A.C. 0
20 Princeton 10

**1896**

6 Trinity 0
12 Amherst 0
18 Brown 0
12 Orange A.C. 0
22 Williams 0
42 Dartmouth 0
16 Wesleyan 0
12 Carlisle 6
12 Elizabeth A.C. 6
16 U.S. Military Academy 2
10 Boston A.A. 0
18 Brown 6
16 New Jersey A.C. 0
6 Princeton 24

**1897**

10 Trinity 0
30 Wesleyan 0
18 Amherst 0
32 Williams 0
10 Newton A.C. 0
18 Brown 14
24 Carlisle 9
6 U.S. Military Academy 6
16 Chicago 6
0 Harvard 0
6 Princeton 0

**1898**

18 Trinity 0
5 Wesleyan 0
34 Amherst 0
23 Williams 0
6 Newton A.C. 0
22 Brown 6
18 Carlisle 5
10 U.S. Military Academy 0
10 Chicago A.A. 0
0 Princeton 6
0 Harvard 17

**1899**

23 Amherst 0
46 Trinity 0
28 Bates 0
12 Dartmouth 0
6 Wisconsin 0
0 Columbia 5
24 U.S. Military Academy 0
42 Pennsylvania State 0
0 Harvard 0
10 Princeton 11

**1900**

22 Trinity 0
27 Amherst 0
30 Tufts 0
50 Bates 0
17 Dartmouth 0
30 Bowdoin 0
38 Wesleyan 0
12 Columbia 5
18 U.S. Military Academy 0
35 Carlisle 0
29 Princeton 5
28 Harvard 0

**1901**

23 Trinity 0
6 Amherst 0
29 Tufts 5
24 Wesleyan 0
24 U.S. Naval Academy 0
45 Bowdoin 0
22 Pennsylvania State 0
21 Bates 0
10 Columbia 5
5 U.S. Military Academy 5
35 Orange A.C. 0
12 Princeton 0
0 Harvard 22

**1902**

40 Trinity 0
34 Tufts 6
23 Amherst 0
35 Wesleyan 0
10 Brown 0
32 University of Vermont 0
11 Pennsylvania State 0
24 Syracuse 0
6 U.S. Military Academy 6
36 Bucknell 5
12 Princeton 5
23 Harvard 0

**1903**

35 Trinity 0
19 Tufts 0
46 University of Vermont 0
33 Wesleyan 0
22 Springfield Tr. Sc. 0
36 Holy Cross 10
27 Pennsylvania State 0
17 U.S. Military Academy 5
25 Columbia 0
30 Syracuse 0
6 Princeton 11
16 Harvard 0

**1904**

22 Wesleyan 0
42 Trinity 0
23 Holy Cross 0
24 Pennsylvania State 0
6 Springfield Tr. Sc. 0
17 Syracuse 9
6 U.S. Military Academy 11
34 Columbia 0
22 Brown 0
12 Princeton 0
12 Harvard 0

**1905**

27 Wesleyan 0
16 Syracuse 0
24 Springfield Tr. Sc. 0
30 Holy Cross 0
12 Pennsylvania State 0
20 U.S. Military Academy 0
53 Columbia 0
11 Brown 0
23 Princeton 4
6 Harvard 0

**1906**

21 Wesleyan 0
51 Syracuse 0
12 Springfield Tr. Sc. 0
17 Holy Cross 0
10 Pennsylvania State 0
12 Amherst 0
10 U.S. Military Academy 6
5 Brown 0
0 Princeton 0
6 Harvard 0

**1907**

25 Wesleyan 0
11 Syracuse 0
17 Springfield Tr. Sc. 0
52 Holy Cross 0
0 U.S. Military Academy 0
44 Villanova 0
11 Washington and Jeff. 0
22 Brown 0
12 Princeton 10
12 Harvard 0

**1908**

16 Wesleyan 0
5 Syracuse 0
18 Holy Cross 0
6 U.S. Military Academy 0
38 Washington and Jeff. 0
49 Mass. Agri. College 0
10 Brown 10
11 Princeton 6
0 Harvard 4

**1909**

11 Wesleyan 0
15 Syracuse 0
12 Holy Cross 0
36 Springfield Tr. Sc. 0
17 U.S. Military Academy 0
36 Colgate 0
34 Amherst 0
23 Brown 0
17 Princeton 0
8 Harvard 0

**1910**

22 Wesleyan 0
12 Syracuse 6
17 Tufts 0
12 Holy Cross 0
3 U.S. Military Academy 9
0 Vanderbilt 0
19 Colgate 0
0 Brown 21
5 Princeton 3
0 Harvard 0

**1911**

21 Wesleyan 0
26 Holy Cross 0
12 Syracuse 0
33 Virginia Poly. Inst. 0
0 U.S. Military Academy 6
23 Colgate 0
28 New York University 3
15 Brown 0
3 Princeton 6
0 Harvard 0

**1912**

10 Wesleyan 3
7 Holy Cross 0
21 Syracuse 0
16 Lafayette 0
6 U.S. Military Academy 0
13 Washington and Jeff. 3
10 Brown 0
6 Princeton 6
0 Harvard 20

**1913**

21 Wesleyan 0
10 Holy Cross 0
0 University of Maine 0
27 Lafayette 0
37 Lehigh 0
0 Washington and Jeff. 0
6 Colgate 16
17 Brown 0
3 Princeton 3
5 Harvard 15

**1914**

20 University of Maine 0
21 University of Virginia 0
20 Lehigh 3
28 Notre Dame 0
7 Washington and Jeff. 13
49 Colgate 7
14 Brown 6
19 Princeton 14
0 Harvard 36

**1915**

37 University of Maine 0
0 University of Virginia 10
7 Lehigh 6
19 Springfield Tr. Sc. 0
7 Washington and Jeff. 16
0 Colgate 15
0 Brown 3
13 Princeton 7
0 Harvard 41

**1916**

25 Carnegie Tech. 0
61 University of Viriginia 3
12 Lehigh 0
19 Virginia Poly. Inst. 0
36 Washington and Jeff. 14
7 Colgate 3
6 Brown 21
10 Princeton 0
6 Harvard 3

**1917**

*(Informal Team)*

7 Loomis Institute 0
33 New Haven Naval Base 0
7 Trinity 0

**1918**

*No Football*

**1919**

20 Springfield College 0

34 Uni. of North Carolina 7
3 Boston College 5
37 Tufts 0
31 University of Maryland 0
14 Brown 0
6 Princeton 13
3 Harvard 10

**1920**

44 Carnegie Tech. 0
21 Uni. of North Carolina 0
13 Boston College 21
24 Uni. of West Virginia 0
21 Colgate 7
14 Brown 10
0 Princeton 20
0 Harvard 9

**1921**

28 Bates 0
14 University of Vermont 0
34 Uni. of North Carolina 0
23 Williams 0
14 U.S. Military Academy 7
45 Brown 7
28 University of Maryland 0
13 Princeton 7
3 Harvard 10

**1922**

48 Bates 0
13 Carnegie Tech. 0
18 Uni. of North Carolina 0
0 University of Iowa 6
38 Williams 0
7 U.S. Military Academy 7
20 Brown 0
45 University of Maryland 3
0 Princeton 3
3 Harvard 10

**1923**

53 Uni. of North Carolina 0
40 University of Georgia 0
29 Bucknell 14
21 Brown 0
31 U.S. Military Academy 10
16 University of Maryland 14
27 Princeton 0
13 Harvard 0

**1924**

27 Uni. of North Carolina 0
7 University of Georgia 6
14 Dartmouth 14
13 Brown 3
7 U.S. Military Academy 7
47 University of Maryland 0
10 Princeton 0
19 Harvard 6

**1925**

53 Middlebury 0
35 University of Georgia 7
13 Pennsylvania 16
20 Brown 7
28 U.S. Military Academy 7
43 University of Maryland 14
12 Princeton 25
0 Harvard 0

**1926**

51 Boston University 0
19 University of Georgia 0
14 Dartmouth 7
0 Brown 7
0 U.S. Military Academy 33
0 University of Maryland 15
7 Princeton 10
12 Harvard 7

**1927**

41 Bowdoin 0
10 University of Georgia 14
19 Brown 0
10 U.S. Military Academy 6
19 Dartmouth 0
30 University of Maryland 6
14 Princeton 6
14 Harvard 0

**1928**

27 University of Maine 0
21 University of Georgia 6
32 Brown 14
6 U.S. Military Academy 18
18 Dartmouth 0
0 University of Maryland 6
2 Princeton 12
0 Harvard 17

**1929**

89 University of Vermont 0
0 University of Georgia 15
14 Brown 6
21 U.S. Military Academy 13
16 Dartmouth 12
13 University of Maryland 13
13 Princeton 0
6 Harvard 10

**1930**

38 University of Maine 0
40 University of Maryland 13
14 University of Georgia 18
21 Brown 0
7 U.S. Military Academy 7
0 Dartmouth 0
66 Alfred 0
10 Princeton 7
0 Harvard 13

**1931**

19 University of Maine 0
7 University of Georgia 26
27 University of Chicago 0
6 U.S. Military Academy 6
33 Dartmouth 33
52 St. John's (Annapolis) 0
3 Harvard 0
51 Princeton 14

**1932**

0 Bates 0
7 Chicago 7
2 Brown 7
0 U.S. Military Academy 20
6 Dartmouth 0
7 Princeton 7
19 Harvard 0

**1933**

14 University of Maine 7
14 Washington and Lee 0
14 Brown 6
0 U.S. Military Academy 21
14 Dartmouth 13
0 University of Georgia 7
6 Harvard 19
2 Princeton 27

**1934**

6 Columbia 12
14 Pennysylvania 6
37 Brown 0
12 U.S. Military Academy 20
7 Dartmouth 2
7 University of Georgia 14
7 Princeton 0
14 Harvard 0

**1935**

34 Uni. of New Hampshire 0
31 Pennsylvania 20
7 U.S. Naval Academy 6
8 U.S. Military Academy 14
6 Dartmouth 14
20 Brown 0
55 Lafayette 0
14 Harvard 7
7 Princeton 38

*A right halfback on the Billy Rhodes 1890 Yale eleven, Dr. Henry L. Williams later enrolled in the School of Medicine at the University of Pennsylvania and helped pay his way by coaching football and track at William Penn Charter School. He then moved to Minneapolis, where he built great Minnesota football teams (1900–1921) and ranked with Amos Alonzo Stagg and Pop Warner as a leading football innovator.*

**1936**

| | |
|---|---|
| 23 | Cornell 0 |
| 7 | Pennsylvania 0 |
| 12 | U.S. Naval Academy 7 |
| 28 | Rutgers 0 |
| 7 | Dartmouth 11 |
| 14 | Brown 6 |
| 26 | Princeton 23 |
| 14 | Harvard 13 |

**1937**

| | |
|---|---|
| 26 | University of Maine 0 |
| 27 | Pennsylvania 7 |
| 15 | U.S. Military Academy 7 |
| 9 | Cornell 0 |
| 9 | Dartmouth 9 |
| 19 | Brown 0 |
| 26 | Princeton 0 |
| 6 | Harvard 13 |

**1938**

| | |
|---|---|
| 14 | Columbia 27 |
| 0 | Pennsylvania 21 |
| 9 | U.S. Naval Academy 7 |
| 13 | University of Michigan 15 |
| 6 | Dartmouth 24 |
| 20 | Brown 14 |
| 7 | Princeton 20 |
| 0 | Harvard 7 |

**1939**

| | |
|---|---|
| 10 | Columbia 7 |
| 0 | Pennsylvania 6 |
| 20 | U.S. Military Academy 15 |
| 7 | Michigan 27 |
| 0 | Dartmouth 33 |
| 14 | Brown 14 |
| 7 | Princeton 13 |
| 20 | Harvard 7 |

**1940**

| | |
|---|---|
| 14 | University of Virginia 19 |
| 7 | Pennsylvania 50 |
| 13 | Dartmouth 7 |
| 0 | U.S. Naval Academy 21 |
| 2 | Brown 6 |
| 0 | Cornell 21 |
| 7 | Princeton 10 |
| 0 | Harvard 28 |

**1941**

| | |
|---|---|
| 21 | University of Virginia 19 |
| 13 | Pennsylvania 28 |
| 7 | U.S. Military Academy 20 |
| 0 | Dartmouth 7 |
| 0 | Brown 7 |
| 7 | Cornell 21 |
| 6 | Princeton 20 |
| 0 | Harvard 14 |

**1942**

| | |
|---|---|
| 33 | Lehigh 6 |
| 6 | Pennsylvania 35 |
| 6 | U.S. Naval Academy 13 |
| 17 | Dartmouth 7 |
| 27 | Brown 0 |
| 7 | Cornell 13 |
| 13 | Princeton 6 |
| 7 | Harvard 3 |

**1943**

| | |
|---|---|
| 13 | Muhlenberg 6 |
| 12 | Rochester 14 |
| 20 | U.S. Coast Guard 12 |
| 7 | Pennsylvania 41 |
| 20 | Columbia 7 |
| 7 | U.S. Military Academy 39 |
| 6 | Dartmouth 20 |
| 20 | Brown 21 |
| 27 | Princeton 6 |

**1944**

| | |
|---|---|
| 7 | U.S. Coast Guard 3 |
| 16 | Cornell 7 |
| 27 | Columbia 10 |
| 32 | Rochester 0 |
| 6 | Dartmouth 0 |
| 13 | Brown 0 |
| 13 | Uni. of North Carolina 6 |
| 6 | University of Virginia 6 |

**1945**

| | |
|---|---|
| 27 | Tufts 7 |
| 0 | Holy Cross 21 |
| 13 | Columbia 27 |
| 18 | Cornell 7 |
| 6 | Dartmouth 0 |
| 7 | Brown 20 |
| 41 | U.S. Coast Guard 6 |
| 20 | Princeton 14 |
| 28 | Harvard 0 |

**1946**

| | |
|---|---|
| 33 | Kings Point 0 |
| 27 | Colgate 6 |
| 20 | Columbia 28 |
| 6 | Cornell 6 |
| 47 | U.S. Coast Guard 14 |
| 33 | Dartmouth 2 |
| 49 | Brown 0 |
| 30 | Princeton 2 |
| 27 | Harvard 14 |

**1947**

| | |
|---|---|
| 34 | Kings Point 13 |
| 14 | Cornell 0 |
| 17 | Columbia 7 |
| 0 | Wisconsin 9 |
| 49 | Springfield 0 |
| 23 | Dartmouth 14 |
| 14 | Brown 20 |
| 0 | Princeton 17 |
| 31 | Harvard 21 |

**1948**

| | |
|---|---|
| 28 | Brown 13 |
| 7 | Connecticut 0 |
| 28 | Columbia 34 |
| 17 | Wisconsin 7 |
| 0 | Vanderbilt 35 |
| 14 | Dartmouth 41 |
| 52 | Kings Point 0 |
| 14 | Princeton 20 |
| 7 | Harvard 20 |

**1949**

| | |
|---|---|
| 26 | Connecticut 0 |
| 33 | Columbia 7 |
| 14 | Cornell 48 |
| 14 | Holy Cross 7 |
| 13 | Dartmouth 34 |
| 0 | Brown 14 |
| 13 | Princeton 21 |
| 29 | Harvard 6 |

**1950**

| | |
|---|---|
| 25 | Connecticut 0 |
| 36 | Brown 12 |
| 21 | Fordham 14 |
| 20 | Columbia 14 |
| 0 | Cornell 7 |
| 14 | Holy Cross 13 |
| 0 | Dartmouth 7 |
| 12 | Princeton 47 |
| 14 | Harvard 6 |

**1951**

| | |
|---|---|
| 48 | Bates 0 |
| 7 | Navy 7 |
| 13 | Brown 14 |
| 0 | Columbia 14 |
| 0 | Cornell 27 |
| 27 | Colgate 7 |
| 10 | Dartmouth 14 |
| 0 | Princeton 27 |
| 21 | Harvard 21 |

**1952**

| | |
|---|---|
| 34 | Connecticut 13 |
| 0 | Navy 31 |
| 28 | Brown 0 |
| 35 | Columbia 28 |
| 13 | Cornell 0 |
| 47 | Lafayette 0 |
| 21 | Dartmouth 7 |
| 21 | Princeton 27 |
| 41 | Harvard 14 |

**1953**

| | |
|---|---|
| 32 | Connecticut 0 |
| 13 | Brown 0 |
| 13 | Columbia 7 |
| 0 | Cornell 0 |
| 7 | Colgate 7 |
| 0 | Dartmouth 32 |
| 32 | Temple 6 |
| 26 | Princeton 24 |
| 0 | Harvard 13 |

**1954**

| | |
|---|---|
| 27 | Connecticut 0 |
| 26 | Brown 24 |
| 13 | Columbia 7 |
| 47 | Cornell 21 |
| 13 | Colgate 13 |
| 13 | Dartmouth 7 |
| 7 | Army 48 |
| 14 | Princeton 21 |
| 9 | Harvard 13 |

**1955**

| | |
|---|---|
| 14 | Connecticut 0 |
| 27 | Brown 20 |
| 46 | Columbia 14 |
| 34 | Cornell 6 |
| 0 | Colgate 7 |
| 20 | Dartmouth 0 |
| 14 | Army 12 |
| 0 | Princeton 13 |
| 21 | Harvard 7 |

**1956**

| | |
|---|---|
| 19 | Connecticut 14 |
| 20 | Brown 2 |
| 33 | Columbia 19 |
| 25 | Cornell 7 |
| 6 | Colgate 14 |
| 19 | Dartmouth 0 |
| 40 | Pennsylvania 7 |
| 42 | Princeton 20 |
| 42 | Harvard 14 |

**1957**

| | |
|---|---|
| 27 | Connecticut 0 |
| 20 | Brown 21 |
| 19 | Columbia 0 |
| 18 | Cornell 7 |
| 20 | Colgate 0 |
| 14 | Dartmouth 14 |
| 20 | Pennsylvania 33 |
| 20 | Princeton 13 |
| 54 | Harvard 0 |

**1958**

| | |
|---|---|
| 8 | Connecticut 6 |
| 29 | Brown 35 |
| 0 | Columbia 13 |
| 7 | Cornell 12 |
| 14 | Colgate 7 |
| 14 | Dartmouth 22 |
| 6 | Pennsylvania 30 |
| 14 | Princeton 50 |
| 0 | Harvard 28 |

**1959**

| | |
|---|---|
| 20 | Connecticut 0 |
| 17 | Brown 0 |
| 14 | Columbia 0 |
| 23 | Cornell 0 |
| 21 | Colgate 0 |
| 8 | Dartmouth 12 |
| 12 | Pennsylvania 28 |
| 38 | Princeton 20 |
| 6 | Harvard 35 |

**1960**

| | |
|---|---|
| 11 | Connecticut 8 |
| 9 | Brown 0 |
| 30 | Columbia 8 |
| 22 | Cornell 6 |
| 36 | Colgate 14 |
| 29 | Dartmouth 0 |
| 34 | Pennsylvania 9 |
| 43 | Princeton 22 |
| 39 | Harvard 6 |

**1961**

| | |
|---|---|
| 18 | Connecticut 0 |
| 14 | Brown 3 |
| 0 | Columbia 11 |
| 12 | Cornell 0 |
| 8 | Colgate 14 |
| 8 | Dartmouth 24 |
| 23 | Pennsylvania 0 |
| 16 | Princeton 26 |
| 0 | Harvard 27 |

**1962**

| | |
|---|---|
| 18 | Connecticut 14 |
| 6 | Brown 6 |
| 10 | Columbia 14 |
| 26 | Cornell 8 |
| 14 | Colgate 14 |
| 0 | Dartmouth 9 |
| 12 | Pennsylvania 15 |
| 10 | Princeton 14 |
| 6 | Harvard 14 |

**1963**

| | |
|---|---|
| 3 | Connecticut 0 |
| 7 | Brown 12 |
| 19 | Columbia 7 |
| 10 | Cornell 13 |
| 31 | Colgate 0 |
| 10 | Dartmouth 6 |
| 28 | Pennsylvania 7 |
| 7 | Princeton 27 |
| 20 | Harvard 6 |

**1964**

| | |
|---|---|
| 21 | Connecticut 6 |
| 54 | Lehigh 0 |
| 15 | Brown 7 |
| 9 | Columbia 9 |
| 23 | Cornell 21 |
| 24 | Dartmouth 15 |
| 21 | Pennsylvania 9 |
| 14 | Princeton 35 |
| 14 | Harvard 18 |

**1965**

| | |
|---|---|
| 6 | Connecticut 13 |
| 0 | Colgate 7 |
| 3 | Brown 0 |
| 7 | Columbia 21 |
| 24 | Cornell 14 |
| 17 | Dartmouth 20 |
| 21 | Pennsylvania 19 |
| 6 | Princeton 31 |
| 0 | Harvard 13 |

**1966**

| | |
|---|---|
| 16 | Connecticut 0 |
| 14 | Rutgers 17 |
| 24 | Brown 0 |
| 44 | Columbia 21 |
| 14 | Cornell 16 |
| 13 | Dartmouth 28 |
| 17 | Pennsylvania 14 |
| 7 | Princeton 13 |
| 0 | Harvard 17 |

**1967**

| | |
|---|---|
| 14 | Holy Cross 26 |
| 14 | Connecticut 6 |
| 35 | Brown 0 |
| 21 | Columbia 7 |
| 41 | Cornell 7 |
| 56 | Dartmouth 15 |
| 44 | Pennsylvania 22 |

29 Princeton 7
24 Harvard 20

**1968**

31 Connecticut 14
49 Colgate 14
35 Brown 13
29 Columbia 7
25 Cornell 13
47 Dartmouth 27
30 Pennsylvania 13
42 Princeton 17
29 Harvard 29

**1969**

15 Connecticut 19
40 Colgate 21
27 Brown 13
41 Columbia 6
17 Cornell 0
21 Dartmouth 42
21 Pennsylvania 3
17 Princeton 14
7 Harvard 0

**1970**

10 Connecticut 0
39 Colgate 7
28 Brown 0
32 Columbia 15
38 Cornell 7
0 Dartmouth 10
32 Pennsylvania 22
27 Princeton 22
12 Harvard 14

**1971**

23 Connecticut 0
21 Colgate 28
17 Brown 10
14 Columbia 15
10 Cornell 31
15 Dartmouth 17
24 Pennsylvania 14
10 Princeton 6
16 Harvard 35

**1972**

28 Connecticut 7
27 Colgate 7
53 Brown 19
28 Columbia 14
13 Cornell 24
45 Dartmouth 14
30 Pennsylvania 48
31 Princeton 7
28 Harvard 17

**1973**

13 Connecticut 27
24 Colgate 18
25 Brown 34
29 Columbia 0
20 Cornell 3
13 Dartmouth 24
24 Pennsylvania 21
30 Princeton 13
35 Harvard 0

**1974**

20 Connecticut 7
30 Colgate 7
24 Brown 0
42 Columbia 2
27 Cornell 3
14 Dartmouth 9
37 Pennsylvania 12
19 Princeton 6
16 Harvard 21

**1975**

35 Connecticut 14
24 Colgate 10
12 Brown 27
34 Columbia 7
20 Cornell 14
16 Dartmouth 14
24 Pennsylvania 14
24 Princeton 13
7 Harvard 10

**1976**

6 Brown 14
21 Connecticut 10
21 Lehigh 6
18 Dartmouth 14
37 Columbia 6
21 Pennsylvania 7
14 Cornell 6
39 Princeton 7
21 Harvard 7

# Index